Y0-ACJ-051

SAINT
VINCENT DE PAUL

CORRESPONDENCE

VOLUME III

SAINT
VINCENT DE PAUL

CORRESPONDENCE
CONFERENCES, DOCUMENTS

III
CORRESPONDENCE

VOLUME III (August 1646 - March 1650)

NEWLY TRANSLATED, EDITED, AND ANNOTATED

FROM THE 1921 EDITION

OF

PIERRE COSTE, C.M.

Edited by:

SR. MARIE POOLE, D.C., *Editor-in-Chief*
SR. JULIA DENTON, D.C.
SR. PAULE FREEBURG, D.C.
SR. MARIAN HAMWEY, D.C.

Translated by:

SR. MARIE POOLE, D.C.
REV. FRANCIS GERMOVNIK, C.M. (Latin)

Annotated by:

REV. JOHN W. CARVEN, C.M.

NIHIL OBSTAT
Very Rev. Jerome R. Herff, C.M.
Censor Deputatus

IMPRIMATUR
Most Rev. William H. Keeler, D. D., J. C. D.
Archbishop of Baltimore

April 3, 1992

TO
VERY REVEREND RICHARD McCULLEN, C.M.
Superior General (1980-1992)

FOR

HIS EMBODIMENT OF THE SPIRIT OF SAINT VINCENT

AND

HIS ABIDING INTEREST

IN THE TRANSLATION OF HIS WRITINGS

© 1992, Vincentian Conference, U.S.A.
Published in the United States by New City Press
86 Mayflower Avenue, New Rochelle, N.Y. 10801

Printed in the United States of America

Library of Congress Cataloging-in-Publication Data:

Vincent de Paul, Saint, 1581-1660.
    Correspondence, conferences, documents.

    Translation of: Correspondence, entretiens, documents.
    Includes bibliographical references and index.
    Contents: I. Correspondence. v. 1. 1607-1639. —
v. 3. August 1646-March 1650.
    1. Vincent de Paul, Saint, 1581-1660—Correspondence.
2. Christian saints—France—Correspondence.   I. Coste,
Pierre, 1873-1935.   II. Title.
BX4700.V6A4   1985   271'.77'024   [B]   83-63559
ISBN 0-911782-50-8 (v. 1)
ISBN 1-56548-022-8 (v. 3)

TABLE OF CONTENTS

APPENDIX

INTRODUCTION

The correspondence of Saint Vincent de Paul contains a wealth of information about the man, the Saint, and his milieu. To facilitate the informed reading of Volume III, the editors felt it would be useful to preface the work with some explanatory remarks regarding language, style, and placement. In this way, a fuller image of the multifaceted personality and influence of the Saint will emerge from these pages, giving the reader a broader understanding of his life and the world in which he lived and worked.

In placing new letters within the volume or changing the placement of letters we have relied on Coste's corrections given in volumes VIII and XIII, the listings found in the *Annales*,[1] the dates on recently discovered letters or, in the absence of a date, on internal evidence. To facilitate research in Coste's work, we have chosen to keep the letter numbers of the original volumes and to indicate material newly added or relocated within each volume by adding a, b, c, etc., to the number of the preceding item. We have also decided to adhere to the span of years assigned by Coste for each volume.

In some cases, the finding of an original has enabled us to join fragments formerly considered separate letters. Such combined letters have been assigned a single number followed by a letter to

---

[1] *Annales de la Congregation de la Mission* (1937), pp. 234-237.

differentiate the whole from the segments as published in the original Coste volume. Where variations of a single letter exist, only the most correct version has been included in the volume. Likewise, although Coste chose to publish letters originally written in Latin both in that language and in French, the present edition bears only the English translation of the original Latin.

Three different types of letters are presented in these volumes: letters *from* Saint Vincent, letters *to* Saint Vincent and, at times, mere summaries of letters where the existence of a letter is known but no text is available. The letters written by Saint Vincent appear in regular type, while those addressed to him are printed in italics. Smaller type has been used to differentiate the summaries.

As Coste states in his introduction, almost all the letters we now possess are either in Saint Vincent's handwriting or in that of one of his secretaries. The term *original autograph* found in the citation of a letter indicates that the manuscript was written entirely in the Saint's hand. If the citation uses the term *signed letter,* the manuscript was written by a secretary and signed by the Saint. For some letters only a facsimile, a handwritten copy, a photocopy, or a photograph is known. Such indications are given in the citation of the letters for which this information is available.

The citations usually state as well the actual location of the manuscript or copy used for the present edition. Great care has been taken to verify these locations where possible. Letters drawn from other publications and those belonging to special collections, private or museum, have not been checked due to the near impossibility of such a task. However, an attempt has been made to verify all letters belonging to private houses of the Daughters of Charity, the Priests of the Mission, other religious houses, churches, and various religious institutions. In checking these locations and in the search for unpublished letters, we have at times been fortunate enough to locate the originals of letters for which only copies were known formerly. In these instances as well no mention has been made of the correction—the citation simply states that the manuscript is an original.

We have updated as well the department names given in the footnotes. Several departments have had name changes since the time of Coste, while two others have been subdivided.[2]

Although the project has undergone many delays, each has contributed in some way to the overall quality of the work. The appearance, in 1983, of the revised edition of Saint Louise de Marillac's writings[3] has permitted us to check her letters to Saint Vincent and her spiritual writings for any corrections which may have come to light. We have also adjusted all the footnote references to the appropriate indication as given in the new edition.

In any work of translation the question of style invariably arises, so it was not strange that we should be faced with the problem. Should we smooth out clumsy or elliptical phrasing in the interest of producing a more "readable" translation or should we preserve the roughness and unpolished style of the original in order to reflect the flavor and spontaneous quality of Saint Vincent's expression, supplying explanations where needed to make the sense clear? As our response to this question, we have attempted to make our translation as "readable" as possible while adhering closely to the style of each correspondent. For that purpose we have made an effort to give as literal a meaning as we could to the expressions used, while still adapting them to modern terminology. We have tried to reproduce even the grammatical constructions used by each correspondent unless the true meaning of the sentence would suffer thereby. Very long sentences have been shortened and short phrases joined together to render thoughts more readily intelligible, though still preserving the sense of the original. The vocabulary

---

[2]*Department* is the term used to designate each of the principal divisions of French territory. It denotes a geographical area similar to that of the American *state*. In the names of several departments, the word *maritime*, indicating *near the sea*, has replaced the word *inférieure* of the same meaning: Charente-Maritime, Seine-Maritime, Alpes-Maritime. In 1964, the Department of Seine was subdivided into Hauts-de-Seine, Paris, Seine-Saint-Denis, and Val-de-Marne; Seine-et-Oise became Essonne, Val-d'Oise, and Yvelines.

[3][Sr. Elisabeth Charpy, D.C., ed.] *Sainte Louise de Marillac. Ecrits Spirituels* (Tours: Mame, 1983), trans. Sr. Louise Sullivan, D.C., *Spiritual Writings of Louise de Marillac, Correspondence and Thoughts* (New York: New City Press, 1991).

and expression have deliberately been kept simple. Saint Vincent's love for and practice of simplicity are no secret to anyone familiar with his life; therefore, it was judged fitting to follow his own simplicity in the choice of words and style unless he himself opted for more elegant forms.

To retain the French atmosphere of the work we have left certain terms and expressions in the original French. General terms of greeting such as *Monsieur, Madame, etc.*, have not been translated, nor have we attempted an English version for expressions such as *O mon Dieu!, O Jésus!* Land-holding titles which often form part of a proper name—*Comte, Duc, Marquis*—have also been left in French. Other titles have been translated by the closest English equivalent possible. Proper names are given in the original language unless there is a familiar English form. This holds true for both people and places. Therefore, *Sainte Jeanne-Françoise Frémiot de Chantal* has been rendered as *Saint Jane Frances* Frémiot de Chantal, whereas *Pierre Séguier* remains in French. For places, *Brittany* is used instead of *Bretagne,* while *Granada, Villeneuve,* and similar names remain in the original language. Proper foreign names within the text of the manuscripts have been left as written by the correspondents. However, the footnotes and index present the name in its original language form—*Alessandro* Bichi for *Alexandre* Bichi; *Patrick Walsh* for *Patrice Valois.*

An attempt has been made to standardize name variations appearing in the original manuscripts: *Gondi* is always used in this edition although the form *Gondy* is often seen in the manuscripts. We have, however, left the variations *Pollalion* and *Poulaillon.* Although the correct spelling is the former, Saint Vincent always wrote the latter.

We have also standardized the various forms of the phrase used by Saint Vincent after his signature: *unworthy priest of the Congregation of the Mission.* Throughout this edition the abbreviation *i.s.C.M. (indignus sacerdos Congregationis Missionis)* has been used.

The word *fille,* meaning girl, daughter, young woman, appears in many of the manuscripts. In the seventeenth century, this word also denoted a woman religious or nun. We have tried to adjust the meaning of *fille* to the context of the various letters and have sometimes rendered the word as *Sister* rather than *Daughter* when referring to a member of Saint Louise's nascent community.

Monetary terms—*livre, écu,* etc.—have not been translated for it would be difficult to assign them an equivalent value in modern currency. Several other words and phrases have likewise been left in French—*Parlement, Chambre des Comptes, collège*—since English has no corresponding institution. These terms have been explained in footnotes. For other words of foreign origin used in English and found in English dictionaries no explanation has been given, for example, *faubourg.*

Saint Vincent often makes use of scriptural references which, however, are not always direct quotes. Where he has done so, the translation has been adjusted to flow with the meaning of the sentence. The scriptural quotations given in the footnotes are usually taken from the *New American Bible,* unless a passage cannot be found in that edition or a more suitable rendering of the phrase is found elsewhere. In such instances, the *Douay-Rheims Bible* has been used. In the case of the psalms, both versions have been cited because of the variations.

Coste almost always refers to Vincent de Paul as Saint Vincent or the Saint. In the present edition we have added this title to the names of Louise de Marillac and any other individual who has been canonized since Coste's time.

Generally speaking, in the titles of the letters, Coste gave the location of the addressee only when he was sure of it and when the locality was outside the then city of Paris. We have continued this practice and have attempted to make it more consistent. We have also followed Coste's custom of placing within brackets dates that are uncertain or conjectural. Brackets have also been used to indicate words either missing from the manuscript or inserted by the editors.

The capitalization forms of the original manuscripts have been adjusted to American usage as has the punctuation. Number forms—words versus figures—follow common American practice as well.

In addition to our goal of producing a smooth English translation which is faithful insofar as possible to the meaning and style of the original French, we have also purposed to present a work which is interesting and informative with regard to Saint Vincent, his correspondents, and his times. Both the scholar who may wish to use this work as a research tool and the ordinary reader unfamiliar with the Vincentian Family and with the religio-political history of the period have been kept in mind. A great effort has been made to update, correct, and amplify Coste's footnote material. Irrelevant notes have been eliminated and new annotation added whenever this has been deemed necessary or helpful. In the case of new matter, no indication has been given to distinguish Coste's footnotes from the annotation added by our editor.

A biographical sketch of each personage has been supplied throughout the work the first time that he or she appears in a volume. To facilitate reference to this data and also to the explanations of terms and places given throughout the text an index has been added to each book. The index indicates the number of the letter to which the reader should refer for the information sought. A general index will also be provided as an appendix to the entire work.

All references in the indices and the footnotes have been given by citing the volume and the number of the item rather than the page. Since Coste's volume span and his numbering of items have been retained, this practice should facilitate research in both his edition and the present translation.

In order to enjoy these volumes more thoroughly, the reader would do well to keep in mind that, as now, so then, one correspondent did not spell out to the other details that were already known and understood by both. Reading these letters at a distance of some three hundred years will often arouse a curiosity which in many cases must remain unsatisfied. The allusions made will not always be clear, nor can they be. However, a familiarity beforehand with the life of Saint Vincent will greatly aid one's knowledge and understanding of the situations mentioned and the people involved. The three-volume definitive biography written by Coste[4] provides extensive information, but many shorter versions of the Saint's life can be found. Placed against such a background, these writings take on still more a life of their own and make the Saint vividly present once again. The twinkle in his eyes and the smile or tenderness in his voice seep through the words and we meet the delightful, charming man known to his contemporaries. The severe, ascetic Saint takes on a new personality and somehow becomes more human.

Let us not fail to seek the man beyond these words, the man of compassion, warmth, humor, savoir faire, authority, and, most of all, the mystic whose sanctity was carved amid the bustle and involvement of very human situations. He will give us hope that we, too, can find holiness in an ordinary, busy life. May this personal acquaintance with the real Vincent de Paul lead us to encounter the dynamic force behind his life, Jesus Christ, who, for him, was all things.

---

[4]Pierre Coste, C.M., *The Life and Works of Saint Vincent de Paul*, trans. Joseph Leonard, C.M., 3 vols. (Westminster, Maryland: Newman Press, 1952; repr., New York: New City Press, 1987).

— xxiv —

ACKNOWLEDGEMENTS

Special thanks should be given to Vincentian Fathers Raymond Chalumeau, former Archivist of the Congregation of the Mission; Thomas Davitt, Ignatius M. Melito, and John E. Rybolt for their dedication in reading the manuscript of this volume and of the two preceding ones. Their expertise in history, theology, Sacred Scripture, and/or English, and their knowledge of Vincentian history and spirituality have allowed us to correct errors, clarify the text, and make stylistic changes which render it more readable. By the invaluable contribution each has made to this translation of Saint Vincent's correspondence, they have merited the gratitude, not only of the editorial staff, but of all who will be enriched by reflective reading of the Saint's own words.

Monsieur

Je Vous Supplie très humblement vouloir
la peine me Mander Je Se Croy frau —
demain Mercredy que Vassembles là vos
Sœurs pourra Je tenir aste que Je Vey Sage
auter et colley Diey et fontenay
Veulle de la Maison me Maistre hier
de Secouri de Vous grand Elle Pourra
descharger entierement Son Cœur Vous
Vendat premier mais Elle ne descrehey

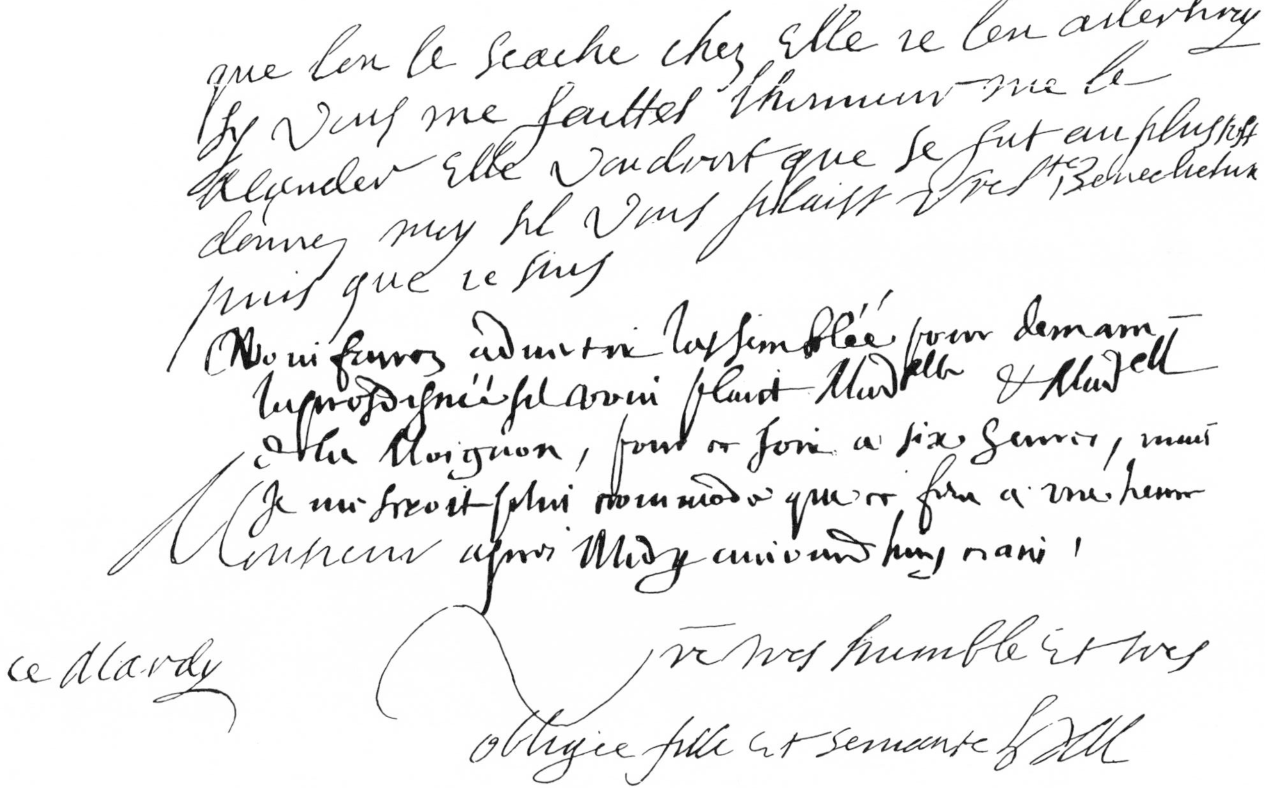

Facsimile of letters 935 and 936

SAINT VINCENT DE PAUL

CORRESPONDENCE

829. - TO ETIENNE BLATIRON,[1] IN GENOA

Paris, August 2, 1646

Monsieur,

The grace of Our Lord be with you forever!

I cannot tell you the consolation my soul experienced in reading your letter; I am in admiration of this good and holy Cardinal[2] and his conduct toward you. As for the difficulties in the establishment, it is legitimate to make some concession regarding time. I do not know why you sent me the plan, which I gather from yours[3] was drawn up by M. Codoing in Genoa.[4]

Letter 829. - Archives of the Mission, Curia Generalitia C.M., Rome, original autograph letter written entirely in the hand of the Saint, except the part which begins: "We sent you a long time ago . . . ."

[1]Etienne Blatiron was born in Saint-Julien-Chapteuil (Haute-Loire) on January 6, 1614. He was received into the Congregation of the Mission on January 6, 1638, ordained a priest in 1639, and placed in Alet (1639-1641), Saintes (1641), Richelieu, Rome (1644-1645), and Genoa (1645-1657). He distinguished himself particularly in the latter post, where as Superior of a new house he had to organize everything. Saint Vincent considered him one of his most competent Missionaries and "a very great servant of God." (Cf. Louis Abelly, *Vie du Vénérable Serviteur de Dieu Vincent de Paul* [3 vols., Paris: Florentin Lambert, 1664], bk. III, p. 70.) Etienne Blatiron died in Genoa on July 24, 1657, a victim of his dedication to the plague-stricken. His biography was published in vol. II of *Notices*, pp. 151-203. (Cf. *Notices sur les prêtres, clercs et frères défunts de la Congrégation de la Mission* [10 vols. in two series, Paris: Dumoulin, 1881-1911].) In the Lyons manuscript there is a report on his virtues addressed to Saint Vincent.

[2]Stefano Durazzo, Legate in Ferraro, then in Bologna, was created a Cardinal in 1633, was Archbishop of Genoa (1635-1664), and died in Rome on July 22, 1667. This pious Prelate was always most gracious and very devoted to Saint Vincent and his priests.

[3]Etienne Blatiron's letter.

[4]Bernard Codoing stayed for a time in Genoa on his return from Rome. Born in Agen on

I am writing again to M. Dehorgny[5] to send you someone other than M. Dunots,[6] and that the person he sends you should be learned, spiritual, discreet, and know how to conduct a seminary, or at least have as many of these qualities as possible.

Monsieur Dufestel[7] has gone home because of his constant

August 11, 1610, he was ordained a priest in December 1635, was received into the Congregation of the Mission on February 10, 1636, and holds an important place among the first companions of Saint Vincent. He was the first Superior of the Annecy Seminary (1640-1642) and directed the house in Rome for two years (1642-1644). Then he was placed at the head of Saint-Charles Seminary (1645-1646), situated on the grounds of Saint-Lazare. From there he went to Saint-Méen under particularly difficult circumstances (1646-1648), then to La Rose (1648-1649), and finally to Richelieu (1649-1650), always as Superior. He was very successful in his missions in France and Italy. His sermons were so appealing that at one point Saint Vincent considered publishing them. Bernard Codoing would have rendered greater service to Saint Vincent had he been less attached to his own ideas and learned to control his tendency to hastiness. We might be tempted to say "Happy faults!" since they merited for us some of the most beautiful letters in Saint Vincent's correspondence.

Sometime between 1651 and 1655 Codoing left the Congregation of the Mission. On July 24, 1654, he was Pastor of Saint-Hilaire in Agen; on January 2, 1673, we find his signature on the baptismal register there. He also acted as Vicar-General of the Bishop of Gap. The last reference to Codoing is October 6, 1675, at which time he was at the seminary in Sens (cf. *Annales de la Congrégation de la Mission*, vol. 114-115 [1949-1950]).

[5]Jean Dehorgny, from Estrées-Saint-Denis (Oise), entered the Congregation of the Mission in August 1627 and was ordained a priest April 22, 1628. In 1632, when Saint Vincent made the move to Saint-Lazare, Dehorgny took over the direction of the Collège des Bons-Enfants, which he retained until 1635, then took up again (1638-1643, 1654-1659). He was Assistant to the Superior General (1642-1644, 1654-1667); Superior of the house in Rome (1644-1647, 1651-1653); and Director of the Daughters of Charity (1660-1667). In 1640, 1641, 1643, 1644, 1659, and 1660, he visited several houses of the Company, reestablishing good order wherever necessary. His sympathy for Jansenist ideas merited for us two beautiful letters from Saint Vincent, who had the joy of seeing him return to sounder beliefs. He died July 7, 1667. We still have twenty-three of his conferences to the Daughters of Charity and several letters.

[6]Humbert Dunots, born near Saint-Claude (Jura), was attracted to the Congregation of the Mission by Bernard Codoing, who received him in Annecy in 1642. At that time he was already a priest and forty years of age. He followed Codoing to Rome and remained there until he died in San Salvatore, near Rome, on September 29, 1649, a few days after hearing the confession of a plague-stricken person, from whom he caught the disease. In a letter written after Dunots' death, Martin Le Vasseur, C.M., praises his great piety, his perfect regularity, and his mortification which led him to use instruments of penance, and adds: "It is very difficult for a man to attain greater purity and innocence in this life than did this good servant of God." (Cf. Bibl. mun. de Lyon, Ms. 774, f°219-223.) Humbert Dunots was scrupulous and ill-suited to teaching. We see in this letter that he suffered from the bad influence of Bernard Codoing; fortunately this lasted only a very short time.

[7]Dufestel's name is scratched out in the original. François Dufestel, born in Oisemont (Somme), entered the Congregation of the Mission in 1633, and was ordained a priest in

opposition to the Rules and regulations of the Company, which he also communicated to others, going so far as to threaten to overthrow it after I am gone and, in fact, he was laying the foundations for this. For rather a long time he had promised me repeatedly that he would set himself straight but instead he was doing just the opposite. He has had the deanery of Lillers in Artois given to him. It is a conquered town.[8] He is satisfied and the Company is at peace.

Monsieur Codoing[9] is still going along as usual. I really fear what you and Monsieur Martin[10] have told me about him, although he seems to be coming around. We shall follow the advice of both of you regarding his place of residence and his duty.[11] He had already done so much harm to M. Dunots[12] that the latter suggested to him that they both go off to Geneva.

But *Mon Dieu!* Monsieur, what is this you tell me about the

September 1636. He was Superior in Troyes (1638-1642), Annecy (1642), Cahors (1643-1644), and Marseilles (1644-1645). He left the Congregation in 1646 to become Dean of Saint-Omer de Lillers (Pas-de-Calais).

[8]Taken from the Spanish.

[9]Codoing's name can barely be deciphered because it has been crossed out.

[10]Jean Martin, born in Paris on May 10, 1620, entered the Congregation of the Mission on October 9, 1638. He was ordained in Rome on April 25, 1645, and that same year was sent to Genoa to found a new house. Saint Vincent probably had no Missionary more gifted in drawing crowds and converting souls. In 1654 Jean Martin was recalled to France and placed in Sedan as Superior and Pastor; then he was sent to Turin in 1655 to direct a new establishment founded by the pious Marchese de Pianezza, Prime Minister of State. There, as in Genoa and Sedan, the zealous Missionary knew how to soften the most hardened hearts. He was given the name "Apostle of Piedmont" and his co-Missionaries were called *Padri santi* (holy Fathers). In 1665 René Alméras asked him to head the house in Rome. This was a painful sacrifice for Jean Martin but he resigned himself to it. He was sent to Genoa (1670), Turin (1674), Rome (1677), Perugia (1680), and back to Turin in 1681, always as Superior. He died in Rome on February 17, 1694. His obituary, written by one of his contemporaries, is in the Archives of the Mission in Paris. It was published, with some corrections, in vol. I of *Notices,* pp. 260-272.

[11]He was named Director of the Saint-Méen Seminary. On July 14, 1645, Achille de Harlay de Sancy, Bishop of Saint-Malo, gave the Priests of the Mission the permanent direction of the seminary he had just established in Saint-Méen Abbey, near Bourseul (Côtes-du-Nord). He guaranteed them a tenth of the yearly annuity of 500 livres and added to the establishment the revenue of the abbey, on condition, among other things, that there be five Missionaries: three for the seminary and two for the missions, that for two or three years they would teach gratis twelve young seminarians, and that they would give a pension to the monks of the abbey until the last one died. As indicated in no. 832, n. 8, Saint-Méen became a troublesome establishment for the Congregation.

[12]An attempt was made to cross out this name on the original to make it illegible.

horrible wickedness of poor B[rother] P[ascal]![13] The evil spirit had the power to make a priest of the Company say what he says[14] and to make him commit this deception! *Bon Dieu!* of what evil is he not capable or the other party guilty! Please send him back to us as soon and as quietly as you can; in the meantime, make use of someone else while you are waiting for the arrival of the person I hope to send off tomorrow or three days from now. It will not be the one about whom I wrote to you previously[15] because we sent him to Le Mans after you told me you could manage without him.

I see clearly that those gentlemen were right in their conclusions but *cui fini* [16] did you send me the plan for the foundation? Is H[is] E[minence] disposed to make the foundation as soon as possible? There are conditions in this project that could change the order of the Company and perhaps upset it in that place. Please let me know the purpose of this document (I have not been able to figure it out very well from reading your letter), and then I shall tell you my little thoughts on these difficulties.

I am writing to you from Orsigny,[17] where I have been since yesterday. In two hours I shall be returning to Paris; I sent your letter from there to the Duchesse d'Aiguillon,[18] who wanted to see it.

I do not recall the other points in your letter to which I should respond.

---

[13]Jean-Pascal Goret, born in Angers in 1613, was received into the Congregation of the Mission as a coadjutor Brother on November 21, 1641. Saint Vincent sent him to Picardy for the relief of the poor, as he had sent Brother Mathieu Régnard to Lorraine.

[14]The Saint had added the words: "*O Jésus,* Monsieur, what wickedness!" which he later scratched out.

[15]Brother Nicolas or Brother Le Rogueux. There were nine Brothers named Nicolas during this period. (Cf. *Notices,* vol. I, pp. 493-509.) It is not possible to identify to which of the nine Saint Vincent was referring. Brother François Le Rogueux (Loroqueux) was born in Hiesville (Manche), and entered the Congregation of the Mission on August 7, 1644, at the age of sixteen.

[16]*Why, for what purpose.*

[17]Farm in the commune of Saclay (Essonne). Saint Vincent accepted this farm from Jacques Norais, notary and Secretary of the King, by a contract dated December 22, 1644. The farm provided food for the Saint-Lazare house. According to Saint Vincent (cf. vol. IV, no. 1467), the farms which supplied Saint-Lazare did not provide a sixth of the needs of the Motherhouse.

[18]Marie de Vignerod de Pontcourlay was born in 1604, in the Château de Glenay near Bressuire, of René de Vignerod and Françoise de Richelieu, the eldest sister of the great Cardinal.

Our little items of news are that, by the grace of God, the Company is doing rather well everywhere,[19] except for what you tell me about this Brother. In Paris there are still about sixty priests in the Bons-Enfants Seminary,[20] and the minor seminary of the Petit

---

While still very young, she married, in the reception room of Anne of Austria, the nephew of the Duc de Luynes, Antoine de Beauvoir de Grimoard de Roure, chevalier, Seigneur de Combalet, whom she had never seen and did not love. During the two years this union lasted, the couple lived together only six months. The Marquis de Combalet, kept away from home by the necessities of war, died in battle at the siege of Montpellier on September 3, 1622. His wife, widowed at the age of eighteen, left the Court and withdrew to the Carmelite convent in Paris. She was admitted to the novitiate and, after a year of enclosure, received the religious habit from the hands of M. de Bérulle and took her first vows. Richelieu, who loved her dearly, did everything he could to bring her back to the Court. It was at his request that the Pope forbade the young Marquise to remain in the cloister, that Marie de Médicis chose her as lady of the bedchamber on January 1, 1625, and that the King elevated her estate of Aiguillon to a duchy-peerage on January 1, 1638.

The Cardinal had her take up residence in a small mansion on rue de Vaugirard, one of the dependencies of the Petit Luxembourg Palace where he himself lived. The Duchesse d'Aiguillon made noble use of her immense wealth and great influence. She frequented and protected men of letters and took charge of all works of charity. She established the Priests of the Mission in Notre-Dame de La Rose, and in Marseilles where she entrusted them with the direction of a hospital she had built for sick galley slaves. The Richelieu and Rome houses subsisted on her generosity. It was she who had the consulates of Algiers and Tunis given to the Congregation of the Mission. She contributed to the foundation of the General Hospital and of the Society of the Foreign Missions, took under her protection the Daughters of the Cross and the Daughters of Providence, and was a great benefactress of Carmel. She was President of the Confraternity of Charity established at Saint-Sulpice, and replaced Madame de Lamoignon as President of the Ladies of Charity of the Hôtel-Dieu. The Duchesse d'Aiguillon must be placed, along with Saint Louise de Marillac, Madame de Gondi, and Madame Goussault, in the first rank of Saint Vincent's collaborators. No one perhaps gave him more; few were as attached to him. She watched over his health with maternal solicitude. The carriage and horses the Saint used in his old age came from her stables. Saint Vincent's death grieved her deeply. She had a silver-gilt reliquary made in the shape of a heart, surmounted by a flame, to enclose his heart. The Duchess died on April 17, 1675 at the age of seventy-one and was buried in the Carmelite habit. Bishops Bresacier and Fléchier preached her funeral oration. (Cf. Comte de Bonneau-Avenant, *La duchesse d'Aiguillon* [2nd ed., Paris 1882].) Le Long mentions, in his *Bibliothèque historique de la France* (Fontette ed., 5 vols., Paris: Hérissant, 1768-1778), vol. III, no. 30.854, a manuscript collection of her letters, which has since been lost. Any further mention in the text of "the Duchess" refers to the Duchesse d'Aiguillon, unless a footnote indicates otherwise.

[19]First redaction: "everywhere, by the grace of God."

[20]On March 1, 1624 Jean-François de Gondi, Archbishop of Paris, had turned over to Saint Vincent the Collège des Bons-Enfants so that he might have a place to lodge the priests wishing to join him in giving missions in the country. This collège, nearly three centuries old and occupying about sixteen acres, was one of the oldest of the University of France; it was almost abandoned and in a pitiable state of decay. It was not a teaching center but simply a hostel where students were provided with shelter and sleeping quarters. When the Missionaries went to the country, which happened often, they entrusted the keys to a neighbor.

Saint-Lazare[21] has about forty; by the grace of God, it is off to a rather good start. We are being asked to go to Notre-Dame de Plancoët, a well-known shrine recently established in Saint-Malo. Monsieur Nouelly[22] and Brother Barreau[23] have left to assist poor Christian slaves in Algiers, and we are about to send a priest and a Brother to Salé, in the kingdom of Morocco, in Barbary.

That, Monsieur, is about all I can tell you. My poor heart which loves yours more than itself is, with unalterable affection, in the love of Our Lord, Monsieur, your most humble servant.

VINCENT DEPAUL

i. p. de la Mission [24]

---

[21]Petit Saint-Lazare, otherwise known as Saint-Charles Seminary. In 1645 Saint Vincent established it within the enclosure of Saint-Lazare for youths completing their studies in the humanities; not all the students, however, aspired to Holy Orders. Before he died, Cardinal Richelieu endowed twelve students; others paid room and board. The seminary stood on the corner, facing rue du faubourg Saint-Denis, which today, on the side of the uneven numbers, meets Boulevard de la Chapelle.

[22]Boniface Nouelly, born in Collanges (Ain), entered the Congregation of the Mission as a priest on November 22, 1643, at twenty-five years of age. In 1644 he was placed in Marseilles, and in 1646 was sent to direct the new mission in Algiers. After a year of hard and dedicated work, he caught the plague at the bedside of a man stricken with the disease and died on July 22, 1647. (Cf. *Notices*, vol. III, pp. 28-34.)

[23]Jean Barreau was born in the parish of Saint-Jean-en-Grève, Paris, on September 26, 1612. While still a young man, he left the position of Parlementary Lawyer to enter the Cistercian Order. Some time later, he asked Saint Vincent to receive him into his Community, and began his novitiate on May 14, 1645. In 1646 Saint Vincent sent him to Algiers to fill the post of French Consul. There his dedication to the slaves was limitless. The goodness of his heart moved him more than once to commit himself for sums he did not possess or which did not belong to him; for this he was badly treated by local authorities and reproved by Saint Vincent. When his companion, Jacques Le Sage, became gravely ill, Barreau took his vows before him, although he was not yet released from the simple vow of religion that he had taken as a Cistercian. This dispensation was not requested until 1652. Finally, on November 1, 1661, he was able to take his vows validly in the Congregation of the Mission. He was in Paris at the time, summoned by René Alméras, the second Superior General, and had only Minor Orders. He was ordained a priest in 1662 or 1663 and spent the remainder of his life at Saint-Lazare as Procurator. In 1672 he was associated with the Procurator General, Nicolas Talec. On May 24, 1675, during a serious illness, he made his will, to which he added a codicil on April 7, 1679. (Cf. Arch. Nat. M 213, N°8.)

[24]Saint Vincent subscribed the initials i.p.d.l.M. (*indigne prêtre de la Mission*) to his signature. It has been traditional in the Congregation of the Mission to append to one's name the Latin of this phrase of Saint Vincent, *indignus sacerdos Congregationis Missionis*, or the initials, *i.s.C.M.* The editors have adopted this traditional practice and have substituted the initials of the Latin phrase for the French used by Saint Vincent.

I am writing M. Dehorgny to drop everything and to send you someone who knows how to conduct a seminary. Please send Brother P[ascal] back to us as soon as you get this letter. We shall have our good Brother[25] leave within three days.

We sent you a long time ago, by way of Marseilles, scissors, penknives, booklets, and devotional leaflets. I think M. Chrétien[26] is delaying sending them on to you, awaiting the person who is supposed to go and visit you. If you need them in a hurry, write to him.

Addressed: Monsieur Blatiron, Priest of the Mission, in Genoa

830. - TO SAINT LOUISE DE MARILLAC[1]

Paris, August 4, 1646

Mademoiselle,

A week and a half have gone by since your departure, and we have heard nothing from you. Everyone here wants some news and I do not know what to say to those who are asking me for it. I myself,

---

[25]Sébastien Nodo, a coadjutor Brother, born around 1603 in the diocese of Rouen. He was received into the Congregation of the Mission in 1633.

[26]Jean Chrétien, born on August 6, 1606 in Oncourt (Vosges), was ordained a priest on April 5, 1631, and received into the Congregation of the Mission on November 26, 1640. He was Superior in Marseilles (1645-1653), sub-Assistant at the Motherhouse (1654), and Superior in La Rose (1655-1662). On November 26, 1667 he was a member of the house in Troyes.

Letter 830. - Saint Paul manuscript, p. 64. Letter 831 informs us that this letter was in Brother Ducournau's handwriting.

[1]Saint Louise de Marillac was born in Paris on August 12, 1591. Her father was Louis de Marillac, brother of the devout Michel de Marillac, Keeper of the Seals (1616-1630), and of Maréchal de Marillac, renowned for his misfortunes and tragic death. She married Antoine Le Gras, secretary of Queen Marie de Médicis, on February 5, 1613, and they had one son, Michel. Antoine Le Gras died on December 21, 1625. The devout widow had implicit confidence in her spiritual director, Vincent de Paul, who employed her in his charitable works, eventually making her his collaborator in the creation and organization of the Confraternities of Charity. The life of Louise de Marillac, whom the Church beatified on May 9, 1920, had been written by Gobillon (1676), the Comtesse de Richemont (1883), Comte de Lambel (n.d.), Monsignor Baunard (1898), and Emmanuel de Broglie (1911). Her letters and other writings were copied and published in

more than all the others, am worried and can only turn to you to find out something. I am so afraid that the intense heat and the discomforts of the coach may have exhausted or at least greatly weakened you that I await the account of your journey with great impatience. I am determined to thank Our Lord fervently if you are still in the same state of health as when you left.[2]

831. - *SAINT LOUISE TO SAINT VINCENT*

Monsieur,

Yesterday I received a letter which seemed to me somehow to come from your charity but, since I did not see any trace of your handwriting in it, I was rather worried, for fear that you were very sick. But I am somewhat relieved by what good Brother Ducournau [1] so kindly told me. In the name

---

part in the work entitled: *Louise de Marillac, veuve de M. Le Gras. Sa vie, ses vertus, son esprit* (4 vols., Bruges, 1886). Saint Louise was canonized on March 11, 1934, and on February 10, 1960, was named the patroness of all who devote themselves to Christian social work. Therefore, in this English edition of the letters of Saint Vincent, "Saint" has been added to her name in titles of letters and in the footnotes. To the above bibliography should be added some of her more recent biographers: Monsignor Jean Calvet, *Louise de Marillac, a Portrait,* translated by G.F. Pullen (1959); Joseph I. Dirvin, *Louise de Marillac* (1970); the compilation by Sister Anne Regnault, D.C., editor: *Louise de Marillac, ses écrits* (1961), of which the section containing the letters was translated by Sister Helen Marie Law, D.C.: *Letters of St. Louise de Marillac* (1972); and the revised edition of this latter work entitled: *Sainte Louise de Marillac. Ecrits spirituels* (1983), ed. Sister Elisabeth Charpy, D.C., trans. Sister Louise Sullivan, D.C., *Spiritual Writings of Louise de Marillac, Correspondence and Thoughts* (New City Press, 1991).

[2]Saint Louise left Paris on July 26, in the company of Sister Elisabeth Turgis who had been assigned to Richelieu, Sister Françoise Noret, Sister Perrette from Sedan, who was going to the Angers hospital, and the Sisters who were to form the little Community of Nantes: Elisabeth Martin, Claude, Marguerite Noret, Catherine Bagard, and Antoinette from Montreuil. The little group arrived in Orléans the next evening, passed the morning of the twenty-eighth there, then left for Meung-sur-Loire, where they spent the night. They made additional stops in Cour-sur-Loire and Mont-Louis. At the port of Ablevoie, Sister Elisabeth Turgis left them to go to Richelieu. They stopped for six or seven hours in Tours before going on to Saumur, and made a pilgrimage to Notre-Dame des Ardilliers. The travelers spent the next night in Ponts-de-Cé at the home of a surgeon's wife. At dawn they took the boat which landed them on August 3 in Angers, where they remained for three days with the Sisters of the hospital. They went by boat from Angers to Nantes, making three brief stops along the way, completing their journey on Wednesday. (Cf. *Ecrits spirituels,* L. 159, pp. 171-178).

Letter 831. - Archives of the Motherhouse of the Daughters of Charity, 140, rue du Bac, Paris, original autograph letter.

[1]Bertrand Ducournau, born in 1614 in Arnou (Landes), was received into the Congregation

of God, Monsieur, you know that you must take a little time to recover your health and to try to keep well for the service of God.

I am quite surprised that you did not receive the letter I wrote to your charity in Orléans, where we spent only Saturday morning so we could reach our destination while our good God still gave me the strength. O Most Honored Father, if your charity were aware of the assistance of His divine guidance, you would be grateful for it to make up for my infidelities and ingratitude. I most humbly beg this of you through the holy love of God.

I do not know what will become of this establishment.[2] As yet, I have not perceived any difficulties, other than a few murmurs among the people, but rather so much praise from everyone that it is unbelievable. We stayed only three days in Angers, where I again had the honor of writing to you, and four or five hours in Tours, but we did not arrive in Nantes until August 8, since we had to stay so long on the water because it is unusually low.

Although we did all we could so that no one would know the day of our arrival, good Mademoiselle La Carisière had given orders for someone to meet us at the boat and to take us, after a visit to the Blessed Sacrament, to Mademoiselle des Rochers' home. She most humbly sends her regards to you and expressed a little regret at not receiving any reply to the two letters she respectfully wrote you after the death of her good husband, who was much loved and esteemed in this town.

I had informed you of some difficulty in asking for Monsieur des Jonchères to be Director of our Sisters, but if I have no further instructions from your charity other than what you gave us, I see no likelihood of making a choice except on your advice and to propose to him that, in his charity, he accept.[3] He is not what people had told me and I do not see how his sister

---

of the Mission on July 28, 1644 as a coadjutor Brother, and took his vows on October 9, 1646. Since he had fine penmanship and common sense, and had learned to be shrewd, frank, and reliable in business affairs, from the various positions he had occupied in the world, Saint Vincent made him his secretary in 1645. The first letter written by Brother Ducournau was that of May 3, 1645. (Cf. vol. II, no. 749.) By his devotion, tact, and love of work, this good Brother rendered inestimable services to Saint Vincent and his Congregation. It can be said that, by his preparation of materials and his personal notes, he contributed more than Abelly himself to the first biography of Saint Vincent. After the death of the Saint, Brother Ducournau remained as secretary to the Superiors General René Alméras and Edme Jolly, and was archivist of Saint-Lazare. He died in Paris on January 3, 1677. His assistant in the secretariat, Brother Chollier, has written his life, which is found in *Notices,* vol. I, p. 377ff.

[2]The establishment in Nantes.

[3]At that time there was at the hospital one of its former chaplains, whom M. des Jonchères, the ordinary confessor of the Visitation nuns, wished to replace. Until that time, Saint Louise had not been much in favor of this choice, for reasons she makes known here, and also because she was afraid of displeasing the Visitandines.

could spoil anything because she is very zealous and sensible and does good not only in this hospital but in all the charitable and needy houses.

Would to God, Most Honored Father, that I had sufficient strength and love to recognize Divine Providence's loving guidance of us. Oh! how loudly would I sing its praises! I must keep this short and be content with inviting the Celestial Court to render to God the glory it can for this, and you, our Most Honored Father, to whom our good God makes known His designs upon us, to supply for our deficiencies.

This Holy Providence, which knows my attachment to my own plans, allowed us to find that the Sister we wanted to bring here had a bad knee. So we had to take another, whom it was necessary to change. Oh! let us bless God forever for His mercies; I bless Him most especially for the grace of being, Monsieur, your most obedient daughter and very grateful servant.

L. DE MARILLAC

I think that a two-week stay here will really improve matters for us.

August 11 [1646] [4]

Addressed: *Monsieur Vincent*

832. - TO ANTOINE PORTAIL,[1] IN RICHELIEU

Paris, August 12, 1646

Monsieur,

The grace of Our Lord be with you forever!
I am writing to you rather hurriedly to tell you that I praise God for your leadership in your work and ask Him to bless it more and more in Richelieu and elsewhere.

---

[4]Year added on the back of the original by Brother Ducournau.

Letter 832. - Archives of the Mission, 95 rue de Sèvres, Paris, original autograph letter.
[1]Antoine Portail, born in Beaucaire (Gard) on November 22, 1590, came to Paris to study at the Sorbonne. He made the acquaintance of Saint Vincent there around 1612 and became devoted to him. From the time of his ordination (1622) to that of his death (1660), he was the Saint's

— 11 —

For a few days now I have been wondering if I should ask you to come back to work on our Rules and to revise, if need be, what you told me should be changed. Because I presume that you will remember it, I ask you to let me know, since I could not give it the requisite attention at the time you informed me about it, and now I would find it difficult to make the change myself. This is because the Coadjutor[2] is going to work on it. He now has the authority to approve our Rules, being the Archbishop's Vicar during his absence. So, let me know again what you think should be changed in our Rules and in those of the Daughters of Charity.

You will find plenty to do in Saintes and in La Rose. We have sent M. Dufour[3] to the former place and have given him M. des

---

auxiliary. Vincent employed him first in the service of the galley slaves, received him as the first member of his new Congregation, initiated him into the ministry of the missions and the work of the ordinands, chose him as First Assistant in 1642, and entrusted to him the direction of the Daughters of Charity. Portail left Paris in 1646 to make visitations in the houses of the Congregation. He began in the West of France, then went south, crossed into Italy, and did not return to Saint-Lazare until September 1649. Except for a fairly long absence in 1655, he hardly ever left the Motherhouse again. He died on February 14, 1660, after an illness of nine days. (Cf. *Notices*, vol. I, pp. 1-94.)

[2]Jean-François-Paul de Gondi, Abbé de Buzay and the future Cardinal de Retz, was the son of Philippe-Emmanuel de Gondi, General of the Galleys, and Françoise-Marguerite de Silly. On June 13, 1643, he was named Coadjutor to his uncle, Jean-François de Gondi, Archbishop of Paris, and was consecrated on January 31, 1644. Although he played an active role in the troubles of the Fronde, the Queen, no doubt to win him over, obtained the Cardinal's hat for him on February 19, 1652. Discontented with his influence and plots, Mazarin had him imprisoned at Vincennes. Becoming Archbishop upon the death of his uncle (1654), and consequently more dangerous to the Prime Minister, Cardinal de Retz was transferred to the château de Nantes, from which he escaped and went into Spain, then on to Italy. In Rome the Priests of the Mission gave him hospitality in their house, upon the order of the Sovereign Pontiff. Because of this, Mazarin very nearly let all the force of his anger fall upon Saint Vincent and his Congregation. After the accession of Pope Alexander VII, who was less benevolent to him than Innocent X, Cardinal de Retz left Rome and undertook a long journey to Franche-Comté, Germany, Belgium, and Holland. He returned to France in 1662, renounced the archbishopric of Paris, and received in exchange Saint-Denis Abbey. Age and trials had made him wiser; during the last four years of his life, some persons even considered him pious. In this peaceful, studious, simple-mannered man, concerned with paying off his numerous creditors, no one would have recognized the ambitious, flighty, and restless Prelate who had stirred up Paris and made the powerful Mazarin tremble. Cardinal de Retz died on August 24, 1679.

[3]Claude Dufour, born in 1618 in Allanche (Cantal), entered the Congregation of the Mission on May 4, 1644, shortly after his ordination to the priesthood. He was first sent to Montmirail (1644), then put in charge of the seminary in Saintes (1646-1648). He was very virtuous but of a rigid and unobliging kind of virtue. In his eyes the life of a Missionary was too soft. He persuaded

Noyelles,[4] who was offended by M. Dufour's spirit to a degree that is quite impressive. Good M. Le Soudier[5] is in agreement with him and has written to me in a way that seems out of sorts. So, it would seem advisable for you to take someone in Richelieu, if possible, in place of M. des Noyelles, whom you will send to them. The man must know how to preach because he will have to conduct the mission in Saintes, while M. Dufour directs the Seminary. M. Bourdet[6] would get along well with M. des Noyelles but I do not see anyone you could take away from him. I make no mention of Saint-Méen because the reformed Benedictines have expelled them from there by a decree of the Parlement.[7] Efforts are being made to reinstate them; there is a Council decree to that effect.[8]

As for M. Le Soudier, it will be easy for you to win him over.

---

himself that the life of a Carthusian was more suited to his love for prayer and mortification. Saint Vincent was of an entirely different opinion, so Claude Dufour, always docile, abandoned his plans. To free him from temptations of this kind, the Saint put his name on the list of priests to be sent to Madagascar. While awaiting the day of departure, the Saint assigned him first to Sedan, then to Paris, entrusting him with the Internal Seminary there during the absence of M. Alméras, and finally to La Rose as Superior (1654-1655). Sea voyages were long in those days; M. Dufour left Nantes in 1655 and arrived in Madagascar in August of the following year. However, he died on August 18, 1656, just a few days after he landed. (Cf. *Notices*, vol. III, pp. 14-23.)

[4]Philippe des Noyelles, born in Arras (Pas-de-Calais), entered the Congregation of the Mission on January 18, 1642, at thirty-three years of age, and took his vows on June 2, 1646.

[5]Samson Le Soudier was born in 1609 in Curson (Calvados), entered the Congregation of the Mission on October 9, 1638, and took his vows in Richelieu on June 14, 1642. He was assigned to Luçon, and later to Saintes where he was in 1646.

[6]Jean Bourdet was born in Saint-Babel (Puy-de-Dôme) on May 14, 1614, entered the Congregation of the Mission at the end of 1636, was ordained a priest in 1640, and took his vows in 1643. He was Superior in Troyes (1642-1644) and in Saint-Méen (1645-1646).

[7]*Parlement* refers to the French judicial system. At the time of Saint Vincent, France had eight Parlements, each with its own legal jurisdiction, chief of which was the Parlement of Paris. They registered or gave sanction to the King's edicts, ordinances, and declarations, and supervised their implementation.

[8]The Benedictines of Saint-Maur had looked askance on the transformation of Saint-Méen Abbey into a seminary. They protested before the Parlement of Brittany, to which the royal letters patent of secularization had been addressed, as was customary, so that they could be verified and registered. When the Bishop of Saint-Malo became aware of the opposition, he feared for his plans and, instead of presenting the letters, turned from the direction of the court and requested that other letters be sent for registration and execution to the Great Council and not to the Parlement. In the meantime, the new requests required time, and the Parlement of Brittany, urged on by the Benedictines of Saint-Mélaine, ordered the Bishop to produce the letters he stated he had received from the King. Confronted with evasive answers time and time again, Parlement forbade him, on June 1, 1646, to change anything within the abbey, and sentenced him to pay

Regarding La Rose, God has taken good M. Jegat,[9] who was a pearl in the Company. He drowned in the Lot River which runs nearby, where he had gone to bathe, on his doctor's orders. Please have the customary prayers said and the usual conferences. Of the seven who should be there, only four Missionaries are left. As soon as possible, we shall send three men to fill the vacancies. If we can, we will send you M. Michel,[10] a parish priest from Normandy. He

---

forty livres in expenses. In addition, the King's attorney was ordered to ask the Superior General of the Congregation of Saint-Maur to send as many monks as were necessary to "carry out the functions and especially the divine service, in line with the devout intentions of the founders." On June 22, after an investigation *de commodo et incommodo* [concerning its advisability], the Great Council handed down its decision in favor of the Bishop. This meant open battle between the two authorities. On July 17, Parlement confirmed its decree of June 1, forbade anyone to put into effect that of the Great Council, under pain of a fine of three thousand livres, and issued an order to the Priests of the Mission to leave the abbey. At dawn on July 23, M. de Montbourcher, Counselor in the Parlement and Commissioner; M. Monneraye, substitute for the Attorney General; an assistant Councillor, a process-server of the court, the Visitor of the Reformed Benedictines, the Priors of Mont-Saint-Michel and Saint-Mélaine, the new Prior of Saint-Méen, five other Benedictine priests, and a lay Brother, presented themselves at the gate of the monastery. All exits were barricaded so thoroughly, wrote Dom Germain Morel, "that it was difficult to imagine that the barricades of Paris, so famous in history, could have been better built." The besieged soon had to give in and take refuge in the guest house of the abbey. The contending parties lived side by side until the beginning of August. Passions were at a boiling point and the slightest provocation resulted in a quarrel. Unbeknown to the directors, the seminarians and the servants took malicious pleasure in exasperating the monks. One day they filled the only well of the enclosure with all kinds of garbage. The monks had had enough and complained to the Parlement. On August 7, 1646 a decree was issued in which the court ordered that humble remonstrances be addressed to the King about the decision of the Great Council, and that the Priests of the Mission, the seminarians, and their partisans should leave the abbey and give back to the Benedictines the holy relics, furniture, and vestments, under pain of imprisonment. The seminary directors and their students obeyed. Such was the situation when Saint Vincent wrote the present letter.

The above information has been drawn from the manuscript of Dom Germain Morel, a Benedictine of the Congregation of Saint-Maur and Prior of Saint-Mélaine in Rennes, one of the main opponents to the entrance of the Priests of the Mission into Saint-Méen Abbey (cf. Bibl. Nat., fr. 19831). M. Ropartz summarized Morel's manuscript in a booklet entitled: *Dom Germain Morel, Histoire de la sécularisation de l'abbaye de Saint-Méen.* If the comments of Dom Morel must be read with a certain circumspection, we can trust the many documents which he has preserved for us in his manuscript.

[9]Bertrand Jegat, born in Vannes (Brittany) in 1610, was ordained a priest on September 20, 1636, and was received into the Congregation of the Mission on October 9, 1638. He died in La Rose in 1646.

[10]Guillaume Michel, born in Esteville (Seine-Maritime), left his parish of Saint-Valery to enter the Congregation of the Mission on June 19, 1646, at thirty-nine years of age. He left the

is a very wise man but has been in the seminary only three or four months.

I ask Our Lord to bless you in that place and everywhere else as well. Things must be hastened a little; M. Dehorgny is in a hurry about Rome.

I cannot write personally to M. Alméras.[11] I cordially greet him and the entire house with the tenderness known to Our Lord. Prostrate in spirit at their feet and yours, I am, in the love of Our Lord, Monsieur, your most humble and obedient servant.

VINCENT DEPAUL
i.s.C.M.

Addressed: Monsieur Portail, Priest of the Mission, in Richelieu

---

Congregation of his own accord before taking vows but later returned. In 1657 he was a member of the house in Sedan, and was in Fontainebleau in 1666.

[11]René Alméras, nephew of Madame Goussault (late President of the Ladies of Charity of the Hôtel-Dieu), was born in Paris on February 5, 1613. A Councillor in the Great Council at the age of twenty-four, he left everything—family, position and hopes—in spite of the opposition of his father (who was to follow him later), to enter the Congregation of the Mission, where he was received on December 24, 1637. He was ordained a priest at Easter in 1639.

Saint Vincent entrusted to him important positions, such as Director of the seminary and Assistant of the Motherhouse. He appointed him to his council and often relied on his prudence to deal with lay persons in delicate matters; he also gave him charge of the retreatants. So much work ruined Alméras' health. The Holy Founder, convinced by personal experience that a change of air could improve one's health, sent him in 1646 to visit several houses in France and Italy. When he reached Rome, Alméras was notified that he had been appointed Superior of the house. He stayed there until 1651. On his return to France he took over the direction of Saint-Charles Seminary. In 1654 we find him engaged in distributing relief to the poor of Picardy and Champagne. He again made visitations of some of the houses of the Congregation and once again became Assistant of the Motherhouse, in which position he remained until the death of Saint Vincent. He was also Visitor of the Province of Poitou. He was in Richelieu when the Saint, realizing that his own death was near, begged him to return to Paris immediately. Alméras was ill, but he came, carried on a stretcher, and had the consolation of receiving a last blessing from the Saint. Appointed Vicar-General by Saint Vincent, then elected Superior General by the Assembly of 1661, he governed wisely the Congregation of the Mission and the Company of the Daughters of Charity, until the day of his death on September 2, 1672.

833. - TO SAINT LOUISE, IN NANTES

Paris, Eve of the Assumption[1] [1646][2]

Mademoiselle,

The grace of Our Lord be with you forever!
I have not yet received any letters from you and cannot believe
you have not sent me any.[3] Just imagine how worried we would be
if we did not have news of you from elsewhere. The former Mother
Superior of the Visitation Monastery in Orléans,[4] who passed
through here on her way to Dieppe, assured us that she had seen
you, and Abbé de Vaux[5] wrote from Angers that you had been there
and had left in good health. That has consoled us somewhat and

---

Letter 833. - Archives of the Motherhouse of the Daughters of Charity, original signed letter.
The postscript is written in the Saint's hand.
[1]August 14.
[2]The year of Saint Louise's journey to Nantes. All the other details confirm this date.
[3]Saint Louise wrote to Saint Vincent on August 11 (cf. *Ecrits spirituels*, L. 147, p. 159) that
she had recently written him from Angers and also when she was in Orléans the previous week
(cf. no. 831).
[4]Marie-Renée Rousseau was Superioress of the Orléans monastery (May 24, 1640-May 21,
1643). Mother Claude-Espérance succeeded her for two straight terms.
[5]Guy Lasnier, Abbé de Vaux, who died on April 21, 1681, was one of the most notable priests
from Anjou in the seventeenth century. For a long time his only ambition was to satisfy his vanity
and his passion for hunting and other worldly amusements. In February 1627 he was appointed
to Saint-Etienne-de-Vaux Abbey in Saintonge, and was named Vicar-General of Angers the
following year, then Canon of Notre-Dame in Paris. Despite the obligations imposed on him by
these dignities, he continued to lead a very worldly life. In 1632 he, like many others, was anxious
to satisfy his curiosity as to what was going on in the Ursuline convent in Loudun. (It was rumored
that some of the nuns were possessed by devils; Richelieu ordered the exorcism of the nuns and
the execution of the Pastor, Urbain Grandier, for the practice of witchcraft.) The Abbé had cause
to rue the day. It is alleged that, to his great confusion, one of the nuns, penetrating into his interior
life, revealed faults he had never mentioned to anyone. From then on he was a new man. In 1635
he made a retreat at Saint-Lazare where he met Saint Vincent, with whom he remained in contact.
He also had dealings with Saint Jane Frances de Chantal, Jean-Jacques Olier, Father Surin, and
Baron de Renty. In his native town of Angers, he established a Visitation convent, richly endowed
the seminary, and founded the ecclesiastical conferences in his diocese. The Daughters of Charity
of the Angers hospital had no protector more dedicated nor counselor more enlightened than
Abbé de Vaux. He gave hospitality to Saint Vincent, Saint Louise and Jean-Jacques Olier.
We have only one of the letters Saint Vincent wrote to him (cf. vol. I, no. 416), but there are
about one hundred addressed to him by Saint Louise. (Cf. François Chamard, *Les vies des saints
personnages d'Anjou* [3 vols., Paris: Lecoffre, 1863], pp. 279-303.)

leads us to hope that you are now in Nantes.⁶ God grant that it is
with the strength needed to work for this establishment. I beg His
Divine Mercy to give you for this purpose an ample share of His
Spirit, so that you can communicate it to your dear daughters and
together with them diffuse in souls the fragrance of holy devotion!

I have nothing particular to say to you on what you will have to
do with these gentlemen,⁷ trusting that O[ur] L[ord] will give you
sufficient light and counsel. He alone knows how ardently I recommend to Him every day your soul and your journey, and what great
blessings I ask Him for you and your little troop, whom I greet in
spirit with all possible tenderness.

I have been able to see your assistants here⁸ only one time. I am
supposed to see them today, please God. Everything is going rather
well, except for a little restlessness apparent in a few Sisters, but
your presence will set everything right again, as will perhaps the
conference I plan to give them next week.⁹

Your son¹⁰ is not feeling well and is in bed at his doctor's¹¹ home.
I offered him our house and anything we could do to make him feel
better, or two Sisters to nurse him, in the event that he wanted to
stay where he is. He preferred the help of the Sisters, who have been
with him for several days now. Monsieur Brin¹² has just been to see

---

⁶She had arrived there August 8.

⁷Administrators of the hospital.

⁸They were Jeanne Lepeintre, to whom Saint Louise had delegated her authority, Julienne
Loret, "a majestic soul in a small body," and Elisabeth Hellot, the very dedicated and intelligent
secretary of the Foundress.

⁹This conference, dealing with mutual respect and cordiality, is still extant (cf. vol. IX, no. 27,
[August 19, 1646]).

¹⁰Saint Louise's son, Michel Le Gras, was born October 19, 1613. The instability of his
character and his vacillation about a vocation to the priesthood were a cause of great anxiety to
his mother. Ultimately he abandoned the soutane at the age of twenty-seven (1640). After ten
years of further wavering, he married Demoiselle Gabrielle Le Clerc on January 18, 1650 in the
Church of Saint-Sauveur. Saint Vincent witnessed the marriage contract.

¹¹M. Vacherot. (Cf. *Ecrits spirituels*, L. 155, p. 168.) Vacherot was a skilled physician who
served the Motherhouses of the Priests of the Mission and the Daughters of Charity (1646-1648).
He was very attached to Cardinal de Retz, whom he helped escape from Mazarin and followed
to Rome in 1654. He died in Commercy in May 1664, at the age of sixty-two.

¹²Gerard Brin, born near Cashel (Ireland), entered the Congregation of the Mission on October

him; he assures me that he is better and that there is nothing to fear. That is why I beg you not to worry about this, but rather see to it that I may soon be rid of my own troubles with the Ladies of Charity of the Hôtel-Dieu, especially Madame de Nesmond,[13] who are waging a fierce war against me for having allowed you to go. If you return in good health, as I hope from God's goodness, peace will soon be made. So please take the best possible care of yourself.

Take all the time you need so as not to rush anything or inconvenience yourself regarding your return. Our Lord will be pleased with this, since you will be doing it for love of Him.

It is in this same love, Mademoiselle, that I am truly your most humble and faithful servant.

VINCENT DEPAUL
i.s.C.M.

Since writing this letter, I have received yours from Angers containing two important matters: first, the problem with Sister Perrette,[14] and the other regarding the confessor for your Daughters in Nantes. For the first, we shall have to see if she changes, and do as you say. I am a little perplexed about the second point; however, all things weighed and considered, I think it better to hold to the

---

14, 1639, at the age of twenty-one. He took his vows on November 2, 1642, and was ordained a priest in 1644. Of all the Irishmen whom Saint Vincent received into his Congregation, Brin was perhaps the most accomplished. He was summoned from Le Mans in 1646 and sent to Ireland where, with several other confreres and compatriots, he did boundless good. Driven back to France by persecution, Brin went as a Missioner to Saint Vincent's native region. Some time later he was named Superior in La Rose (1652-1654). He held the same position in Troyes (1657-1658), Meaux (1658-1660), and Toul (1660-1662). He returned to Ireland in 1663 and there resumed his apostolic work with a zeal that age had not slackened. Neither a month in prison, nor illness which brought him twice to the brink of the tomb, was able to deter this heroic Missionary.

[13]Madame de Nesmond, born Anne de Lamoignon, was the wife of Théodore de Nesmond, Presiding Judge of the Parlement of Paris, and sister-in-law of Madame de Lamoignon (Marie de Landes).

[14]Sister Perrette was a source of great anxiety to Saint Louise (cf. *Ecrits spirituels,* L. 178bis. p. 200, and L. 182bis p. 205). In the hope that a change of residence might be beneficial to her, she was assigned to Nantes. In the end, she ran away from Nantes and returned to her family in Sedan.

decision we made here, because this is the beginning and because there is some thought of using him elsewhere after a while. So then, you could take the spiritual Father of the Visitation,[15] unless you think it better to act otherwise, based on the knowledge you have there. That is what I ask you to do.

I have just learned that your son is almost cured, and I am going to send word to your officers to come here immediately after dinner to discuss with them what will have to be done.

Please look after your health and pray to God for the greatest sinner in the world who is y[our] s[ervant].

V. D.

Once again I ask you to follow the inspiration Our Lord will give you concerning the Sisters' confessor.

Addressed: Mademoiselle Le Gras, Superioress of the Daughters of Charity, in care of the Administrators of the Nantes Hospital, in Nantes

834. - JULIEN GUERIN [1] TO SAINT VINCENT

[Tunis,] August 1646

I feel obliged to inform you that, on the feast of Saint Ann, a second Joseph [2] was sacrificed in this town of Tunis for the preservation of his

---

[15]M. des Jonchères.

Letter 834. - Abelly, *op.cit.*, bk.II, chap. I, sect. VII, §8, p. 125.

[1]Julien Guérin, born in Lacelle (Orne), had lived some time in the army before entering the priesthood. The reception of his brother, Jean, into the Congregation of the Mission on November 7, 1639, left vacant the parish of Saint-Manvieu which Julien administered for three months. He resigned it at the age of thirty-five to come to Saint-Lazare, where he was received on January 30, 1640. In 1641 he went to assist the unfortunate population of Lorraine, but his health failed and he was sent to Richelieu, where he took his vows on June 14, 1642. The missions he preached in the diocese of Saintes in 1643-1644 were a great success. Saint Vincent suggested to him in 1645 that he go to establish the Mission in Tunis. The valiant Missionary died in that city on May 13, 1648. His biography has been published in vol. III of *Notices*, pp. 57-82.

[2]Antonin de la Paix. The patriarch Joseph (Gn 39:6-21) had been imprisoned for spurning the

chastity, after resisting for more than a year the violent solicitations of his lewd owner and receiving more than five hundred strokes with a rod because of the false reports this she-wolf was making. In the end he gained the victory by dying gloriously for refusing to offend his God. For three days he was bound by a heavy chain. I went to visit and console him and to exhort him to suffer all the torments in the world rather than act contrary to the fidelity he owed to God. After making his confession and receiving Holy Communion, he said to me: "Monsieur, they can make me suffer all they want; I intend to die a Christian." When they came to take him to his execution, he made his confession once again, and for his consolation God permitted that we be allowed to assist him at his death, something that had never been granted by these inhumane beings. His last words, uttered with his eyes raised to heaven, were: "O my God, I die innocent." He died very courageously without ever showing any sign of impatience in the midst of the cruel torments he was made to undergo. Afterward, we had a very honorable funeral for him.

His wicked and lewd owner was not long in suffering the punishment due to her perfidy because, when the master returned home, he promptly had her strangled as the final measure in giving vent to his anger.

That saintly young man was Portuguese by birth and twenty-two years of age. I invoke his assistance, and since he loved us on earth, I hope he will not love us any less in heaven.[3]

---

advances of the wife of Potiphar, his first master during his captivity in Egypt.

[3]This martyrdom is recounted in greater detail in the obituary of Julien Guérin (cf. *Notices*, vol. III, pp. 67ff).

835. - TO CARDINAL MAZARIN[1]

Paris, August 20, 1646

Your Eminence,

The Bishop of Saintes[2] is going to see [Your Eminence]. He will confirm what I had the h[onor] of writing to Y[our] E[minence] regarding Bordeaux and M[aillezais][3] for La Rochelle, and will tell him that the par[tisans] of the Bishop of Maillezais[4] accept this treaty[5] and will thank Y[our] E[minence] for it, and that the Bishop [of] Maillezais desires that it might please the goodness [of Your Eminence] to lead him to hope for some abbey with [a benefice], to make up for the loss of revenue [he] suffers because of this treaty. [He does this] in such a way, however, that he submits to the will of Y[our] E[minence]. He has done very well in [Maillezais] and intends to do even better in Bordeaux.

Letter 835. - Archives of the Mission, Paris, signed letter. This is a first draft with some additions inserted in the Saint's handwriting.

[1]Jules Mazarin (Giulio Mazarini) was born in Pescina in Abruzzi (Italy) in 1602, studied in Spain as a youth, and served in the Papal army and the Papal diplomatic corps. He met Richelieu for the first time in 1630, and represented the Pope in negotiating the peace of Cherasco with France in 1631. He had hardly begun preparing for the priesthood (he received tonsure in 1632, but never became a priest) when he was assigned to other important diplomatic positions: Vice-Legate of Avignon (1634), then Nuncio in France (1635-1636), in which positions he demonstrated the ability and flexibility of the most subtle statesman. He became a French citizen in 1639, and Richelieu obtained a Cardinal's hat for him in 1641. Before his death (1642), Richelieu recommended Mazarin to Louis XIII. He became the principal minister of Queen Anne of Austria during the regency of Louis XIV (1642-1661) and, until his own death in 1661, was the absolute master of France.

[2]Jacques-Raoul de la Guibourgère, born in 1589, was the widower of Yvonne de Charette and father of several children when he entered the priesthood. In 1631 he became Bishop of Saintes, succeeding his uncle; then he went to the diocese of Maillezais, and finally to La Rochelle, when the See was transferred there. Very few other bishops were so intimately associated with Saint Vincent. He died in 1661.

[3]Today, principal town of a canton in Vendée, in the district of Fontenay.

[4]Henri de Béthune, Bishop of Maillezais.

[5]An important treaty by which the See of Maillezais was transferred to La Rochelle, the Bishop of Maillezais appointed Bishop of Bordeaux, and the Bishop of Saintes named for La Rochelle. It was hoped that a decisive thrust would be effected against Protestantism by erecting a diocese in one of its main bulwarks. (Cf. L. Bertrand, *La vie de Messire Henri de Béthune, archévêque de Bordeaux* [2 vols., Paris, 1902].)

And I, Eminence, continue my [poor] prayers for the preservation of Y[our] E[minence], [for the] welfare of this State and for the sanctification of your dear soul. I am, by the grace [of God], Eminence, your most humble and very obedient servant.

VINCENT DEPAUL

i.s.C.M.

836. - TO SAINT LOUISE

Paris, August 21, 1646

Mademoiselle,

I received the letter you wrote me from Nantes.[1] I praise God for all you tell me, particularly for your good health which I ask His Divine Goodness to preserve, and I ask you, for your part, to do all you can for this purpose.

I am glad you found that the lady you mentioned to me[2] is different from what you had imagined her to be. Since this is the case, you will do well to abide by your first decision regarding the direction of our Sisters, provided however that nothing has occurred to cause you to change your mind.[3]

M. de Vaux has informed me that one of the Sisters in Angers[4] is seriously ill. Perhaps he has also notified you of this, and you have been able to think of someone we could send in her place, if need be.

The Queen has commanded us to send her two Sisters for the Charity in Fontainebleau. We have complied with this and chose

Letter 836. - Saint Paul manuscript, p. 64.

[1]Cf. no. 831.

[2]Mademoiselle des Jonchères.

[3]The first person proposed to direct the Sisters was M. des Jonchères.

[4]Sister Marie-Marthe Trumeau. She recovered, and subsequently served in various houses of the Company: Nantes, where she was Superior; La Fère, and Cahors, in addition to her work in Saint-Paul parish in Paris.

Sister Barbe[5] and another Sister,[6] whom I think we shall have to recall because she is too young.[7]

837. - SAINT LOUISE TO SAINT VINCENT

Nantes, Tuesday, August 22, [1646] [1]

Monsieur,

I think you have received the letter in which I told you I felt Divine Providence wanted us to follow the order your charity had given us about the direction of our Sisters, and the grace His goodness has granted us regarding the difficulties with Sister Perrette about which I had written you. I think our Sisters will have as their ordinary confessor the confessor [2] *of the Visitation nuns, who would like to devote himself as hospital chaplain, in place of the one who has been there for a long time. I greatly fear that those good nuns are going to blame us for their displeasure at this. They do not know about it yet, and I shall do my best to have the honor of seeing them beforehand, lest they reproach me for it, even though I had no part in it.*

I thank you very humbly, Most Honored Father, for your kindness to my son. This gave me great peace of mind. The day I had the honor of receiving your dear letter, I had a very strong desire to offer him to God and to surrender him entirely to Him. That helped me to bear the news your charity gave me.

---

[5]Sister Barbe Angiboust, who was placed in charge of the poor and the sick. She occupies an important place in the first twenty-five years of the history of the Daughters of Charity. Barbe entered the Community on July 1, 1634, at the age of twenty-nine, and was admitted to vows March 25, 1642. She was put in charge of the foundations in Saint-Germain-en-Laye (1638), Richelieu (1638), Saint-Denis (1645), Fontainebleau (1646), Brienne (1652), Bernay (1655), and Châteaudun (1657) where she died on December 27, 1658. In 1641 she was in charge of the Sisters serving the galley slaves. The conference on her virtues held in the Motherhouse on April 27, 1659 is very edifying (cf. vol. X, no. 109).

[6]Sister Anne Scoliège, born in Nantes, entered the Company in 1646. She was principal of the girls' school.

[7]A few months later, three more Sisters were sent to staff the hospital in Fontainebleau.

Letter 837. - Archives of the Motherhouse of the Daughters of Charity, original autograph letter.
[1]Year added on the back of the original by Brother Ducournau.
[2]M. des Jonchères.

*I hope that our business with these gentlemen [3] will be completed
tomorrow. All that will remain is to see that the arrangements I requested
of these gentlemen have been finalized, and a little time to see that each of
our Sisters is exact in the practice of the Rules in her particular duty.
However, the fear of satisfying myself unnecessarily and of remaining ill
causes me to resolve to leave next week to take the Angers coach, if I still
have the good health God is now giving me. Sister Jeanne Lepeintre [4] told
me that a clergyman was at our house to tell me to pass through Le Mans.
I will not do this, at least not make a stop there, unless your charity instructs
me to do so and informs me what I should do there.*

*I am very annoyed that my son did not accept the honor you did him of
taking him into your house. Mon Dieu! I think my prayer for his total
conversion will never be answered! It seems to me that the illness he had
is more dangerous than he realizes. However, I am really afraid he is
turning a deaf ear and is unwilling to allow fear to enter his mind, lest it
urge him to a felicitous change of heart.*

*I know nothing about your health and that causes me a little concern.
For the love of God, Monsieur, please reassure me.*

*I think the Ladies of the Hôtel-Dieu will be quite satisfied with me when
they see that I did not fail to write. I am surprised at so much anxiety, since
I know well that I do not deserve it. God knows this, and why does He permit
it? It is to humble me.*

*I attribute to your charity some of the honors bestowed on us here. In
the name of God, do not mislead anyone about me any longer. People take
me for a great lady. I think there is scarcely a lady of rank who has not
come to see us, and some people have even come from the country just for
that. Oh! how I shall burn [for this] some day, and how greatly embarrassed*

[3] Administrators of the hospital.

[4] Jeanne Lepeintre had been sent to the Daughters of Charity by her mistress, Madame
Goussault. Saint Vincent says elsewhere that she was "a very fine, wise, and gentle girl." Both
he and Saint Louise had great confidence in her because of her intelligence and organizing ability.
She was first sent to the school of the Charity in Saint-Germain-en-Laye (1642). In the spring of
1646, after installing the Sisters in the Le Mans hospital, she returned to Paris, where she was
put in charge of the Motherhouse while Saint Louise was establishing the house in Nantes. Jeanne
then became Superior in Nantes (1646), where great difficulties were being encountered. In 1654
she headed the foundation in Châteaudun, and in 1657 at the Salpetrière (cf. *Ecrits spirituels*, L.
64, p. 77, n. 1). In the manuscript *Recueil de Pièces relatives aux Filles de la Charité* (p. 24), we
read: "During the lifetime of Mademoiselle Le Gras, she seemed to be a hypochondriac.
Moreover, she could not be made to do anything she did not like, nor would she accept opinions
other than her own." She was reprimanded for this fault more than once by Saint Vincent. Her
last years were sad ones spent at the Nom-de-Jésus, where she had to be committed because of
mental illness.

I shall be! May God's Will be done; in it I am, Monsieur, your very obedient servant and unworthy daughter.

L. DE MARILLAC

Addressed: *Monsieur Vincent*

838. - TO SOME RELATIVES[1]

It is not without some special design of Providence that you have been slandered. God has permitted this for His glory and your own good: for His glory, so that you may be conformed to His Son, who was calumniated to the point of being called a seducer, an ambitious man, one possessed by the devil; for your own good, so that you may satisfy God's justice for other sins you may have committed and of which you perhaps are unaware but which God knows.

839. - TO JEAN BARREAU, IN ALGIERS

Paris, Feast of St. Bartholemew,[1] 1646

Blessed be God, Monsieur, for bringing you safely to your consulate in Algiers! I ask His Divine Goodness to bestow His Spirit on you in order to serve Her Majesty and the people there in this same spirit, under the guidance of His Son and of the guardian angel He has given you.

Letter 838. - Abelly, *op. cit.*, bk. III, chap. XIX, p. 291.
    [1]Abelly states that, because of the accusations of despicable calumniators, a celebrated Parlement, probably that of Bordeaux, instituted a suit against some relatives of Saint Vincent. Despite the entreaties of his friends, the Saint refused to intervene, except to moderate the severity of the judges who censured the slanderers, and, by this letter, to persuade his kinsmen to bear courageously this painful trial.

Letter 839. - Archives of the Mission, Paris, original autograph letter.
    [1]August 24.

I cannot express to you the consolation my soul experienced on receiving your letter. Oh! how fervently I ask God to bless your stay in that place and all you will do there, as he has blessed your arrival!

I am writing to M. Nouelly about what is being done for those poor ransomed persons and the captives, which is nothing as yet.

Your good aunt came to see us to get some news of you. She was delighted with what I told her of your arrival, as was I with the goodness I saw in that dear soul. She recommends herself to your prayers and I, Monsieur, recommend my soul to you that God may be pleased to make it a sharer in the good you are doing there. I am waiting faithfully for news about this. In the meantime, I ask Our Lord to bless and sanctify your own dear soul more and more.

We have nothing worth writing to you at the present, except the blessing Our Lord has been pleased to give to the humble works of the Little Company. A mission that lasted three or four months has just been given by M. Gallais.[2] I cannot express to you the extraordinary blessings Our Lord bestowed on it and on the one in Genoa as well.

His Divine Goodness, which fortifies and humbles, has subjected us to suffering and shame because of the persecution we are undergoing in the Saint-Méen foundation, or rather the Bishop of Saint-Malo,[3] who established us there. Blessed be His Divine Goodness who arranges things in this way!

I am, in His love, your most humble servant.

VINCENT DEPAUL
i.s.C.M.

Addressed: Monsieur Barreau, Consul of Algiers, in Algiers

---

[2]Guillaume Gallais, a very talented Missioner, was born in Plouguenast (Côtes-du-Nord), was received into the Congregation of the Mission on April 7, 1639, at the age of twenty-four, was ordained a priest in 1641, and took his vows in 1645. He was Superior in Sedan (1643-1644), Crécy (1644-1645), and Le Mans (1645-1647).

[3]Achille de Harlay de Sancy was born in Paris in 1581, entered the Oratory in 1620, and in 1631 was named Bishop of Saint-Malo where he died on September 20, 1646.

840. - TO ETIENNE BLATIRON, SUPERIOR, IN GENOA

Paris, Feast of St. Bartholemew,[1] 1646

Monsieur,

Only God alone could express to you the consolation you and M. Martin give me in all you are doing. O Monsieur, how gladly I am going to say Holy Mass that His Divine Goodness may sanctify your dear souls more and more! I have just written to M. Dehorgny what I just told you, asking him to send you the man he has designated for you,[2] if he has not already done so.

Good M. Jegat, whom M. Martin knew, has died in La Rose. I recommend him to your prayers.

Our foundation[3] in Saint-Méen is undergoing persecution from the reformed monks.[4] They want to expel us from an abbey, a source of revenue for the monks, which the Bishop gave to the Company for its seminary, with the permission of the King and his Great Council. Help us to honor in this the expulsion of Our Lord from certain provinces and the acts of virtue He practiced. Please pray for these Fathers, whom I cherish more than myself and whom I have tried to serve at every opportunity, as our own Little Company.

At the same time, Our Lord, who fortifies and humbles, has consoled us by the marvelous and almost miraculous blessings He bestowed on a mission, lasting four months, that M. Gallais has just given in the same place, deep in the heart of Maine. I am sending the letter about it to M. Guérin in Tunis.

The things you requested were sent to you quite a long time ago. I think you will have received them and that the good Brother[5] we sent you will be with you as soon as this letter.

Letter 840. - Archives of the Mission, Paris, original autograph letter.
[1]August 24.
[2]François Richard, born in Metz on February 3, 1622, was admitted to the Congregation of the Mission on September 24, 1641, took his vows in 1643, and was ordained a priest in Rome on March 31, 1646.
[3]The Saint had first written "our house."
[4]The Saint had added, "Benedictine," then he scratched out these words.
[5]Sébastien Nodo or Sébastien Drugeon. The latter was born in Brienon-sur-Armançon

I think it is better for you to send Brother Pascal[6] back to us and to hire instead some young boy to serve you, while waiting for us to send you someone else.

I warmly embrace good M. Martin and you, Monsieur, whom I cherish more than myself. I am, Monsieur, your most humble servant.

VINCENT DEPAUL

i.s.C.M.

Keep Brother Pascal as long as you [need him].[7]

841. - TO SAINT LOUISE

Paris, Feast of St. Louis,[1] 1646

Mademoiselle,

M. des Jonchères wrote that he accedes to the request you made him about the direction of our dear Sisters. It is impossible for me to write to him; the mail is just going out. Please assure him of my devotedness.

You will find the number of your Sisters increased by three, two of whom seem very good to me. I am not so sure about the third. *Mais quoi!* she came from a place one hundred leagues[2] away. I told all of them we would try them out. They are from Poitou.

Your son was here yesterday. He is completely cured. I did not see him because I did not get down in time.

But when are you coming, Mademoiselle?

(Yonne), entered the Congregation of the Mission at Saint-Lazare on November 1, 1645, and took his vows in November 1648.

[6]Jean-Pascal Goret.

[7]These or similar words are missing from the original because the edges of the paper were cut carelessly.

Letter 841. - Archives of the Mission, Paris, copy made from the original letter owned by M. Butel, a lawyer in Pau (14 rue Marca).

[1]August 25.

[2]One league equals about two and one half miles or four kilometers. Therefore, these three aspirants came some 250 miles to present themselves to Saint Louise.

Enclosed is a summary of the conference of our dear Sisters, written out by dear Sister Hellot.[3] I have just read part of it and must confess that I shed a few tears in two or three places. If you are not coming soon, send it back to us after you have read it.

We await you with God knows what affection. I am, in His love. . . .

842. - TO GILBERT CUISSOT[1]

Paris, Feast of St. Louis,[2] 1646

Monsieur,

The grace of Our Lord be with you forever!

I most humbly ask your pardon, prostrate in spirit at your feet, for not having replied sooner to the question about which you wrote me on the first of this month.

M. Vasse's affair involves an indemnity he has the right to take from Coëffort[3] when the Superior is changed. We have made

---

[3]Sister Elisabeth Hellot, a native of Paris, entered the Daughters of Charity in 1645. She was secretary to Saint Louise until her death in 1651 and used to draft the letters of the Foundress. During the conferences of Saint Vincent, she took notes which she immediately transcribed and verified.

Letter 842. - Archives of the Mission, Paris, original autograph letter.

[1]Gilbert Cuissot, born November 5, 1607, had been a priest for six years when he entered the Congregation of the Mission on May 14, 1637. After directing the Luçon house, he was appointed Superior in La Rose (1640-1644), then at the Collège des Bons-Enfants (1644-1646), where he took his vows November 11, 1644. We find him next at the Le Mans Seminary (1646), and at Saint-Lazare (1646-1647). He was Director of the Cahors Seminary (1647-1662), and was in charge of the Richelieu house (1662-1666). He declared in writing that, at the time of the election of Saint Vincent's successor, he was hesitant about voting for René Alméras, who was in poor health. The Saint, however, appeared to him and determined his choice. He also declared that in 1662, while exorcising a possessed woman, he drew from the demon precious avowals concerning the Founder's holiness and the reward reserved by God for Missionaries faithful to their vocation. Gilbert Cuissot died in 1666.

[2]August 25.

[3]Notre-Dame de Coëffort, collegiate church in Le Mans, entrusted to the Congregation of the Mission.

arrangements with a Canon of Le Mans and Master of Requests for
four hundred livres[4] to be given him living or dead. M. Gallais will
explain that to you, and he must be paid as soon as possible. I did
not know about all these debts. What we can do is to try to pay Abbé
Lucas[5] here, and you could get some help from what the Farmer-
General[6] owes him. I am writing all this to M. Gallais.

I shall tell M. Bajoue[7] what you told me about our Brothers
learning to serve Holy Mass.

M. Gallais will be able to inform you about M. Pousset's business; you can decide together what is to be done, and then let me
know.

M. Alain[8] is suffering from tertian fever. He had his fifth attack
yesterday. We are hoping that this will not amount to anything. As
soon as he is better, I will ask him to answer your letter.

M. Gallais and you, Monsieur, can decide whether it is advisable
to give the internal and external direction of the seminary to
M. Leblanc.[9]

---

[4]Throughout this edition the various denominations of foreign money have been left in French,
since no adequate, unchanging value in modern currency can be assigned. One écu equals three
livres; one thousand livres could support two priests and one Brother for a year on the missions
and "it hardly takes less for those who stay at home." (Cf. vol. V, no. 1972.)

[5]Councillor and chaplain of the King, Commendatory Abbot of Saint-Hilaire in the Carcas-
sonne diocese. He lived in Paris, rue Neuve-Saint-Honoré, in Saint-Roch parish. It is from him
that the Priests of the Mission held the provostship of the collegiate church of Notre-Dame de
Coëffort, and their titles with respect to the Hôtel-Dieu.

[6]Farmers-General was a syndicate of financiers who bought from the State for a lump sum the
right to collect taxes. Whatever profit they could make was used in other financial endeavors
such as lending money.

[7]Emerand Bajoue, born in Céaux (Vienne), entered the Congregation of the Mission as a priest
on December 1, 1640 at thirty-one years of age, took his vows on April 24, 1657, in the presence
of Antoine Portail, and died on February 28, 1671. He was Superior in La Rose (1649-1652),
and Notre-Dame de Lorm (1652-1654).

[8]Jean Alain, born in Dreux, entered Saint-Lazare as a priest on May 20, 1643, at the age of
thirty-one, took his vows on April 20, 1646, and died around April 6, 1649. The tertian fever
from which he suffered was a type of malaria marked by a recurrence of symptoms at forty-eight
hour intervals.

[9]Georges Le Blanc (George White), born in the diocese of Limerick (Ireland), was thirty-seven
years old when he entered the Congregation of the Mission as a priest on November 7, 1645.
Saint Vincent sent him to Ireland at the end of 1646, and recalled him to France in 1648 to place
him in Saint-Méen; in 1649 he sent him to Paris. In 1651 a certain Georges Le Blanc, with a
degree in theology, was involved in an affair concerning Irish students of the Sorbonne, who

Your nephew[10] is well, thank God. He returned to the seminary
of his own accord and is doing well there.

I ask Our Lord to strengthen you more and more. I am, in His
love, more tenderly than I could express to you, Monsieur, your
most humble and obedient servant.

VINCENT DEPAUL
i.s.C.M.

At the bottom of the first page: M. Cuissot

843. - TO ANTOINE PORTAIL, IN SAINTES

Paris, August 25, 1646

Monsieur,

The grace of Our Lord be with you forever!

I cannot tell you how consoled I am by the success of your
visitation of Richelieu. I ask Our Lord to bless the others in the same
way and to strengthen M. Alméras and you. I greet M. Alméras and
ask him to apologize to his father[1] for himself and for me because

---

signed a declaration against Jansenism. (Cf. Patrick Boyle, "Les relations de saint Vincent de
Paul avec l'Irlande," in *Annales C. M.* [1907], vol. LXXII, p. 190.) According to Father Thomas
Davitt, C.M., these are one and the same person. (Cf. Thomas Davitt, "Jansenism and the Irish
Student-Priests in Paris 1650-1651" in *Colloque,* the Journal of the Irish Province of the
Congregation of the Mission, no. 15, Spring 1987.) There were three Irish confreres named White:
George, Francis and John, and one Frenchman named Charles Le Blanc. So, identification of
"Monsieur Le Blanc" is difficult, and at times can be clarified only by the date or context of the
letter.
[10]Jean Cuissot, born in Moulins (Allier), entered the Congregation of the Mission on
November 28, 1642 at twenty-three years of age, and took his vows on November 11, 1644. He
had left the Congregation and been readmitted.

Letter 843. - Archives of the Mission, Paris, original autograph letter.
[1]René Alméras the elder, born in Paris on November 12, 1575, first married Marguerite Fayet
and then Marie Leclerc, the mother of his six children. He was secretary to the King, became

he did not go to take leave of him, for which he is more annoyed with me than I can tell you.

You will find plenty of work in Saintes, since Messrs. Soudier and Noyelles[2] are not living a very orderly life, nor getting along with M. Dufour.

The latter's deep recollection has grated upon them. It may be that M. Dufour is going to excess. Not everyone can adapt to such holy exactitude as his. However, the principal fault stems from the freedom, though reasonable, of the others. Try to get them to settle their differences. If M. des Noyelles gives you no hope of adapting himself to the exact observance of regularity, it would be better to send him to Saint-Méen. M. Bourdet will be quite pleased with that. However, I do not know of anyone who can speak in public, who could replace him in Saintes. Please give this some thought, Monsieur.

I have just written to M. du Coudray[3] that you will soon be with him, once you have taken care of matters in Saintes; I asked him to give you a warm reception and to make good use of your recom-

Treasurer of France in Paris on January 19, 1608, secretary to Marie de Médicis, Comptroller (1622-1656), Postmaster General (1629-1632), and secretary for the execution of the orders of Marie de Médicis. He filled all these positions worthily. After he had given his son to the Congregation of the Mission, he himself entered it on March 2, 1657, at the age of eighty-one. He died at Saint-Lazare on January 4, 1658. (Cf. *Notices,* vol. II, pp. 453-461.)

[2]Samson Le Soudier and Philippe des Noyelles.

[3]François du Coudray, Superior in La Rose. Born in 1586 in Amiens, he was ordained a priest in September 1618, and in March 1626 was received into the Congregation of the Mission, of which the only other members were as yet Saint Vincent and Antoine Portail. He was gifted with extraordinary intelligence and knew Hebrew well enough to be judged capable of doing a new translation of the Bible.

The Saint chose him to go to Rome to negotiate the approbation of the nascent Congregation. He remained there from 1631 to 1635. We find him next in Paris; from there he went into various areas to relieve the poor, to assist soldiers, or to give missions. In 1638 the Saint put him in charge of the house in Toul. He was recalled to Saint-Lazare in 1641, spent part of 1643 in Marseilles evangelizing the galley slaves and founding a house, and in 1644 took over as Superior in La Rose.

Unfortunately, his vast erudition was not based on sufficiently solid theological knowledge. He maintained some unorthodox opinions and persevered in them despite several admonitions. The measures Saint Vincent was obliged to take to prevent him from spreading his errors darkened the last years of his life. In 1646 he went from La Rose to Richelieu where he ended his days in February 1649, in his sixty-third year.

mendations. I requested that he then go to make the visitation in
Cahors in the same way he will observe you make it. The Bishop of
Cahors[4] is dissatisfied with M. Delattre[5] and asks for someone to
replace him, and this is what is causing me difficulty.

I do not know if you heard about M. Jegat's death. On his
doctor's orders he had gone to bathe, and drowned in a river that
flows near La Rose. I cannot tell you what a loss we have suffered.
When you get there, have the conference on him, if M. du Coudray
has not had one, as I instructed him. Have someone write down what
is said about his virtues and send it to us so we can have our own
based on it. Only a few men here [knew] him.

I do not know if I wrote you about M. Le Soudier's[6] departure
for Salé in Africa, beyond the strait, on the Oceanic Sea,[7] and that

---

[4]Alain de Solminihac was born in the château of Belet in Périgord on November 25, 1593. He
was only twenty-two when one of his uncles resigned in his favor Chancelade Abbey (Dordogne),
which depended on the Order of Canons Regular of Saint Augustine. He replaced the old buildings
and had discipline restored. On January 21, 1630 Cardinal de la Rochefoucauld sent him full
powers to visit the houses belonging to the Canons of Saint Augustine in the dioceses of
Périgueux, Limoges, Saintes, Angoulême, and Maillezais. Alain de Solminihac was sought after
in many places to establish the reform. Appointed to the Cahors diocese on June 17, 1636, he
devoted himself body and soul to the Church of which he was the shepherd. He procured for his
people the benefit of missions, visited the parishes of his diocese regularly, created a seminary
for the formation of his clergy, and entrusted its direction to the sons of Saint Vincent. At the
time of his death on December 21, 1659, the Cahors diocese was completely renewed. Since God
had manifested the sanctity of Alain by several miracles, his cause was introduced in Rome at
the request of the clergy of France. (Cf. Leonard Chastenet, *La vie de Mgr Alain de Solminihac*
[new ed., Saint-Brieuc: Prud'homme, 1817]; Abel de Valon, *Histoire d'Alain de Solminihac,
évêque de Cahors* [Cahors: Delsaud, 1900].) He was beatified by Pope John Paul II on October
4, 1981.
[5]Born in Amiens, Guillaume Delattre was received into the Congregation of the Mission on
August 10, 1642, at the age of thirty-two. He became Superior in Cahors (1644-1646), La Rose
(1646-1648), and Agen (1648-1650), and died in Bordeaux in 1650.
[6]Jacques Le Soudier. He got only as far as Marseilles. Born in Vire (Calvados) on October
28, 1619, Jacques Le Soudier entered the Congregation of the Mission on May 16, 1638, was
ordained a priest in 1642, and took his vows in Richelieu on June 14, 1642. In 1646 Saint Vincent
considered him for the foundation of the mission in Salé (Morocco). The project was abandoned,
however, when Saint Vincent discovered that the Order of Recollects (Franciscans) had already
made a commitment to that mission. In 1651 Le Soudier was in Saint-Quentin, where he remained
for two years. He became Superior in Crécy (1652-1654), and Montmirail (1655-1656). A long
illness interrupted his work and he died in Montauban on May 17, 1663.
[7]The Atlantic Ocean; Salé is north of Rabat in Morocco.

the reformed Benedictine monks have expelled us from Saint-Méen on the authority of the Parlement. I have just received a letter from the Bishop of Saint-Malo,[8] informing me that he has been notified that our men have been reinstated by order of the King, with the help of the captain of the guards of the Governor of the province.[9] If the matter depended on us, we would recall our men, but it is the Bishop's affair. He has acted in his own name and interdicted the Saint-Méen Church, forbidding his people, under penalty of excommunication, to enter it while those Fathers are there. *Mon Dieu,* Monsieur, how this has grieved me! Would you ever have said that we would be tried in this way by those good Fathers, whom we have tried to serve with as much zeal as if it were question of our own affairs? I hope Our Lord will look upon the little we have attempted to do for them as proceeding from charity, *quae patiens est.*[10] May it please the mercy of God that this be so and give me the means of serving them in future! I intend to do this more zealously than ever, with the help of God and I beg you to ask this of Him for me.

I am ending here, after recommending myself to your prayers and to those of the confreres, whom I embrace, prostrate in spirit at their feet and yours, and I am, Monsieur, your most humble servant.

VINCENT DEPAUL
i.s.C.M.

Addressed: Monsieur Portail, Priest of the Mission, presently at the Mission of Saintes

---

[8]Achille de Harlay de Sancy.

[9]At the request of Achille de Harlay de Sancy, the Governor of Brittany, Maréchal de la Meilleraye, had sent fifteen cavaliers, under the command of Grand-Maisons, to rout the Benedictines from the abbey.

[10]*Which is patient.* Cf. 1 Cor 13:4. (NAB)

Throughout this edition use is made of the *New American Bible* (NAB) translation. However, when necessary, the Douay-Rheims (D-RB) translation of the Vulgate will be utilized, since the NAB omits some passages which the D-RB contains.

844. - *CARDINAL MAZARIN TO SAINT VINCENT*

August 27 [1646]

Monsieur,

I have reported to the Queen what you and the Bishop of Maillezais [1] have decided. She gives it her full approval and wishes all of it to be put into effect, point by point. To this end I am sending you the official letter of the appointment she has made of the Bishop of Maillezais to the archbishopric of Bordeaux,[2] with the assurance that, on his part, he will be very glad to place his resignation into your hands.

As for the two thousand livres in pension and four hundred in benefices which you agreed upon, Her Majesty has ordered me, on her part, to assure you of them, so that nothing may delay the conclusion of this affair. In the meantime, I am. . . .

845. - *JEAN GARRON TO SAINT VINCENT*

(Now Vol. VI, 2128a.)

Letter 844. - Archives des Affaires Etrangères, *Mémoires et documents*, France, 1646-1647, Letters of Mazarin, Reg. 261, f°186 v°, copy.

[1]Henri de Béthune, Bishop of Maillezais.

[2]Upon being appointed Archbishop of Bordeaux, Henri de Béthune resigned the See of Maillezais which was then joined to the diocese of La Rochelle. Jacques-Raoul de la Guibourgère was appointed Bishop of La Rochelle.

Letter 845. - It is the opinion of the editors that Coste erred in transcribing the date for this letter (August 26, 1646). Abelly, *op. cit.*, bk. I, chap. XI, pp. 48-49, clearly dates this letter August 27, 1656. The editors, therefore, have placed it in its correct chronological order (Vol. VI, no. 2128a).

846. - *SAINT LOUISE TO SAINT VINCENT*

Monsieur,

We have almost nothing to do, and yet I would not know how to get these gentlemen to move. They are keeping me here again for this week. We have one great difficulty: the custom of this town is to have a supplier who advances money gratuitously for the hospital dispensary, where his wife had been accustomed to come and prepare the portions of the sick; she still comes to distribute them whenever she wishes, although that is contrary to our regulations.

I presented this difficulty to the Administrators, who have been granting me all that I ask of them. I greatly fear that this will delay us and hold things up a little longer than I thought. I foresee great drawbacks to the peace and union of our Sisters, all the more so because this woman is unhappy with their way of doing things and is trying to connive, first with one Sister, then with another; I do not think I should leave them until they are free of this obstacle.

If matters can be settled this week, we shall leave on Monday, I hope. However, since that is not very certain, I beg you most humbly, Monsieur, kindly to let me know what I should do. This woman and her husband will finish their term in three or four months, and the Administrators plan to do away with this duty because of several other inconveniences. I need to know whether I should leave them with this hope, even though I fear that the disorders, complaints, and lack of proper service to the poor during that period might give people the impression that all these failings stem from our Sisters.

If you do me the honor of writing to me, I beg you most humbly, Monsieur, to address the letter to Sainte-Marie,[1] lest it fall into the wrong hands, in the event that all these difficulties are really and truly removed and I leave on the day I indicated to you.

It is true that Abbé de Vaux informed me of the illness and relapse of our good Sister Marie-Marthe [2] in Angers; I have had no news since last week. Even if God has taken her, I do not think it necessary, Monsieur, to send another Sister yet, all the more so since our Sisters have made clear to me their need for the four Sisters they have been requesting for a long time. The Fathers of the Poor [3] asked me for them on their own initiative, when

---

Letter 846. - Archives of the Motherhouse of the Daughters of Charity, original autograph letter.
[1]The Visitation Convent.
[2]Marie-Marthe Trumeau.
[3]The Administrators or Directors of the hospital.

*they saw that I was on the point of leaving Angers without discussing it with
them, promising me anything I thought necessary to ask for their convenience. I promised them I would speak to you about it on my return and
assured them we would send them someone as soon as possible, likewise
two for this hospital here in Nantes. So, Monsieur, that makes seven Sisters
we must ask of Divine Providence. May God be eternally glorified for the
blessings He gives to our Little Company! I am always hopeful that it will
grow, since your charity works so hard for its perfection. I cannot express
to you the consolation my heart experiences from this, since God is showing
me that I am in no way necessary to it and of very little use.*

*I felt very deeply the sorrow of Monsieur and Madame de Liancourt but
am very much afraid that the way their son died [4] will be a great affliction
for this good mother for a long time to come.*

*I was hoping that the illness of M. Vacherot's boarder [5] would have
taught him a lesson but, from what I hear, he wanders about and even sleeps
out of the house. He wrote to me and seems resentful again of having been
put out of action and, in my humble opinion, he has placed and is placing
a wall around his heart to prevent him from becoming aware of the state
of his soul. I see all this evil but remain rather tranquil about it and no
longer seem to be disturbed by it, although I greatly desire his salvation. I
most humbly entreat your charity to ask this of our good God through the
merits of His Son. It is, I believe, a matter for the Almighty.*

*My health is a little better than when I had the honor of last writing to
you. You know all my needs but not my infidelities, which keep me from
almost any exercise of devotion. I am always with people or taking care of
my health. Poor me! However, Monsieur, I truly am—and God grant that
it not be to my great shame—your most humble and very grateful daughter
and servant.*

L. DE MARILLAC

[Nantes,] August 28, [1646] [6]

Addressed: *Monsieur Vincent*

---

[4]Henri-Roger du Plessis, Comte de la Roche-Guyon, Marquis de Montfort, killed at the siege
of Mardick on August 6, 1646.

[5]Her son, Michel Le Gras.

[6]Year added on the back of the original letter by Brother Ducournau.

Paris, August 28, 1646

Monsieur,

The grace of Our Lord be with you forever!
I thank God for the grace you lead us to expect, of your coming
soon to rest after your heavy labors. O Monsieur, how welcome you
will be and how gladly I will embrace you! Please come then,
Monsieur, and do not delay. I assure you that we will take very
special care of your health; you will be the master of the house, free
to say and do whatever you please, and my [master] in particular, I
who have always loved you more tenderly than my own father.

If you need the four thousand livres in revenue you gave to the
Feuillants[2] and allocated to the Mission, we will return it to you most
willingly, since it only seems fair to me that a founder who is in
need should be assisted from the income of the foundation he has
made. In addition, we will do more because if you need the capital

---

Letter 847. - Collection for the process of beatification.
  [1]Louis Callon, Doctor of the Sorbonne, was one of those men "in whom holiness, learning,
zeal, and simplicity were beautifully allied." (Cf. Placide Gallemant, *La vie du vénérable prestre
de J.-C., M. Jacques Gallemant,* [Paris, C. Couterot, 1653, p. 231].) To these gifts were added
that of fortune, for his parents had left him between fifty thousand and sixty thousand livres, a
large sum for that period. In July 1626 he left the parish of Aumale, his native place, to enter the
Congregation of the Mission. After a rather short stay at the Collège des Bons-Enfants, he returned
to Aumale with the consent of Saint Vincent, who continued to regard him as one of his own
men. The good he did in Aumale was considerable. He established a college in his paternal home,
bought a house for a girls' school, assisted the parish church, the hospital, and the convent for
penitent religious. The Feuillants (a branch of Cistercians) of Rouen, and other Communities,
likewise benefited from his generosity. On August 23, 1629 he gave Saint Vincent four thousand
livres to establish missions to be given every two years by two priests of the Congregation in the
Rouen diocese, and more particularly in the deanery of Aumale. He himself preached in the
dioceses of Rouen, Paris, Meaux, Chartres, and Senlis. In the midst of his labors, he found time
to write various works of piety: among others, *Traité pour la préparation à la sainte communion*
(Rouen: Laur-Maury, n.d.), and *Le catéchisme de la chasteté honorable* (Paris: Thierry, 1639).
Conscious that his end was near, he left Rouen to go to die at Saint-Lazare, but his illness
prevented him from getting beyond Vernon, where he died on August 26, 1647, in the convent
of the Third Order of Saint Francis.
  [2]In 1630 Pope Urban VIII divided the reformed religious of the Order of Cîteaux (Cistercians)
into two groups. The French group became known as the Congregation of Notre-Dame des

to support you in your old age, we will transfer it to you as we did for the pastor of Vernon.[3] He had given us six hundred livres in revenue and, when he later asked us to return it, assuring us that he needed it, we gave him back both the interest and the principal. However, if you do not need it, you can still use the interest, Monsieur, as you have done up until now, and we will continue the missions we have begun and carried on with so many blessings.

We have been approached about an establishment in that area, which could be useful there. For my part, Monsieur, I shall never have a consolation greater than that of being able to please you, as my good and very dear father whom I cherish more than myself. I am, in the love of Our Lord, Monsieur, your most humble servant.

VINCENT DEPAUL
i.s.C.M.

848. - TO JEAN MARTIN, IN GENOA

[Late August 1646][1]

Monsieur,

The grace of Our Lord be with you forever!

Your letter, like all the others you write me, has consoled me infinitely because of all the matters about which you inform me and

---

Feuillants, popularly called Feuillants. The money referred to here was returned to the Feuillants on November 23, 1650. (Cf. Arch. Nat. M 211, f°1.)

[3]Today, principal town of a canton in Eure.

Letter 848. - Archives of the Mission, St. Louis Province, presently at St. Mary's Seminary, Perryville, Missouri (USA), original acc. no. 091-HA-4. The letter used here was available to Coste only from a copy and contains two lines not found in his text: ". . .because of all the matters of which you inform me and the spirit in which you have written."

[1]This letter evidently belongs somewhere between nos. 840 and 853, i.e., between August 24 and September 6, 1646. Since Saint Vincent was accustomed to writing every week, it is rather probable that this one was written on August 31.

the spirit in which you have written. I thank God for this and ask Him to sanctify your dear soul more and more.

I am worried about M. Blatiron's little journey in the intense heat, although I am greatly consoled that he has rendered this small service to God in the person of Madame de Guébriant,[2] a person of considerable importance.

I have just now written to tell M. Dehorgny to hurry and send you M. Richard. I think you will have welcomed our Brother Bastien[3] before receiving this letter. You will find him a very fine young man.

That, Monsieur, is all that my pressing business allows me to tell you now, in very great haste and with the assurance once again of my fidelity, which I give you with all possible humility and affection. I am, in the love of Our Lord, your most humble servant.

VINCENT DEPAUL

849. - TO JEAN DEHORGNY, SUPERIOR, IN ROME

Paris, August 31, 1646

Monsieur,

The grace of Our Lord be with you forever!

I did not receive your packet this week. Nevertheless, I am sending you these lines to keep up our correspondence by all the regular mails, and also to tell you that I saw Father Charlet,[1] who

---

[2]Renée du Bec-Crespin was the widow of Jean-Baptiste de Budes, Comte de Guébriant, Maréchal of France, who died November 24, 1643, as a result of a wound received in the siege of Rotweil. He was buried at Saint-Lazare. In 1645 Queen Anne of Austria had entrusted to Madame de Guébriant the difficult mission of bringing to the King of Poland Princess Marie-Louise de Gonzague, whom he had married by proxy. Madame de Guébriant returned to Paris in 1646, and died in Périgueux September 2, 1659.

[3]As indicated in no. 840, this could be either Sébastien Nodo or Sébastien Drugeon.

Letter 849. - Bibliothèque Nationale, Rothschild collection, original autograph letter.

[1]Etienne Charlet, French Assistant to the General of the Jesuits.

told me, with regard to our vows, that we should leave them as they are for the present.

I would be glad to know the thinking there, as to whether the perpetuity of the General[2] requires the authorization of the Pope, or if that of the Archbishop of Paris is sufficient.

I am hampered by the refusal you received for granting faculties to the Missionaries in Algiers. I had a letter from them saying that they were well received and have already done much good there.

M. Le Soudier[3] has left for Salé, an African coastal town on the Oceanic Sea, beyond the strait.

What shall we do about this? Will matters continue in this way after Bishop Ingoli?[4]

The Capuchins here are requesting that no other Community be allowed to open houses in the towns of Greece, Africa, and Asia, where the King has Consuls and they themselves have houses, unless letters from the King are brought to the Consul. I have negotiated that but since the affair has not yet been settled, I will think it over.

I must admit that I am, I think, extremely attached to and zealous for the propagation of the Church in infidel lands, for fear that God might gradually do away with it here and that nothing or little of it will remain in a hundred years because of our depraved morals, those new opinions[5] which are spreading more and more, and the general state of affairs. In the past hundred years, [the Church] has lost, through two new heresies,[6] the greater part of the Empire and the Kingdoms of Sweden, Denmark and Norway, Scotland,

---

[2]Until 1968 the Superior General of the Congregation of the Mission was elected for life. In accordance with the 1984 revision of the Constitutions and Statutes of the Congregation, the Superior General is now elected for a term of six years, and he can be reelected for a second term of six years (cf. C. 105).

[3]Jacques Le Soudier.

[4]Bishop Ingoli was Secretary of the Congregation for the Propagation of the Faith (Propaganda Fide) from 1622 to 1649. For certain activities within France, it was necessary for Saint Vincent to deal with Propaganda Fide.

[5]Jansenism.

[6]The heresies of Luther and Calvin.

England, Ireland, Bohemia, and Hungary, so that she has only Italy, France, Spain, and Poland, and there are many heresies in France and Poland.

Now, these losses of the Church in the past hundred years give us reason to fear in the present misfortune that in another hundred years we may lose the Church entirely in Europe. So, keeping this fear in mind, blessed are those who cooperate in extending the Church elsewhere.

M. Martin informs me that you told M. Blatiron you are sending him M. Richard, and they are happy about this. I ask you to carry this out as soon as possible and to pray to God for me who am, in the love of Our Lord, Monsieur, your most humble and obedient servant.

VINCENT DEPAUL
i.s.C.M.

At the bottom of the first page: M. Dehorgny

850. - TO JEAN BOURDET, SUPERIOR, IN SAINT-MEEN[1]

Paris, September 1, 1646

Monsieur,

The grace of Our Lord be with you forever!

[Your letter] of last month consoled me on the one hand and worried me on the other. [The consolation] came from the fact that you suffered none of the violence you expected on the following day; [the worry] stemmed from what you wrote me about not [being able to maintain] the Company, in its present danger. [With regard

---

Letter 850. - Archives of the Mission, Paris, original autograph draft of a letter. The document is in very poor condition. Where the text is illegible we have reconstituted it from a copy in Reg. 2, p. 287.

[1]To understand Jean Bourdet's state of mind at the time Saint Vincent wrote this letter, it is

to this, I shall say] that, if the affair depended on the Company, [we would have] recalled [you] at the first summons. However, we are [partners with] a Prelate who is party to the suit, and the affair involves the welfare of [other persons]. If, then, we thought we were observing the evangelical counsel by not going to court, [we would fall] into ingratitude, the crime of crimes. Moreover, the cause is just.

Furthermore, what risk does the Company run in all that? It means going to prison, you will tell me, for that is the worst one. Alas! [Monsieur,] of what else are we capable if not of doing that for [God]? Is it possible for us to see a hundred thousand men, from the lowliest of the common people [to Princes] of the blood, exposing themselves to danger, not only of imprisonment but of death, for the service of the State, and that Our Lord will not find five or six faithful servants courageous enough for His service?

Yes, but that is contrary to the Gospel maxim which forbids us to go to court and contrary to the custom of the Company. Saint Paul and Our Lord have advised us to suffer the loss of everything rather than go to court. But both of them were obliged to come to that in the end, and they lost their case and their lives in the process. The maxim of the Company is to prefer to suffer a loss rather than go to court. That is true, and I ask God to grant you the grace of being very faithful to the practice of this maxim, but that [is] when the

---

essential to know that the Benedictine monks, driven from the abbey on August 20 by the soldiers of Maréchal de la Meilleraye, had requested help and protection from the Parlement of Brittany. On August 22 the Court opened an investigation. On August 28 it ordered the arrest of Fathers Orgeville, the Vicar-General; Bourdet, de Beaumont, Grand-Maisons, and several others. Maréchal de la Meilleraye recalled his troops, probably to avoid bloodshed. Pierre de Beaumont remained alone to guard the abbey. "Jean Bourdet," wrote Dom Morel, a somewhat prejudiced observer (cf. Ropartz, *op. cit.*, p. 195), "was seized with panic and terror, causing him to put his foot immediately into the stirrup and ride for a day and a night without halting. He did not dare to dismount for fear of falling into the hands of the law. Finally, when man and horse could go no farther, he dismounted in front of an inn, which he found in a village in the Vannes diocese. He intended to stay there for a time to catch his breath and to rest when, unfortunately, he discovered two horses in the stable, and was informed that they belonged to two bailiffs who had just arrived. He was so taken aback that, without waiting to find out from where they had come, where they were going, or their mission, he packed up, mounted his horse, and galloped off until, I was told, the horse fell dead under him."

matter depends on us. *Mais quoi!* we are not the ones involved; it is a Prelate who has called us to serve God along [with him] in his diocese, whereas persons who have no right are driving you out of it. A Benedictine Abbey that is not part of the reformed Congregation, nor of any other, depends in no way on any other. No abbot has the right to enter the abbey of another nor the benefice of another Order. In addition, these good Fathers have no permission to go into an abbey to set up their reform there, except with the consent of the monks, the abbot or the bishop. Now, the monks have negotiated with the Bishop of Saint-Malo, in whom, as Abbot—which he is—and as Bishop, their right resides, [and the Bishop of Saint-Malo][2] has forbidden their entrance. *In qua ergo potestate?* [3]

Yes, but the Parlement [supports them] and has brought them in. True, but this sovereign Senate [does not have the auth]ority either to bring into or maintain an individual in a property, if it does not belong [to him] by right. Furthermore, it seems likely that the one in Brittany, [which] has the reputation of having some of the best lawyers in the kingdom, [will not uphold] these monks, once [it is well] informed. Besides, the King [has given us the per]mission, and he has sovereign authority [over] the authority of the Parlements, and the power to overrule them. How can [you][4] know better the Will of [God in] temporal matters than by the orders of Princes, and in spiritual matters than by those of our prelates, each in his own diocese?

Yes, but this is the property of Saint Benedict, and consequently his children have the right to claim it when people try to alienate it from his Order and apply it to other uses. [I reply] that Church property belongs to the Church. If Saint Benedict were still alive, being a child of the Church, he would be very loath to deny this statement, especially since his Order's property was given to it by

---

[2]These words, required for the meaning, were not found in the text. Achille de Harlay de Sancy was Bishop of Saint-Malo.

[3]*On what authority, therefore?* "On what authority are you doing these things?" Cf. Mt 21:23. (NAB)

[4]A word left out of the original.

the Church because of the assistance he rendered it at that time through seminaries of clerics, which he erected for the service of the Church and to fill up its benefices. Now they no longer do this, and the Church has ordered it to be done by the bishops. The King's edicts also oblige them to do likewise and to use benefices and other revenues for it. Is it not just that the same Church which gave that property to this Order for the creation of the above-mentioned seminaries—which it is no longer doing nor is in any condition to do—that the same Church should have the use of this small part of property, by authority of the Prince and the Prelate, to substitute for what these Fathers did formerly and do no longer, provided they do this with the consent of the rightful owners?

Accordingly, Monsieur, you are in the right, with proper authorization, based on a need of the Church and in line with its intention. And after all that, there will be some among us who are unwilling to suffer anything for this cause! Well! *bon Dieu!* what better opportunity awaits you to suffer something for God? I certainly see none. In the name of God, Monsieur, let us not be so little attached to God's service that we yield to a useless fear which may cause us to abandon the task He has given us.

Yes, but the Company will be blamed and discredited. O Monsieur, what pri[de there would be] if, under the guise of deference and humility, we [were to abandon] the honor of God so as not to risk our own! Oh! how far Saint Paul was from that, when he said that God must be served *[per] infamiam et bonam famam, quasi seductores et tamen veraces!* [5] I just said that you [have a just cause] and, since this is so, as everyone thinks, hap[py will you be] to suffer something *propter justitiam,* [6] [since by this] means the kingdom of heaven is yours. This is the [end for] which you have been called by God for the establishment and continuance of things pertaining

---

[5] *Whether honored or dishonored, taken for impostors and yet we are truthful.* Cf. 2 Cor 6:8. (NAB)
[6] *For justice' sake.* Cf. Mt 5:10. (NAB)

to His glory, surely not like lions among sheep but like sheep among the [lions], to be torn to pieces and devoured.

May [His] Goodness grant us this grace!

I am, in His love. . . .

851.- TO CARDINAL MAZARIN

Paris, September 4, 1646

My Lord,

This letter is to inform Your Eminence that a theology professor at the Sorbonne has died recently, and they are talking about proceeding to a new election in the same Faculty. The Penitentiary[1] told me that the Jansenists are busy intriguing to have one of their party elected. Those who hold the common opinion of the Church are working in concert against them and have cast their eyes on a man named M. Le Maistre,[2] who is very learned, preaches well, is one of the best writers in the world and belongs to the good party. He was asked whether he would accept the nomination, if he were elected. He raised an objection to this because a prelate is offering him a much more advantageous position. Because of this, My Lord, those gentlemen in the good party wanted me to ask Y[our] E[minence] if you would agree to guarantee him at present twelve hundred livres annuity on some benefice, or promise him that you will do so soon.

The advantages that will accrue from this for the Church, My Lord, are that Y[our] E[minence] will prevent this dangerous

Letter 851. - Archives of the Mission, Paris, original signed letter.

[1]Jacques Charton, Doctor of Theology, member of the Council of Conscience and Director of the Trente-Trois Seminary (which took its name from the thirty-three men it educated each year for the priesthood). A Penitentiary is an officer in a diocese, who is vested with power from the bishop to absolve in cases normally reserved to the bishop.

[2]Nicolas Le Maistre accepted the post offered to him. He was nominated for the Lombez diocese on July 4, 1661 and died on October 14 of the same year.

opinion from being taught openly at the Sorbonne, will match a powerful genius against those persons, and will act with your usual providence in all matters of importance, in a question that concerns the glory of God and the welfare of His Church. Finally, you will be appointing a person on the side of the King and Y[our] E[minence]. The election is to take place next Monday. I need to know Y[our] E[minence's] will by Friday evening.[3]

In the meantime, My Lord, I ask God to preserve Y[our] E[minence] and to sanctify your dear soul more and more. I am, in His love, My Lord, your most humble and very obedient servant.

VINCENT DEPAUL
i.s.C.M.

852. - TO JEAN BARREAU, IN ALGIERS

Paris, September 6, 1646

Monsieur,

Only God Himself could make you understand how consoled we are by your successful voyage and the beginnings and progress you have made since your arrival. I thank the infinite goodness of Jesus Christ who has granted you this [grace], and ask Him to sanctify your dear soul more [and more] so that, always and in all things, you may act in a holy manner.

Here is a little advice I think I should give you. It seems that you were somewhat too hasty in promising the postal tax money: (1) because it could happen that you might not find this money by the appointed time; (2) it could be that, if you borrowed this amount from merchants there, to be repaid to them in Marseilles, it could happen that the money would not be ready by the time they arrived in Marseilles, and this would bring discredit both to you and to your

---

[3]September 7.

Letter 852. - This letter was published in the *Revue des documents historiques,* June 1873, p. 45, taken from the original which had been put on sale by Charavay.

office. However, this was not the case because Providence allowed you to win the confidence of the reformed Mathurins[1] to advance twelve thousand livres in ten to twelve days in Marseilles to the person to whom you sent the order to withdraw them.

The second piece of advice is never to write or speak about conversions there and, what is more, not to support those that take place contrary to the law of the country. You have reason to fear that someone may feign conversion in order to provoke an affront. Please remember, Monsieur, what I told you the Jesuits formerly did in Pera[2] in similar circumstances. We should really have a code, if you know how to use one, or perhaps I could send you one.

The heart of your affair is the intention of the pure glory of God; the continual state of interior humiliation, since you cannot devote yourself very much to exterior ones; and interior submission of the judgment and will to the person given you as adviser. As much as possible, do nothing without consulting him, if you are not obliged to give an immediate reply. Jesus Christ was the sovereign Lord [of Mary] and Saint Joseph; nevertheless, He did nothing without their advice. It is this mystery, Monsieur, that you must honor in a special way, so that His Infinite Goodness may be pleased to guide you in your present situation.

I wrote you that I saw your good aunt and how much she edified me. I am, in the love of Our Lord, Monsieur, your most humble servant.

VINCENT DEPAUL
i.s.C.M.

I plan to send you someone to act as Chancellor. We are urging the Fathers of Mercy[3] to do this but, from what I hear, the disorder

---

[1]The Order of Mathurins, founded by Saint John de Matha, dates back to the twelfth century. It took its name from the Paris convent built on the site of an old chapel dedicated to Saint Mathurin. It is also called the Order of the Trinitarians.

[2]A district in Constantinople.

[3]The Order of Redemption (Order of Mercy) was founded for the redemption of captives by Saint Peter Nolasco in the thirteenth century. Its members are commonly known as Mercedarians.

among them is so great that there is no likelihood of our being able to arrange anything with them. The King has commissioned M. de Morangis[4] to look into the matter. That is going. . . .We shall see what we can do about it. I praise God that you have taken that Father into your house.

Addressed: Monsieur Barreau, Consul in Algiers[5]

853. - TO JEAN MARTIN, IN GENOA

September 6, 1646

Monsieur,

The grace of Our Lord be with you forever!

I cannot tell you the consolation your letters bring me, particularly the last I received, dated August 17. Please write to me often.

I am worried because M. Blatiron has not yet returned from his service to Maréchal de Guébriant's wife. I am afraid he may have fallen ill or that the lady's ailment has gotten worse, God forbid!

I have word from M. Dehorgny regarding my request to him a long time ago to send you someone. He wrote me that he was waiting for the first rainfall to send off M. Richard, who is a fine man and from whom I hope you will receive great comfort. I truly experience the grief of the long labors you are enduring and feel none greater. I have continually asked M. Blatiron to do something to get the C[ardinal]-Arch[bishop][1] to moderate his zeal and your occupations, and I am planning to write plainly to him about this by

---

[4]Antoine Barillon, Sieur de Morangis, was made Master of Requests in 1625 and Councillor of State in 1648.

[5]A note written by Brother Barreau tells us that this letter was received on January 22 and answered on January 25.

Letter 853. - Archives of the Mission, Turin, original signed letter.
[1]Stefano Cardinal Durazzo.

the next regular mail. Meanwhile, Monsieur, please take the best possible care of yourself.

I praise God for the disposition he has granted those two priests who are with you to give themselves to the Company; I ask Our Lord to give them an ever greater share of His own Spirit. Please greet them most cordially for me as I greet your own dear soul, which my humble one embraces with special tenderness and affection.

I sent your letter to your mother; if she sends me a reply, I shall forward it to you.

We here are praying constantly for you and your work. Do the same for me who am, Monsieur, with all my heart, in the love of Our Lord, your most humble servant.

VINCENT DEPAUL
i.s.C.M.

Addressed: Monsieur Martin, Priest of the Mission, in Genoa

854. - CARDINAL MAZARIN TO SAINT VINCENT

Monsieur,

In reply to your letter of the fourth of this month,[1] which you took the trouble to write me, I shall tell you that I have only praise for the zeal you manifest in all that regards the glory of God and the good of His Church. The care you are taking to put an end to the intrigues of the Jansenists, by the election of M. Le Maistre, is a fresh proof of this to me.

I am pleased with the choice being made of a person who, according to your testimony, is worthy of filling the vacancy at the Sorbonne. In the meantime, you may assure him, on my part, of the twelve hundred livres annuity which you deem appropriate to be given him from some benefice, and this will become effective at my first opportunity.

Letter 854. - Archives of the Mission, Paris, original signed letter.
[1]Cf. no. 851.

Believe, Monsieur, that I shall always be most faithful in rendering you service.

CARDINAL MAZARINI

Fontainebleau, September 7, 1646

Addressed: *Monsieur Vincent, Superior General of the Mission, at Saint-Lazare, faubourg Saint-Denis, in Paris*

854a. - TO BONIFACE NOUELLY, IN ALGIERS

Paris, September 7, 1646

Monsieur,

The grace of Our Lord be with you forever!

I beg Our Lord to make known to you the incomparable consolation your letters have brought me. I ask His Divine Goodness, who has chosen you from all eternity for a work as important as this to give you His Spirit of interior fidelity in His exterior submission to Saint Joseph.

O Monsieur, how many demons the prince of demons has assigned to tempt you in this situation! The work of our dear Brother,[1] the differences of opinion, the mutual and reciprocal disapproval, and our natural inclination to have everything go our way—all these things have a devil that is forever at work to break the bond of charity with which God has united your hearts! But be steadfast, Monsieur; humble yourself profoundly for both of you; make many interior acts toward your dear other half, and you will rout those wicked phantoms and cast them headlong into the very depths of hell, so that they will never tempt you again. Just imagine,

---

Letter 854a. - The original autograph letter was put on sale in 1925 or 1926 by M. Lemasle, a dealer in antiquities. The text was published in the *Annales C. M.* (1926), pp. 233-235, and reprinted in *Mission et Charité*, 19-20, pp. 59-61. This edition uses the latter text.
[1]Brother Jean Barreau.

Monsieur, how much the holiness of your duty and the progress achieved in your way of acting enrages the demons.

In the meantime, apply yourself to your principal work, Monsieur. Visit, console, strengthen, and animate your poor slaves[2] with the Spirit of God. That is the main and only reason for your work; everything else is subordinate to it.

O Monsieur, how well M. Chrétien is doing, just as everyone would wish! Everybody recognizes that the Spirit of God is animating and guiding his own. Could you not write to one another? If there is any way to do so, I would be consoled by it, in order that this reciprocal communication might animate both of you and be of mutual assistance. If you do it, it should be done with such discretion that no one may find fault with your letters if they are intercepted.

I am writing two small pieces of advice to the Consul. The information in his letter, which you will anticipate with your own, will fill you in on what I am saying to you. Besides, I am extremely pressured.

Here is some news I have to tell you, to share with you our deep sorrow at M. de Beaumont's[3] imprisonment at the Parlement of Rennes, where his life is at stake. The Bishop of Saint-Malo established us at Saint-Méen in his diocese, where he opened a seminary for priests. With the King's consent, he added to it the revenue of the monks in the abbey, with their consent as well, in conformity with the Council of Trent and the edicts of our Kings. The reformed Benedictine monks complained to the Parlement and incited them so much that they expelled us from that place. When we were reestablished there by the King's authority, they took Monsieur de Beaumont prisoner and gave orders that we should be

---

[2]Boniface Nouelly had been sent to Algiers to minister to the Christian slaves held captive there. Brother Barreau was sent to Algiers as French Consul, for the diplomatic service of the captives.

[3]Pierre de Beaumont, born in Puiseaux (Loiret) on February 24, 1617, entered the Congregation of the Mission on February 23, took his vows on October 4, 1643, and was ordained a priest in March 1644. He was imprisoned as the result of the lawsuit which took place when the house in Saint-Méen was established. He became Director of the Internal Seminary in Richelieu, and afterward was twice Superior of that house (1656-1660, 1661-1662).

expelled from the province, contrary to the King's decrees, which are maintaining us there.

That, Monsieur, is why we have reason to honor the expulsion of Our Lord and the Apostles from certain provinces, and how our Little Company has begun to suffer in prison without having done any wrong. In this way, God has blessed its work, especially that of M. de Beaumont, in a particular way. He is one of the finest men I have ever known and one of the best workers in the Company. We are suffering in consequence of what is apparently their hatred of the Bishop of Saint-Malo because he had recourse to the Great Council instead of to them for the registration of our letters of establishment with the Parlement.

I share my sorrow with you so that you may see that you find your safety working among the infidels, while we suffer all these things in the midst of the faithful.

I am in a hurry to finish, while recommending myself to your prayers. I am, in the love of Our Lord, Monsieur, your most humble and obedient servant.

VINCENT DEPAUL
i.s.C.M.

Addressed: Monsieur Nouelly, Priest of the Mission, in Algiers

855. - TO CLAUDE DE MARBEUF[1]

September 8, 1646

My Lord,

I am the unworthy Superior of the Congregation of the Mis[sion and I] take the liberty of writing you this letter, pros[trate] at your

---

Letter 855. - Archives of the Mission, Paris, unsigned draft in the secretary's handwriting. The document is in very poor condition.
[1]Chief Justice of the Parlement of Rennes.

feet and those of the members of your Par[lement], to beg you, by
the compassion of Our Lord, [kindly to] protect the innocence of
one of the [finest] men in the world, who is working for the salvation
of the po[or common people with] great blessings from God. He is
M[onsieur de] Beaumont, one of the priests of our Com[pany. The]
reformed Benedictine [monks] have had him put in your p[rison],
where his feet are in chains because he was found [at Saint-Méen].[2]

I beg you, My Lord, to consider that he [and his] confreres were
called to that place by the Bishop of [Saint-Malo] for the purpose
of establishing a seminary of young clergymen, in order to have
them instructed in all things necessary [for their] state in life, in
conformity with the Council of Trent [and the] orders of our Kings,
who want the [bishops] to set up seminaries of priests in [their
dioceses], where they may be trained according to the ancient
custom of the Church, and to designate benefices for their maintenance. The Bishop of Saint-Malo established his [seminary] in
Saint-Méen Abbey and appropriated to this work the revenue of the
monks, with their consent, except for the pensions mentioned in the
agreement made with them. The King confirmed this by his letters
patent and by various decrees.

I am of the opinion, My Lord, that, once you and the members
of the Court have been well in[formed] about the affair, you will

---

[2]We have already seen in no. 850 that, following an arrest order issued by the Parlement of
Rennes, Pierre de Beaumont remained alone in Saint-Méen Abbey. When the royal sergeant, La
Fontaine, came to the area with a small group of men to see that the orders of Parlement were
carried out, he seized de Beaumont and took him to the Rennes prison. Disappointed at not having
caught the important persons he thought he would find at the abbey, La Fontaine vented his anger
on his one and only prisoner, and ordered the jailer to chain his feet brutally in irons. Dom Morel,
who gave this account, adds that, at his personal intervention, de Beaumont received preferential
treatment and was released after interrogation in the criminal chamber on September 4. The
prisoner's detention lasted only four or five days, and he was already free when Saint Vincent
wrote this letter. (Cf. Pierre Collet, *La vie de Saint Vincent de Paul,* [2 vols., Nancy: A. Leseure,
1748], p. 416.)

Saint Vincent's behavior during the Saint-Méen incident was one of the main objections raised
by the Devil's Advocate at the process of beatification. (Cf. *Novae animadversationes R.P.D.
Fidei promotoris super dubio virtutum tam theologalium quam cardinalium, quarta difficultas,*
p. 9; and *Ultimae animadversationes,* p. 3.) The Procurator of the cause had no difficulty proving
not only that his actions were irreprehensible but that he had conducted himself as a true saint.
This admirable letter is the proof.

find no fault with it, except perhaps that these good Fathers are saying that the B[ishop] of Saint-Malo could not bring about the union of the said revenue nor approve it, seeing that it belongs to the Benedictine Order and not to the above-mentioned Bishop of Saint-Malo. The reply to this, My Lord, is that it belongs to the Benedictines in such a way that it depends on the Bishop's jurisdiction. Therefore, the General of the Re[gulars] has jurisdiction only over monks of the abbeys of his Congregation, and no authority over the others who [are not]. Consequently, neither he nor anyone else in the Order had any right to oppose the union of the said revenue with that seminary, considering that it does not depend on any Congregation.

To this, My Lord, I add another reason: since Saint-Méen Abbey is under the jurisdiction of the Bishops of Saint-Malo, it is probable that the Bishops are the [founders] of this abbey and gave it the tithes [it] possesses and a large part of the property, in consideration [of the fact] that this house served as a diocesan seminary for the training of young clergymen and furnished good pastors to the parishes that depended on it. This being the case, does it [not] seem reasonable, My Lord, that, since the reformed monks no longer do either of these things, they have, in fact, changed their status of workers in the Lord's vineyard to something lesser, and the Church should recover its rights and apply the revenue it gave them to workers who are striving to do what they do not do?

Let us add to that, My Lord, that they could not ask the Congregation's permission to enter the said abbey, seeing that the Bull of erection of their Congregation did not allow them to enter any abbey, even though they may have been called there by the monks, unless the Abbot and the Bishops consented to this. And far from asking the permission of the Bishop of Saint-Malo, who is the Abbot and who has jurisdiction over Saint-Méen, he has, on the contrary, in his possession a letter from the General of Saint-Maur, in which it seems as though the Bishop of Saint-Malo had asked him to put some of his reformed monks into that abbey, and this good Father excused himself from doing so because he lacked subjects to put there. Seeing this, the Bishop of Saint-Malo acted as he did both to he did both to remedy the disorders existing in that abbey and to set up his seminary for the good of his diocese. After that, My Lord, were those good Fathers right to proceed so heatedly against their Prelate and the workers he placed in his vineyard, and [to have them] imprisoned and shackled? I do [not say] this, My Lord, by way of complaint against them. [There is no] man in the world who honors or [cherishes] them [as] affectionately as I try to do, by [the grace of God], as they themselves could tell you.

But if people find fault with the fact [that M. de Beaumont] returned to Saint-Méen contrary to the [Parlement's decrees], rest assured, My Lord, that he did [so with the] simplicity of a poor Priest of the Mission [who does not] know what a lawsuit is, and who thought he was [doing the right thing] in following the orders of his Bishop and the King. You may believe, My Lord, that if the matter had depended on us, who are not involved in the case, we [would have] recalled [them] at the first writ issued.

This being the situation, My Lord, I have [recourse to] your goodness, since you are the principal [minister] of God's sovereign justice in your [province], to request most humbly your protection for M. de Beaumont and for our Company. Besides the merit you will have for this before God, you will merit from all of us a perpetual obligation that will cause us to seek opportunities of rendering you our most humble services. I beg you, My Lord, with all possible humility and affection, to accept these offers for you and your family. I shall begin the prayers I plan to offer all my life for you, My Lord, and for the sanctification of your dear soul. I am, My Lord, in the love of Our Lord, your most humble and very obedient servant.

856. - TO N.

September 12, 1646

Saint Vincent de Paul announces to his correspondent that a priest of the Saint-Méen house has been released from prison, after spending four or five days there.

857. - TO JEAN DE FONTENEIL[1]

Paris, September 13, 1646

Monsieur,

I beg you, in the name of Our Lord, to address this packet so that it can be sent and delivered to M. du Coudray in La Rose. I know I am imposing on you, but you know also that my services are at your disposition, and my heart as well. It greets yours with all possible humility and affection, because I am truly, in the love of Our Lord, Monsieur, your most humble and obedient servant.

VINCENT DEPAUL
i.s.C.M.

Addressed: Monsieur Fonteneil

Letter 856. - Collet, *op. cit.,* vol. I, p. 415. The recipient was probably Antoine Portail. Through Charavay we learn that on September 12, 1646 Saint Vincent wrote him a three-page letter.

Letter 857. - Archives of the Mission, Paris, original signed letter.

[1]Jean de Fonteneil, born in Bordeaux around 1605, was a friend and imitator of Saint Vincent. His outstanding qualities procured for him the highest positions in the diocese. He was appointed Canon of Saint-Seurin in July 1623, special archiepiscopal Vicar-General on November 1, 1639, Vicar in perpetuity of the parish church of Sainte-Colombe, then of Saint-Siméon in Bordeaux, Grand Archdeacon, Chancellor of the University of Bordeaux in 1650, and Vicar-General of the diocese on September 10, 1655. Like his friend, Saint Vincent, he was convinced of the great good that would result from seminaries, missions, retreats, and weekly meetings of priests to discuss questions of theology, discipline, or piety. For this purpose, he founded the Congregation of the Missionaries of the Clergy, who directed the ordinands' seminary in Bordeaux and the seminaries in Aire and Sarlat. They were given the chapels of Notre-Dame-de-Montuzet, and the parishes of Saint-Louis-du-Marais and Saint-Simon-Cardonnat (Gironde). This Congregation

858. - TO CLAUDE DUFOUR, IN SAINTES

Paris, September 13, 1646

Monsieur,

The grace of Our Lord be with you forever!

I hope to write to you in more detail in my own hand, at the first opportunity. I cannot do so now because it is late and the mail is about to leave.

I cannot express to you my consolation at what M. Portail has written me about you, of which I was already aware. I ask Our Lord to give you an ever greater share of His own guidance and Spirit.

I am writing to Messrs. Le Soudier[1] and des Noyelles. Please give them my letters unopened, as is done elsewhere. I am informing the latter, in view of the difficulties he is encountering in Saintes, to go to La Rose. So I ask you, Monsieur, to give him what he will need for that. As for M. Le Soudier, I am exhorting him to do his utmost to unite his heart with yours and to live with you with the requisite understanding and submission. If he were to act otherwise, and if in the end you are not satisfied with him, please send him to me; I will send someone to replace him. In fact, we shall send you a priest and a student Brother[2] at the first opportunity.

I humbly recommend myself to your prayers and greet you with all the affection of my heart. I am, in the love of Our Lord, Monsieur, your most humble servant.

VINCENT DEPAUL
i.s.C.M.

Addressed: Monsieur Dufour, Superior of the Priests of the Mission, in Saintes

---

was short-lived, surviving its founder by only three years. He died in Bordeaux on March 2, 1679. (Cf. Louis Bertrand, *Histoire des Séminaires de Bordeaux et de Bazas* [3 vols., Bordeaux: Féret, 1894], vol. I, pp. 207ff.)

Letter 858. - Archives of the Mission, Paris, original signed letter.
[1]Samson Le Soudier.
[2]Clerical seminarians were frequently entitled "Brother." The context of the letter often dictates

859. - TO JEAN MARTIN, IN GENOA

Paris, September 14, 1646

Monsieur,

The grace of Our Lord be with you forever! I am so consoled at receiving your letters that I cannot refrain from complaining when I do not receive any, as happened this week, because this deprivation causes me to worry about you and M. Blatiron. I have not heard a word from him since he went to help Madame de Guébriant. As for myself, I shall try as far as possible to keep up the correspondence by all the regular mails. At present I still have nothing more to tell you except what I wrote a week ago, which is that M. Dehorgny is only waiting for the first rainfall to send you M. Richard, as he has assured me twice. This leads me to think that, if he is not already in Genoa, he will arrive there soon. The man is so good that M. Dehorgny is very reluctant to let him go. Since we cannot give you someone else suitable, we have also sent you from here a coadjutor Brother who is both exemplary and very supportive. Please let me know if he has arrived and what you think of him.

I now have high hopes that your work load will be a little lighter, especially if Monsieur Blatiron explains to the Cardinal-Archbishop[1] the danger to which he exposes you by obliging you to work so continually and, in so doing, causes you to act contrary to the usual custom of the Company and the recommendation I have so often repeated to you to take a rest from time to time. I ask Monsieur Blatiron to make him understand this clearly, once and for all, because I hope he will take it into consideration.

Monsieur Guérin, who is in Tunis, informs me that he can easily communicate with you by letter, because ships from the principality of Genoa dock there frequently. I would be pleased if that were the

whether Saint Vincent is referring to a lay (coadjutor) Brother or a clerical student.

Letter 859. - Archives of the Mission, Turin, original signed letter.
[1]Stefano Cardinal Durazzo.

case, both to serve as a diversion for Monsieur Guérin who has almost none, and for the consolation you would experience in reading his letters. Whenever I receive any, it is always with particular satisfaction.

I am not writing to M. Blatiron because I am not sure he has returned. If perchance he has, please let this letter be for both you and him.

I greet the two of you, prostrate in spirit at your feet, while humbly recommending myself to your prayers. Mine are intended to ask God to be pleased to preserve you, to grant you an ever increasing share in His Spirit, and to grant me the grace of letting you know how much I am, in the love of Our Lord, Monsieur, your most humble servant.

VINCENT DEPAUL

i.s.C.M.

Addressed: Monsieur Martin, Priest of the Mission of Genoa, in Genoa

860. - TO JEAN-FRANCOIS DE GONDI,[1] ARCHBISHOP OF PARIS

[Between August and November 1646][2]

Vincent Depaul, Superior General of the Congregation of the Priests of the Mission, humbly petitions, stating that, since it has pleased your pastoral charity to authorize the said Priests of the Mission to establish the Confraternity of Charity for the assistance

---

Letter 860. - Archives of the Motherhouse of the Daughters of Charity, copy of the period. Saint Louise personally wrote on the back of this document: "A copy of a petition presented to the Archbishop of Paris for the establishment of the Daughters of Charity." This petition is a second version; the first was published in vol. II, no. 773.

[1]Archbishop of Paris (1622-1654).

[2]The first date is that of the Sisters' entrance into the hospital at Nantes; the second is that of the approbation of the petition.

of the sick poor in all the parishes of your diocese where it can be conveniently established, after having successfully made the establishment in several villages, some charitable ladies of Paris have been so touched by it that they have brought about, through their own pastors, a similar establishment in their own parishes. These include Saint-Germain-l'Auxerrois, Saint-Nicolas-du-Chardonnet, Saint-Leu, Saint-Sauveur, Saint-Médéric,[3] Saint-Etienne, Saint-Sulpice, Saint-Gervais, Saint-Paul, and others, where the Charity has been established and is functioning successfully.

But because the Ladies who are members belong, for the most part, to a social class that does not allow them to perform the most menial and abject services that must be rendered, such as carrying the soup pot through the city, doing the bleeding, giving enemas, dressing wounds, making beds, and watching at night over the sick who are alone and near death, they have taken some good country girls to whom God has given the desire to assist the sick poor. These [girls] attend to all these little services, after having been trained for this purpose by a virtuous widow named Mademoiselle Le Gras. They have been supported, while living in the house of the above-mentioned lady, by the assistance of some charitable widows and other persons, who have contributed their alms to this. The result is that, in the thirteen or fourteen years since this work was begun, God has so blessed it that at present there are in each of those parishes two or three of these girls who work every day assisting the said sick poor, and even sometimes instructing poor girls when they can. They live at the expense of the Confraternity of the parishes where they are employed, but so frugally that they spend only one hundred livres a year at the most for food and clothing, and in some parishes, only twenty-five écus.

Besides the work these girls do in the parishes, three of them are employed by the Ladies of Charity of the Hôtel-Dieu to serve the sick poor there, and to prepare the little delicacies that they bring them every day to the Hôtel-Dieu. In addition, there are ordinarily

[3]Saint-Merry.

at least ten or twelve engaged in raising the little foundlings of this city, and two or three for the assistance of the poor convicts. Besides those employed in the aforementioned works in this city, there are also some serving in the hospitals in Angers, Nantes, Richelieu, Saint-Germain-en-Laye, the Hôtel-Dieu of Saint-Denis-en-France, and in other places in the country. There, they perform more or less the same tasks with regard to the care of the sick, healing wounds, and educating little girls.

And in order to provide these girls for all these places and all the others where they are being requested, the above-mentioned lady trains others in her own home and ordinarily has more than thirty of them, some of whom she employs to teach the poor little girls who go to school in her home; some to visit the sick of the parish to bring them food or medicine, or to nurse them; some to dress the wounds of the poor who come to them from the outside for this purpose; some to learn to read and write; and others to do the housekeeping.

She also supports them partly with the money the girls earn from their handwork when they have some leisure time after their ordinary work; partly with the assistance of the above-mentioned widows who contribute according to their means; partly with ordinary alms, but especially with the revenue that the late King[4] and the Duchesse d'Aiguillon have charitably donated to them in perpetuity, amounting to around two thousand livres a year.

And what is still more noteworthy in the work of these poor girls is that, besides the corporal services they render to the sick poor, they try to contribute as best they can to their spiritual welfare, particularly by saying some good word to them from time to time, counseling those who are going to die, that they might leave this world in a good state; and those who are recovering, in order to help them to lead a good life. And Our Lord so blesses the little service

---

[4]Louis XIII died on May 14, 1643.

they render in their simplicity that there is good reason to glorify Him for its successful results.[5]

Because, however, works pertaining to the service of God come to an end ordinarily with those who begin them, if there is no spiritual bond among the persons involved in them, the petitioner fears that the same thing may happen to this company, if it is not erected as a Confraternity. That is why he represents to Your Most Illustrious Lordship, with all possible respect, that it seems desirable that you be pleased to erect as a Confraternity this company of girls and widows, under the title of *Confraternity of Charity of the Servants of the Sick Poor in the Parishes,* and to give them as regulations the following articles, according to which they have lived until now, and are resolved to live by for the rest of their days.[6]

VINCENT DEPAUL
Most unworthy Superior General
of the Congregation of the Mission

Addressed: His Excellency, the Most Illustrious and Most Reverend Archbishop of Paris

861. - TO ANTOINE PORTAIL, IN LA ROSE

September 22, 1646

Monsieur,

The grace of Our Lord be with you forever!
I am writing to you in haste from Fontainebleau,[1] where I have

---

[5]At this point the Saint deleted a rather long passage of the first petition, probably because it contained an encomium of his works.

[6]The Rule is published with other documents in vol. XIII, no. 145.

Letter 861. - Archives of the Mission, Paris, original signed letter. The postscript is in the Saint's handwriting.

[1]The residence of the Court.

come to take care of the business entrusted to me. [I write also] to keep up my correspondence with you, to give you renewed assurance of my poor heart's affection for your own most dear one, and to tell you, Monsieur, that the Bishop of Cahors[2] informs me that he will be very happy to have you make a journey to Cahors to see the state of our house and how things are going there. This is what I wanted to ask you by these lines, so you can set out as soon as possible.

I send Monsieur Alméras, Monsieur du Coudray, and the rest of the family my warmest greetings, humbly recommending myself to your prayers and theirs. I am, in the love of Our Lord, Monsieur, your most humble servant.

VINCENT DEPAUL
i.s.C.M.

Since this is the Bishop's wish, consult with good M. du Coudray whom I greet warmly, as to whether it is expedient for him to join you. If it is, I ask him to do so.

Addressed: Monsieur Portail, Priest of the Mission, presently at Notre-Dame de la Rose, in La Rose

---

[2]Alain de Solminihac.

862. - TO JEAN DEHORGNY, SUPERIOR, IN ROME

Orsigny,[1] September 27, 1646

Monsieur,

The grace of Our Lord be with you forever!

You did well not to attempt the ch. . .since affairs are in the state they are, Father Co. . . . . . .the Dominican feels we should be content. . .of M. from Paris, and he thinks that suffices and that. . .and which, supposing our intention of keeping ourselves in the. . .is better, because those of the Pope would be a dispo. . .to enter the religious state.

Messrs. Portail and Alméras are still in La Rose[2] and will leave from there for Marseilles;[3] they are trying to see that the entire little Rule,[4] as it is written, is observed by everyone. You will see to this, since you are there.

I am very consoled by what you tell my about Bishop Ingoli's idea of making Messrs. Guérin and Nouelly Vicars Forane.[5]

Letter 862. - Provincial House of the Daughters of Charity, 80 rue du Noyer, Brussels (Belgium). This letter was put on sale in 1951 by M. Degrange, a dealer in antiquities in Paris. A description of this letter had been given in the Laverdet catalogue for January 1854, item no. 1060. Coste published two extracts from this catalogue in his edition (no. 862) and cited Laverdet's description: "A signed, two-page letter with a tear in the top outer margin, eliminating the end of seven lines on the front of the page and the beginning of four lines on the back." The text was published in the *Annales C. M.* (1951), pp. 373-374, and reprinted in *Mission et Charité,* 19-20, pp. 62-63. This edition uses the latter text; ellipses indicate the missing words.

[1]Saint Vincent was spending some time at the Orsigny farm, which the Congregation had been given in 1644.

[2]Notre-Dame de La Rose, near Sainte-Livrade, in the Agen diocese. The Missionaries had been established there since 1639, serving the pilgrims and giving missions in the rural areas. M. Portail was making the canonical visitation of the house at the time, and Vincent was considering asking him to do the same for the houses in Annecy and in Rome, and lastly to take over the direction of the house in Rome.

[3]Fathers Portail and Alméras were supposed to pass through Marseilles, which they did. M. Portail went to make the canonical visitation of the house in Rome, where M. Alméras was appointed Superior.

[4]The first draft of the Common Rules was completed in 1642; their approbation was being sought in Paris and then in Rome. The first paragraph of this letter, in spite of the gaps, seems to be dealing with this question of approbation.

[5]In order to add weight to the authority of the Missionaries in Barbary (Julien Guérin in Tunis,

I am also consoled that you have sent M. Richard to Genoa; that little Community is held in high regard, according to what was told me by the Intendant of Justice of the King's army in Italy.

I share your view regarding the establishment of the Company in that Republic,[6] as also your way of conducting yourself with Cardinal Ludovisi,[7] and think you did well to limit yourself to the smallest space for your lodging.

Act as God inspires you regarding San Salvatore;[8] the opportunity to withdraw is very timely, since you deem that establishment in that place has certain disadvantages. . .would be very desirable to find some. . .they say about Saint-Esprit in Toul;[9] they are beginning. . .the rural mission afterward with the odor. . .the Company in the administration of Saint-Amand parish.[10]

The little persecution in Brittany[11] has not yet abated, although the Bishop and the Coadjutor of Saint-Malo[12] went right to the spot for that very purpose. Our prisoner was set free five days later. The Company is scattered here and there. Our Lord will bring them together when He chooses. As for me, I conclude by recommending

Boniface Nouelly in Algiers), Bishop Ingoli, Secretary of Propaganda Fide, had them appointed Vicars-General of the Archbishop of Carthage.

[6]Republic of Genoa.

[7]Nicolò Albergati-Ludovisi became Cardinal-Archbishop of Bologna in 1645. He served as Grand Penitentiary from 1649 to 1687, the year in which he died.

[8]Perhaps San Salvatore Abbey, located some thirty-eight miles from Rome, where the Missionaries went to rest from time to time.

[9]The Missionaries were established in Toul in 1637. The allusion here is to the difficulty encountered by them with regard to the missions and retreats for ordinands. The Holy Spirit Brothers, who were serving in the hospital, felt threatened by the foundation.

[10]Undoubtedly the parish in the town of Toul, which had been entrusted temporarily to the Missionaries.

[11]Allusions to the difficulties in Saint-Méen.

[12]Ferdinand de Neufville de Villeroy had been Coadjutor to his uncle Achille de Harlay de Sancy since 1644. The latter died on November 20, 1646. Neufville succeeded him and remained Bishop of Saint-Malo until 1657, when he was named Bishop of Chartres.

myself to your prayers and am, in the love of Our Lord, Monsieur, your most humble and very obedient servant.

VINCENT DEPAUL
i.s.C.M.

Addressed: Monsieur Dehorgny

863. - TO JEAN MARTIN, IN GENOA

Orsigny, September 27, 1646

Monsieur,

The grace of Our Lord be with you forever!

I received your letter of the eleventh of this month with the usual consolation your letters give me, because your soul is so dear to me and whatever comes from it is a pleasure.

I praise God for Brother Sébastien's[1] arrival and for the warm welcome given him by the priests with you and the Cardinal himself. I ask Our Lord to grant him the grace always to satisfy them and to edify them by his good example. M. Dehorgny sent me word that M. Richard had also left for Genoa. I think he must be with you today, and that he arrived in time to help you with the ordination work, in the absence of M. Blatiron, who you say is still being detained by Maréchal de Guébriant's wife. I also praise God that she is satisfied with his services, and fully approve of his continuing to render them for as long as she needs them.

With God's help, you will continue to succeed in your leadership and in your duties, because Our Lord's work is accomplished not so much by the multitude of workers as by the fidelity of the small

Letter 863. - Archives of the Mission, Turin, original signed letter.
[1]Either Sébastien Nodo or Sébastien Drugeon.

number whom He calls. And because I know you are full of zeal and charity, I also expect to see great blessings resulting from your efforts, if our common Master is pleased to grant you the graces I ask of Him. I entreat you, Monsieur, to recommend my poor soul to Him, since I am, in His love, Monsieur, your most humble servant.

VINCENT DEPAUL
i.s.C.M.

Addressed: Monsieur Martin, Priest of the Mission, in Genoa

864. - TO RENE ALMERAS THE ELDER

Saint-Lazare, [September 28, 29, or 30, 1646][1]

Monsieur,

The grace of Our Lord be with you forever!

I prostrate myself in spirit at your feet and ask your pardon, with all the humility and affection in my power, for having inadvertently given you reason to complain about me because M. Alméras, your son, did not go to take leave of you before his departure. I told you, Monsieur, that I committed this fault without thinking; it is true that I did not reflect on it at all before he left.

This is how that happened. For a long time, we were not sure whether he should go to the country, because he was not feeling well and because we were uncertain about the places to which he should go. We had first thought of sending him to make the visitation of the few houses we have, beginning with Sedan, then

---

Letter 864. - The original autograph letter belonged to M. Morel, a contractor in Rouen.

[1]An unknown hand added beside the addressee: "September 1646." In fact, this is the only date which fits. Since the letter was written after the journey from Fontainebleau, and since the Saint had not yet returned on September 27, we can choose only from among the last three days of the month.

on to Toul, Troyes, Annecy, Marseilles, and Rome; not so much to make visitations as to try and see if this diversion might restore his health. We consulted the doctors, and they were strongly of the opinion that he should be sent to the country, but not to Rome, unless he was in perfect health when he reached Marseilles. A good deal of time was spent considering the route to Sedan, but when the very hot weather was upon us, we were fearful of sending him by that route because there are no coaches that can be covered, until after Troyes. This caused us to change our plans overnight, when the opportunity presented itself to send him to Angers, where he could go by covered coach as far as Orléans, and from there by river. The decision was made in the evening and he left the next day, without my giving a thought to his filial obligation to go and receive your instructions. I think the same holds true of him; at least he never mentioned it to me at all. From this you see, Monsieur, that my fault was not deliberate but a want of reflection on what I should do.

The letter I am sending you from your son will point out another failure to you, Monsieur. I received it some twenty days ago and am sending it on to you only now. This is another fault, but it is not so much my doing as it is of one of our Brothers, to whom I had given it before my departure for Fontainebleau and who forgot to forward it to you. I was quite surprised when I asked him on my return if he had sent it and he said no. Although, thank God, he is very careful, he was not so on this occasion. I think our sudden departure for Fontainebleau, where he accompanied me, was the reason. I am telling you all this, Monsieur, that you may kindly believe that on this occasion I was not lacking good will but memory, and, consequently, you may be more willing to grant me the pardon I ask for your son and for myself.

Monsieur Portail wrote me on the eighth of this month from our house in La Rose in the Agen diocese that your son and he have never felt better—those are his very words—and that they will be leaving there in a week for Marseilles. From there, one will head for Genoa and Rome, and the other for Annecy in the Geneva diocese, according to the instructions I am sending to them in Marseilles. Now, I am not certain which of the two will go to Rome, or whether they will both go. I assure you, Monsieur, that your son will not go to Rome if Monsieur Merlet and our doctor, Monsieur Vacherot, think there is the slightest drawback in this. Your son's life is too dear to us, Monsieur, as is your own satisfaction. Even should the doctors judge that he can go, I shall nevertheless send word for him not to do so if, when he reaches Marseilles, his health is not as good as it was when he arrived in La Rose.

That, Monsieur, is our humble manner of acting with regard to your son, whom I honor, as God knows, and cherish more than myself. I am, in the love of Our Lord and His holy Mother, Monsieur, your most humble and very obedient servant.

VINCENT DEPAUL
i.s.C.M.

Addressed: Monsieur Alméras, Councillor of the King and his Master of the Chambre des Comptes

865. - TO THE SUPERIOR OF THE HOUSE IN TOUL[1]

1646

We go to court as little as possible and, when we are obliged to do so, it is only after having sought advice both within and outside [the Community]. We prefer to relinquish what belongs to us rather than scandalize our neighbor.[2]

Letter 865. - Collet, *op. cit.,* vol. II, p. 236.

[1]The house in Toul had two Superiors in 1646: Jean Bécu (1642-1646) and Charles Aulent (1646-1647). The person to whom this letter is addressed, states Collet, "had undertaken some business matter in which he failed." We think this person was Jean Bécu.

[2]Having recorded these words of the Saint, Collet added: "Nevertheless, God did permit him to have a few lawsuits, some of which he won and some he lost; but this was because Providence had chosen him as a model for all states of life, and those who go to law need a good example." As a matter of fact, the only time Saint Vincent initiated a lawsuit was when he was driven to it, not for his own interest but for the interest of others. (Cf. no. 850.)

866. - TO A VISITATION NUN[1]

[Between October 1 and 6, 1646][2]

My dear Sister,

I praise God for what you tell me about our Mother's[3] frame of mind, and for her sending me word that she will do nothing in Chartres,[4] unless her daughters strictly enjoin her to do so. With

---

Letter 866. - Reg. 1, f°23 v°, copy made from autograph rough draft.

[1]Letter 873 leads us to think that this letter was addressed to a Sister in the first Visitation Monastery in Paris, most probably Sister Louise-Eugénie de Fonteines, who had previously been its Superior.

Louise-Eugénie de Fonteines was born in Paris of Huguenot parents on March 13, 1608, and was received into the Visitation Monastery (rue Saint-Antoine) in 1630, seven years after her abjuration of heresy. She soon became Mistress of Novices there. After her election as Superior in 1641, she was reelected so often that the convent had her as its head for almost thirty-nine years. In 1644 she went to La Perrine Abbey near Le Mans to establish the renewal there. On her return, the Archbishop of Paris asked her to work on the Rule of the Port-Royal Abbey. Saint Vincent, who observed her behavior in certain difficult situations, stated that "an angel could not have comported herself with more virtue." (Cf. *Sainte Jeanne-Françoise Frémyot de Chantal. Sa Vie et ses oeuvres* [8 vols., Paris: Plon, 1874-1880], vol. VIII, p. 446, n.) She died September 29, 1694, at the age of eighty-six, leaving the reputation of a holy religious. "God always blessed her leadership and her undertakings," said the *Book of Professions* (Arch. Nat. LL 1718). Her biography has been written by Jacqueline-Marie du Plessis, *Vie de la vénérable Mère Louise-Eugénie de Fonteines, religieuse du monastère de la Visitation de Sainte-Marie* (Paris: n. p., 1693).

[2]The announcement of the impending return of Hippolyte Féret, the very subject matter of this letter, and the fact that it was written towards the end of the annual retreat, which closed October 6, 1646, leave no doubt about the date given here.

[3]Hélène-Angélique Lhuillier was born in 1592, the daughter of François, Seigneur d'Interville, and Anne Brachet, Dame de Frouville. In 1608 she married Thomas Gobelin, Seigneur du Val, Master-in-Ordinary of the Chambre des Comptes [sovereign court for the examination, registration, and auditing of taxes]. After her marriage was annulled, and on the advice of Saint Francis de Sales, she was accepted into the Visitation convent in Paris on July 2, 1622, and was elected Superior several times. Saint Vincent used to say that she was one of the holiest souls he had known. (Cf. *Sainte Jeanne-Françoise*, vol. V, p. 65, n.) He put her in contact with Commandeur de Sillery in the hope that she would finish the work of bringing him back to God. She died March 25, 1655, at the Chaillot monastery, where she was the first Superior. Her name is often mentioned in the biography of her sister, Madame de Villeneuve: R.P. Salines, *Madame de Villeneuve* (Paris: Beauchesne, 1918). [Cf. manuscript life of Mother Hélène-Angélique Lhuillier, in the Archives of the Daughters of the Cross of Tréguier.]

[4]Efforts were being made to establish a Visitation monastery in this town.

regard to La Perrine,[5] I shall consider the resolution that will be taken on it as coming from God.

As for what you said to me about going to your house to be present at your conference before your Mother comes, I beg you, dear Sister, to hold me excused from this, because I would scandalize our men if I were to go out during the retreat. I go further, my dear Sister, and ask you to offer my excuses to our Mother and to your dear Community for no longer having the joy of continuing my humble services to it, because this retreat has made me see as plain as day that I am neglecting our Company in order to devote myself to concerns other than theirs, for which I shall have to give an account before God.

There is also another reason which is no less compelling, namely, that the Company has a Rule that we not be involved in the care of nuns, so as to devote ourselves entirely to the service of poor country people. Yet, here I am in contravention of this Rule. And because it is to be feared that, after me, attention will be paid not so much to the text of the Rules as to the way I practiced them, I am obliged in conscience to resign.[6] If I have acted otherwise, it has not been without qualms of conscience. I have even greater involvements,[7] and I hope Our Lord will release me from them as well.

There are other persons in Paris who will serve you very well. For example, there is M. Féret, who is going to be Pastor of

---

[5]Abbey in the Le Mans diocese. Sister Louise-Eugénie de Fonteines had previously restored monastic observance there.

[6]For eighteen months subsequent to this letter, Saint Vincent did not fulfill the functions of Director of the Visitation nuns. At the insistence of Marguerite de Gondi, Marquise de Maignelay, Jean-François-Paul de Gondi, Cardinal de Retz, obliged him to resume these functions. Whenever Saint Vincent counseled members of his Community against assuming the direction of nuns, he referred to the Rules of the Congregation of the Mission and the obligation forced on him by Cardinal de Retz.

[7]His position on the Council of Conscience, or Royal Council for Ecclesiastical Affairs. Saint Vincent became a member in 1643 and was dismissed by Cardinal Mazarin in 1652. This Council discussed and decided all questions dealing with religion in France, e.g., episcopal appointments.

Saint-Nicolas-du-Chardonnet,[8] and there is also M. Abelly.[9] These
are men who will serve you in the spirit of our blessed Father[10] and
with incomparably more grace than I. I will even be happy to ask
them to do this, on condition that neither you nor your Mother will
write to me, nor have anyone else write to me, about taking up this
duty again. You will likewise dispense me from going to your
house, because I have taken the resolution not to go there any more,
assuring you, my dear Sister, that this is not due to any dissatisfaction. Oh no! I assure you of this before God; it is, rather, a matter
of conscience, for the reasons I have given you. You have had only
too much charity and forbearance with my wretchedness. I ask Our
Lord to reward you for it and to forgive the faults I have committed
in this regard.

Rest assured, my dear Sister, that I shall honor and cherish you
in O[ur] L[ord] as much and more than ever, and I shall remain, in
life and in death. . . .

[8]Hippolyte Féret, Doctor of Theology, was born in Pontoise (Val-d'Oise). For several years
he had been in Alet, where he had become Vicar-General. Saint Vincent, who had sent him to
live with Bishop Nicolas Pavillon of Alet, recalled him to Paris to become Pastor of Saint-Nicolas-
du-Chardonnet, probably at the request of Archbishop Jean-François de Gondi. Saint Vincent
thought so highly of Féret that he proposed him as Coadjutor Bishop of Babylon.

[9]Louis Abelly was born in Paris in 1604. From the earliest years of his priesthood he took part
in Saint Vincent's apostolic labors. The Saint spoke so highly of him to François Fouquet,
Bishop-elect of Bayonne, that he appointed him his Vicar-General. His stay in Bayonne was not
long. He accepted a simple village parish near Paris, and shortly afterward (1644) was given
charge of Saint-Josse, a parish in the capital, where he formed an ecclesiastical community. He
later became Director of the Sisters of the Cross (1650), chaplain of the General Hospital (1657),
and Bishop of Rodez (1664). In 1666 he resigned his diocese for reasons of health and retired to
Saint-Lazare, where he spent the last twenty-five years of his life in recollection and study. We
have almost thirty of his books on devotion, history, and theology, among them the *Vie du
Vénérable Vincent de Paul*. He is not merely the sponsor of this work, as has been asserted, but
is truly its author. His task was greatly facilitated by Brother Ducournau, who collected and
classified the documents. Abelly made a donation to the Saint-Lazare house of some property he
owned in Pantin, which became the country house of the students. He died October 4, 1691, and,
according to his wish, was buried in the church of Saint-Lazare, under the Sainte-Agnès chapel.
(Cf. Collet, *op. cit.*, vol. I, pp. 5ff.)

[10]Saint Francis de Sales.

867. - TO CARDINAL GRIMALDI[1]

Paris, October 4, 1646

My Lord,

The purpose of this letter is to renew my obedience to Y[our] E[minence] and to request you most humbly to allow me to send you some writings concerning the two leaders, Saint Peter and Saint Paul. They have been composed by one of the most learned theologians we have, a very fine man, who wishes to remain anonymous.[2] He prepared these writings, not knowing whether he would have them printed. He learned from the Rome Gazette that the author's book on those two leaders is being examined there,[3] and that two Doctors of the Sorbonne presently in Rome[4] are maintaining that it is the teaching of their department. Furthermore, when that same department learned that this opinion was being attributed to it, it met and sent a deputation to the Nuncio to disclaim

---

Letter 867. - Reg. 1, f°14 v°, copy made from an autograph rough draft. Another autograph draft of the same letter is extant in the Archives of the Mission, Paris. Because the latter has several gaps, we chose to follow the text of Reg. 1 and place in the notes the divergencies between the two drafts.

[1]The name of the recipient was made known to us though the *Mémoires* of Father René Rapin (3 vols., Paris, 1865), vol. I, p. 115. Gerolamo Cardinal Grimaldi was born in Genoa in 1597. Vice-Legate of Romagna in 1625, Governor of Rome in 1628, Nuncio in France in 1641, he became a Cardinal in 1643, and Archbishop of Aix in 1648, where he died on November 4, 1685.

[2]Raoul Allier erroneously claims in *La cabale des dévots* (Paris, 1902), p. 168, that the Saint was referring to François de Raconis, Bishop of Lavaur, who defended orthodox doctrine in two works: *Examen et jugement du livre de la fréquente communion* (Paris, 1644), and *De la primauté et souveraineté singulière de saint Pierre* (Paris, 1645). François de Raconis had died on July 16, 1646 and had signed his writings.

[3]The doctrine of the equality of Saints Peter and Paul, upheld for the first time in the preface to the book entitled *De la fréquénte communion*, had been opposed by François de Raconis. In 1645 it was taken up again by an anonymous author in two books which some persons attribute to Barcos, nephew of Abbé de Saint-Cyran, and others to Antoine Arnauld: *De l'autorité de S. Pierre et S. Paul, qui réside dans le Pape, successeur de ces apôtres,* and *La grandeur de l'Eglise romaine établie sur l'autorité de S. Pierre et de S. Paul.* The intervention of Isaac Habert, Theologian of Paris, and of Dom Pierre de Saint-Joseph, a Cistercian, on behalf of the traditional doctrine, gave rise, in 1646, to a book entitled: *Esclaircissements de quelques objections qu'on a formées contre le livre de* La grandeur de l'Eglise romaine.

[4]The bishops who had approved *De la fréquente communion* sent Jean Bourgeois and Jérôme Duchesne to Rome to prevent the condemnation of this work.

these Doctors,[5] to assure him of the contrary, and to entreat him to see to it that the next Gazette mentions that this teaching is falsely attributed to it.[6] That is what prompted this good, virtuous person to bring me these writings today, so that I might send them to Rome to serve as a thesis for those whom His Holiness has designated to examine the said book. They will find in this work all the authors, quoted in favor of the so-called equality of Saint Peter and Saint Paul, refuted by the same authors whose excerpts they quote, one after the other.[7]

Now, to whom can I better address this work than to Y[our] E[minence], My Lord, to have it used as this good Doctor wishes,[8] since Y[our] E[minence] is the prince and protector of things pertaining to our holy religion, and has done me the honor of telling me that I should turn to Y[our] E[minence] in all matters concerning the service of God? This leads me to hope, My Lord, that you will have no objection to this nor to the fact that I claim always the title

---

[5]The words "disclaim these doctors" are missing in the rough draft.

[6]Nicolas Cornet, Doctor of the Navarre and trustee of the University, was informed by the Nuncio, Nicolò di Bagno, that Jean Bourgeois and Jérôme Duchesne were stating in Rome that the doctrine of Barcos' book had the approval of the Sorbonne. When Cornet informed his colleagues of this imputation, they became very upset, and immediately condemned the error attributed to them.

[7]This sentence, with a slight change in the French verbs (*on trouvera* instead of *ils trouveront*), was written personally by the Saint on the back of the letter addressed to him by Cardinal Mazarin on September 7, 1646. The following was added at the bottom: "Note that these words were written by Vincent de Paul himself. It seems that the work of which the Servant of God speaks was published by D. Le Maître, mentioned in Dupin's books, . . .the book of Maître Morel, Doctor of the Sorbonne, published by Recolet in 1646, in which the falsified text. . . ." (Cf. Rapin, *op. cit.,* vol. I, pp. 114-115.)

[8]Following these words, the Saint had written in the rough draft a few lines that he then scratched out so as to reconstruct his sentence. They are: "That this good Doctor. . .the author claims that I. . .once again, by all accounts among the most learned men in the world and one of the best, I very humbly implore you to accept, Eminence, and to allow me always the disposition that Your Eminence has led me to hope for, which is to consider myself your most humble and obedient servant."

you allow me to have, that of your most humble and very obedient servant.[9]

VINCENT DEPAUL
i.s.C.M.

It would be a consolation to this good Doctor if Y[our] E[minence] would kindly do me the honor of having someone write to me about the reception and outcome of his thesis.[10]

868. - TO MONSIEUR DESGORDES

Saint-Lazare, October 4, 1646

Monsieur,

The grace of Our Lord be with you forever!

Since your mother, Madame Desgordes, and your relatives have asked me to send them and you, Monsieur, a clergyman to be with you and to direct your studies, I have had introduced to your mother a clergyman of this city, M. Le Noir, the bearer of this letter, and she approves of him. He has the necessary qualifications for this position, and I hope, Monsieur, that you will be fully satisfied, once you get to know him.

---

[9]Here again three lines have been scratched out in the rough draft: "These opinions, Eminence, still trouble somewhat the Church here, but not so vehemently, it seems to me, as they did in the beginning; and, after God, what appears to have contributed most effectively to this is the Bull of His Holiness."

[10]The doctrine of the two leaders was censured by Innocent X on January 24, 1647 as dangerous and in opposition to the fundamental principles of the Church, but the condemnation of Rome did not put an end to the dispute. (Cf. Louis Ellies Dupin, *Histoire ecclésiastique du XVII siècle* [5 vols., Paris: A. Pralard, 1714], vol. II, pp. 145 ff.)

Letter 868. - The original rough draft of this letter is the property of the Daughters of Charity of Castelsarrasin.

In the name of God, Monsieur, accept him and obey your mother in this matter. Nature obliges you to do so, God orders you, and you know, Monsieur, that this is the intention of the Court. I can also assure you that the Queen will be especially pleased and that, if there is ever an opportunity to serve you, I shall do so most willingly. I am, in the love of Our Lord, Monsieur, your most humble and obedient servant.

VINCENT DEPAUL
i.s.C.M.

868a. - TO GUILLAUME DELVILLE,[1] IN MONTMIRAIL

Saint-Lazare, October 4, 1646

M. Delville will be assured by this note, which I am writing in haste because the mail coach is here, that we have received the letters he wrote to M. Codoing and me. I shall forward his to Rouy[2] in Brittany, where he is—I mean M. Codoing—and on his part I ask M. Delville to send back to me as soon as possible the sermons he left him. He has great need of them in the place he now is.

The Bishop of Soissons[3] is most anxious for us to be established in Montmirail,[4] on the conditions already known. We have written

---

Letter 868a. - The original autograph letter was put on sale in Paris in 1932. The text was published in the *Annales C. M.* (1933), pp. 217-219, and reprinted in *Mission et Charité*, 19-20, pp. 64-65. This edition uses the latter text.

[1]Guillaume Delville, born at Tilloy-lez-Bapaume, today Ligny-Tilloy (Pas-de-Calais), entered the Congregation of the Mission as a priest on January 19, 1641, at thirty-three years of age. He was Superior in Crécy (1644) and in Montmirail (1644-1646, 1650-1651). He then retired to Arras, where for several years he continued his missionary work with Saint Vincent's permission. He died in Arras in 1658.

[2]The exact location of Rouy is unknown to us.

[3]Simon Le Gras, born in Paris in 1598, was appointed Bishop of Soissons in 1623, and died at the château de Sept-Mons, near Soissons, in 1656.

[4]The Priests of the Mission had been established in Montmirail (Soissons diocese) in 1644.

to him. I think the Prior[5] told me that you went to see him and that he gave you his consent. If that is the case, it would be well for you to go and see M. Nacquart,[6] and to accept the gift of the house he wishes to make, even though the Bishop may not have given you the word. What cannot be done at one time can be done at another. So please do not lose any time in this[7]. . . . However, it does not appear to me that he will do what he had intended to do and it is even out of the question.

If we were able to give the missions and open the seminary you mentioned, Monsieur, we would have to do it, provided those young men were aspiring to the priesthood. But we cannot do the former, which is our principal duty, and how can we do the latter! Not to give missions, *O Jésus,* Monsieur, God forbid! We shall see, with time, if we can give you two of our students to teach the classes, while you give the mission with M. Royer[8] and the man we will send you.

---

[5]The Prior of the Hôtel-Dieu in La Chaussée (faubourg of Montmirail), which was part of the Troyes diocese.

[6]Charles Nacquart, born in Treslon (Marne) in 1617, entered the Congregation of the Mission on April 6, 1640. After his ordination he was sent to Richelieu. Designated for the first group of Lazarists (Vincentians) to be sent to Madagascar, he arrived there on December 4, 1648. He had learned the native language so well on the voyage to Madagascar that in a short time he was able to draft a brief summary of Christian doctrine, *Petit catéchisme, avec les prières du matin et du soir. . .* , (Paris: Georges Josse, l657). (Cf. also Abelly, *op.cit.,* bk. II, chap. I, sect. 9, §5 and §6.) A new edition of Nacquart's work, edited by Ludwig Munthe, Elie Rajaonarison and Désiré Ranaivosoa, has been published under the title of *Le catéchisme malgache de 1657,* (Antananarivo; Egede Instituttet, 1987). He converted several Protestants, baptized seventy-seven Malagasy, and regularized the situation of the French who were living in concubinage with native women. He evangelized not only Fort-Dauphin, but all the interior within a radius of ten leagues. Exhausted by so much work, Nacquart died on May 29, 1650. *Mémoires de la Congrégation de la Mission* (11 vols., Paris, 1863-1899), published in vol. IX his letters, diary, and testament from the old copies preserved in the archives of the Congregation.

Since Nacquart was born in the Soissons diocese, his desire to give a house he owned to the Community in Montmirail is understandable.

[7]A two-line tear occurs here. The first line starts with *M. le Pri. . .* ; the second with *Delville. . . .*

[8]The person referred to here is either Nicolas Royer or Ponce Royer. Nicolas Royer was born in Chenières (Trèves diocese) in 1613, entered the Congregation of the Mission on August 24, 1639, and was ordained a priest in 1642. Ponce Royer was born in Thor (Cavaillon diocese) in 1615, and entered the Congregation of the Mission as a priest on October 25, 1645.

My most humble thanks for your kind treatment of the Prior and his men. We are grateful for this.

I am writing to you during my retreat. There are about forty of us making it [in several groups; besides] seven priests [. . .], there are two or three clerics with us, part of the seminary in the other, and the coadjutor Brothers separately. When will you make yours? Please recommend ours to God, and God knows how wholeheartedly we shall recommend yours to Him. He also knows how cordially I cherish you. Truly, only He can make you realize this.

My most humble greetings to M. Royer as well. I promise you both that I shall send you a priest at the first opportunity. I am, in the love of the same Lord, Monsieur, your most humble servant.

VINCENT DEPAUL
i.s.C.M.

Addressed: Monsieur Delville, Superior of the Mission of Fontaine-Essarts,[9] in Montmirail

869. - TO ANDRE PRAT, CONSUL OF FRANCE, IN SALE

Paris, October 5, 1646

Monsieur,

The grace of Our Lord be with you forever!

I cannot express to you, Monsieur, my gratitude for the charity with which you are pleased to honor our Little Company, by wishing to employ it in God's service and yours, to assist our poor slaves in Salé. I thank you most humbly for this, Monsieur, and offer you the

---

[9]A hamlet near Montmirail, where the Missionaries established themselves after they left La Chaussée, which had become uninhabitable.

Letter 869. - Original autograph draft of a letter, Bibl. Nat. n. a. f. 3533, pièce 395.

humble services of our Little Company, along with my own, with all the humility and affection in my power.

I do not know what to say about the conduct of that good Father who forged ahead,[1] Monsieur, except that one of our maxims is that we should relinquish to others the good works they offer to do, in the belief, with good reason, that they will do them better than we. Furthermore, we are afraid that some local dispute might arise, and that would be a scandal rather than an edification to both Christians and unbelievers. Should it happen that your son[2] has not welcomed this good Father, or if his journey is concerned only with the ransom of slaves, as he said when he was leaving, so people tell me, in that case or a similar one, we shall do most willingly whatever you order. You have been chosen by the King and consequently by God to make His Will known through your own in these circumstances. If, in recognition of this obligati[on], any opportunity to honor you should arise, we shall do this most willingly, Monsieur.

In the meantime, we shall pray to God for the p[reservation] of your person and that of your [son, who] is your representative in Salé. May He preserve you both, and sanctify more and more your dear soul and those of the rest of your family. I am, in His love, Monsieur, your most humble and obedient servant.

VINCENT DEPAUL
i.s.C.M.

---

[1] A Reformed Franciscan, the Recollect mentioned in no. 870.
[2] Henri Prat. He succeeded his father on October 20, 1648.

Paris, October 6 [1646][1]

Monsieur,

The grace of Our Lord be with you forever!
Yesterday I received two of your letters, one dated September
21 and [the other] September 22. I am going to write to M. de [. . .
I] am sending you this letter by express messenger.

Mon Dieu, Monsieur! what shall we do [about] what you told
us? It does not seem probable that that person[2] will retract his
opinions, because of his state of mind. He has already reached the
point of judging that the Councils have not fully understood Sacred
Scripture. It is impossible to retire a man with a mind like his. The
other man[3] is subject to catarrh and is unstable; the former[4] a little
melancholy and set in his ways. It is awkward to keep him, and
awkward also to send him away. Nevertheless, all things considered, we shall be obliged to come to that.

You will see from the letter I am writing to him, which I am
sending you open and which you will seal afterward with our seal,
that I am asking him to go to Richelieu, where I plan to go and see

Letter 870. - Original autograph letter. In 1931 it was in the Library of the State of Prussia, Berlin.
Pémartin (no. 3040) had published a text taken from a copy, which at times was defective and
incomplete; Coste reproduced it, but with some conjectural corrections. The text was published
in *Annales C. M.* (1931), pp. 696-699, and reprinted in *Mission et Charité,* 19-20, pp. 65-69. This
edition uses the latter text, although some reference to the Coste text has been made.
[1]The context establishes the certainty of this year.
[2]François du Coudray was a scholar, but for a time he professed certain heterodox ideas. As
mentioned in no. 885, some of these included the belief that Our Lord was not yet exalted in
heaven, and that Rome, the Councils, and the Fathers of the Church had not understood Holy
Scripture very well. Saint Vincent had to remove him from La Rose; he found a place for him in
Richelieu, where he died in 1649.
[3]Léonard Boucher, born on August 29, 1610, was admitted to the Congregation of the Mission
on November 12, 1632, and ordained a priest on September 23, 1634. He took vows on November
6, 1642, and renewed them on October 3, 1656, in the presence of Antoine Portail. At the time
of this letter, he was stationed in La Rose and manifested an attachment to the person and ideas
of his Superior, M. du Coudray.
[4]From here to the end of the following paragraph the pronouns refer to M. du Coudray.

him, and to advise him as to what will have to be done. Give it to him at the time and in the manner you think best. And no matter what he says or does, remain always in the spirit of gentleness and humility.

Regarding M. Boucher, if he wants to follow him, tell him that an order from me is required for that. It is not advisable for him to go with him. If he does it on his own, we shall look into it.

As for the person you will put in his place, what you tell me about M. Dufour[5] in Cahors and M. Delattre in La Rose is not feasible for M. Dufour; that would be too humiliating for the Bishop of Saintes.[6] However, the thought that has come to my mind is to put M. Testacy[7] in Cahors, if the Bishop agrees to it and you see no disadvantage, given his leadership and the fact that his mother is close by.[8] He seems like a man with common sense, faithful enough in his practices, educated and knowledgeable about business affairs. [It is] unfortunate that he has just become a priest and that [the fami]ly[9] will find it difficult to see him [go] straight away [to] his post as superior. But, since Messrs. Water and Treffort[10] are good and not ambitious, you might be able to get them to approve, in

[5]Claude Dufour was Superior of the Saintes Seminary in 1646, and remained there until 1648. He died in Madagascar in 1656. M. Portail had proposed to send him to Cahors when Guillaume Delattre was to be changed from there to La Rose.

[6]Jacques-Raoul de la Guibourgère, who was transferred that same year to Maillezais-La Rochelle. His successor for the Saintes diocese, Louis de Bassompierre, was named at the end of 1646.

[7]Charles Testacy, born in Condom (Gers), entered the Congregation of the Mission on March 27, 1643 at thirty years of age, took his vows on January 9, 1646, and was ordained a priest that same year. As mentioned here, he became Superior in Cahors at the end of 1646; in 1647 he was sent to the house in Saintes.

[8]Cahors was only about 125 miles from Condom.

[9]The confreres in the house.

[10]The Coste text does not have either of these names. James Water, born in Cork (Ireland) in 1616, entered the Congregation of the Mission at Saint-Lazare on October 9, 1638. He was ordained a priest in 1642, took his vows in 1644, and was sent to the Cahors Seminary, where he was in 1646, 1654 and 1662. He returned to Ireland in 1662.

Simon Treffort, born in Villiers-Herbisse (Aube) on October 2, 1611, entered the Congregation of the Mission on October 5, 1642, and took vows on October 7, 1645. In 1646 he was at the Cahors Seminary. He was Superior in La Rose (1668-1677), then returned to Cahors, where he died in 1682. Some days after his death, Edme Jolly, the Superior General, wrote a letter in which he greatly eulogized his virtues.

consideration of his business acumen. As for the Bishop of Cahors, perhaps you will find him well disposed to this; if not, we shall try to send you M. Grimal or M. Berthe.[11] I had thought of M. Bourdet, but I think we will send him to Ireland, where we are anxious to send some Missionaries native to the country, under the direction of a French superior. They will be able to leave in two weeks, if M. Bourdet is ready.

That will leave you Messrs. Riou,[12] a good little priest from Normandy,[13] M. des Noyelles,[14] and M. Le Soudier,[15] since the other man[16] has left for Barbary and is still in Marseilles, wondering if he will make it, because of an incident with a Recollect Father, who usurped his place. Also, we were not sure which one, he or M. Le Sage,[17] would be leaving.

---

[11]François Grimal, born in Paris on March 6, 1605, began his Internal Seminary on June 6, 1640, and took his vows on October 9, 1646. He rendered outstanding service to his Congregation, as Superior of the houses in Crécy (1645-1646), Montmirail (1646-1649, 1654-1655), and Agen (1650-1651); as Second Assistant to Saint Vincent (1652); and in more humble positions in Fontainebleau and elsewhere. The introduction of vows into the Company corresponded to his wishes, and he made every effort to have this measure accepted by those around him. He renewed his vows on October 3, 1665, in the presence of M. Portail.

Thomas Berthe, Superior of the Missionaries sent to Picardy and Champagne. Born in Donchery (Ardennes), he was admitted to the Congregation of the Mission on December 26, 1640 at the age of eighteen, took his vows on December 8, 1645, and was ordained a priest in 1646. He served the Community in many important positions: Superior in various houses, Secretary of the Congregation, and Assistant to the Superior General (1661-1667). In October 1659 Saint Vincent decided that among his Missionaries none was more suitable to succeed him as head of the Congregation than René Alméras or Thomas Berthe. These were the two names which he proposed in advance, in writing, to the General Assembly which was to choose his successor. (René Alméras was elected.) There were some clashes between Berthe and Edme Jolly, Superior General at the time, which clouded his last years. Thomas Berthe died in 1697. (Cf. *Notices,* vol. II, pp. 247-313.)

In his text Coste inserted the name of Dufestel (François) before that of Berthe. He observed that the name was not found in the defective text he used.

[12]M. Riou is not listed on any of the available personnel lists of the Congregation of the Mission, so he cannot be identified.

[13]Guillaume Michel.

[14]Philippe des Noyelles.

[15]Samson Le Soudier.

[16]The person referred to is Jacques Le Soudier, whom Saint Vincent sometimes called Le Soudier the younger.

[17]Jacques Lesage, born around 1614 in Auffay (Seine-Maritime), entered the Congregation of the Mission as a priest on October 7, 1639, and took his vows on November 26, 1645. He embarked for Algiers in January or February 1648, and dedicated himself entirely, with no regard

If M. Le Soudier does not go to La Rose, M. Cuissot the younger,[18] who is replacing him and is doing very well at present, will go to La Rose, and M. Perraud[19] will go to Saintes. We shall try to send the other two as soon as possible.

Here we are, reestablished at Saint-Méen for the second time, by a decree of the Council. However, the Parlement, from whom the Commissioner,[20] who expelled our men, and the Procurator General[21] have a personal writ of summons, has put them in such a fury that we shall never have any peace of mind in that province if we do not come to a compromise. M. Codoing, whom we have sent there, is working on that.

When this good priest[22] leaves, dealings with those women will have to be stopped and those boys sent away, if they are not paying a reasonable amount for room and board.

The Bishop of Cahors has informed me that he wants you to make the visitation there. He will unburden [his heart] to you. I think he is a little annoyed with [me] because I have not [served] him enough to the liking of those good Fathers[23] in the lawsuit he had there.

You have never done anything more timely than to remain in La Rose until you can put everything in the best state possible.

I think we shall have no difficulty changing what M. Dehorgny and you judge appropriate to change in the functions[24] you point out

---

for hardships and dangers, to ministering to the poor slaves. After a visit to the plague-stricken, he himself contracted this terrible disease, and died on May 12, 1648.

[18]Jean Cuissot, the younger brother of Gilbert Cuissot.

[19]Hugues Perraud, born in Arguel (Doubs) on October 3, 1615, entered the Congregation of the Mission on January 5, 1640, took his vows on March 23, 1644, and was ordained a priest in 1646. He was placed in Saintes (1646), and in Richelieu (1651), and died in Paris on December 26, 1659.

[20]M. Huchet de la Bédoyère.

[21]M. de la Touche-Frélon, Counselor in the Parlement.

[22]M. du Coudray.

[23]The monks of the Chancelade reform, whose Superior was Alain de Solminihac, had a lawsuit in process aginst the Augustinian monks of Sainte-Geneviève.

[24]This refers to a part of the Rules and Constitutions of the Congregation of the Mission, whose approbation Saint Vincent was endeavoring to obtain, first from the Archbishop of Paris and then from the Holy See. The Saint was seeking the advice of M. Portail with regard to these Rules.

to me, nor in the others. I will continue to pressure the Coadjutor,[25] who is very slow getting things done.

There are about forty of us on retreat. I am with the group of priests. God has given me strength for that. This is the eighth day. Only our visit remains, and I am thinking of putting it off until you return, which I pray God will be as soon as possible.

I will write to you in Marseilles and send you there the Common Rules in Latin.[26]

Meanwhile, I embrace that little Community with all the humility and affection in my power, and I am, Monsieur, your most humble servant.

VINCENT DEPAUL
i.s.C.M.

Monsieur Bourdet has apologized profoundly to me for contradicting you, and promised to have your recommendations observed.[27] If he does not go to Ireland, we will be able to send him to La Rose, if you do not decide on one or the other I mentioned to you.

I wrote to the Bishop of Cahors, in consequence of what he had said about recalling M. Delattre. I told him I had thought of representing to him that we had no one else but him who understood business, but that we would nevertheless do what he orders.

Addressed: Monsieur Portail, Priest of the Mission, in La Rose

---

[25]Jean-François-Paul de Gondi, who, since 1643, had been Coadjutor to his uncle, Jean-François de Gondi, Archbishop of Paris. He was created a Cardinal in 1652 [Cardinal de Retz], and succeeded his uncle in 1654.

[26]Saint Vincent was referring to the text of the Rules of the Company, which would not be definitively established until 1658.

[27]The visitation recommendations left by M. Portail in Saint-Méen.

871. - TO FRANCOIS DU COUDRAY[1]

[October 6, 1646][2]

I cannot, no, I cannot express to you, my dear little Father, my sorrow at grieving you. I implore you to believe that, were it not for the importance of the matters, I would prefer a thousand times to bear the pain of this myself rather than upset you by it.

872. - *ETIENNE BLATIRON, SUPERIOR, TO SAINT VINCENT*

Genoa, 1646

On behalf of Cardinal Durazzo, Archbishop of this city, we have written to all the archpriests of the places where missions are given, to notify all the pastors and priests in their deanery that the spiritual exercises are to begin on a certain day in the house of the Mission, and that all those who wish to take advantage of this fine opportunity should be there at a given time. A good number have already come and gone. I cannot express to you the tremendous consolation they received, the abundant graces Our Lord bestowed on them, the great modesty and exact silence they observed, their humility and sincerity in giving an account of their prayer, and the admirable and almost miraculous conversions that have taken place there.

Among others there was a pastor who told me, almost in public, that he had come so that the Cardinal would have his income increased. He came with the intention of ridiculing things and more out of hypocrisy than devotion. He said also that the Mission had no greater enemy than he, and that he had said all the evil that could be imagined about it and even about His Eminence. He was a man strongly addicted to vice; he had obtained a benefice by simony, was ordained without any title except this benefice, carried out the functions of a priest, administered the sacraments, and

---

Letter 871. - Collet, *op. cit.,* vol. II, p. 162.

[1]Collet states that the letter of which this is an extract was addressed to a Missionary. The expression, "My dear little Father," allows us to identify the Missionary as François du Coudray.

[2]The above extract ties in with the circumstances in the letter of October 6, 1646, addressed to François du Coudray and announced to M. Portail in no. 870.

Letter 872. - Abelly, *op.cit.,* bk. II, chap. IV, p. 290.

performed every parochial duty. He remained in this state for several years,
a man given to scheming and enterprising, etc. However, God finally
touched him, and touched him in a most efficacious way. He was converted,
he wept, he humbled himself, and gave notable proofs of his change. All
who saw him during that retreat, or have heard about him, have been
extremely edified, and we no less than all the others, who have produced
good fruits, each according to his needs.

Better than any words I could use, Monsieur, to express the great joy
and consolation His Eminence experienced because of this, are surely the
tears he shed when some of those priests told him how they felt. This caused
such a stir in the city and even in the environs that a number of other men
have presented themselves to come and do likewise.

873. - TO A VISITATION NUN[1]

Feast of Saint Denis[2] [1646][3]

My dear Mother,

The grace of Our Lord be with you forever!
The reason I asked you, dear Mother, to offer my excuses to

Letter 873. - Reg. 1, f°34, copy made from an autograph rough draft.

[1]Very probably Mother Marie-Agnès Le Roy, Superioress of the Second Monastery of Paris.
Born in Mons (Nord) in 1603, she was, through her mother, the niece of Philippe de Cospéan,
Bishop of Lisieux. In 1624 she entered the First Monastery, which she left at the request of the
Marquise de Dampierre to join the group of Sisters who were sent to the monastery in the faubourg
Saint-Jacques at the time of its foundation. She became Directress there and then Assistant. Three
times the votes of the Sisters entrusted to her the duty of Superior (June 11, 1634 to May 24,
1640; May 27, 1646 to May 13, 1652; and June 6, 1658 to 1664). She went in person to inaugurate
the monasteries in Amiens, and in Mons where she remained three months, and founded one in
Angers and the Third Monastery in Paris. She also played a prominent role in the establishment
of the monastery in Warsaw. She died May 18, 1669. (Cf. *Année sainte des religieuses de la*
Visitation Sainte-Marie [12 vols., Annecy: Ch. Burdet, 1867-1871], vol. V, p. 547.)

[2]October 9.

[3]In his letter of May 19, 1647 (no. 949) to Mother Catherine de Beaumont, Saint Vincent says
that he has tried for the preceding seven or eight months to resign his functions in the Visitation
monasteries. From this we may deduce that the present letter was written in 1646. This conclusion
is strengthened by the fact that Sister Madeleine-Augustine, the last of Madame Fouquet's
daughters, who was a nun in the Second Monastery, was professed in 1646.

Madame Fouquet[4] for being unable to assist at the profession of our
dear Sister, her daughter,[5] and to get someone else whom you and
she would choose, is that the retreat I have just made has caused me
to see clearly that I cannot reconcile my obligation toward our
Company with the service I owe to your house. Moreover, since it
is a Rule of our little Congregation that we should not devote
ourselves to the service of nuns, so as not to be diverted from the
service we owe to the poor country people, I feel obliged in
conscience to observe it because, in future, the practice of our Rules
will be regulated not so much by the text of the Rules as by the way
I will have observed them. If I have acted otherwise because of the
affection I have for your holy Order, it has not been without qualms
of conscience, even though I had been promised that it would be
temporary. If I have even greater involvements,[6] I hope Our Lord
will release me from them as well.

That is why, dear Mother, I most humbly entreat you to accept
willingly the resolution I have taken to resign, and to think about
someone else who might act as your spiritual Father. There are
plenty of persons in Paris, filled with the Spirit of God and of our

---

[4]Marie de Maupeou had married François Fouquet, Vicomte de Vaux, Master of Requests,
and then Councillor of State. Among her eight children were Nicolas Fouquet, the celebrated
Superintendent of Finance; François, the Bishop of Narbonne; Louis, the Bishop of Agde; and
several daughters who entered the Visitation Order. One of her daughters, Marie-Thérèse, became
Superioress of the Visitation in Toulouse. Marie de Maupeou was a lady of exceptional piety and
immense charity, of whom Saint Vincent said that "if through some mischance the Gospels were
lost, their spirit and maxims would be found in the conduct and sentiments of Madame Fouquet."
He added, "She makes devotion so attractive that she encourages everyone to be devout." (Cf.
Année sainte, vol. I, p. 627.) When she heard that her son Nicolas had fallen into disgrace, she
exclaimed: "I thank you, O my God. I have asked You for the salvation of my son, and this is
the way to obtain it." She died in 1681, at the age of ninety-one, mourned by everyone, but
especially by the poor, who called her their mother. In the catalogue of the Ladies of Charity she
is listed under the name of President Fouquet.

[5]Madeleine-Augustine Fouquet was sixteen years old at the time. She went from the Second
to the Third Monastery when the latter was established. She was Councillor for thirty years and
held in succession the offices of Directress, Assistant, and Treasurer. Three of her sisters,
Anne-Madeleine, Elisabeth-Angélique, and Marie-Thérèse, were nuns in the First Monastery.
Another, Louise-Agnès, was with her in the Second Monastery, then in the Third. She died in
1705, at the age of seventy-five. An account of her virtues is found in *Année sainte.*

[6]His position on the Council of Conscience.

blessed Father,[7] who will serve you with far greater grace from God than I.

874. - *RENE ALMERAS THE ELDER TO SAINT VINCENT*

[October 1646] [1]

When I consider the manner and acquiescence with which I consented to my son's vocation; that natural affection did not prevent me from placing him in your hands; that for almost ten years now I have never demanded a visit from him, nor any of the duties that children owe to their fathers; that I have never mentioned his vocation to him except to approve it, rejoicing at having so well confirmed him in it; I declare to you before God, the Searcher of hearts, that I find no fault with your plans for my son. Neither do I have any objections regarding the work you give him or the journeys you have him take, even should they be to the Indies, because I firmly believe that you are acting in all this only for the glory of God. The first time I brought him to you, I placed in God's hands and yours my paternal authority over him, making you his absolute master. I cannot and must not now take back the offering I so voluntarily made of him. So, all that remains to me is to ask God to bless his actions and prosper his journeys, and you, Monsieur, to give me some share in your prayers.

[7]Saint Francis de Sales.

Letter 874. - Manuscript life of M. Alméras, p. 15, quoted in *Notices*, vol. III, p. 234.
[1]The author of *Notices* dated this letter 1647. The author of the manuscript life simply stated that René Alméras the elder wrote this letter "to reply to the excuses" that Saint Vincent "offered him, because his son had left for Rome without notifying him or taking leave of him." So this letter belongs near no. 864.

875. - TO ANTOINE PORTAIL, IN LA ROSE

Paris, October 13 [1646][1]

Monsieur,

The grace of Our Lord be [with you for]ever!

This letter is to [confirm what] I told you in my last [letter regarding] the person in question,[2] and [also because] I have written to Richelieu asking that he be [welcomed with] the respect and cordiality he deserves. Act in this and in all else as your prudence dictates. Brother Champion[3] told me the same thing as you about the Ascension and the Cross of Our Lord. It would be well if you wrote in your own name a little informative note about this, mentioning the errors of the person and that you were receiving depositions from M. Alméras and others who heard him state and maintain this error. You and they will have to sign it and send it to me sealed.

You did well to accept the one hundred écus that were placed in your hands; we shall pay them back in this city.

You will also have to make the visitation in Cahors. Let me know whether M. Delattre is assigned to La Rose and M. Testacy to Cahors, so we can praise God, if you have done it; if not, so that we can send you someone to take charge in La Rose.

That is all I can tell you for now in my haste. I am, for you and for M. Alméras, Monsieur, your most humble and obedient servant.

VINCENT DEPAUL
i.s.C.M.

Addressed: Monsieur Portail, Priest of the Mission, in La Rose

---

Letter 875. - Archives of the Mission, Paris, original autograph letter.
[1]The contents of the letter require this date.
[2]François du Coudray.
[3]Louis Champion, born in Le Mans, entered the Congregation of the Mission on April 12, 1643, at twenty years of age, and took his vows on June 17, 1646. In 1650 he had only received tonsure but was nevertheless teaching moral theology at the Bons-Enfants. He was Superior in Montmirail (1652-1654), and from there went to the house in Marseilles, where he was in 1655.

876. - TO EDMUND DWYER, BISHOP OF LIMERICK[1]

FIRST DRAFT

Paris, 15 [October 1646][2]

Excellency,

Here at last are the eight Missionaries[3] who [are going] to Ireland. Five of them are Irish, [one is a French priest, one a French seminarian,] and one an English Brother. The [French priest is going to] be in charge of the group, on the advice of the late M. Skyddie,[4] who told me before he died that he thought this is how it should be done. The French seminarian has [learned] chant. All of them fear and love God and, by the grace of Our Lord, are zealous for the salvation of their neighbor. They are going to cast themselves at your feet, Excellency, to offer themselves for the service of Y[our] Most Illustrious L[ordship] and the prelates to whom they will, with time, be able to render some small service. We are preparing others here, whom we will be able to send once they have been trained, if there is any way of finding a means of subsistence for them by the attribution of some benefice. In this way, they will not be a burden on the people to whom they will go to give missions. And would to God, Excellency, that I were worthy to be among them! God knows how willingly I would go, and how ardently I offer Him this little band, and to you, Excellency, my perpetual obedience![5] I most humbly entreat you, Excellency, to accept this.

Letter 876. - Archives of the Mission, Paris, original autograph letter.

[1]Richard Arthur, Bishop of Limerick, died May 23, 1646, and was succeeded by his Coadjutor, Edmund Dwyer. The latter lived through the worst period of the Cromwellian religious persecution, giving an example of unequaled faith and courage. Forced to leave Ireland after the siege of Limerick, he died in Brussels two years later in 1654.

[2]The month and year of the Missionaries' departure for Ireland.

[3]The names are given in no. 877.

[4]John Skyddie was born in Cork (Ireland) in 1609, entered the Congregation of the Mission on October 9, 1638, and was ordained a priest in 1640. He died before 1646.

[5]Saint Vincent found it hard to hit upon the right phrase. He had first written, "how willingly

SECOND DRAFT

When you were in this city, I took the honor of telling Your Most Illustrious L[ordship] that I had received an order from the Holy Father to send some Missionaries of our Company to Ireland. Various unforeseen circumstances have prevented us from sending them sooner. Here now are eight of them, Excellency, who are going to prostrate themselves at your feet to ask your holy blessing.[6]

Marvelous things have been said of the leadership of Y[our] L[ordship], Excellency, and that, after God, it is to this alone that the good relations of Church and State in those regions are to be attributed. Alas! Excellency, this is not difficult to believe for those who, like myself, have had the happiness of approaching Y[our] L[ordship]. I have never come away from you without reflecting that the Spirit of God and His holy workings reside in you. If Our Lord chooses to have this affair succeed according to your holy intentions, your memory will be immortalized on earth and in heaven. This, Excellency, is what I, prostrate in spirit at your feet, ask of Him who grants me the honor of kissing the sacred hands of Y[our] Illustrious L[ordship]. I am, in the love of Our Lord and His holy Mother. . . .

I would work, according to the orders which Your Illustrious Lordship might be pleased to honor me;" then changed it to "how willingly I would submit to you, Excellency," before he finally decided on the words used in the present letter.

[6]When he had finished his second draft, the Saint was dissatisfied and deleted all he had written, with the exception of the paragraph given above. He replaced the deleted part with what follows in the letter.

877. - TO ANTOINE PORTAIL, IN LA ROSE

Paris, 18 [October 1646][1]

Monsieur,

The grace of Our [Lord be with you] forever!

I was greatly consoled by y[our letter and] am awaiting some good results. I [already wrote you] twice, [in addition to this letter, about what I] think you should do in La Rose, and especially that you should see to it that the person in question[2] come to Richelieu; [we] will send word whether he should be brought here.

I see clearly from the way you speak to me about M. Testacy that we should not attempt to do what I mentioned to you in my last letter, namely, to put him in charge either in La Rose or in Cahors. We must hope that Our Lord will do whatever is best. I had thought of sending M. Lucas[3] or M. Grimal there, or else M. Le Soudier the younger.[4] I doubt he will go to Barbary, since there is a Recollect Father who has usurped his place there, forged ahead, and taken the

---

Letter 877. - Original autograph letter in the château of Clavières-Ayrens near Aurillac (Cantal). Coste published a text based on the Pémartin edition (vol. I, no. 505, pp. 591-592) and preserved Pémartin's interpolations of a defective text. Since the publication of the Coste edition, the original was found in 1937 and put on sale at the Hôtel des Ventes in Paris. The text was published in *Annales C. M.* (1937), pp. 730-731, and reprinted in *Mission et Charité,* 19-20, pp. 69-71.

The original manuscript is badly torn at the top right hand corner; it affects the front and back of the page and makes it difficult to make sense out of some of the fragments. Because of the expertise of both Pémartin and Coste, the editors of this edition have been able to fill in the lacunae in the text by adding, in brackets, the educated conjectures found in the Coste text.

[1]There can be no doubt that this letter was written either in October or November 1646. Father Raymond Chalumeau, C.M., archivist at Saint-Lazare, has established October 18, 1646 as the date for this letter. Coste speculated that it could be October 20.

[2]François du Coudray.

[3]Antoine Lucas, born in Paris on January 20, 1600, had pursued higher studies at the Sorbonne. He entered the Congregation of the Mission in December 1626 and was ordained a priest in September 1628. His zeal, his talent for preaching, and his skill in debate made him much appreciated by Father de Condren and by Jean-Jacques Olier, who one day asked Saint Vincent for him for his personal instruction and for the conversion of a heretic. Antoine Lucas was in the La Rose house in 1645, Superior of the Le Mans house (1647-1651), and then placed in Sedan. He died in November 1656, a victim of his zeal for the plague-stricken. (Cf. *Notices,* vol. I, pp. 135-146.)

[4]Jacques Le Soudier.

position that was destined for him in Salé. Please send me your opinion about all this as soon as you can.

M. Brin, M. Barry,[5] Brother [O'Brien], a seminarian,[6] and Brother Patriarche[7] have left for Ireland and are to pick up Messrs. Le Blanc[8] and Duiguin[9] and Brother Le Vacher[10] in Le Mans, and perhaps M. Bourdet in Brittany.[11] We have been pressured about this both by Rome and by the prelates of that country; that is why we shall not be making any other foundation for a long time.

[I think you are] right to have [M. Alméras] leave [for] Annecy, if his health permits, [for the reasons] you point out to me. You [can tell him] that if he shows any signs [of what he had] last year, it is better [for him to stay] only a short time in La Rose and to go to

---

[5]Edmund Barry, born in the Cloyne diocese (Ireland) on June 24, 1613, was ordained a priest in Cahors in 1639 and admitted into the Congregation of the Mission on July 21, 1641. He took his vows at Saint-Lazare a few days before his departure for Ireland, returning to France in 1652, after Limerick had been captured by Cromwell's army. He was placed in Richelieu (1652-1653), and Montauban (1653-1680). While in Montauban, he directed the seminary (1657-1664, 1675-1680). He died there in 1680.

[6]Dermot O'Brien, born in Emly (Ireland) in 1621, entered the Congregation of the Mission on October 23, 1645, at the age of twenty-four, and died a priest in November 1649.

[7]Salomon Patriarche, born on the Isle of Jersey in 1620, entered the Congregation of the Mission as a coadjutor Brother on July 24, 1642, at the age of twenty-two, and took his vows in 1646. He returned to France in 1649 because of mental problems and was assigned to Saint-Méen. He lost his mind completely in 1651.

[8]Georges Le Blanc (George White).

[9]Dermot Duiguin (Duggan), born in Ireland in 1620, was a priest when he entered the Congregation of the Mission on August 26, 1645, at the age of twenty-five. In November 1646 he was sent back to Ireland, returning to France in 1648. Two years later he left for Scotland, where he spent the rest of his life amidst great perils, animated with the zeal of an apostle and the courage of a martyr. He died May 17, 1657 on the isle of Uist, where an ancient chapel still bears his name and recalls his memory. (Cf. *Notices*, vol. III, pp. 114-121)

[10]Philippe Le Vacher, born in Ecouen (Val-d'Oise) on March 23, 1622, entered the Congregation of the Mission on October 5, 1643 and took his vows on August 5, 1646. He was recalled to France in 1649 and was sent to Marseilles, where he was ordained a priest on April 2, 1650, and sailed for Algiers as Vicar Apostolic and Vicar-General of Carthage. In 1657 he returned to France in order to collect alms for the slaves. His absence, which was intended to last a few months, was prolonged for two years. He set out again in September 1659, reached Barbary, and in 1661 accompanied Brother Dubourdieu to Algiers, where the latter was destined to replace Brother Barreau, French Consul of that city. Le Vacher paid Barreau's debts, settled a number of business matters, and finally left Barbary in 1662, accompanied by the seventy slaves whom he had ransomed. He was assigned to the house in Fontainebleau, where he led a most exemplary life till the day of his death, August 5, 1679. (Cf. *Notices*, vol. III, pp. 595-606.)

[11]Abelly has preserved for us the instructions which Saint Vincent gave orally to the

Richelieu from where [he will be able] to come back. [You can] send someone else to Annecy and to the other houses, where they are continually asking for someone to visit them.[12] Health is the main thing I ask you to consider here; Our Lord will provide for everything else.

You will learn in Marseilles about the mistake made by Brother Barreau, the Consul in Algiers, of committing himself to pay forty thousand livres for the ransom of some captive, contrary to the explicit prohibition he was given in this regard.[13] This affair places us in a painful position; what is more unfortunate is that one hour previously good M. Nouelly[14] had begged him not to do it. Please have Mass celebrated by each member of the family in La Rose, and also for the mission in Ireland.

We have been reestablished in Saint-Méen by the King's order, but I do not know if this will last.[15]

We have just made our retreat with good results, by the grace of God. In his love I am, Monsieur, your most humble and obedient servant.

VINCENT DEPAUL
i.s.C.M.

Addressed: Monsieur Portail, Priest of the Mission, in La Rose

---

Missionaries who were leaving him to go to work in Ireland. After a forced stop in Nantes, where they spent their spare time in the service of the sick and the poor, they embarked on a Dutch ship, which brought them to the end of their journey without incident. There they divided into two groups; one to preach in the diocese of Limerick and the other in that of Cashel. (Cf. Abelly, *op.cit.,* bk. II, p. 187.) The Missionaries sent to Ireland by Saint Vincent risked their lives there, in the midst of persecutions, from 1646 to 1652.

[12]Make a canonical visitation.

[13]Brother Barreau had had the misfortune to post bail for Father Sébastien Brugière, a religious of the Order of Mercy [Trinitarians]. After having imprudently gone into debt in order to ransom slaves, Brugière was prosecuted by his creditors and thrown into prison. Because his health was bad, he was transferred to the Consul's residence under house arrest. (Cf. Pierre Dan, *Histoire de Barbarie et de ses corsaires* [Paris: P. Rocolet, 1649], p. 151; also, "Documents algériens, Certificat des souffrances du Père Sébastien," *Revue Africaine* [1891], vol. XXXV)

[14]Brother Barreau's Superior.

[15]The Congregation of the Mission staffed the Saint-Méen Seminary until the time of the French Revolution.

878. - TO THE MARQUIS DE MIREPOIX,[1] GOVERNOR OF THE FIEFDOM OF FOIX

Paris, 20 [October 1646][2]

Monsieur,

The grace of Our Lord be [with you forever!]

I hereby renew to you the [offer of my] obedience with all the humility and affection of which I am capable. I most humbly entreat you to accept it, Monsieur, together with my humble request that you esteem the Bishop of Pamiers,[3] whom I know to be one of the most zealous bishops in the kingdom with regard to the glory of God. He is aware of the honor you pay me by acknowledging me as your servant. He is also most anxious for me to inform you that he esteems and respects you far more highly than I could express to you, and wants to come to an arrangement with you, Monsieur, about matters that concern the service of God in his diocese, which

---

Letter 878. - Archives of the Mission, Paris, autograph draft.

[1]Armand Dupeyré, Comte de Troisvilles (Tréville), Marquis de Mirepoix, was named Governor of the region of Foix on February 10, 1646, and Governor and Captain of the Château and town of Foix on March 16 of the same year.

[2]The outline of those parts of the original document which have been damaged by dampness shows that this letter is connected with those written on October 20 of the same year. The parts in brackets are suggested emendations of the defective text.

[3]François-Etienne de Caulet, born in Toulouse on May 19, 1610, was endowed in 1627 with Saint-Volusien Abbey in Foix. He became attached to Jean-Jacques Olier and accompanied him on his missions in Auvergne, in the Chartres diocese, and in other places in the kingdom. He supported him in his parish ministry and, together with him and M. du Ferrier, founded the Vaugirard Seminary. Saint Vincent, who knew the Abbot of Saint-Volusien, thought that he would do well at the head of a diocese. Thanks to him, François de Caulet was consecrated Bishop of Pamiers on March 5, 1645. In 1638 he had testified against Saint-Cyran. As Bishop, he continued for a long time to combat Jansenism, forbade in his diocese the reading of books by adherents of the movement, and made every effort to bring back those who had strayed from the path of truth. However, his association with Nicolas Pavillon, Bishop of Alet, succeeded in winning him over to Jansenism. The Bishop of Pamiers died on August 7, 1680, without having made an act of submission to the Church. (Cf. Jérôme Besoigne, *Vies des quatres évesques engagés dans la cause de Port-Royal* [2 vols., Cologne: n.p., 1756]; Georges Doublet, *Un prélat janseniste, F. de Caulet, réformateur des chapitres de Foix et de Pamiers* [Paris: A. Picard, 1895].) M. Gazier, an authority on Jansenism, had in his library, rich in books and rare manuscripts, a manuscript entitled *Histoire abrégée de la vie de M. François de Caulet, évêque de Pamiers*, by Father Gabaret.

comes under your jurisdiction. Although I assured him that he has no need of a mediator [because you are the] most church-minded person [there is], nevertheless, I do not hesitate [to write] to you, [in accordance with the wi]shes of the above-mentioned Bishop. Experience [shows that], as long as Bishops and Governors [have a good] understanding, the reign of Jesus Christ is firmly [established] in souls, and [when they do] not, God's affairs go [badly].

He has a dispute with the [organized] clergy in his diocese, and with one man in particular,[4] who is [strong]ly supported by some influential persons, who are in favor of these scandals going unpunished. It would be worthy of your incomparable piety, Monsieur, if you were kind enough to have someone tell that man, on your behalf, that he should submit to the orders of the Prelate, and should live in such a way that His Excellency would not be obliged in conscience to take action against him. And perhaps, Monsieur, God will bless your intervention, not only with regard to this priest, but to many others who are in nearly the same state.

It certainly seems to me, Monsieur, that this is as good as done, and I am already thanking God for it. I beg you, Monsieur, to regard me as someone [over whom you have] absolute authority. [If I can be of service to you in] anything, please honor me [with your orders].

In the meantime, I shall ask Our Lord [to bless you] more and more. I am, in His love, your servant.

---

[4]Probably the Archpriest of Ax-les-Thermes. (Cf. Georges Doublet, *François de Caulet, évêque de Pamiers, et la vie ecclésiastique dans son diocèse ariégeois sous Louis XIV* [Foix: Pomiès, 1896], pp. 39ff.)

879. - TO A PRIEST OF THE MISSION[1]

Paris, October. . ., 1646[2]

Monsieur,

The grace of Our Lord be with you forever!

You can imagine the sorrow your letters have brought me because of the affection I have had for you and will have all my life. All the reasons you allege to me are based on your poor health and on the hope you have of improving it in the air of your native land; in which case, you propose to return to fulfill the promises[3] you made to God. Allow me to tell you, Monsieur, that it is not so important for us to live a long time as to continue in the vocation to which God has called us, according to the Apostle's advice, and to abide by what we have promised God. *Vovete et reddite Deo vestro.*[4] Moreover, do you think[5] your native air will lengthen the days of

---

Letter 879. - Reg. 2, p. 289. The Archives of the Mission has an autograph draft, which has suffered the ravages of time. Since the copyist of Register 2 most probably made his copy from the original, this is the text we follow here, although variants from the draft are placed in the notes.

[1]The rough draft does not give any clue as to the recipient of the letter. Register 2 states that it is addressed "to a priest of the Company who had left under the pretext of illness." The Avignon manuscript, which also reproduced it, states "to M. N. in Le Mans." If this indication is correct, the only priests then in Le Mans, as far as we know, were Fathers Gallais, Le Blanc, and Cuissot. As the contents indicate, the recipient had taken his vows and was not a Superior, so the description seems to fit Gilbert Cuissot. The author of his obituary seems to concur (cf. *Notices,* vol. II, p. 87). This conclusion, however, does not agree with Register 2. In fact, it is evident that this letter and no. 896 of November 24 were written to the same person. However, no. 896 could not have been written to Gilbert Cuissot, who was then living at Saint-Lazare, as is evident from nos. 891, 899, and 900.

Two Missionaries left the Company in November: Jean Bourdet, Superior of Saint-Méen, and Thomas Berthe. Letters 879 and 896 cannot refer to Jean Bourdet, to whom Saint Vincent offered the direction of the mission to Ireland. But is it not possible that it might have been written to Thomas Berthe, whom Saint Vincent considered sending to Cahors and who, assigned to Sedan, returned to his family out of vexation at not being named Superior? (Cf. no. 888.)

[2]In the rough draft, the corner where the date was written has disappeared. Register 2 gives only the month and year. The Avignon manuscript alone indicates the day, but we strongly suspect that the copyist chose October 1 without any reliable basis for doing so. It would seem that the date is more appropriately placed at the end of the month than at the beginning.

[3]Text of the rough draft: "to put yourself in a position to fulfill the promise."

[4]*Make vows to God and fulfill them.* Cf. Ps 76:12. (NAB) Ps 75:12. (D-RB)

[5]Rough draft: "do you think, Monsieur."

your life beyond the reckoning God has made of them? *O Dieu!*
Monsieur, how a little of the courage of those who go in search of
illness and those who get themselves killed in a battle through vanity
would well suit our piety! Three men of the Company[6] were under
this illusion, that they would be in better health in their native
region. The first[7] hastened his death there and died three days after
his return. That was M. Perdu.[8] M. Senaux[9] spent four months with
his relatives,[10] and was no better there, and M. Dubuc,[11] who is with
his family right now, has sent me word[12] that he is ill in mind and
body there. Perhaps things will be different with you.

Be that as it may, from what I just told you I see no reason[13] for
a dispensation in this instance, nor consequently any assurance for
you. And you must beware of this all the more because the basis for
your decision is that you were flattered by the expectation of being
made a Superior. When things turned out differently, your thoughts
turned first of all to leaving the place where we had sent you;[14]
secondly, temptation drove you further to consider leaving the
Congregation, for this is really the heart of the matter, although
deceitful nature may have caused you to see the contrary. And if
you had revealed[15] this innermost recess of your soul to those whose

---

[6]Rough draft: "of the house."

[7]Rough draft: "with this hope that in their native place they would be better, the first of
whom. . . ."

[8]Jacques Perdu, born in Grandvilliers (Oise) on April 9, 1607. He entered the Congregation
of the Mission in 1630, was ordained a priest in 1632, was placed in Richelieu in January 1638,
and died in September 1644.

[9]Nicolas Senaux, born in Auffay (Seine-Maritime) on May 9, 1619, entered the Congregation
of the Mission on June 22, 1639, was ordained a priest February 20, 1644, took his vows on
March 23 of the same year, and died in Troyes on March 28, 1658. Saint Vincent praised his
regularity, resignation, and spirit of indifference in a letter of April 12, 1658 (vol. VII, no. 2570)
and in a conference on the following June 28 (vol. XII, no. 184).

[10]Rough draft: "four months in his native place."

[11]Louis Dubuc, born in Eu (Seine-Maritime), was received into the Congregation of the
Mission after Easter in 1636.

[12]Rough draft: "and at present, M. Dubuc is there, who sends me word."

[13]Rough draft: "Perhaps it will be different for you. I beg Our Lord Jesus Christ that it may
be so, and shall continue to ask this all the days of my life. In line with what I have just told you,
I see no reason in that for a dispensation."

[14]Sedan. This word is written out in the rough draft, but was scratched out.

[15]Rough draft: "and if you had shown."

advice you sought, they probably would have counseled you to stay,[16] especially if you had told them what care is taken of the sick here in this house, thank God, not only with regard to food and remedies, but also with regard to changes of place and duties. In line with that, I wrote to the Bishop of Cahors,[17] the day before I received your letter, that we were assigning you to take charge of his seminary.[18] Since this is so, I beg you to return, Monsieur, by the promise you made to God to live and die in the Company, and by the divine judgment He must make of your soul at the hour of death. You have in the same Company two outstanding examples of persons who, having yielded to the temptation of leaving, soon recovered and came back.[19] One has gone to establish a house in his own country;[20] he is the seventh or eighth, and the other[21] is working with good results. We have the same confidence in him as before, and will have the same in you because I know the goodness of your dear heart, which I ask God to sanctify more and more. I am, in His love. . . .

---

[16]Rough draft: "They would have advised you otherwise."

[17]Alain de Solminihac.

[18]Rough draft: "of his mission."

[19]Rough draft: "Who, having yielded to the temptation, soon recovered and came back to the Company."

[20]In Ireland.

[21]Marc Coglée (Cogley), born in Carrick-on-Suir, Lismore diocese (Ireland), on April 25, 1614, was ordained a priest on May 30, 1643, and was received into the Congregation of the Mission on the following July 24. In a period of distress and discouragement, he had the good fortune to meet Gerard Brin, a fellow countryman, who induced him to remain in the Congregation. After having given him time to make up his mind definitely by spending some time in the novitiate, Saint Vincent sent him to Sedan (1646). Marc Coglée took his vows there on December 13, 1649, and the following year was named Pastor of the parish and Superior of the house. Replaced in 1654 by Jean Martin, he resumed these same functions in 1655 and kept them for another year. For a few months in 1659 he was Superior of the Annecy Seminary, and from there he returned to Saint-Lazare.

880. - *NICOLAS PAVILLON,[1] BISHOP OF ALET,*
TO SAINT VINCENT

Monsieur,

I am sending back to you M. Féret, whom you kindly lent us for a few years. I thank you most humbly, sincerely acknowledging that I am much obliged to you for this. He has rendered great service to God in this diocese and, by his instructions and the example of his virtues, has spread there the fragrance of edification in all circumstances. Consequently, he has been generally loved and will be missed by everyone. He goes off to throw himself into your arms, in a spirit of indifference, to be assigned by your counsel and decision to wherever you think he should be employed. He can only be successful in this and promote favorably the service of God and of the Church.

I hope you will see in this experience much more than I could tell you. Although the loss for this poor diocese will be severe, we accept it, nevertheless, meekly and patiently, as coming from the good, paternal hand of God, who gives and takes away from us as He chooses. He will speak to you about all our little needs, with which I most humbly entreat you to assist us. I trust you will do this all the more willingly, Monsieur, since it concerns the restoration of God's service and the discipline of His Church.

Monsieur Féret will inform you more clearly about all these matters and of the means that could be used to succeed in doing something about them. I have no doubt, Monsieur, that your zeal and tact, together with the influence God has given you, will contribute greatly to their advancement. That is why I feel obliged to make the request on this occasion, and to ask your prayers and sacrifices for our urgent spiritual needs. I shall beg Our

---

Letter 880. - Archives of the Mission, original autograph letter.

[1]Nicolas Pavillon was born on November 17, 1597. As a very young priest he placed himself under the direction of Saint Vincent, who had him teach catechism, employed him in the work of the missions, and sent him to the Charities, where his presence was deemed useful. More than once he entrusted him with the conferences and retreats for priests. Appointed to the diocese of Alet in 1637, Pavillon accepted it only upon the Saint's entreaties. This elevation did not deter him from his apostolic works. He gave a mission in Rueil at Richelieu's invitation, then in Saint-Germain-en-Laye at the King's request. He was consecrated at Saint-Lazare on August 22, 1639, and went to his diocese accompanied by Etienne Blatiron, a Priest of the Mission. A zealous, intelligent Bishop, dedicated to reform, he justified the expectation placed on him. His episcopate would have been more fruitful had he been more on his guard against Jansenistic ideas. Saint Vincent begged him in vain to sign the formulary against Jansenism. The Bishop of Alet died December 8, 1677. There are several biographies of him, notably that of M. Etienne Dejean, *Un prélat indépendant au XVII* siècle, Nicolas Pavillon, évêque d'Alet* (Paris: Plon-Nourrit, 1909).

Lord in exchange to fill you with His most holy blessings, and I ask you to do me the honor of believing that I am, more and more, in His love, Monsieur, your very humble and most obedient servant.

NICOLAS,
B[ishop] of Alet

Alet, October 25, 1646

Addressed: *Monsieur Vincent, Superior General of the Congregation of the Mission*

881. - TO ETIENNE BLATIRON, IN GENOA

Paris, October 26, 1646

Monsieur,

The grace of Our Lord be with you forever!

I have received no letters from you this week and yet I cannot discontinue mine to you. I enjoy so much reading yours and finding out what is happening in your work that I ask you, Monsieur, to write me by every ordinary mail. This joy is not just for myself; I share it with the whole Company when there is something special, and use that opportunity to ask everyone for prayers for you.

I can appreciate the C[ardinal]-Archbishop's[1] reason for not granting you any respite in your work, on the grounds of his zeal or[2] the disposition and present fervor of the people. However, we must look ahead and preserve the workers, so that the work will endure. So please make some effort toward this moderation. If His Eminence insists, at least be careful to go easier in the pulpit and in the services. Speak to the people more familiarly and in a softer tone, making them come closer to you, for, in the final analysis,

---

Letter 881. - Archives of the Mission, Paris, original signed letter.
[1]Stefano Cardinal Durazzo.
[2]At first the Saint wrote "or even," but on second thought he scratched out the "even."

virtue is not found in extremes, but in prudence, which I recommend as strongly as I can, both to you and to Monsieur Martin.

M. Portail will be going to see you soon. He is still in La Rose, but is on the point of leaving there to go to Marseilles and then on to Genoa.

Brother Pascal[3] has not yet arrived. When he does, we shall welcome him in the way you want and as he desires.

Prostrate at the adorable feet of Our Lord, I greet your dear soul and your little flock with a most extraordinary consolation and tenderness of heart. I ask Him to take all of you under His protection, and to animate you more and more with His Spirit and His love, in which I am, Monsieur, your most humble servant.

VINCENT DEPAUL
i.s.C.M.

Addressed: Monsieur Blatiron, Priest of the Mission, in Genoa

882. - TO ANTOINE PORTAIL, IN CAHORS

Paris, October 27, 1646

Monsieur,

The grace of Our Lord be with you forever!

I received your letter written from Cahors, which obliges me to thank God for all the things you told me and for all the good that God is doing through you. I ask His Divine Goodness to continue to enlighten and guide you, so that you will succeed in what remains for you to do, as you have in what you have done.

I have written to Richelieu, asking that M. du Coudray be made welcome and remain there until circumstances cause us to act

---

[3]Jean-Pascal Goret.

Letter 882. - Archives of the Mission, Paris, original signed letter.

otherwise in his regard. For the rest, concerning La Rose and Cahors, I cannot come to any decision until you have done everything and I know your views.

I ask M. Alméras to go to Annecy, since his health allows it, and you, Monsieur, to Marseilles, but only after you have finished where you are.

M. Brin and four or five of our other Irishmen[1] have left for Ireland, and M. Bourdet is supposed to go and join them in Nantes to be their Superior. B[rother] Vacher,[2] who was in Le Mans, is also one of their number, as is Brother Patriarche. I recommend them to your prayers.

M. Lambert[3] is now Superior at the collège,[4] and M. du Chesne[5]

---

[1]In no. 877 Saint Vincent mentioned Edmund Barry, Dermot O'Brien, Dermot Duiguin (Duggan) and Georges Le Blanc (White).

[2]Philippe Le Vacher.

[3]Lambert aux Couteaux, born in Fossemanant (Somme) in 1606, had been a member of the Congregation of the Mission since August 1629. In the early 1630s he preached in the South of France with Robert de Sergis. He founded the house in Toul in 1635 and remained there as Superior until 1637. In January 1638 he began the establishment in Richelieu (Indre-et-Loire), where he was Pastor and Superior for four years. The General Assembly of 1642 named him Assistant to the Superior General. For a brief period he was Superior at the Bons-Enfants (1646-1649), as mentioned in this letter, then at Saint-Charles. In 1650-1651 he was again in Richelieu. The Saint had such confidence in him that he had him make the visitation of Saint-Lazare. He sent him to render the same service to the Missionaries in La Rose and Toul, as well as to the Sisters in Angers and Nantes. Urged by Propaganda Fide in 1647 to designate someone as Coadjutor Bishop of Babylon, Saint Vincent could think of no one more worthy than Lambert aux Couteaux. In his response to Bishop Ingoli he expressed himself as follows: "I must admit, Excellency, that the loss of this man is like having me pluck out one of my eyes or cut off one of my arms." The plan, however, did not materialize. He was also the Saint's choice for establishing the Congregation in Poland, where the Queen was asking for the Missionaries. Lambert aux Couteaux went there in 1651. Everything had to be organized in that war-torn and plague-stricken country. His efforts were blessed by God but short-lived; he died January 31, 1653, a victim of his dedication to the plague-stricken. (Cf. *Notices,* vol. II, pp. 1-28.)

[4]The Bons-Enfants Seminary.

[5]Pierre du Chesne entered the Congregation of the Mission in 1637. He was to become one of the best Missionaries of Saint Vincent, who entrusted him with the direction of the house in Crécy (1641-1644), the Bons-Enfants (1644), the mission of Ireland and Scotland (1646-1648), Marseilles (1653-1654), and Agde (1654). He also summoned him to attend the two General Assemblies convoked at Saint-Lazare during his lifetime. Pierre du Chesne died in Agde on November 3, 1654.

is giving a mission with the Bishop of Tréguier.[6] M. Bécu[7] is helping us here, where most of our priests are presently leaving for the missions. M. Bajoue is staying for the seminary.

We sent M. Alain and a few other men back to Le Mans, and are recalling M. Cuissot because of his ailment.[8] His nephew[9] has gone to Saintes with M. Perraud and B[rother] David.[10]

I cannot tell you anything else, since I am hurrying off to the Council. I entreat you, Monsieur, to recommend my soul to Our Lord. I am, in the love of Our Lord, Monsieur, your most humble and obedient servant.

VINCENT DEPAUL
i.s.C.M.

Addressed: Monsieur Portail, Priest of the Mission, in Cahors

883. - TO FRANCOIS PERROCHEL,[1] BISHOP OF BOULOGNE

Paris, October 31, 1646

Excellency,

I thank God for all the graces He has given you, Excellency, and

---

[6]Balthazar Grangier de Liverdi.

[7]Jean Bécu was from Braches (Somme), where he was born on April 24, 1592. He was ordained a priest in September 1616, and in September 1626 came to join the first companions of Saint Vincent. Two of his brothers, Benoît and Hubert, followed him into the Congregation, the latter as a lay Brother; one of his sisters became Sister Marie, a Daughter of Charity. He was Superior of the house in Toul (1642-1646). He spent the rest of his life in Paris, where he died on January 19, 1667, having been Vice-Visitor, then Visitor of the Province of France. (Cf. *Notices,* vol. I, pp. 125-133.)

[8]Gilbert Cuissot was subject to attacks of quartan fever, a form of malaria in which the fever recurs every seventy-two hours.

[9]Jean Cuissot.

[10]David Levasseur, coadjutor Brother, born in Dancé (Orne) in 1608, entered the Congregation of the Mission on January 2, 1638.

Letter 883. - Original autograph letter owned by the Priests of the Mission in Panningen (Holland); photograph in the Archives of the Mission, Curia Generalitia, Rome.

[1]François Perrochel, born in Paris on October 18, 1602, was a cousin of Jean-Jacques Olier.

through you to the souls He has entrusted to you, and in general to His entire Church. I ask His Divine Goodness to sanctify it more and more.

Monsieur de Villequier[2] has said marvelous things here about his Bishop to the Queen and to the Cardinal,[3] so much so that, when they talk about good bishops, they usually name the Bishops of Boulogne and Alet.[4] That is why, Excellency, I think you will make use of every imaginable means to preserve this good understanding between the two of you and, because of him, with those who inquire into your Hôtel-Dieu. I have expressed my humble thoughts on this to good Abbé de Colugri, who can tell you about them.

Your latest letter refers to your added financial burden in the conquered regions,[5] and the difficulty of doing what has to be done there, owing to the small income. I will speak to the Queen about this, so that she might be pleased to give you assistance from another source.

When I mention here that you are making your visitation with six persons and only one horse, everyone is surprised and in admira-

He was one of the pious and zealous priests who gathered around Saint Vincent to be animated by his spirit and to work under his direction. He gave missions in several places, especially in Auvergne, Joigny, and the faubourg Saint-Germain. He was a member of the Tuesday Conferences and was present at the meetings in which retreats for ordinands were organized. As Bishop-elect of Boulogne, he was invited to give the conferences for the ordinands at the Bons-Enfants and was so successful that the Queen wished to hear him. Moved by his words, she left generous alms for the Saint to help him defray part of the expenses incurred by the retreats. François Perrochel was consecrated in the church of Saint-Lazare on June 11, 1645. The episcopate of this holy Prelate was one of the most fruitful and glorious known to the Boulogne diocese. When, in 1675, worn out by age and infirmity, the Bishop of Boulogne saw that he could not govern his diocese properly, he resigned. He crowned his career on April 8, 1682 by a death worthy of his life. (Cf. Van Drival, *Histoire des évêques de Boulogne* [Boulogne-sur-Mer: Berger frères, 1852].)

[2]Antoine, Marquis de Villequier, later Duc d'Aumont, Governor of the city and territory of Boulogne, was born in 1601. In 1638 he became a Brigadier-General, a Lieutenant General in 1645, and Maréchal of France in 1651; he was created a Duke and Peer in 1665 and died on January 11,1669.

[3]Cardinal Mazarin

[4]Nicolas Pavillon. Perrochel and Pavillon became acquainted in Paris because they had attended the Tuesday Conferences at Saint-Lazare and had given more than one mission together.

[5]Taken from the Spaniards. This part of the Boulogne diocese was very poor and was often ravaged by the Spanish garrisons from Saint-Omer, Aire, and Renty, who pillaged the churches and even put them to the torch.

tion. Oh! how rich is the bishop who wins the admiration, not only of all those who see him, but even of those who hear of the treasures of their virtues! It is no small matter that the world itself proclaims more worthy of esteem the holy poverty of a bishop who models his life on that of Our Lord, the Bishop of bishops, than the riches, retinue, and pomp of a bishop who possesses great wealth.

What I have said, Excellency, will not prevent me from taking the opportunity to represent your needs, when the occasion arises.

I prostrate myself in spirit at your sacred feet and ask for your holy blessing. I am, in the love of Our Lord, Excellency, your most humble and most obedient servant.

VINCENT DEPAUL
i.s.C.M.

884. - TO JEAN MARTIN, IN GENOA

Paris, All Souls' Day[1] [1646][2]

Monsieur,

The grace of Our Lord be with you forever!

I write you in haste, but not without great consolation for all the good things you wrote to me, for which I thank you. I ask Our Lord to give you the fullness of His Spirit, so you can share it with all those good seminarians whom His Divine Providence has given you to guide. Believe me, have great confidence in Him and do not be surprised at the sight of your own inadequacy. This is a good sign and a necessary means for the operation of the grace God has destined for you. We shall continue to pray for you, and I will have the rules and practices of the seminary sent to you to make things easier for you in the beginning. I beg you above all to take care of

---

Letter 884. - Archives of the Mission, Turin, original signed letter.
[1]November 2.
[2]In 1646 Jean Martin began to work with the ordinands in Genoa.

yourself and to take the same care of M. Blatiron and the others, whom I greet affectionately, particularly your dear [self].³ God knows in what esteem I hold you. I ask Our Lord to shower upon you His graces and His love, in which and by which I am, Monsieur, your most humble servant.

VINCENT DEPAUL
i.s.C.M.

Addressed: Monsieur Martin, Priest of the Mission, in Genoa

885. - TO ETIENNE BLATIRON, IN GENOA

Paris, November 2 [1646]¹

Blessed be God, Monsieur, for all the things [you] recounted to me and which you had already written to me! [I ask Him] to be His own thanks for al[l the good] He has done for you in all the ways you [tell me]. *Mon Dieu!* Monsieur, how good that seems to me, by [the grace of] God, who guides your family through you!

My only concern is your dear heal[th. In the name of] God, Monsieur, take care of it in the lengthy [labors in which He] wishes you to be engaged, and console me by [your news] every chance you get.

We have sent off seven Missi[onaries to] Ireland, and I had written M. Bourdet in B[rittany] to be the eighth. I am not sure he will be able to go.

More and more, God is blessing the leadership and labors of M. Guérin in Tunis. Our Consul in Algiers² took on an obligation

---

³This word was left out in the original.

Letter 885. - The original autograph letter is the property of the Daughters of Charity, Calle de Jesus, Madrid. The upper right corner was damaged by humidity.
¹There is no doubt about the year; it was written long ago on the back of the letter, and the contents call for it.
²Brother Jean Barreau.

for about seven thousand piastres for the ransom of several captives, which was effected but not paid. This worries us, but we are more concerned about a certain person in the Company,[3] other than M. C[odoing], who has allowed himself to be carried away by certain unorthodox opinions and, what is worse, is holding to them. He believes that Our Lord has not yet ascended into heaven, and says that neither Rome, nor the Councils, nor the Fathers have understood Holy Scripture clearly, and he has other similar strange ideas. We are worried about what to do with him. Curiosity about the Hebrew language and the Rabbis has led him to these extravagant views he upholds. It is thought[4] that he should be dismissed from the Company if he does not retract these errors, and we will be obliged to do this. O Monsieur, what a strange demon is vanity of the mind! I recommend this matter to your prayers.

We have seventy priests in our Bons-Enfants Seminary, among whom there is even a Bachelor of Theology, and in our own for the Company, here in this house, there are about thirty. God is blessing both of them. I ask Him to bless yours in Genoa. I am, in His love and that of His holy Mother, for you and for M. Martin whom I embrace, prostrate at his feet and yours, Monsieur, your most humble and obedient servant.

VINCENT DEPAUL
i.s.C.M.

Addressed: Monsieur Blatiron, Priest of the Mission, in Genoa

---

[3]François du Coudray.
[4]First redaction: "The Penitentiary says."

886. - TO ANTOINE PORTAIL, IN LA ROSE

Paris, November 3, 1646

Monsieur,

The grace of Our Lord be with you forever!

[I am] surprised at not receiving any letters from you concerning [what] you did in Cahors, both with the Bishop [as well as what regards the good] order and direction of the house. I can[not] believe that you have not sent me the report, [unless] matters are not yet finished [and you] are waiting until the end. Be that as it may, I [am anxious] to know what you did there. If you have returned to La Rose, what [arrangements did you make] for what remains to be done to restore [order] in that house?

I heard that M. du Coudray has arrived. . . .When he is in Richelieu, I will let you know what will be done about him.[1]

In the meantime, I await news from you and the assistance of your prayers and Holy Sacrifices for me and for all the needs of the Company.

Prostrate at your feet, I embrace in spirit your dear soul, which is in special esteem with me before God, in whose love I am, Monsieur, your most humble servant.

VINCENT DEPAUL
i.s.C.M.

Addressed: Monsieur Portail, Priest of the Mission, in La Rose

---

Letter 886. - Archives of the Mission, Paris, original signed letter.

[1]The secretary had first written: "When he is in Richelieu and when I know what will be done there about him, I shall let you know." The sentence did not satisfy the Saint, and he crossed out the words: "and when I know what will be done there about him" and added in his own hand: "what will be done about him."

887. - TO JEAN DEHORGNY, SUPERIOR, IN ROME

Paris, November 8, 1646

Monsieur,

The grace of Our Lord be [with] you forever!

I did not get a letter from you this week. [Here] is the subject of this one. The Parlement of Rennes [is in] an awkward position because of the Council decrees, which annul theirs and provide for a personal subpoena for the P[rocurator] General and the Commissioners who executed the decrees [of this] Parlement against us. Lastly, a d[ecree] was issued [in] which it is stated, among other things, that the Bishop of Saint-Malo could not esta[blish] us at Saint-Méen except by Papal Bulls, presented to the Estates of the Province[1] and verified i[n the Parlement] of Rennes.[2] M. Codoing, presently at S[aint-Méen, is the head] of the family, which has been established there by a decree [of the Council], executed by a bailiff of the Council of State[3] in presence of the Bishop of Augustopolis, Coadjutor of Saint-Malo,[4] and brother of Maréchal de Villeroi, the King's tutor,[5] who is in charge of this affair. In order to be fully at peace, there is talk of obtaining Bulls from Rome for the union of the Saint-Méen revenues to the seminary erected by the Bishop of Saint-Malo, the perpetual direction of which has been given to the[6]

Letter 887. - Archives of the Mission, Paris, original autograph letter.

[1] Each province in France had a local Estate or Provincial Assembly similar to the Assembly or the Estates-General in which representatives from the entire nation met. Saint Vincent refers here to the Estate for the Province of Brittany.

[2] This edict was dated October 8; it was confirmed by another issued on the twenty-eighth.

[3] His name was Quiqueboeuf.

[4] Since 1644 Ferdinand de Neufville had been Coadjutor to his uncle, Achille de Harlay, who would die on November 20, 1646. Ferdinand de Neufville succeeded him and remained Bishop of Saint-Malo until 1657.

[5] Nicolas de Neufville, Marquis de Villeroi, born on October 14, 1598, served successfully in the army. He won the confidence of Mazarin, became Maréchal of France (October 20, 1646), tutor of Louis XIV (1646), and Duc de Villeroi (September 1663). He died in Paris on November 28, 1685.

[6] First redaction: "to the priests of the."

Congregation of the Priests of the Mission.[7] Here is the story followed by the reasons.

The Bishop of Saint-Malo, seeing the wretched state of most of the priests of his diocese, obtained the King's permission, in conformity with the ordinances of our Kings and of the Council of Trent, to unite the monks' revenue to the priests' seminary which he had set up at Saint-Méen. There were twelve priests there, and he had entrusted its direction to the Priests of the Mission. Letters patent from the King had been addressed to the Great Council and verified by it, and the union was effected by the Bishop of Saint-Malo. The Parlement, at the urging of the reformed Benedictine monks, and annoyed because the Bishop of Saint-Malo had had the letters patent addressed to the Great Council, committed all the acts of violence about which I have written you. Finally, having seen that the [King's] Council was very much opposed, they found [the me]ans of safeguarding themselves, in a sense. [They] found this means so as to give us the opportunity to make some arrangement with those Fathers, or to establish ourselves according to [their] way of thinking. That is what the Chief Justice told the Bishop of Rennes,[8] who wrote it to me.

Besides the disinclination of Rome toward unions, you will meet with opposition there from those good Fathers. They will claim that the Council[9] and the Kings of France prescribe that Bishops shall unite benefices to their seminaries, not meaning that these be benefices that depend on Orders, but only those that depend on themselves.

To this it may be replied that this abbey depends on the Bishop of Saint-Malo and not on any Congregation or any other Superior whomsoever; (2) that most likely the Bishops gave Saint-Méen the tithes they possess, in consideration of the fact that they were then operating seminaries and were doing what we are trying to do. This

---

[7]Pope Alexander VII issued the Bull, *Ad apicem apostolicae dignitatis*, on April 4, 1658 (cf. vol. XIII, no. 117).
[8]Henri de la Motte-Haudancourt (1642-1662).
[9]Council of Trent.

last reason will be out of place, so do not bring it forward. State only that monks of the abbey, who were in a state of very great disorder, had consented to that and were content with the conditions offered them; there is no advantage in it for anyone else.

You will be told that only the Pope, and not the bishops, can suppress what belongs to a religious Order by union with another body. To this it is replied that, generally speaking, that is true, but since the Councils give authority to the bishops [regarding] ordinary benefices and do not limit the [number] of benefices, it is probable that the [Bishop] could effect this union, seeing, as I said, that this abbey is under his jurisdiction and is presumed to be dependent on him.

If they say that it is the property of the Benedictines and [that the] General of the reformed monks[10] had the right to appeal [in favor of his] Community, the reply is that the Bull [of institution] of their Congregation states that they shall establish themselves [in] abbeys where the monks, the abbot, and the bishop [ask for them]. Now, the monks of this abbey are not requesting this reform, nor does the Abbot or the Bishop, who is the Bishop of Saint-Malo and Abbot and Superior of the house, [consent] to it. Consequently, neither the General nor the reformed monks have any right to oppose the Bulls you will request, nor to do what they have done.

Add to this that a monk's revenue[11] is not a benefice, and that the Court of Rome has no interest in this union because, since it is not a benefice, the Pope never gives Bulls for such revenues.

These, Monsieur, are more or less the reasons for this union. There are two ways to settle the question: either have Rome decide if the union effected by the Bishop of Saint-Malo is valid or not and, in the event it is not, have His Holiness approve it and compensate for what is lacking; or else issue a Bull that makes no mention of the one that has already been issued.

---

[10]Dom Grégoire Tarrisse. He governed the Congregation of Saint-Maur for eighteen years and died in Paris on September 24, 1648. Collet notes that the Benedictines were the first to request of the Holy See the beatification of Vincent de Paul.

[11]First redaction: "an abbatial revenue."

I beg you, Monsieur, to seek advice [on] this affair, and let me know as soon as possible what you find out about it. And, if [need] be, we shall have someone from here write to His Holiness. The gentlemen from Saint-Malo [are] very determined to use every means in their power for this matter. To tell the truth, I think Our Lord will be greatly glorified and the Church will receive not a little assistance from it because of the seminaries that could be established by this means and scarcely by any other.

The Assembly of the Clergy[12] has raised the question of the importance of priestly seminaries and discussed the means of maintaining them. They have found none more advantageous than that of uniting certain benefices, where the monks are in a state of disorder and are not at all disposed to calling in the reformed monks, or in which the reformed monks are unwilling to be established because of the meagerness of the revenues, which they do not want.[13]

Enclosed is the paper with the name, surname, and diocese of that young Polish gentleman,[14] whom the Queen of Poland[15] left here with us, and who entered the students' seminary at the Petit Saint-Lazare.[16] Please procure a dimissorial letter *ad omnes ordines*[17] for him, Monsieur. He has some inclination toward joining the Company, and I to remain all my life, in the love of Our Lord, your most humble servant.

VINCENT DEPAUL
i.s.C.M.

---

[12]The periodic national meeting of the representatives of the clergy, who formed the First Estate in France; it might be analogous to a national synod.

[13]The seminary question was discussed the day before in the Assembly of the Clergy, as a result of a memorandum presented by the priests of the Caen Seminary. (Cf. *Collection des procès-verbaux des assemblées générales du clergé de France* [Paris, 1769], vol. III, p. 372.)

[14]Probably Stanislas-Casimir Zelazewski. Born in Warsaw, he was received at Saint-Lazare on October 19, 1647, at the age of eighteen. Because of his instability, he was always a trial to his Superiors. After trying to retain him in the Company, which he wished to leave, Saint Vincent himself was obliged in 1655 to ask him to withdraw.

[15]Louise-Marie de Gonzague.

[16]At Saint-Charles Seminary.

[17]*For all orders.* Saint Vincent apparently wanted to obtain a general permission for the one needed each time a candidate is promoted to the various orders leading to the priesthood.

888. - TO ANTOINE PORTAIL, IN LA ROSE

Paris, November 10 [1646][1]

Monsieur,

The grace of Our Lord be with you forever!

I received your letter and those y[ou wrote me] from La Rose, together with the document [I had] requested [of you]. I heard about the regulations [established] in La Rose by M. Alméras [and the ones] he gave in Cahors. I am [very pleased] about that and thank God for it, [asking Him to] be ever mindful of your constant prayers for the guidance you ask of Him during your visitations.

I shall tell you the first of my humble thoughts concerning what is to be done with regard to M. B[oucher], although I think it is a good thing to settle the problem of M. du C[oudray] before his. The latter is still in Richelieu. I have written to him, asking him to wait awhile, because I judged it advisable to act in this way, while awaiting the document pertaining to him, which you sent me. My idea right now is to have him come to Fréneville[2] and to discuss his affair with him there, since I judge it a little inconvenient to have him come to this city. However, we shall study the matter again. It may perhaps be [well] to act with him as we did with M. C[odoing], who no longer holds those opinions. He is now successfully [doing the work] entrusted to him [in Bri]ttany, where he is replacing M. [Bourdet],[3] who is in Nantes making his retreat. The latter is [waiting] for my permission to leave, which he has sought [because]

Letter 888. - Archives of the Mission, Paris, original autograph letter.

[1]All the details in this letter indicate the year 1646: M. Portail's visit to La Rose, René Alméras' presence in that house, the business concerning François du Coudray and Leonard Boucher, etc.

[2]In 1635 Madame de Herse gave two farms to the Saint-Lazare house: one in Mespuits, the other in Fréneville, a little village in the commune of Valpuiseaux (Essonne). Saint Vincent stayed at the latter from time to time. In return for her gift, Madame de Herse asked that a mission be given in perpetuity on her estates every five years, and that two Missionaries be placed at her disposal or that of her son, Félix Vialart, the Prior of Bu. These priests were to work in the localities indicated to them for three months every four years.

[3]The original read: "Brunet," but it is evident that the Saint wrote one name for another. Jean Bourdet left the Company; Dom Morel informs us that Saint Vincent obtained for him an excellent

of an unfortunate encounter [he had] with the Bishop of Saint-Malo, whose sentiments are shared by M. Codoing and a few members of the family who find fault with the way he is handling matters. This is confidential. Apart from M. Alméras, please do not mention it to anyone else. We had named him for Ireland to be in charge of the group we are sending there; he would make the eighth one, but he is begging off. We shall see the outcome of his retreat. I have implored him by every imaginable means to remain in the Company and come here.

Twelve hundred livres is a lot for La Rose. You would find it hard to imagine our poverty. Please dispose the family to honor the discomforts of Our Lord. The expenses incurred in Le Mans have reduced this house and the one there to a state of need. Things arrange themselves with time. Only God can have everything to His liking; His servants should act as Our Lord did. Have a letter of[exchange for] five or six hundred livres drawn up, please. If that is a small amount for the house, rest ass[ured] that it is a great deal for us.

Bon Dieu! Monsieur, how well you [acted in giving] the order you did with regard [to. . . .]

I think I wro[te you that] Monsieur Berthe has left because he could not [tolerate] the opinion [held by more than] one lay person in the [place] where we had sent him.[4] He had had a rumor circul[ated around] town that he was going there to be the Superior. When he was set straight about that and told to come here, he pretended he was ill in Rheims, and from there he returned to his parents' home in Donchery, about one league from Sedan.

So, you will soon be on the point of leaving for Rome. God knows what a cordial welcome awaits you there and in the other

---

benefice belonging to the Abbey of Marmoutiers (cf. S. Ropartz, *op. cit.,* p. 196). Had M. Ropartz read the Saint's correspondence, he would not have added, after reporting the fact: "This is the only intervention of Saint Vincent in the entire business (the Saint-Méen affair), and the only occasion on which Dom Morel mentioned his name. Need I say that I felt very happy about this?"

[4]The Sedan house.

houses, and M. Alméras in Annecy. I ask Our Lord to bless you both and to sanctify your dear souls more and more.

I remain in His love and most humbly greet the little family of La Rose, where I think this letter will reach you. Prostrate in spirit at its feet and yours, I am, in the love of Our Lord, your most humble and obedient servant.

VINCENT DEPAUL
i.s.C.M.

I find it hard to send you the two persons you are requesting for Cahors and La Rose.

Addressed: Monsieur Portail, Priest of the Mission, in La Rose

889. - *SAINT LOUISE TO SAINT VINCENT*

[November 1646] [1]

Monsieur,

We have great need of your charity's guidance concerning a rather serious fault of one of our Sisters. Her name is Marthe,[2] *and she is the daughter of a gardener who lives on the road from the village of Issy. She was in Saint-Leu parish for quite a long time and seemed a rather simple, good girl. However, I am afraid she is rather a little sly and stand-offish, if anything.*

Letter 889. - Archives of the Motherhouse of the Daughters of Charity, original autograph letter.
[1]Date added on the back of the original by Brother Ducournau.
[2]Sister Marthe Dauteuil, born in 1626 in Clamart (Hauts-de-Seine), entered the Company of the Daughters of Charity on January 1, 1642. She served the poor in Saint-Leu parish, then at Saint-Paul in Paris where she was at the time of this letter. In 1650 she was sent to Nantes; in August 1653 she set out for Hennebont. In the conference on her virtues, after her unexpected death on November 10, 1675, her departure from Nantes was explained in this way: Saint Vincent had requested the Sister Servant in Nantes to send one of her companions to Hennebont, but the Administrator formally opposed it. Sister Marthe decided to proceed to Hennebont without saying anything, so that the orders of her Superiors would be carried out. The Administrators of the Nantes hospital and those of Hennebont wrangled over her. In the end, Sister Marthe stayed at Hennebont and remained there for more than twelve years.

Not long after she was in the parishes, curiosity led her to want to know many things, and on her own she made progress in surgery. Her mother, the poor woman, told us that she gave her a large case of instruments. After she was placed at Saint-Paul, she still had a lancet, and said that her mother had given it to her again. Unknown to her Sister Servant, she let blood, although no one had ever shown her how, unless it was one of the surgeons in the parishes. When her Sister asked her for the lancet, she refused, saying that she would give it to me. She told me that she had thrown it away because she never again wanted to see the object that had caused her to offend God.

I have kept her here in this house, Monsieur, to find out from you what we should do about such faults. I think that these examples are very necessary for the good of the Company in the future, and so that we will know how to proceed in such matters with justice and charity.

Do me the charity of asking our good God that, through His mercy, my son, and I also, wretched and unfaithful to God, may one day share in the merits of the life and death of Jesus crucified, the living source of all holiness. I am, though most unworthy, Monsieur, your very grateful daughter and obedient servant.

L. DE MARILLAC

I forgot to tell you that I kept this Sister from confessing and receiving Communion today, and I await the orders your charity will give me before sending her.

Addressed: *Monsieur Vincent*

889a. - *SAINT LOUISE TO SAINT VINCENT*

[Before 1647]

Monsieur,

I forgot to ask you yesterday if our Sister Renée should remain this time

---

Letter **889a**. - Original autograph letter belonging to the Daughters of Charity of the Hôtel-Dieu in Nogent-le-Rotrou. It was published in the *Annales C. M.* (1931), p. 293. Following the observations of the editors of the *Annales C. M.*, it has been placed here and dated "Before 1647." *Ecrits spirituels* reprints it as no. 136bis, p. 339, in a section of letters lacking precise dates, but written before 1650.

to make her retreat; it is around the time your charity had indicated to her. If she does remain, do you think it would be a good idea for our Sister Claude from Chinon to go and replace her during this period? She teaches school here rather often and does it well.

I beg you most humbly to remember the need we have of a conference. If it could be this week to help us make a better preparation for the feast of the Blessed Virgin, do us the charity of letting us know the day. All our Sisters greatly desire it. Our Sisters, who hope they will not be delayed any longer from giving themselves entirely to God, beg you to consent to this, as do I, who call myself, Monsieur, your most humble and very grateful daughter and servant.

L. M.

889b. - SAINT VINCENT TO SAINT LOUISE

[Before 1647]

I think it is a good idea for you to have this fine girl make her retreat now and to send the other one to replace her during that period.

It will be possible for me to give the conference on Friday or Saturday, I hope, but no sooner.

Addressed: Mademoiselle Le Gras

Letter 889b. - Original autograph letter belonging to the Daughters of Charity of the Hôtel-Dieu in Nogent-le-Rotrou. This note, which is Saint Vincent's response to the previous letter, and is written on the bottom of it, was printed with it in the *Annales C. M.* (1931), p. 293.

890. - *SAINT LOUISE TO SAINT VINCENT*

[Before 1650] [1]

Monsieur,

My son's little servant came to tell me that he [Michel] sent him away yesterday and he [the servant] does not know where he is. You can imagine my anxiety, which I most humbly entreat your charity to relieve and allay before God, and to commend to His mercy the state he may be in now and in the future. If you would kindly do me the charity of sending someone from your house to find out if he said anything and what he has done, without revealing my apprehensions nor the dispositions he mentioned to you, it would be a great relief to me to hear something. Since I fear everything, I am wondering if he has taken his bedroom funiture, to leave altogether without my knowing where he went.

I am really sorry to be giving you so much trouble, but it is impossible for me to seek help elsewhere. Not only that, but I am so afraid that my chagrin may be known, and I fear that someone may come to say something to me about it. This would add to my suffering. My sorrow is so great! If God does not assist me, I do not know what I will do. Help me to remain strongly attached to Jesus crucified, in whom I am, Monsieur, your most humble daughter and very grateful servant.

L. DE M.

Something I said to my son is the cause of my great anxiety.

Addressed: *Monsieur Vincent*

Letter 890. - Archives of the Motherhouse of the Daughters of Charity, original autograph letter.
   [1]The year of Michel Le Gras' marriage.

891. - TO MICHEL ALIX, IN AUMONE[1]

Paris, November 23 [1646][2]

Monsieur,

The grace of Our Lord be with you [forever!]

I received your letter with great joy. [However, it] left me sad because [you] are suffering from fever and the w[orries people] are causing [you]. But, thanks be to God! He [is full of goodness] both for you and for me; fo[r you] because of the [good use] you make of this in all [He] asks of you for the greater [perfection and] sanctification of your dear soul. [This is apparent] because such trials bear the s[pecial] mark of God's goodness to you, by giving you reason to honor the most loving actions of the life and death of His Son, Our Lord. Oh, then, Monsieur, practice that divine virtue of patience and submission to His good pleasure! It is the touchstone by which He tries you, and by it He leads you in His own pure love. While you are asking Him for the strength to suffer well, I shall be asking Him for the grace to comfort you and, right now, prostrate in spirit before His infinite mercy, I humbly beg Him to restore to you health of body and the interior peace[3] of your heart.[4]

We have two persons in the Company who also have quartan fever; one is here in this house just now,[5] but the other did not fail to undertake the journey to Ireland with the same courage as the rest, who are in the best of health. I have no doubt that God will soon deliver him from it, so pleased is He to do good for those who detach themselves from self in order to serve Him. Would to God, Monsieur, that I had the means of contributing [to yo]ur relief! He

---

Letter 891. - Archives of the Mission, Paris, original signed letter. The postscript is in the Saint's own handwriting.

[1]Saint-Ouen-l'Aumône, near Pontoise (Val-d'Oise).

[2]This year is required both by the date of the dedication mentioned by Saint Vincent (November 22, 1646) and by the contents of the letter.

[3]First redaction: "peace of mind."

[4]First redaction: "of your soul."

[5]Gilbert Cuissot.

knows how lovingly I would [work] at this. And if the opportunity
arises of giving you a change of residence, you will see that I shall
spare [noth]ing that depends on me.

[I] would also have gladly rendered you my service [with rega]rd
to the foundation people are trying to make in your parish, [if I ha]d
known the name of the foundress or what sort [of re]ligious Order
she wants to establish there. In the absence of that, [I shall be]
content with the means you suggest to me, [by speaking] to the
Duchesse d'Aiguillon [and al]so to the magistrates of Pontoise,
which I shall do as soon as possible.

But what are you telling me, Monsieur, when you inform me that
you have dedicated a book[6] to me? If you had reflected that I am the
son of a poor plowman, you would not have given me this embarrassment, nor done your book the injustice of putting on its title page
the name of a poor priest, who has no other renown than his
wretchedness and sins. In the name of Our Lord, Monsieur, if this
work is still at a stage where it could be dedicated to someone else,
do not burden me with this obligation. For a long time, I have been
aware of your good will toward me, and you must know that I am
filled with gratitude to you and with the desire to be always,
Monsieur, your most humble and obedient servant.

VINCENT DEPAUL
i.s.C.M.

I shall consider it a blessing to be of service to you in the change
you mention, and promise to think it over, although I see nothing at
present and have reason to fear that my sins may render me unworthy.

Addressed: Monsieur Alix, Pastor of Aumône

---

[6]A new edition of *Hortus pastorum* by Jacques Marchant.

892. - TO ETIENNE BLATIRON, IN GENOA

Paris, November 23, 1646

Monsieur,

The grace of Our Lord be with you f[orever!]

I received two of your letters at the same time. Both have helped to con[sole] me by informing me that your health [and your] leadership continue to be good. I thank G[od] for this [and] ask Him to preserve and bless you [where you are].

My soul received additional [consolation] from the fact that the Cardinal[1] [is leaving you] free to take the rest that is [necessary] after each mission. Please make use of this, then, and take care of yourself, for you are a person very dear to the Company, and especially to my own heart, which has an extraordinary affection for you.

My most cordial greetings to Messrs. Martin and Richard. I humbly recommend myself to their prayers and yours, as well as to those of the good priests who are going to work with you. I entreat you to offer my services to them once again.

A week ago I sent you the contract for your establishment, with a few of my comments on it. Let me know what you will do about it, and please believe that I am, in the love of Our Lord, Monsieur, your most humble servant.

VINCENT DEPAUL
i.s.C.M.

Addressed: Monsieur Blatiron, Priest of the Mission, in Genoa

Letter 892. - Archives of the Mission, Paris, original signed letter.
[1]Stefano Cardinal Durazzo.

893. - TO GUILLAUME DELATTRE, IN CAHORS

Paris, November 23, 1646

Monsieur,

The grace of Our Lord be w[ith you] forever!

I am writing these li[nes] to tell you I received y[our] last letter and will not be able to reply [to you] in detail on [its contents], except to say that we [can fall into] excess in the practice of the v[irtues and that] excess is sometimes a [greater] evil than the failure to practice them. There are persons, and I know some, who find sensual and shameful pleasure in that sort of thing, and it will be enough for you to make use of it as I have allowed you to do, once a day, for the space of a *Miserere, absque emissione sanguinis; non enim meritum tam in dolore quam in amore consistit.*[1] In the name of God, Monsieur, take that as an example, follow the advice M. Portail gives you and, in general, do whatever he instructs you to do. I make this request of you all the more gladly because I know that holy obedience is the soul of your soul, and I am, in the love of Our Lord, Monsieur, your most humble and obedient servant.

VINCENT DEPAUL
i.s.C.M.

Addressed: Monsieur Delattre, Superior of the Priests of the Mission, in Cahors

---

Letter 893. - Archives of the Mission, Paris, original autograph letter.

[1]*Miserere, without drawing blood; merit consists not so much in pain as in love.* As becomes clear from no. 894, Saint Vincent permitted Delattre to flagellate himself, but set limits for his practice of this penance: he was to do it only once a day, and only for the length of time it would take to pray the *Miserere* (Ps 51 in NAB; Ps 50 in D-RB); in addition, no blood was to be drawn.

894. - TO ANTOINE PORTAIL, IN CAHORS

Paris, November 23 [1646][1]

Monsieur,

The grace of Our Lord be with you forever!

Yesterday I received your letter dated. . . ; and I think I have [also received and] answered all the others you wrote me.

If you have not finished in Ca[hors, please] do so as soon as possible and [go] to La Rose to conclude what you began there. [Visitations] which drag on like that are not usually very successful. Minds tire [easily]. The person who wants to cure bodily ills and restore health must administer the remedies gradually; otherwise, it is to be feared that more harm than good will be done. It suffices for one visitation that we discover the disorder, prescribe and order the remedies, and leave it to the Superior to see that they are applied. You were right to take only two or three days to explain the Rules to them and to see how they were observed. After that, however, the matter should be left to God and the Superior. Eight to ten days at the most in any one place is sufficient.

You did well to point out the excess in the use of the discipline, to moderate its frequency. and to prescribe the length of time and the manner of taking it. You may easily allow M. Delattre to take it daily for the space of a *Miserere,* but it must be simple and without points. As for the others, allow them less, console them for their fidelity to rigorous practices of penance such as this, and moderate them.

I also ask you, Monsieur, to have Monsieur Alméras leave for Annecy as soon as possible. He cannot cross the mountains of

---

Letter 894. - Original autograph letter. Bibl. Nat. n.a.f. 1473. The document is in poor condition; an old copy has helped us to complete the damaged phrases.

[1] The year M. Portail made the visitations of La Rose and Cahors.

Auvergne. He will have to head straight for Béziers, on to Montpellier and through Nîmes, and from there to Saint-Esprit,[2] to Lyons, and then to Annecy.

I say nothing here about the order you have to establish in La Rose because Monsieur Delattre[3] will carry it out.

We have not given missions [in Ai]guillon for a long time. I ask you to make it the first [to be] given in that area, to do everything possible to arrange them with the Duchess and her [people] and among themselves, and to spend this Advent there until the Christmastide celebrations, so as to do a thorough job of it. [May God shower] graces on those who will have to speak, who give. . .stronger and who have the grace to vi[sit en]emies! They will tell no one that this is on my orders; they will say that we are obliged to go there every five years, and that we do not count as a mission what Monsieur du Coudray did when he went there with Monsieur Drouard.[4]

You tell me that we owe three hundred livres to Cahors. I do not know why we here gave four hundred livres to the Bishop of Cahors, which he was supposed to send back to us on his arrival. I do not know if he did, and we will not mention it to him.

That, Monsieur, is all I can tell you for now, except that I embrace you, prostrate in spirit at your feet, and I do the same for the little family of La Rose. I am, for you and for them, Monsieur, your most humble and obedient servant.

VINCENT DEPAUL
i.s.C.M.

---

[2]In Pont-Saint-Esprit, a district near Uzès (Gard).

[3]The recently appointed Superior of the La Rose house.

[4]Bertrand Drouard, overseer of the estates of the Duchesse d'Aiguillon.

895. - TO BONIFACE NOUELLY, IN ALGIERS

Paris, 2[. . .November, 1646][1]

Monsieur,

The grace of Our Lord be [with you forever!]

I am writing to tell the Consul[2] [how difficult it is for us] to get the money for [which he has committed himself]. The council has decided that it will be p[aid with the] money raised as soon as [the collection has been taken up] in Paris for the slaves. . .is willing to be responsible for the collec[tions. . .] of the Mercedarians nor of the Mathurins, [who] lead us to hope for more help than the [others]. We are trying to make arrangements with them. Please God, we shall lose no time; as soon as the money is ready, we shall send it via Tunis, as you have told us.

I beg M. Barreau never to commit himself for anything again, nor even to become involved in the ransom of any slave, but to do his own duties well. I also ask him not to undertake any business, great or small, without letting you know. And I ask you, Monsieur, to do likewise, living together with great deference, openness of heart, and full confidence, as two persons united in Jesus Christ.

I have also written by this same ordinary mail to M. Guérin in Tunis, that he should write you something about his method and manner of acting with the poor slaves, so that you may model yourselves on that as far as [possi]ble.

I am writing to you in great haste because [it] is night. I ask Our Lord to be increasingly your light, your strength, and your spirit, and, in the end, your reward.

Letter 895. - Archives of the Mission, Paris, original signed letter.

[1]The right hand corner of this letter, which included the date, has disappeared because of the ravages of humidity; only the first digit of the month remains. On the back of this letter is written "March 8, 1647." However, this does not fit with the number 2 that appears at the beginning [Paris, 2. . .]. Moreover, the remaining outlines of the damaged part are strangely similar to letters dated November 23, 1646, and from the contents it seems better to place it near no. 877.

[2]Brother Jean Barreau.

[I am], in Him, with all the strength of my soul, Monsieur, your most humble servant.

VINCENT DEPAUL
i.s.C.M.

Addressed: Monsieur Nouelly, Priest of the Mission, in Algiers

896. - TO A PRIEST OF THE MISSION[1]

November 24, 1646

I have received two letters from you which have redoubled my grief, seeing that you persist in separating yourself from us. This obliges me to persist also in pointing out to you the danger to which you are exposing yourself, but I do so with all the humility and affection of which I am capable, and filled with the desire for your salvation. So, with these sentiments, I shall tell you:

(1) That I see no reason for dispensing you from your vows, and for the one that you allege, which is very weak, there are a number of strong ones that convince me you should return. You are not well, it is true; but is this pretext strong enough to oblige God to release you from the promise you made Him? You were not unaware then that you might be subject to bodily infirmities like the rest of men. And since you took the step, should a slight ailment discourage you now?

(2) Returning to your own home will not cure you. Of what remedies will you avail yourself that you do not have here? The air of your native place is no better than that of Paris, and you know quite well that you will not find among your relatives more rest and good care than our sick receive in the Company.

Letter 896. - Reg. 2, p. 290.
[1]Probably Thomas Berthe, based on the line of reasoning presented in no. 879, n. 1.

(3) I ask you to consider God's goodness in calling you from the world. How many souls will be lost for want of such a grace! But how many more will deserve to be lost for having made light of it after having received it!

(4) You have admitted time and time again that you were moved to gratitude to God for the blessing of your vocation. Why are you now rejecting it?

(5) God has endowed you rather liberally with talents for all the works of the Company. By withdrawing from it, you will deprive the people and priests of the spiritual assistance for which perhaps He gave them to you. And although you think you may make good use of them by assisting your neighbor on your own, nevertheless, this will not be very effective because the grace of vocation will be lacking. The experience of others makes me fear that for you.

(6) How many victories will you lose if you lose your vocation, since with it you can overcome the devil, the world, and the flesh, and at the same time enrich your soul with Christian perfection, for which the angels would become incarnate if they could, so that they might come to earth to imitate the example and virtues of the Son of God!

(7) I would like to believe that you think your departure does not proceed from the motive I mentioned, although you have reason to believe the contrary. For, if that were so, how could such an abrupt change take place? In leaving for that house, you were as contented as you could be with your vocation, and I was very edified by this. But even if it were true that this evil stemmed from some other cause and not from that one, as you say I shall see on Judgment Day, what will you say on that great day, when you are asked to render an account of your promises, of the lights you have received, and the use you have made of your time and talents? Do you think that the care of your health will excuse you, since it is God who gives it and takes it away when He pleases, and it is said that the person who wishes to save his life will lose it?

In the name of Our Lord, Monsieur, reflect on all this and do not resist the reproaches of your conscience. Place yourself in the state in which you would want to die, and I hope that God in His goodness will give you the strength to overcome nature, which seeks only its own freedom, to the prejudice of your poor soul, for which God has given me an inexplicable, tender affection. That is why I implore you once again, in the name of Jesus Christ and by the love He has for you, to come back here. I will have greater confidence in you than ever because I shall no longer be afraid of losing you, seeing you protected against such a dangerous pitfall. Choose whatever house you would like; you will be welcomed everywhere with open arms, and you will give me the opportunity of proving to you that I am, in His love, Monsieur, your. . . .

897. - TO A PRIEST OF THE MISSION

Paris, November 27 [1646][1]

Monsieur,

The grace of Our Lord be with you [forever!]

I was consoled to see in your letter [that] the Pastor has relented a little in his deter[mination] not to allow chil[dren's] Communion. [I hope] he will give in completely, once yo[u take care to] point out [to him]: (1) that [we are bound] to this by our Rules; (2) that it has always been [done this way] in all the missions we have [given; (3) that the children] are well instructed and in a state to [prepare] well [for] Communion, which serves to dis[pose] them later to make other [Communions well]; (4) that this is one of the princi[pal means] we have to reach older persons, whose hearts are obdurate and hardened, and who allow themselves to be won over by the devotion of the children and the care that is taken with them. With regard to this, I have learned from Genoa that the Cardinal-

---

Letter 897. - Archives of the Mission, Paris, original signed letter.

[1]What is said in this letter about Louis Thibault leads us to place it near no. 900, dated December 2, 1646. The damaged state of the original, compared with the condition of the originals that precede and follow this one, removes all doubt.

Archbishop[2] is so attached to children's Communion that he is there for most of them and weeps with emotion, as if he were a child himself. Lastly, our experience with the blessing God bestows on this act should serve as a motive to the Pastor to give his approval to it in his own parish.

If he says he wants to do it himself, and that he will instruct them during Lent so they can receive Communion at Easter, you could reply to him that he will do a much better job of it than we, that is true, but what we will do will not prevent him from doing the same thing then. If he is afraid we might admit to Communion children who may not be adequately prepared and do not have the other dispositions necessary, please tell him that it is our custom to examine them all [in] presence of the pastors, who will judge for [them]selves whether or not they should be allowed to receive this sacrament, and the Pastor could put off to another time [those] he does not find ready. Lastly, if he objects to the solemnity of the procession, [we shall make it as] simple as possible, without [show and with]out dressing up some of the children like [angels], as is done in certain places. I do not think we can [oppose him] in that.[3]

So please explain all these things clearly to him, and I hope he will give you full liberty in this regard; otherwise, we shall consult the Company to see whether it is advisable to continue the mission without this Communion.[4]

Regarding confessions, nothing will be lost by postponing them until Monday. As to having the mission last until the end of the year, fine, we will do that as well, if necessary.

We shall send some money to M. Thibault,[5] and notify him to do as you say with regard to M. Raisin, to see if anything has been left by mistake in his house.

---

[2]Stefano Cardinal Durazzo.

[3]Abbé Villien, a learned professor at the Institut Catholique de Paris, is of the opinion that Saint Vincent was the first to introduce the custom of solemnizing First Communion. (Cf. "La discipline des sacrements" in *Revue du clergé*, vol. LXIX [January 1, 1912], p. 30.)

[4]The end of the sentence, from "otherwise we shall consult," is written in the Saint's hand.

[5]Louis Thibault was born in Ferrières-Gâtinais (Loiret) on March 29, 1618. After the death of their daughter, his parents decided to leave the world to serve God; the father with the Priests of

Since you do not have enough beds, Monsieur, see if you could send a few of the men to sleep at the Bons-Enfants.[6]

We will sent Brother Laisné[7] back to you. If he is not needed, you can send him back in two or three days.

We will send you some surplices and birettas tomorrow.

The two pistoles you sent have been received.

I greet the whole Company, and you in particular, Monsieur. I am, in the love of Our Lord, Monsieur, your most humble servant.

VINCENT DEPAUL
i.s.C.M.

---

the Mission, the mother with the Daughters of Charity. Louis was received at Saint-Lazare on August 21, 1637 and was ordained a priest in April 1642. From his post as Superior of the house in Saintes, he was recalled to Paris in 1646, where he took his vows and dedicated himself zealously and successfully to the missions. From 1648 to his death in February 1655, he was Superior of the Saint-Méen house. During his missions he would seek out pious persons wishing to detach themselves from the world, and assist them in the choice of a religious community. The Company of the Daughters of Charity greatly benefited from his zeal. (Cf. *Notices,* vol. III, pp. 124-128.)

[6]On March 1, 1624, Jean-François de Gondi, Archbishop of Paris, had turned over to Saint Vincent the direction of the Collège des Bons-Enfants so that he might have a place to lodge the priests wishing to join him in giving missions in the country. The Collège, dating back nearly three centuries, was one of the oldest in the University; it was almost abandoned and in a pitiable state of decay. It occupied an area of about sixteen acres, near the Porte Saint-Victor, at the corner of rue des Ecoles and rue du Cardinal Lemoine. It was not a teaching center, but simply a hostel in which students were provided with shelter and sleeping quarters. The Saint waited until after Madame de Gondi's death to go and live there.

[7]*Notices,* (vol. V, p. 343) lists two Missionaries named Laisné, both born in Dreux (Eure-et-Loir): Pierre, on November 9, 1623, and Nicolas in 1625. They entered the Congregation of the Mission on September 24, 1641 and took their vows on October 4, 1643. Pierre received all the Sacred Orders in December 1648, with a dispensation *extra tempora*. He is probably the person in question here. In 1657 he was a member of the Saint-Méen house.

898. - *SAINT LOUISE TO SAINT VINCENT*

[1646] [1]

Monsieur,

I did not think to ask you if I should share this [2] *with our Sisters, and I have not done it. Allow me to tell your charity that the explanation given in our Rule of Daughters of Charity causes me to want to retain this title, which has been left out, inadvertently perhaps, in the text of the terms of the Establishment.* [3]

Could not this uncompromising wording "dependence on the Archbishop" [4] *be harmful to us in future, by the liberty it gives to draw us away from the direction of the Superior General of the Mission? Is it not necessary, Monsieur, that by this Act of Establishment your charity be given to us as perpetual Director? And regarding these regulations we are to be given, is it the Archbishop's intention that they be indicated after the request? Does that require a separate act, or should others be formulated, since it mentions them separately?*

In the name of God, Monsieur, do not let anything happen that would, even in the slightest, draw the Company away from that direction God has given it, because you can be sure that immediately it would no longer be what it is, and the sick poor would no longer be assisted. And thus, I believe that God's Will would no longer be done among us, through which I have the happiness of being, Monsieur, your most obedient daughter and most grateful servant. [5]

Letter 898. - Archives of the Motherhouse of the Daughters of Charity, original autograph letter.

[1]The word "Monsieur" in the salutation shows that the letter was written before 1650, since after 1649 all the letters of Saint Louise to Saint Vincent begin with "Most honored Father." The contents of the letter also enable us to pinpoint the year more clearly.

[2]The Act of November 20, 1646 by which Jean-François de Gondi, Archbishop of Paris, established the Company of the Daughters of Charity as a confraternity. (Cf. vol. XIII, no. 146.)

[3]The Coadjutor, Jean-François-Paul de Gondi, who signed the Act of Establishment in the name of his uncle, the Archbishop of Paris, gives the Sisters the name of "Servants of the Poor of the Charity."

[4]The Coadjutor, Jean-François-Paul de Gondi, the future Cardinal de Retz, specified in 1646 that the Company "will remain in perpetuity under the authority and dependence" of the Archbishops of Paris. He added that he "confides and entrusts to Vincent de Paul the guidance and direction of the above-mentioned society and confraternity, as long as God allows him to live." In 1655 Cardinal de Retz, now Archbishop of Paris, while maintaining his authority and that of his successors over the Daughters of Charity, confided the governance and direction of the Institute to Saint Vincent, as long as he lived, and to his successors as Superiors General of the Congregation of the Mission. (Cf. vol. XIII, no. 149.)

[5]Saint Louise's apprehension was justified. During the reign of Napoleon Bonaparte, the

— 133 —

899. - TO ANTOINE PORTAIL, IN CAHORS

Paris, December 1 [1646][1]

Monsieur,

The grace of Our Lord be with [you forever!]

I received your letter and was greatly co[nsoled at seeing] all that you wrote me. I u[nceasingly thank] God for the good order you ha[ve established] in our houses. I beg His Divine [Goodness to grant His] blessing for the h[ouses still to be visited, in what]ever you [will prescribe for them. So now,] Monsieur, I see by your letter that you are [ready to leave]. I cannot tell you what [a consolation this is to me] be[cause you] are awaited patiently elsewhere, and are needed, especially in Rome. I ask Our Lord Jesus Christ to conduct you there, and to continue to grant you the same grace to restore things to the point He desires, in what remains for you to do, as in what you have done.

M. B[oucher] has written twice from La Rose about the good sentiments and gratitude God is giving him. Please let me know, Monsieur, if I can rely on this.

I have nothing more to tell you except to assure you that everything is going well here, thank God. I have no other news to give you. I can just add that M. Cuissot has quartan fever, M. Bécu has

---

Vicars-General of the Archdiocese of Paris, basing their action on the very terms of the approbation given in 1646 and, as they interpreted it, again in 1655, asserted that they had the right to direct the Company of the Daughters of Charity. Within the Community, this caused a schism which lasted about eight years. (Cf. John W. Carven, C.M., *Napoleon and the Lazarists* [The Hague: Martinus Nijhoff, 1974], pp. 156-161; pp. 174-175.) The question of the traditional authority of the Superiors General of the Mission over the Sisters was definitively settled by Pope Leo XIII in 1882. On July 8, 1882, the Congregation of Bishops and Regulars, speaking on behalf of the Pope, stated that nothing was to be changed in the government of the Daughters of Charity which, according to pontifical indults, pertained to the Superior General of the Mission instituted by Saint Vincent de Paul. (Cf. Miguel Pérez Flores, C.M., "The Superior General of the Congregation of the Mission and the Daughters of Charity," *Vincentian Heritage*, vol. V, no. 2 [1984], p. 35.)

Letter 899. - Archives of the Mission, Paris, original signed letter.
[1]The year M. Portail made a visitation in Cahors.

gout, and I have the grace to be, in the love of Our Lord, Monsieur, your most humble servant.

VINCENT DEPAUL
i.s.C.M.

Addressed: Monsieur Portail, Priest of the Mission, in Cahors

900. - TO LOUIS THIBAULT, IN MONTGERON[1]

Paris, 2 [December 1646][2]

Monsieur,

The grace of Our Lord be with [you forever!]

We are sending this messenger to g[et] news [of you] and to give you ours, [which is] good, thank God. The Com[munity enjoys good] health, except for M. [Bécu, who has gout, and] M. Cuissot, who has quar[tan fever. And what about you? Are you] we[ll after] such long la[bors? Perhaps you have some slight] ailment, but I [ask Our Lord] to preserve you for His glory. I [thank Him for] your success in [accomplishing] them; we have heard about it here. May it please His Infinite Goodness to grant to so many poor souls the grace to make use of it for their salvation!

Enclosed are one hundred livres we are sending you to pay what you owe to Villeneuve-Saint-Georges, if perchance M. Gentil[3] has not sent you the wherewithal for that, and also to cover expenses and other debts you have since contracted, and give you the means

Letter 900. - Archives of the Mission, Paris, original signed letter.

[1]Commune in the district of Corbeil (Essonne).

[2]Because of its contents, this letter should be placed near no. 899.

[3]Mathurin Gentil, born in Brou (Eure-et-Loir) in May 1604, entered the Congregation of the Mission on November 11, 1639, and took his vows on October 7, 1642. At the time of this letter he was Treasurer at Saint-Lazare; in 1647 he assumed the same position in the Le Mans Seminary. He died in that town on April 13, 1673, mourned by everyone, especially his Superior General, Edme Jolly, who announced his death to the Company in a most laudatory letter.

of returning, which I beg you to do so as soon as possible, by Thursday at the latest. You have done enough for now. Besides, we have some business for you here. We shall send someone else to Villejuif,[4] and the Orsay[5] mission can be put off until Christmas. I await you then with the desire to embrace you affectionately and with the hope of seeing you take a good rest after such fatigue.

May God grant us the grace to rest eternally in Him, in whose love I am, Monsieur, your most humble servant.

VINCENT DEPAUL
i.s.C.M.

Addressed: Monsieur Thibault, Priest [of the Mission, in Mont]geron

901. - TO JEAN MARTIN, IN GENOA

Paris, December 7 [1646][1]

Monsieur,

The grace of Our Lord be with you forever!

So there you are, Monsieur, all alone in your new duty! Oh! blessed be God for having given you such a fitting means of taking counsel of Him on how to promote in His love those He has entrusted to you! Where human assistance is lacking, His abounds, and blessed forever be His Loving Kindness in wishing to be served, at one and the same time in town and country, by only three persons, in such important affairs as His! This is a sign that He Himself wants a hand in this and desires to make their labors result in bringing forth fruits of eternal blessing.

---

[4]Large commune near Paris.
[5]Place in the district of Versailles (Essonne).

Letter 901. - Archives of the Mission, Turin, original signed letter.
[1]Jean Martin was put in charge of the seminary at the end of 1646.

My soul is deeply moved when I think of you and of the choice He made of placing you, young as you are, in such a lofty ministry as that of leading priests to perfection. I thank Our Lord for having merited this grace for you, and ask Him to fulfill in you His eternal plans. As for you, Monsieur, humble yourself profoundly, considering the virtue and competence needed to teach others and to train the children of the King of Heaven in the army of Christ. But trust fearlessly in Him who has called you, and you will see that all will go well. It would seem that, in this time of beginning, God has willed to facilitate your entry into this holy work by giving your seminarians an inclination toward piety and the spiritual exercises, obliging you to undertake it with greater courage. His guidance is to be adored; nevertheless, do not expect that you will always find persons so compliant and easy to direct; be hopeful, however, that in proportion as difficulties increase, God will increase His grace for you.

And in order that you, Monsieur, may be armed on your part with all sorts of weapons, practice meekness and patience, virtues that are most suited to win over cantankerous and harsh persons. You can be sure that, for my part, I shall pray earnestly to Our Lord to obtain for you the fullness of His Spirit. Please recommend my soul to Him, and give the enclosed to Brother Sébastien,[2] to whom I am writing, on your advice. I am, in the love of Our Lord, Monsieur, your most humble servant.

VINCENT DEPAUL
i.s.C.M.

Addressed: Monsieur Martin, Priest of the Mission, in Genoa

---

[2]Probably Brother Sébastien Nodo.

902. - TO ANTOINE PORTAIL, IN CAHORS

Paris, December 8 [1646][1]

Monsieur,

The grace of Our Lord be with you [forever!]

Although I am not sure whether this [will reach] you in Cahors or in La Rose, I am still [writing to you] to be present by means of this letter at your departure [from there, if] it catches up with you, and [to wish] you [God's speci]al protection [on your journey.]

[I have writ]ten to Mars[eilles to announce your impending arrival, but], M[onsieur, I think it would be a good idea for you] not to make the visitation there un[til your return. You should] go where it is most urgent, namely, to Rome. For that reason, [do not stop] even in Genoa, ex[cept to] see M. Martin, who is in charge of the seminary, and [to say] a word of greeting to M. Blatiron and M. Richard in the place where they will be giving the mission, unless you can see them in passing without going out of your way. I will write you in more detail between now and then.

The next ordination is to take place at Saint-Lazare. I recommend it to your prayers, and ask you not to forget my own poor soul nor the Company, which, thank God, is doing well.

I am quite worried about M. du Chesne, whom, as you know, we have sent to Nantes to lead the mission to Ireland. Since he left three weeks ago, we do not know where he is, having had no news of him. May God give us some good news and may He preserve you, Monsieur, for whom His Divine Goodness has given me extraordi-

---

Letter 902. - Archives of the Mission, Paris, original signed letter.
[1]The year is written on the back of the original and the contents confirm it.

nary sentiments of affection and esteem, and has made me, in His love, Monsieur, your most humble servant.

VINCENT DEPAUL
i.s.C.M.

Addressed: Monsieur Portail, Priest of the Mission, in Cahors

903. - TO JACQUES THOLARD,[1] IN VILLEJUIF

Saint-Lazare, 8 [December 1646][2]

Monsieur,

The grace of O[ur Lord be with you] forever!

It must be said, Monsieur, that, by [inflicting on the demon the] harsh treatment you are ma[king him undergo, and] waging the fierce war on him that you a[re doing,] ex[pelling him from the souls he] has stirred to rebellion and whom you. . . .[3] Our [Lord Jesus Christ blesses] the [assistance] you give [to souls He has] redeemed by His Precious Blood. [In the name of God], hold fast, and do not surrender your weapons. The glory of God is at stake, as well as the salvation of perhaps a million [souls] and the sanctification of your own. Remember, Monsieur, that you have God with you, that He fights along with you, and that you will certainly overcome. He [the

---

Letter 903. - Archives of the Mission, Paris, original autograph letter.

[1]Jacques Tholard was born in Auxerre (Yonne) on June 10, 1615, and was received into the Congregation of the Mission on November 20, 1638. He was ordained a priest on December 17, 1639, and died after 1671. Throughout his life, in Annecy (1640-1646), Tréguier, where he was Superior (1648-1653), Troyes (1658-1660), Saint-Lazare, Fontainebleau, and elsewhere, he manifested the qualities of an excellent Missionary. During the Generalate of René Alméras, he was Visitor of the Province of France and of Lyons.

[2]The damage which humidity caused to the original document is so similar to the state of no. 902 that it, too, can only be dated December 8, 1646. Moreover, a study of the contents leads to the same conclusion.

[3]Only a few scattered words remain of the following two lines, and it is impossible to put them together to make sense.

demon] can bark but he cannot bite; he can frighten you but not harm you, and I can assure you of that before God, in whose presence I speak to you. Otherwise, I would be very doubtful about your salvation, or at least that you might render yourself unworthy of the crown Our Lord is preparing for you, while you are laboring so successfully for Him. Confidence in God and humility will obtain the grace you need. If, however, you are so strongly assailed by temptation, stop hearing confessions for a while and work hard at the reconciliations. Tell M. Gentil[4] that I have asked you to do this and, if need be, I will send you one or two priests from the Bons-Enfants to hear confessions in your place.

In the meantime, I renew to you the offering of my heart, and I greet M. Gentil[5] and the rest of the family, prostrate at its feet and yours. I am, in the love of Our Lord, Monsieur, your most humble servant.

VINCENT DEPAUL
i.s.C.M.

Addressed: Monsieur Tholard,[6] Priest of the Mission, in Villejuif[7]

---

[4]The name is scratched out in the original, probably to hide the name of the recipient.
[5]The name is scratched out in the original.
[6]The name is scratched out in the original.
[7]This word is scratched out in the original.

904. - TO JEAN MARTIN, IN GENOA

Paris, December 14, 1646

Monsieur,

The grace of Our Lord be with you forever!

This is a very short letter, but it brings my dear Monsieur Martin the assurance of the great affection God has given me for him. I cannot put it into words, and yet I feel it intensely, deep in my heart. May He who sees it make you understand it, just as He has caused me to understand the goodness of your soul and the graces with which He has filled it, and these are the subject of my most usual consolations! Often, and especially right now, I beg Our Lord to be entirely yours and you His, and to bless your work so that it may honor and glorify Him in Himself and in those young seminarians whom Providence has entrusted to you. May your words be like seeds sown in their hearts, bearing a hundredfold the fruits of charity and good example to the poor faithful, in order that they may do works worthy of this name. You can see clearly, Monsieur, that, if my wishes are fulfilled, the good you will do will go on to infinity and continue after you. I hope for this from the goodness of God, who wills to make use of you in such important[1] matters. For this reason, humble yourself and put your trust in Him.

I am, in His love, Monsieur, your most humble servant.

VINCENT DEPAUL
i.s.C.M.

At the bottom of the first page: M. Martin

Letter 904. - Archives of the Mission, Turin, original signed letter.

[1]The secretary had written "great." The Saint crossed out this word and replaced it in his own handwriting by "such important."

905. - TO BERNARD CODOING, SUPERIOR, IN SAINT-MEEN

Paris, December 15 [1646][1]

Monsieur,

The grace of Our Lord be wi[th you forever!]

I received two of your letters [which] soon caused me to share the difficulties [you are experiencing], and [have made] me ask Our [Lord to grant you the grace] of [being freed of them]. . . .[2] [I had the] opportunity [to] disclose the [needs of the] Company to him.[3] He promised me that he would co[ntinue to provide the] same assistance as his predecessor [and to do us] whatever good he can.

I also discussed Plancoët[4] with him. He wants to be on the scene before granting you permission for the withdrawal of the men who are there, and he is supposed to go there in a month or six weeks. In the meantime, Monsieur, please be patient and do whatever you can. All the same, it would be desirable for you to continue the missions and the seminary at the same time. I am well aware that there are too few of you, but you can join forces with some priests, who will be a help to you, even if only to pray the Office. I already wrote you that we have an example of this in a house[5] where there are only three of our men, one of whom directs the seminary and the others are almost always out giving missions. I would be relieved if you could do the same. However, I leave that to your discretion, knowing well that you are incomparably more zealous than I for the welfare and promotion of the neighbor.

Letter 905. - Archives of the Mission, Paris, original signed letter. The document is in very poor condition.

[1]This seems the most likely date. It was, in fact, at the end of 1646 that Bernard Codoing became Superior of the Saint-Méen house and Ferdinand de Neufville succeeded his uncle as Bishop of Saint-Malo.

[2]Very few words could be deciphered in the three lines omitted here.

[3]Ferdinand de Neufville, the new Bishop of Saint-Malo.

[4]Saint Vincent did not approve the commitment made by Jean Bourdet to serve the Plancoët chapel. (Cf. no. 815.) He was taking steps to be released from this promise.

[5]The house in Genoa.

I was unable to send you the help you requested of me bec[ause we have no] extra men here, and also [because of my fear lest] the storm [return. N]ow I am [obliged] to put him off. . .[6] in his[7] willingness to [do us go]od.

Adieu, Monsieur. I beg you to take care of yourself for the greater glory of Our Lord. My most affectionate greetings to your little band, whom I ask the Divine Goodness to bless with His everlasting blessings, and your own dear soul in particular, which mine embraces cordially.

I am, in the love of Our Lord, Monsieur, your most humble servant.

VINCENT DEPAUL
i.s.C.M.

At the bottom of the first page: M. Codoing

906. - TO LOUIS RIVET, IN RICHELIEU[1]

Paris, December 19, 1646[2]

Monsieur,

The grace [of Our Lord] be wi[th you forever!

---

[6]The two lines following are too incomplete to be reconstructed.

[7]Probably the new Bishop of Saint-Malo.

Letter 906. - Archives of the Mission, Paris, seventeenth century copy; Pémartin, *op. cit.,* vol. III, p. 221, l. 1183. In his corrections in vol. XIII, p. 849, Coste states that the first part of no. 1978 (vol. V, p. 488) is really no. 906. Although no. 906 is based on a seventeenth century copy, the Pémartin text was used for no. 1978. Since this latter text is more complete than the copy, it has been used to amend no. 906.

[1]Register 2 (p. 107) erroneously addressed the letter to "M. Rivet, Superior in Saintes." In 1646 Louis Rivet was in Richelieu. Born in Houdan (Yvelines) on February 19, 1618, he entered the Congregation of the Mission on June 13, 1640, took his vows on October 16, 1642, and was ordained a priest on September 19, 1643. He was placed in Richelieu in 1646, then at the seminary in Saintes, which he directed for several years (1648-1650, 1656-1662, 1665-1673).

[2]In the copy we are using, a tear in the top right corner obliterated the last digit of the year. We know the date from Register 2.

It has] already been several [days since] I received [your reply, and I am] still filled with the consolation it [brought me, seeing the sentiments] you have of yourself, which are very necessary in [the work] God has given you in M. Gautier's[3] absence. I [am most grateful] to His Divine Goodness for the insight He has granted you, and beg Him to accomplish His divine plans in you. However, Monsieur, you know that this mistrust of your own strength must be the basis for the trust you should have in God; without it we are often worse than we think, and with it we accomplish a great deal, or rather God Himself does what He expects of us. So, do not dwell any longer on what you are, but consider Our Lord close by you and within you, ready to put His hand to the work as soon as you call upon Him for help, and you will see that all will go well. Do you think that, since the order of His Providence has established you in this duty, He has not also given you the appropriate graces to carry it out well, if you undertake it courageously for love of Him? Have no doubt about this, Monsieur, no more than about the sincere affection of my heart for yours, which is such that I cannot convey it in words to you. May God be pleased to make it known to you, and fill you increasingly with His Spirit, so that through you it may be poured into the souls you guide, and your own soul may be more greatly sanctified!

I embrace in spirit the whole family and am, in the love of Our Lord, Monsieur, your most humble servant.

VINCENT DEPAUL
i.s.C.M.

---

[3]Denis Gautier, born in Langres (Haute-Marne) in 1610, was already a priest when he entered the Congregation of the Mission on July 19, 1639, at the age of twenty-nine. He was Superior in Richelieu (1642-1646, 1648-1649).

907. - TO DENIS GAUTIER, SUPERIOR, IN RICHELIEU

Paris, December 23 [1646][1]

Monsieur,

The grace of Our Lord be wi[th you forever!]

I do not know if this letter wi[ll reach you during the] work of the missions. . . .[2] Blessed [be God] forever, then! [I pray that you will be more and] more animated with His Spirit, in order [to labor for His] glory.

Your letter, which I received last evening, informed me of the special blessing God has been pleased to give to His work; I cannot thank Him enough for this. May it please His Divine Mercy to draw His gratitude from the fruit of this mission, granting to these poor souls the grace to know and acknowledge His liberalities, and to us the grace to continue our humble services in all things that can extend and strengthen the influence of Jesus Christ!

The proposal you made to me of taking in as boarders students who intend to become priests, and no others, has made me think that perhaps God wishes to use us in your house to help these young plants take root, and has caused me at the same time to hope that He might be pleased to grant us the grace to do it profitably. So, you can [give it] a try, but the fee should be fifty [écus]; you cannot take them for a lower fee, [and sti]ll less, for nothing, for fear of using for that purpose [what is necessary] for the maintenance of priests destined [to evangelize the peop]le and for [the administration of] the parish. . . .[3]

I have finally acquiesced to the requests of those who want to

---

Letter 907. - Archives of the Mission, Paris, original signed letter.

[1]The year had been written on the back of the original and indicated in Register 2 (p. 176); humidity caused it to fade out.

[2]The next four lines are missing.

[3]Of the next seven lines of the original, there remain only isolated words with no apparent connection.

have us in Luçon.[4] The request made by the Bishop of Luçon[5] and his Chapter, and the Archdeacon's[6] new proposal are signs that God wills this, and are means that facilitate making this establishment. I ask M. Chiroye to go there, accompanied only by one of the Brothers, to decide with these priests what will be required. When the time comes, we shall send the necessary workers. I already have my eye on one of our priests who seems quite suitable, and on two good clerics from the Bons-Enfants Seminary, who want to go for a year or two to give glory to God by serving with us. I shall await news of the outcome of M. Chiroye's journey. Please give him my letter.

I find [Monsieur] Lucas's[7] request for some relief a reasonable one, and there is as much jus[tice as charity] in granting him this. So I ask you, [Monsieur, to] dispense him from any kind of work [and office], other than to hear a few [confessions] on Sundays and feast days. . . .[8]

Continue [your kindness] to M. du C[oudray.] You and the Company [have been very good] to him, [and I] thank [you for this]. I have been very pleased that you [acted] that way. So, let him do what he wants, for I hope there will be nothing objectionable in his conduct. I am writing to him also and, if I can, I will write to

---

[4]As early as 1640 a few Priests of the Mission were established in Luçon, under the direction of Gilbert Cuissot. He was succeeded by Jacques Chiroye, who was still head of the house on May 3, 1645. (Cf. no. 749.) Chiroye had been named Superior of Luçon by a letter dated October 6, 1640. (Cf. vol. II, no. 488.) We have no information as to why he and his men left Luçon and went to Richelieu. It is quite probable that it was because the house was in financial difficulty.

Jacques Chiroye was born in Auppegard (Seine-Maritime) on March 14, 1614, entered the Congregation of the Mission on June 25, 1638, and took his vows on March 9, 1660. He served as Superior in Luçon (1640-1650, 1654-1660, 1662-1666) and in Crécy (1660-1662). He died on May 3, 1680.

[5]Pierre Nivelle (1637-1662).

[6]Claude Thouvant, Archdeacon of Aizenay, chaplain and Councillor of the King. Discussion of his proposition was to culminate in the contract of March 7, 1647 (cf. Arch. Nat. S 6706), by which he gave the Superior, Jacques Chiroye, a sum of eighteen hundred livres, and returned to him his rights on the Hôtel de Pont-de-Vie, a house bought by the Priests of the Mission in December 1641. All of this was on condition that the above-mentioned Priests of the Mission would give an annual mission of three weeks in his archdeaconry.

[7]Antoine Lucas.

[8]Four lines of the original are omitted; all that remains are a few scattered words.

Monsieur Gobert[9] to express my joy at his good health, and how touched I was by his fervor when I saw him so soon at work. May God bless both him and the whole Company, whom I embrace in spirit with great tenderness and consolation, especially your own dear soul, for which only God knows the affection I have, and which I would like you to know. I am, in His love, Monsieur, your most humble servant.

VINCENT DEPAUL
i.s.C.M.

We will send you someone in M. Chiroye's place as soon as possible.

At the bottom of the first page: M. Gautier

908. - TO JACQUES CHIROYE, IN RICHELIEU

Paris, December 23, 1646

Monsieur,

The grace of Our Lord be with [you forever!]

Who would not be glad to receive the letters [you write,] and who would not be consoled to [see that you never stop] s[eekin]g the salvation [of souls? Your zeal has touched] me [and] produced [such joy in me that I cannot express] it [to you. I constantly] th[ank God and as]k [Him to continue to grant] you [the graces He is] giving [you for the foun]da[tion in Luçon. Confidence], Monsieur! That's the [spirit! You are going to] begin a work from [which Our Lord] wants to draw the salvation of an infinite number of [souls and] the complete

---

[9]Evrard Gobert, born at Vendresse (Ardennes), entered the Congregation of the Mission as a priest on July 1, 1641, at the age of thirty-four.

Letter 908. - Archives of the Mission, Paris, original signed letter.

sanctification of your own. While you are negotiating this business, we shall prepare the workers you will need, namely, one of our priests whom I already had in mind, along with a Brother seminarian[1] and two good priests from our Bons-Enfants Seminary who want to spend a year or two in the service of the poor country people. They will, I hope, give you great satisfaction. But, before we send you anyone, please put things in order without, however, taking a decision on the conditions proposed to you by either the Bishop or his clergy, or by the Archdeacon, until I have first been informed about them.

Since Our Lord Jesus Christ has been pleased to entrust to you the care of a matter that concerns Him, I ask Him to give you the fullness of His Spirit and guidance to deal with it for His honor and according to His plan.

The Archdeacon [would like to have the] mission every [year] in his archdeaconry. . . .[2] You can easily make a commitment [for the first, but] not for the second, except for two or three villages at the most. Please explain to me what he has in mind. I shall write to him and indicate our submission to his wishes and to those of these priests, and my gratitude for the favor he offers us. Please give him all possible assurance of this, as I assure you of my heart's affection for yours. May it please God to unite them with His love for time and for eternity! I am in Him, Monsieur, your most humble servant.

VINCENT DEPAUL
i.s.C.M.

I have delayed sending the letter to the Archdeacon and the others until the first opportunity I find to send them to you in Richelieu or Luçon. Do not mention that these priests are not members of the Company.

At the bottom of the first page: M. Chiroye

---

[1]Candidates for the priesthood in the Congregation of the Mission. Saint Vincent often sent seminarians to various houses and works during their seminary training, as needs dictated. Also available to him at times were diocesan clergy living at the Bons-Enfants, while studying in Paris.

[2]The Archdeacon's wishes were listed here, but so few words of the original remain in this

909. - JULIEN GUERIN TO SAINT VINCENT

[Tunis, between 1645 and May 1648] [1]

We are expecting a large number of sick persons when the galleys return. If these poor people endure great miseries while they are at sea, those who remain here do not put up with any less. They are forced to toil every day at sawing marble, exposed to the burning sun, which is so hot that I can only compare it to a fiery furnace. It is amazing to see the work they endure, and the excessive heat which is enough to kill a horse. Yet, these poor Christians continue to survive, losing only their skin, which they surrender to the devouring heat. We see them like poor dogs with their tongues hanging out because of the unbearable heat in which they have to breathe. And yesterday a poor slave, who was quite elderly, became very ill and could hardly continue. When he asked permission to leave, the only reply he received was that, even if he were to drop dead on the stone, he still had to keep on working. I leave you to imagine how deeply these cruelties touch my heart and cause me pain.

And yet, these poor slaves bear their sufferings with incredible patience, and bless God in the midst of all the cruelties inflicted on them. I can also tell you truthfully that our Frenchmen surpass all the other nations in goodness and virtue. We have two patients who are at death's door and who, to all appearances, cannot escape it. We have given them all the sacraments. Last week two others died like true Christians, and it can be said of them: Pretiosa in conspectu Domini mors sanctorum ejus.[2] My compassion toward these poor afflicted beings, who labor at sawing marble, compels me to give them a share of the little refreshments I would give them if they were sick, etc.

There are other slaves who are not so badly treated; some of them remain in their masters' houses and are at their service for everything night and day; for example, to bake bread, wash clothes, prepare the food and drink, and do other small household chores. Others are used by their masters for business outside the house. Still others are free to work for themselves, giving a certain amount each month to their masters; they try to earn a little something and save it.

---

place that it is impossible to reconstruct the text.

Letter 909. - Abelly, *op.cit.*, bk. II, chap. I, sect. VII, §7, p. 118.

[1]The length of Julien Guérin's sojourn in Tunis.

[2]*Precious in the sight of the Lord is the death of his faithful ones.* Ps 116:15. (NAB) Ps 115:15. (D-RB)

— 149 —

910. - TO SAINT LOUISE

[Between 1645 and 1651][1]

Mademoiselle Le Gras is requested to inform Mademoiselle de Lamoignon[2] that she must go and ask Madame de Brienne[3] to be present at the meeting, where they need her advice and that of the Duchesse d'Aiguillon as well. Because the latter is engaged in urgent business matters today, you will have to insist on the first named, at least.

VINCENT DEPAUL

Addressed: Mademoiselle Le Gras

Letter 910. - Archives of the Motherhouse of the Daughters of Charity, original autograph letter. Saint Louise gave this letter to Mademoiselle de Lamoignon, who wrote in the margin: "Please notify me of this. I am at your disposition. M. de L. Wednesday at one o'clock."

[1]This letter seems to belong to the period when Madame de Lamoignon was President of the Ladies of Charity.

Madame de Lamoignon, born Marie de Landes on September 28, 1576, married Chrétien de Lamoignon on June 10, 1597, and died December 31, 1651. In 1647 Antoine Portail wrote from Rome to Saint Louise, telling her of the indulgences obtained from the Holy Father for the Ladies of Charity. In this letter, Madame de Lamoignon was named as one of those who merited this because of her great zeal and devotedness in all good works. Mademoiselle de Lamoignon (Madeleine) was her daughter.

[2]Madeleine de Lamoignon was born in Paris, September 14, 1608 of Chrétien de Lamoignon, a Presiding Judge of the Parlement of Paris, and of Marie de Landes, who initiated her from childhood in the traditions of the Confraternity of Charity. Mother and daughter were both very zealous in their dedication to the unfortunate. They often went to visit them in their homes, dressed their wounds, cleaned their rooms, made their beds, and gave them clothing, linen, food, and money. Saint Vincent used to say that Mademoiselle de Lamoignon forged ahead so fast with her charitable works that nobody could keep up with her. She supported and took an active part in all the works the Saint founded. She died on April 14, 1687, at seventy-nine years of age.

[3]Louise de Béon, a Lady of Charity very devoted to Saint Vincent and his work, was the daughter of Louise de Luxembourg-Brienne and Bernard de Béon who was Intendant of Saintonge, Angoulême, and the territory of Aunis. She was the wife of Henri-Auguste de Loménie, Comte de Brienne, Secretary of State. Louise de Béon died September 2, 1665.

911. - TO ETIENNE BLATIRON, SUPERIOR, IN GENOA

Paris, December 28 [1646][1]

Monsieur,

The grace of Our Lord be with [you for]ever!

I received your letter of [. . . . I thank] God for [all] you [tell me about the success of your missions. . .],[2] for, from what I can see, [he is one of the greatest] saints in His [Church.[3]

I am] deeply grateful for the modera[tion you have shown] in the clause for the foundation, which you mentioned to me. I am sending it in the form in which it will have to be drawn up, if this is agreeable to him.

I have indeed been greatly consoled to hear about the good order in the seminary and the progress being made there. This is a special grace from God, for which I ask His Divine Goodness to be Himself glorified and to accept my gratitude to Him, especially for the sound leadership of good M. Martin, who needs to be supported and strengthened by the Holy Spirit in his various duties. God knows how much I fear he may give way beneath the burden, and you beneath yours.

By this same mail I am writing to ask M. Dehorgny to send you without delay the man you are requesting, or some other worthwhile person. And to put more pressure on him to do so, I am sending him your letter, so that your reasons will help him understand the need for this. I hope he will give you cause for satisfaction.

I do not know whether you recall that Saint-Nicolas-de Champvant priory[4] in the Poitiers diocese was previously given to

---

Letter 911. - Archives of the Mission, Paris, original signed letter.

[1]The year was added on the back of the original but has disappeared because of the damage caused by humidity.

[2]The few words remaining in the following eight lines of the original are not sufficient to reconstruct the text.

[3]This probably refers to Cardinal Durazzo.

[4]This priory remained in the possession of the Congregation of the Mission until the French Revolution.

the Richelieu [house,] and the letters of confirmation were sent to [Rome fo]r immed[iate] possession of the said [priory] by the Con[gregation of] the Priests of the [Mission established in] Ri[chelieu. You] must make a [renunciatio]n of it before a [notary] to [have it] handed over to [M. . . .], and. . . , in line with [what] has been [determined by the] abbots and monks [of Notre]-Dame-des-Noyers[5] on whom the priory [depends], the right of nomination being theirs by an edict of last November 6, in presence of Girard, the royal notary. Send this resignation promptly to M. Dehorgny, so that, with it and the copy of the agreement I am supposed to send him, he may obtain the Brief for this union.

I would like to think that this letter will find you nearing the close of your extensive mission. Please God it will also find you in the best of health and with a happy outcome to your labors for the salvation of the poor whom you instruct, and the sanctification of your own soul! I wish the same for those priests working with you, for whom God has given me a special, tender affection, seeing their goodness and the good example they give to our whole Congregation, whom I often tell about their virtue and zeal. I beg you to greet them humbly and cordially for me, rene[wing the] offer of my obedience. I [also] embrace M. Richard and Brother Sébastien,[6] and as[k Our Lord] to bless them more and more.

I am, [in His love, Monsieur], your most humble servant.

VINCENT DEPAUL
i.s.C.M.

---

[5]An abbey of Reformed Benedictines of the Congregation of Saint-Maur in the Tours diocese.
[6]François Richard and either Sébastien Nodo or Sébastien Drugeon.

911a. - *DEDICATION TO SAINT VINCENT BY CHARLES AUBERT* [1]

To Monsieur Vincent, Superior General of the Priests of the Mission

Monsieur, people will perhaps find it strange that, although I do not have the happiness of knowing you personally, I so readily offer you this humble Discours in the simplicity of our spirit and language. However, the great progress being made daily by worthy and pious persons whom God, through you, has raised up in this region, and who are working so successfully for the welfare and salvation of souls, [2] clearly manifests your ardent zeal for His service, His honor, and His glory.

This knowledge has given us the courage to present it to you simply, judging it unworthy and improper in our day to use skill to cloud or even conceal the truth in all things. This acts as an enticement to sin rather than a sure guide for walking straight in the path of virtue, which of itself has very effective means to attract the spirit of a good foundation without seeking external embellishments.

I offer you, then, Monsieur, this little work, submitting most humbly to the reception of any correction you are pleased to give it. I am, for the rest of my days, Monsieur, your most humble and very obedient servant in Our Lord.

C. AUBERT
Unworthy priest

912. - TO ETIENNE BLATIRON, SUPERIOR, IN GENOA

January 4, 1647

You can tell the Cardinal [1] that the prelates are our masters for all

---

Letter 911a. - Letter printed at the beginning of *Brief Discours de Charles Aubert, prêtre, du respect et honneur des enfants envers leurs pères et mères* (Le Mans: n.p., 1646). (Cf. Bibl. Nat. D 21298.) The text was published in the *Annales C. M.* (1941-1942), p. 274, and reprinted in *Mission et Charité*, 19-20, pp. 71-72. This edition uses the latter text.

[1]Charles Aubert (ca.1567-ca.1653), lawyer and priest in Le Mans; author of works of a religious character.

[2]Allusion to the apostolic works of the Priests of the Mission, who had been in Le Mans since 1645 (major seminary and missions).

Letter 912. - Reg. 2, p. 76.
[1]Stefano Cardinal Durazzo.

our external works, and we are obliged to obey them, as the servants of the Gospel obeyed their master. If they command us to go, we are obliged to go; to stay, we are obliged to stay; if to work, we are obliged to do that, and if we fail to do so, they have the right to punish us. In a word, we owe obedience to the bishops in all things pertaining to our work in the missions, with ordinands, etc., but the spiritual and internal direction belongs to the Superior General.

913. - *ALAIN DE SOLMINIHAC TO SAINT VINCENT*

[1647] [1]

I really wish that M. Testacy and the others in our seminary would stop worrying you about many things, as they are now doing, since there is no need for this. The bursar of my house has always told me that the boarders could be fed for one hundred livres, and I think this is so. However, even were it not the case, since they had been made to understand that this is a synodal decision taken on the advice of our entire synod, they will have to wait until the next synod to get it changed.

There are twenty-five clerics in our seminary, and in a few days there will be nearly thirty-five of them. That is why it is absolutely necessary to send one of your men to assist the others, especially for the chant; this is very necessary. I had asked M. Portail to tell you that. I hope you will make provision for this.

In the meantime, believe me to be your most humble servant.

ALAIN
Bishop of Cahors

Letter 913. - Archives of the Diocese of Cahors, Alain de Solminihac collection, file 5, no. 6, original.

[1] The letter was written while Charles Testacy was Superior of the Cahors Seminary and shortly after Antoine Portail passed through that town in December, 1646.

914. - TO JEAN MARTIN, IN GENOA

Paris, January 11, 1647

Monsieur,

The grace of Our Lord be with you forever!

I received your dear letter with a very sincere and tender affection for your dear soul, which seems to me more and more blessed and chosen by the hand of God to procure His glory in those whom you guide and, through them, in an infinite number of others, who will praise Him in time and in eternity. So let us work courageously and lovingly for such a good Master as ours; let us imitate Him in His virtues; above all, in His humility, gentleness, and patience. Then you will see good results in your manner of directing.

I certainly speak to you with compassion about your heavy labors, but I am consoled by the confidence I have that God is increasing your strength and preserving your heart in peace. This is the grace I ask of Him, while awaiting the arrival of the help that is supposed to come to you from Rome. It has already been two weeks since I asked M. Dehorgny to send you someone posthaste, and by the next regular mail I will send you the rules of our Bons-Enfants Seminary. I gave this errand to someone a long time ago. Excuse his forgetfulness and mine.

M. Portail will soon be going to see you. He is already in Marseilles and is only waiting for a means of transport to leave. M. Alméras will go to Rome with him.

I recommend them to your prayers, and myself along with them. I am, with all my heart, in the love of Our Lord, Monsieur, your most humble servant.

VINCENT DEPAUL
i.s.C.M.

Addressed: Monsieur Martin, Priest of the Mission, in Genoa

Letter 914. - Archives of the Mission, Turin, original signed letter.

915. - *SAINT LOUISE TO SAINT VINCENT*

Wednesday [Between 1643 and 1649] [1]

Monsieur,

I sent your note, which was delivered to Madame de Lamoignon, since Mademoiselle was not there. Madame sent me word that the day of the meeting depended on you, and that Mademoiselle Viole [2] *would really have liked it to be on Friday.*

I am, Monsieur, your most obedient daughter and servant.

L. DE MARILLAC

916. - TO JEAN MARTIN, IN GENOA

Paris, February 1, 1647

Monsieur,

The grace of Our Lord be with you forever!

You give me special pleasure by consoling me with your letters, because of the effect they have on me. I never read any of them without being moved by gratitude to God and affection for you, seeing the sentiments of humility and confidence He gives you. From these springs the holy generosity with which you bear the burden of a seminary. Please God, Monsieur, you will be strengthened more and more, and be given the fullness of His Spirit to animate this little body and shape it according to the maxims of

---

Letter 915. - Original autograph letter made available by Abbé Le Gras, 8 avenue du Parc, Lyons.

[1]Before 1643 Madame de Lamoignon was not yet President of the Ladies of Charity; after 1649 Saint Louise no longer addressed Saint Vincent as "Monsieur" at the beginning of her letters.

[2]Mademoiselle Viole, born Madeleine Deffita, was the widow of Jacques Viole, Counselor at the Châtelet in Paris. Among the Ladies of Charity of the Hôtel-Dieu, she held the office of Treasurer. Her name recurs often in the correspondence of Saint Vincent, who greatly appreciated her charity, intelligence, and activity. She died in Paris on April 4, 1678.

Letter 916. - Archives of the Mission, Turin, original signed letter.

Jesus Christ! I never think of you without offering you to Him, thanking Him for the graces He gives you. Did I not see God's special assistance to you, I would think I was dreaming when I reflect that a young man like you[1] directs several others so successfully, both interiorly and exteriorly. I beg Our Lord once again to carry out His plans in you and through you, and to grant me mercy through your prayers.

I am, in His love, Monsieur, your most humble servant.

VINCENT DEPAUL
i.s.C.M.

Addressed: Monsieur Martin, Priest of the Mission in Genoa

917. - TO JEAN MARTIN, IN GENOA

Paris, February 18, 1647

Monsieur,

The grace of Our Lord be with you forever!

O Monsieur, what a comfort your letters always are to me! In fact, Monsieur, this is so much the case that I cannot express it to you.

Alas! Monsieur, how right you are in your description to me of your interior state! But, blessed be God for the good use you make of it! Even were we saints, as long as we are in this valley of tears, we will always experience what you are feeling. God permits this to keep us ever on the alert in the practice of holy mortification and humility. Let us be steadfast in this, and Our Lord will remain the victor over our passions, reign sovereignly within us, and, through

---

[1]Jean Martin was born on May 10, 1620; therefore, he was twenty-seven years old.

Letter 917. - Casa della Pace, Chieri (Italy). In 1886 Pietro Marietti gave this original autograph letter to the Priests of the Mission in gratitude for their hospitality to him when he made his

us, in the souls for whose service His Providence has destined us. So then, let us be steadfast, and always walk in the ways of God without coming to a standstill.

O Monsieur, what shall we say about your holy Prelate,[1] of whom you tell me so much! I certainly admire that, and hope, if Our Lord preserves him for ten years in His Church, that he will renew his whole diocese, as did the Bishop of Alet.[2]

I am writing to M. Blatiron that it is desirable that the establishment of conferences among the pastors and other priests in the rural areas should be suggested to this holy Prelate. I hope that, if Our Lord is pleased to continue to give His holy blessing to the labors of this holy Prelate, as He has done up to the present, and especially with regard to conferences of this sort, with which M. Blatiron is familiar, since he was one of the first to work in them, great benefits will result. *Mais quoi!* things have to be done gradually. Grace has its small beginnings and its progress.

As for the mission in the town, you were right to tell him how we go about it.

I ask you, Monsieur, to renew to him, from time to time, the assurance of my obedience, and to ask his blessing for me, which I request, prostrate in spirit at the feet of His Eminence. I am, in the love of Our Lord, your most humble and obedient servant.

VINCENT DEPAUL
i.s.C.M.

Addressed: Monsieur Martin, Priest of the Mission, in Genoa

---

ordination retreat in their house in Chieri. The letter is still in the house, where it has been framed and is held in great veneration.
[1]Stefano Cardinal Durazzo.
[2]Nicolas Pavillon.

— 158 —

918. - *SAINT LOUISE TO SAINT VINCENT*

[Between 1639 and 1649] [1]

Monsieur,

I do not know what to tell you about my health, but I assure you that I really must speak to you about the needs of several Sisters, before thinking about anything else.

We have Sister Charlotte [2] *here, who has been very sick for a long time. She is the sister of Sister Geneviève* [3] *of the Hôtel-Dieu, who also used to serve light meals there. I greatly fear that she will be like our late Sister Bécu. Several times a bloodletting had been ordered for her foot, but no one was able to draw blood. If your charity were willing to send us good Brother Alexandre,* [4] *perhaps he could get some. Her fever is usually higher in the evening than in the morning.*

Our Sisters on retreat will make their confession whenever you wish. It will not be a general one for either of them.

The woman from Lorraine, who spoke to you Saturday at the Hôtel-Dieu, cannot find work. That is why she has been at the Hôtel-Dieu for two weeks. What shall we do about her? Please do not send her any money. I told Sister Geneviève to give her what she needs. She would like nothing better than to live there with nothing to do, and to have some money.

I see such disorder everywhere that I feel overwhelmed by it. Neverthe-

---

Letter 918. - Archives of the Motherhouse of the Daughters of Charity, original autograph letter.

[1]Sister Marie Bécu was still alive in 1639 (cf. vol. I, no. 387); after 1649, all the letters written by Saint Louise to Saint Vincent began with "Most honored Father."

[2]Sister Charlotte Poisson.

[3]Sister Geneviève Poisson entered the Company of the Daughters of Charity before 1636. She was first placed at the Hôtel-Dieu in Paris. In July 1647 she was present at the installation of the foundlings in Bicêtre, where she devoted herself to them for many years. She showed great prudence and astuteness, especially during the first war of the Fronde (1648-1649), when upheavals made it very difficult to obtain the means of subsistence for the house with its eleven hundred children, mostly under seven years of age, and twelve Sisters. In 1651 she participated in the Council as a senior Sister. On August 8, 1655 she signed the Act of Establishment of the Company. She was named Treasurer on May 22, 1657.

[4]Alexandre Véronne, a coadjutor Brother, born May 15, 1610 in Avignon, was received into the Congregation of the Mission on July 22, 1630. He was infirmarian at Saint-Lazare and was so dedicated and capable that he won the esteem of all, particularly of Saint Vincent. His death on November 18, 1686 was announced to the whole Company in a circular letter from Edme Jolly, Superior General (1673-1697). Brother Chollier wrote his life, which was published in *Miroir du frère coadjuteur de la Congrégation de la Mission* (Paris, 1875), pp. 145ff. This work

less, I continue to hope, and I wish to place my trust in Divine Providence, with Saints Martha and Mary.

It is in the love of our good Jesus that I am, Monsieur, your most humble daughter and very grateful servant.

L. DE M.

Addressed: *Monsieur Vincent*

919. - TO JEAN MARTIN, IN GENOA

Paris, February 28, 1647

Monsieur,

The grace of Our Lord be with you forever!

I received a letter from you this week, but none from M. Blatiron, who cannot do everything, because he is away and very busy. I certainly am in admiration at the care you have taken, in the midst of running a house and seminary, not to fail to give me this consolation, which is extraordinary this time because it tells me of the blessings God has been pleased to continue to give to M. Blatiron and his work. What is happening in and through him seems like a little miracle.

[I see also] the special graces this same Lord gives you as well, blessing your leadership and filling your dear heart with perfect trust in His help, the best means to carry out His work successfully. You have discovered the secret; anyone who will not act in this spirit, no matter how competent he may be, will never succeed either for himself or for others. So then, let us be steadfast, Monsieur, let us be steadfast in this precious trust in God, the Strength of the weak and the Eye of the blind. And, although things may not go according

---

also served as the basis for his biography in *Notices,* vol. III, pp. 528-548.

Letter 919. - Archives of the Mission, Turin, original signed letter.

to our views and way of thinking, let us have no doubt that Providence will bring them to the point necessary for our greater good.

Do not be at all surprised at the reports you hear. That good priest,[1] who first worked in the missions and who has expressed to you his distaste for them now, should not measure others by himself, nor think they are engaged in this holy work simply to please the Cardinal. Even if this were the case, God will still be glorified by these wrong intentions, and a number of souls saved. If they are discontinued, as will happen if they do not take God into account, the Cardinal will realize that, for a stable establishment, he needs persons who have given themselves to Our Lord in these duties, and not local priests who have other aspirations.

May it please His Infinite Goodness to grant us the grace that all our men may strive for the advancement of His glory and our own self-emptying!

I am, in His love, Monsieur, your most humble servant.

VINCENT DEPAUL
i.s.C.M.

Addressed: Monsieur Martin, Priest of the Mission, in Genoa

---

[1]Perhaps in a letter which is not extant, M. Martin had informed Saint Vincent of a certain priest who abandoned the task of preaching missions. From the context of the present letter, he appears not to have been a member of the Congregation of the Mission, but some priest from the Genoa area.

920. - TO FRANCOIS ADHEMAR DE MONTEIL, ARCHBISHOP OF ARLES

Paris, February 29,[1] 1647

Excellency,

I received, with all the respect I owe to such a worthy Prelate, the letter with which you have honored me. I had already heard, from public report and from one of the Marseilles deputies, of the happy outcome of your mediation in the pacification of that town, which acknowledges that, after God, it is indebted for this to your prudent guidance. As for me, I have thanked Our Lord for it, and have no doubt that, as a reward, He will give you the perfection and attribute of this beatitude. I ask Him also to preserve you for many years for His glory and for the welfare of His Church.

As for Saint-Césaire Abbey, rest assured, Excellency, that I will most willingly give my support to your plan both because you order me to do so, and because of my devotion to the great Saint Caesarius. Besides, I have long been aware of the need in this monastery, since your predecessor tried to remedy it.[2] By his death, however, God has reserved to you the execution and merit of this good work. May it please His Infinite Goodness to carry out His eternal designs in you! I should offer you only my poor prayers, since that is all I can do for your service. Nevertheless, Excellency, I take the liberty of renewing to you here the offer of my obedience, with all possible

---

Letter 920. - Original signed letter in the Municipal Library of Arles, Ms. 142, vol. III. This manuscript came from the library of Laurent Bonnemant, a priest from Arles, and is entitled *Actes anciens et modernes concernant l'archevêché d'Arles.*

[1]A distraction of the secretary; it was most likely March 1.

[2]In order to restore regularity in the monastery of Saint-Césaire, where the most deplorable abuses had crept in, Jaubert de Barrault, Archbishop of Arles, brought in some nuns from Billom (Auvergne) in 1639. (Cf.*Gallia christiana novissima* [Arles: Valence, 1901], col. 967, no. 2259, taken from the Archives of Bouches-du-Rhône, S. Césaire d'Arles, Reg. XXXVI, pièce 2.) Their companions were jealous and disliked them, and the Abbess persecuted them to the point of depriving them of food. In spite of the remonstrances of the Archbishop and the insistence of the King, the unfortunate reformers were never able to remedy the disorders to which they were daily the sorrowful witnesses. (Arch. Nat. V[6] 187, no. 36.)

humility and affection, confident that you will not be displeased by this, since Our Lord has brought me to the point of being, in His love, Excellency, your most humble and obedient servant.

VINCENT DEPAUL
i.s.C.M.

Addressed: His Excellency, the Archbishop of Arles, in Arles

921. - *ALAIN DE SOLMINIHAC TO SAINT VINCENT*

Mercuès, March 3, 1647

Monsieur,

I have raised the same objection as you about receiving into the seminary those two boys of whom I wrote you. I had said this to M. Testacy, but I felt obliged to write to you, leaving everything to your judgment. Meanwhile, the local Seigneur and some of the inhabitants who were resisting came to an agreement. I shall encourage them in this good intention, while waiting for God to make known to us His Will about having a collège in Cahors to train and instruct those who devote themselves to His service in the ecclesiastical state, and to furnish us with the means of putting this into execution, as He will do if this is His Will. The foundation of a thousand écus for those two young men is a start.

You were right not to tell M. de la Marguerie [1] *what I wrote you concerning his son,* [2] *since he is of the opinion you mentioned to me.*

You do not know the Provincial of the Capuchins very well. He did not tell you the complaints his men are making to me, not only by letter, but in person. I am sending you a copy of the letter the King wrote me about him, and another from the Nuncio, [3] *for you to read at your leisure. This will give*

Letter 921. - Archives of the Diocese of Cahors, Alain de Solminihac collection, notebook, copy.

[1] Elie Laisné, Sieur de la Marguerie et de la Dourville, Ordinary State Councillor. On October 31, 1633 he had given Saint Vincent two hundred livres out of the town hall revenues "on condition that every five years he would send three priests and a Brother to give missions for four months, round trip included, in the Angoulême diocese." (Arch. Nat. M 211, f°1.) After the death of his wife, Elie Laisné entered the priesthood. He died October 3, 1656.

[2] Louis Laisné.

[3] Nicolò di Bagno, Archbishop of Athens, Nuncio in France from June 25, 1643 to 1657. He

you an idea of that mentality. Please disregard all that, and let people talk. You know my maxim about this, which I still maintain.

I ask you to admit these two good monks [4] *as boarders at the Bons-Enfants like the others, during their stay in Paris. They are coming to have the Sainte-Geneviève case tried, for which I beg your continued assistance.*

You would be overjoyed if you knew the good our seminary is doing. Good M. Testacy is ecstatic over it. He is a very fine priest. I would be glad if he were as experienced as he is good.

In the name of God, I implore you to have pity on the dioceses of Montauban and Sarlat, and on my own which is suffering from their turmoil.

A word of recommendation to M. de Morangis on behalf of our good monks would be very helpful to them.

ALAIN,
Bishop of Cahors

922. - TO JEAN DEHORGNY, SUPERIOR, IN ROME

March 1647

God will provide you with other workers when the time comes. You have had no urgent need of them up until now, since you have not had an ordination, and you have a fairly good number for the missions, although not as many as you would like. Here and elsewhere we do what we can. Would it be reasonable for us to have men in large numbers, making them superfluous part of the time, while God is short of them in other places where He calls us? Did not Saint Ignatius make a hundred foundations before his death, with two or three men in each? This was not done without great inconvenience, since he sent some novices and was obliged at times

---

was made a Cardinal with the titular church of San Eusebio, and Bishop of Senigallia on April 9, 1657. He died in Rome on August 23, 1663, at the age of seventy-nine. Saint Vincent, with whom he had a close relationship, could only be pleased with his benevolence.

[4]Probably Fathers Vitet and Parrot, Reformed Augustinians of Chancelade Abbey, which Alain de Solminihac directed. The Bishop was engaged in a protracted dispute with the Canons Regular of Sainte-Geneviève, who opposed the establishment of the Congregation of Chancelade.

Letter 922. - Reg. 2, p. 72.

to make them Superiors, but neither was it fruitless nor without providence. If we have begun a few, thank God it has not been with any desire to advance ourselves, as His Divine Goodness is aware, but solely to correspond to His plans. Nor was this done by our own choosing or at our request, but only by disposition from on high, which our indifference has given us the leisure to learn from experience, and to acknowledge.

Who will assure us that God is not calling us right now to Persia? This must not be conjectured from the fact that our houses are not full, for the ones that have more men do not produce the most fruit. Do we not rather have good reason to believe the contrary, even to fear that God may abandon Europe to the mercy of the heresies which have been waging war against the Church for a century, and have wrought such great havoc that they have reduced it to what seems like a mere speck? And to make matters worse, what now remains of it seems ripe for dissension because of the new opinions[1] proliferating daily. How do we know, I say, whether God does not wish to transfer the Church to the lands of unbelievers, who perhaps preserve greater innocence in their morals than the majority of Christians, who have nothing less at heart than the holy Mysteries of our religion? On my part, I am aware that this feeling has been with me for a long time. But even if God does not have this in mind, should we not contribute to the extension of the Church? Doubtless, yes, and that being the case, in whom does the authority of sending persons *ad Gentes*[2] reside? It must be the prerogative of the Pope, or the Councils, or the Bishops. Now, the last mentioned have jurisdiction only in their own dioceses, and there are no Councils at present, so it must reside in the person of the first-named. If then, he has the right to send us, we also have the obligation to go; otherwise his authority would be pointless.

You know, Monsieur, how long the Sacred Congregation has had its eyes on us, how often it has approached us, and how slowly

---

[1]Jansenism.
[2]*To the peoples.* This term refers to the sending of missionaries to non-evangelized territories.

we have moved so as not to involve anything human in the decision on this holy endeavor. However, since we are being pressured once again both by letter and by the Nuncio,[3] I no longer have any doubt that this must be done. I had prepared M. Féret for Babylon, but the Archbishop of Paris wanted him for Saint-Nicolas-du-Chardonnet,[4] and complained to me that I was trying to take him away from him. I told you that, not knowing anyone to whom I could turn outside the Company, I had thought of M. Gilles,[5] but that was not judged appropriate. I have sounded out other priests, who are members of our conference, but have not found any either sufficiently determined or suitable. I have only M. Brandon to see. If he fails,[6] I am obliged to go back to the Company for someone. I will let you know. Meanwhile, I await the report M. de Montheron promised you about that journey.

I am. . . .

---

[3]Nicolò di Bagno.

[4]He resided in that parish from September 7, 1646 to January 16, 1676.

[5]Jean-Baptiste Gilles, of the Avranches diocese, had been headmaster and professor of philosophy at the Collège de Lisieux, situated on rue de Beauvais in Paris. He was received into the Congregation of the Mission on November 28, 1642, and took his vows on October 11, 1645. After Gilles had served at the Cahors Seminary for some time, Saint Vincent entrusted to him the chair of moral theology at Saint-Lazare. As mentioned in this letter, when the Nuncio asked Saint Vincent to propose a candidate for Coadjutor Bishop of Babylon, the Saint thought of Jean-Baptiste Gilles. At the second General Assembly (1651), of which he was a member, he took part in the debate on the vows, which he insisted on maintaining. His ardent opposition to the Jansenists was manifest mainly in his lectures and conferences to seminarians preparing for ordination. However, his insistence on attacking them ran the danger of producing the opposite effect. The Saint understood this and transferred him from Saint-Lazare in 1651. For a short time, Gilles was Superior of the Crécy house, where he died on August 22, 1652. He received a well-deserved place in *Notices*, vol. III, pp. 110-114. His will, drawn up on April 30, 1643, showed the high esteem in which he held Saint Vincent (cf. Arch. Nat. M 211, f°1).

[6]Philibert Brandon, Seigneur du Laurent, became a Counselor in the Parlement on February 18, 1622. On the advice of Father de Condren, he left this position after the death of his wife, Marie de Ligny, niece of Chancellor Séguier, to enter the priesthood. He was one of the founders of Saint-Sulpice Seminary. Brandon had offered his house in Saint-Maur-les-Fosses (Val-de-Marne) to M. Olier and his first companions. It was there that this pious phalanx of apostolic men spent part of the years 1640-1641. In 1648 Brandon became Bishop of Périgueux, after having refused the Babylon diocese offered to him by Saint Vincent. He stayed in Périgueux until his death on July 11, 1652. His relationship with Abbé de Saint-Cyran did not affect his orthodoxy.

923. - TO JEAN MARTIN, IN GENOA

Paris, March 8, 1647

Monsieur,

The grace of Our Lord be with you forever!

This letter is simply to glorify God for the blessings He gives to your direction of the seminary and to the good dispositions of your soul, which cause you to act with such trust in Our Lord that seeing this in your letters fills me with its perfume. This virtue, together with humility and gentleness, practiced toward these good seminarians, will produce admirable effects in their souls because God Himself will animate your example and words with His own Spirit, and will fill yours with His light and strength. In the end, He will shower His eternal consolations on you. This is the prayer I offer Him, prostrate before Him, and will offer Him all my life because He has made you so dear to my poor soul, and has made me your most humble servant.

VINCENT DEPAUL
i.s.C.M.

Addressed: Monsieur Martin, Priest of the Mission, in Genoa

924. TO ETIENNE BLATIRON, SUPERIOR, IN GENOA[1]

March 8, 1647

Three of your letters to me arrived at the same time. I received

---

Letter 923. - Archives of the Mission, Turin, original signed letter.

Letter 924. - Reg. 2, p. 198.

[1]The Avignon manuscript gives as recipient of this letter "M. N., Superior in Richelieu." This was obviously a distraction of the copyist because Register 2, which ordinarily follows the Avignon manuscript, states it is addressed to Etienne Blatiron, and several passages would be inexplicable if the recipient were the Superior in Richelieu.

them as coming from you, Monsieur, that is, with joy and consolation, and certainly with gratitude to God for preserving you in the midst of so much work, and for blessing this same work, despite the obstacles the evil spirit tries to put in its way. You can imagine how often I thank His Infinite Goodness for all this and, offering Him the good results He produces through you, present to Him also the desires and affections of your charitable heart, even your entire dear heart, that He might bathe it in the sweetness of His love. Because I am filled with tender love for you, and with dread that you may be overwhelmed by these painful duties, I also find myself continually urged to invoke the Divine Assistance for you, even though my sins cause me to fear the inefficacy of my prayers.

925. - SAINT LOUISE TO SAINT VINCENT

March 10 [1647] [1]

Monsieur,

The awkward position in which you are placed because of the important guests you have makes me hesitate to send you Monsieur des Jonchères' [2] *letter. I also have a few others to share with your charity so as to get your advice on them.*

I do not think that what my son said was taken amiss because, in my opinion, it did not go beyond the bounds of the respect he owes. However, I find it absolutely impossible for this matter to be settled, unless you give your consent. I also foresee that the delay will be very prejudicial to my son, for several reasons I cannot put in writing. I must resign myself to all the consequences I dread from this, however painful they may be.

What I told you had been said to me was said to put a stop to abuses and slander against the morals of those whose doctrine is suspect. It had been remarked that those who sided with them had protested from the pulpit that

Letter 925. - Archives of the Motherhouse of the Daughters of Charity, original autograph letter.
[1]Year added on the back of the original by Brother Ducournau.
[2]A diocesan priest in Nantes who had recently assumed the duty of confessor for the Daughters of Charity at the hospital in Nantes.

they were involved in this only in a spirit of union and charity and were speaking only in those terms.

The Comtesse de Maure [3] told me to take care to return to her a book she sent you, the Apologie de Jansénius[4]. *She is also sending you this one to look at, as she promised you.*

If I thought I could have a little time to speak to you tomorrow about a certain situation in our Company, in addition to the serious one in Nantes, I would beg you to give it to me.

Sister Madeleine [5] is much better, thank God, and all is going rather well in Angers. I cause so much disorder everywhere. I fear that your charity is forgetting my needs, which cause me to hope more than ever that your charity believes me to be, by God's Will, Monsieur, your most obedient and very grateful daughter.

L. DE M.

Addressed: *Monsieur Vincent*

926. - TO BISHOP INGOLI[1]

Paris, March 15, 1647

Excellency,

With all the respect and devotion Our Lord gives me for one of the Prelates of the Church who labor the most for the extension of the empire of Jesus Christ throughout the earth, I have received the letter with which your Most Illustrious Lordship has been pleased

[3]Anne Doni d'Attichy, Comtesse de Maure, and niece of Saint Louise de Marillac.

[4]Work published by Arnauld in 1644.

[5]Madeleine Mongert, from Sucy-en-Brie, was sent to Angers in March 1640 and named Sister Servant in October 1641, succeeding Sister Elisabeth Martin. She experienced some difficulties in directing this little Community. Saint Louise had her stay in Paris for a few months in 1644. After several changes of Sisters at the Angers hospital, she resumed responsibility for the Community until 1648, when the state of her health required that she be replaced by Cécile Angiboust. She died in Angers toward the end of 1648.

Letter 926. - Original signed letter, Archives of Propaganda Fide, VI, *Lettere di Francia, Inghilterra, Scozia, Ibernia ed India,* 1647, n°145, f°81.

[1]The Secretary of Propaganda Fide.

to honor me. I have given myself to God to obey Him with regard to Your Illustrious Lordship's command that I designate a member of the Company as Coadjutor of Babylon. Since I have found no one outside of it who seems to have the requisite qualities, and who is willing or able to undertake this good work, the person I am designating for this purpose, Excellency, is one of the two Assistants[2] given me by the Company as Councillors in governing it. It seems to me that the Divine Goodness has been pleased to bestow on him almost all the qualities necessary for this holy ministry. I must confess, Excellency, that losing this person is like plucking out one of my own eyes or cutting off my arm. However, my attachment to the authority Our Lord has given to His Church to send men *ad gentes,* which resides in the person of our Holy Father, and, consequently, the obligation of all priests in the Church to obey him in this; the thought that Abraham was ready to sacrifice his only son, and that the Eternal Father has given us His own Son—all this has induced me to designate this good Missionary for such a work and to offer myself, were I worthy of it.

That, Excellency, is our disposition regarding this affair, about which I hope to speak to the Queen[3] and the Cardinal[4] to find out Her Majesty's intention, of which I shall inform Your Illustrious Lordship. I offer you the obedience of our Little Company, and my own, and I am, in the love of Our Lord Jesus Christ, Excellency, your most humble and obedient servant.

VINCENT DEPAUL
Unworthy Superior of the Congregation of the Mission

At the bottom of the first page: Bishop Ingoli

---

[2]Lambert aux Couteaux. The other Assistant was Antoine Portail.
[3]Anne of Austria, mother of Louis XIV.
[4]Jules Cardinal Mazarin.

927. - A PRIEST OF THE MISSION TO SAINT VINCENT

Marseilles, 1647

We have just finished a mission that, for the space of five weeks, has kept us tied down to the confessionals, the pulpit, and the settling of lawsuits, with such successful results that I can say without exaggeration that we could not ask for more. We rectified nine or ten invalid marriages and settled about twenty-five to thirty lawsuits where, in some cases, very large sums of money were at stake; in others, honor; and in still others, lives. Almost all of them were settled by mutual agreement with no mediator. Some persons even did this publicly in church during the sermon, with so much emotion and tears that the preacher was interrupted by it.

It also happened that a man of modest condition, in a fit of anger, answered one of our men with a lack of discretion, and publicly added a blasphemous remark to his reply at the door of the church. Two weeks later he had such remorse that, in order to make satisfaction for this sin, of his own accord he made it his duty to pay one hundred écus for the reparation of the church before which he had uttered that blasphemy.

928. - TO JEAN MARTIN, IN GENOA

Paris, March 15, 1647

Monsieur,

The grace of Our Lord be with you forever!

This is simply that I may continue to be comforted by you through our exchange of letters. Yours give me more joy than anything else because it seems to me that I see your heart in them, as well as a great desire and disposition to love our good Lord. He will not fail on His part to give you an ever-increasing share in His love and virtues so as to fill your soul with them. This is what I shall beg of Him all my life.

Letter 927. - Abelly, *op.cit.*, bk. II, chap. I, sect. II, §4, p. 38.

Letter 928. - Archives of the Mission, Turin, original signed letter.

I am not writing to Messrs. Portail and Alméras because I think they are closer to Rome than to Genoa at the time of this writing. I have no doubt that you were consoled to see them. I await news of their departure and of what they have done. What you asked me about having one of them stay in Genoa is not feasible now because they have things to do elsewhere, and also because God will give you and the others the grace to correspond to His plan for our establishment in the place where you are, as He has done up to the present.

We should not want the Company to be talked about and esteemed for its extension. Humility and shame are more appropriate for us, and God does not need either the favor of men or our influence to call us where He pleases. I beg you to recommend my soul to Him, and to believe that yours is very dear to me. I am, in His love, Monsieur, your most humble servant.

VINCENT DEPAUL

i.s.C.M.

Addressed: Monsieur Martin, Priest of the Mission, in Genoa

929. - TO A PRIEST OF THE MISSION, IN ROME

(Now Vol. VI, no. 2197a.)

Letter 929. - In vol. VIII (p. 626) Coste corrected the date he had placed on this letter, stating that it belongs in vol. VI. The editors have placed it there as no. 2197a.

930. - *A PRIEST OF THE MISSION TO SAINT VINCENT*

1647

The mission of Gémozac[1] had most consoling results. Seven or eight heretics abjured their errors, and others would have imitated them, had they not feared a surcharge on their taxes by the local leaders, who belong to the reformed religion. Those inhabitants who, out of human respect, do not go to Mass, would be pleased if the King obliged them to carry out this duty.

One of these converts is an old man, whom we had exhorted several times, but in vain. After we had made one last effort shortly before our departure and saw that we were unable to get anywhere with him, the thought came to us to have recourse to the Blessed Virgin and beg her intercession to obtain the conversion of this poor black sheep. For this intention, we went and prostrated ourselves on our knees to recite the litanies, and when we had finished them, lo and behold, we saw our elderly man returning to us to acknowledge that he recognized the truth, and was willing to abjure his heresy. We had him do this and make his general confession afterward; then we gave him Holy Communion. As he was saying good-bye to us, he begged us earnestly to recommend him to the prayers of all the Catholics.

931. - TO CLAUDE DUFOUR

March 31, 1647

I thank God, Monsieur, for the many, many blessings God gives to your work of the missions and with the ordinands. I ask Him to give the same blessings to the seminary you are beginning and not to allow the temptation you are experiencing against your vocation to trouble your peace of mind. I am well aware that the Carthusian

Letter 930. - Abelly, *op.cit.,* bk. II, chap. I, sect. II, §2, p. 28. The paragraph in italics is a portion of the letter which Abelly summarizes above.
[1]Chief canton town in the district of Saintes.

Letter 931. - Reg. 2, p. 291. In the Archives of the Motherhouse of the Daughters of Charity, the Register entitled *Recueil de pièces relatives aux Filles de la Charité,* p. 675, presents us with a somewhat different text.

Order is more perfect in itself, but I do not think God wants you there, after calling you here. You responded and acquiesced to the inspiration of this call, and His Goodness blessed you in it with a very special blessing, with the result that, if you esteem it, it will strengthen you unalterably in the Congregation, particularly if you place yourself in the state in which you would wish to be found at the time of God's judgment. Please weigh in the balance the benefits of solitude on the one hand, and on the other, those Our Lord effects and will effect more and more through you. You will see that the latter will prevail.

Take also into consideration the conformity of your present life with that which Our Lord led on earth. This is your vocation, and the greatest need of the Church today is to have workers who labor to lead the majority of its children from the ignorance and vice in which they are, and to give it good priests and good pastors. That is what the Son of God came to do in the world, and you will consider yourself only too happy to be, like Him and through Him, engaged in this holy work.

You know, Monsieur, that, although the contemplative life is more perfect than the active life, it is not, however, more so than one which embraces at the same time contemplation and action, as does yours, by God's grace. But even if the contrary were true, it is certain that God does not call everyone to what is more perfect. All the members of the body are not the head, and all the angels do not belong to the first hierarchy. Those belonging to the inferior ones would not want to belong to the superior ones; they are satisfied with where God has placed them. And the blessed who have less glory do not envy those who have more. In like manner, we should be satisfied with the state in which we have been placed by the designs of Providence, and in which God blesses us. Indeed, the child of a poor woman disregards all other mothers in order to cling to its own mother's breast.

You say you experience great difficulty in the Mission. Alas! Monsieur, there is no lot in life where there is nothing to be endured. What person does not encounter difficulties and contradictions in most circumstances in his situation and does not think he would be happier in some work other than his own? Rest assured, Monsieur, that this is a ruse of the devil to turn you away from the good you are doing for the Church. One of his tricks is to tempt very good people to greater perfection, in order to make them abandon that in which God wishes them to be. So, remain steadfastly in your state *et ambula vocatione qua vocatus es,*[1] and *noli flectere ad dexteram neque ad sinistram.*[2] You can be sure that your vocation will bring about your sanctification and, in the end, your glorification. Let me know what can be done to comfort you in all this, for if one of our men is disturbing your peace, we will send someone else in his place. I ask you to make an hour's prayer on what I am saying to you, and tell me the sentiments God gives you on the subject. Please do not forget me there, so that God will deign to have mercy on my poor soul.

I am, in the love. . . .

932. - TO A SUPERIOR[1]

April 9, 1647

Five or six months ago I received two packets of letters from you, and a short while ago I received another. I did not answer the first ones because I did not know what to say to so many of the things you were suggesting. The regard I have always had for your piety caused me to respect the things you have said and written to me, so much so that I read these two packets on my knees, before the Blessed Sacrament, and asked God to grant me the grace to know

---

[1]*And walk in the vocation to which you are called.* Cf. Eph 4:1. (NAB)
[2]*And do not deviate to the right or to the left.* Cf. 2 Par 34:2. (D-RB)

Letter 932. - Reg. 2, p. 293.
[1]The recipient of the letter is undoubtedly Bernard Codoing. The Superior to whom it was addressed was most likely a seminary director. Now, among the Superiors of the six seminaries confided to the Congregation outside of Paris, only Bernard Codoing, at that time in Saint-Méen, had ideas like those which Saint Vincent censures in this letter.

whether the things you were saying came from Him, and, if so, to adopt them. But I must confess, Monsieur, that, if this is the case, my sins have made me unworthy of recognizing it. On the contrary, it seems to me we would destroy the little good God is pleased to do for those seminarians, since it is evident that, when things reach the point you are proposing, there is no difference between such seminarians and the scholarship holders in the collèges. We have attempted this in several ways, but experience has shown us that the way we do it now is the one that succeeds best.

We have sixty priests in the collège des Bons-Enfants, forty minor seminarians at Saint-Charles Seminary, and thirty seminarians in the Cahors Seminary, and the Bishop informs me that he is satisfied with them, by the grace of God. There are eight in Annecy, who are also starting out well, the same in Le Mans, and ten or twelve in Saint-Méen. These little attempts cause us to hope that Our Lord will bless His work, if it pleases His mercy not to consider the abomination of my life.

If I may venture to say so, Monsieur, what makes me the most wary of your views is the spirit of slander and insult apparent in them, which seems to me so far removed from the genuine charity of which we have a true-to-life picture represented in the blessed Bishop of Geneva.[2]

Do not think, Monsieur, that I am offended by what you tell me about myself. *O Jésus!* no, no, but only what you say about the Church in general and of several persons in particular, which is directly opposed to kindness, the second condition of charity. Moreover, Monsieur, did Our Lord reveal to you these methods you are proposing?

---

[2] Saint Francis de Sales.

933. - TO FRANCOIS ADHEMAR DE MONTEIL, ARCHBISHOP OF ARLES

[1647]

Since God has given me entire and perpetual obedience in your regard, I feel obliged to renew my offer of it to you from time to time. I did so recently[1] when, in reply to the honor of your letter, I assured you that I would gladly do my best to get an order from the Queen directed to the reform of Saint-Césaire. I continue to do so at present, Excellency, with all due reverence, begging you to accept this, since it is to accompany the letter Her Majesty has written to you concerning the reform. It can only be well done, since it is in M. de Verthamon's style.

In the name of God, Excellency, make use of your authority over me on all occasions. I am, in His sacred love, Excellency, your. . . .

934. - JULIEN GUERIN TO SAINT VINCENT

[Tunis, between 1645 and May 1648] [1]

You would be delighted to hear the Exaudiat sung, along with the other prayers, for the King of France, for whom even the foreigners manifest respect and affection, and to see with what devotion these poor captives offer prayers for all their benefactors, whom they know are in France or come from France for the most part. It is likewise no small source of consolation to see here persons in fetters and chains, from almost every nation, praying to God for the French.

Letter 933. - *Lettres et Conférences de Saint Vincent de Paul (Supplément)* [Paris, 1888], p. 526, 1. 3133.

[1]In the letter of February 29, 1647. (Cf. no. 920, n. 1, where the date is corrected to March 1, 1647.) Saint Vincent's reference to a previous letter prompted Coste to assign 1647 as the date for the present letter.

Letter 934. - Abelly, *op.cit.,* bk. II, chap. I, sect. VII, §7, p. 122.

[1]The period during which Julien Guérin was in Tunis.

935. - SAINT LOUISE TO SAINT VINCENT

[Between 1642 and 1649] [1]

Monsieur,

I ask you most humbly to take the trouble to let me know if the meeting of our Sisters can be tomorrow, Wednesday, so that I can inform them, as well as the Sisters of Issy and Fontenay. [2]

Mademoiselle de Lamoignon sent word to me yesterday to find out from you when she could come and see you to unburden her heart entirely to you. However, she does not want anyone in her home to know this. I will notify her about it, if you do me the honor of letting me know. She would like it to be as soon as possible.

Please give me your holy blessing, since I am, Monsieur, your most humble and very grateful daughter and servant.

L. DE M.

Tuesday

Addressed: *Monsieur Vincent*

936. - TO SAINT LOUISE

[Between 1642 and 1649][1]

Please call the meeting for tomorrow afternoon, Mademoiselle, and for Mademoiselle de Lamoignon, six o'clock this evening. However, it would be more convenient for me here at one o'clock this afternoon.

Letter 935. - Archives of the Motherhouse of the Daughters of Charity, original autograph letter.
[1]The letter was written after the houses in Issy and Fontenay-aux-Roses were opened (1642), and before the closing of the Issy house (1649).
[2]Two sections in the suburbs of Paris.

Letter 936. - Archives of the Motherhouse of the Daughters of Charity, original autograph letter.
[1]This letter answers the preceding one and was written immediately after Saint Vincent received it.

937. - *SAINT LOUISE TO SAINT VINCENT*

Easter [April 21, 1647] [1]

Monsieur,

I thought it necessary for your charity to take the trouble to look at this letter from Monsieur d'Annemont [2] *before our Sisters leave for Nantes. I think there are two things we also need to know from you: whether our thought about changing Sister Catherine* [3] *should be shared with Messieurs des Jonchères and d'Annemont, and even with Mademoiselle de la Carisière, or, if things were to remain calm, would it not be advisable to send away Sister Elisabeth,* [4] *who is still sick, as you will see; or else, should we leave it to Sister Jeanne* [5] *to handle this change, according to the instructions your charity gives her about it.*

Another thing I think most necessary and useful is for your charity to take the trouble to write a letter to all the Sisters, if you deem it appropriate, to express a little dissatisfaction with them and also to encourage them.

What is also true, Most Honored Father, is that this poor Company suffers greatly under my miserable guidance. I think, therefore, that God will soon deliver it from this captivity, which is such a great hindrance to the perfection of His work. I myself have good reason to fear dying in my callousness, unless your charity helps me.

During this holy season, can we not hope for the benefit of a conference to complete the instruction on the duties of Sisters toward their Sister Servants and the guidance and support of Sister Servants with regard to their companions? [6] *If this were well understood and practiced, I think it*

Letter 937. - Archives of the Motherhouse of the Daughters of Charity, original autograph letter.
[1]Date added on the back of the original by Brother Ducournau.
[2]Chaplain to the Maréchal de la Meilleraye in Nantes. D'Annemont had recommended that the Administrators of the hospital in Nantes invite the Daughters of Charity to this hospital.
[3]Sister Catherine Bagard entered the Company of the Daughters of Charity between 1636 and 1638. In 1646 she accompanied Saint Louise to Nantes. Her inappropriate behavior, her bad spirit, and her relationship with the chaplain there caused considerable difficulties for her Superiors and her companions. She returned to Paris in August 1647 and left the Company shortly after.
[4]Isabelle or Elisabeth Martin was among the first Daughters of Charity and one of the most talented, although she was often in poor health. She was Sister Servant at the Angers hospital (1640), Richelieu (1641), and at the Nantes hospital (1646). She returned to Richelieu in 1648 and died there the following year.
[5]Jeanne Lepeintre. A few days later she was named Sister Servant in Nantes.
[6]Saint Vincent had treated this subject the preceding February 2 in a conference which has come down to us. (Cf. vol. IX, no. 29.)

would prevent all the little disorders in the Company, as would having our little Rules,[7] *so that we could read them from time to time in the Company.*

A Lady asked me to find out whether there were fifty acres of land for sale between the house where the foundlings are lodged[8] *and La Chapelle. I suggested to her your house near the Recollect Fathers,*[9] *in the hope that something might be found close to the property she wants, including the house. I beg you most humbly, Monsieur, if you think this is feasible, kindly to take the trouble to let me know through Brother Ducournau because after the feast days this Lady is supposed to send a man to inspect the place.*

Will your charity please remember the Comtesse de Maure with regard to my son, because the other affair is quickly leaking out. It seems to me that you are hearing about nothing else but this affair. Mon Dieu! how my pride causes me to suffer because of it, and what a great relief it would have been had I been spared it! The most holy Will of God has not permitted this. May He be forever blessed for it! I have the honor to be, Monsieur, your most obedient and very grateful daughter and servant.

LOUISE DE MARILLAC

Addressed: *Monsieur Vincent*

---

[7]The Regulations or Statutes of the Company, approved November 20, 1646 by Jean-François-Paul de Gondi, Coadjutor to his uncle, the Archbishop of Paris. Saint Vincent read them to his Daughters during his conference of May 30, 1647 (cf. vol. IX, no. 30). To what might this delay of six months be attributed? Apparently, it would have been longer without the insistence of Saint Louise. It was not due, at least not entirely, to the important duties of the Founder, since he took the time to assemble the Sisters on February 2. Perhaps he entertained for a time the hope of procuring certain modifications in the details; perhaps also, the pontifical document was not given to him until several months after the approbation. It is evident from no. 898 that Saint Louise also desired some modifications in the Rules as approved by the Archbishop of Paris.

[8]The Foundling Home faced rue du Faubourg-Saint-Denis; it stood opposite the enclosure of Saint-Lazare, near the site now occupied by the Gare du Nord. Boulevard de la Chapelle, located close by, runs along the boundary of what was then the village of La Chapelle.

[9]This convent has given its name to the present rue des Récollets. It became the Saint-Martin Military Hospital.

938. - TO CLAUDE DUFOUR, SUPERIOR, IN SAINTES

April 23, 1647

Thank you most humbly, Monsieur, for the confidence you show in me by asking my advice on your thought of entering the Carthusians. I will tell you quite simply what I would wish to advise you at the hour of my death, namely, that you should continue in the vocation to which God has been pleased to call you, without listening in future to the suggestions of the spirit that is strongly averse to final perseverance in the good already begun. Under pretext of greater assurance of your salvation, his intention is to lure you away from where God has placed you, so that you may fall into greater danger. If he entices you from the place where you now are, he will then prevent you from going where you aspire, or else he will cause you to leave after you get there. Someone told me that there are a hundred Jesuits in Paris who have left the bosom of their holy mother, under pretext of working wonders elsewhere, and most of them are a source of scandal and in great peril of being lost.

In the name of God, Monsieur, remain steadfast in the state in which Our Lord has placed you, and reject the contrary idea as hostile to God's eternal plan for you and for the many souls whom His Divine Majesty wishes to save through you. If staying in Saintes, or the duty you have, does not suit you, please let me know; we will assign you somewhere else.

I tell you once again, Monsieur, that I offer myself to God to answer for you and for me to His Divine Majesty for the advice I am giving you. In the meantime, I ask Our Lord to let you see, as I think I see it, the wickedness of this temptation, which is leading you to sacrifice certainty for uncertainty, and causing you to mistake a point of view for inspiration, and weariness for anxiety.

Letter 938. - Reg. 2, p. 294.

939. - TO THE DAUGHTERS OF CHARITY AT THE HOSPITAL IN NANTES

Orsigny, four leagues from Paris, April 24, 1647

Dear Sisters,

I never think about you and the happiness you have to be Daughters of Charity and the first to be engaged in assisting the poor where you are, without feeling consoled. However, when I hear that you are living as true Daughters of Charity, which is to say, as true daughters of God, my consolation is increased to the extent that only God alone can make you realize. Keep this up, dear Sisters, and strive more and more toward perfection in your holy state. Here are the reasons which should urge you to do so.

In the first place, there is the sanctity of your state, which consists in being true daughters of God, spouses of His Son, and true mothers of the poor. This state is so noble, dear Sisters, that human understanding can conceive of nothing greater in a simple creature on earth.

The second reason is that, in order to elevate you to this happiness, God has withdrawn you from the corrupt mass of the world.

The third is your fidelity in corresponding to the holy inspiration Our Lord has given you in calling you to this state, the ardor with which you asked to be accepted in the beginning, and the resolutions you took at that time to live and die in a holy manner.

In the fourth place, my dear Daughters, consider the blessing God has been pleased to give to your spiritual exercises and to the assistance of the poor, how much good example you have given in

---

Letter 939. - Archives of the Motherhouse of the Daughters of Charity, copy made by Sister Hellot, who died in 1650. This letter, written at the request of Saint Louise, following the observations made by M. d'Annemont (cf.*Ecrits spirituels*, L. 173, p. 193), was sent by the Foundress, who added a note to it and some advice (cf. *ibid.,* L. 174, pp. 195-197): "O Sisters! the gentle tone in which it was written, the remark about the graces God has granted you and us, and the instructions his charity gives you so graciously, have filled me with inexpressible awe, when I recall that God has so often warned us through him of our obligations; he has so often been aware of our faults and deliberately overlooked them, never tiring of animating us nor of taking paternal care of us."

the house, how many fine girls you have attracted and who are living in a holy manner, how many sick poor you are leading to a good life, how many others you have reconciled with God by your good advice during their illnesses, and again, how many others who are now blessed in heaven and pray unceasingly for the sanctification of your dear souls. These are some of the reasons, dear Sisters, among an infinity of others, which several reams of paper could not contain, that should animate you more and more to persevere and to perfect yourselves in your holy vocation.

It seems to me, dear Sisters, that all of you tell me that you really want this, but that you are shaken by an infinite number of temptations which weigh you down. To this I reply, dear Sisters, that all these temptations are sent to you, or permitted by God, for the same reasons He sent and permitted those which His Son suffered, namely, to give proof of His infinite love for the glory of His Father and for the sanctification of His Church.

Yes, you will say, but it seems to me that so many other good souls in the world and in religious communities, and even in your own Community, are not tried interiorly to the extent you are. Well, my reply is that there are no souls professing to belong entirely to God and His poor members, who undergo as many interior and exterior trials as you do, for it is a decree given by God, not against but in favor of good and holy souls, that every one of them will suffer temptation and persecution.

It is bad enough to be tempted at times, you will say to me, dear Sisters, but always and everywhere and by almost all those with whom I live is unbearable! God's good pleasure, dear Sisters, is that those blessed, chosen souls, whom He loves so dearly, should be tempted and afflicted daily. This is what He points out and to what He exhorts us, when He says in the Gospel that those who wish to come after Him must renounce themselves and carry the cross,[1]

---

[1]Cf. Lk 9:23, which includes the notion of "daily," to which Saint Vincent refers here; cf. also Mt 16:24. (NAB)

which means that they must suffer afflictions daily. Ponder this word "daily," dear Sisters.

Monsieur, you will say, I willingly put up with that from persons on the outside, but why does it come from my own Sisters, who should be a consolation to me, and are a trial, a cross, and an affliction in all they say, and do, and fail to do!

Alas! dear Sisters, from whom shall we suffer if not from those with whom we live? Will it be from persons who are far away, or from those whom we have not seen and never will see? What causes a member of the body to suffer, if not the pain caused by another member? From whom and by whom did Our Lord suffer, if not His Apostles, disciples, and those among whom He lived, the people of God? One day, while making his confession, a good man said to his confessor, who asked him what use he made of the afflictions brought on him by his neighbor, "Alas! Father, I have nothing to suffer in that area. Since my wife and children have died, I am all alone and could not get angry with anyone, even if I wanted." This goes to show you, dear Sisters, that our daily crosses caused by others can come only from those with whom we live.

Well, you will say to me, I endure more willingly trials coming from my Sisters, rather than when they come from our Sister Servant.[2] Her coldness, her ailments, her silences, and the fact that she never says a kind word to me—and if she does speak, it is always abruptly and peevishly—that is what I cannot stand. That is what makes me seek consolation from some of our Sisters who experience the same suffering as I, and what causes me to talk as often as possible to my confessor and to tell my troubles to outsiders.

To that I reply, dear Sister, that this is a sign that we are very weak or sick, since we need to be flattered by our Superiors in whatever they say to us or order us to do. Far from considering this cajolery advantageous, a Daughter of Charity should, on the contrary, have reason to think that, when the Sister Servant flatters

---

[2] Elisabeth Martin. Her poor health was probably the main cause of the disorders that had slipped into the little Community in Nantes.

them, she is treating them like children or sick persons. Our Lord guided His followers in a firm and severe manner, and sometimes even used apparently harsh and insulting words, even calling some of them hypocrites and others Satan. Another time He took a whip and struck those who were selling things at the temple gate, and what is more, He foretold to them only the extreme afflictions that were to befall them. And after that, we want to be flattered by our Superiors, and we draw away from them, like the unfortunate man who betrayed Our Lord, to form a separate group with a few malcontents and with our confessors! *O Jésus!* my very dear Sisters, may God preserve you from this!

It seems to me, my very dear Sisters, that you are telling me you have not fallen into this wretched state, by God's grace, or that you are asking me for advice on how to extricate yourself from it if you have fallen into it, and to be reunited with your leader, with each Sister in your family, and consequently with Our Lord. He will not allow any union with Him if there is none with those who represent Him and with His members. If you have not fallen into this miserable state, I thank God and shall celebrate Mass for that intention. However, if you have fallen into it, dear Sisters, here are the means to get out of it, with God's help, and I am going to ask this of Him at Holy Mass.

The first means is to make your prayer two or three times on what I have written to you. The first will be made on the first part of the letter, the second, on the second, and the third, on the third.

The second means is for all of you to confess to Monsieur des Jonchères all the faults you have committed in this regard, not only since your last confession, but also since you have been in Nantes, to resolve to accept willingly the good advice he will give you and carry it out.

The third is for all of you to embrace one another after Holy Communion, ask pardon of one another, and assure one another of your affection.

The fourth is to make your prayer every month for a year on this same subject.

The fifth is not to follow the impulse of your affection in the choice of Sisters with whom you associate, and instead to avoid communication with those to whom you might be inclined, so as to bind yourselves closer to the others.

The sixth is not to speak with your confessor except in the confessional, unless it is just a word or two for necessary matters and not otherwise, acting in this case as do the Sisters in your house in Paris with their confessors from Saint-Lazare.

The seventh is for each of you to write me the sentiments Our Lord gives you as a result of your three meditations and the confession and communion you will make for this intention, as I mentioned to you.

The eighth is for the Superioress to write each month to Mademoiselle Le Gras to tell her how her family is progressing in these practices.

The last means is for you to make your interior communication to Monsieur des Jonchères every month, particularly regarding the faults contrary to the above-mentioned matters.

These, dear Sisters, are my humble thoughts on the reasons you have to praise God for your vocation, to persevere in it, and to work at your perfection in it. They are also a reminder of the faults into which a family of Charity can fall in its new foundation, and the means to remedy this. I beg you most humbly, dear Sisters, to accept what I have told you, for the love of Our Lord Jesus Christ. I am, in His same love, dear Sisters, your most humble servant.[3]

VINCENT DEPAUL
i.s.C.M.

Addressed: Our very dear Sisters, the Daughters of Charity, Servants of the Sick Poor, at the Hospital in Nantes

---

[3]Lambert aux Couteaux and Sister Jeanne Lepeintre went to make a visitation of the Nantes hospital; the latter remained as Superior in place of Sister Elisabeth Martin, who went to the Richelieu hospital.

940. - *JACQUES LESCOT,[1] BISHOP OF CHARTRES,*
TO SAINT VINCENT

1647

I could receive no more pleasant or favorable news than what has been sent to me, namely, that you wish to have the missions continued in my diocese, if I think it worthwhile. There is no diocese in France more entirely at your disposition, and I do not know if there is anywhere the missions may be more useful and necessary, given the amazing ignorance I encounter in my visitations, which horrifies me. I make no decisions regarding the place, the time, nor the authority; this is entirely up to you. To borrow the expression of Abraham: ecce universa coram te sunt.[2] *I am, personally and cordially, yours truly, . . .*

941. - TO JEAN MARTIN, IN GENOA

Orsigny, four leagues from Paris, April 26, 1647

Monsieur,

The grace of Our Lord be with you forever!

I have only two words to say to you, since I have been in the country for four or five days. I simply want to assure you that, wherever I am, the thought of you is very dear to me and very frequent, and my heart is always entirely yours. God knows how ardently I pray to Him for you and my consolation in offering you completely to Him, knowing how much you belong to Him and how faithfully you correspond to His eternal plans.

Take care of your health and give my cordial greetings to

Letter 940. - Abelly, *op.cit.,* bk. II, chap. I, sect. I, p. 2.

[1]Jacques Lescot, born in Saint-Quentin in 1593, was a professor at the Sorbonne, Canon of Notre-Dame, and Richelieu's confessor before becoming Bishop of Chartres where he remained from November 13, 1643 until August 22, 1656, the day of his death.

[2]*Behold! everything is open before you.* Cf. Gn 13:9. (NAB)

Letter 941. - Archives of the Mission, Turin, original signed letter.

M. Richard and B[rother] Sébastien.

I told you I had your letter delivered to your mother. If she has sent her reply to the house, I will forward it to you.

I have been told that your brother has gone to Toulouse with the Archbishop and is still with him.

May God grant us the grace of remaining steadfast in His love by which I am, Monsieur, your most humble servant.

VINCENT DEPAUL
i.s.C.M.

Addressed: Monsieur Martin, Priest of the Mission in Genoa

942. - TO JEAN DEHORGNY, SUPERIOR, IN ROME

May 2, 1647

As you can imagine, I seek only God's Will in the Persia affair. I have written you all the details of this.[1] I did my best to get someone from the outside for the See of Babylon, which has been offered to us, and no one is willing or able to accept it because of personal inclination, or because of his situation or the state of his affairs. This work seems to me to be very important for the glory of God. He is calling us to it through the Pope, who alone has the authority to send men *ad gentes,* and not to obey him is a matter of conscience. I feel interiorly urged to do so, because I think that this authority, which God has given His Church to go and preach the Gospel throughout the earth, would reside in vain in its head, if his subjects were not equally obliged to go to the places he sends them to labor for the extension of the empire of Jesus Christ. Furthermore (perhaps I am mistaken), I strongly fear that God may permit the annihilation of the Church in Europe because of our depraved

---

Letter 942. - Reg. 2, p. 74.

[1]Saint Vincent is probably referring to no. 922.

morals, the various strange opinions we see cropping up on all sides, and the little progress being made by those who are at work striving to remedy all those evils. The new opinions are creating such havoc that it seems like half the world is involved. It is also to be feared that, if some faction were to arise in the Kingdom, it might devote itself to protecting the latter. What do we not have to fear in view of all that, Monsieur, and what should we not do to save the Spouse of Jesus Christ from this shipwreck! If, in all this, we cannot do as much as did Noah in preserving the human race during the universal deluge, we shall at least be contributing to the means which God can use for the preservation of His Church by placing, like the poor widow, a mite in the poor box.[2] Even if I were wrong—as I hope from the wisdom of God, who seems to will to destroy, the better to save—we will make a sacrifice to God, like Abraham who, in place of Isaac, sacrificed a sheep, in holy ignorance of the reason why He seemed to demand the former in order to have the latter.

These and several other motives have led me to decide on this holy endeavor and to disregard the consideration of our small number of workers and the need we have here of the man we are designating for that place. What impels me in this difficulty is the thought of the sacrifice Abraham intended to make of his son, although he was his only one and he knew that God had destined him to be the source of His people's blessing.

I have also disregarded the danger that this example might cause some persons in the Company to aspire to becoming bishops, because I thought that the remoteness of that place, the risks to be run in going and in residing there, and the apostolic humility with which the one sent there should act, which is like that of the Bishops of Ireland, will, along with several other inconveniences, dispel any ambitions for these duties.

Perhaps people will say that, if the bishop does not act in that country *in magnis*,[3] the Prince's Court, the Christians, and the

---

[2]Cf. Lk 21:1-4. (NAB)
[3]*With noble bearing.*

members of the religious Orders will despise him; in addition, he will not have, to the extent His Holiness perhaps expects of him, authority to negotiate, with the requisite propriety, the union between the King of France and that Prince against the common enemy of the Christians. To this I reply that I hope he will make up in virtue for the lack of this splendor and this pompous state, and that the Armenian Bishops there, who, no more than their Patriarch, appear anything other than the simple priests here, will not be so averse to our bishop as they would if they found him pompous.

Our Lord and the holy Apostles renounced and had all the Christians renounce pomp, and Christians are almost instinctively aware of the differences between this pompous state and that of the humble Jesus Christ, and are scandalized by it.

If it is being said that I have been considering M. Lambert[4] for this office, it is true that I did think of him. However, I did not decide on it and, although I have spoken to him of the plan in general and asked his advice about it, and although he has often volunteered to go to the ends of the earth if we send him there, I never told him I had thought of him, and he still knows nothing about it.

As for temporalities, this diocese has an income of nine hundred écus and, in order that the former Bishop, who is in possession of it and does not reside there, may transfer half of it to his successor, he will be given thirteen or fourteen hundred livres from another source as a benefice or lifetime annuity in compensation for that half.

That is the state of the affair. I shall, however, defer making a decision, until I have seen what you wish to write me about it, so as to accept your reasons, if they are better than mine.

[4]Lambert aux Couteaux.

943. - TO JEAN MARTIN, IN GENOA

Paris, May 3, 1647

Monsieur,

The grace of Our Lord be with you forever!

I thank God for the blessing he has given the Quarto[1] mission, and I thank you for your assistance to M. Blatiron in this; he has expressed to me his great satisfaction and gratitude. Now he is back in Genoa, and you are in a position to assist him in another way, taking care to have him rest as much and as long as he can. I have no doubt he will render you the same charity because he has told me his fear that the work is too much for you. I certainly have no less [fear of this] than he, which is why I very often pray and have others pray for your health, and I beg you yourself to take the best possible care of it. I hope that, since Messieurs Portail and Alméras have seen the need you all have of a little help, they will hasten the departure of the person M. Dehorgny is supposed to send you. I requested him to do this a long time ago and am doing so again today in order to contribute what I can to your relief. Would to God I could do it in person! I would willingly go to join you so as to share in the happiness that is yours of being constantly devoted to the practice of divine[2] love. Oh! May your heart ever taste the sweetness of that of Our Lord! I ask Him to fill you with it in order to communicate it to those to whom you render service.

As for me, Monsieur, I am entirely, in Him, your most humble servant.

VINCENT DEPAUL

Addressed: Monsieur Martin, Priest of the Mission, in Genoa

Letter 943. - Archives of the Mission, Turin, original signed letter.
[1]Quarto al Mare, a town about six miles from Genoa.
[2]Saint Vincent inserted this word between the lines.

944. - *ETIENNE BLATIRON, SUPERIOR IN GENOA,*
TO SAINT VINCENT

May 6, 1647

We are now back from the mission in. . . .It covered five parishes, in addition to the crowd from the surrounding areas. There was a very large number of conversions and general confessions, despite the callousness of the people, who were so very hard to move that we almost lost heart in the beginning. However, Our Lord willed to console us toward the end of the mission, touching those hardened hearts and showering such abundant graces on them that those, who in the beginning were loathe to listen to us, could not, at the close of the mission, tear themselves away from us. So, on the day of our departure, when we went to the church to receive the pastor's blessing, all the people came to the church and began to weep, crying out "Have mercy!" as if we were killing them by our leaving, so much so, that we had a hard time getting away.

Many members of the nobility of the town of Genoa came to this place and took part in the mission, which edified them greatly. The Cardinal-Archbishop of Genoa [1] came to administer Confirmation. Afterward, while he was eating with the Missionaries and some gentlemen who had accompanied him, a Seigneur of a nearby place sent a gift for him, but he excused himself from accepting it, saying that it was a rule of the Missionaries not to take anything during the mission, and he sent it back.

945. - TO JEAN DEHORGNY, IN ROME

May 9, 1647

I admit that the office of Superior is not carried out well in our houses. However, rest assured that this is what usually happens in Companies that are starting out, and the Jesuits, except for the first nine Fathers and a few others, were in a similar situation in the beginning. Grace imitates nature in many things, making them ugly

---

Letter 944. - Abelly, *op.cit.*, bk. II, chap. I, sect. IV, p. 70.
 [1] Stefano Cardinal Durazzo.

Letter 945. - Reg. 2, p. 27.

and unpleasant, but with time she perfects them. Who would have said that the limited knowledge, the poverty of possessions and position, and the holy rusticity of the prelates in the first century of the Church would bring about what they accomplished? Who would have thought that our puny Company, which is only a miserable specimen of the others in the Church, would do what God is pleased to accomplish through it, not only in France but also in foreign countries? The blessing Our Lord gives to our Missionaries in Ireland, Genoa, Tunis, and Algiers is admirable. Now, since that is being done with the grace God has given to the same Company, we have good reason to hope that His Divine Goodness will also give it the proper persons to govern it. This being the case, we should not judge God's designs on it according to human reasoning, to which, nevertheless, our limited minds are subject.

946. - TO RENE ALMERAS, IN ROME

Paris, May 10, 1647

Monsieur,

The grace of Our Lord be with you forever!

I praise God that you have arrived in perfect health, and I ask Him to give you His Spirit of direction for governing the Company there. O Monsieur, how I hope it is far removed from the maxims of the world and entirely abandoned into the arms of God's Providence. At times, when I think about the government of the Little Company, I experience a very tangible consolation from the fact that it seems to me we have tried to follow that same Providence in all its humble direction, so that we rely on human means no more than we do on reeds. I can also tell you, Monsieur, that I trust them no more than I would our enemy, and if the Company believes me

---

Letter 946. - Collection for the process of beatification. In his deposition in 1710, Brother Chollier states that the original was in the Saint's own handwriting.

in this, it will never act otherwise. O Monsieur, what a happiness to will nothing but what God wills, to do nothing but what is in accord with the occasion Providence presents, and to have nothing but what God in His Providence has given us!

The human intellect will tell you that things are not the same in Rome as they are elsewhere, that people have to worm their way into things, to assume authority, to act in a human way with human beings, and to use human means with them. But do not believe this, Monsieur; all these maxims are irrelevant with regard to a Company which Our Lord has raised up for Himself and animates with His own maxims, and which claims to act according to His Spirit. What I am telling you may seem paradoxical; rest assured, Monsieur, that experience will cause you to understand it.

I am writing to Monsieur Dehorgny, asking him to remain with you this summer to help you. Please put your trust in him, Monsieur, and in the good advice Monsieur Portail will leave with you. But, what am I saying? Alas! Monsieur, I am wrong to ask this of you, since I know, by God's grace, that this is your spirit.

It would be a consolation to me if I could say more to you, but the Bishop of Chalcedon[1] has been waiting almost an hour for me, so I must close, recommending myself, prostrate in spirit at your feet and at those of the Company. I am, with the cordiality of which His Divine Goodness is aware, Monsieur, your most humble and obedient servant.

VINCENT DEPAUL
i.s.C.M.

Addressed: Monsieur Alméras, Superior of the Priests of the Mission, in Rome

---

[1]Richard Smith, Bishop *in partibus* [i.e.,in infidel lands] of Chalcedon, and former Vicar Apostolic of England, where he had been sent by Pope Urban VIII.

947. - TO JEAN MARTIN, IN GENOA

Paris, May 10, 1647

Monsieur,

The grace of Our Lord be with you forever!

No, I cannot stop writing to you, even though I have no new reason to do so. For now, I use that of recommending that you take care of your health and of M. Blatiron's. I already said this in my last letter, and will keep it up as long as I fear that your excessive work may be too much for you. In truth, Monsieur, there is nothing in the world you can do that would please me more than that. It should suffice for you that God wills it, since the progress of a number of persons depends on your good health. I ask God earnestly for this, along with His continued favors and consolation for your dear soul, which mine embraces tenderly.

Yesterday I received some letters from M. Guérin in Tunis. God is blessing him in an extraordinary way. He wrote me that the men in Algiers are also doing very well. I cannot tell you how that, and what we hear about your little family, consoles and encourages the entire Company.

We also have news of our men in Ireland. They tell me that war and the poverty in their country are great obstacles to them. Nevertheless, when they gave a mission, the crowd of people was so big that, although there were five or six confessors, there were not enough of them to hear confessions because a number of persons from the surrounding areas flocked there, when it was rumored that the Gospel was being preached. Some of them, from places about ten leagues away, waited four or five days in order to be able to go to confession. I recommend them to the prayers of all your Company, and my poor soul in particular to your Holy Sacrifices.

Letter 947. - Archives of the Mission, Turin, original signed letter.

I am, above all, in the love of Our Lord, Monsieur, your most humble servant.

VINCENT DEPAUL
i.s.C.M.

Addressed: Monsieur Martin, Priest of the Mission, in Genoa

948. - TO BERNARD CODOING, SUPERIOR, IN SAINT-MEEN

May 11, 1647

The Bishop of Tréguier[1] wants a member of our Company for a month or two to encourage him and help him to apply himself to his episcopal duties before he enters his diocese; he has to be there eight to ten days before Pentecost.

As yet, he has spoken in public only two or three times, because of the tact of M. du Chesne, who purposely has brought him to a mission and trained him in our little method, with the result that he never wants to speak any other way. He is a good, sensible, intelligent person. He has a great love for the Company, which he has thought of establishing in his diocese, if he can find the means to do so. If he does not have the support of this assistance in such spiritual exercises as visitations, exhortations, sermons, and catechetical instructions, he fears he will neither begin nor continue anything. Now, I am writing to you for this purpose, and I ask you to go to Tréguier before Pentecost, taking Brother. . .with you as assistant. I am not telling you what is the best way to proceed with this good Bishop; the humility, gentleness, zeal, and respect Our Lord has given you will accomplish in you whatever is needed.

Letter 948. - Reg. 2, p. 173.
[1]Balthazar Grangier de Liverdi (1646-1679).

949. - TO MOTHER CATHERINE DE BEAUMONT,[1]
IN TOULOUSE

Paris, May 19, 1647

My very dear Mother,

The grace of Our Lord be with you forever!

I was greatly consoled by the reception of your two cherished letters, as you can imagine, dear Mother, and I thank God that His Providence has entrusted you to one of the most excellent Bishops in the Church[2] and to one of the most devout towns under the sun, as I heard the Bishop of Lisieux[3] say; he was the Bishop of Nantes when you were in that town.[4]

So there you are in our region, dear Mother, or very near it. Oh! how gladly I praise God for this! I pray also that He will sanctify

---

Letter 949. - The original autograph letter is in the Visitation Convent in Toulouse. Bishop Célestin Douais gave a facsimile of it in his book, *La Visitation de Toulouse: Etudes, souvenirs et documents* (Paris: E. Poussielgue, 1905).

[1]Anne-Catherine de Beaumont-Carra was one of the pillars of the Visitation Order. Born in Chambéry, the daughter of Paul de Beaumont-Carra and Antoinette-Charlotte de Divonne, she took the habit at the First Monastery of the Visitation in Annecy on April 23, 1617. From the Annecy Monastery, where she spent the first years of her religious life, she went with Saint Jane Frances to make a new foundation in Bourges. She was elected Superioress of the First Monastery in Paris in 1622 and again in 1625. In 1626 she opened the Second Monastery in Paris, in the faubourg Saint-Jacques, and was its Superioress. Subsequently she was twice elected Superioress in Grenoble (1629 and 1632) and in Pignerol (1637 and 1641), then made a new foundation in Toulouse (1647). She died there on January 30, 1656, at age of sixty-eight. Mother Faber has written an account, published by Bishop Douais, of the time Mother de Beaumont spent in Toulouse. *Année Sainte* (vol. V, p. 533) states: "Saint Vincent de Paul had great respect for her, and this fact was brought to the knowledge of the Queen, Anne of Austria. This great Princess favored the humble Mother with her kindness and did not think it unworthy of Her Majesty to honor her with her visits." Saint Jane Frances frequently consulted Mother de Beaumont, as her correspondence shows. We see from these letters that Mother de Beaumont was "cold, too firm, and serious," and that her energetic character sometimes led her to neglect spiritual exercises.

[2]Charles de Montchal (1628-1651). He was one of the most remarkable Prelates of the seventeenth century because of his piety, zeal, learning, and his firmness in defending the rights of the Church against encroachments of the State.

[3]Philippe Cospéan was Bishop of Aire from February 18, 1607 to March 18, 1622, of Nantes from March 18, 1622 to 1635, and of Lisieux from July 25, 1636 to May 8, 1646, the day of his death. He had also administered the Toulouse diocese for a time.

[4]When Mother de Beaumont was Superioress in Grenoble, she had to go to Nantes to make arrangements for establishing a convent, and left several of her nuns there.

your dear soul more and more, and through you the souls of so many good Sisters, whom this same Providence has destined for you.

The matter you mentioned to me, dear Mother, I mean the question of the Maguelonne collège,[5] seems an impossibility to me because it was intended for the training of seminarians, and consent will never be given to put it to any other use. It is of no avail to say it is in a state of great disorder; you will be told that a time will perhaps come when it will be reformed. Also, dear Mother, take my word that, although in the past the Bishop of Toulouse had some thought about it for us, and the head of the collège met with me several times for that purpose, I most willingly renounce it, and will praise God if matters can be worked out as you desire. I offer you my most humble services for this with all possible affection, although, as I told you, the question seems impossible to me, according to my understanding of the attitude of the King's Council, and the outcome of affairs in similar situations. Alas! dear Mother, it is not through our own interest that we are not of service to you in this! Are you fully aware, dear Mother, that we have the maxim and practice of not requesting any foundations, and that Our Lord alone has established us in the places where we now are? If the Company takes my word in this, it will always act in this way. The Archbishop himself can tell you with what indifference he has seen me act in this affair, but perhaps we have given him reason to think we were not sufficiently grateful for the favor his goodness was offering us, because we failed to tell him what I am telling you, namely, that we strive to follow God's adorable Providence in all things and not to anticipate it. I beg you before God, dear Mother, help me to establish us firmly in this practice.

It is true, dear Mother, that I asked our dear Sisters[6] to excuse me for being unable to serve them any longer as spiritual Father because of the pressure of business, preventing me from doing the things I

---

[5]Collège founded in Toulouse in 1363. Like other collèges in that town, it served as a hostel for university students.
[6]The Visitation nuns in Paris.

am obligated to do. I made this request seven or eight months ago,[7] and God knows that it is not from any want of affection, nor have I ever experienced any reason for dissatisfaction with them, but rather gentleness, kindness, and charity of every sort. His Divine Goodness is also aware that I am tearing off my own skin by doing this; *mais quoi!* conscience urges me to limit myself to what I can do and to honor the omnipotence of God by the recognition of my own powerlessness. They have not yet found anyone else. I have tried up to now to do what is necessary without going to their house, while waiting for them to find someone. You may believe, dear Mother, that no one has greater power to help me get over my difficulties than you do, if only for the reason I gave you. I renew to you here the offer of my humble services, with all possible affection and humility. I am, in the love of Our Lord, dear Mother, your most humble and obedient servant.

VINCENT DEPAUL
i.s.C.M.

Addressed: Reverend Mother Anne-Catherine de Beaumont, Superioress of the Visitation Sainte-Marie of Toulouse, in Toulouse

950. - TO ETIENNE BLATIRON, SUPERIOR, IN GENOA

May 24, 1647

I do not know if it is necessary for me to urge you to take a rest, since you know that the greatest satisfaction you could wish for me in this world is your good health. So, take care of it for the love of Our Lord, and, while others are pushing you to do too much, allow me to invite you not to work so hard. Speak up courageously in my name and, without complaining, say that it is too much.

---

[7]Cf. nos. 866 and 873.

Letter 950. - Reg. 2, p. 218.

951. - JULIEN GUERIN TO SAINT VINCENT

Tunis, 1647

On Easter Sunday I received word that a galley ship from Algiers had arrived in Bizerte, and I left immediately to go and visit the poor Christians who were in chains. I found about three hundred of them, and the captain allowed me to give them a little ten-day mission. I had taken with me a priest to help me catechize and hear the confessions of those poor people, who all made their duty,[1] with the exception of a few Greek schismatics. O great God! what a consolation to see the devotion of those poor captives, most of whom had been unable to get to confession for a long time! Some had not approached this sacrament for eight or ten years, and others for even twenty years. I had them all unchained every day and brought ashore from the galleys to receive Holy Communion in a private home, where I celebrated Holy Mass. After the mission was over, I gave them fifty-three écus worth of provisions.

I was lodged in the house of a Turk, who fed me during the time of the mission; yet, he would never take any money from me, saying that alms should be given to those who give them to others. This is certainly a most noteworthy action for an unbeliever. What will amaze you even more is that almost all the Turks in that place were so moved and edified by this mission that several of them came to kiss my face and hands, and I have no doubt that your dear heart would have been overjoyed to see this. However, if the fruit of this little mission in Bizerte was sweet to me, the path to reach it was very rough and thorny because, since I did not want to take any janissaries[2] with me as attendants, I had an encounter with some Arabs, who beat me up. One of them grabbed me by the throat, squeezing so hard that I thought he was going to strangle me. I felt I was surely going to die but, since I am only a miserable sinner, Our Lord did not judge me worthy of dying in His service.

Letter 951. - Abelly, *op.cit.,* bk. II, chap. I, sect. VII, §9, p. 130.

[1]Reference to the Easter duty: confession at least once a year, if necessary, and reception of Holy Communion between the beginning of Lent and Trinity Sunday.

[2]Select corps of Turkish soldiers. Originally they were boys taken from the homes of people, principally Christians, subjugated by the Turks, and raised to constitute the Sultan's elite guard.

952. - TO JEAN MARTIN, IN GENOA

Paris, May 31, 1647

Monsieur,

The grace of Our Lord be with you forever!

Your letter had two opposite effects on me: it made me happy because it came from you, whom my soul cherishes tenderly, and it made me sad to see that poor M. Blatiron has been left on his feet. I fear, and with good reason, that his health may fail unless God preserves him, as I hope He will, since so much work can be done only through sheer obedience.

I am no less apprehensive about you because, according to what this same M. Blatiron says, you are overwhelmed with worry and work. However, I ask Our Lord unceasingly to be your strength in the midst of such difficulties, and your eternal reward.

I thought you had already received help from Rome, so my mind was at ease, thinking you had some relief. But why has it not come, since I requested Rome so long ago to send it to you? Well now, Monsieur, let us ask Our Lord that all things may be done in accord with His Providence, and that our wills may be so submissive to Him that between Him and us there may be only one will, causing us to enjoy His unrivaled love in time and in eternity.

With this desire, I am, Monsieur, your most humble servant.

VINCENT DEPAUL
i.s.C.M.

Addressed: Monsieur Martin, Priest of the Mission, in Genoa

Letter 952. - Archives of the Mission, Turin, original signed letter.

953. - *SAINT LOUISE TO SAINT VINCENT*

[June 1647] [1]

Monsieur,

If your charity thought fit to suggest to the owner of the house near Saint-Laurent that he might live in the apartment he leased to the beer brewer, that would arrange matters for the little children, provided the Ladies are willing to compensate him.

I cannot refrain from telling you that I was greatly troubled today by the fear of predestination, because of a thought I had at prayer. It weighed so much on my mind that it caused me to make an act of acquiescence to God's plan for my son and me to be forever the object of His justice.

I forgot to ask your permission to go to Communion throughout the novena of Masses being said to the Holy Spirit, which began on Friday. Using the permission your charity gave me to receive Communion when my health permitted, I also went to Communion during that part of the novena. I do not dare continue without a more specific permission from you, which I ask you for the love of God, along with the help we need. I am, Monsieur, your most grateful daughter and very humble servant.

L. DE M.

Addressed: *Monsieur Vincent*

954. - TO SAINT LOUISE

Mademoiselle Le Gras is requested to send this packet to the Duchesse d'Aiguillon; it is for those good nuns.[1] If she is not in town, give it to the Swiss porter for me, and ask him to send it with the first person going to Rueil, where she now is.

Letter 953. - Archives of the Motherhouse of the Daughters of Charity, original autograph letter.
[1]This letter was written between Ascension and Pentecost; it seems to be from the same year as no. 937.

Letter 954. - Archives of the Motherhouse of the Daughters of Charity, original autograph letter.
[1]The Duchesse d'Aiguillon had taken under her protection both the Daughters of the Cross and the Daughters of Providence. It is not clear to which of these two Communities Saint Vincent refers, if either. As is evident from succeeding letters, they had fled to Paris from Lorraine.

955. - TO SAINT LOUISE

[Around 1647][1]

Mademoiselle,

The Duchess has acquired one hundred écus from the Superintendent for those good nuns. They will be [given] to them on condition that they return home. In the meantime, please have them teach in your school, and see how they do. They have God's blessing for that. Please say nothing to them about the one hundred écus.

956. - TO SAINT LOUISE

Mademoiselle,

I will see those good nuns in two or three days, God willing. Could you not induce them to retire to their monastery?

957. - TO SAINT LOUISE

[Around 1647][1]

Mademoiselle,

The Duchesse d'Aiguillon wants those good nuns to go back to Lorraine, and has had this sum given to them with [that] in view, and not otherwise. She has also sent me two hundred livres for the same purpose, and agrees that they should carry on their person only

---

Letter 955. - Saint Paul manuscript, p. 70.
[1]This letter was written toward the end of the trouble in Lorraine.

Letter 956. - Saint Paul manuscript, p. 70.

Letter 957. - Saint Paul manuscript, p. 71.
[1]This letter followed no. 955 by a few days.

what is necessary for their food. We will have someone in Toul hold for them the one hundred écus they withdrew and the two hundred livres we have. Please tell them to let me know when they will be ready to go home, and that not a single one of all those who came to Paris is taking back so much; at least, not as far as I know.

958. - TO JEAN MARTIN, IN GENOA

Paris, June 7, 1647

Monsieur,

The grace of Our Lord be with you forever!

This letter is simply to rejoice with you at the help that has reached you; I have no doubt that M. Patrice[1] is now in Genoa, since he left Rome more than a month ago, according to what M. Portail has written me. Please embrace him for me, as I embrace all of you in spirit, begging Our Lord to bind all of us together in His pure love, so that together we may love Him uniquely, strongly, and eternally. *Mon Dieu!* Monsieur, how my soul desires the perfection of yours! Yes indeed, as much as its own advancement, since I do not know how to ask for one without the other. I also continually implore for you and your works the effects of the special protection of Our Lord, who has made me, invariably, Monsieur, your most humble servant.

VINCENT DEPAUL
i.s.C.M.

Addressed: Monsieur Martin, Priest of the Mission, in Genoa

Letter 958. - Archives of the Mission, Turin, original signed letter.

[1]Patrice Valois (Patrick Walsh—Valois was the usual French transliteration for Walsh) was born in Limerick (Ireland), received into the Congregation of the Mission on December 21, 1644, at the age of twenty-five, and ordained a priest in 1646.

959. - TO ANTOINE PORTAIL, IN ROME

June 14, 1647

According to your letter, from now on we should consider Messieurs. . .and. . .[1] only as persons weakened by temptation, and we can no longer be sure of them, since the former has the venom of temporal possessions in his heart, and the other has his heart in the corruption of flesh and blood. So, let us await God's disposition in this and remain in peace.

960. - TO CLAUDE DUFOUR, SUPERIOR, IN SAINTES

June 15, 1647

I cannot express to you the consolation my soul received from the last letter you wrote me, and from the strength of will Our Lord has given you. Indeed, Monsieur, I think that heaven itself rejoices in this for, alas! the Church has enough solitaries, by His mercy, and too many useless ones, and even more who tear her apart. Her great need is evangelical men who work to purge, enlighten, and unite her to her Divine Spouse. This is what you are doing, through His Divine Goodness. Recently I was touched by the fact that the R[everend] Prior of the Carthusian Monastery of Mont-Dieu[1] had come to spend an entire day here in this house during the time of ordination, to observe the exercises that are carried out. He was so moved by them, and said such flattering things to me about the happiness of this work, that modesty does not permit me to repeat them. I cannot describe to you how he sighed during the Pontifical,[2]

Letter 959. - Reg. 2, p. 101.

[1]Perhaps M. de Restal, and Pierre de Fondimare who, according to no. 1068, did not persevere in the Congregation of the Mission.

Letter 960. - Reg. 2, p. 292.

[1]A commune in the district of Sedan (Ardennes).

[2]During the explanation of the Pontifical, the book of ceremonies used in the administration of the Sacraments.

on hearing what was said about the duty of a deacon. I assure you, Monsieur, that this good Father has more of the missionary spirit than I, and if he were allowed, he would leave his cell to go and proclaim Jesus Christ to the poor people, and work at training priests.

I beg you, Monsieur, let us labor at that with all our might, confident that Our Lord, who has called us to His manner of life, will give us a greater share in His Spirit and, in the end, in His glory. So, reject all those thoughts[3] resolutely, and when you grow weary of residing in the place you now are, let me know; I will do all in my power to contribute to your consolation. You know the esteem and affection Our Lord has given me for you, and that I cherish you more than myself.

961. - JULIEN GUERIN TO SAINT VINCENT

Tunis, June 1647

We have put the money you sent me to such good use that we ransomed that poor Frenchwoman who has suffered the tyranny of a cruel master for such a long time. It is truly a miracle to have extricated her from the hands of that tiger, who did not want to give her up for either gold or silver. One morning he took it into his head to send for me. While I was in his home, we came to an agreement on three hundred écus, which I gave him immediately. I had him draw up her release paper, and I took her at once to a safe place. Two hours later, that wretch repented of having done this and almost went out of his mind with regret. This is truly a stroke of the hand of God.

We also ransomed a boy from Sables-d'Olonne, who was on the point of abjuring his faith. I think I wrote you how we have prevented him two or three times from doing this. He cost one hundred fifty écus. I gave thirty-six as my share; we begged the rest from wherever we could.

---

[3]Claude Dufour was being tempted to leave the Congregation of the Mission in order to enter the Carthusians.

Letter 961. - Abelly, *op.cit.*, bk. II, chap. I, sect. VII, §12, p. 139.

I also rescued that young Sicilian woman who was a slave in Bizerte and whose husband had become a Turk. For three whole years she endured indescribable torments rather than imitate her husband's apostasy. Around Christmas of last year, I wrote you about the pitiful condition in which I found her, all covered with sores. She cost two hundred fifty écus, which had been given as alms and of which I contributed a part.

962. - TO ETIENNE BLATIRON, SUPERIOR, IN GENOA

June 21, 1647

Yes, yes, Monsieur, we shall pray to God for you and for the reconciliation of those persons so bent on vengeance, and will have Masses said for that intention. If possible, mine will be celebrated at Notre-Dame, according to your wishes but, after all, are you not willing to accept that our efforts and prayers may be ineffectual, if such is God's good pleasure? For, Monsieur, what would it be like if everything was favorable to us, and what right have poor people like us to expect that we shall always be successful? We have even less reason to be upset when someone offers resistance to our humble opinions. Since God is satisfied with our good will and honest efforts, let us also be satisfied with the outcome He gives to them, and our actions will never be without good results. I say all this to you because of your distress that no one is profiting from your missions, for we should not be surprised at this; rather, Monsieur, let us believe that all is going along the best in the world when we take no satisfaction in it, provided we humble ourselves for this and redouble our confidence in God. It is true, however, that we have good reason to praise God for His continued blessings on you. So, I thank Him for this, and ask Him to preserve both your good health and your desire for the advancement of His glory.

Letter 962. - Reg. 2, p. 218.

963. - TO JEAN MARTIN, IN GENOA

Paris, June 21, 1647

Monsieur,

The grace of Our Lord be with you forever!

Did you have in mind anything more definite than to will invariably what God wills? I think not. What reason can you have then, Monsieur, for becoming discouraged when things do not turn out right for you? Up until now, you have had good reason to thank God for this, and I, on my part, certainly help you as best I can to do it, so grateful am I for the graces He has granted you. I know your fidelity and concern for God's work. So what remains for you except to be at peace? This is all He asks of you, along with the humble recognition of the success He gives to it, and I have no doubt that this is total in your heart. Why then these misgivings? You tell me your weaknesses; alas! and who is not filled with them? The important thing is to be aware of them and to love the humiliation coming from them, as you do, without dwelling on them except to lay on them the foundation of a firm confidence in God. Then the building is established on a rock, so that when the storm arises, it remains firm. So, do not be afraid, Monsieur; you are founded on that, I know. The fears and mistrust you experience come from nature, and only from a distance do they have access to your heart, which is much more generous than that. Therefore, let God do as He pleases with us and our works, even if the trouble we take for men is to no avail; and if the same men show only ingratitude and contempt toward us, we will not, for all that, fail to continue our occupations, knowing that through them we are fulfilling the law of loving God with our whole heart and our neighbor as ourselves.

Letter 963. - Archives of the Mission, Turin, original signed letter.

I ask this grace of God for you, and for me who am, in His love, Monsieur, your most humble and affectionate servant.

VINCENT DEPAUL
i.s.C.M.

Addressed: Monsieur Martin, Priest of the Mission, in Genoa

964. - *SAINT LOUISE TO SAINT VINCENT*

Most Honored Father,

I was quite surprised that you left before giving us the orders necessary for our Sisters' departure for Montreuil.[1] Were it not for the fact that the places in the coach have been reserved, we would postpone it. However, it has to be this Wednesday, and what will they do without your charity's blessing and instruction, which they so badly need? Unless our good God inspires you to inform us of how they should conduct themselves in all things, we shall really be at a loss. I assure you, Monsieur, my spirit is so overwhelmed that I admit to being the cause of this distress which our poor Sisters will suffer.

As for our Sisters' departure for Nantes,[2] there is no way for us to do this without getting your charity's advice on the word we received not to change Sister Cathe[rine] Ba[gard], the one who started the trouble in the hospital, and that she thinks it absolutely necessary to recall Sister Elisabeth,[3] and to send a Sister to be in charge.[4]

Letter 964. - Archives of the Motherhouse of the Daughters of Charity, original autograph letter.

[1]The Daughters of Charity had been called to Montreuil-sur-Mer (Pas-de-Calais) by Comte Charles de Lannoy, Governor of that town. Saint Louise sent Anne Hardemont and Marie Lullen there from Le Mans. They left on June 26, after receiving the instructions of their Foundress (cf. *Ecrits spirituels,* L. 213, p. 204). Saint Vincent had already given them his at the Council of June 19, 1647.

[2]Two Sisters, Jeanne de Saint-Albin and Jacquette, were sent to Nantes.

[3]Elisabeth Martin, Sister Servant in Nantes.

[4]Sister Jeanne Lepeintre was going to Nantes to make a visitation of the hospital and then on to Angers for the same purpose. She remained in Nantes as Sister Servant. In the Council of June 19, Saint Vincent said of her: "Now, Sister Jeanne would need four minds; if she could take along that of Mademoiselle Le Gras, she would be quite happy. Isn't that true, my Daughter?"

I think you are aware of the arrival of our Sisters who returned from Angers. The accused, however, appears the most innocent person in the world.[5] I dared not write to her father without hearing from your charity what we should do with her. I think he will not be long in coming. I beg our good God that your charity might return in good health before that time.

Please, Father, give our Sisters and us your holy blessing!

Sister Marguerite Tourneton went off Sunday without saying a word; the Mother Prioress[6] wrote me that she had gone to the Hôtel-Dieu this morning and she had received her. She is asking for another habit so she can return ours.[7] I have not given any answer and will not do so until your return. God alone knows the state of my poor mind amidst all these disorders, for it seems as if our good God wants to destroy us entirely. I deserve this and am surprised that His justice is so long in being carried out. Provided His mercy saves my soul, that is enough for me.

Obtain this grace for me through your charity, since I am, Monsieur, your most obedient daughter and very humble servant.

June 24 [1647][8]

L. DE MARILLAC

Addressed: *Monsieur Vincent, Superior General of the Priests of the Mission*

---

[5]Sisters Marie-Marthe Trumeau and Perrette from Sedan. The accused was probably Sister Perrette, whose frivolous manner worried Saint Louise. She subsequently left the Company (cf. no. 971).

[6]The Prioress of the Augustinian Sisters of the Hôtel-Dieu.

[7]Marguerite regretted her action and returned; she died the following year.

[8]Year added on the back of the original by Brother Ducournau.

965. - TO SAINT LOUISE

Fréneville,[1] June 26, 1647

Mademoiselle,

The grace of Our Lord be with you forever!

I left so unexpectedly that it was impossible for me to say good-bye to you. I hope that in your goodness you will excuse me for this. Please God, I will be back Monday or Tuesday morning. In the meantime, I ask you to send news of yourself with one of our Brothers, who will be leaving for here tomorrow.

I am sending you one or two letters, which I received before leaving but was unable to read until I got here.

I ask Our Lord to keep you in good health. I am fine and am entirely, in His love, Mademoiselle, your most humble servant.

VINCENT DEPAUL
i.s.C.M.

966. - *SAINT LOUISE TO SAINT VINCENT*

June 26 [1647] [1]

Monsieur,

Our poor Sisters [2] *left this morning, very chagrined at not having your blessing, but submissive nevertheless to the guidance of Divine Providence. Please God, through His goodness, you will return soon in good health!*

Letter 965. - Archives of the Mission, Paris, original autograph letter.

[1]In 1635 Madame de Herse gave two farms to the Saint-Lazare house: one in Mespuits, the other in Fréneville, a little village in the commune of Valpuiseaux (Essonne). In return, she asked that a mission be given in perpetuity on her estates every five years, and that two Missionaries be placed at her disposal or that of her second son, Félix Vialart, the Prior of Bus. These priests were to work for three months every four years in the places assigned to them.

Letter 966. - Archives of the Motherhouse of the Daughters of Charity, original autograph letter.

[1]This year corresponds to the contents of the letter.

[2]Anne Hardemont and Marie Lullen, the Sisters designated for the foundation in Montreuil.

Our entire Little Company is in a state of great sorrow, shock, and fear at the loss of our Sister.[3] They are making veiled comments because no one dares to talk about it. I await your charity's return to make them understand how they should view this change.

It seems to me, Monsieur, that I am beginning to get a little stronger, provided nothing else happens to me! However, I am taking exceptionally good care of myself and have no more important concern than to be good to myself. It is not the same for the interests of my soul, although, by the grace of God, I am a little calmer than when I had the honor of writing to you to reveal to your charity the state of the one whose only consolation is the happiness of being, Monsieur, your most obedient and very grateful daughter and servant.

LOUISE DE MARILLAC

I think there is something to be said against the freedom of our Sisters in Serqueux.[4]

Addressed: *Monsieur Vincent, Superior General of the Priests of the Mission*

967. - TO LOUIS SERRE,[1] IN CRECY

July 2, 1647

When those gentlemen who wish to devote themselves to the Company are ready to come here, we will accept them into the seminary, through which they must pass, no matter how good they are. Experience has shown us that virtue puts down only shallow roots in those who are there for just a short time. A number of men,

---

[3]Sister Marguerite Tourneton, who had just left the Company of the Daughters of Charity.

[4]Commune of the district of Neufchâtel (Seine-Maritime). The Daughters of Charity had been there since 1645.

Letter 967. - Reg. 2, p. 40.

[1]Louis Serre, born in Epinal (Vosges), was ordained a priest in September 1643. He entered the Congregation of the Mission on March 23, 1644 at the age of twenty-six, and took his vows in July 1646. His first assignment was Crécy, where he was Superior (1646-1648). From there he was sent to Saint-Méen, where he spent nearly his whole missionary life. He directed this house (1655-1665, 1671-1675, and 1676-1681).

who seemed very regular to us in the seminary and were sent to work elsewhere too soon, lost their vocation because of this. So then, you can see the necessity of their going through this testing period.

968. - TO A PRIEST OF THE MISSION IN RICHELIEU

July 7, 1647

You spoke to us of three young women who are applying to enter the Charity. If they are suitable and have really set their minds to this, please send them along. If others present themselves, write to me about them; this Little Company is short of subjects because there are so many requests for them from everywhere.

Remind Monsieur. . .of what you told him about the Daughters of Charity, their financial difficulty, and how much it is to be desired that their modest means should be assured.

969. - TO SAINT LOUISE

[July 7, 1647][1]

Mademoiselle Le Gras is requested by the Ladies of Charity to send four children, two boys and two girls, with two Daughters of Charity, to the château of Bicêtre,[2] at one o'clock tomorrow, Sun-

---

Letter 968. - The text of this letter is taken from a manuscript entitled: *Lettres choisies du Bienh. Vincent de Paul, instituteur et premier supérieur général de la congrégation de la Mission.* This collection, compiled between 1729 and 1737, is preserved at the Motherhouse of the Daughters of Charity. It is from the same family as the Avignon manuscript (cf. vol. I, p. xxxvii), and reprints all the letters in the same order, adding a ninth part which contains nineteen letters, all pertaining to the direction of the Daughters of Charity.

Letter 969. - Archives of the Motherhouse of the Daughters of Charity, original autograph letter.
   [1]The date on which the foundlings were transferred to Bicêtre.
   [2]It would seem that the four children mentioned here were the first ones placed in Bicêtre.

day, with their personal belongings and what they will need for that day and the next, but not the babies' beds. Madame Truluy will go with a carriage to get the children and the linen they need, at the time indicated above, and will take them either to Madame de Romilly's[3] or to the home of the Chancellor's wife.[4] The other Ladies will pick them up and take them. They have a particular reason for acting this way, and really hope that Mademoiselle might be disposed to join in this course of action, but I do not think we should consider it.

970. - SAINT LOUISE TO SAINT VINCENT

[July 1647] [1]

Monsieur,

In the end, experience will cause us to see that my fears about the living quarters at Bicêtre were justified. Those Ladies are trying to make our Sisters do the impossible. They choose for lodgings little rooms, where the air is quickly tainted, and leave the large ones empty; however, our Sisters dare not say anything. They do not want Mass to be said, but for our Sisters to go to Gentilly to hear it. And what will the children be doing in the meantime, and who will do the work?

You have Sister Geneviève [2] *there. Please take the trouble to talk with her. She will explain to you all the trouble they are having and the expectations of the Ladies. I strongly fear that we will have to abandon the service of these poor little children.*

---

[3]Louise Goulas, Madame de Romilly, a Lady of Charity. Her husband was Treasurer General of Wars and a Councillor of the King.

[4]Madeleine Fabri, wife of Pierre Séguier, Keeper of the Seals. She was born on November 22, 1597 and died in Paris on February 6, 1683. She assisted Saint Vincent and Saint Louise with her influence and her fortune.

Letter 970. - Archives of the Motherhouse of the Daughters of Charity, original autograph letter.
[1]Date added on the back of the original by Brother Ducournau.
[2]Sister Geneviève Poisson directed the Foundling Home.

May God's Will be done! In it I am, Monsieur, your most obedient and very grateful daughter and servant.

L. DE MARILLAC

Will your charity please remember our two Ladies, who will be ready to go to confession tomorrow morning, if possible?

Addressed: *Monsieur Vincent*

971. - THE SISTERS OF THE MOTHERHOUSE TO SAINT VINCENT

Monsieur,

This note is to inform your charity that two of our Sisters went off this morning without saying a word. One is Perrette, back from Angers, and the other is Marguerite, back from Fontainebleau. We have sent someone to the Sedan coach, thinking they might be there. However, since our Sister has no authority to stop them by force, in the event that she does locate them, and since Mademoiselle judges it necessary, she begs your charity to lend us one of your Brothers, if you think it well. Otherwise, for the love of God, kindly let us know what we are supposed to do. While awaiting this, we remain, Monsieur, your most humble and obedient servants.

THE DAUGHTERS OF CHARITY

July 23 [1647] [1]

Addressed: *Monsieur Vincent*

Letter 971. - Archives of the Motherhouse of the Daughters of Charity, original autograph letter.
[1]Year added on the back of the original by Brother Ducournau.

972. - TO SAINT LOUISE

[July 1647][1]

Let us bless God, Mademoiselle, for purging the Company of subjects like that, and let us honor the disposition of Our Lord when His disciples were abandoning Him. He said to those who remained, "Do you not wish to go after them?"[2]

I do not see what can be done about those girls when they are found. We have no authority to stop them. They are free; let them go. I am sending someone to the Sedan coach, which does not leave until nine o'clock. M. Gallais[3] is not here; he has been in Picardy for the last ten days. They will not both head that way. Perrette's father will have to be notified of what she did both in Angers and in Nantes.

I do not think you have to say anything else to Jeanne Lepeintre,[4] other than a few words of encouragement and of sympathy for her ailment,[5] telling her also to do her best to send C[atherine] Bagard back. And if [something][6] should happen, all right! In the name of God, let us not be surprised at anything. God will do everything for the best.

Letter 972. - Archives of the Motherhouse of the Daughters of Charity, original autograph letter.

[1]Saint Vincent wrote these words on the same letter from the Sisters of the Motherhouse, which letter he was sharing with Saint Louise, who was in Bicêtre at the time.

[2]Cf. Jn 6:67. (NAB)

[3]Guillaume Gallais had been Superior in Sedan, the home of Sister Perrette; he may even have sent her to the Company.

[4]Superior in Nantes at the time.

[5]An inflammation. (Cf. *Ecrits spirituels*, L. 189, p. 214.)

[6]Because the original is damaged, we are not certain of the reading of these words and of the words "be surprised."

973. - *LAMBERT AUX COUTEAUX TO SAINT VINCENT*

Nantes, July 26, 1647

Monsieur,

Your blessing, please!
Here we are, on the point of leaving Nantes, after doing the things I am now going to report to you.

I can assure you that our Sisters have been very upset, and if indeed they have committed some minor faults, the circumstances in which Providence has placed them have been strong reasons for trying their souls. The Sister Servant had been at variance with the confessor, and he with her; this was public knowledge. Each had supporters inside and outside the house. It is enough to tell you this much to make you understand all the rest, and especially that what was said by both of them was not always based on truth but rather on feelings.

We have sent off three of our Sisters: two to Paris, Sisters Catherine Bagard and Antoinette Larcher; [1] *and the other, Sister Isabelle,* [2] *to Richelieu. We have given them Sisters Claude* [3] *and Brigitte to divert them as far as Saumur, and have left orders for Sister de Turgis* [4] *to go to the Saumur fountain. She will be there next Sunday evening to meet our two Sisters, Catherine and Antoinette. The other two will come back home. I have authorized Sister Brigitte to make her vows.*

It was necessary to change not only our two Sisters but our Sister Isabelle as well. She is an excellent Sister, but has also, through imprudence, contributed greatly to all the little disorders that have occurred. That still leaves Sister Henriette [5] *here; she has a terrible infatuation for the*

Letter 973. - Archives of the Motherhouse of the Daughters of Charity, original autograph letter.

[1] A native of Montreuil-sur-Mer, Sister Antoinette Larcher traveled to Nantes with Saint Louise in July 1646. She returned to Paris in 1647 when she left the Company and returned home.

[2] Elisabeth Martin.

[3] Claude Carré, from Neuville near Pontoise, (Val-d'Oise) arrived at the Nantes hospital in August 1646 and became the Assistant there. She went back to Paris around 1652-1653, returning in August 1656 to Angers, where she was named Sister Servant after the departure of Cécile Angiboust.

[4] Elisabeth Le Goutteux, the widow of M. Turgis, left a high position in the world to consecrate herself to God in the Company of the Daughters of Charity. She was Superior of the Angers hospital (1639-1640, 1644), at the Foundlings (1642), in Saint-Denis (1645), in Chars near Pontoise (1645, 1647), and in Richelieu (1646-1647). She died in Chantilly in October 1648, after a long and painful illness.

[5] Henriette Gesseaume, a very intelligent and resourceful Daughter of Charity, but too independent. A skilled pharmacist, she was of great assistance at the Nantes hospital, where she

chaplain, even though it is quite innocent both in its results and in its source because the chaplain is a very upright man, and she is a very good Sister. Nevertheless, the poor girl is upset by the instructions I am leaving for her to have no more contact with this good priest. We will have to see how that works out. In any case, if she cannot refrain from this, she can be recalled, although it will be very difficult to uproot her from here. I hope, however, that this will all be settled, and that Sister Jeanne Lepeintre will take care of everything.

I have stipulated that the Fathers of the Poor [6] should go to the Vicar-General to request or suggest a confessor from somewhere else. I have had the chaplain and the Vicar-General agree to this. In addition, they promised me to dismiss the good Brother that either you or Mademoiselle sent.

That, Monsieur, is more or less what we have done. I hope that God in His goodness will forgive me the harm I have put in the way of things, and will procure His glory in everything else. Furthermore, Monsieur, I could not tell you how much the entire Little Company is obliged to good Monsieur des Jonchères in particular and to his whole family in general for the affection he shows toward our poor Sisters, and for their kindness in our regard during our stay here. We were lodged at the home of Monsieur des Jonchères' mother. They are also most outstanding in piety and goodness.

Those Fathers of the Poor are likewise very good to our Sisters. To be sure, if God granted us the grace of their being able to live together in true harmony, the little establishment here would greatly sanctify the Daughters of Charity, for I think God will still grant them for a long time to come the grace to suffer from things outside. I recommend this blessing to your prayers, Monsieur, and to those of Mademoiselle Le Gras.

If God grants our Sisters the grace of going as far as Paris, oh! they should be warmly welcomed because they have done none of the evil of which they have been suspected, and if things had been handled properly, I think the blame would not have fallen on them.

I am not writing to Mademoiselle Le Gras, even though she has written to me. If you think well of it, I hope this letter will do for her also.

I am going now to say good-bye to our Sisters, and I ask you, Monsieur, to continue to pray for us. I hope we will be in Luçon early in the month of

---

remained from 1646 to 1655. Two of her nieces, Françoise Gesseaume and Perrette Chefdeville, also became Daughters of Charity. Claude, one of her brothers, and a nephew, Nicolas Chefdeville, were coadjutor Brothers in the Congregation of the Mission.

[6]Administrators of the hospital.

August, and from there will go to Saintes, where we expect to receive some news of you. Once again, I ask your blessing on your most humble and very obedient servant.

LAMBERT,

i.s.C.M.

Addressed: *Monsieur Vincent, Superior General of the Congregation of the Mission, at the Collège des Bons-Enfants, near Saint-Victor Gate, in Paris.*

974. - *JEAN BARREAU, CONSUL IN ALGIERS, TO SAINT VINCENT*

Algiers, July 27, 1647

Monsieur,

From the last letter good Monsieur Nouelly wrote you by way of Genoa and Leghorn, you were able to learn how, this past June 26, the recently arrived bacha [1] had me put in prison because of the bond I had to post for the Fathers of Mercy. This letter is to reconfirm that and to inform you that I got out on the twentieth of this month, by the grace of Our Lord, feeling as if I had made a retreat. What greatly contributed to this was the conference Monsieur Nouelly gave me at that time on conformity to the Will of God. Doubtless, it was only by a very special inspiration that he gave me this, to prepare me for the storm that has broken over me since, and from which I still have not escaped.

Now, the means Our Lord was pleased to [use] to get me out was the fact that, as the contagious disease increased, so did the burning desire of the above-named priest to bring relief to the poor sick Christians through the administration of the Sacraments and through other temporal assistance. In the end he was finally stricken by it himself on Wednesday, the nineteenth of this month, between nine and ten in the morning, and returned to the house. A great feeling of weariness came over him and he was drenched with perspiration. This was reported to me while I was still in

---

Letter 974. - Lyons manuscript, f°208ff.

[1]The spelling used today is "pasha." The pasha was the Governor of a province within the Turkish kingdom and was usually appointed for three years.

prison. At that news I resolved to get out at all costs, so as to go to his aid. Finally, in return for forty-five piastres, which I had to give to certain persons who had influence with the King and to a few of his officers, the order was given that I should be released, and it was put into effect immediately. So, I went home on Saturday, the twentieth, around three o'clock in the afternoon, and found that he was not as delirious as he had been during the night and morning. This consoled me greatly because everyone was telling me that, if I did not hurry and get out, I would not find him alive, since he had had Holy Viaticum and the holy oils brought to him in the morning.

My presence gave him some sort of consolation. He embraced me very tenderly at first, without saying a word, scarcely recognizing me. Nevertheless, some time later, when he recovered consciousness, he told me he thought that it was all over for him and that Our Lord wanted to take him. He had no regret in dying, except that he foresaw that the poor Christians would be abandoned and helpless. After encouraging him as best I could, I asked him about his illness and what remedies had been given him during the night and on the preceding day.

I did not ask the cause of it because the tears and sighs of the Christians were sure proof that the care with which he assisted them, particularly the most abandoned, as were those stricken by the plague, was, after God, the primary cause. And it would be a grave insult to his memory for me not to make public the truth. What played a major role in this was the little care he took of himself, not even allowing himself a drop of wine or something else in the morning, before taking the Blessed Sacrament to the sick, so strong was his desire to help his children. Shortly before his illness, when he was having a meal with me in prison, as was his custom, I asked him what precautions he was taking against the disease, which was so violent that the sick did not last forty-eight hours with it. He answered that he had none except confidence in God. When I replied that this was truly an excellent remedy but that God did not forbid us to to take, along with it, a little drop of wine before going out, he replied that, when he saw all the people leaving the chapel as soon as he had finished saying Mass, it seemed to him he would be committing a serious act of irreverence if he were to leave Him alone. To this we can add his fear that this disease might attack the sick too quickly and he might arrive too late to help them. Although I explained to him that he was extremely necessary here and that, if he was unwilling to take care of his health for his own sake, he might at least take care of it for others and for me who needed him so much in the situation in which I was, I even had the temerity to go so far as to tell him that it was tempting God to risk his life in that way. But it was useless because his respect for the Blessed Sacrament and his love for the poor were incom-

parably greater than his love for himself, and no advice his friends could give him was capable of lessening the one or changing the other.

He made this clear again before he died. Signor Ortensio Gualteri, who is acting Vicar-General here for the Bishop of Carthage, told him that, if God granted him the grace of being restored to health, he would forbid him, even under pain of excommunication, to have so much contact with the sick, but rather he should be informed about them and assist them through a third party. He replied, with a deep sigh, that this could not be, so great was his zeal for the salvation of souls, of which you see yet another proof.

About a week before falling ill, he had gone to dine with Father Sébastien, of the Order of Our Lady of Mercy,[2] because of whom I was a prisoner. As we were washing our hands, a poor man from Provence arrived to implore his help for a man named Pierre Boquit, who had been a slave for twenty-five years and who used to help bury the dead, and he begged him to come and hear his confession. Immediately, he put down the towel and followed him, preferring the good of this poor Christian's soul to his own wants and needs.

I do not give you this example as being something unique but rather as an ordinary and daily occurrence. How often have we seen him, drenched with perspiration after racing around all morning, looking for some dose, as he used to call this exercise. Thinking he would give himself a rest of half an hour, he would instead immediately go rushing off at that very moment, with no respite, to the house of another Christian, who was seeking

---

[2]Sébastien Brugière, a Father of Mercy, had come to Algiers in March 1644 with his confreres, François Faure and François Faisan, for the ransom of slaves. The amount of money entrusted to him was sufficient to ransom two hundred slaves. Ninety-six other Christians were freed on the promise of 8990 piastres and the exchange of twenty-two Turks. Brugière was held hostage while his companions returned to France to raise the promised sum, which they were not able to collect. He had to have recourse to heavy loans at fifty percent interest to quiet his most pressing creditors, while his debts went on accumulating. In May 1645 a renegade Christian, who was trying in vain to obtain fifty piastres from him for the price of a slave, attacked him with a knife and was about to kill him. Father Brugière escaped but fell, broke two ribs, and burst his spleen. Complaints were lodged at the custom house of the town. He was seized, condemned, and thrown into a horrible prison, where he was confined for two months. Then, because his health gave cause for concern, he was granted permission to go and live in the French Consul's residence under house arrest. He was still there on November 25, 1645 when, before François Constans, Chancellor of the Consul of Algiers, he made the statement which *Revue africaine*, vol. XXXV, published under the title "Certificat des souffrances du Père Sébastien."

help for someone else. I can assure you it was not in vain that he called this exercise a race, because he went to it with as much and even more enthusiasm as do the pirates of Algiers to seize some merchant ship. And as they make no exception of persons and capture everything in sight, so did our fine pirate, for there was no Spaniard, Italian, or person from any other nation, whom he did not try to win over to Our Lord and put in a good disposition.

His illness began with severe pain in his stomach and kidneys, extreme weariness in his arms and legs, and with such a violent fever that everyone thought he would not make it through the day. Then he began to vomit, which immediately revealed the nature of his illness. This fever lasted until Sunday evening, accompanied by great agitation, hallucinations, and extreme sweating. He had them all of Sunday, and they brought down the fever. Toward evening, he became rational again, so we thought he was out of danger of dying. I stayed with him all night, and since I was alone with him, I had the happiness of enjoying his conversation for the space of two or three hours, during which he gave me some advice on how to behave when I would be alone in this country. He made me see the consolation received by a soul who dies while carrying out the duties of his vocation. He displayed admirable fortitude in accepting death, which he had been expecting from the moment we embarked in Marseilles to come to this town, even, as he told me several times, to be burned or impaled, with perfect resignation to God's Will, but with such immense tenderness that I wished I were in his place.

Finally, on Monday morning, his fever intensified. Note that when a little rain, lasting a quarter of an hour, fell after a year of drought, this day was so difficult that they say that 8250 persons died. So, at the outset of the bad weather, which began around two o'clock in the afternoon, he went into agony again, with great stress and violence. He sat up in bed, crucifix in hand, imagining he was in the pulpit to preach. In this state, he said a few words which we could not understand. From time to time, I had him kiss the crucifix and say Sancta Maria, *etc., or* Maria mater, *etc., but I cannot express to you how ardently and affectionately he uttered them as best he could. After making this effort for about an hour his strength failed him, and a short time later he began to grow cold. After a peaceful quarter of an hour he expired, or rather, fell asleep, so gently did he pass away. This, more or less, is how his illness progressed.*

As soon as he had expired, news of his death spread so rapidly throughout the town that the house was immediately filled with French, Italian, and Spanish Christians, and those from other nations as well, who testified by their tears how keenly they felt his loss. Several attempts were made to get them to leave because of the infected air, but there was no way.

Finally, we brought him to be buried in a place called Bab-Azoun,[3] near the seashore, where he was laid to rest close to the late Father Lucien.[4] Seven or eight hundred Christians from various nations were present there, all with tears in their eyes. There were also many Turks, who mourned him even more because of the help he gave their slaves when they were ill. This was a great consolation to me in the state I was in. Indeed, they would have been very ungrateful had they not done this. He had won their confidence because of the special graces God had granted him to move the hearts of those barbarians to have compassion on their slaves.

He entered their homes as freely as he would our own, and the blessing God gave his labors, by the recovery of some, caused him to pass for a doctor. Under this guise he went freely to visit, console, and assist poor Christians, no matter how hidden they were, and he administered the Sacraments to them right in front of their owners, leading them to believe that they were remedies. In this he was not in any way being deceitful, since they worked more effectively than bodily remedies.

After paying our last respects to him, we turned our thoughts to preserving his remains and to give this all possible care and attention. Father Sébastien Brugière, of the Order of Our Lady of Mercy, advised me to make some perfumes and to burn a large quantity of aromatic wood in the house, particularly in the room where he had died.

The day after his death, my heart felt very weak and I perspired a great deal with no respite. My imagination, which was even more affected, had me picturing myself already dead. In this frame of mind, I began to dispose of everything as if I were to die that very day. Having done this, I began to detach myself from all earthly things and to place myself in the hands of our good God. It was then I remembered what I had read in prison in the treatise on conformity to the Will of God. At times, reflecting on the inspiration of the late M. Nouelly to give me this treatise, I thought that it was an effect of his holy and exceptional prudence, by which he was trying to dispose me to accept death patiently, even though deprived of my principal mainstay, far from my nearest or closest friends, with no consolation in a country where I had been so fiercely persecuted. Nevertheless, I felt that all these considerations gave me greater courage, since I believed

---

[3]The site of a Christian cemetery.

[4]Father Lucien Hérault, a Trinitarian. During his first trip to Algiers in January 1643, he had ransomed forty-eight slaves. He returned in 1645, ransomed others, and offered himself as guarantee. Since the promised money was delayed in coming, he was imprisoned. He died shortly afterward, on January 28, 1646 and his body was interred outside the city in the Christian cemetery, near the Gate called Bab-el-Oued. (Cf. Dan, *op. cit.*, p. 151.)

I was even more in conformity with His Will, which was ordaining things in this way. However, for a day now, it would appear that He wants to keep me for another occasion.

The day after his death, a solemn service was sung in the King's prison, where a crowd as large as the place and time would permit had gathered. A eulogy was given there by the Carmelite, Father Pierre, who enlarged on the cause of his illness. Then, having come upon the psalm Beatus qui intelligit super egenum et pauperem,[5] *he so exaggerated the help he had given to priests as well as to the laity, that he made him out to be a saint. Two days later another service was sung in Cheleby's* [6] *prison, where a eulogy was also given by the Franciscan, Father Ange, who took as his subject the way Saint Jerome mourned the death of Saint Paula, and he used as a reference* in morte ejus omnes defecisse virtutes.[7] *He expounded on his charity toward the poor Christians, his gentleness and kindness which were such that no Christian ever left him without being satisfied, his modesty by which he won all hearts, and so on for the others.*

Among the persons who charitably and cordially assisted him, I cannot keep from telling you of the zeal of Father Sébastien and of Father Corse, director of the deceased. They assisted him to his last breath, never leaving his side, in spite of the danger there was in this. I would be ungrateful not to mention Gabriel Mirsane, a surgeon from La Flèche in Anjou, for whose ransom the Duchesse d'Aiguillon told me to go as high as 500 livres. His care and diligence were indescribable as was his attentiveness in watching over him, always sleeping in the house so as to be prompt in coming to his aid.

It was on this occasion that I witnessed the fidelity of René Duchesne, an impoverished gentleman from Poitou,[8] who has been rowing on the galleys for twelve years and has been living in the house for a year as our secretary, and of Jean Benoît, who has been our cook for the same length of time; they vied with one another in showing their affection. He was also aided by three other Christians: Jean Petit, from Boulogne; Lepine, from Picardy; and Guillaume Mobavec, from the Coutances diocese. These men have assisted us and still continue to offer their services.

This, then, is more or less the happy outcome of what happened in Algiers with the late M. Nouelly. I say "more or less" because it would be too much

---

[5]*Blessed is he who thinks of the needy and the poor.* Cf. Ps 41:2. (NAB) Ps 40:2. (D-RB)
[6]Overseer of the convict prison.
[7]*At his death all virtues cease.*
[8]René Duchesne was born in Saint-Juire-Champgillon (Vendée) in August 1607. He entered the Congregation of the Mission in Richelieu on February 16, 1654 as a coadjutor Brother, and took his vows November 1, 1658.

for me to try to spell out the services he rendered to the poor sick and needy. They were too extensive before God to have his reward deferred.

As for me, I thank God for the grace of the time He has still given me to do penance. May this be to God's greater glory, as I think it is, and the truth is that I have the honor, Monsieur, to call myself your most humble and very obedient servant.

BARREAU

975. - JULIEN GUERIN TO SAINT VINCENT

[Tunis, between 1645 and May 1648] [1]

We have here a little thirteen-year-old boy from Marseilles, who, from the time he was captured and sold by corsairs, was dealt more than a thousand blows with a stick for the faith of Jesus Christ, which they were trying by force to make him deny. For this same reason, they tore the flesh off one arm, as if they were making strips of meat to grill on charcoal. After this, he was condemned to receive four hundred blows with a stick, that is, either to die or to become a Turk, so I went immediately to his owner and got down on my knees three or four times before him, with hands joined, to ask for him. He gave him to me for two hundred piastres. Since I had no money, I borrowed a hundred écus at interest, and a merchant donated the rest.

976. - TO ALAIN DE SOLMINIHAC, BISHOP OF CAHORS

July 30, 1647

Excellency,

Your good monks from Chancelade have returned home with their decree. They worked wonders in the application to the judge

---

Letter 975. - Abelly, *op.cit.*, bk. II, chap. I, sect. VII, §12, p. 140.
  [1]The length of Julien Guérin's stay in Tunis.

Letter 976. - Reg. 1, f°2, copy made from the rough draft which was in the Saint's handwriting.

in this affair and greatly edified all those with whom they had to deal. There is a clause in the decree which gives you a good opening to obtain the erection of your Congregation. The Council ordains that the monks of Chancelade, Sablonceaux,[1] and Saint-Girard[2] shall live under the guidance of the Superior or Abbot of Chancelade. Strictly speaking, that means the erection of one Congregation composed of these three houses. Since the temporal magistrate cannot give the spiritual jurisdiction required for a superior of several houses, and since this must be given by the Pope, in whom this right resides, the monks of the above-mentioned houses must go back to His Holiness and ask him to authorize the Abbot of Chancelade to govern the three houses spiritually. The Abbot of Chancelade, the Bishop of Cahors, has founded a house in the Cahors diocese for men to live under the direction of the Superior or Abbot of Chancelade,[3] and there are several other houses of the same Order asking to live under the direction of the Superior of Chancelade. His Holiness is, therefore, being petitioned to erect as a Congregation the union of those three houses created by the King's Council, so that they can live under the direction of the Superior of Chancelade, and to confer on this Congregation the rights and privileges conferred on other religious Congregations, with authority to receive into the above-mentioned Congregation houses that are not reformed nor belonging to another Congregation, of the Order of Canons Regular of Saint Augustine, who will ask to be united to it. This is in conformity with what is stated by the holy Council of Trent, which ordains that religious houses not belonging to any Congregation shall be bound to be incorporated into a Congregation.

---

[1] A small locality in Charente-Maritime. Alain de Solminihac had sent two of his monks there at the request of M. de Sourdis, Archbishop of Bordeaux, commendatory Abbot of the abbey.

[2] In Limoges.

[3] A month earlier the Bishop of Cahors had called to this town twelve Canons Regular of the Chancelade reform. Three of them, including their Superior, Father Garat, were lodged at the Bishop's palace; five or six of them were living in a rented house in the faubourg of Barre; the others were to give missions all year long, except during harvest time. A few years later, they were established in Cahors, in a building erected for them by the Bishop.

These, Excellency, are my humble thoughts on this question. And because the presence of a man hastens the outcome of an affair and makes a success of it sooner and more assuredly, I think the matter merits your sending someone there who will not appear in the habit,[4] so that the question may be settled before their agents in that place are informed about it.

It is being said that the Bishop of Puy[5] is supposed to go to Rome for the beatification of the blessed Bishop of Geneva this fall or next spring. If this is so, I shall ask him to work on the case.

This, Excellency, is what I can offer you, along with my poor heart, which I am folding up into this letter to send it to you. I am, in the love of Our Lord, Excellency, your most humble and very obedient servant.

VINCENT DEPAUL
i.s.C.M.

977. - TO A PRIEST OF THE MISSION

[1647][1]

We have no news except the death of Monsieur Aulent, Superior of our house in Toul, where he ended his days with almost infallible

---

[4]By advising that Bishop Solminihac's delegate to Rome not wear his religious habit, Saint Vincent was advocating what he thought was prudent in order to avoid opposition in Rome. However, Father Vitet, one of the monks who was sent to Rome, informed Saint Vincent on September 5, 1650 (cf. no. 1256) that any monk in Rome who did not wear his religious habit was excommunicated.

[5]Henri Cauchon de Maupas du Tour, a member of the Tuesday Conferences, was Bishop of Le Puy (1641-1661), and then of Evreux from 1661 to August 8, 1680, the day of his death. He was a renowned orator and preached the funeral panegyrics for Saint Jane Frances de Chantal and Saint Vincent. He also wrote biographies of Saint Francis de Sales and Saint Jane Frances, and was one of the two Bishops who approved Abelly's life of Saint Vincent.

Letter 977. - Lyons manuscript.
[1]The year Charles Aulent died. Born February 1, 1614, in Ath, a town in Hainaut (Belgium), he entered the Congregation of the Mission at the end of 1636, was ordained a priest in 1640, and took his vows on December 11, 1644. He directed the house in Toul from 1646 to 1647, the year he died.

indications of his eternal happiness. But then, he had lived as a true servant of God and in as holy a manner as is possible for a true Missionary. I cannot give you the details, but you can form a picture of him by imagining a man in whom no faults are evident and who practices all the virtues. That can be said of him without exaggeration, and I say it to you with a deep feeling of sorrow at the loss the Company has suffered in him. May God grant us the grace to imitate him, and me that of obtaining mercy through his prayers and yours!

978. - JULIEN GUERIN TO SAINT VINCENT

[Tunis, between 1645 and May 1648] [1]

I cannot refrain from letting you know what a Turk told me recently, to the shame of the bad Christians. I was trying to reconcile two Christians who had a grudge against one another. When he saw that I was having a hard time getting them to agree, he said to me in front of them, in his own language: "Father, among us Turks, it is not permitted for us to remain three days at odds with our neighbor, even though he may have killed one of our closest relatives." And, as a matter of fact, I have several times remarked this practice among them, seeing them embrace one another immediately after a fight. I do not know whether the interior corresponds to the exterior, but there is no doubt that on judgment day these unbelievers will condemn those Christians who are unwilling to be reconciled either interiorly or exteriorly, and, harboring their hatred against the neighbor in their hearts, manifest it scandalously on the outside as well, even glorying in the vengeance they have taken, or desire to take, on their enemies. Yet, these people, whom we judge to be barbarians, consider it a great shame to nurture any hatred in their hearts and to be unwilling to be reconciled with those who have done them wrong.

Letter 978. - Abelly, *op.cit.*, bk. II, chap. I, sect. VII, §8, p. 124.
[1] The period during which Julien Guérin was in Tunis.

979. - SAINT LOUISE TO SAINT VINCENT

[Bicêtre, August 1647] [1]

Monsieur,

Yesterday I apologized to Monsieur Le Roy for not giving you a message from him. Nevertheless, I think it my duty to tell you everything he had told me and what I replied to him, which would be very difficult to send you by letter. However, the main point is that he is bringing forward the fact that he is Director and Administrator of the children's hospital. [2] *As such, he claims the right to go there and give instructions whenever he feels like it, to place a priest there, and to have the entire spiritual care of it; he also wants us to do him the favor of finding a priest and present him for his approval. [He said] he was more jealous of this than of a bishopric or cardinalate and, if it were refused him, he would take his complaints to the Attorney General* [3] *and resign from the administrative post that had been given him.*

I acted surprised that he had not mentioned this sooner, telling him that up until now the Ladies [4] *had always been equally concerned for spiritual as well as temporal needs, as is obvious from the baptisms, Easter confessions, and instructions for First Communion. They have also had Holy Mass said for the children and the wet nurses. I said also that I thought the Priests of the Chapter had turned over full responsibility for this work to the care of these Ladies, with the exception of the twelve hundred livres for which the latter were accountable to them, and that for more than fifty years since the Priests of the Chapter had this responsibility, no other administrative matters were involved except for that sum. [I told him] that I was speaking, however, without having heard anything about all that from the Ladies, of whom I saw very little, and what I was saying to him was only in a general sense. He complained of not having been informed about Bicêtre. I pointed out to him that I thought it would not even have occurred to the Ladies to have to do so, and that things happened very quickly. He told me many other things, and I him, which I cannot put in writing to you. He did not fail*

Letter 979. - Archives of the Motherhouse of the Daughters of Charity, original autograph letter.
    [1]Date added on the back of the original by Brother Ducournau.
    [2]The foundlings had originally been associated with the Hôtel-Dieu, which led this Administrator to claim that his authority extended to their care.
    [3]Blaise Méliand (1641-1650).
    [4]The Ladies of Charity.

to cite Sister Geneviève's [5] reply to those priests at their request, and I made him understand why she said it.

If some distinguished person could get this place from the Queen for an establishment of the Mission, it would put a stop to many arguments, and great good would be done.

I almost forgot to tell you that, upon my refusal to speak to you, Monsieur Le Roy decided to go to those Ladies and to speak to them in strong terms.

Will your charity please take the trouble to look at Madame de Romilly's letter? I will send it, if you think it a good idea.

Please bless us, and believe that I am, Monsieur, your most obedient servant and very grateful daughter.

L. DE MARILLAC

Since the great need came to my mind, I told him that I think the Ladies will soon be obliged to turn the entire work over to someone else who could do it. We still remain good friends because I spoke to him as a neutral party.

I believe we should think about the wine as soon as possible.

980. - ALAIN DE SOLMINIHAC TO SAINT VINCENT

Toulouse, August 20, 1647

Monsieur,

I received the letter you took the trouble to write me on the fourth of this month. There is nothing to be said against the commissioners you have named for the affair concerning my monks.

Ever since Abbé d'Estrades [1] has been named for the Périgueux diocese, I have never ceased exhorting, begging, and pressuring him to use all possible diligence to get the Bulls quickly and go to his diocese. In the end, seeing from his letters that he was allowing himself to be influenced by his

[5]Geneviève Poisson.

Letter 980. - Archives of the Diocese of Cahors, Alain de Solminihac collection, notebook copy made from the original.

[1]Jean d'Estrades, named Bishop of Périgueux in July 1646, never took possession of his diocese. He was transferred to Condom and replaced in Périgueux in 1648 by Philibert de Brandon, Bishop Solminihac's candidate.

brother's urging to get them free of charge and not to hurry their expedition because he was hoping to obtain it in this way, I wrote to him in these terms about two months ago. I asked him to put before his brother this truth of which he should have no doubt, namely, that since the time he has been requesting the Bulls gratis, a number of souls in that diocese have been lost. This would not have happened had he been there and, until he gets his Bulls free of charge, many who would have been saved if he had been in his diocese will be lost. I asked if he wanted to answer to God for them, which I do not think; and even if his brother were willing to answer for them, would he be freed of responsibility for them before God? I [told him] I was writing that with considerable feeling, etc.

About five weeks later, he wrote back that he was determined to attend to the needs of the Périgueux diocese in one way or another, and was in contact with the Bishop of Condom [2] *to obtain his resignation. A few days after, he wrote me that the contract had been settled, and he was giving his abbey to the nephew of the Bishop of Condom, who would hand over to him his resignation from the bishopric, with the exception of twelve thousand livres pension. He asked me to write this to you, requesting you to have this resignation accepted, which I am now doing since he desires this, although I feel there is no need for it, knowing how zealously you wish that this afflicted diocese of Périgueux be promptly occupied by someone having the requisite qualifications to govern it. It is feared that the Bishop of Condom's nephew is aspiring to it, and people wanted me to inform you so that, if it is the case, you will do your utmost to oppose it. He is the one who had been negotiating with the Bishop of Agde* [3] *for the Bayonne diocese, and*

---

[2] Antoine de Cous, who died February 15, 1648.

[3] François Fouquet was the son of François Fouquet, Comte de Vaux, and of the devout Marie de Maupeou, one of the Ladies of Charity most admirable for her zeal and her devotedness to Saint Vincent. Fouquet's brothers were Nicolas Fouquet, Superintendent of Finances, and Louis Fouquet, Bishop of Agde. His sister, Louise-Agnès, became a nun in the First Monastery of the Visitation. François Fouquet, named Bishop of Bayonne in 1636, was not consecrated until March 15, 1639. He was transferred to the diocese of Agde in 1643, appointed Coadjutor of Narbonne on December 18, 1656, and Archbishop of that diocese in 1659. Relegated to Alençon in 1661, he died in his exile on October 19, 1673. He brought the Priests of the Mission to Agde and Narbonne, and established the Daughters of Charity in the latter town. A very zealous Prelate, too zealous perhaps, he found Saint Vincent's slowness hard to understand, but greatly admired his virtue. He felt deeply the Saint's death, and as soon as he received news of it, he wrote to the priests of Saint-Lazare: "However prepared I may have been for M. Vincent's death, since he was advanced in age, I assure you that I did not hear the news of his passing without surprise and without being moved with great sorrow, humanly speaking, at seeing the Church deprived of a most worthy subject, the Congregation of its very dear Father, and me of a very charitable friend, to whom I am so greatly obligated. I think that of all those whom his charity caused him to

whom you judged undeserving because of something he did, unworthy of his calling, on leaving your house after his retreat.

The Bishop of Valence [4] has been informed that you used your influence in his favor at the Council of Conscience; he is much obliged to you for this. He asks you, as do I, to continue to render him this service at the Council, so that His Eminence [5] will make it possible for him to go and carry out his functions freely in his diocese. It is quite easy to find good governors for towns but very difficult to find good bishops as zealous for the salvation of souls as he is. And since this governor cannot refrain from committing acts of violence against him or his officers, it is quite right and more reasonable to give this governor some other post than to oblige the Bishop of Valence to leave his diocese.

I have been here for two months, prosecuting the important case I mentioned to you against the Comte de Rastignac,[6] my vassal, but I have been unable to get an adjudication. It is possible that I will not obtain it from this Parlement because there is so much chicanery in the law courts. Whether I get it or not, I shall return to my diocese in a few days. In the meantime, I am, Monsieur, etc.

ALAIN DE SOLMINIHAC
Bishop of Cahors

981. - *SAINT LOUISE TO SAINT VINCENT*

[Bicêtre, August 22, 1647][1]

Monsieur,

If your charity permits, provided there is no need for me to hurry home, I think it is advisable for me not to return, leaving here only a school-mistress, who is busy teaching the children how to sew and to read. Speaking of that, Monsieur, I very humbly make a request of your charity,

---

embrace as his children, there is no one to whom he showed more affection and gave more signs of friendship than to me."

[4]Charles-Jacques de Gelas de Leberon (1624-1654).

[5]Jules Cardinal Mazarin.

[6]Jean-François Chapt, Marquis de Rastignac, Brigadier General of the royal armies.

Letter 981. - Archives of the Motherhouse of the Daughters of Charity, original autograph letter.

[1]Brother Ducournau added "August 1647" on the back of the letter; the postscript permits us to pinpoint the day.

for the love of God: it is that you would kindly go and visit our five Sisters whom I left on retreat without having done much for them. I had led them to hope for my return this evening or tomorrow morning. One is from Saint-Germain-en-Laye, one from Nanteuil,[2] and one from the village of Issy, as well as the girl I think we will have to send back to Saint-Denis because we do not feel she is suitable for us. The others are in a big hurry to go back home, and they should leave by next Saturday at the latest. The fifth is the girl I am sending as one of the teachers for our little children.

I think it is most necessary, Monsieur, for your charity to give us a priest immediately, for two reasons: one, so he can instruct the boys; the other, Monsieur, is that it seems to me that the first one able to fill this need will be the one to stay.

One of our children died this morning. I took the liberty of having someone ask the good priest to come and bury him and, if it is inconvenient for him to come and bury him this evening, to do us the kindness of coming tomorrow and to say Mass for us on the same occasion.

If you think it necessary for our Sisters to go to your house to speak to you, rather than your not speaking to them at all, I most humbly beg you kindly to let me know. Nevertheless, it would be a great consolation for the whole family if it were at the house.

If your charity thinks our Sisters should go and speak to the Procurator General [3] to remind him of the needs you pointed out to him, I think Sister Geneviève [4] should be the one; the others are not so well suited for this. He should be told that the entire supply of wood must be provided.

Our Ladies gave no thought to arranging a place for the school. We inspected one downstairs that would be quite suitable for the boys, who must be separated from the girls. It seems that the only thing that has to be done is to make a doorway and close up the windows. The girls will be taught upstairs. I really would like us to have some of those alphabet charts. We will put them against the walls; that is the method the Ursulines use wherever they are. I am not mentioning writing because I do not think it advisable for the girls to learn how to write.

It is true, Most Honored Father, that there is reason to hope that much good will come from this work, if our good God is pleased to continue to give it His holy blessing. I ask you with all my heart to give me yours, for

---

[2]Nanteuil-le-Haudoin (Oise).
[3]Blaise Méliand.
[4]Geneviève Poisson.

the holy love of Him, so that His holy Will in this matter may be accomplished in me. I am, Monsieur, your most obedient and very grateful daughter and servant.

LOUISE DE MARILLAC

I forgot to ask your permission to fast and abstain tomorrow, Friday, because I think I am up to it. I will do it, unless your charity forbids me.

982. - *SAINT LOUISE TO SAINT VINCENT*

Monsieur,

My heart is still filled with joy at the understanding our good God seems to have given it of the words "God is my God," and the awareness I had of the glory which all the blessed render Him in consequence of this truth. I cannot refrain from speaking to you this evening to entreat you to help me make good use of these excesses of joy and indicate to me some practice for tomorrow, the feast day of the Saint whose name [1] I have the honor to bear. It is also the day for the renewal of my vows.[2] For both of these intentions, I hope to assist at your Holy Mass, if your charity will please let me know the time. I most humbly ask this of you in the hope, Most Honored Father, that you are aware that all that I am is in your hands, to be given to this good God whose love has made me, through His great mercy, your most humble and very grateful daughter and servant.

LOUISE DE MARILLAC

Feast of Saint Bartholemew [3]

Letter 982. - Original autograph letter at Saint-Sulpice Seminary, Paris.

[1]Saint Louis, whose feast is August 25. He is known in history as King Louis IX of France.

[2]On May 4, 1623, feast of Saint Monica, Saint Louise had made a vow to remain a widow, if she should outlive her husband. (Cf. *Ecrits spirituels,* A. 2, p. 3.) She renewed this vow annually on that day (cf. Abbé Gobillon, *La vie de Mademoiselle Le Gras, fondatrice et première supérieure de la Compagnie des Filles de la Charité* [Paris: A. Pralard, 1676], p. 27; Eng. trans., *The Life of Mademoiselle Le Gras* [London: Sisters of Charity, Provincial House, Mill Hill, 1984], p. 10). She also renewed this vow on the first Saturday of each month (cf. *Ecrits spirituels,* A. 1, p. 688) and on important anniversaries. Later she added another vow, of consecrating herself to the service of the poor.

[3]August 24.

983. - TO SAINT LOUISE

[August 25][1]

Blessed be God, Mademoiselle, for the caresses with which His Divine Majesty honors you! They must be welcomed with respect and devotion and in view of some cross He is now preparing for you. His Goodness is accustomed to forewarn in this way souls He loves, when He wishes to crucify them. Oh! what a happiness to have such a paternal Divine Providence watching over you; how that should make you increase your faith and trust in God, and to love Him more than ever! So, do it, Mademoiselle. The action you are about to perform today will mean a great deal to you. I shall share in your consolation, as I intend to share in your cross, by the Holy Sacrifice I hope to offer to Him today, between eight and nine o'clock.

Good day, Mademoiselle. Y[our] s[ervant].

V. D.

984. - TO JEAN-FRANCOIS DE GONDI, ARCHBISHOP OF PARIS

September 3, 1647

Excellency,

I hereby renew to you, with all the humility and devotion in my power, the pledge of my obedience. I most humbly entreat you to accept it, Excellency, together with the most humble request which M. Ribier, the bearer of this letter, is going to make of you regarding the union of his priory of Brière-le-Château.[1] Three reasons seem

---

Letter 983. - Original autograph letter at Saint-Sulpice Seminary, Paris.
[1]This is a reply to the preceding note and is written in its margin.

Letter 984. - Reg. 1, f°63 v°, copy made from the original in the Saint's own handwriting.
[1]This is the name used in the copy. Should it be Bruyères-le-Châtel (Essonne), or rather

to invite this of your goodness, Excellency, in addition to the fact that we are your poor lowly creatures. The first is that the Prior has desired this for a long time now, six or seven years, plus the fact that his late father on his deathbed advised him to do it. The second reason is our own need because of our excessive workload. We have in the Bons-Enfants Seminary forty extern priests, who pay only about one-third of what they cost us, seven sous a day; and we have the ordinands, whose number is about to double with the reception of all those taking Minor Orders in your diocese, whom you wanted us to accept. The third, Excellency, is that the right to assign this benefice belongs to the the Abbot of Saint-Florent-lez-Saumur,[2] and does not depend on you, Excellency, so you are not detracting anything from the rights of your dignity. Add to that, Excellency, the fact that it will serve us as a stopover for members of the Company who will go to give missions in those parts. Your goodness, Excellency, brought us into existence in establishing us at Saint-Lazare and, by doing us the favor in question, you will give us the means of improving the situation and of doing more work in your service.

I admit, Excellency, that I am unworthy of your taking my request into consideration, but the paternal kindness Our Lord has given you for your Mission and for the welfare of the souls in your diocese will make up for my unworthiness. I am, in the love of Our Lord, Excellency, your. . . .

Brienne-le-Château (Aube), as Pémartin believed? The priory of which Saint Vincent is speaking had M. Ribier as its titular head and was part of the archdiocese of Paris, and the Abbot of Saint-Florent-lez-Saumur had the right of assigning it as a benefice. The priory of Brienne-le-Château fulfilled only the first condition; Bruyères-le-Châtel fulfilled all three. There is, therefore, no doubt about it. As intimated here, Ribier wished to entrust the priory, property, and income to the Congregation of the Mission.

[2]Saint-Florent had been united to the Benedictine Congregation of Saint-Maur in 1637. Mazarin was the Abbot of Saint-Florent. Today it is part of the town of Saumur in the Angers diocese.

985. - TO MATHURIN GENTIL, IN LE MANS

Paris, September 17, 1647

Monsieur,

The grace of Our Lord be with you forever!

I am completing the answer to two of your letters because in my last one I spoke to you about many things contained in them. With regard particularly to lightening the burden of your house, I asked you to send back to us Brothers Laisné,[1] Dupont,[2] and Denis,[3] and the two little schoolboys. I repeat this, in the event that they have not left.

I am indeed surprised at Brother Laisné's liberty in taking money, and also at the way he spent it. We will reflect a little on what to do regarding him.

We shall send you Brother Gurlet[4] to be schoolmaster, after his retreat, which he is about to begin. He could take M. Prudhomme's children and any others who may present themselves.[5]

I informed you that if you would let us know where M. Gautier lives, or to whom we should go for the repurchase of Valobron, we will try to have some time given to you to pay for it.

If the Provost of La Couture[6] agrees that Madame Gremy should be given the lease for twenty-nine years, with a certain increase in the cost, and that the building be handed over at the end in good

---

Letter 985. - Archives of the Mission, Turin, original signed letter.

[1]Probably Nicolas Laisné.

[2]Louis Dupont, born in Nemours (Seine-et-Marne), entered the Congregation of the Mission on October 23, 1641 at twenty-two years of age, and took his vows in November 1644. He was Superior in Toul (1652-1653), Tréguier (1654-1661), Annecy (1662-1663), and at Saint-Charles (1664-1671).

[3]Perhaps Denis Gigot, who was born in Donnemarie (Seine-et-Marne), entered the Congregation of the Mission on July 22, 1647 at the age of twenty-two, and took his vows in Troyes on October 9, 1649, with M. Bourdet present.

[4]Claude Gurlet, born in Lyons, entered the Congregation of the Mission on June 12, 1646 at twenty-four years of age, and died on February 2, 1653.

[5]Probably for the Bons-Enfants Seminary.

[6]A parish in Le Mans.

condition, I am satisfied with that and leave it to the Provost to arrange matters.

M. Aubert[7] is wrong to be asking two pistoles for the manure he put in the gardens. M. Gallais assures me they have been deducted for him since the first year, and he himself has paid them. With regard to the four pistoles you said you promised him for not using the gardens, M. Gallais does not admit to that, because M. Aubert cannot claim any prevention of possession by the contract of his lease. As for me, I do [not] know; please discuss it with the Provost.

For the exchange you are being asked to make of the little house and the quarter of the vineyard of the late M. de Saint-Jacques. . . .[8]

Monsieur, your most humble servant.

VINCENT DEPAUL
i.s.C.M.

Addressed: Monsieur Gentil, Priest of the Mission, in Le Mans

986. - TO ANTOINE PORTAIL, IN ROME

September 20, 1647

I entreat you, Monsieur, to leave Saint-Sauveur[1] and not to spend more than six days to complete the visitation in Rome.[2] That is more than enough, because the shorter you make it, the less trouble you will have, and also because we need you here. I am alone in

---

[7]Pierre Aubert, a tradesman of Le Mans. (Cf. Arch. Nat. S 6707.)

[8]This is how the sentence was written in the original; the secretary must have inadvertently left it unfinished.

Letter 986. - Reg. 2, p. 104.

[1]San Salvatore Abbey in the Sabine region, about fifty-three miles from Rome. Antoine Portail had gone there to escape the intense Roman heat, which bothered him greatly.

[2]The visitation, which began on April 23, did not end until November 16. The very hot weather caused several interruptions. (Cf. *Notices,* vol. I, pp. 55, 59.)

shouldering the burden, with only M. Cuissot to help me.[3] I likewise entreat you to be satisfied with another six days to review our Rules with Messieurs Dehorgny and Alméras, and then start back for France. If, in passing through Genoa, you think a second visitation there is needed, you could make it, but only for a week, please. Marseilles could be done in eight to ten days. Although I realize that several considerations might demand more time, nevertheless, I have good reason to want absolutely and to implore you in the name of Our Lord, as I am now doing, Monsieur, not to spend any more time in any of these places, not only for the reasons I have mentioned but also because greater good results from a visitation of short duration, while people are still zealous about the action, than when it drags on too long. Time that goes beyond what I have said serves to weary the persons visited and diminishes the fervor of the work rather than produce any fruit. We have a certain experience of this, and the practice of other Communities causes us to think this way. I entreat you once more to act in this manner; it will give me special consolation.[4]

987. - TO CHARLES TESTACY, SUPERIOR,[1] IN CAHORS

Paris, September 21, 1647

Monsieur,

The grace of Our Lord be with you forever!

This letter is simply to ask you for news concerning three matters: first, the state of your health and the effectiveness of the

---

[3]Lambert aux Couteaux was making visitations also. (Cf. no. 987.) Gilbert Cuissot was one of Saint Vincent's Assistants.

[4]Circumstances were not favorable to the Saint's wishes; he would not see Antoine Portail for two more years.

Letter 987. - Archives of the Mission, Paris, original signed letter.
[1]The content of the letter gives us the clue to the recipient.

remedies you are taking; second, the success of your ordination; and third, what has become of M. Lambert and what route did he take?[2] I thought I would get a letter from him in this latest mail and even one of yours, as usual; but since I received neither, I am worried about all the above-mentioned matters, especially the one which concerns you, and that is why I beg you to let me know something. It is not because I do not have great hope that all is going well; we have asked this of God in the prayers of the Company and in those of the one who is, in the love of Our Lord, Monsieur, your most humble servant.

VINCENT DEPAUL
i.s.C.M.

988. - ALAIN DE SOLMINIHAC TO SAINT VINCENT

Mercuès, September 21, 1647

Monsieur,

I sent you a note yesterday with good M. Lambert, who made the visitation of our seminary with excellent results. He will give you details of it.

I have just received the letter you took the trouble to write me on the seventh of this month. I am pleased that the election of the Prioress of Le Pouget was approved. She is a good nun, who will reestablish and maintain

---

[2]The preceding August 6, Lambert aux Couteaux was making a visitation of the house in Saintes; on September 20 he was in Cahors.

Letter 988. - Archives of the Diocese of Cahors, Alain de Solminihac collection, notebook copy made from the original.

the reform there, if the Queen grants her the patent necessary to do it. The nun about whom a stir was made is the one the Bishop of Utica [1] mentioned to you in my presence. In addition to the general faults common to all the nuns of that house, of knowing neither in theory, nor still less in practice, what religious life is, she has some others of her own. So I beg you to oppose this scheme and to remind Her Majesty of what she has so often assured me, namely, that she would appoint an apostolic man to the diocese of Périgueux, where pillage is rampant. Souls are being lost by the thousands and non est qui recogitet.[2] Oh! how rare is faith in this century! Clama, ne cesses.[3] Remember that the harder the struggle, the more glorious the victory and the greater the reward, which I know well that you are not considering.

I was ready to go to the altar when I received your letter. I immediately announced to our ordinands that henceforth I wanted those taking the four Minor Orders to assist at the ordinations, since it was only just that our seminary should model itself on its mother.

I shall notify the Bishop of Valence [4] of the trouble you have taken to procure some satisfaction for him. He is very piqued at the fact that, by a Council decree, the place he occupied for the sermon in his Church has been given to the President or Seneschal. It is essential for him to be in his diocese, but I also think we should try to give him some satisfaction. If you think it advisable for the King to write him about this, it seems to me it would be advantageous for His Majesty to tell him he had given express orders to the Governor of Valence not to interfere in his office and in what is due to his dignity, etc.

We received word from Sarlat that the business of Monsieur Sevin [5] regarding that bishopric has been settled, and that the documents were to be delivered on the twentieth of this month. This has given me great joy. I

---

[1] Pierre de Bertier, Doctor of the Sorbonne, former Canon and Archdeacon of Toulouse, Coadjutor of Bishop Anne de Murviel and then his successor (1652). In 1636 he was consecrated Bishop *in partibus* of Utica. He had to put up with a great deal of trouble from the elderly Bishop of Montauban, and several times was on the point of resigning. Some time before the Prelate's death, he wrote to Mazarin: "His health is so good and his humor so bad that I cannot hope for his succession nor even his favor. Therefore, my Lord, not only am I unemployed in my ministry and deprived of sufficient revenues for my position, I am in addition constantly persecuted and believed guilty without any reason."

[2] *No one cares.*

[3] *Cry out, do not desist.*

[4] Charles-Jacques de Gelas de Leberon.

[5] Nicolas Sevin.

leave tomorrow morning to go and visit the part of my diocese in that area and Chancelade during the grape harvest.

When you see the Queen, I beg you to tell Her Majesty that the diocese of Couserans, now vacant,[6] is in an extremely deplorable state.

I am, Monsieur, etc.

ALAIN,
Bishop of Cahors

989. - TO ETIENNE BLATIRON, SUPERIOR, IN GENOA

September 27, 1647

I never think of you or one of your men without great consolation. All of you desire to belong entirely to God, and God also wants all of you to belong to Him. You are the first He called to Genoa for the work He wishes the Company to do there. He will give you special graces for this, which will serve as a foundation for all those He will ever bestow on this new house. Oh! what a motive for praising His goodness! What confidence should you not have in His protection, but also what humility, union, and respect for one another! O God my Lord, please be the bond of their hearts; bring to flower the effects of so many holy affections You cause them to form, and give growth to the fruits of their labors for the salvation of souls. Water with Your eternal blessings this establishment, like a new tree planted by Your hand. Strengthen these poor Missionaries in their fatigue. Lastly, my God, be Yourself their reward, and through their prayers spread over me Your immense mercy.

I come back to you, Monsieur, only to assure you that I am, in Our Lord. . . .

---

[6]Pierre de Marca was promoted to the bishopric of Couserans in 1648.

Letter 989. - Reg. 2, p. 198.

990. - TO JEAN BARREAU, CONSUL OF FRANCE, IN ALGIERS

[End of September or beginning of October 1647][1]

Yesterday I received the sad yet happy news of the death of the late M. Nouelly. It caused me to shed many tears several times, but they were tears of gratitude for God's goodness to the Company in having given it a priest who loved Our Lord so perfectly and who had such a happy death.

Oh! how fortunate you are that God has chosen you for such a holy work, to the exclusion of so many other people who are useless to the world!

So there you are, practically a prisoner for charity, or, to put it better, for Jesus Christ. What a happiness to suffer for this great Monarch, and how many crowns await you if you persevere to the end!

991. - TO A PRIEST OF THE MISSION

[End of September or beginning of October 1647][1]

Although I am on retreat, I am still writing to you to recommend to your prayers a deceased member of the Company. Monsieur Nouelly, the priest, has died in Algiers, where he had been sent to assist the poor Christian slaves. He accomplished this so worthily that he preferred to expose himself to the danger of a contagious disease, rampant among these poor afflicted persons, rather than fail to comfort them even to their last breath, with the result that he

---

Letter 990. - Abelly, *op.cit.*, bk. II, chap. I, sect. VII, §3, p. 102.

[1]This is a reply to Jean Barreau's letter of July 27, 1647 (cf. no. 974) and had reached Paris during the annual retreat or just a few days before (cf. no. 991).

Letter 991. - Lyons manuscript.

[1]This letter was written the year M. Nouelly died and during the eight days of Saint Vincent's annual retreat.

caught the same disease and died from it. His companion, Brother
Barreau, has written me some very touching and edifying things
about him.

992. - TO JACQUES DESCLAUX, BISHOP OF DAX

October 2, 1647

Excellency,

I have received with great joy, as always, the honor you have
been pleased to do me of informing me of your arrangement with
the priests of your Chapter.[1] I ask O[ur] L[ord] to cement this union
with that in which He is, and will be, eternally united to His Father.
I ask His Divine Goodness to do likewise with regard to M. de
Poyanne.[2]

The Orthez benefice is still there, although I spoke of it at the
last Council. O[ur] L[ord] will dispose of it as and when He pleases.
M. de Vignoles from Béarn and his friends are petitioning for it in
favor of one of his nephews; another man from Béarn,[3] the secretary

---

Letter 992. - Reg. 1, f°26, copy made from an autograph draft.

[1]The Bishop of Dax was at law with his Canons on the wording of the titles of nomination to
choral prebends, the appropriate salary for the senior chaplain, and the honors to which the
Chapter claimed a right during pontifical functions. The Parlement of Bordeaux, before which
the case was being tried, handed down its decision by a decree of April 4, 1647. An appeal was
made to the King's Council. The Canons, however, fearing they might lose their case, suggested
a settlement to Jacques Desclaux, to be arbitrated by the Bishops of Aire and Bazas. The two
Bishops announced their decision on July 13, 1647, and the arrangement was ratified by the
drawing up of new statutes. (Cf. Antoine Degert, *Histoire des évêques de Dax* [Paris: Poussielgue,
1903], p. 328; and Pierre Coste, "Histoire des Cathédráles de Dax," in *Bulletin de la Société de
Borda* [1908], p. 275.)

[2]Jean-Henri-Gabriel de Baylens, Marquis de Poyanne, Commander of the King's Orders,
Governor of Dax, Saint-Sever, and Navarrenx; Lieutenant-General of the King in Béarn and
Navarre. He died in Saint-Sever on February 3, 1667, leaving behind him the reputation of a
brave leader.

[3]Isaac Bartet. He became Cabinet Secretary, Counselor to the King, and Agent for Poland in
France. On November 25, 1669, Mademoiselle de Montpensier sold to him the marquisate de
Mézières-en-Brenne (Indre), which he resold on March 17, 1692 to Louis de Rochechouart, Duc
de Mortemart. He died in September 1707.

of Prince Casimir, Cardinal of Poland,[4] is asking most insistently for it. They hold the views of the person who can do everything in this matter.[5]

The ardent desire you manifest to me in most of your letters, Excellency, to have a mission established in your diocese, has made me reflect more seriously on this since receiving your last letter during my retreat, which I am still making. It leads me to propose to you whether a simple little priory we have, two leagues from Orléans, might be useful for this purpose, provided the Pastor of Poy[6] or someone else from there would be willing to exchange posts and come to some arrangement. It consists of a farm, where there are two farmers, each having two plows for tilling about four hundred [arpents][7] of land, in one piece all around.

The service you can draw from this will be missions from All Saints' Day to Easter, in whatever parishes in the diocese you, Excellency, will send them, [and] the ordinands. If you, Excellency, give orders that no one will be admitted to Holy Orders without spending at least six months in your seminary, in fifteen years you will have the consolation of seeing that the face of your clergy has changed, if O[ur] L[ord] is pleased to give His blessing to His work and its consequences, and not consider the weakness of the workers. The Bishop of Cahors[8] does this and it costs him nothing. Each seminarian pays his room and board according to the amount

---

[4]Few princes experienced as many vicissitudes of fortune as did Cardinal Jan-Casimir. Born in 1609, he went to France in his youth and was thrown into prison by Richelieu. He became a Jesuit, received the Cardinal's hat, and ascended the throne of Poland on the untimely death of his brother, Ladislaus IV. Obtaining a dispensation from his vows, he married his brother's widow, Louise-Marie, and ruled Poland under the title of Jan-Casimir V. His reign was unfortunate. Poland, attacked in turn by the Cossacks, Sweden, Brandenburg, Russia, and Transylvania, and torn assunder by internal dissensions, was forced to surrender a large part of its territory to its enemies. Jan-Casimir lost his wife in 1667; he abdicated and withdrew to Flanders. From there he went to Saint-Germain-des-Prés Abbey and afterward to Saint-Martin Abbey in Nevers. He died in that city in 1672.

[5]Jules Cardinal Mazarin.

[6]Pierre de Larroque (1634-1655). The pastors of Poy, or Pouy, were also Directors of the Buglose chapel.

[7]This word was left out of the original. An arpent is about one and a half acres.

[8]Alain de Solminihac.

prescribed by the Bishop; they pay only one hundred livres or forty écus a year. Moreover, there is no province in France where people can live more cheaply than in that place, where all the food must be consumed right there; there is no transport at all. What might be costly are the buildings and furnishings, if there are not enough in Burglosse[9] or wherever you, Excellency, establish them. As for the maintenance of the Missionaries, it seems to me that it will amount only to sixteen or eighteen hundred livres. I have been told that the parish of Poy is worth one thousand livres. Perhaps the Masses which will be said in Burglosse could make up the difference.[10]

These, Excellency, are my humble thoughts on the subject; I propose them to you at random because you do me the honor of instructing me to reflect on the matter.

I just remembered that M. Sanguinet, the Pastor near Tartas,[11] told me he had some thought of coming to live in Paris; it seems to me it was someone from there who told me that. If the value of the parish is similar to that of Poy and is part of your diocese, perhaps he would be glad to discuss the matter. I say this to you haphazardly, Excellency, and I also say that you have no one on earth to whom God has given greater esteem and affection for you than I, who am, in His love. . . .

---

[9]Burglosse or Buglose was, and still is, part of the old commune of Pouy, which has been renamed Saint-Vincent-de-Paul. In the Saint's childhood, as all local historians agree, there was neither a chapel at Buglose, nor any pilgrimage there. Jean-Jacques du Sault, Bishop of Dax, moved by the rumors of miracles worked in that place, held an inquiry and had a small chapel built in honor of the Blessed Virgin. He solemnly blessed it on May 16, 1622, and in the course of time it became a center of devotion to Our Lady in this district. On a passing visit to his native place two or three months after this unforgettable event, Saint Vincent went to pray before Our Lady of the Landes and said Mass in her chapel. (Cf. Collet, *op. cit.,* vol. I, p. 109.) The history of Our Lady of Buglose (*Histoire de la sainte chapelle et des miracles de Notre-Dame de Buglose* [Bordeaux: Boudé, 1726]) was written by Raymond de Mauriol, C.M.; later, by Abbé Pierre Danos (*Le pèlerinage de Saint-Vincent-de-Paul et de Notre-Dame de Buglose, suivi de l'art de sanctifier le pèlerinage* [Buglose, 1844]); and by Canon Labarrère (*Histoire de Notre-Dame de Buglose et Souvenir du Berceau de Saint-Vincent-de-Paul* [Paris: Frayet de Surcy, 1857]). A clear, correct idea of the origin of this pilgrimage is given in Abbé Jean-Baptiste Gabarra's article, "Pontonx-sur-l'Adour et la prieuré de S. Caprais" in *Revue catholique d'Aire et de Dax* [1874], Abbé Degert (*op. cit.,* pp. 313ff), and in Jules Bonhomme's, "L'origine de Buglose" in *Revue de Gascogne* [1882], vol. XXIII, pp. 373-383.

[10]The Priests of the Mission were not established in Buglose until 1706.

[11]Joseph Sanguinet, Pastor of Saint-Yaguen near Tartas, in the Dax diocese, Saint-Sever district.

993. - TO ANTOINE PORTAIL, IN ROME

October 4, 1647

We are coming out of retreat. There were eighteen of us in one group and thirty-two in another. We have just renewed our vows, and because a few men said they are null, and found some difficulty in renewing them (M. . .and a cleric were the principal ones), I did not allow the latter to renew them. Monsieur. . .came to find me to tell me that all his difficulties had vanished after a little conference I gave all of them last evening. This morning he asked me sincerely for permission to renew them and, in fact, brought me a number of things he had been keeping, to divest himself of them. However, I let him keep them and gave him permission to renew his vows with the others.

The little exhortation I gave had two points: first, the reasons we have for making this renewal, so that God might be pleased to grant us the grace which accompanies the vows; second, the means, about which I said two things: first, that I begged those who did not feel resolved to persevere in them to leave; and second, that a sign of having this grace was to be determined never to speak contrary to this holy action, and to defend it against those who disapprove of it on occasion, because there is no doubt that some will do whatever they can to attack these vows within [the Company] and outside it.

I think God has blessed this talk. I have never seen greater sentiments of devotion apparent in everyone, except my miserable self, the greatest sinner in the world. So, if the question is attacked, it will be because the granting of a dispensation is reserved to the Pope. Nevertheless, the Doctors here tell us it can be done, and that each man can renounce his right to have recourse to the Ordinary, and apply to His Holiness for a dispensation. It is primarily the prerogative of the Pope to dispense one from the vows, and privately with regard to vows of chastity and the pilgrimage to Rome.

Letter 993. - Reg. 2, p. 6, copy made from the original autograph letter.

Never, better than today, have I seen the importance of the vows. Bishop Ingoli[1] can be a great help to us in getting the approbation, as he did for our Bull and for our house in Rome. I ask M. Dehorgny, M. Alméras, and you, Monsieur, to make him understand clearly that we have been anxious concerning the consolidation of our Institute, about which he is rather well informed. The prelates do not want us to be religious, and the religious advise us to the contrary, based on human instability and the heavy labors of our state; God in His Providence has finally inspired the Company with this holy, ingenious means of placing us in a state in which we have the happiness of the religious state through simple vows, and of remaining, nevertheless, among the clergy and obeying the prelates, with regard to our works, as the lowliest priests in their diocese. I shall try to send you today or Friday the opinion of the Doctors, the Penitentiary,[2] and Messieurs Duval,[3] Péreyret,[4] Cornet,[5] and Coqueret.[6] I am confident that, if this holy Prelate is well instructed,

---

[1] Secretary of Propaganda Fide.

[2] Jacques Charton.

[3] André Duval, renowned Doctor of the Sorbonne, author of several learned works, friend and adviser of Saint Vincent, was born in Pontoise on January 15, 1564, and died in Paris on September 9, 1638. The Saint never made an important decision without having recourse to his wisdom. He asked his advice before accepting Saint-Lazare (cf. Abelly, *op. cit.*, bk. I, chap. XXII, p. 97) and before establishing vows in the Congregation, as this letter shows. The humble Doctor got upset one day, when he saw his portrait in one of the rooms at Saint-Lazare. He insisted so much that Saint Vincent had to remove it. (Cf. Robert Duval, *Vie d'André Duval, docteur de Sorbonne*, manuscript copy [Robert Duval was the nephew of André Duval]; J. Calvet, "Un confesseur de Saint Vincent," in *Petites Annales de Saint Vincent*, May 1903, p. 135.)

[4] Jacques Péreyret, born in 1580 in Billom (Puy-de-Dôme), first served as Canon Theologian in Mende. He was a brilliant professor of philosophy and theology at the Collège de Navarre and was raised to the dignity of Grand Master. He was sent to Clermont as Vicar-General and, until the day of his death on July 15, 1658, strove actively to reform abuses there. In 1650 he wrote a Latin treatise on grace against the Jansenists (*Apparatus ad tractatum de gratia*).

[5] Nicolas Cornet, born in Amiens on October 12, 1592, was also Grand Master of the house and society of Navarre. He refused the archbishopric of Bourges and the honor of being Richelieu's confessor. He died at the Collège de Boncourt on April 18, 1663. Bossuet preached his funeral oration, and his biography has been published. For his obituary see Joseph Grandet, *Les saints prêtres français du XVIIe siècle*, ed., G. Letourneau [2 vols., Angers: Germain et G. Grassin, 1897], vol. I, pp. 82-88.

[6] Jean Coqueret, Doctor of the Collège de Navarre, was head of the Collège des Grassins and Superior of the Discalced Carmelites of France. He was a friend of Saint Francis de Sales, André Duval, and Saint Vincent with whom he had given a mission in Villepreux in 1618. Born in Pontoise in 1592, he died in Marseilles on October 7, 1655. Saint Vincent consulted him before

he alone can inform His Holiness and the Congregation of Regulars, and take care of our business; for who could reasonably attack something that is not contrary to the Councils, the Canons, or papal decrees, but is, rather, in conformity with the Church's custom before solemn vows in the days when people made simple ones, which were, consequently, subject to dispensation?

If someone says that those vows were considered religious, a good reply is that, although, at the time, those vows constituted the religious state, they cannot do so now because the Church forbids the institution of new religious Orders, unless they profess one of the four Rules approved by the Church, which include solemn vows; or unless the Pope authorizes it, such as in the case of the Jesuits.[7] Now, we do not adopt any of those four Rules of religious Orders, and the Holy Father has not erected us in the religious state, but rather as secular priests. It follows that we do not belong to the religious state, since we declare that, even though we make those simple vows, we do not intend to be religious, but to remain always in the ranks of the clergy.

If the objection is raised that the vows alone, by their very nature, establish a person in the religious state, I reply that this is true of solemn vows but not of simple vows, because a private individual, even several of them, can make the three simple vows privately without being on that account a religious. So, if private individuals may do this, why not a Company?

In the name of God, Monsieur, ponder this truth and have others ponder it. Pray to God for this affair and lose no time about it. If Bishop Ingoli approves and undertakes it, I have perfect confidence that he will see it through.

---

introducing vows into the Company, as mentioned here, and invited him to the conferences on Jansenism given at Saint-Lazare.

[7]The interdiction against founding a Religious Order of any kind without authorization from the Holy See, handed down by the thirteenth and fourteenth Ecumenical Councils [Fourth Lateran (1215) and Second Lyons (1274)], is not accompanied by any restriction. Nevertheless, many canonists agree with Arthur Vermeersch that this rule did not apply to Institutes which embraced the Rules of Saint Basil, Saint Augustine, Saint Benedict, or Saint Francis. (Cf. *De religiosis institutis et personis* [2 vols., Bruges, 1902], vol. I, p. 45.) Dominique Bouix was not of this opinion. (Cf. *Tractatus de jure Regularium* [2 vols., Paris: Lecoffre, 1857], vol. I, p. 205.)

994. - *CARDINAL MAZARIN TO SAINT VINCENT*

October 10, 1647

Monsieur,

I saw the letter you wrote to de Lionne [1] regarding the promotion of the Abbot of Chailli to the episcopate.[2] As the difficulty you find with this consists in a question of fact, about which I made a careful inquiry, I discovered that the situation of which you were informed never existed, and am assured of this every day by persons worthy of credence. For your part, I ask you, please, to lose no time in taking the steps you think necessary to satisfy your own mind, so that you may be fully enlightened. Write me what you will have learned, since, for a number of important reasons which I shall tell you as soon as I see you, Her Majesty wants to put an end to this business without further delay.[3]

In the meantime, I remain. . . .

995. - TO GUILLAUME DELVILLE, IN COULOMMIERS

Paris, October 11, 1647

Monsieur,

The grace of Our Lord be with you forever!

We are sending you six or seven priests, five from the Company

---

Letter 994. - Mazarin Library, Ms. 2216, f°404, copy.

[1]Hugues de Lionne, a confidant of Mazarin, whom he had met in Rome. After being secretary of the Orders of the Queen Regent, he became Grand Master of Ceremonies and Commander of the King's Orders. He was sent to Italy (1654-1656), where he participated in the election of Pope Alexander VII, and to Germany as extraordinary Ambassador (1658). He negotiated the preliminaries for the Treaty of the Pyrenees for peace between France and Spain (1659), and was appointed Minister of State. He continued to hold this position after Mazarin's death, and died in Paris on September 1, 1671, at sixty years of age.

[2]Charles-Louis de Lorraine had been proposed for the bishopric of Condom. He was Abbot of Chailli, a renowned Cistercian abbey in the Senlis diocese, and died in Paris on June 1, 1668.

[3]Saint Vincent stood fast. The Condom diocese was given to Jean d'Estrades, Bishop of Périgueux who, in 1658, when the Saint was no longer on the Council of Conscience, gave his bishopric to Charles-Louis de Lorraine in exchange for Chailli Abbey.

Letter 995. - Collection for the process of beatification.

and the other two from the Bons-Enfants Seminary. Of the five, two are from Montmirail, and one of the remaining three is Monsieur Watebled,[1] of whose goodness you are aware. He will be able to see to the observance of regularity under you, since you do not lack other occupations. It is important for the Rules to be observed well because several of these men are destined for other houses, where it is important that they bring with them what is being done in the missions. For this purpose, it will be well for you to have read immediately at table the Rules that should be read at the beginning of missions. The Theologian[2] is capable of doing that; he has done it other times. However, you must ask him not to tie himself down to the time of retiring or to other duties.

You informed me that the Theologian will preach only three times a week and that you have to do the rest for the evening and the morning sermon. That seems difficult to me. I hope to send you M. Tholard in three or four days; he could relieve you and take the mornings. God has given him the grace to dispose people for receiving the mercies He showers on missions that are well made, which is equivalent to saying missions where regularity is observed. He will not be hearing confessions;[3] he can be helpful with reconciliations. If his cold allows it and God blesses a bloodletting he had today, he will be able to leave in three days.

You told me that Madame de Longueville[4] wants to pay the expenses. *O mon Dieu!* Monsieur, are we to begin in Monsieur Delville's time and mine, and through Monsieur Delville, the dissipation and destruction of the spirit of the Mission! *O Jésus!* God

[1]Pierre Watebled, born in Tully (Somme) in 1622, entered the Congregation of the Mission on January 19, 1641 at nineteen years of age, and took his vows on June 14, 1643. He was Superior of the Saintes Seminary (1650-1651), and died a victim of his dedication in Villeneuve-Saint-Georges (Val-de-Marne) in October 1652.

[2]Antoine Caignet, Doctor in Theology; Canon, Chancellor, Theologian and Vicar-General of Meaux, and a renowned preacher, died in 1669. He is the author of two reputable works: *L'Année pastorale* (7 vols., Paris, 1657) and *Le Dominical des Pasteurs ou le Triple emploi des curés* (2nd ed., Paris, 1675).

[3]For the reason indicated in vol. II, no. 424. Tholard was suffering from a serious case of scruples.

[4]Anne-Geneviève de Bourbon, Duchesse de Longueville.

forbid that you should be the instrument of such a misfortune! We are no less obliged to give our missions gratis than the Capuchins are obliged to live on alms. *Eh! bon Dieu!* what would people say of a Capuchin who would draw a salary, and what do they not have the right to say of Missionaries who would allow their expenses to be defrayed by certain people during the mission, and to have Monsieur Delville allow this, and in my time! *O Jésus! absit hoc a nobis!* [5]

Enclosed are twenty écus which I said were to be given to you after travel expenses were deducted. You will provide what is needed. This is to give you time to send for what will be needed for the total expenses. That is your department. If anyone prevents you from doing this, leave, Monsieur, after asking permission of the Bishop of Meaux. [6] Change your residence and find one where you are free to take care of your own expenses. You should know, Monsieur, that I found myself in a similar situation, and I said quite frankly to the lady who had provided the mission that, if she did not allow us to be united, we would return home that very day. In fact, we would have done so, if that good lady had not told us that she consented to our doing what we would like. She was very edified by all that, and I can assure you of the same thing in the case of Madame de Longueville. Furthermore, she and everyone who hears about it will be edified by your fidelity to the observance of our Rules; but you would disedify everyone, if you went so far as to allow yourself to be tempted by the effect of her kindness.

In the name of God, Monsieur, act as I am telling you, now and always. If you do not have what you need, let me know; we will provide it. I say this to you with great sorrow at seeing this misfortune befalling our Company in my time and through M. Delville,

---

[5] *Let us be firmly opposed to this!*
[6] Dominique Séguier, Bishop of Meaux.

whom I cherish a million times more than myself. I am, in the love of Our Lord, Monsieur, your most humble and obedient servant.

VINCENT DEPAUL
i.s.C.M.

Addressed: Monsieur Delville, Superior of the Priests of the Mission of Crécy, in Coulommiers

996. - TO JEAN CHRETIEN, SUPERIOR, IN MARSEILLES

[Between September and November 1647][1]

Informed by Jean Chrétien that Jean Le Vacher[2] was ill and in no condition to travel from Marseilles to Tunis, Vincent de Paul replies that the voyage must not be postponed.[3]

Letter 996. - Archives of the Mission, Paris, manuscript life of Jean Le Vacher, p.3.

[1]Jean Le Vacher's departure for Tunis necessitates this date.

[2]Jean Le Vacher, born in Ecouen (Val-d'Oise) on March 15, 1619, entered the Congregation of the Mission with his brother Philippe on October 5, 1643. He took his vows in 1646 and was ordained a priest in 1647. Julien Guérin, a Missionary in Tunis, needed assistance, and Saint Vincent sent him Jean Le Vacher. On August 23, 1647, as the Founder and his young disciple were leaving Saint-Lazare together, they met Nicolò di Bagno, the Nuncio. "Excellency," said the Saint, "you are just in time to give your blessing to this good priest who is leaving for the Tunis mission." "What! this child!" exclaimed the astonished Nuncio. "Excellency," replied the Saint, "he has the vocation for that."

Jean Le Vacher arrived in Tunis on November 22, 1647. Julien Guérin's death on May 13, 1648, followed two months later by that of the Consul, Martin de Lange, placed on Le Vacher the double burden of head of the Mission and of Consul. In 1650 he added Vicar Apostolic to these titles. Since the Holy See would not allow priests to be in charge of the consulate, Saint Vincent sent a layman, Martin Husson, a parlementary lawyer, who arrived in Tunis in 1653 and left in April 1657, expelled by the Bey. For two more years Le Vacher carried out the functions of Consul. He returned to France in 1666, and was sent to Algiers in 1668 as Vicar-General of Carthage and Vicar Apostolic of Algiers and Tunis. His life in Algiers was that of an apostle and his death that of a martyr. On July 16, 1683, the town of Algiers was being bombarded by Duquesne. The Turks, having used every device to make Le Vacher apostatize, tied him to the mouth of a cannon, which shot his body into the sea. (Cf. Raymond Gleizes, *Jean Le Vacher, vicaire apostolique et consul de France à Tunis et à Alger* [Paris: Gabalda, 1914].)

[3]According to Jean Le Vacher's first biographer, the substance of the Saint's reply was as follows: "If M. Le Vacher is too weak to go as far as the ship, have him carried there! If during the crossing he cannot stand the sea air, then throw him into the sea!" This way of speaking is so strange coming from the Saint's pen that we are inclined to wonder if his thought was correctly expressed.

997. - TO JEAN LE VACHER, IN MARSEILLES

[Between September and November 1647][1]

Vincent de Paul urges Jean Le Vacher to take the precautions his state of health requires and to set sail without fear.

998. - *SAINT LOUISE TO SAINT VINCENT*

October 19, [1647] [1]

Monsieur,

I was very annoyed that someone had gone to see you without my knowledge, to tell you that, by the grace of God, my health was no worse than when your charity left me, and continues to improve. For that reason I went to Mass on the feast of Saint Luke.

Mesdames de Herse,[2] Traversay,[3] de Saint-Mandé,[4] and Viole met again yesterday here in this house without my knowing why, nor that they were going to do this, until about an hour beforehand. I think it was to rejoice

---

Letter 997. - Manuscript life of Jean Le Vacher, p. 3.

[1]This letter is from the same date as the preceding one.

Letter 998. - Archives of the Motherhouse of the Daughters of Charity, original autograph letter.

[1]Year added on the back of the original by Brother Ducournau.

[2]Madame de Herse, née Charlotte de Ligny, was the daughter of Jean de Ligny, Seigneur de Ranticey, Master of Requests. She was the widow of Michel Vialart, Seigneur de la Forest de Herse, Counselor to the King in his Parlement Court, President of Requests of the palace, then Ambassador to Switzerland. He died in Solothurn, on October 26, 1634. Madame de Herse was also the mother of Félix Vialart, Bishop of Châlons, as well as a relative of Jean-Jacques Olier. She was dear to Saint Francis de Sales, who was her son's godfather. As a Lady of Charity, she became one of Saint Vincent's chief auxiliaries and was a great benefactress of the poor of Paris, Picardy, and Champagne. She generously supported the works for ordinands and for abandoned children, and established the Daughters of Charity in Chars (Val-d'Oise). During the wars that ravaged the capital, the Queen Mother entrusted to Madame de Herse and some other Ladies the distribution of her personal alms. Madame de Herse died in 1662.

[3]Anne Petau, widow of René Regnault, Seigneur de Traversay and Counselor in the Paris Parlement. She was the sister of President Méliand, and one of the Ladies of Charity most devoted to Saint Vincent and his works. She founded the Monastery of the Conception, rue Saint-Honoré, and was responsible for the Daughters of the Cross after the death of their Foundress, Madame de Villeneuve.

[4]Marie de Fortia, wife of Jérôme de l'Arche, Seigneur de Saint-Mandé, Lieutenant-General for civil and criminal cases in the jurisdiction of the palace in Paris.

that Providence had made it apparent that the poor little children should be taken care of. Several small donations have come in, and the best aid is the five thousand livres they are supposed to receive today. I think this is part of the eight thousand because it is the collection officer of the Hôtel-Dieu who is supposed to get the receipt.

The Ladies anxiously await the conference your [charity] decided to give before your departure.

Their hearts have been completely renewed in light of this aid, and they are determined to have their work continue at Bicêtre. Madame Traversay and Mademoiselle Viole are supposed to go and spend the day there on Monday. They gave me the responsibility of applying to Monsieur Drouard for five hundred livres from one source and two hundred from another, by order of the Duchesse d'Aiguillon.

I hope your return will succeed in bringing a respite to the great needs of this work of Our Lord, in whose love I am, Monsieur, your most obedient daughter and very grateful servant.

LOUISE DE MARILLAC

Addressed: Monsieur Vincent, Superior General of the Priests of the Congregation of the Mission.

999. - *SAINT LOUISE TO SAINT VINCENT*

[October 1647] [1]

Monsieur,

A good lady, moved by Mademoiselle de Lamoignon and by the guidance of Divine Providence, sent us one hundred écus for those poor little children. Please thank her for us, Monsieur, and allow me to remind your charity about our Sister Jeanne Lepeintre.

If you think it appropriate, I beg you to leave us the three reports we sent you for the Ladies' meeting, lest they get mixed up during your absence.

I am still not feeling well and I thought that, in these frequent changes of ups and downs, God wants me to make use of them to reveal to your

Letter 999. - Archives of the Motherhouse of the Daughters of Charity, original autograph letter.
[1]Date added on the back of the original by Brother Ducournau.

charity the inconstancy of my passions. I am so conditioned by them that, whatever resolution I take, they give me no freedom to subject them to reason. I am better for a few days and immediately I get carried away.

If, in one of your books, your charity has a picture similar to the Lord of Charity,[2] *I most humbly entreat you to do me the kindness of giving me one. I apologize for taking this liberty. It is simply that I am not able to recover as I would like and am hoping this might be a great help to me, with the assistance also of your charity's prayers. I am, Most Honored Father, your most obedient servant and all-unworthy daughter.*

Please do me the favor of giving me our good God's blessing and your own at Holy Mass.

Addressed: Monsieur Vincent

1000. - *SAINT LOUISE TO SAINT VINCENT*

[November 1647][1]

Monsieur,

It seemed to me that God gave my soul great peace and simplicity at prayer, which I made very imperfectly on the necessity for the Company of Daughters of Charity always to be uninterruptedly under the guidance which Divine Providence has given them, both for spiritual and temporal matters. I think I have understood that it would be more favorable for His glory if the Company were to fail completely than to be under any other guidance, since that would seem contrary to God's Will. The indications of this are that there is reason to believe that, when God makes known His plans in the beginning, He inspires and makes known His Will for the perfection of the works His Goodness wishes to accomplish. You know, Monsieur, that in the early stages of this one it was suggested that, if it were to fail through misconduct, the temporal goods of the Company would

[2]Cf. vol. II, no. 421, n. 6. In the Motherhouse of the Daughters of Charity, there is a painting of Christ standing barefoot on a globe, with his hands extended in appeal. Above His head is the title: *DEUS CHARITAS EST.* Saint Vincent and Saint Louise had great reverence for this picture of "The Lord of Charity."

Letter 1000. - Archives of the Motherhouse of the Daughters of Charity, original autograph letter.
[1]Date added on the back of the original by Brother Ducournau.

revert to the Mission, to be used for the instruction of the country people.

I hope that, if your charity has understood from Our Lord what I think He has told you in the person of Saint Peter, namely, that He wanted to build this Company on you, it will persevere in the service you request of it for the instruction of children and the relief of the sick.

As for the parlor,[2] I have not made up my mind. However, with regard to the election of the Ladies, oh! I see it ever more necessary to have the one I mentioned to your charity. I am, Monsieur, your most obedient daughter and very grateful servant.

LOUISE DE MARILLAC

I most humbly beg your charity to give us a conference tomorrow, if possible, and kindly let us know about this.

Addressed: *Monsieur Vincent*

1001. - *ALAIN DE SOLMINIHAC TO SAINT VINCENT*

Mercuès, December 4, 1647

Monsieur,

I thank you with my whole heart for all the trouble you have taken to give us Monsieur de Sevin as Bishop of Sarlat. This work is of inexpressible merit. May God be your reward! Not having his address, I have put in your packet the reply to a letter he wrote me. I thought you would be kind enough to have it delivered to him.

Monsieur d'Estrades, appointed to the See of Condom, wrote me recently that you had put up strong resistance at the Council so that the Abbot, about whom I wrote you on his advice,[1] would not be named Bishop of Périgueux. I cannot conceive how they can possibly think of giving

---

[2]The plan of building a parlor was adopted at the Council of June 28, 1646. Saint Vincent earnestly requested that the parlor not have a grill, for fear that the Sisters might get the idea of becoming nuns (cf. Vol. II, no. 814).

Letter 1001. - Archives of the Diocese of Cahors, Alain de Solminihac collection, copy made from the original.

[1]The nephew of Antoine de Cous, Bishop of Condom. (Cf. no. 980.)

bishoprics to persons like that, and such an important diocese as Périgueux. Its present situation is well known, since it has been stated so often, as has the need of placing an apostolic man there. I beg you to use your influence in this and never grow weary of doing so on behalf of such a holy work.

Mother de Laroque, who was elected Prioress of the Pouget Monastery by the nuns of that house, is fulfilling her duty well. I told one of her brothers-in-law, whom she had sent to visit me on her behalf, that the King's patent was needed, according to what you had written me. They will send someone, or give instructions to someone in Paris, to ask for it. The person who has this responsibility will go to you to find out what steps he must take to get it.

I am always, Monsieur, etc.

ALAIN,
Bishop of Cahors

1002. - TO ETIENNE BLATIRON, SUPERIOR, IN GENOA

December 13, 1647

I thank God that your health has improved in the midst of so much work. You are frail and weak and constantly engaged in hard work; nevertheless, His Divine Goodness is pleased to preserve you. This is not without good reason and causes me to think that in this you are almost like Mademoiselle Le Gras, whom I consider as dead, according to nature, for ten years now. To see her, one would say she has just stepped out of the tomb because her body is so frail and her face so pale. However, God knows the strength of spirit she possesses. Not so long ago she made a journey of one hundred leagues.[1] Were it not for her frequent illnesses and her respect for obedience, she would often be going in every direction to visit her Daughters and work with them, although the only life she has is the one she receives from grace. That same grace

---

Letter 1002. - Reg. 2, p. 218.
[1]To accompany the Daughters of Charity assigned to the Nantes hospital.

strengthens you also, Monsieur, in order to sanctify you, and sanctifies you so that you might encourage others in the ways of salvation.

I very much approve the little assistance you and M. Martin offer one another in the daily sermons and catechism lessons you and he give. O Divine Goodness, unite in this way all hearts in the Little Company of the Mission, then order whatever You please. Labor will be sweet to them and every task easy; the strong person will relieve the weak one, and the weak will cherish the strong and obtain increased strength for him from God. And so, Lord, Your work will be done as You would like, for the building up of Your Church, and Your workers will multiply, attracted by the perfume of such charity.

1003. - ETIENNE BLATIRON, SUPERIOR IN GENOA, TO SAINT VINCENT

December 16, 1647

The mission in . . . was a great success. Seven bandits were converted, and a Turk working for a gentleman asked for Baptism, which was given him, after a suitable preparation.

1004. - TO ANTOINE PORTAIL, IN GENOA

December 20, 1647

What shall we say about the Marseilles house? It really needs your help, so please go there as soon as possible. You will find a lack of workers and, as you know, of a good Superior,[1] especially now that they are planning to open a seminary there, which will

---

Letter 1003. - Abelly, *op.cit.*, bk. II, chap. I, sect. IV, p. 70.

Letter 1004. - Reg. 2, p. 102.
[1]The Superior was Jean Chrétien.

undoubtedly be very useful. But how can these needs be remedied? We are certainly going to send two or three persons there after the ordinations. Our Brother Get,[2] who presents the morning conference to the ordinands with great clarity, giving many indications of his ability, will be one of them, and, I hope, will be in charge of the seminary. However, it is impossible for us to send a capable superior there now. We had thought of M. [Cuissot],[3] who is careful about external affairs but has little unction for internal ones, although he is totally given to God; but, lo and behold, the Bishop of Cahors has taken him away from us, since he was unable to appreciate M. [Testacy], who is now in Saintes. M. du Chesne would be quite suitable if he were here, because the diversity of the works of that house requires an active person. However, we have not had a letter from him for six months,[4] which really worries us. On the other hand, Providence is depriving us of the means of leaving M. Dehorgny there for a time, as we had planned, and is, in fact, obliging us to keep M. [Chrétien] there for now.[5]

This being the case, I beg you to deal tactfully with him and to consider two things: first, that there is someone with him who, through antipathy, makes his faults seem greater than perhaps they are; the other thing is that it is difficult to master one's feelings and be exact in everything in the midst of many affairs. Please bear this in mind and treat him as gently as possible, so as not to discourage him. If, nevertheless, you judge that M. . . . is more likely to succeed better as Superior than the other man, you can give him a try.

It would be well for you to be very circumspect with the

---

[2]Firmin Get, born in Chépy (Somme) on January 19, 1621, entered the Congregation of the Mission on January 6, 1641 and took his vows in January 1643. He was placed in the Marseilles house in 1648; in 1654 he became Superior there, remaining in office until 1662, except for a very short time spent in Montpellier to open a seminary, which lasted only a few months (1659-1660). Later he became Superior in Sedan (1663-1666, 1673-1681), and in Le Mans (1670-1673), and Visitor of the Province of Poitou, an office he held until April 4, 1682.

[3]Gilbert Cuissot.

[4]Not long after, Saint Vincent heard from Pierre du Chesne, who had been sick in Ireland.

[5]He remained in authority until 1653.

Administrators regarding the hospital, and, above all, in everything that concerns the Bishop of Marseilles.[6] Our Lord will inspire you in all else and will give you a share in His Spirit. I hope for this all the more, since this visitation is more important than the preceding ones, and this house is the most difficult one we have because of the extraordinary diversity of its works: the hospital, missions on the galleys, rural missions, chaplaincies, the seminary, Barbary affairs, letters to be sent and received, and other engagements.

1005. - TO NICOLAS PAVILLON, BISHOP OF ALET

Paris, January [3][1] 1648

Excellency,

At the beginning of this year, please accept my renewal of the offer of my perpetual obedience to you. Prostrate at your feet, Excellency, I ask your blessing, that God may be pleased to have mercy on my soul, now that its separation from this wretched body is near. I do so, Excellency, with all the humility and confidence a poor priest could have with regard to one of the worthiest Prelates he knows in this world.

More and more, Excellency, I hear about the blessing God is giving to your leadership, so completely apostolic and diffusing everywhere such sweet perfume that my poor heart cannot contain the joy it experiences from this. I ask Our Lord to continue to be glorified by it.

I have been requested by M. de Benjamin, son of the late M. de Benjamin who was a member of the Royal Academy, to speak to

---

[6]Etienne du Puget (1644-1668).

Letter 1005. - Jules Gossin, *Saint Vincent de Paul peint par ses écrits* (Paris: J. J. Blaise, 1834), p. 453, from the original letter, made available by the Marquise de Périer.
[1]The Gossin text has "31." This date is obviously erroneous because the reply is dated January 29. (Cf. no. 1011 for Pavillon's refusal of the Saint's request.)

you about him and to beg you, as I now do, Excellency, to admit him for a time near your sacred person. He is a seminarian, a deacon around twenty-eight or thirty years of age. He is devout and learned, has a good spirit, and seeks only to perfect himself in his calling. He gives proof of this especially in the choice he makes of such a fine school.[2] I mention this to you, Excellency, only on condition that you can do it without inconveniencing yourself. He will in no way be a burden to you with regard to expenses because he has an income of five or six thousand livres from his patrimony. Please do me the favor, Excellency, of informing me of your wishes and of honoring me with your orders. You know they will be very dear to me and that I am, in life and in death, in the love of Our Lord and of His glorious Mother, Excellency, your most humble and very obedient servant.

VINCENT DEPAUL
i.s.C.M.

1006. - SAINT LOUISE TO SAINT VINCENT

[Between 1644 and 1649] [1]

Remember to warn the Ladies to be careful in their instructions not to talk too much to the seriously ill, even if the latter have not made a general confession, but simply to advise them to confess the sins they might formerly have forgotten or held back, if they recall any, with the intention of confessing all those they have committed against God and the neighbor.

---

[2]M. de Benjamin became Vicar-General of Paris and succeeded M. Féret as Pastor of Saint Nicolas-du-Chardonnet.

Letter 1006. - Archives of the Motherhouse of the Daughters of Charity, original autograph letter. In this letter Saint Louise suggests to Saint Vincent the advice it would be well to give the Ladies of Charity at the next day's meeting.

[1]The seal on the wax that secured this letter is not to be found on any letters before 1644. Saint Louise's use of the expression "Monsieur" in addressing Saint Vincent indicates that it should be placed before 1650. *Ecrits spirituels* has assigned "around 1647" to this letter (cf. L. 196bis. p. 232).

If possible, they should have them make acts of faith, hope, and charity necessary for salvation, and spend a long time disposing those who are getting better to resolve to live as good Christians, showing them how they should go about it.

This, Monsieur, is the advice of the nun they call "Mother of the Sacraments," [2] *which was given to Mademoiselle de Villenant. However, I just received this letter from Mademoiselle de Lamoignon, who says that Mademoiselle de Saint-Mandé suggests that nothing be said about this at the general meeting.*

Will your charity please remember, Monsieur, to point out how good it is, after one's death as well as during one's life, to assist in the continuation of a good work that has begun, when it is undertaken for the love of God, like that of the Foundlings. Also, those who do good by means of their bequests have the same merit as those who have done so during their lifetime, when this is done in perfect charity, since they had the intention of doing it, had they been able, provided they are sincere in this. I think this could be useful, pointing out the danger of everything of coming to a standstill.

Will your charity also please tell me the address of the President's wife, Madame du Sault, [3] *so I can send her a note informing her about tomorrow's meeting. Please do not forget it yourself.*

The Ladies are really remiss about being at the collation, but a few of them deserve to be praised for being so conscientious about being there.

Pardon, Monsieur, your very humble daughter and servant.

L. DE MARILLAC

Addressed: *Monsieur Vincent*

---

[2] The Augustinian nun of the Hôtel-Dieu whose duty it was to notify the chaplain when a patient requested the Sacraments.

[3] A Lady of Charity of the Hôtel-Dieu.

1007. - *SAINT LOUISE TO SAINT VINCENT*

Wednesday morning [January 15, 1648] [1]

Monsieur,

We arrived at Bicêtre in good health, thank God, but are not doing much. I most humbly beg your charity to send us tomorrow the Brother baker to whom I spoke, so he can teach us and help get a good oven prepared and find us someone who is skilled at this.

We really should also start selling the wine. There is quite a big market for it in barrels and large bottles in this neighborhood because of the soldiers. If we wait any longer, it is to be feared that sales will not go so well. [2] *Sister Geneviève* [3] *says that she thinks those Ladies want to wait so they can get some cheaper wine to mix in with it.*

I do not think this would be good business because a boy would be needed for it, and he might make off with all the profits. In addition, it would be a great burden for our Sisters, who would have to be on the watch that no one does any cheating, which would be hard to avoid.

I most humbly entreat your charity to remember that you promised us a conference for a week from today. [4]

Yesterday I saw Monsieur Vacherot's sister who is quite seriously ill. She asked me to recommend her to your holy prayers and told me that, if she dared, she would beg you to do her the charity of kindly going to see her. If she gets any worse, I would certainly entreat you to do so. I am asking Sister Julienne [5] *to keep you informed about this, if you think fit.*

Letter 1007. - Archives of the Motherhouse of the Daughters of Charity, original autograph letter.
[1]Date added on the back of the original by Brother Ducournau.
[2]The innkeepers of Paris did not look favorably on this venture. They vented their anger on the Sisters, insulting and maltreating them. The guilty parties, handed over to justice, escaped punishment only through the intervention of Saint Vincent. (Cf. Testimony of Sister Geneviève Doinel, seventeenth witness at the cause of beatification of Saint Vincent.)
[3]Geneviève Poisson.
[4]Saint Vincent gave this conference on January 22. (Cf. vol. IX, no. 34.)
[5]Julienne Loret was born in Paris on October 7, 1622 and baptized the same day. Orphaned at an early age, she was taken in by the parents of Jacques de la Fosse who later became a Priest of the Mission. "She had a tiny body which enclosed a great soul," it was said in a conference after her death. (Cf. *Recueil des principales circulaires des supérieurs généraux de la Mission*, [3 vols., Paris, 1877-1880], vol. II, p. 524.) She entered the Company of the Daughters of Charity on June 9, 1644 and made her vows on December 25, 1649. Her merit and virtue were so remarkable that, on October 30, 1647, scarcely three years after her own admission to the Community, she was entrusted with the formation of the new Sisters. At the same time, Saint

I think it would do our Sisters much good if you took the trouble to visit the Sisters at the house, to make Sister Hellot understand how beneficial it can be for the Company for the Sisters to accustom themselves to submit to one another, and for those who seem to have some influence to serve as an example.

The work of our poor Sisters in this house is almost unbelievable, not only because of its great difficulty but also because of their natural repugnance for this work. That is why it is most fitting to help them, to encourage them, and to make known what they are doing and that this is part of their work before God. They should also be assisted by prayer.

I, more than anyone else, need this, since I am the weakest in body and spirit, although I have the happiness of being, Monsieur, your most humble servant and very grateful daughter.

L. DE MARILLAC

Addressed: *Monsieur Vincent, Superior General of the Mission.*

1008. - TO SEVERAL PRIESTS[1]

Paris, January 17, 1648

Messieurs,

The grace of Our Lord be with you forever!

Louise took her as her Assistant. "It was she who directed the whole Community," Sister Mathurine Guérin would later say, "because Mademoiselle was in no state to assist at any exercise." (Cf. *Recueil*, vol. II, p. 530.) Julienne Loret also carried out the duties of secretary. In this capacity she was responsible for taking down Saint Vincent's talks, to which she listened pen in hand. In 1651, she was sent to Chars, a village some sixty miles from Paris, to settle a particularly delicate situation: the new pastor subscribed to Jansenist ideas and was attempting to impose these practices upon the Sisters. Returning to Paris in 1653, after two years of difficult trials, she received her appointment as Superior in Fontenay-aux-Roses (Hauts-de-Seine), where she remained until 1655. Recalled to the Motherhouse, she was again named Assistant, remaining in office under Mother Marguerite Chétif after the death of the Foundress and again under Mother Nicole Haran. She died in Fontainebleau on August 9, 1699. Her manuscript life, by Antoine Durand, C.M., is found at the Motherhouse of the Daughters of Charity.

Letter 1008. - Archives of the Daughters of Charity, Provincial House, Marseilles, original signed letter.
[1]Perhaps some Priests of the Most Blessed Sacrament, a Congregation founded by Christophe

Having heard of the pains you have taken during the mission on the galleys, and the large share you had in the blessings God was pleased to grant it, I could not refuse my heart the expression of gratitude I owe to your zeal. What a happiness, Messieurs, to imitate so closely Our Lord, who came into this world for the same ends for which you have given yourself to Him in your work, which is all the greater because of the extreme needs of these poor souls! Your crown will surely be great, and even greater if you acquire it through perseverance.

I ask Our Lord to animate you more and more with His Spirit and to give me opportunities to render you my services. I desire wholeheartedly to prove to you that I am, in the love of Our Lord, Messieurs, your most humble and obedient servant.

VINCENT DEPAUL
i.s.C.M.

1009. - SAINT LOUISE TO SAINT VINCENT

January 23 [1648] [1]

Monsieur,

Enclosed is the letter from Mademoiselle Poulaillon [2] attesting to the

---

d'Authier de Sisgau, Bishop of Bethlehem. This Congregation was established in 1632 and approved by Pope Innocent X in 1647. Its end was the work of missions and the direction of seminaries. Initially, the priests were called Missionaries of the Blessed Sacrament.

Letter 1009. - Archives of the Motherhouse of the Daughters of Charity, original autograph letter.

[1]The letter from Mademoiselle de Pollalion (Saint Vincent always wrote "Poulaillon"), after which Saint Louise wrote hers, is dated January 22, 1648.

[2]Marie de Lumague was the widow of François de Pollalion, a gentleman-in-ordinary of Louis XIII's household. She was among those devout widows whom Saint Vincent put to work in the apostolate. Born in Paris on November 29, 1599, married at the age of eighteen, and widowed shortly after, she made a vow of celibacy and placed herself under Saint Vincent's direction. Together with Saint Louise and other charitable Ladies, she visited the Charities, instructed little girls, and took alms to the poor. She especially wanted to gather together and reform delinquent girls; to this end she founded the Daughters of Providence. Saint Vincent

uprightness of that man who is applying for work at Bicêtre.[3] He says that, besides this, he knows how to bake bread well, do the gardening, plow, and drive a cart. All of this has to be done at that place, and is quite expensive when we have to hire someone by the day.

If your charity thinks it advisable, mention the impossibility of putting in a door in order to sell wine in the place where the President, Madame de Herse, had designated, because it would require steps at least two toises [4] wide, or nearly that.

Fifty-two children have died at Bicêtre since we have been there, and fifteen or sixteen others are not much better off. I hope they will not go so quickly, once everything is settled as those good Ladies wish.

Perhaps they will say that I have spoken of the need to have the Blessed Sacrament there, not only because of the necessity, but so that Our Lord may take possession of that house in the eyes of the people who, in a certain way, have an interest in the work. This leads me to take the liberty of telling you that it occurred to me that not only should the Ladies be advised of the day, but it should also be announced effectively at the homily in the parishes, so as to oblige people to do some good for it. When people see this magnificent place, which they think belongs to the little children, and that everyone in charge of it is of high social standing, most of them believe there is great wealth there. However, we have to borrow money in order to buy provisions, in addition to all the other necessities of which you are aware.

Would your charity please remember to ask for some girls for us? We have an urgent need of them, for the work at the house and elsewhere increases daily.

Do me always the honor of believing, Monsieur, that I am your most obedient servant and very grateful daughter.

LOUISE DE MARILLAC

Addressed: *Monsieur Vincent*

---

worked on the Rules of this Institute, procured funds and good directors for it, and obtained its approbation by the King and the Archbishop of Paris. Mademoiselle de Pollalion died on September 4, 1657. (Cf. Hyacinthe Collin, *Vie de la Vénérable Servante de Dieu Marie Lumague, veuve de M. Pollalion* [Paris: Cl. J. B. Hérissant fils, 1744]; Abbé L. Teillet, *Histoire de l'Union chrétienne de Fontenay-le-Comte* [Fontenay-le-Comte: L. P. Gouraud, 1898].)

[3]The original of this letter is in the Archives of the Motherhouse of the Daughters of Charity, Document 78, p. 79, and has been published in *La Compagnie des Filles de la Charité aux Origines*, ed. Sister Elisabeth Charpy, D.C., (Tours: Mame, 1989), D. 464, p. 507.

[4]An old French unit of measure equal to approximately two meters or six and a half feet.

1010. - TO THE DUCHESSE D'AIGUILLON

January 24, 1648

Only Our Lord Himself can make you understand the consolation I received from the blessing He bestowed on the Duc de
Richelieu's[1] armies, and the love with which I ask Him for the
preservation and infinite sanctification of your dear soul.

Enclosed are some letters from Marseilles. For many reasons,
it is very difficult for me to send M. Lambert there.[2] M. Codoing
is seriously ill and is perhaps now before God. He became ill at
Saint-Méen. We have here in this house a man with certain qualifications more suited for external affairs than M. Delattre; he is
Superior in La Rose—M. Delattre, I mean. It is true that M. Delattre is more spiritual and regular. We shall see about this after
M. Portail's visitation; he is supposed to send me the report on it
by the first mail.

In the letter I wrote him last night, I told him to leave for Annecy
as soon as he finished the visitation in Marseilles, but after rereading his letter, which I am sending you this morning, I thought it
advisable for him to remain until the business regarding the house
and the seminary is settled,[3] and I am now telling him to stay.

Letter 1010. - Reg. 1, f° 67, copy made from an autograph rough draft.

[1]Armand-Jean du Plessis, Duc de Richelieu, born on October 2, 1631, had succeeded his
father, François de Vignerod, brother of the Duchesse d'Aiguillon, as General of the galleys.
During the battle which Saint Vincent mentions here, the Duke was in command of about thirty
French ships, three Portuguese vessels, and four fire ships. He set fire to five Spanish ships that
had dropped anchor off Castellamare. As the main body of the fleet approached, he opened fire,
forcing it to retreat to Baia and Castel dell'Ovo and he sank three or four ships. This victory had
no follow-up because the food supply ran out, obliging the fleet to return to the French coast.
The Duc de Richelieu died May 10, 1715.

[2]Saint Vincent had been considering sending Lambert aux Couteaux to Marseilles as
Superior.

[3]The Marseilles Seminary opened in 1648. This was one of the reasons why Antoine Portail
stayed so long in that city looking for a suitable dwelling for the Missionaries, who were crowded
in a rented house near the arsenal. He bought a vast stretch of land for them, located today in
the center of town, between rue du Tapis-Vert, rue Thubaneau, boulevard Dugommier, and rue
Longue-des-Capucines. He had the buildings started but it took about ten years to complete the
construction. (Cf. Henri Simard, *Saint Vincent de Paul et ses oeuvres à Marseille* [Lyon: E.
Vitte, 1894], p. 95.)

The Princess[4] is supposed to be present at the meeting at exactly three o'clock today at Madame de Lamoignon's house. Will you be there, Madame? If so, we shall have the pleasure of discussing all these matters with you. You will find enclosed a letter from M. Barreau.

1011. - *NICOLAS PAVILLON TO SAINT VINCENT*

Alet, January 29, 1648 [1]

Dearest and most honored Father,

I cherish and respect all the more the letters that come to me from you, now that I know that they are drawn, as it were, from the press of your holy and very important occupations for the service of God and of the Church, which I hear are increasing day by day. So, when this happiness comes my way, I receive it as an effect of your paternal charity toward me and, consequently, feel obligated to thank you in a very particular way with all the humility, affection, and reverence in my power.

If the state of our poor, insignificant family and the situation of our various humble works would allow me to receive some priests to serve among us in them, other than those men we need for the administration of the diocese and the business pertaining to it, I would gladly welcome an opportunity such as you are pleased to propose to me and which, in my opinion, could only contribute to the general edification of all our servants and our clergy. However, for these same reasons, finding myself obliged in the past to make my excuses to several persons from the leading, most noteworthy families in this region, who had presented themselves for this very purpose, I think I should fear giving them some cause for dissatisfaction by bringing in persons from somewhere else and setting a precedent for similar circumstances in future. Consider for yourself, Monsieur, the grounds for this difficulty.

---

[4]Charlotte-Marguerite de Montmorency was the wife of Henri II de Bourbon, First Prince of the royal blood, Prince de Condé, Duc d'Enghien, Peer and Grand Master of France. This charitable Princess, mother of the Grand Condé, lost her husband on December 26, 1646; she herself died in Châtillon-sur-Loing on December 2, 1650.

Letter 1011. - Archives of the Mission, Paris, original autograph letter.
[1]This is the Bishop of Alet's reply to Saint Vincent's request in no. 1005.

In the meantime, dearest and most honored Father, I cannot hide from you that one of the greatest desires I might still have in this life would be to have the honor of seeing you again and to enjoy, for a short time at least, your holy and amiable conversation, which would doubtless be a particular consolation for me and most helpful spiritually. But if Divine Providence arranges things otherwise, as seems likely, I most humbly entreat [God] not to consider my extreme unworthiness and deprive me of this grace in eternity. By your holy prayers and sacrifices, dearest Father, you can obtain this mercy. I earnestly implore you to do so and to believe that I am, more than ever, dearest and most honored Father, in the love of our dear Savior and of His holy Mother, your most humble, obedient, and grateful servant and son.

NICOLAS,
unworthy B[ishop] of Alet

Addressed: *Monsieur Vincent, Superior General of the Priests of the Mission, at Saint-Lazare-lez-Paris*

1012. - A PRIEST OF THE MISSION TO SAINT VINCENT

1648

The people in the commune of Saché,[1] with six hundred regular communicants, followed the exercises of the mission in an edifying manner. Twelve hundred of the faithful were there for the general Communion, and there were numerous reconciliations, restitutions, and conversions. The Pastor, his curate, and five other priests made their general confession. One of the richest men in the area, whose heart had been closed to compassion up until then, had an announcement made during the sermon that three times a week he would distribute bread to the poor who would come to his door.

Letter 1012. - Abelly, *op.cit.,* bk. II, chap. I, sect. II, §8, p. 53.
[1]A commune in the district of Chinon (Indre-et-Loire).

1013. - *BALTHAZAR GRANGIER,[1] BISHOP OF TREGUIER, TO SAINT VINCENT*

Guingamp, 1648

Your letter found us all busy with our mission, from which I have great hopes. One of your priests preaches in the evening in an admirable and devout manner; another has the main catechism class at one o'clock in the afternoon, where he makes himself admired and loved by children and adults alike. Another teaches the children's catechism class, and my Canon Theologian preaches in the morning in the Breton dialect. In a word, everyone is working, and even I have not been allowed to remain idle, for I preach two days a week. Tomorrow we will all begin to hear confessions, God willing. The people of this region are quite astounded because they are not accustomed to missions. Each one expresses his opinion in a different way, but respectfully. I hope, with the grace of God, that all will go well.

1014. - TO A PRIEST OF THE MISSION

[1648][1]

We are about to go and bury the body of our good Monsieur du Chastel, who died yesterday at one o'clock in the afternoon, after edifying us for so long a time by his patience during such a painful illness as his. Please render him the assistance of the Holy Sacrifices and prayers of your Community.

Letter 1013. - Abelly, *op.cit.*, bk. II, chap. I, sect. II, §6, p. 44.

[1]Balthazar Grangier de Liverdi.

Letter 1014. - Lyons manuscript.

[1]The year Pierre du Chastel died. Born in Courcelles-le-Comte (Pas-de-Calais), he entered the Congregation of the Mission as a priest on October 9, 1641, at the age of twenty-five, and died at Saint-Lazare in 1648.

1015. - TO ANTOINE PORTAIL, IN MARSEILLES

Paris, February 7, 1648

Monsieur,

The grace of Our Lord be with you forever!

Mon Dieu! Monsieur, how consoled I have been by the conference you had on the shortcomings of the missions for the galleys! The good results are a sign that God has been pleased with this action. With all my heart I thank Him for it, and [I thank] you, Monsieur, for being present at the Administrators'[1] meeting. I have not been able to finish reading the articles they proposed to you; I shall look them over, God willing, together with the foundation of the Duchess. So that I might be able to tell you my thoughts on the obligations entailed in the latter, I ask you, before you draw up any regulations regarding the hospital, to send us a copy of the patent for the foundation, which will be very useful to us—I mean the foundation or declaration of the King regarding the hospital.[2] It is a good idea for you to explain to the Administrators that the Company has no general Visitor, but only one for each province.

I am not sorry that M. Tyrry is not going to Algiers, and would be pleased to know whether M. Lesage has gone there and how he fared.

In five or six days, God willing, we will be sending you a fine coachload of people, most of them being for Rome and the remainder for Marseilles. Please expect them and recommend me to Our Lord, in whose love I am, Monsieur, your most humble and obedient servant.

VINCENT DEPAUL
i.s.C.M.

Letter 1015. - Archives of the Mission, Turin, original signed letter.
[1]The Administrators of the hospital for the galley slaves.
[2]This part of the sentence is in the Saint's handwriting.

Has the Bishop of Marseilles[3] returned? Did you deliver my letter to him and make the proposal about the seminary? If so, what sort of reception and what disposition did you remark?

At the bottom of the first page: M. Portail

1016. - TO ANTOINE PORTAIL, IN MARSEILLES

Paris, February 14 [1648][1]

Monsieur,

The grace of Our Lord be with you forever!

I have no doubt that the Administrators[2] intend to have the upper hand in everything. When they speak to you again about the rules for the hospital, please tell them, as if it were coming from you, that a good maxim for those whom God uses to establish holy and new works is to defer as long as possible making the regulations. Experience teaches that what is feasible at the beginning is sometimes harmful as things go on, or subject to troublesome inconveniences and, on this account, some Communities, like the Carthusians, did not draw up their Constitutions until a hundred years had passed. Saint Ignatius made only a brief draft of his, but his Company has since put them into their present state, according to the lights time has revealed to them. Because the Bishop of Geneva was in too great a hurry to make the Regulations of the Sisters of Sainte-Marie, he was obliged to have a Directory.[3]

---

[3]Etienne du Puget.

Letter 1016. - Archives of the Mission, Turin, original signed letter.

[1]The letter is from 1648, although the secretary inadvertently dated it 1647. Three reasons lead us to make this modification in the text: (a) The Missionaries in Ireland could not have written to the Saint in September 1646 because they did not leave France until November (cf. no. 902); (b) Firmin Get was not a priest on December 20, 1647 (cf. no. 1004); (c) Louis Callon was still alive on February 14, 1647. So we must reject 1647; only 1648 suits the circumstances.

[2]The Administrators of the hospital for the galley slaves.

[3]The Directory for the Visitation nuns was drawn up at a General Assembly held in Annecy

If, after this general argument, the Administrators press you, please come down to particulars and tell them we cannot obligate ourselves to maintain two priests of the Company[4] in the hospital because: (1) the foundation of the Duchess does not stipulate this; (2) the revenue is insufficient for this and the other expenses; (3) our Institute has only two principal ends, namely, the instruction of poor people in rural areas, and seminaries; therein lies our duty and not in the management of hospitals, which is merely accessory. Nevertheless, we have taken on the one in question, with the idea of putting priests from the outside there when our own men cannot suffice, as we do during missions. I am sending you a summary of the points of what the foundation obliges us to do. The maintenance of two priests at the hospital would certainly be a great hardship for us since, if one of them were to fall sick, as would often happen, a third man would be required. God will inspire you for the rest.

Our people will leave, God willing, on the first Lyons coach. I hope M. Gallais will be among them. M. Get is good and wise enough to act as Assistant.

It was not my intention to provide for the Armenian priest for so long a time but, since it is an act of charity, *in nomine Domini!*

Two or three seminarians from the collège[5] were all set to go on the galleys, but, since M. Chrétien wrote us not to send them and that he would find enough local priests for that end, we discouraged and dissuaded them from their resolution, with the result that I fear no one will be found now who is willing to go. Nevertheless, I have asked M. Berthe[6] to sound out a few of them. I have received the

---

in May 1623, with Saint Jane Frances de Chantal presiding. The Foundress took her inspiration particularly from notes left by Saint Francis de Sales, who died on December 28, 1622. This Directory was edited in 1850 under the title: *Coutumier et directoire pour les soeurs religieuses de la Visitation Sainte-Marie.*

[4]The words "of the Company" are written between the lines in the Saint's handwriting.
[5]The Collège des Bons-Enfants.
[6]Superior of the Collège des Bons-Enfants.

documents from the Bishop of Trebizond[7] and the indulgence requested by the late M. Callon.[8]

There is nothing new here, except some old news from Ireland, which arrived two days ago, and dates back to the months of September and November.

M. du Chesne was suffering from dysentery for a month prior to his last letter, and our Brother Le Vacher[9] ever since he has been in Ireland. The others are in good health, thanks be to God. The country is sorely afflicted in every way, and the enemy has surrounded the place where our men are living, so that when they go to give a mission they are in danger.[10] I recommend them, and my own soul in particular, to your prayers.

I am, in the love of Our Lord, Monsieur, your most humble servant.

VINCENT DEPAUL
i.s.C.M.

Addressed: Monsieur Portail, Priest of the Mission, in Marseilles

1017. - TO ETIENNE BLATIRON, SUPERIOR, IN GENOA

February 14, 1648

The graces God is showering on your labors are the result of His

---

[7]Augustin Fracioti, Bishop *in partibus* (1654-1659) of Trabzon (Trebizond), a port city on the Black Sea.

[8]He had died in Aumale on August 26, 1647.

[9]Philippe Le Vacher.

[10]Cromwell's troops had entered Tipperary and Caher in September 1647. Then they went to Cashel, took the town, and massacred a part of the population. On November 13, they inflicted a bloody defeat on the Irish army massed at Kanturk. The Irish Catholics who escaped the battles and massacre were not able to escape dire poverty. The priests ran the greatest risk and had to go into hiding to practice their religion, under pain of prison or death.

Letter 1017. - Reg. 2, p. 199.

pure mercy and not of our wretched prayers. We are poor people, more liable to turn aside His blessings than to draw them down. I thank His Divine Goodness for the zeal and fidelity He gives your heart and those who are with you. In fact, Monsieur, I am so touched by the use you make of these virtues and of many others that, when the opportunity arises to animate the Saint-Lazare community to its own perfection, I relate to it the examples that yours gives us of this. I tell them of your long labors, despite the weaknesses of some of your men, your patience in difficulties, your charity and support for one another, the gracious welcome, courtesy, and consideration outsiders find in each of you. So you see, Monsieur, that honey from your hive flows even into this house and serves as food for its children. *O Dieu!* what a source of consolation for the whole Company, but also what a motive for our little family to humble itself before God and to do ever better and better, since He is pleased to extend and multiply in this way the good it is doing even in places where it is not present!

You may accept the gifts people bring to you in Genoa, although they come from places where you have given the mission. However, refuse courteously any that might be offered to you while giving the missions.

1018. - TO THE MARQUISE DE MAIGNELAY[1]

Saint-Lazare, Saturday morning [1647 or 1648][2]

Madame,

With all possible humility and respect, Madame, prostrate in spirit at your feet, I beg you to forgive me for not going today to Monsieur du Fresne's[3] house as you ordered because, since I cannot do immediately what he has proposed, for the reasons of conscience I mentioned to you, it would be too distressing for me to give a refusal, face to face, to the person to whom I have the greatest obligation and desire to obey in this world, regarding the matter in question. I solemnly declare to you, Madame, that I would rather die than disobey you, were it a question of anything less than my own salvation and, far from this being a lack of affection for those good Sisters,[4] if I yielded to my natural inclinations, I would go to see them at this very moment I am speaking to you.

As for Mademoiselle d'Anse,[5] I shall not fail, Madame, to go

---

Letter 1018. - The original autograph letter is in the British Museum, Egerton Ms. 1609, f° 35-36 v°.

[1]Claude-Marguerite de Gondi, sister of Philippe-Emmanuel de Gondi and widow of Florimond d'Halluin, Marquis de Maignelay, whom she had married on January 7, 1588. Her husband was assassinated three years after their marriage, her son died in the flower of his youth, and she had a daughter whose husband, Bernard, the eldest son of the Duc d'Epernon, brutalized her. Prevented by her family and Pope Paul V from entering religious life, the Marquise de Maignelay devoted herself to the service of the poor. She faithfully visited hospitals, prisons, churches, and convents. The Capuchins, Carmelites, Daughters of Providence, Oratorians, and her parish church all benefited from her generosity. To Saint Vincent she gave her time, service, and money, contributing to all his works, especially that of the ordinands. She died on August 26, 1650, and was buried in the convent of the Capuchin nuns, clothed in their habit.

[2]The context of this letter prompts us to assign the dates within which this letter could have been written, since Saint Vincent had taken the resolution in 1646 to withdraw as Director of the Visitation nuns, which he did for eighteen months.

[3]Charles du Fresne, Sieur de Villeneuve, former secretary of Queen Marguerite de Valois. After her death in 1615, he entered the house of Philippe-Emmanuel de Gondi, for whom he was secretary, then intendant. He was one of Saint Vincent's closest friends.

[4]We know from a conference, preached to his Missionaries on November 3, 1654 (cf. vol. XI, no. 111), that the Visitation nuns had recourse to the Marquise de Maignelay to induce Saint Vincent to change his mind about being their Director. In the end the nuns had their way.

[5]Marie Lambert, Demoiselle d'Anse and maid of honor to Queen Anne of Austria, was also

and receive your orders tomorrow or the day after, God willing. In His love I am, Madame, your most humble and very obedient servant.

VINCENT DEPAUL
i.s.C.M.

Addressed: The Marquise de Maignelay

1019. - *SAINT LOUISE TO SAINT VINCENT*

Monsieur,

More than a month ago we were informed that Abbé de Vaux [1] *was supposed to be coming to this city at the beginning of the month of May, and it is necessary for him to name a Director for our Sisters, which he will not do until I have presented all his propositions to you before he leaves and the change of Sisters takes place. My limited experience and ability hinder me from being able to give your charity reason for making provision for the dangers into which I often imagine the entire Company gradually declining, instead of becoming settled. This often makes me think of Hagar's fear of her son's death because she did not want to see him perish, but with greater reason than she, since my sins are the source of all the disorders.*

I most humbly ask your pardon for the added trouble I am giving you. If only I could believe that this was God's Will, I would try to view all these dangers peacefully. I beg His Goodness to remedy them and your charity

---

a Lady of Charity. Disgraced and banished from Court during the Fronde for having shown her feelings toward Mazarin, she succeeded so well in regaining the Queen's favor that the latter bequeathed her ten thousand livres. On more than one occasion, Saint Louise and Saint Vincent turned to her for assistance.

Letter 1019. - Archives of the Motherhouse of the Daughters of Charity, original autograph letter. Coste did not assign a date to this letter, but he placed it among those written in 1648. *Ecrits Spirituels* dates it "around March 1644" (cf. L. 39, p. 107).

[1]Guy Lasnier, Abbé de Vaux, Vicar-General of Angers. Saint Louise apparently feared that a Director appointed by Abbé de Vaux would separate the Sisters in Angers from the guidance of Saint Vincent and thus divide the Company.

to believe always that I am your most humble daughter and very grateful
servant.

L. DE M.

Addressed: *Monsieur Vincent*

1020. - TO CHARLES NACQUART, IN RICHELIEU

Paris, March 22, 1648[1]

Monsieur,

For a long time now, Monsieur, Our Lord has given your heart the desire to render Him some special service. When the opening of missions to the gentiles and idolaters was given in Richelieu,[2] I think Our Lord made your soul aware that He was calling you there, along with another member of the Community in Richelieu, as you then wrote me. It is now time for this seed of the divine call to take effect in you. For behold, by authority of the Sacred Congregation of the Propagation of the Faith, of which the Holy Father the Pope is head, the Nuncio has chosen the Company to go and serve God on Saint-Laurent Island, also called Madagascar.[3] The Company has cast its eyes on you, as the best offering it has, to do homage

---

Letter 1020. - Archives of the Mission, Paris, Madagascar file, an old copy.

[1]Abelly, who reproduced this letter in its entirety (*op.cit.*, bk. II, chap. I, sect. IX, §1, p. 156), making several "improvements," dated it "April 1648."

[2]When the opening of the mission in Madagascar was announced in the Richelieu house.

[3]The departure of the Missionaries was so hasty that Saint Vincent, lacking time for recourse to Rome, was content to request faculties from Nicolò di Bagno, Nuncio to France. The Nuncio did not know that Propaganda Fide had reserved the Madagascar mission to the Discalced Carmelites and had already given them the necessary faculties. By a decree of July 20, 1648, Propaganda Fide suspended the faculties granted by the Nuncio to Charles Nacquart and Nicolas Gondrée. Nevertheless, so that they would not be condemned to enforced idleness, they were given authority to exercise all parish functions, but only for the Catholics of the island, until the Carmelites renounced their rights. The situation was regularized by a formal renunciation by these religious and a new decree from Propaganda Fide.

to our Sovereign Creator and to render Him this service, together with another good priest of the Company.

O my more than dearest Father, what does your heart say to this news? Does it have the shame and confusion suitable for receiving such a grace from heaven, a vocation as lofty and adorable as that of the greatest Apostles and Saints of the Church of God, and the fulfillment in you, in time, of eternal plans? Humility alone, Monsieur, is capable of bearing this grace, and perfect abandonment of all that you are and can be, in exuberant trust in your Sovereign Creator, must follow. You will need generosity and sublime courage. You also need faith as great as Abraham's and the charity of Saint Paul. Zeal, patience, deference, poverty, solicitude, discretion, moral integrity, and an ardent desire to be entirely consumed for God are as appropriate for you as for the great Saint Francis Xavier.

This island [lies][4] below the Tropic of Capricorn. It is four hundred leagues long and approximately one hundred sixty wide.[5] There are poor people there who do not know there is a God; they are, however, very simple, intelligent, and quite clever. To get there, you have to cross the equator. The persons who govern the island are merchants from Paris, who are like the kings of the country.[6]

---

[4]This word is omitted in the copy.

[5]According to Encyclopaedia Britannica, Madagascar covers 227,760 square miles: 995 miles from Cap Sainte-Marie to Cap d'Ambre and 360 miles at its widest, with a coastline of some 3000 miles. It is 250 miles off the eastern coast of Mozambique in southern Africa.

[6]On January 22, 1652, the *Société de l'Orient*, a partnership of moneyed men composed of twenty-four members, had obtained from Richelieu the exclusive rights for doing business in Madagascar and the neighboring islands for ten years. They had sent settlers to the island, under the authority of M. de Pronis, whom the Company had to replace because of continued abuses. Etienne de Flacourt was chosen as his successor and traveled to his new post on the same ship which conveyed Messrs. Nacquart and Gondrée. (Cf. *Mémoire sur la Compagnie des Indes Orientales, 1642-1720*, Bibl. Nat. f.f. 6231.)

Etienne de Flacourt, born in Orléans in 1607, governed the colony of Madagascar (1648-1655) amidst innumerable difficulties, caused especially by the colonists, who made several attempts to kill him. After his return to France, he was employed in the administration of the company. He has left the following works: *Histoire de la grande isle de Madagascar* (Paris, 1654), and *Dictionnaire de la langue de Madagascar* (Paris, 1658), which he dedicated to Saint Vincent.

The first thing you must do is model your voyage on that of the great Saint Francis Xavier, serving and edifying those on the ships which will take you there; arranging for public prayer, if that can be done; taking great care of those who are uncomfortable, always inconveniencing yourself to accommodate others; and contributing to the success of the voyage, which lasts four or five months,[7] as much by your prayers and the practice of every virtue, as the sailors will do by their labors and skill. With regard to those gentlemen,[8] always be very respectful to them. Remain, however, faithful to God, so as not to fail in what concerns Him. Never betray His principles for any reason whatsoever, and take great care not to spoil God's affairs by too much haste in them. Take His own good time and know how to wait for it.

When you arrive on that island,[9] you will first have to get settled as best you can. Perhaps you will have to separate in order to serve in different places. Visit each other as often as possible to console and strengthen one another. Carry out all your priestly functions for the French and the converted idolaters. Follow in everything the practice of the Council of Trent and use the Roman Ritual. Do not permit any other custom to be introduced. If there is already one in existence, try gently to restore things to this practice. In order to do this, it would be a good idea to take with you at least two Roman Rituals.

Your chief concern, after striving to live among those with whom you will have to get along amicably and in an exemplary way, will be to help these poor people, born in the darkness of ignorance of their Creator, to understand the truths of our faith, not by subtle theological reasoning, but by arguments taken from nature. You have to begin in that way, trying to let them see that you are only developing in them the signs of Himself that God has left on them and which corrupt nature, long accustomed to evil, had

---

[7]It lasted more than six months.
[8]De Flacourt, de Bloye, Galiot, Ruffin, and other traveling companions.
[9]The copyist inadvertently wrote *ville* (city) instead of *île* (island).

effaced in them. To do this, Monsieur, you will often have to turn to the Father of Lights, repeating to Him what you say to Him every day: *Da mihi intellectum ut sciam testimonia tua.*[10] In your meditation, set in order the lights He will give you, in order to demonstrate the truth of the First and Sovereign Being, the appropriateness of the mystery of the Trinity, and the necessity of the mystery of the Incarnation, which causes a second, perfect man to be born in us, after the corruption of the first, so that we may improve and reform ourselves on Him. I would like to make them see the weaknesses of human nature in the disorders which they themselves condemn, for they have laws, kings, and punishments.

Although there are a few books dealing with these matters, such as Granada's catechism[11] or some other which we will try to send you, I can only repeat to you, Monsieur, that the best one will be the prayer, *Accedite ad eum et illuminamini,*[12] abandoning yourself to the Spirit of God, who speaks in these circumstances. If His Divine Goodness is pleased to give you the grace to cultivate the seed of the Christians who are already there, living with these good people in Christian charity, I have no doubt whatsoever, Monsieur, that Our Lord will make use of you there to prepare an abundant harvest for the Company. Go then, Monsieur, and since your mission is from God, through those who represent Him for you on earth, cast your nets boldly.

I know how much your heart loves purity. You will need to make good use of it there, [seeing that these people],[13] tainted in many respects, are especially so in that area, to such a degree that it is even said that husbands bring their own wives to the Europeans to have children by them. The unfailing grace of your vocation will protect you from all these dangers.

---

[10]*Give me discernment that I may know your decrees.* Ps 119:125. (NAB) Ps 118:125. (D-RB)

[11]*Catéchisme ou instruction du symbole de la foy,* translated by Canon Nicole Colin (Paris: Chaudières, 1587) from the Spanish of Luis de Granada.

[12]*Come to Him and be enlightened.* Cf. Ps 34:6. (NAB) Ps 33:6. (D-RB)

[13]These words, required by the context, are not found in the copy; we have taken them from Abelly's text.

We shall have news of you every year, and shall send you our news. Even though no money is needed to live in those countries, nevertheless, Monsieur, the Company is arranging to have one hundred gold écus sent to you for any necessity that may arise. We shall also send you a complete chapel kit, two Roman Rituals, two small Bibles, two Councils of Trent,[14] two Binsfelds,[15] and pictures of all our Mysteries, which are wonderful for helping these good people understand what we are trying to teach them, and they like to look at them.

We have here a young man, about twenty years old, from that country; the Nuncio is supposed to baptize him today. I use pictures to instruct him, and I think that helps him to fix his attention.

I wonder if it might not be necessary to take with you some irons to make altar breads for Holy Mass, pins, needle-cases—three or four of each—holy oils for Baptism and Extreme Unction, a Busée[16] for each of you, a few copies of *The Introduction to a Devout Life,*[17] and some abridged lives of the saints.

You have an obedience[18] from us and full powers from the Nuncio, who has this work very much at heart.

With all that, I give myself absolutely to you, if not actually to follow you, inasmuch as I am unworthy to do so, at least to pray every day that God will be pleased to leave me on earth for you and, if God is pleased to have mercy on me, to see you again in eternity and honor you there as one who, by the dignity of his calling, will be placed among apostolic men.

I conclude, prostrate in spirit at your feet, asking you also, please, to offer me to our common Lord, so that I may be faithful

---

[14]The first edition of the Canons and Decrees of the Council of Trent appeared in Rome in 1564. More recent editions were those of Antwerp (1640) and Cologne (1644).

[15]Binsfeld was the author of *Enchiridion theologiae pastoralis* [Trèves (Trier), 1591], republished in Paris in 1646.

[16]*Manuel des Méditations dévotes sur tous les évangiles des dimanches et fêtes de l'année.* This work, composed in Latin by the Jesuit, Jean Busée, had been translated and revised by René Alméras in 1644.

[17]A beautiful edition of the *Introduction* had just appeared in Paris in 1641.

[18]The obedience letter was sent on March 28 to Messrs. Nacquart and Gondrée. It was published in *Mémoires*, vol. IX, p. 42, n. 1.

to Him and finish the journey to eternity in His love. I am in time and will be forever, Monsieur, your most humble and obedient servant.

VINCENT DEPAUL
i.s.C.M.

The man we are assigning to go with you is M. Gondrée,[19] whom you may have seen in Saintes, where he lived while still a seminarian. He is one of the best men in the Company and is still as devout as when he entered it. He is humble, charitable, cordial, and zealous. In a word, he is such that I cannot tell you all the good I think of him.

Some merchants will be leaving here Wednesday or Thursday for La Rochelle, from where the ship is supposed to leave. If they are willing to pass through Richelieu, Monsieur Gondrée could go with them and join you there. They could go on ahead to prepare their ship and wait for you around the fifteenth or twentieth of next month, when they are supposed to set sail.[20] I beg you, Monsieur, to keep yourself ready.

We will add to the above-mentioned books the life and letters of the Apostle of the Indies.[21]

Please do not make this public; we have not yet announced it here.

One of the gentlemen[22] to whom this island has been granted by

---

[19]Nicolas Gondrée, born in Assigny (Seine-Maritime), entered the Congregation of the Mission as a sub-deacon on April 11, 1644, at twenty-four years of age. During his novitiate he was ordained a deacon and was sent to Saintes. In 1646 he returned to Paris and was ordained a priest. In 1648 he volunteered for Madagascar, where he arrived on December 4. God was satisfied with his good will and called him to Himself on May 26, 1649. Saint Vincent esteemed highly the virtue of M. Gondrée and considered him "one of the best subjects in the Company." (Cf. *Notices*, vol. III, pp. 43-56.)

[20]The ship did not weigh anchor until Ascension Thursday, May 21.

[21]Among the French biographies of Saint Francis Xavier which Saint Vincent may have known were those by Martin Christophe (1608), Michel Coissard (1612), Etienne Binet (1622), one by Balinghem and one by an anonymous author published in Mons (1619). The first French edition of his letters came out in Paris in 1628.

[22]M. de Flacourt. The *Société de l'Orient* had promised to find clothing, room, and board for the Missionaries. The new governor did not fulfill his obligations.

the King is making the voyage. He will pay your expenses on board and when you land. You will see on your arrival whether, in the course of time, you will be able to find some land there to take care of your maintenance. Living is so cheap that five sous worth of rice, which takes the place of bread, is sufficient to feed one hundred men a day.

What more can I say to you, Monsieur, except that I beg Our Lord, who has given you a share in His charity, to give you also a share in His patience, and that there is nothing on earth I would like better, if it were allowed me, than to go as your companion in place of M. Gondrée.

1021. - TO DENIS GAUTIER, SUPERIOR, IN RICHELIEU

Paris, March 29, 1648

Monsieur,

The grace of Our Lord be with you forever!

I am writing to M. Nacquart by way of M. Gondrée, who leaves today by coach for Richelieu so as to travel to La Rochelle together with these gentlemen, who are supposed to take them to the Indies around the twentieth of next month.

The Archbishop of Rheims[1] is in your neighborhood; he wrote me that you have not paid him a visit. Please go and see him, Monsieur, and, prostrate at his feet, ask his pardon for not having gone to pay your respects to him sooner. Say that you have come to offer him your obedience and that of the Company, since he is the one who established you in Richelieu and, for that reason, you owe him all respect and submission. Please offer him also, on my part, a renewal of my perpetual obedience. I have recommended

---

Letter 1021. - Archives of the Mission, Turin, original signed letter.

[1]Léonor d'Estampes de Valençay had been Bishop of Chartres (1620-1641) and was transferred to Rheims, where he died in April 1651.

M. du Coudray to you and I do so again. I cannot do it sufficiently to the extent of the affection God has given me for him.[2] Please show him proof of this and let me know his present state. We have asked Our Lord for his preservation and good health.

I do not know if M. Chiroye[3] has recovered his health; I asked for news of him a week ago. Please write to me about him, in case he does not do it himself, and greet the whole Community for me. I am, for it, and for you in particular, Monsieur, in the love of Our Lord, your most humble and obedient servant.

VINCENT DEPAUL
i.s.C.M.

M. Gondrée left without M. Nacquart's letter; I am sending it to you.[4] Read the letter for Brother Cruoly[5] and give it to him, if you judge it appropriate.

At the bottom of the first page: M. Gautier

---

[2]It is a fact that François du Coudray had unusual ideas about certain dogmatic points.
[3]Jacques Chiroye, Superior in Luçon.
[4]Cf. no. 1020.
[5]Donat Cruoly (Crowley), born in Cork (Ireland) on July 24, 1623, entered the Congregation of the Mission on May 9, 1643, took his vows in November 1645, and was ordained a priest in 1650. He was among the group of Missionaries sent to Picardy in 1651 for the relief of the people reduced to destitution by the war. Saint Vincent afterward appointed him Director of Students and theology professor at Saint-Lazare (1653-1654). He next sent him to Le Mans as Superior. In 1657 he returned to Saint-Lazare to teach moral theology. Later he filled the office of Superior in Richelieu (1660-1661), Saint-Charles (1662-1664), Montauban (1664-1665), Agen (1665-1666), and Saint-Brieuc (1667-1670). Sent to Le Mans in 1676, he was Superior there from 1687 to 1690. There is no trace of him after 1690.

1022. - *CHARLES NACQUART TO SAINT VINCENT*

April 1, 1648

Monsieur,

Your holy blessing, please!

In reading and rereading your letter, it seems to me that the expressions in it do not come from a man, but are the words of the Spirit of God, which communicate to me, in truth, that His good pleasure is to make use of me in such a noble and exalted vocation, of which I truly know I am unworthy. I have felt no repugnance for it except that I would have preferred, and still desire, to be under someone else's leadership, and not to be in charge. I consider myself totally incapable of this because of a lack of virtue, prudence, and knowledge. This makes me very fearful of spoiling God's work and of being an obstacle to His glory, which someone else would procure far more favorably; I would be much more at ease having only to obey.

Alas! I find it very difficult to convince myself that it is to me, poor Charles Nacquart, that this indication of God's plan is addressed. Oh well! since, however, on earth you hold the place of father to me, after the one I have in heaven, I have no doubt about it. Let M. Gondrée come whenever he pleases. I will go with him blindly, like a lost child, to find out whether this is the Promised Land. Even though I have contemplated my leprous hand, I am confident that God will give us His all-powerful staff to accomplish what He wishes.[1] However, if you are not sending a Superior, at least please add a third companion so that this three-stranded rope will be stronger and indissoluble. You say perhaps that you have no one to give us. All you have to do is send a letter here to M. Maillard [2] who, if you recall, also requested this of you two years ago as earnestly as anyone could. Just now, as I was writing, since he had suspected something and surmised it because of something he learned from M. Gautier, he earnestly begged me to tell you that his heart is still set on this, more than ever, if you think well of it. And to tell the truth, I, too, think he would do very well because of his virtue, his gentleness, and his other qualities through which

---

Letter 1022. - Archives of the Mission, Paris, Madagascar file, copy.

[1]Cf. Ex 4:1-9. (NAB)

[2]Antoine Maillard, born in Veney (Meurthe), entered the Congregation of the Mission on May 21, 1644, at twenty-six years of age, took his vows in 1646, was Procurator of Saint-Lazare for a long time, and Procurator General (1679-1686).

we would be of only one heart. If you say he is too much in demand as Procurator in Richelieu, he has put things in such good order that someone else could easily take his place. Brother Vageot, who has no inclinations for studies,[3] might perhaps do a good job of it. Give him [4] to us as Superior; he is incapable of being vain.

Some men get drunk on one glass of wine and drown in four fingers of water. The slightest whiff of honor is capable of making my head spin. I can say, qui datus est mihi stimulus carnis,[5] *meaning the opposite sex; this makes me fearful of being alone at times. As you say, three cost no more than two; however,* fiat voluntas Domini! [6]

However, in the event that you confirm your first proposal of me, here are some questions. Should we choose a place of residence to serve as a center from which we would go around the island to give missions and then return, as is done in this country? Are there towns, parishes, churches, and priests other than us there,[7] or any other controversial religion? Are there Seigneurs other than the French on whom we may have to depend? How are our priestly functions to be carried out? The same way as in this country? Must our ceremonies be observed in entirely the same way, and is there a plainchant book? Should we say Mass every day on the ship? Will we be able to find matter for consecration everywhere? If we have only one chapel kit, what shall we do when we separate? Are there any obstacles to our religion, with regard to our functions and our priestly clothing? Do we need square birettas and surplices? Will we be able to establish Confraternities of Charity and receive retreatants? How shall we regulate our time without clocks or watches? Could you send us the Rule of the Mission with the finishing touches on it? [8] Will we be able to admit companions from that country to become priests and to be educated? Are there any Bishops there, or will we have coadjutors from here or from there? Brother J. Bance [9] had volunteered, as you know. Should we accept,

---

[3]Philippe Vageot, born in Bellegarde (Ain), entered the Congregation of the Mission as a cleric on May 3, 1645, at twenty-three years of age, and took his vows on October 12, 1647. In September 1648 he was ordained a priest and placed in the house in Saintes shortly after his ordination. He was Superior there from 1651 to 1655, the year he left the Company.

[4]Antoine Maillard.

[5]*I was given a thorn in the flesh.* 2 Cor 12:7. (NAB)

[6]*May the Lord's Will be done!*

[7]There was only one priest, M. de Bellebarbe, in that part of the island where the Missionaries would be living.

[8]With the latest modifications.

[9]Jean Bance, born in Ménonval (Seine-Maritime) in 1611, entered the Congregation of the Mission as a coadjutor Brother on November 9, 1637.

on our own, some foundation for our maintenance and have it set up, without writing to you about it? That would take a long time.

There might perhaps be something else to propose to you that you could take care of by giving us new recommendations, if you have not already done so through M. Gondrée. You will have sufficient time to reply to this letter before we leave, if you will kindly do so by the next mail; we will be looking forward to it. Will we have a thurible, incense, and a monstrance to honor O[ur] L[ord] in the Blessed Sacrament of the altar? Should we always reserve the Blessed Sacrament on board? Shall we try to have everyone on the ship make a general confession? Should we have reading at table en route and there? Will we be free to follow the order of the day for Missionaries while we are traveling, and to give conferences among ourselves and to those gentlemen on the ship if they are so disposed, as well as to the children and men, when we get there? [10]

If we had a number of indulgences to distribute, Privileged Masses, the Forty Hours prayers, etc., that would encourage devotion.

I await your letter before saying good-bye and making my will, [11] *before dying to the whole country, to all intents and purposes. Please ask the Company once again to pray for us; without this I would be much less self-confident about such an undertaking.*

The merchants going there for temporal affairs will act as a stimulus or a subject of humiliation to me, if I do not do, for the glory of God and the salvation of souls, as much as they do for their business, although I am extremely fearful of being lost, knowing my own weaknesses and my inability to direct souls. May O[ur] L[ord] take me by the hand and grant me what you have already wished for me, and will ask of Him, along with so many other good souls whose help I beg through you.

I am, in His love and in that of His holy Mother and Saint Joseph, Monsieur and Most Honored Father, inviolably and wholeheartedly, your most humble and affectionate son.

CHARLES NACQUART
i.s.C.M.

Is there any harm in writing a little note to my father to ask for his blessing and prayers for me?

---

[10]Saint Vincent answered in the affirmative and Charles Nacquart had the joy of seeing the sailors and passengers respond to his efforts.

[11]The only existing will of Charles Nacquart is dated June 24, 1649. It was published in *Mémoires*, vol. IX, p. 137.

1023. - *NICOLAS GONDREE TO SAINT VINCENT*

Tours, April 3, 1648

Monsieur,

Your blessing!

I arrived safely in Tours with Monsieur de Bloye, who is accompanying us by order of M. de Flacourt.[1] *He could not have given us a better leader, not only for temporal matters but also for the spiritual as well. I assure you that he has edified me as much as anyone in his position has ever done. Morning, evening, and at all hours, he sings and encourages others to devotion. I hope God wills to make use of him in Madagascar, for he has proved to me to be as fervent as I could hope for. He is also desirous of increasing God's glory in these people, not only through others, by upholding them with his authority, but also through the familiar instructions he plans to give them. He has already begun his mission by teaching people how to go to Communion, and how to say the* Pater *and the* Credo. *In short, he is like the sun in the midst of many stars, and I, because of my imperfections, am only darkness in the midst of these luminaries. He expressed to me the wish that many priests might be willing to give themselves to God for the conversion of the island. He met an upright priest in search of a position, and was delighted to learn of his willingness to serve God in that country. He also scrutinized his motives, which are very good, for he assures us that it is not from self-interest that he is going to that area, but purely for the glory of God, with the desire to suffer, obey, work, and, if need be, undergo martyrdom. May God be blessed for having given him this spirit! He hopes to hear from you as soon as possible because he could buy some supplies for there, provided you get the approval of the Nuncio,*[2] *for whom, as for you, Monsieur, [I am] your most humble servant.*

N. GONDREE
i.s.C.M.

Letter 1023. - Archives of the Mission, Paris, seventeenth century copy.
[1]Etienne de Flacourt. (Cf. no. 1020, n.6.)
[2]Nicolò di Bagno.

Monsieur de Bloye, M. Galiot, M. Rufin, and the rest of our group recommend themselves to your holy prayers and to those of the whole Company. You think that only two Missionaries are going, but they have assured us that we will not be alone, and they will willingly do all they can to help us. To crown their work, some have promised me that they will go to see you to thank God for their journey by making a good retreat, as some have already done. Please God that they will be able to put their plans into execution!

Monsieur de Bloye requests that you kindly send your letters to M. Henry in La Rochelle, where he has taken this good priest, who showed me all his papers, which are in good order. This good priest has asked me to tell you that he eagerly awaits your reply; we, too, are anxious to learn the outcome of this affair. This good priest is named Abraham Louvel, and he is from the Le Mans diocese.

Monsieur, I send you this letter only to satisfy the wishes of M. de Bloye, who desired it in order to find out what you want to do about this good priest, who has been a curate in a number of towns. He seems too crafty, a little ignorant, and has been refused in Orléans.³ To make a long story short, I do not think we could get along with him. We await your reply.

1024. - TO SAINT LOUISE

[Between 1645 and 1649]¹

Mademoiselle,

I approve, and promise to do, everything you told me.

I am going to tell that Sister that I think it is a good idea for her to remain here, and that this is in conformity with the Gospel.

---

³This appears to imply that Abraham Louvel had been denied incardination in the Orléans diocese. In this context, incardination is the necessary formal acceptance by a diocese of a priest transferring from another diocese or from a religious Community.

Letter 1024. - Archives of the Motherhouse of the Daughters of Charity, original autograph letter.

¹Internal evidence and the information in note 3 provide the reason for the approximate date of this letter.

Since the Sister in this parish[2] wants to leave, fine! Put Sister Jeanne de la Croix[3] in her place and speak to her in the way you mentioned.

I am taking care of my health, and I promise I will take even better care of it. I am, in the love of Our Lord, y[our] s[ervant].

V. D.

Addressed: Mademoiselle Le Gras

---

[2]Saint-Laurent parish.

[3]Sister Jeanne de la Croix, born in Le Mans (Sarthe), entered the Daughters of Charity in 1645 or 1646. She was in Serqueux in November 1648, and became Assistant to Saint Louise in 1651. At the end of 1653 she returned to Serqueux, and was still there in 1657 when she again became Assistant. Early in 1659 she was sent to Châteaudun to replace Sister Barbe Angiboust, who had just died (December 27, 1658). In 1664 she opened the mission of Chartres; later she served the Company as Treasurer General (1668-1671).

1025. - *JEAN-JACQUES OLIER* [1] *TO SAINT VINCENT*

[April 1648] [2]

He who has God has everything!

Monsieur,

I am writing to inform you that Father Maurice [3] *had a visit from M. du Bosquet* [4] *and that Abbé de Cérisy* [5] *remains on good terms with him through the intermediary of Madame Seguin, the devoted penitent of Father Maurice. She will violently oppose the removal of the good priest from her and, in order to keep him, she will do her utmost to influence the Chancellor* [6] *through these gentlemen and on her own. This good lady is as zealous regarding the new party* [7] *as anyone could be. A few days ago, I had one of our men notify the Chancellor's wife to inform her husband*

Letter 1025. - Archives of Saint-Sulpice Seminary, original autograph letter.

[1]Jean-Jacques Olier, the celebrated founder of Saint-Sulpice Seminary, was one of the principal restorers of ecclesiastical discipline in the seventeenth century. Saint Vincent calls him "a man given over to the grace of God and completely apostolic." He was born in Paris on September 20, 1608. After a few hesitations, which Saint Vincent succeeded in dissipating, he decided to become a priest and was ordained on May 21, 1633. The first years of his priestly career were dedicated to the work of missions. He participated in the labors of the priests of Saint-Lazare, whom he edified by his zeal and humility. For reasons still unexplained, perhaps because of a divergence of views on the question of whether he should accept becoming a Bishop, Olier changed from the direction of Saint Vincent, who had been his confessor for three years (1632-1635), to that of Father de Condren. This was not a desertion—far from it. In 1649 he wrote, "For extraordinary affairs, we do not fail to see Monsieur Vincent, and for ordinary matters, all our brothers assembled." He did not begin the Vaugirard Seminary or accept the pastorate of Saint-Sulpice until he had consulted the Saint. "M. Vincent is our father," he often used to say to his seminarians. Jean-Jacques Olier died on April 2, 1657, assisted by his holy friend. The latter consoled the priests of Saint-Sulpice in their sorrow, and we still have a fragment of the address to them on this occasion, which has been attributed to Saint Vincent (cf. vol. XIII, no. 51).

[2]Date added on the back of the original.

[3]A Discalced Carmelite of the Paris house in Saint-Sulpice parish.

[4]François de Bosquet, Administrator for Justice in Languedoc, who later became Bishop of Lodève and then of Montpellier.

[5]Germain Habert, Abbé de Cérisy (Manche), member of the French Academy, author of a life of Cardinal de Bérulle; he died in 1655.

[6]Pierre Séguier.

[7]The Jansenists.

that they were trying to bring Father Séguenot [8] *into this city, which would be dangerous. Good Madame Seguin declared that she found it hard to accept the fact that there was opposition to this party and its members. It might perhaps be important, Monsieur, that you see the Chancellor and forewarn him of this, depending on whether Divine Wisdom opens the way for you to do so.*

I am at liberty to inform you of these matters as affairs necessary for discerning in them God's work, which you love and which He commissions you to maintain.

OLIER

Addressed: *Monsieur Vincent, Superior General of the Mission*

1026. - *ALAIN DE SOLMINIHAC TO SAINT VINCENT*

April 1648

Monsieur,

I am writing to the Marquise de Senecey [1] *to entreat her to represent to the Queen the deplorable situation of the Rodez diocese. It is in a state almost as ruinous as Périgueux, except that the churches there are not so run down and there are more priests. Their morals, however, are so depraved that, as soon as the Bishop of Rodez* [2] *died, they removed their*

---

[8]Claude Séguenot, born in Avallon (Yonne) on May 6, 1596, left the law courts to enter the Oratory in 1624. He soon struck up a friendship with Abbé de Saint-Cyran. His translation into French of Saint Augustine's book on virginity earned him four years' imprisonment in the Bastille (1638-1643) and the censure of the Sorbonne. He was Superior in Nancy, Dijon, Rouen, Saumur, and Tours, and was appointed Assistant to the General in 1661, 1666, and 1669. He governed the Oratory of Paris (1667-1673) and died in that city on March 7, 1676. Several of his works are still in manuscript form.

Letter 1026. - Archives of the Diocese of Cahors, Alain de Solminihac collection, copy made from the original.

[1]Marie-Catherine de la Rochefoucauld, Comtesse and then Duchesse de Rendan, first lady of honor to the Queen, Anne of Austria; governess of Louis XIV during his early childhood; wife of Henri de Bauffremont, Baron de Senecey, whom she lost in 1622. She died on April 10, 1677, at the age of eighty-nine.

[2]Charles de Noailles, who died on March 27, 1648. On June 10, 1648 he was succeeded by Hardouin de Péréfixe, future Archbishop of Paris (1664-1670).

clerical dress. Some hung their cassocks from the windows of cabarets, others drank to his health, and those who had left their mistresses took up with them again.

The first act of the Vicars-General was to rescind all the orders issued by that Prelate for the reform of his diocese. That has caused so much scandal throughout this province that I am at a loss to describe it. It is one of the largest dioceses in this kingdom and one of the most difficult to govern that could be imagined because of the mentality of the people in that region, who are very troublesome. It [is] imperative that Her Majesty appoint an apostolic man for that place, and I implore her to tell His Majesty this, either on her own part or because she has been entreated to do so.

I wanted to put down here for you what I have written to her so that you might make use of it, if the opportunity arises. In the name of God, I beg you to do your utmost to see that this diocese is provided with a shepherd such as is demanded by the state to which it is reduced. Not only must he be an apostolic person, but he must also be endowed with great strength of character and great courage. Is it possible that the Queen, because of some reason of State, would be willing to place there someone lacking the requisite qualities for the reform of this diocese? I cannot believe that of this good Princess and would be deeply grieved if it were to happen. If you wish to tell her what I have written to you, you can assure Her Majesty that all that is quite true. Very few persons know the state of that diocese better than I. It borders mine for more than twenty leagues in France, and I cannot tell you the trouble it is causing. No matter how hard I try to put good Vicars Forane in the border areas, to make frequent visits there, and to send our missionaries there often, this still does not prevent it from suffering great harm because the morals of the priests in that region are so scandalous and corrupt.

Good Monsieur Ferrier [3] *has left. In the short time he was there, he worked hard at the reform of the clergy and earned a fine reputation for himself as well as credibility in this entire area.*

Will the poor diocese of Périgueux still be left in a state of wretchedness? I felt urged to write to the Marquise of Senecey. Please say so to the

---

[3]A disciple of Father de Condren and collaborator of Jean-Jacques Olier, one of the founders of the Saint-Sulpice Seminary. He came to Rodez at the request of the Bishop, Charles de Noailles, who conferred on him the titles of Vicar-General and Officialis (Ecclesiastical Judge). It was due to his efforts that the Villefranche Seminary, founded by Raymond Bonal, was recognized as a diocesan seminary. He worked so effectively for the reform of the diocese that, after a stay of six months, he considered his work completed and returned to Paris.

Queen; tell her I asked you to do so and that there is nothing of which she will have to render a greater account to God than of not providing dioceses with shepherds having the requisite qualities, and of not doing so soon enough. May God inspire Her Majesty to choose persons after His own heart!

I am, in the meantime, Monsieur, etc.

ALAIN,
Bishop of Cahors

1027. - TO ANTOINE PORTAIL, IN MARSEILLES

April 24, 1648

Please conclude all business with the Administrators of the hospital before your return. From what I can see, there will be no major difficulties. They have already approved our retaining the entire spiritual direction. In so doing they are modeling themselves on the Administrators of the Hôtel-Dieu in Paris, who concern themselves only with temporal affairs, leaving everything else to the care of the priests from Notre-Dame.[1] These latter do not serve that Hôtel-Dieu themselves but have it served by others. They are content to designate one of their men to see in general if all is going well. We shall gladly do the same, and I am assuring Monsieur de la Coste[2] that I never intended to do otherwise because the service of hospitals is not in accord with our duties. In the hospital for galley slaves we shall put secular priests whom we will choose from the seminaries; one of our priests will supervise them and work with them.

Letter 1027. - Reg. 2, p. 103.

[1]The Canons of Notre-Dame in Paris.

[2]Gaspard de Simiane de la Coste, born in Aix in 1607, turned to God because of the premature death of a person whom he loved. He came to Paris, where he studied the art of controversy under Father Véron and struck up a friendship with Vincent de Paul, who developed in his heart a love for the unfortunate; most especially, he got him interested in the condition of the poor galley slaves. It is to Saint Vincent, to Bishop Jean-Baptiste Gault of Marseilles, and to de la Coste in particular, that is due the establishment of the hospital for galley slaves in Marseilles.

1028. - TO DENIS GAUTIER, SUPERIOR, IN RICHELIEU

Paris, April 26, 1648

Monsieur,

The grace of Our Lord be with you forever!

Yes, Monsieur, please go and thank the Archbishop of Tours; his charity and courtesy toward your men certainly warrant this journey. In expressing your gratitude to him, convey mine to him and beg him to accept my renewed offer of obedience, which I make to him through you with all possible humility.

I thank God for the new dignity of Messrs. Constantin[1] and Manceau.[2] Please greet them for me; tell them I have begged Our Lord and will continue to beg Him to grant them always renewed dispositions for the [Holy] Sacrifice and the grace never to offer it through routine. I entreat them to remember me when they say *Nobis quoque peccatoribus,*[3] as for the greatest sinner on earth. With this in mind, Monsieur, I recommend myself to your prayers also and to those of your Community. To them, and to you in particular, I make the gift of my heart and of all that I am, even though I am such as I have just mentioned.

He also founded the *Oeuvre des femmes bohèmes* for women who followed the galleys, either so as not to abandon their husbands or for less admissible reasons. This pious gentleman loved to quote the maxims of Saint Vincent. As far as he could, he conformed to the Rule of the Missionaries: he rose at 4:00 A.M., spent an hour in prayer, read a chapter of the New Testament on his knees with his head uncovered, read a spiritual book for half an hour, visited the Blessed Sacrament on leaving and returning to the house, and made a monthly retreat and an annual eight-day retreat. Most of his time was taken up with the convicts in the hospital, to whom he was pleased to bring consolation and care. The Missionaries could not have had a better auxiliary. He died of the plague on July 24, 1649, a victim of his dedication to the sick galley slaves.

Letter 1028. - Archives of the Mission, Turin, original signed letter.

[1]François Constantin, born in Limoges (Haute-Vienne), entered the Congregation of the Mission on December 19, 1643, at twenty years of age, took his vows on December 25, 1645, and was ordained a priest on March 31, 1648.

[2]Simon Manceau, born in Kalembourg, a village in the commune of Laumesfeld (Moselle), entered the Congregation of the Mission on January 17, 1645, at twenty-four years of age, and was ordained a priest on March 31, 1648. He died in Richelieu in May 1651.

[3]*For us who are also sinners* (from the present Eucharistic Prayer I [Roman Canon] in the Mass).

I am glad M. du Coudray is better and that you are allowing him to stay at Bois-Bouchard.[4] I beg you, Monsieur, to bear with him in that and in all else as best you can,[5] and especially with me who am, in the love of Our Lord, Monsieur, your most humble and obedient servant.

VINCENT DEPAUL
i.s.C.M.

M. Lambert has not answered you because, on leaving his retreat, in which he honored that of Our Lord in the womb of His incomparable Mother, he wished also to honor His childhood by remaining in the seminary, where he has been for four or five days. God knows what humility and edification he has shown the Company in this.

At the bottom of the first page: M. Gautier

1029. - *SAINT LOUISE TO SAINT VINCENT*

Feast of Saint Monica [May 4,1648] [1]

Monsieur,

I believe Mademoiselle Viole is going to suggest a baker to do the cooking in Bicêtre. Would your charity think it well to say that there is already one who bakes quite well, and we are satisfied with the way he works? I really would fear another being brought in, who might not be so suitable for the good of the children and for our Sisters as well.

---

[4]The fief, Bois-Bouchard, situated near Marie-de-l'Etoile, belonged to the Richelieu Missionaries, whose country house was there.

[5]François du Coudray maintained some unusual ideas with regard to certain points of dogmatic theology.

Letter 1029. - Original autograph letter in the residence of the Visitatrix of the Daughters of Charity, Province of Marseilles, 104 Chemin du Roucas Blanc, Marseilles.

[1]Date added on the back of the letter by Brother Ducournau.

The Pastor of Saint-Laurent [2] is still complaining about not getting what is his right from the baptisms. The Ladies want him to take the Pastor of Saint-Christophe [3] to court but, since he does not have any copy of the foundation contract, he cannot do so. Furthermore, the Pastor of Saint-Christophe was complaining of being unable to get anything out of it. I think, Monsieur, that the Ladies should take the trouble to find out the reason for this; it would also be quite easy to have the necessary papers given to the Pastor of Saint-Laurent.

So as not to offend the Pastor of Chars [4] too much, I have been thinking since yesterday about suggesting to your charity, if you think fit, to send Sister Jeanne-Christine [5] in place of Sister Turgis [6] and to keep Sister Jacquette for Chantilly; [7] I foresee that we will still have to remove the Sister who has remained in Chars, so as not to ignore that anonymous warning. However, for a long time now, both of these Sisters have been asking to make vows, and I think it would distress them too much to put them off. It seems very likely that this would be to good purpose, since both are older and sufficiently mature.

Please take the trouble to give us a reply on this matter as soon as possible because time is getting short for Chars. I am, Monsieur, your most obedient servant and unworthy daughter.

LOUISE DE MARILLAC

Addressed: *Monsieur Vincent*

---

[2]Guillaume de Lestocq was Pastor from 1628 to May 9, 1661, the day of his death. He was the principal instrument in the union of the Congregation of the Mission and the Priory of Saint-Lazare.

[3]A parish in Paris. It included within its boundaries near the Hôtel-Dieu the house where the newborn foundlings were brought. There was another home for the foundlings in Saint-Laurent Parish.

[4]Commune in the district of Pontoise. The Daughters of Charity, who had been there since 1647, had suffered greatly from the Jansenistic tendencies of the Pastor, M. Pouvot.

[5]Jeanne-Christine Prévost, who was in Fontainebleau in 1648. In 1651 she went to Liancourt, and to Sedan in 1654.

[6]Sister Elisabeth Turgis.

[7]The Daughters of Charity opened a house there the preceding year.

1030. - TO ANTOINE PORTAIL, IN MARSEILLES

May 8, 1648

You are right, Monsieur, to have said that the Superior of the Marseilles house does not have to ask the advice of the Administrators when there is question of placing or changing secular priests in the hospital. I mean he must not be under any obligation to do so. He will have the right to bring them in and to dismiss them on his own, just as a pastor does with his curates. So, arrange everything in compliance with the document I sent you and put the agreement in writing, if those gentlemen wish to do so, particularly in the case where the foundation patents or the regulations they have made might bind us either to something else or to act otherwise than that document states. What is put in writing can be inserted after their regulations, if you judge it appropriate.

You can also settle other points such as time and duties, not, however, obliging us to conduct any solemn service in the chapel, though we may preach there once a month and teach catechism there occasionally. Our house is too poor to maintain the priests who would be needed, if we had to assure the chant and do all that those Administrators are requesting. Tell them we will do the best we can and accommodate ourselves as far as possible to what they desire. After that, let us not waste time trying to figure out their intentions for the future because, even though they seem so circumspect to us in the beginning, we must not imagine that they are planning to encroach on spiritual matters but only to do things properly, according to their present lights.

Letter 1030. - Reg. 2, p. 104.

1031. - *JULIEN GUERIN TO SAINT VINCENT*

Tunis, May 1648

It is impossible for me to describe to you the great weeping and wailing of the poor slaves, of all the merchants, and of the Consul,[1] *and how consoled we have been by them. Even the Turks come to visit us in our distress, and the most prominent men in the city of Tunis have offered me their help and service. In a word, Monsieur, I see clearly how good it is to serve God faithfully, since in the midst of tribulation He raises up even His enemies to relieve and assist His poor servants. We are afflicted, even excessively so, by war, plague, and famine, and along with all that we have no money. However, our courage is very firm, thank God. We no longer fear the plague; it is as if it did not exist. The joy that our Brother*[2] *and I have because of good M. Le Vacher's state of health has made us as strong as the lions in our mountains.*

1032. - *SAINT LOUISE TO SAINT VINCENT*

May 13, 1648

Monsieur,

We are in a hurry to send out two of our Sisters, one to Crespières,[1] *the other to Maule. They are among the ones who asked your charity some time ago if they could give themselves to God by the vows. They have been in the Company a good six or seven years, without ever showing any distaste but, on the contrary, have always given very good example. Will your charity please allow them to hear Mass and perform this holy action tomorrow morning before they leave? They will not be departing until*

Letter 1031. - Abelly, *op.cit.,* bk. II, chap. I, sect. VII, §1, p. 94.

[1]Martin de Lange. The cause of this sorrow was the fear of losing Jean Le Vacher, who had almost died of the plague.

[2]François Francillon, born in Céaux (Vienne) in January 1621, was received into the Congregation of the Mission as a coadjutor Brother in April 1645. He accompanied Julien Guérin to Tunis, returned to France, and was sent to Algiers where he devoted himself to his work until July 6, 1688, the day the Turks tied him to the mouth of a cannon.

Letter 1032. - Hospice of Dourdan (Essonne), copy.

[1]Commune in the district of Versailles, where the Sisters had just opened a house.

around noon. Please do us the charity of letting us know if this is agreeable to you and if we shall have the happiness of hearing your Holy Mass for this intention.

I have a very great need for God to grant me the grace of speaking with you and for your charity to believe that I am always, Monsieur, your most obedient daughter and very humble servant.

LOUISE DE MARILLAC

One of our Sisters is named Andrée; she is near Tours; the other is Catherine de Gesse, who used to serve the poor at Saint-Gervais.

1033. - TO JEAN MARTIN, IN GENOA

Paris, May 15, 1648

I cannot refrain from advising you, Monsieur, to take care of your health. It is so precious to me and so useful to souls that I beg you once again to do all in your power to recover it, suspending every kind of work and following exactly the doctors' instructions. Remember, Monsieur, that Saint Augustine says that a person who does not obey the doctors is doing his best to kill himself; we shall be reading that in the Office one of these days. So, I hope you will be faithful to their orders and will give the Company this consolation, after so many others it has received from you. I am, in the love of Our Lord, Monsieur, your most humble and obedient servant.

VINCENT DEPAUL
i.s.C.M.

The Chief Justice of the Court of Aids has spoken very highly of your brother to me.

At the bottom of the first page: M. Martin

Letter 1033. - Archives of the Mission, Turin, original signed letter.

1033a. - *SAINT LOUISE TO SAINT VINCENT*

[May, between 1646 and 1648] [1]

Monsieur,

I think it is essential for us early today to remove that poor young woman whom God seems to want to rescue, withdrawing her from the most lamentable danger. I only hope she is not wanton. If we allow her to go free, however, she will be lost completely, for several reasons which I will tell your charity when God grants me the grace of being able to speak with you. . . .

Monday

Addressed: *Monsieur Vincent*

1033b. - TO SAINT LOUISE

[May, between 1646 and 1648][1]

I was at the Madeleine yesterday. The Mother[2] absolutely

Letter 1033a. - Archives of the Motherhouse of the Daughters of Charity, original autograph letter. This letter and Saint Vincent's reply which follows it, were placed by Coste in his First Supplement (cf. vol. VIII, nos. 3304 and 3305). Their content and Coste's notes for no. 1033b account for their relocation by the editors.

[1]Only the first page of this letter has been preserved. Of the second page all that remains is the first word, or sometimes the first two words, of each line. We can ascertain that at the end of the letter Saint Louise calls Saint Vincent "Monsieur," as she did at the beginning, allowing us to arrive at the conjectured date of the letter.

Letter 1033b. - Archives of the Motherhouse of the Daughters of Charity, original autograph letter. Saint Vincent's reply to Saint Louise's letter (no. 1033a) was penned on that same letter.

[1]As noted below (n. 4), this letter was written on Rogation Monday after the Sisters were established in Saint-Denis (August 1645), at the time when Saint Louise was in the habit of calling Saint Vincent "Monsieur" (before 1650). The year 1649 is to be excluded because on May 10, 1649, Monday of Rogation Week, Saint Vincent was not in Paris. So the above letter must have been written either on May 7, 1646, May 27, 1647, or May 18, 1648. It was most probably in 1648, given the illness of Mother Hélène-Angélique, who had been reelected Superioress of the First Monastery in Paris on June 6, 1647 but, because of poor health, was replaced on May 16, 1649, before the end of her three-year term.

[2]Anne-Marie Bollain was born on September 30, 1599. One time, when Saint Francis de

refused to take that creature. All that remains is to write and ask Madame Traversay to use her influence to put her in the Pitié.[3] I cannot go there; this morning we will have the Notre-Dame procession,[4] which I have to welcome, and a person of quality is waiting for me. It would be well for you to write to her. If need be, M. Lambert[5] will go to see her immediately after dinner, while I go to Saint-Denis to see Hélène-Angélique,[6] who is ill, and also for an urgent matter there that cannot be put off. I strongly fear that I shall not be able to see our dear Sisters of Charity there.

The thought has occurred to me that there may be some complicity between this creature and the young man in order to become more worthy of consideration. This may be a rash judgment, but the wretched state in which she is makes me suspicious, except that she might have promised the young man she would make him rich in England and, once she was on the point of leaving, she found this pretext to get away from him.

Sales was in Paris, she presented herself to him to be received into the First Monastery of the Visitation. He asked her name and she replied, "Bollain." "My daughter," the Saint said to her, using a wordplay on her name, "the flaxseed [lin] is tiny but it multiplies extremely well; so must you be in the soil of religious life, where I promise you a place." She was so mature, even as early as the novitiate, that Saint Jane Frances followed her advice and moderated various articles in the Book of Customs. In 1629 she was sent as Superioress to the Madeleine convent, which she left in 1633, summoned to the First Monastery by the vote of the Sisters, who wanted her as their head. Three years later she returned to the Madeleine as Superioress. In 1664 she absented herself for six years in order to govern the Community in Chaillot. The First Monastery requested her again in 1673. She died there on January 15, 1683, having served God in the cloister for sixty-three years. Saint Jane Frances said of her that she was "a very fervent and virtuous soul, who would go straight to God." (Cf. *Année Sainte*, vol. I, pp. 360-375.)

[3]A hospital in Paris.

[4]Saint-Lazare Church was one of the stations assigned for the procession of Monday of Rogation Week. The old custom book, preserved in the Archives of the Mission, describes the ceremonial used on that occasion, when the clergy of Notre-Dame would honor the Priests of the Mission with a visit. This ceremonial was used until the end of the eighteenth century.

[5]Lambert aux Couteaux.

[6]Hélène-Angélique Lhuillier.

1034. - DENIS GAUTIER TO SAINT VINCENT

1648

In the course of two missions given in Bas-Poitou, three Missionaries had the happiness of converting prominent heretics.

1035. - *JEAN BARREAU TO SAINT VINCENT*

[Algiers, May 1648] [1]

Here is a story you will find no less beautiful than last year's. You can see from its outcome the help I have received from the all-powerful hand of our good God, who has cured me once again, this time of the contagious disease which continues to spread daily. I cannot fathom the deliberations of His promptings,[2] but I fear, and rightly so, that He may throw the chaff into the fire after plucking the wheat from it.

It seemed like the great and important services which the late Monsieur Lesage, my dearest beloved father and master, rendered to our good God in the person of the poor Christian slaves in this town of Algiers should have merited for him a century of life, and that acts of cowardice should have soon found their end in the end of my life. To my confusion, I see quite the contrary.

He made his appearance in this town only like a flash of lightning; however, it left some very tangible signs of its effects and made him all the more respected since they were more extensive.

His mission did not last as long as that of the late Monsieur Nouelly, but his work was just as important because of the many opportunities Our Lord offered him from last Ash Wednesday, when he came to town, until the twelfth of this month, when he went to his glory. That entire period was but one continual succession of care and solicitude for both the spiritual and temporal assistance of the poor who were sick with the plague or with some other illness.

Letter 1034. - Abelly, *op.cit.*, bk. II, chap. I, sect. II, §8, p. 53.

Letter 1035. - Lyons manuscript, f° 203ff.

[1]Jean Barreau wrote this letter in May 1648, some time after May 12, the day Jacques Lesage died.

[2]Perhaps an allusion to Rm 11:34: "For who has known the mind of the Lord?" (NAB)

His first concern after his arrival was to find out exactly how Monsieur Nouelly acted with regard to the poor Christian slaves. He also asked about his method of assisting them and then of prompting them to worthy fruits of penance by the salutary exhortations he used to give, both at the end of Mass and of Vespers, in the prisons under Cheleby and Collorgli, two powerful persons in the town. He would sometimes have them say evening prayers at the end of Vespers, as he had done at the beginning of Mass for morning prayers. This had not yet been a practice in this town. To oblige everyone to adopt this holy custom, he had the prayers translated into Spanish, the most common language in this town. We were working on this at the very time the severity of his illness obliged him to take to his bed.

At the end of his exhortations, he would ask all those present to let him know when one of them or someone they knew became ill of the plague or of some other disease and that he would go to assist them, even at the risk of his own life. This plea was made so lovingly that it brought tears to the eyes of all. But that was nothing compared to his zeal in doing what he had promised them. This gave him such credibility among the poor Christians that they would flock to him from all sides to be assisted either spiritually or corporally, according to their needs.

Since he feared that his words might not have enough effect on them, he promised a monetary reward to those who would do him the favor for which he so greatly thirsted, and he always had some Christians in his pay who did nothing but comb the town to find out where there were any sick persons. In this way, what his own weakness did not allow him to do himself, he accomplished through others, carrying out his ministry with great ardor in the administration of the sacraments as well as the other assistance he gave.

He knew how to accompany his zeal with such discretion and prudence that he would send ahead Monsieur Claude Didier, the apothecary he had brought with him from France, to find some way of talking with the sick persons. If, in fact, there was any difficulty gaining entry, he would make it clear to the master that he could give no remedy to his slave unless the doctor had seen him and that he had brought one with him for this purpose. In this way, he gained entry to places where his life was in danger.

So, thanks to this ingenious method, they both entered the home of a Turk who rudely turned them away at first but, when he was told that one of them was a doctor and the other a surgeon and that they were there to visit his sick Christian, he allowed them to come in and wanted to accompany them. When Monsieur Didier saw that this man's presence would hinder them, he began to talk with him and steered him imperceptibly out of the hole where the poor patient was lying, while our doctor was performing his pious duty. The Turk believed quite simply everything said to him about the man who was with his slave. At that point in time, however, the women suddenly appeared, and they realized that this was a papas, as they call the priests. Yet, our good God, who was viewing this whole trick favorably, gave them sufficient restraint not to reveal this because there was grave danger for both sides. So, their inventiveness was successful, to the advantage of the poor Christian and to the greater glory of God.

Another time, he used the same trick to get inside the house of a powerful Turk, where a poor Christian and a Spanish renegade were both stricken with the plague. Despite the two obvious dangers of plague and fire, he was determined to enter at all costs. In fact, he succeeded so well in this that, when the renegade, who was lying beside the Christian, heard his exhortations to him and the regrets being expressed by the latter, he was moved with very deep sorrow for having abandoned our holy faith and earnestly requested the sacrament of Penance. Our good doctor thought it advisable to put this off until evening, so he could seek a little advice and counsel on what had to be done in such a case. In the meantime, he had him make some acts of contrition, in the hope that he could return that evening. He did not fail to do so, although I told him he was risking the fire in this, and if, on the point of dying, the renegade refused to say certain words proper to them, this would be attributed to his visit; or if he recovered, there was still danger. None of this prevented him from going back that very evening. But, alas! how impartial are the judgments of God! He discovered that Our Lord had already taken care of matters and the man had died.

There was no less danger regarding the Christian because the master was planning to make a Turk of him. Several times Monsieur Didier went back there but was never allowed to see him again. Our good doctor wanted to try one more time to exhort this poor Christian to remain steadfast in the faith. However, the very day he was to carry out his plan, he fell ill. Since then, we have heard nothing more of him. What gives us reason to fear is that a few women were taking good care of him during his illness and, profiting by his weakness, may have corrupted him.

That, Monsieur, seems to me sufficient to make him a martyr by desire. This is not the only occasion on which he exposed himself to death. There are many others which, through humility, he kept hidden from us. Shortly before he fell ill, his zeal prompted him to enter a house where there were some plague-stricken persons, so that he could assist a poor dying Christian. This same zeal led him to go into another house from which everyone had fled and, finding there, stone dead, the person he was seeking, he knelt fearlessly at his feet, said a De profundis *for his soul, and went off to his next venture. O Monsieur! how I admire that!*

Had his strength equaled his courage, he would have given us much more matter on which to reflect, even though I am not wanting for any, by the grace of God. If I tried to spell out in detail all his heroic actions, since there were very few days when something noteworthy did not happen to him, or if I could resurrect the Christians who died of the plague in the Cheleby hospital or the Customs Office prison, they would reveal to us many things which he kept hidden from us. In a word, I think I have said it all when I say that no Christian of any nationality, with any illness whatsoever, who sought his help, was not assisted by him with unbelievable charity.

Amidst his lofty occupations, he always remembered his prisons. He used to preach there so effectively that we have seen slaves who had not been to confession for ten, twelve, or fourteen years come and cast themselves at his feet and make their Easter duty with generous resolutions to rid themselves of their bad habits.

With the arrival of Holy Week, he intensified his exhortations after Tenebrae, which we chanted on these three days, as is customary. On Holy Thursday he performed the ceremony of the washing of the feet so devoutly that everyone had tears in his eyes. Since I too was present, I shed a few as well.

The next day, he preached the Passion, crucifix in hand, and at the end he asked for justice against those who might neglect their duty. Then he had all his listeners declare that they would put themselves in the disposition of good Christians; most of them have been faithful to this. To make things easier for them, since there were only two priests, he decided to sleep in the prison at night in order to hear the confessions of those who might present themselves. The following day he celebrated the Office with all the ceremonies and devotion that time and place allowed.

After having spoken, to the best of my ability but not as the importance of the subject deserves, of the way he dealt with strangers, I do not think it out of place to say a few words about his gentleness in settling matters in the house. By this means he was able to lead me gradually to do what he thought advisable, as he did with everyone else in the house.

I had the honor of writing to you previously about how I prepared to welcome him and the great peace this gave me. That is why I shall not speak of it here. No one ever heard him contradict anything whatsoever. He approved with flattering words all that was done, and the affinity between us was so strong that, when he was out, I was worried, and when he did not see me, he had no rest. We were so united in affection that the two of us had but one heart, with the difference, however, that mine was *very far from the perfection of his. But alas! this happiness did not last! It seems to me that it was only a dream.*

From all of the above, it is easy to imagine that his illness was due only to his assiduity in assisting those poor persons stricken with plague and other diseases, which forced him to take to his bed on Friday, the fifth of this month. The night before, he had felt some pain in his right groin, obliging him to send for Monsieur Didier, who advised him to go back to bed. However, since he preferred the salvation of souls to that of his own body, he did not have enough influence over him to prevent him from going to say Mass at the Customs Office prison or from stopping on his way home at the Cheleby prison at the insistence of the prison supervisors. The Prefect of the Capuchins had gone there to sing High Mass in honor of Saint Roch, and he was supposed to take the office of deacon. Once the Mass was over, which was very fatiguing for him, we returned to the house, where he told me he was in pain. After working with him for quite a long time on the translation of the prayers I mentioned above, he had to take to his bed at two o'clock in the afternoon, which he did with a certain joy and cheerfulness at seeing himself come to a halt for such a beautiful reason. This caused me to shed tears of sweet consolation, reflecting that M. Nouelly had fallen ill on a similar Friday.

We visited him afterward and found that the plague had already made him quite swollen. About an hour later the carbuncle appeared on the outside, about the width of a finger, which at first we took for a good sign.

Immediately Monsieur Didier applied remedies to assist nature, which seemed to want to take its own course. Meanwhile, we had him take some stimulants with some broth, but his weak stomach caused him to vomit. This obliged Monsieur Didier to apply a poultice of treacle and other things to his stomach. He had only a slight fever and no nausea or headache, which led us to hope that nothing would come of this or at least that he would come out of it.

We did not fail to have his confession heard in the evening, and on the following day he received Holy Viaticum. Nevertheless, since he was sleeping fitfully, we felt that his illness had already affected his heart. For this reason, we thought it advisable on Sunday morning to give him Extreme Unction, while his mind was still clear. After this he asked me to read, one word at a time, the formula of the vows which the members of the Company make before you and he repeated it most fervently. He also asked me to assure you that he was dying with all the sentiments the Company asks of its members and declared that, if our good God should choose to restore his health, he would use it for the salvation of souls, even to his last breath.

That, I assure you, brought tears to my eyes. After receiving his blessing, which I had knelt down to ask of him, I repeated the same vow formula one word at a time and begged him, when he would appear before God in heaven, to bear the same testimony before His Divine Majesty as he was instructing me to bear before others. I embraced him at that very moment as cordially as possible, declaring that I would die at his feet rather than abandon him. Remembering a silver cross he had around his neck, in which there were some relics, he himself pulled it off saying that he had scruples about dying while wearing this treasure, and he placed it in my hands to dispose of it as you would like. When I asked him if he was wearing it without permission, he said that you had in fact given it to him, but you did not realize how valuable it was. You can see, Monsieur, how great was his detachment.

Meanwhile, his weak stomach caused him to reject even the restoratives we had given him, and he could not keep down the broth. Finally, on Tuesday, the twelfth of this month, he began with a slight sweat lasting for about a quarter of an hour, and we thought this was the crisis. After that, his extremities turned cold. Then we asked him how he was, and he told us he felt rested. While we were thinking that this was the case, a quarter of an hour later he entered into his agony. Immediately I took his crucifix and had him kiss it while making an act of contrition, which he repeated one word at a time. Then I had him say Maria mater gratiae [3] *and ten or twelve times the Holy Names of Jesus and Mary. Following this, Father Sébastien,[4] a religious of Our Lady of Mercy, gave him a plenary indulgence in virtue of his Order, and general absolution. A moment later he died, hands joined, without a struggle and without losing his faculties.*

So that, Monsieur, was a death to be hoped for, inasmuch as his life was exemplary and worthy of imitation, causing us to recognize clearly that in brevi explevit tempora multa [5] *because he died at the age of thirty-six, the age he had given me shortly before.*

If people mourned the late Monsieur Nouelly, they did no less for him. The tears of the poor Christians are the genuine proof of this, and they say openly that they have lost their father.

The next day we took him to Bab-Azoun, near the late Monsieur Nouelly. We were accompanied by four or five hundred Christians, who were weeping, thinking they were being abandoned in the danger they were running, especially since the other priests are unwilling to take such risks.

---

[3]*Mary, Mother of Grace.* Opening words of the Latin hymn.
[4]Sébastien Brugière.
[5]*In a brief space he made up a great deal of time.*

Unless there are some as courageous as those two priests, they will not get much assistance.

That same day, the first Mass in our chapel was said with his body present. I had him laid out in another place because it was too small. The Mass was said by a Benedictine monk, the only priest we have left of those three said to be of the regular observance, who were taken recently. Our deceased had an advantage over the others because as soon as a Christian dies, he is put into the ground.

This morning a solemn service was sung in the King's prison, at which a good number of those Christians whose free time allowed were present. The Capuchin Father summarized briefly some of his principal accomplishments but, since he has only been in this town a short time, he could not know all that had happened to him. Here, more or less, is what I have been able to recall of what he said: that the more perfect things are, the more we should miss them when we lose them. He proved his perfection by his mortification, having died to himself, since, with no concern for his own health, he risked his life for the salvation of his brothers. He quoted the passage of the Apocalypse, Beati mortui,[6] *with the application given by Saint Ambrose. He gave proof of this also by his simplicity and gentleness, comparing him to that little child in the Gospel to whom Our Lord, repeating the commandments of God, replied,* hac hora,[7] *etc., and when it comes to judgment, our deceased might very well say the same thing. He proved it also by his charity, risking his life so magnanimously by coming to this town, well aware that the disease was so rampant.* Majorem caritatem,[8] *etc. Finally, he concluded by saying that this was sufficient to make him a martyr. But what might he have said had he known all that I mentioned above!*

Father Sébastien gave him all the help he could. All I can say is that he has very great charity since, as soon as he heard about his illness, he came and offered his services, never leaving him until he had buried him.

Monsieur Didier, who was especially impressed by his virtues, did all that was humanly possible to restore him to health, always sleeping in his room in order to be more prompt in assisting him, regardless of the danger.

---

[6]*Happy are the dead.* "I heard a voice from heaven say to me, 'Write this down: Happy now are the dead who die in the Lord!' The Spirit added, 'Yes, they shall find rest from their labors, for their good works accompany them.'" Rev 14:13. (NAB)

[7]*In this hour.*

[8]*Greater love.* "There is no greater love than this: to lay down one's life for one's friends." Jn 15:13. (NAB)

Poor René Duchesne and Jean Benoît,[9] whose only hope of freedom lies in your assistance, looked after him with all possible affection.

In a word, Monsieur, everyone did his duty in this situation. I am the only one who acquitted himself badly of it, for which I most humbly ask your pardon. It is with these sentiments that I feel obliged to close this letter, which is going on the galley ship. I assure you that I will consider myself blessed if, after such a beautiful life, I could have such a beautiful death. I beg you to obtain this from our good God for me and am, in His love, with my whole heart, Monsieur, your most humble and obedient servant.

BARREAU

I ask pardon for my haste in concluding this letter. We thought that the galley was not to leave until tomorrow; an order has just arrived to have it leave shortly. The Capuchin Father is very ill; we do not know what is wrong with him. The other priest is on the galley where René Duchesne and Jean Benoît have gone. At present, I am alone.

1036. - *SAINT LOUISE TO SAINT VINCENT*

[Before 1650][1]

Monsieur,

It is true that I have a very special affection for the feast of Pentecost and that the period preceding it is very dear to me. I remember being greatly consoled some time ago on hearing a preacher say that it was on that day God gave His written law to Moses and, in the law of grace, on that same day He had given to His Church the law of His love which had the power to effect it. And because on that same day God was pleased to place in my heart a law that has never left it [2] despite all my bad qualities,

---

[9]Both were slaves in Algiers. Duchesne entered the Congregation of the Mission as a coadjutor Brother in 1654. (Cf. no. 974.)

Letter 1036. - Archives of the Motherhouse of the Daughters of Charity, original autograph letter.

[1]After 1649 Saint Louise always used the salutation "Most honored Father."

[2]Saint Louise alludes here to her "Light of Pentecost" experience in 1623. In no. 753, n. 2, she refers to Divine Providence showing her that she would embrace the vows of poverty,

I would gladly hope, if it were allowed me, that on that same day His goodness might make me understand the means of observing this law in accordance with His holy Will. I do not know if that is why I had the thought of asking your permission for us to prepare ourselves for this feast by abstaining from Holy Communion on those eleven days during which the Blessed Virgin, the Apostles, and the holy women were separated from their dear Master. We might also profit from this occasion to reflect on the poor use we have made of our Communions during the year, in order to stir up within us a renewed desire of receiving Communion more fervently and profitably for the glory of God, and to share with the Apostles the baptism of love and fervor for the service of the neighbor.

I beg you most humbly, Monsieur, not to let the weaknesses of my spirit, which I have manifested to you, exact of your charity the condescension that might cause you to think I want you to defer to my way of thinking. This is completely foreign to my desire, and I have no greater pleasure than when I am reasonably thwarted, since God almost always gives me the grace to acknowledge and value the advice of others, particularly when this is a charity. I am certain of seeing this truth clearly, even in matters that may be obscure to me for a time.

1037. - TO JEAN MARTIN, IN GENOA

Paris, May 22, 1648

The grace of Our Lord be with you forever!

I received your letter written in M. Blatiron's absence. It gave me special joy by informing me that your health has improved, but I am still saddened to see that you are determined to go back to work already, where I fear you will relapse into a worse state. I beg you to be patient and to build up your strength as much as you can with rest and remedies. You can give me no greater consolation nor render greater service to your neighbor than to place yourself in a condition to serve him for a long time. Those priests, whom

---

chastity, and obedience in a small Community dedicated to the service of the neighbor. This is the "law" which God put in her heart and which "has never left it."

Letter 1037. - Archives of the Mission, Turin, original signed letter.

you think you will be scandalizing, will, on the contrary, be edified to know you are most obedient in this, as you are on important and difficult occasions.

I have written M. Blatiron to keep M. Brunet[1] for a while, even though we need him badly elsewhere.

I beg you to recommend my soul to Our Lord, since I am, in His love, Monsieur, your most humble servant.

VINCENT DEPAUL
i.s.C.M.

At the bottom of the first page: M. Martin

1038. - TO JEAN MARTIN, IN GENOA

Paris, June 12, 1648

Monsieur,

The grace of Our Lord be with you forever!

Thank you for taking the trouble to write me in M. Blatiron's absence. I am trying to find a way to get our letters to you without any cost to you. It is not right that the postage is being paid twice.

I am writing M. Alméras to give you one of his Brothers, if possible, in exchange for another whom you will send to him.

You know that the Community in Genoa is very dear to me. I am greatly consoled when its members are content and when, generally speaking, things are going well there. To this end I recommend it quite often to Our Lord, and especially your own dear soul, Monsieur, to which mine is so closely united.

---

[1]Jean-Joseph Brunet was born in Riom (Puy-de-Dôme) in 1597, joined the companions of Saint Vincent in 1627, and gave missions in the Bordelais region. He was stationed in Alet, in Genoa, and in Marseilles where he died on August 6, 1649, a victim of his dedication to the plague-stricken.

Letter 1038. - Archives of the Mission, Turin, original signed letter.

I am seriously considering sending you an older man who, as you and M. Blatiron have written me, is needed so that those who come to the house will have confidence in him.

You tell me nothing about your health; please God it will improve more and more for His glory and my consolation. I am, Monsieur, your most humble servant.

VINCENT DEPAUL
i.s.C.M.

At the bottom of the first page: M. Martin

1039. - TO MATHURIN GENTIL, IN LE MANS

Paris, June 14, 1648

Monsieur,

The grace of Our Lord be with you forever!

Since M. Lucas[1] has gone to give a mission, I ask you to send the enclosed letter by express messenger to Monsieur de Saint-Aignan,[2] who will hand deliver it to him. Also, give M. Charpentier the one I am writing to him. Perhaps he could be the bearer of the first one.

We have no one to give you to play the organ because Brother Dufresne[3] is needed here.

Since it is customary to offer lunch to the Lieutenant General, the officers, and others who are with him on the feast of Corpus Christi, this is an established tradition and consequently it must be respected. It would be difficult to dispense with it.

Letter 1039. - Archives of the Mission, Turin, original signed letter.

[1]Antoine Lucas, Superior of the house.

[2]Paul Chevalier, who had been Canon of Saint-Aignan at Notre-Dame de Paris since 1638. Later he was Vicar-General for Cardinal de Retz. He died in 1674.

[3]Perhaps Denis Dufresne, coadjutor Brother, born in Argenteuil (Val-d'Oise), entered the Congregation of the Mission on November 1, 1642, at forty-one years of age.

I am writing to you in haste but not without the consolation of assuring you that your heart is dear to me and that I am, with all my heart, Monsieur, your most humble servant.

VINCENT DEPAUL
i.s.C.M.

At the bottom of the first page: M. Gentil

1040. - *TOMMASO TURCO, MASTER GENERAL OF THE DOMINICANS, TO SAINT VINCENT*

Most Reverend Father and Lord,

The loyal attachment of your Most Reverend Paternity to me and to my Order gives you so many claims to my gratitude that, when I reflect on your acts of kindness, I am often impelled to come with my thanks to distract you from your holy and public occupations and to offend your modesty.

What especially urges me to express my gratitude to you is the establishment of a chair of theology, for the benefit of both regular and secular clergy, at the university directed by our Order in Cashel, Ireland. This was done at the request of our confrere, Father Fabian Ryan, an Irishman of our Order, delegated by his Provincial for this purpose. I have appreciated this kindness toward our Order all the more deeply because, since it is public in nature, it is also profitable for the knowledge and glory of God, for the instruction and salvation of many, as well as being a help and an honor for our Institute. I hope and pray that this holy work may be sustained by the hand that established it and that, having begun under the inspiration of such great charity, it may be brought to completion by the glowing flames of that same virtue.

In return for the services rendered and the one for which I am hoping, I offer Your Most Reverend Paternity the good wishes which I and my Order here and everywhere, particularly in Ireland, formulate for the preservation of your person and that of your holy Society. It will have everywhere the gratitude of one who will always be indebted to it. I await

---

Letter 1040. - Archives of the Mission, Paris, copy made at the Generalate of the Dominicans, *Epistolae R. P. Turchi*, IV, p. 91. The original was written in Latin.

the opportunity of offering you something more than good wishes and of proving to you effectively that I am truly and sincerely Your Most Reverend Paternity's most humble and very devoted servant in Our Lord.

Rome, Convent of Santa Maria sopra Minerva, June 15, 1648.

1041. - *SAINT LOUISE TO SAINT VINCENT*

[June 1648] [1]

Monsieur,

Monsieur Lambert will tell you about the grave illness of our dear Sister Louise from Saint-Jacques. [2] *I entreat your charity most humbly to explain to him the blessing our Holy Father has granted us and how it is applied, so that our poor Sister may share in this great benefit.* [3]

I beg you most humbly to allow me to visit her tomorrow, and Madame de Marillac, [4] *if I can find transportation, and by the same means, to make the three holy stations that are quite close to one another on rue Saint-Denis. I would also be glad if your charity would kindly talk with me on Saturday, so that I may receive Holy Communion on Sunday, with the intention of gaining the Jubilee.*

I beg you most humbly to take the trouble of informing me whether I should write to Sister Barbe [5] *concerning the little girl she sent us, in view of what she has told me about her.* [6] *Also, what shall I tell her about that*

Letter 1041. - Saint-Paul manuscript, p. 24.

[1]The presence in Paris of Lambert aux Couteaux, Superior at the Collège des Bons-Enfants, and Louis Thibault; and the mention of the Jubilee, leave no doubt as to the year. Moreover, the letter was written just a few days before June 24, the date of Saint Louise's letter to Sister Barbe Angiboust (cf. *Ecrits spirituels*, L. 181bis, p. 246).

[2]Saint-Jacques de la Boucherie. L. 181bis refers to the illness and death of this Sister.

[3]1648 was a Jubilee Year and Saint Louise was referring to the special Jubilee indulgences.

[4]Jeanne Potier, wife of Michel de Marillac, the grandson of the Keeper of the Seals of the same name.

[5]Barbe Angiboust, who was then in Fontainebleau.

[6]This "good little girl," as the Foundress calls her, came to Paris and, because Mademoiselle found her too young, she sent her back to Barbe Angiboust, to whom she wrote on June 24, 1648, "I think you would do well to place her in service, provided it be with good people, with a farmer perhaps, even if, in the beginning, she only minded the cows; then, as she grows up, she could be given something else to do. When she has worked for three or four years, if God grants her the will to serve among us, we will accept her. It is far better that she should wish to do so once she has reached the right age than to come now when she does not know what she

*woman and the two girls she mentions in her letter, which I received
yesterday and am sending on to you?*

*If Monsieur Lambert does me the charity of telling you all the com-
plaints made to him about me, you will see clearly the need I have of your
granting my request to you for Saturday.*

*Mademoiselle's [7] chaplain has just informed me himself that he would
take the trouble to come to this neighborhood to share Sister Barbe's letter
with you, and would show it to me as well. I had not said anything to him
on your part.*

1042. - TO SAINT LOUISE

[June 1648]

Yesterday Monsieur Lambert went to see our good Sister from
Saint-Jacques and found her in very grave danger but equally
resigned to God's good pleasure. I do not yet know what is usually
done with that type of indulgence granted to you by our Holy
Father; I shall make inquiries about it. Moreover, this good Sister
has gained the Jubilee, during which all other indulgences are
suspended. If your health permits and you have a carriage, you
could pay her a visit and make your stations in two or three places
at the most.

It would be well to send word to Sister Barbe to send you those
two girls, if M. Thibault thinks they are suitable. Say nothing to her
about the girl who accompanied that Sister.

---

wants." (Cf. *Ecrits spirituels*, L. 181bis, p. 247.)

[7]Anne-Marie d'Orléans, Duchesse de Montpensier, daughter of Gaston d'Orléans, brother of
Louis XIII. "Mademoiselle" was the stylized official title given to the eldest niece of Louis XIII;
Gaston d'Orléans bore the title "Monsieur." The Duchesse de Montpensier is usually referred
to as "La Grande Mademoiselle."

Letter 1042. - Saint-Paul manuscript, p. 24. This letter is Saint Vincent's reply to the preceding
one.

1043. - TO JEAN DEHORGNY, IN ROME

Paris, June 25, 1648

Monsieur,

The grace of O[ur] L[ord] be with you forever!

Your last letter stated two things: first, that we give our coadjutor Brothers duties of too great importance; and the other, that we have done wrong by declaring ourselves opposed to the new opinions.[1]

On the first point, Monsieur, I will tell you that I thank Our Lord most humbly for directing your attention to the way the Company is governed. I ask you to continue to do so, even though I think we are right in acting as we do regarding the two points mentioned above.

In the entire Company, only Brother Alexandre[2] receives and is responsible for money. We gave him this duty when we sent M. Gentil to Le Mans[3] because we had no priest whom we could assign to it, and he has fulfilled this duty in such a way that we have good reason to praise God for it.

That good Brother Nicolas[4] of the Crécy house, whom you mention to me, did not have charge of the money, regardless of what you have been told. The money is kept there in a coffer with two locks on it. M. Tournisson[5] had the key to one of them and his assistant had the other. The same is done everywhere, especially in the places where M. Portail has made his visitation. This does not mean that we will not entrust this duty to a priest at a later date or that we are not making note of what you tell me.

Letter 1043. - Archives of the Department of Vaucluse, D 296, an old copy made from the original. *Mémoires de Trévoux* also reprints it with slight variants so minor that it was deemed expedient to point out only two.

[1]Jansenism.

[2]Alexandre Véronne.

[3]*Mémoires de Trévoux* had "Maine."

[4]Several coadjutor Brothers had this Christian name.

[5]This name is not found in the catalogue of personnel; it is probably a misreading of "Louis Serre."

I think the trouble caused in religious Orders by the Brothers arises from the fact that they are kept in too lowly a position. Saint Francis gives instructions that the lay Brothers should have a voice in the election of Guardians; however, the Capuchins and the Recollects[6] have abolished this. That is what is dispiriting those poor Brothers and has obliged them to complain of it to the Pope. The Son of God treated His Apostles as friends, although they were not yet priests, and here we want to treat our Brothers as servants, even though it is true to say that most of them are more virtuous than most of us, at least more than I.[7]

As for your second point, concerning the fault we have committed in declaring ourselves opposed to the new opinions, here, Monsieur, are the reasons which have led me to do so.

The first is my position on the Council of Ecclesiastical Affairs, where every member—the Queen, the Cardinal,[8] the Chancellor,[9] and the Penitentiary[10]—has declared opposition to them. Judge from that whether I could remain neutral. The outcome has revealed that it was expedient to act as we have done.

The second reason is my knowledge of the intention of the author of these new opinions,[11] which is to ruin the present state of

---

[6]Reformed Franciscans.

[7]This whole section is omitted in *Mémoires de Trévoux*.

[8]Jules Cardinal Mazarin.

[9]Pierre Séguier, son of Jean Séguier, Seigneur d'Autry, and Marie Tudert de la Bournalière, was born in Paris on May 29, 1588. In 1633 he was named Keeper of the Seals, and Chancellor in 1635. In 1649 the Seals were taken from him only to be returned in 1656, at the death of Mathieu Molé. He retained them until his death in Saint-Germain-en-Laye, January 28, 1672.

[10]Jacques Charton.

[11]Jean du Verger de Hauranne, Abbé de Saint-Cyran, was born in Bayonne in 1581. He had met Saint Vincent in Paris around 1622 and was not long in striking up a friendship with him. According to his nephew, Barcos (*Défense de feu M. Vincent de Paul*), he had supposedly rendered some important services to the Saint, and the Congregation of the Mission was in some measure indebted to him for the possession of the Collège des Bons-Enfants and for Saint-Laz-are, as well as for the Bull of approbation obtained from the Roman Court. What is certain is that their meetings, rather frequent while the Saint was living at the Bons-Enfants, became more rare after 1632 and almost ceased from 1634 on. In 1638 Saint-Cyran was arrested on the authority of Richelieu and imprisoned at the Château de Vincennes. As soon as the Cardinal was dead (1643), Louis XIII allowed the prisoner to communicate with people outside. This measure of clemency was soon followed by a second: on February 16, 1643, Saint-Cyran was

the Church and put it under his own power. He told me one day that God's intention was to destroy the present Church and that those who were working to maintain it were doing so contrary to His plan. When I said to him that this was the pretext ordinarily used by heresiarchs, such as Calvin, he replied that Calvin was not wrong in all he had attempted but had defended himself poorly.[12]

The third is that I noted that three or four Popes[13] had condemned the opinions of Baius,[14] maintained by Jansenius. The Sorbonne had done likewise in 1560, and the most devout part of the same faculty, composed of all the older men, declared themselves opposed to these new opinions,[15] and our Holy Father has condemned the doctrine about the two Heads of the Church, which certain ill-intentioned persons were trying to establish.[16]

The fourth, which I place last here, apart from several others, is what Pope Celestine says in *Epistola 2 ad Episcopos Galliae* against some priests who were advancing certain errors against grace, which those Bishops had condemned. This good Pope, after praising the latter for their opposition to the teaching of those priests, said in these very words: *Timeo ne connivere sit hoc tacere; timeo ne illi magis loquantur qui permittunt illis taliter loqui; in*

---

set free. He did not enjoy the royal favor for long; he died of a cerebral hemorrhage on October 11, 1643.

[12]Abelly gives an account of this conversation, *op. cit.,* bk. II. chap. XII, p. 410.

[13]Saint Pius V (1566-1572), Gregory XIII (1572-1585), and Urban VIII (1623-1644).

[14]Michel Baius (de Bay) was born in Melin (Belgium) in 1513. Appointed Professor of Sacred Scripture, then Chancellor, at the University of Louvain, he was so highly esteemed by his colleagues that they sent him as a representative to the Council of Trent. He was also appointed to the office of Inquisitor General. His peculiar views on the state of redeemed nature, justification, the efficacy of the Sacraments, and the merit of good works, which he spread through his writings and public lectures, disturbed several Doctors of Theology at the University and provoked attacks on his teachings. Eighteen of his propositions were condemned by the Faculty of Paris (June 27, 1560) and seventy-six by Saint Pius V (October 1, 1567 and May 13, 1569). Gregory XIII was compelled to intervene again on January 29, 1579. Baius died on September 19, 1589, after retracting his errors verbally and in writing. His *Oeuvres* were printed in Cologne in 1696 by the Jansenists, Quesnel and Gerberon, and were put on the Index on May 8, 1697.

[15]Jansenism had adherents in the Sorbonne, especially among the younger Doctors of Theology. (Cf. Rapin, *Mémoires,* vol. I, pp. 43-46.)

[16]Condemned by Innocent X on January 24, 1647.

*talibus causis non caret suspicione taciturnitas, quia occurreret
veritas, si falsitas displiceret; merito namque causa non respicit,
si silentio faveamus errori.*[17] If anyone tells me that this is true for
bishops but not for private individuals, I reply that in all probability
it applies not only to bishops but also to those who see evil and, as
far as in them lies, do nothing to prevent it.

Let us see now what is involved here. You tell me that it is a
question of the book *De la fréquente communion* of Jansenius[18]
which, to begin with, you have read twice, and that the misuse of
this Divine Sacrament has perhaps led to that.

It is true, Monsieur, that only too many persons abuse this
Divine Sacrament. I, wretch that I am, do this more than anyone
else in the world, and I beg you to help me to ask God's forgiveness
for it. Instead of inclining people toward frequent Communion, the
reading of this book, in fact, turns them away from it. No longer
do we see people with this great desire for the Sacraments as we
formerly did, not even during the Easter season. Many pastors in
Paris complain that they have far fewer communicants than in past
years. Saint-Sulpice has three thousand fewer. After Easter, the
Pastor of Saint-Nicolas-du-Chardonnet[19] visited, personally and by
proxy, the families in his parish, and he told us recently that he
discovered fifteen hundred parishioners who had not been to
Communion. The same is true of others. Almost no one, or very
few persons, can be seen any more receiving the Sacrament on the
first Sunday of the month and on big feast days, and scarcely more

---

[17]*I am afraid that to be silent is tantamount to consent. I am afraid that those who allow them
to speak as they do, speak even louder; in such matters silence is not without suspicion because
the truth would come forth if falsehood were disliked; indeed we are under indictment if we
favor error by silence.* Migne, ed., *Patrologiae Cursus completus,* (221 vols., Paris, 1857-1864),
vol. IV, col. 529. Migne prefers the reading *foveamus errorem.*

[18]Seldom did a book cause more of a stir and prove to be such a success as Antoine Arnauld's
De la fréquente communion [On Frequent Communion], written according to the spirit of
Jansenius and published in Paris in 1643. By 1648 it had already reached its sixth edition.
M. Dehorgny was presented with a copy by his Jansenist friend Bourgeois, a Doctor of
Theology, who had come to Rome to prevent its condemnation. He had read it and was imbued
with its teaching, which he found excellent. (Cf. Godefroy Hermant, *Mémoires sur l'histoire
ecclésiastique du XVIIᵉ siècle (1630-1663)* [6 vols., Paris: Plon, 1905-1910], vol. I, p. 389.

[19]Hippolyte Féret, a Doctor of Theology.

in religious Orders, except a few in the Jesuits. Moreover, that is what the late M. de Saint-Cyran claimed in order to discredit the Jesuits.

Some days ago M. de Chavigny[20] was telling a close friend that this good priest had told him that Jansenius and he had made it their intention to discredit that holy Order in the matter of the doctrine and administration of the Sacraments. I myself heard him almost every day hold a number of conversations along these lines.

As soon as M. Arnauld,[21] the author of that book, saw the opposition he encountered on many sides concerning public penance and the penance he was trying to introduce before Communion, he explained that absolution was simply declaratory. Be that as it may, there are, however, still errors in this, as the Grand Master of Navarre,[22] one of the wisest men of the day, recently told us. The Penitentiary and Messrs. Cornet and Coqueret, who were meeting here for matters of this kind, did the same, saying also that this declaration is captious and contains a number of things that are scarcely any better than what he says in the first book.

Is he not erroneous in stating, Monsieur, that the Church which, in the beginning, observed the practice of public penance before absolution, has always desired to reestablish this custom; other-

---

[20]Léon Bouthillier, Comte de Chavigny and Besançois, kinsman of Jean-Jacques Olier, was born in Paris on March 28, 1608. Although he had been personally appointed by Louis XIII to be a member of the Regency Council for Louis XIV during his minority, Mazarin pushed him aside. During the troubles of the Fronde, he sided with the Princes against Mazarin. His sincere piety was allied with his love for pleasure. He died in Paris on October 11, 1652. His wife, Anne Phelippeaux, was an ardent Jansenist.

[21]Antoine Arnauld, born in Paris on February 6, 1612, was ordained a priest in 1641 and admitted into the Sorbonne community in 1643. On the death of Saint-Cyran, he became the leader of the Jansenist party, whose apostle and theologian he had already been. His first controversial work, *De la fréquente communion,* gave him a great deal of notoriety. Subsequently he wrote *Grammaire générale, La Logique ou l'Art de penser [Logic or the Art of Thinking],* and such a large number of other treatises that, combined with his letters, they form a collection of forty-five volumes. He died in exile in Brussels on August 8, 1694. His brothers and sisters were all ardent Jansenists; some of them, Arnauld d'Andilly; Henri Arnauld, Bishop of Angers; Catherine Arnauld, the mother of Le Maistre de Sacy; Mother Angélique, and Mother Agnès, even played important roles in the party. (Cf. Pierre Varin, *La Vérité sur les Arnauld,* [2 vols., Paris: Poussielgue, 1847].)

[22]Jacques Péreyret, Grand Master of the Collège de Navarre.

wise, she would not be the pillar of truth, always consistent with herself, but would be instead a synagogue of errors? Cannot the Church, which never changes in matters of faith, do so with regard to discipline? Has not God, who is immutable in Himself, changed His manner of acting with regard to men? Did not His Son, Our Lord, sometimes change His way of acting, and the Apostles theirs? Why then does this man say that the Church would be in error if she did not retain the desire to restore those forms of penance which she practiced in the past? Is that orthodox?

As for Jansenius, he must be regarded either as upholding the opinions of Baius, so often condemned by the Popes and the Sorbonne, as I have said, or as upholding other doctrines which he treats in his book.

With regard to the first, are we not obliged to respect the censures of the Popes and this learned body against those opinions and to declare ourselves opposed to them? As for the rest of the book, since the Pope has forbidden us to read it, should not the Council of Ecclesiastical Affairs have advised the Queen to use her authority so that the orders of Pope Urban VIII be carried out, and make public profession of being opposed to the censured opinions of Baius and these kinds of new opinions coming from this Doctor, who rashly upholds those concerning grace, about which the Church has not yet made a decision?

You tell me in your letter that Jansenius read the complete works of Saint Augustine ten times and the treatises on grace thirty times, and that it is unlikely that the Missionaries will presume to make a judgment on the opinions of this great man. To this I reply, Monsieur, that ordinarily those who want to establish new doctrines are very learned men who study assiduously and earnestly the authors they wish to use. We have to admit that this Prelate was very learned and, with the intention of discrediting the Jesuits, as I have said, he may well have read Saint Augustine the number of times you mentioned. That does not mean, however, that he did not fall into error, and it would be inexcusable for us to adhere to his opinions, which are contrary to the censures given against his teachings. Priests have the obligation of not accepting and of refuting the teachings of Calvin and the other heresiarchs, although they may have never read the authors on whom these men relied, or even his books.

You tell me in addition that the opinions we call ancient are modern, and that about seventy years ago Molina[23] formulated the opinions which people say are ancient, setting off the quarrel. I admit, Monsieur, that Molina is the author of what is called *scientia media*.[24] Strictly speaking, this is simply the method showing how it happens that two men may have the same intelligence, the same dispositions and a similar degree of grace to work out their salvation and, nevertheless, one does so and the other does not; one is saved and the other is lost. *Mais quoi!* Monsieur, it is not a question of that, which is not an article of faith. Is the teaching that Jesus Christ died for all, which he is attacking, a new doctrine? Does it not come from Saint Paul and from Saint John? Was not the contrary opinion condemned at the Council of Mainz[25] and at several others[26] where Godeschalcus[27] was condemned? Does not Saint Leo say in the Lessons for Christmas that Our Lord was born *pro liberandis hominibus?* [28] Do not most of the holy Fathers use

---

[23]Luis de Molina, the celebrated Spanish Jesuit, was born around 1535 in Cuenca, Spain, and died on October 12, 1600. He is known chiefly for his book *De concordia gratiae et liberi arbitrii [Of The Harmony Between Grace and Free Will]*, in which he develops his theory of *scientia media* (cf. n. 24 below). Attacked from the outset of its appearance, this work gave rise to violent controversies between the Jesuits and the Dominicans. The question was referred to Rome, and Pope Clement VIII (1592-1605) established an ad hoc congregation, *de Auxiliis*, to judge the controversy. After prolonged and fruitless discussions, Pope Paul V (1605-1621) allowed each of the opposing views to be taught freely and forbade both schools, under threat of severe penalties, to indulge in reciprocal condemnations.

[24]*Scientia media*, so called because it keeps in some way the middle path between divine knowledge of possible things and those which must absolutely come to pass. It is the knowledge whereby God knows infallibly, before each and every absolute decree of His Will, what a person will do in every situation and with every assistance of divine grace.

[25]In the year 848.

[26]For example, at the Council of Quiercy-sur-Oise in 849.

[27]Godescalc or Gottschalk, a learned Benedictine, born in Germany around 803, taught heterodox doctrines on predestination. Condemned by several Councils, he was defrocked, publicly whipped, and imprisoned in the Abbey of Hautvillers. He died in his prison in 868, without renouncing his opinions.

[28]*To free men.*

similar language? In the sixth session of the Council of Trent, *De Justificatione*, chapter 2, do they not bring forward Saint John's words on this point: *Hunc proposuit Deus propitiationem per fidem in sanguine ipsius pro peccatis nostris, non solum autem pro nostris, sed etiam pro totius mundi?* [29] And in the third: *Verum etsi ille pro omnibus mortuus est,*[30] and it goes on to say that, although this is so, *non omnes tamen mortis ejus beneficium recipiunt, sed ii dumtaxat quibus meritum passionis ejus communicatur.*[31] After that, Monsieur, can we say that this is a new doctrine?

Shall we also call "new" the doctrine he attacks, against the possibility of observing the Commandments of God? This is contrary to Canon 18 of the same Council and session, which states: *Si quis dixerit Dei praecepta homini etiam justificato et sub gratia constituto esse ad observandum impossibilia, anathema sit.*[32]

And the one you mention, Monsieur, that it is of little importance for us to know whether there are sufficient graces or whether they are all efficacious, is that new? Is it not contained in chapter 25 of the second Council of Orange? Here, Monsieur, are the words of that Council, by which you will see, if not the exact words, "sufficient grace," at least what is equivalent to their meaning: *Hoc etiam secundum fidem catholicam credimus quod, accepta per baptismum gratia, omnes baptizati, Christo auxiliante et cooperante, quae ad salutem pertinent, possint et debeant, si fideliter laborare voluerint, adimplere.*[33]

As for your saying that it is of little importance for us to know that, I beg you, Monsieur, to allow me to tell you that I think it most important for all Christians to know and believe that God is so good

---

[29]*Him has God proposed as the propitiation through faith in His Blood for our sins, and not for ours only, but also for those of the whole world.* Cf. I Jn 2:2.

[30]*But though He died for all.*

[31] . . . *yet all do not receive the benefit of His death, but those only to whom the merit of His passion is communicated.*

[32]*If anyone would say that the Commandments of God are impossible to observe, even for one who is justified and in the state of grace, let him be anathema.*

[33]*According to Catholic faith we also believe that, after grace has been received through Baptism, all the baptized, if they are willing to labor faithfully, can and should accomplish, with Christ's help and cooperation, what pertains to salvation.*

that all Christians can, with the grace of Jesus Christ, work out their salvation; that He gives them the means through Jesus Christ; and that this strongly manifests and magnifies the infinite goodness of God.

Furthermore, we cannot call "new" the opinion of the Church which believes that all graces are not efficacious, since we can refuse them, as in *De Justificatione,* chapter 4.

You say that Clement VIII and Paul V have forbidden any discussions concerning grace.[34] I reply, Monsieur, that this refers to matters which have not been decided, such as those I just mentioned. For the others which have not been decided by the Church, why does Jansenius attack it? In that case, is it not according to natural law to defend the Church and to uphold the censures fulminated against this?

You say that these are questions for the schools to treat. That is true for some and, even if it were the same for others, is this any reason to remain silent about them, allowing the substratum of the truths to deteriorate by means of these subtle arguments? Are not our poor people obliged to believe in and consequently to be instructed in matters concerning the Trinity and the Blessed Sacrament, which are so difficult to define?

This, Monsieur, is what has come into my mind to make you see our reasons for declaring ourselves on this occasion opposed to these new opinions. I see no objections to them, except for two. First, there is the reason to fear that, by attempting to stem this flood of new opinions, we may stir people up more. My reply to this is that, if this were the case, heresies should not be opposed nor should those who are determined to rob people of life or property, and the shepherd would do wrong to cry "Wolf!" when he sees one about to enter the sheepfold.

---

[34]To put an end to the discussions which were disturbing the two famous Orders in the Church, after Molina's book had come out, Clement VIII (1592-1605), as was noted above, reserved the matter to himself and forbade both parties to discuss the disputed issues, until he had made known his own decision.

The other reason is prudence, purely human, since it is based on what people will say. We will make enemies. *O Jésus!* Monsieur, God forbid that Missionaries should defend the interests of God and of the Church for these despicable and wretched motives, which are ruining the interests of God and of His Church and filling hell with souls.

Yes, you will tell me, but must Missionaries preach against the opinions of the day and the world? Must they discuss them with one another, debate, attack, and raise a hue and cry in defending the old opinions? *O Jésus,* no, not at all! Here is how we act: we never debate these matters, we never preach on them, we never bring them up in Companies if others do not mention them to us. However, if they do, we try to speak about them with the greatest possible discretion. M. G[illes] is the exception to this; he gets a little carried away by his zeal. Please God, I shall try to remedy that.[35]

Well then, you will say to me, do you forbid discussion on these matters? My reply is yes and that none of them are ever discussed here in this house.

What! do you want them not to be mentioned at our Mission in Rome or elsewhere? I am asking the officers to enforce this and to give a penance to those to who do so, except in the circumstances I cited.

As for what you say to me, Monsieur, that each member of the Company should be allowed to believe what he likes in these matters, *O Jésus!* Monsieur, it is not proper to maintain contrary opinions in the Company. We must always be *unius labii;* [36] otherwise, we would all be tearing one another apart in the same Company.

And how can a person subject himself to the opinion of a superior? I reply that it is not to the superior that he is subjecting

---

[35]M. Gilles taught theology at Saint-Lazare and gave conferences to the ordinands. Saint Vincent gave him several warnings but, unable to mitigate the professor's excessive zeal against the new opinions, had to transfer him from Saint-Lazare.
[36]*Of one tongue.*

himself but rather to God and to the thinking of the Popes, Councils, and saints. And if someone is unwilling to defer, it would be better for him to withdraw and for the Company to ask him to do so. Many Companies in the Church of God give us the example of that. At the Chapter the Discalced Carmelites had last year, it was decreed that their theology professors should teach the ancient opinions of the Church and react against the new ones. Everyone knows that the Jesuit Fathers act in this way, while the Congregation of Sainte-Geneviève, on the contrary, orders its Doctors to uphold the opinions of Saint Augustine. We claim also to do this in explaining Saint Augustine by the Council of Trent, and not the Council by Saint Augustine because the former is infallible and the latter is not. If people say that some Popes have ordered us to believe Saint Augustine on matters of grace, that is to be understood, at most, of questions that were debated and decided at that time.[37] However, since new ones appear from time to time, we must, in their regard, abide by the decision of a Council,[38] which has determined all things according to the true meaning of Saint Augustine, whom it understood better than Jansenius and his followers.[39]

That, Monsieur, is my reply to your letter, which I have shared with no one whomsoever, nor shall I ever do so. I tell you further that I have not mentioned it to anyone whomsoever, nor have I sought the assistance of anyone whomsoever in the world about what I am saying to you, as you can clearly judge by my poor style and by my ignorance which is only too apparent. If there is anything that seems beyond that, I admit, Monsieur, that I have made a

---

[37]In a letter to Saint Caesarius, Bishop of Arles, Pope Boniface II reckons Saint Augustine among the Fathers who have explained the true doctrine of divine grace: "Since many Fathers, especially Bishop Augustine of blessed memory, but also our former high priests of the Apostolic See, are proved to have discussed this with such detailed reasoning that there should be no further doubt that faith itself also comes to us from grace, we have thought that we should abstain from a complex response." (Migne, *op. cit.*, vol. LXV, col. 31.)

[38]The Council of Trent.

[39]Among the propositions condemned by the Holy Office on December 7, 1690 was the following: "Whenever one finds a doctrine clearly founded in Augustine, he may keep and teach it absolutely, regardless of any official document of the Pope" (Prop. 30).

modest study of these questions, and this has been the usual subject of my poor prayers.[40]

I beg you, Monsieur, to share this reply with M. Alméras[41] and those members of the Company whom you judge fit, so that my reasons for upholding the ancient thinking of the Church and for declaring that I am opposed to the new [opinions] may be understood. Let us ask God and do all in our power to have *cor unum et anima una* [42] in this as in everything else. I shall live in this hope and would be more distressed than I could tell you if anyone, forsaking the living springs of the truths of the Church, were to make for himself cisterns of the new opinions, of whose danger scarcely anyone has been better informed by the author than I. I am in the love of Our Lord, Monsieur, your most humble and obedient servant.

VINCENT DEPAUL
i.s.C.M.

I venture to tell you, Monsieur, that M. Féret,[43] who had been caught up in these new opinions, told the Pastor of Saint-Josse[44] that what led him to abandon them was the firmness he witnessed in this miserable sinner's opposition to them in two or three conferences we had on this subject. As soon as the Pastor of Saint-Nicolas-du-Chardonnet returned from Alet, everyone told him he was on the side of these opinions. He is so far from these sentiments that he suggested to the Pastor of Saint-Josse that we should form some kind of secret committee to defend the ancient truths. I beg you to keep this secret.

---

[40]Saint Vincent wrote a very substantial treatise on grace. (Cf. vol. XIII, no. 48.)
[41]From what will be seen later (cf. no. 1068), it is quite probable that M. Dehorgny preferred not to share this letter with his Superior.
[42] . . . *one heart and one mind.* Cf. Acts 4:32. (NAB)
[43]Collet mistakenly wrote the name "Froger" and gave in the notes a quotation from his work. Froger, however, had died in September 1646.
[44]Louis Abelly, Saint Vincent's first biographer.

I have not had the leisure to reread my letter, and I dared not have it copied. You will find it hard to read; excuse me.

Addressed: Monsieur Dehorgny, Priest of the Mission, in Rome

1044. - *CHARLES NACQUART TO SAINT VINCENT*

Saint-Vincent Island,[1] *Cape Verde, [June 25, 1648]* [2]

Monsieur,

Your holy blessing, please!
We have been ashore here for four or five days to take on fresh water. We raised anchor and left La Rochelle on the feast of the Ascension. We are in good health, thank God, after a little seasickness or vomiting in the beginning. We have had the consolation of witnessing the piety of the crew members, who did their duty to gain the Jubilee, which I learned had been granted by His Holiness. We had its opening from Pentecost to Corpus Christi. We reached this island on the eve of the feast of Saint John and have celebrated Mass every day, as we did on the ship, whenever the weather permitted.

We have met here some Portuguese, who are very good Christians, although they are slaves; they have been sent here to hunt goats. We hope to hear their confessions through an interpreter and to give them Holy Communion tomorrow so they can share in the Jubilee. We did this yesterday and today for about twelve men from a ship from Dieppe, which came to this same island to get water. What we have admired in these Portuguese is the fact that they are fine musicians and chant the Psalms in good harmony.

But now we are ready to put out to sea again for about four more months. Ask Our Lord to help us, like the chosen people, reach the goal He desires. We hope for great success in that country, especially since our commander [3] *(who sends you his humble regards) expresses a strong*

Letter 1044. - Archives of the Mission, Paris, seventeenth century copy.
[1]Island in the western part of the Cape Verde archipelago, located in the Atlantic off the coast of Senegal.
[2]The letter was certainly written between June 23 and 29, 1648. The choice of June 25 seems to be the result of a comparison between what is said here and the contents of no. 1179.
[3]M. de Flacourt.

desire to have some part in it. We shall write you from that country. If you want to write to us and send something when a ship leaves for these gentlemen . . . .

We usually celebrate Mass for you in particular and for the Company in general, as well as for Monsieur Lambert and other persons whom we know. Nor do we forget the seminary, that it may increase in numbers and in virtue and help young plants to grow, so that they might come and live on Saint-Laurent Island [4] and in other places so sorely in need of workers.

Among other things, I ask you, if possible, to contact a certain Monsieur Rozée, a merchant from Rouen, living on rue aux Ours. He is the French representative for the Senegal islands, where it is said that there are many souls to be won for Jesus Christ, as well as in the Cape Verde Islands and in Gambia. There are no priests there, except perhaps a chaplain for the ship which is sent there. All that depends on this M. Rozée, who is said to be a virtuous man and a good Christian. Our ship's captain says there is as much security and freedom to preach the Gospel there as there is in Paris. All those poor people are Mohammedans, good and very docile. May God be pleased to provide for this!

Adieu, Monsieur. We are learning the Malagasy language. Please recommend us once again to the prayers of the whole Company and especially to Monsieur Lambert and Monsieur Gautier, to whom I would write if time permitted.

The bearer of this letter is a captain from Dieppe.

I am, with all my heart, in the sacred love of Our Lord and of His holy Mother, Monsieur and most honored Father, your most humble and obedient son.

C. NACQUART, i.s.C.M.
of the Mission of Saint-Laurent Island

---

[4] The former name for Madagascar.

1045. - TO JEAN MARTIN, IN GENOA

Paris, June 26, 1648

Monsieur,

The grace of Our Lord be with you forever!

I received your letter of the first of this month together with the ones from M. Blatiron. Today we have earnestly recommended the Cardinal[1] to the prayers of the Company, that God may be pleased to grant him peace in his diocese and give him a long life for the good of this same diocese. God knows we have not forgotten you, neither you nor our dear confreres, and shall continue to ask Him faithfully for His abundant blessings on each and every one of you in particular.

Like you, Monsieur, I think it would be beneficial to return to places where the mission has been given, preach there from time to time in passing, and reestablish the Confraternity of Charity if it has fallen off. All this, however, must be planned ahead of time and something better must not be neglected.

I thank God for restoring Signor Baliano's[2] health. I rejoice greatly in this and ask Our Lord to preserve him both for His own glory and for our consolation. My consolation will always be to give evidence to you that I am, in the love of this same Lord, Monsieur, your most humble servant.

VINCENT DEPAUL
i.s.C.M.

At the bottom of the first page: M. Martin

Letter 1045. - Archives of the Mission, Turin, original signed letter.

[1]Stefano Cardinal Durazzo, Archbishop of Genoa.

[2]Pietro Paulo Baliano, born on February 3, 1628 in Genoa, entered the Congregation of the Mission on November 1, 1649, and took his vows on September 8, 1652. Perhaps the person in question here is his father or a relative.

— 333 —

1046. - TO PROPAGANDA FIDE

[1648][1]

Most Eminent and Reverend Lords,

Since the three parts of Arabia known as Arabia Felix, Arabia Petrea, and Arabia Deserta have not yet been assigned to any religious Order or secular priests to be evangelized and led to the Christian faith, Vincent Depaul, Superior of the Congregation of the Mission, offers to send several of his priests to these parts of Arabia, whenever Your Eminences are willing to entrust this to him to be evangelized by the Mission *sub nomine proprio*,[2] which he can provide from time to time with what is necessary. He entreats them to grant him the customary faculties, with authority to appoint a vice-prefect, who would reside at the entrance to a port on the border of Arabia Felix, where Missionaries could be sent on Dutch and English ships. At present, there are six priests of his Congregation to be proposed for approval to the Nuncio of France, after which the list of those selected will be given to the Sacred Congregation, who can declare them Missionaries and approve as vice-prefect the most suitable man among them.[3]

Letter 1046. - Archives of Propaganda Fide; original unsigned petition in Italian.
[1]Cf. no. 1068.
[2]*In its own name.*
[3]The plan never materialized.

1046a. - *DEDICATION TO SAINT VINCENT BY J.-B. DE LA PLACE* [1]

[1648]

To Monsieur Vincent de Paul, Founder and Superior General of the Congregation of the Mission.

Monsieur,

I would fail in my duty if I did not offer you this Union. *I approach the original in order to judge the fidelity of my copy; I planned this piece of work while observing how you act. All that the public owes to me is a little cloth and color and many shadows which conceal more of its beauty than is revealed in it. From the time your zeal has consolidated devotion in order to share it with a whole Christian world, ignorance has left the altar, shanties as well as palaces have their Doctors, and golden mouths make themselves heard where sacrifice is offered only in lead.*

Before the most just among our Monarchs had placed her Church in your hands, men were born wearing miter and ring. You govern the goods of that illustrious minor with impartial blindness. You make a choice of plebeian knowledge rather than of noble ignorance, and virtue which might pity itself for its lowly birth is indebted to you for the throne where it is elevated in defiance of partiality. [2]

Your humility, Monsieur, equals your zeal; it is covered with brilliance and remains in obscurity, laden with grandeur and does not depart from its lowliness. France regards you as Antiquity did its heroes, who reserved for themselves from their conquests only the glory of achieving them. So many virtues, which you gather together in yourself, justify the patronage of my work, which does not deviate from my purpose if it attaches me to your person, Monsieur, as your most humble and obedient servant.

DE LA PLACE

Letter 1046a. - This dedication was printed at the beginning of *Union mystique ou exercices spirituels pour s'unir à Jésus-Christ, Notre-Seigneur, dans tous les temps de l'année selon l'ordre ecclésiastique* ... (Paris, 1648). The text was published in *Annales C. M.*, 1947-1948, p. 323, and reprinted in *Mission et Charité*, 19-20, p. 75. This edition uses the latter text.

[1]Jean-Baptiste de la Place (1612-1678), Doctor of the Sorbonne and Commendatory Abbot of Val-Richer, a Cistercian abbey in the Bayeux diocese (Calvados), which he restored to regular observance in 1645. He resigned in 1651 but returned to Val-Richer, where he stayed some years before he died, wearing the Cistercian habit.

[2]Allusion to the zeal displayed by Saint Vincent in the Council of Conscience to fill episcopal Sees with bishops worthy of their pastoral office.

1047. - TO ETIENNE BLATIRON, SUPERIOR, IN GENOA

July 3, 1648

Is not our poor nature miserable? Everyone in Genoa is satisfied with Brother [Sébastien].[1] Only he cannot put up with himself. He wants to leave to satisfy himself, although he sees clearly that he cannot do this without displeasing and inconveniencing those toward whom he could exercise constant charity, as he has done until now. It could be, however, that God will draw His glory from such a fault; I ask Him to do so with all my heart, etc.

It is true, Monsieur, that those persons will do good for the poor and captives in foreign lands if they are content to do the same things here for the sick and afflicted. I praise God that you are testing Brother Sébastien's eagerness to go to Barbary.

1048. - JEAN LE VACHER TO SAINT VINCENT

Tunis, 1648

Among the slaves captured by the corsairs and brought to Tunis are two boys around fifteen years of age. One is French, the other English. Since their masters' homes were close to one another, they were able to see each other often. They loved one another like brothers. The English boy, converted from Lutheranism by the French boy, had been instructed by Jean Le Vacher. He was so strongly attached to his new faith that he declared to some heretic English traders, who had come to ransom slaves from their own country and religion, that he preferred slavery to apostasy.

The two friends continued to see and encourage one another in their good dispositions. More than once, after their masters had tried in vain to entice them into Mohammedanism, they tortured them to the point of causing them to faint and fall to the ground.

One day the English boy came to the French boy's house and found him

---

Letter 1047. - Reg. 2, p. 199.
[1]Brother Sébastien Nodo.
Letter 1048. - Abelly, *op.cit.*, bk. II, chap. I, sect. VII, §11, p. 135.

lying there unconscious. He called out to him. "I am a Christian for life," replied the French boy, who was beginning to regain consciousness. The young visitor bent down to kiss his friend's bleeding feet. Just at this moment some Turks came in. To their questions he replied, "I am honoring the members that have just suffered for Jesus Christ, my Savior and my God." The furious infidels began to insult him and chased him away.

Some time after that, the French boy, in his turn, found the English boy lying on a rattan mat, his body bruised from the beating his master had just given him. Nearby, some Turks were chatting with the master himself. The French boy came close to his friend and asked, "Whom do you love more, Jesus Christ or Mohammed?" The English boy answered, "Jesus Christ. I am a Christian and I want to die a Christian." These words infuriated the Turks. One of them, wearing two knives at his sides, acted as if he was going to cut off the French boy's ears. The boy seized one of the knives himself and, without hesitation, sliced off his own ear. To prevent him from going any further, they hastened to disarm him.

From that day on, the Turks stopped their entreaties; they felt that any attempt was doomed to failure. The two young martyrs died the following year, carried off by a contagious disease.

1049. - TO BERNARD CODOING, SUPERIOR, IN SAINT-MEEN

July 11, 1648

Monsieur,

The grace of Our Lord be with you forever!

Enclosed in a note is the reply of Mademoiselle Le Gras and my own regarding the girls from Moncontour[1] and Saint-Méen, who want to give themselves to God in the Company of the Daughters of Charity.

The good example given by the three deceased Sisters, during the short time they lived after their arrival, cannot be expressed. At

---

Letter 1049. - Archives of the Motherhouse of the Daughters of Charity, copy from a collection of selected letters.

[1]Today chief town of a canton in Côtes-du-Nord. Mathurine Guérin was one of these girls, and the only one who persevered.

the conferences concerning them, such wonderful things were said about those good Sisters that their life and death have left us indications and sentiments of their sanctification.

1050. - TO THE BUREAU OF FINANCES OF THE CITY OF PARIS

[Around July 14, 1648][1]

The said petitioners represent to you that, since the said Saint-Maur road[2] is merely a lane, it must be only thirty feet wide, in conformity with your regulations. Furthermore, in several places the above-mentioned road is only four toises[3] wide, even where it merges with la Vallée de Fécamp[4] and becomes part of the main road of Porte Saint-Antoine.[5] In the area from la Vallée de Fécamp up to the entry to Picpus, this Saint-Maur road is only the width of a cart and is not even a track road, which is supposed to be fifteen feet wide. This was reported to you by Jacques Bouzauct, Commissioner of Roads of the city and faubourg of Paris, in conformity with your order of November 8, 1645.

In consideration of all this, Gentlemen, may it please you to allow the aforementioned petitioners to have summoned before you the said Vincent Thibaut, to have it declared and ordered that, since he has moved back from the Saint-Maur road four toises at its upper end, near its opening onto the chaussée du Bourget[6] and four toises two feet at the lower end, and in this way has encroached on the lands of the petitioners to the extent of ninety-three and a

---

Letter 1050. - Original signed petition; property of the Daughters of Charity, 3 rue Oudinot, Paris.

[1]A note written at the end of this petition supplies the date.

[2]Today it is rue Saint-Maur.

[3]A "toise" equals 1.949 meters or 6.4 feet. The road is, therefore, about twenty-five feet wide.

[4]There used to be a street in Paris named rue de la Vallée-de-Fécamp. Today it is part of rue de Charenton near rue de Montgallet.

[5]Porte Saint-Antoine was located near the Bastille.

[6]This was the name of the section of rue du faubourg Saint-Martin which runs from Saint- Laurent Church to rue de Flandre.

half toises of the terrain, the petitioners shall recover a similar tract of land lying between the Saint-Maur road and the enclosure of the said Thibaut, to use and dispose of as belonging to them and to the former domain of Saint-Lazare; and to order that, where the Saint-Maur road opens onto the chaussée du Bourget, it shall be as broad as is stated in your regulations, that is, thirty feet in width; and to ordain that hereafter no alignment shall be granted to private individuals wishing to build on the other side of the Saint-Maur road facing the estate of the petitioners, unless the latter be summoned, so that in future no one may be allowed to encroach upon their lands, and that the roads be as wide as your regulations require. And you will do justice.[7]

VINCENT DEPAUL

1051. - TO A SEMINARIAN OF THE MISSION

July 15, 1648

I intend to suspend my judgment on your letter until I hear something from M. . . about it. I find it hard to believe that his behavior is as you describe it or that what he said, which you found so offensive, was spoken without good reason. I know that his manner of acting is rather gentle, thank God; no one but you has ever complained to me about it. I find your complaint all the more

---

[7]At the end of the petition the following is written: "The present petition is to be presented to Thibaut and served him as soon as possible in our presence, to be heard and answered. On that day Thibaut will give a report on the alignment granted him for his enclosure and building.—Given at the Bureau of Finances of Paris on the fourteenth day of July in the year one thousand, six hundred and forty-eight, and the erection of any building there without our permission is prohibited to all other persons.—Devavoquier, Hard, Longuer.—By the above-mentioned gentlemen . . . Sensier.—In the year one thousand, six hundred and forty-eight, on the sixth day of August, at the request of the venerable Priests of the Congregation of the Mission."

Letter 1051. - Reg. 2, p. 296.

strange because of his extraordinary gentleness toward you, not only in bearing with your faults but in concealing them from others, as he tried to do even with me, when you wrote me a letter on which you did not reflect as much as you should have, for he wrote me one to make excuses for you.

Let us suppose, however, that he forgot himself, as it seems to you. Should we be alarmed at such a trifle? With whose imperfections will you bear, and what insult are you capable of enduring, if a thoughtless word from your own Superior is unbearable? Perhaps he said it deliberately to test you. In that case, the test was rather successful, since your unfriendly disposition was immediately apparent in several respects: (1) you excuse your fault by comparing it with that of your brother; (2) you complain that teaching children is a heavy added burden for you; (3) you ask for a change of house; (4) you show that you are full of self-importance and presume that the entire Community will testify that it has never remarked anything in you deserving of the correction you received.

All these things are very far from the sentiments of the poor publican and from those a good Missionary should have. Yet, you are writing them to me, so you say, to preserve your vocation. Would to God, dear Brother, that this is your intention, but that is hardly the way to go about it! The practice of patience, humility, and exact observance of the Rule is the true sign of our perseverance. We shall see if you will work in future at the acquisition of these virtues and give your Superior greater satisfaction than in the past. This, I assure you, dear Brother, would be one of my greatest consolations. I shall ask God to grant you this grace, for your soul is dearer to me than I can express.

1052. - *ALAIN DE SOLMINIHAC TO SAINT VINCENT*

Mercuès, July 15, 1648

After I have thanked you most humbly, as I do with this letter, for your zealous assistance in the business which we and our monks of Chancelade have with the men of Saint-Geneviève and which I beg you to continue, allow me to tell you that, far from any thought of not wanting you to receive priests from my diocese into your Congregation, I have, on the contrary, always believed that it is just and necessary for you to accept some of them. It is just because your Congregation serves it well; it is necessary because your men who conduct our seminary could not give missions effectively if no one from my diocese were with them, because of the local dialect, which they do not know and must use in order to be effective.

You may also recall that one of the reasons I gave you for counting on our seminary is that you can draw from it, as is the case, many men to give missions throughout this region and in Languedoc because the language is almost the same. It is true that I felt it necessary to set down certain conditions: first, because of the eight hundred livres foundation which my clergy gives annually for the maintenance of six seminarians destined for the service of our diocese. I felt that this quota had to be filled before you thought about taking any others. You agreed with me on this, as did M. Lambert when he was here. The other, which is more a suggestion than a condition, is that you might consider the need of priests for this diocese. You could not believe how great it was when I came. Presently, it has almost as many as it needs, or will have in a short time, and there would be some to spare, if the other dioceses were not taking them.

You would be delighted to see my clergy and would bless God a thousand times, if you knew the good your men have accomplished in our seminary and which has spread throughout the province. So, I beg you to reconsider how just this stipulation is and not accept any men until this quota of six is filled. There are only two; moveover, they are foreigners, converts to our religion, who want to become priests. Up until now, I did not want your men to go to the trouble of trying to see that this quota was filled but quite the contrary, at least during the time when M. Delattre and M. Testacy were the directors.

In conclusion, I have only two things to say to you. One is that my attachment to your Congregation, which will never give place to that of

---

Letter 1052. - Archives of the Diocese of Cahors, Alain de Solminihac collection, notebook, copy made from the original.

any of your own men, causes me to beg you to consider very carefully whether or not you should put some stipulation on the authority you will give your men to accept priests from the dioceses where you will be established. I have always believed—and what your men have done in my regard makes me believe it even more—that this is absolutely necessary in order to be on good terms with bishops who will invite you into their dioceses. I beg you not to measure others by your own yardstick; you would surely be mistaken in this. Would to God, though it cost part of my blood, which I would give willingly for your Company, that they had your spirit! God grant, by His grace, that they might have a portion of it, if not all! I really think M. Lambert is striving to acquire it; I ardently hope the others will do likewise.

The other thing I have to say to you is that there will be no stipulations for you. You will always have full authority over whatever is in my control. I beg you, however, to keep this just between you and me, and to believe that I am, Monsieur, etc.

ALAIN,
Bishop of Cahors

1053. - ALAIN DE SOLMINIHAC TO SAINT VINCENT

Mercuès, July 22, 1648

Monsieur,

A thousand thanks for your continued efforts on behalf of our monks and me in our business with the monks of Sainte-Geneviève.

Since you were unable to obtain the perpetual confirmation for Mother de Laroque,[1] we shall try to get it extended through the Superiors of the Order.

I have written to you at length about receiving priests from my diocese into your Congregation. You will understand that I did not mean you should accept absolutely none of them; that did not enter my mind. Allow me, nevertheless, to say that it seems to me you will not be making provision for the inconveniences that will arise, unless you add to this rule some

Letter 1053. - Archives of the Diocese of Cahors, Alain de Solminihac collection, notebook, copy made from the original.
[1]As Prioress of the Pouget Monastery.

stipulation which you find just, so that those in the seminary will not be received during their time there. M. Delattre did that for me; he kept his word while he was there and put off accepting them until they were out. Please make provision for this difficulty; I have never raised any objection for those who are studying with you or elsewhere, or who are out of the seminary and have not lived there, but merely said by way of suggestion that discretion should be exercised in receiving them, until the diocese has been provided with those it needs. These are my humble opinions which I submit to yours.

In the meantime, I offer you a thousand million thanks for all the trouble you have taken to give us M. Brandon [2] for Périgueux, which God has finally blessed. I hope He will be glorified and you rewarded for this. And because my diocese also benefits from neighboring on it, I beg you, if you see fit when you see the Queen, to tell Her Majesty that I thank her most humbly. I ask God to grant her the grace of always providing good shepherds for the dioceses in this kingdom.

I am always, Monsieur, etc.

ALAIN,
Bishop of Cahors

1054. - TO CLAUDE DUFOUR, IN SAINTES

July 24, 1648

I received your letter with joy, seeing how faithful you have been in disclosing to me the thoughts troubling your heart. It is no wonder that you are tempted; on the contrary, it would be strange if you were not, because man's life is nothing but temptation, and no one is exempt from it, especially those who have given themselves to God. Even His own Son passed through this trial. But if it is necessary for everyone, it is also a source of merit for those to whom God grants the grace of turning all things to good, as you do.

---

[2]Philibert de Brandon had been named Bishop of Périgueux.

Letter 1054. - Reg. 2, p. 31.

You are well aware, Monsieur, that without disorders there would be no rules, but our inclinations tend toward evil in so many ways that divine and human prudence had to offer specific remedies for them. That is why the Old and the New Testaments are filled with commandments, counsels, and rules for salvation; why the Church has made so many ordinances and decrees, and jurists have established laws for civil matters.

Your Rules are evangelical maxims and the means to observe them, almost the same ones we practice here, and no one here, thank God, has yet complained of them. If their number seems excessive to you, please consider the large number of divine precepts, canons, decrees, laws, and admonitions of which I have just spoken. Several thick volumes cannot contain them.

It may be, however, that you are having difficulty with the diversity of things recommended to you and are perhaps being pressured too much to observe them. I am glad you wrote to me about this because I shall ask the Visitors to be careful in future to give only orders that are truly relevant. I am also asking your Superior[1] to see that you are treated gently, in the event that people have failed to do so in the past, and even to have you changed, if you so wish.

The Company has always been most satisfied with your exactness. Those who have seen you here have been very edified by it and, from what I hear, those who live with you now are no less so. This causes me to think that the slight repugnance you are experiencing is the work of the evil spirit, who is trying to make you grow weary on such a beautiful path. I beg you, Monsieur, not to listen to him, for if two or three Rules displease you because they seem superfluous in your regard, someone else may like them because they suit him.

The children of Our Lord walk simply in His ways; they trust Him. So, when they fall, He lifts them up and if, instead of stopping to grumble about the stone over which they tripped, they humble

---

[1]Louis Rivet.

themselves at their fall, He helps them to make great strides in His love. This, Monsieur, is what I hope from you who, by His mercy, belong entirely to Him and who ardently desire only His holy Will.

There is a vast difference between the apostolic life and the solitude of the Carthusians. The latter is truly very holy but is not suited to those whom God has called to the former, which is in itself more excellent. Otherwise, Saint John the Baptist and Jesus Christ Himself would not have preferred it to the other, as they did by leaving the desert to preach to the people. Furthermore, the apostolic life does not exclude contemplation but encompasses it and profits by it to know better the eternal truths it must proclaim. In addition, it is more helpful to our neighbor, whom we are obliged to love as ourselves and consequently to assist in a way solitaries do not.

Although it may seem to you that you would carry out the duties of this holy religious state more willingly than those of our humble Institute, you would undoubtedly be mistaken, like many others who have abandoned their true vocation to enter a different way of life, in which they found less satisfaction. Why? Because the difficulties they thought to escape did not lie in what they left behind but in their own illusions, since one's state of mind remains the same everywhere, for want of correcting it by constant mortification. Moreover, Monsieur, you know that we are not a religious Order and have no intention of being one; God has not judged us suited to that state. Let us ask Him to make us worthy of the one in which He has placed us.

1055. - TO A PRIEST OF THE MISSION, IN ROME

July 24, 1648

I am really sorry about your ailments. I think a change of air will

---

do you good. Before returning to the air of France, however, I ask you to try that of the Roman countryside by means of the missions to be given there this winter. If this remedy is ineffective, I assure you, Monsieur, that we shall ask you to come back. I would do so right now, did I not fear interfering with God's plan for you by calling you here before trying every possible means to improve your health there.

As for your second reason for returning to France, believe me, Monsieur, the heat of the climate has very little to do with unruly inclinations; the flesh drags its weakness along with it everywhere. Even if you were here, you would experience its miseries the same as in Italy. This is a trial God is permitting you to undergo, as he did with Saint Paul, and perhaps for the same purpose, or at least to give you an opportunity for merit.

1056. - ALAIN DE SOLMINIHAC TO SAINT VINCENT

Mercuès, July 28, 1648

Monsieur,

The care I had taken to see that those new opinions not be discussed in this town of Cahors nor in any other part of my diocese is the reason why we have lived in great peace up to the present. But, since the common enemy of peace never ceases to work at sowing disturbances, it has happened recently that one of the theology professors in our university [1] has been teaching the doctrine and opinions of Jansenius. Being advised of this during my retreat, I sent word to the Grand Archdeacon of my cathedral church,[2] a well-qualified man and a great enemy of all these innovations, to go and tell him on my part that I was very surprised that he was teaching this doctrine and to order him to desist. He did this at

---

Letter 1056. - Archives of the Diocese of Cahors, Alain de Solminihac collection, notebook, copy made from the original.

[1]Father Louis Mesplède, a Dominican. The proceedings drawn up against the views of this friar are preserved in the archives of the Cahors diocese.

[2]Claude-Antoine Hébrard de Saint-Sulpice.

once but, instead of obeying, that Doctor answered him arrogantly that he had already given this treatise, and he said many things to him to back these opinions.

When the Grand Archdeacon reported that to me, I informed my Promoter [3] at once to order all the students, on my part, to bring me their notes and to forbid them, under pain of disobedience, to study any more under this professor, a Dominican friar. They obeyed immediately and he had to discontinue for lack of students.

When the Canon Theologian of my church, who does not like him, heard about this, he preached against those opinions; this drove the other wild. When I learned of this, I instructed my Promoter to forbid the Theologian to preach again in that manner and that I wanted to handle the matter quietly, as is best; to go tell that professor that I did not approve of what the Theologian had done, and that, if he, on his part, did not talk about it and acknowledged his error, I would try to hush up the affair and preserve his honor. He thanked me profusely through my Promoter. At the same time, however, hearing that the university faculty was meeting, he left his convent and went to the hall where they were assembled. He informed them that I had confiscated his writings, forbidden his students to attend his lectures any more and, although I had apologized to him through my Promoter, he was still not satisfied and was asking them to join him in going to court against me, offering to provide all the money needed.

The faculty had him leave so that they could deliberate. They agreed unanimously not to allow this doctrine to be taught at the university, and they all sided with me. When they had him brought back in, they rebuked him sharply. I notified all the convents of this and they likewise sided with me. All the prominent persons who heard about his conduct strongly censured it, so he found himself all alone. He was scarcely able to find a few persons interested in learning what this was all about. He did not, for all that, stop there but protested boldly that he would have these opinions printed in order to defend them.

In the meantime, the Bishops of Bazas [4] and Condom [5] did me the honor of coming to see me. I sent word to the Grand Archdeacon and the Chancellor [6] to come here. They did so and reported to them the opinions

---

[3]Promoter of Justice. A diocesan official who serves the interests of justice. He forestalls the influence or possibility of scandal, intervening in contentious cases which, in the judgment of the Ordinary, may involve the public welfare.

[4]Samuel Martineau.

[5]Jean d'Estrades.

[6]Pierre Parriel, Chancellor of the University of Cahors.

of the other professors. When they saw that these were the same opinions of Jansenius, it was decided that I should send for him and, if he came, I was to reprimand him severely for having taught that doctrine. I was also to forbid and prohibit him strictly from ever teaching it again and order him to give evidence to anyone with whom he had discussed it that he was truly sorry for this. If he did not obey, I was to issue a decree forbidding and prohibiting him from teaching it ever again, under penalty of proceedings being brought against him with the full force of the law, and the students were to be forbidden to listen to him any more or to keep his notes, under pain of excommunication. The university was to issue another decree, whereby it would deprive him of active and passive voice and prohibit him from teaching any longer.

When he learned of this decision, he came to his senses. Yesterday he came here to this house with the Chancellor and expressed his regret for having taught this doctrine and incurring my displeasure. I reprimanded him soundly and made him acknowledge his fault. So, by the grace of God, this fire which was about to break out in our town has been put out, and I hope that very shortly there will be no further talk of it.

This affair grieved me deeply in the beginning but has been nipped in the bud, thank God. I wanted to write to you about it because I want you to know about affairs of this kind which occur in my diocese and so that you may recall what I have said to you so often about my presence being so essential in my diocese that I should never leave it except for very important and urgent matters.

I also wanted to tell you that the Bishops of Bazas and Condom have put a great deal of pressure on me to go and defend them in court against the violent attacks of Monsieur d'Epernon,[7] particularly on the Bishop of Bazas and several others in the province. The prelates there [8] have written to them saying that all of them in the province should converge there, and they mention me in particular. I replied that I will always be inseparably united with them in the defense of their dignity and their persons, but I did not think I could go to Paris because my presence was required in my diocese for four important matters, the least of which demanded that I be here. So, I could not make up my mind to this, although I shall perhaps be obliged to do so. I pointed out many things with regard to this and told them I would write to you about it. They told me to recommend the matter to Our Lord and that they would leave it up to me.

So, I shall tell you that I have never been able to see that it was God's

---

[7]Bernard de Nogaret de La Valette, Duc d'Epernon (1592-1661) and Governor of Guyenne.
[8]In Paris.

Will for me to go there for that purpose. On the contrary, I think it would be against His Will because I do not remember ever having seen any example in Church history where all the bishops in a province left it to go and lodge their complaints to Princes about the persecution of governors, not even of tyrants. Instead, they sent a deputation while the others remained in their dioceses or, if they were unable to live there in safety, they withdrew to neighboring ones and ministered to their people from there. I also do not see how that could be approved at court, especially in the times in which we are living, which would oblige us, if we were there, to leave and return to our dioceses. I, for one, would not on my life want to have been absent while that Doctor was teaching that false doctrine, which I might never have been able to root out, particularly since all Toulouse is afire.

Please let me know how you feel about all this. In the meantime, I will tell you that, since the Bishop of Bazas has seen that the attacks of d'Epernon are increasing from one day to the next and that he is taking advantage of the times, he has decided to go to Paris for a while, but he has no intention of registering a complaint during these disturbances.[9] He is a fine Prelate, truly deserving of assistance and of being supported by the Queen. That is why I beg you to dispose Her Majesty's mind to this so that, in due time, she will take up the cause. In the name of God, use all your authority and influence to prevent Monsieur de Lavardin from becoming Bishop of Le Mans,[10] for the reasons the Bishop of Bazas will explain to you.

In the meantime, believe me, etc.

ALAIN,
Bishop of Cahors

---

[9]During the Fronde.

[10]Philibert-Emmanuel de Beaumanoir de Lavardin had a rather bad reputation. Despite Saint Vincent's objections, he was, nevertheless, appointed Bishop of Le Mans on February 20, 1649.

1057. - TO DENIS GAUTIER, SUPERIOR, IN RICHELIEU

[July 1648]¹

Monsieur,

The grace of Our Lord be with you forever!

Here is some very sad news mingled, however, with great consolation. God has taken to Himself good M. Guérin in Tunis and perhaps M. Lesage in Algiers.² Both of them were stricken with the plague that has been raging in those places for a long time. M. Le Vacher and Brother François³ have also experienced its venom, but the Divine Goodness has been pleased to preserve them almost miraculously.

We were expecting news of M. Le Vacher's death, when he himself sent us word of M. Guérin's, which occurred this past May.⁴ His end, like his life, bore tangible witness to his zeal and charity, giving us a morally certain assurance of his soul's reception into a blessed eternity. Nevertheless, please render him the customary assistance.

All we know about M. Lesage is that our Brother Barreau, his companion, told us in letters written on May 4 that he had fallen ill of the plague two days previously. In a letter of June 20, M. Le Vacher spoke of this in the following words: "I think," he said, "that you have now received letters from Algiers about M. Le-sage's death." Now, even though we have not received any, other

---

Letter 1057. - Archives of the Mission, Turin, original signed letter. This letter was sent to the various houses of the Congregation of the Mission.

¹There is no doubt about the year because Julien Guérin died on May 25, 1648. The month is not quite as certain. Preference has been given to July because the Saint could not have received Jean Le Vacher's letter of June 20 before July, and it appears that he had received before August the letter from Brother Barreau, written May 12 or during the following week.

²He had, in fact, died on May 12, a victim of his dedication to the plague-stricken, whom he visited and consoled with no regard for his own health.

³François Francillon.

⁴May 25 is the date given by Jean Le Vacher himself in his letter of June 22, 1648, written from Tunis to René Alméras.

than the ones about his illness, we still fear that his death has followed and that, since M. Le Vacher has heard about it, the brief news he gave us is only too true. It may also be just a false rumor because he is a hundred leagues away from Algiers.

Whereas, Monsieur, we await the latest news, M. Le Vacher is then in good health, thank God. However, his condition was so serious that people gave him up for dead, and good M. Guérin, who was not yet ill, had given instructions for his burial. Everyone had left his room, except for our Brother François. Every now and then he would look at him. Two hours later, he noticed some signs of life in him and went out at once to notify those who had left him for dead, and they rushed back in to ascertain the truth of this. Recognizing that it was so, they too were amazed and consoled by it.

A few days later, this good Brother was attacked by two kinds of plague and unremitting fever. Next, M. Guérin fell ill, so all three of them were in bed. When Brother François was informed of this, his charity impelled him so strongly that he got up at once to look after the others. When people tried to stop him because he was so sick, he replied, "God will do what He pleases with me, but in their present state, I must do them all the good I can." In fact, he continued to nurse them, giving them broth and medicine, going sometimes into town, sometimes elsewhere. In a word, he did whatever he could to relieve them, as if he were not ill at all.

A few days later, as a reward for his charity, God allowed him to be cured of one of these plagues. His appetite returned and little by little the other plague also disappeared, without his taking any remedy until M. Le Vacher was well, when the latter had him bled and purged. He speaks of this Brother as a wonder, and good M. Guérin never mentioned him to me except with words of praise.

These, Monsieur, are strong reasons for praising God both for the good health of some and for the death of the others; for the former because it allows those two good servants of God to continue serving Him in the person of the sick and abandoned slaves, which is the highest degree of charity that can be practiced in this world, and for the latter because such a death is precious in heaven and on earth and, with God's help, will be the seed of Missionaries, as the blood of martyrs has been the seed of Christians. It is also a martyrdom of love to die in the corporal and spiritual assistance of the living members of J[esus] C[hrist].

Friday evening we had a conference on the virtues of the late M. Guérin and will continue at the next one. We are compiling what is said about him, to share it with all our houses. The subject certainly merits this. He was one of the purest, most detached souls, closest to God and the neighbor, whom I have ever known. O Monsieur, what a loss for the poor, but what a loss for us no longer to have this model of zeal and charity! I often used it as one of the most efficacious ones to animate the Company to the practice of these virtues. We no longer have this; God has deprived us of it. Perhaps this is to punish us for the misuse we made of it. However, since it is true that the greater number have profited by it, God wants to incite us to greater emulation to go and establish everywhere the empire of His Son, Our Lord, as did our good M. Guérin, who now enjoys the reward due to his labors. He will obtain for us the grace to imitate him, if we really begin right now with the opportunities we have each day. This good servant of God did not wait until he was in Barbary to love and console the poor; he always did his utmost to do so in France and in Lorraine. It was this that merited for him the happiness of going to die in the service of the poor slaves, as several men remarked in our conference.

I beg Our Lord to be the life of our hearts and to make me worthy of the grace I have received to be, in His divine mercy, for you and your little Community, which I embrace tenderly in spirit, Monsieur, your most humble and obedient servant.

VINCENT DEPAUL
i.s.C.M.

At the bottom of the first page: M. Gautier

1057a. - TO FRANCOIS BOULART [1]

Saint-Lazare, August 7, 1648

Reverend Father Boulart is assured by his servant, Vincent, that he has given the agreement for Nieuil Abbey[2] in favor of Father Beurrier and has sent it to M. de La Rose,[3] the Cardinal's secretary, to have it forwarded.

VINCENT DEPAUL
i.s.C.M.

1058. - TO ETIENNE BLATIRON, SUPERIOR, IN GENOA

August 15, 1648

I praise God for your vigilance and good influence in arranging that those priests from Genoa who are called "Missionaries" shall not be so called any more, to prevent the confusion of identical names and to forestall the inconveniences arising from having a large number with the same title. It would be well for you to insist also that the Cardinal might be pleased to change the name of the works they do, for fear lest, if these are called "missions," in time people will begin again to call those who give them, "Missionaries," because workers often get their name from the works they do, and it is easy to pass from one to the other. In addition, it is

---

Letter 1057a. - Archives of the Motherhouse of the Sisters of Charity of Nazareth, Kentucky (USA), original signed letter. Coste inserted this letter in vol. XIII (no. 3320). Because of its certain date and for chronological reasons, the editors have repositioned it here.

[1]François Boulart, born in Senlis (Oise) in 1605, received the Augustinian habit in 1620 in Saint-Vincent Abbey and took his vows the following year. He became secretary to Cardinal de la Rochefoucauld, directed the Congregation of France as Superior General (1640-1643, 1665-1667), and was named Assistant in 1647 and 1650. He was Coadjutor of the Sainte-Geneviève Abbey during his first generalate and Abbot during the second.

[2]Abbey of the Augustinian Order in the former diocese of La Rochelle.

[3]Later Secretary of the King's Council and member of the French Academy. He was over eighty-six years of age when he died in January 1701.

Letter 1058. - Reg. 2, p. 85.

customary in the Church to assign distinct names to all Companies
and their functions in order to distinguish one from the other.

1059. - EDMUND DWYER, BISHOP OF LIMERICK, TO SAINT VINCENT

[Around August 1648] [1]

*It is only just, Monsieur, that I should thank you with all my heart for
the benefit I have received from you through your priests and to tell you
how much we need them in this country. I can assure you in all confidence
that their labors have produced more fruit and they have converted more
souls than all the other priests. Furthermore, because of their example and
good conduct, most of the nobility of both sexes have become models of
virtue and devotion. This was in no way apparent among us before the
arrival of your Missionaries in these parts. True, the troubles and the
armies in this kingdom have been a great hindrance to their work.
Nevertheless, through them, the memory of matters concerning God and
salvation is so engraved on the minds of city and country dwellers that
they bless God equally in times of adversity and prosperity. I hope to be
saved myself through their assistance.*

1060. - THOMAS WALSH, ARCHBISHOP OF CASHEL,[1] TO SAINT VINCENT

August 16 [1648] [2]

The departure of your Missionaries provides me with the opportunity

---

Letter 1059. - Abelly, *op.cit.*, bk. II, chap. I, sect. VIII, p. 149.

[1]Abelly states that this letter was written around the same time as no. 1060.

Letter 1060. - Abelly, *op.cit.*, bk. II, chap. I, sect. VIII, p. 148. Abelly remarks that the letter
was written in Latin, although he gave only the French translation.

[1]Thomas Walsh, born in the Waterford diocese (Ireland) in 1580, was appointed Archbishop
of Cashel in 1626. He was imprisoned for the faith at the end of 1652 and, after a captivity of
nine months, was exiled to Spain, where he died on May 5, 1654.

[2]Abelly dates this letter "1658;" the necessary rectification has been made.

of expressing to you my humble gratitude and thanks. By your great charity you have deigned, through your Missionary priests, to come to the aid of the little flock God has entrusted to me. This has been done not only at a most opportune time for meeting our needs but also during a real emergency. So, it is true that through their labors and works the people have been stimulated to devotion, which is increasing daily. Although these good priests have put up with many inconveniences since their arrival in this country, they have not, for all that, failed to apply themselves constantly to the labors of their mission, like indefatigable workers who, aided by grace, have gloriously extended and increased the worship and glory of God.

I hope that this same good and all-powerful God will be Himself your generous recompense, and theirs as well. For my part, I shall ask Him to preserve you for a long time, since He has chosen you for the welfare and service of His Church.

1061. - JEAN LE VACHER TO SAINT VINCENT

[Tunis, 1648] [1]

In return for some money I gave to the owners or guardians of these poor slaves, I was able to gather them together in each place, and there, by God's grace, I instructed and consoled them, heard their confessions, and confirmed them in the faith. Arranging the place as respectably as possible, I celebrated Holy Mass, at which they all received Communion. We were both filled with the consolation which God was pleased to dispense to these poor slaves amidst the wretchedness of their captivity, painful and burdensome beyond anything free persons can imagine. Consequently, the joys and consolations they have tasted in the midst of their hardships can only be the result of God's grace. I embraced them all and, to revive them a little from their fatigues, gave them as much of a treat as our poverty allowed. In addition to that, I gave each of the poorest a fourth of a piastre.

Letter 1061. - Abelly, *op.cit.*, bk. II, chap. I, sect. VIII, §9, p. 131.

[1]Jean Le Vacher doubtless wrote this letter in the year of his arrival in Tunis, on his return from his first trip to the small farms and field habitats.

1062. - TO SISTER MADELEINE-ELISABETH DE MAUPEOU, VISITATION NUN[1]

Dear Sister,

The grace of Our Lord be with you forever!

Your presence is desired here; you are being asked for there, and you are indifferent, as a good servant of God and a good daughter of Sainte-Marie should be. Your monastery here is asking for you for the Compiègne foundation;[2] your dear Sisters in Bayonne feel that they need you and are insisting that you remain with them. Do whatever you judge best before God—come or stay.

My conviction, that you seek only God and His holy Will, leads me to think that I also am doing this by leaving the discernment up to you. If you come, which is to be desired, I ask you to inform me of this, after you have received this letter and, unless you are detained by something important, to come as soon as possible so that matters pertaining to the foundation may be settled. Oh! dear Sister, what a warm welcome you will receive, if you come! If you do not come because you cannot, we shall leave the matter to God's good pleasure, which will be made known to us by the choice you

---

Letter 1062. - *Année sainte,* vol. VII, p. 253.

[1]Madeleine-Elisabeth de Maupeou, daughter of Gilles de Maupeou, Intendant and Comptroller-General of Finances under Henri IV. She entered the First Monastery of the Visitation in Paris in January 1628, at thirty-two years of age. The nuns of the Caen convent elected her Superioress on May 24, 1635, and reelected her on May 20, 1638. In 1641 she went to Bayonne to found a monastery of her Order, at the request of her nephew, François Fouquet, Bishop of that town. Her second three-year term of office had expired a year before Saint Vincent wrote her this letter. She remained in Bayonne and was again elected Superioress there on June 2, 1650. On her return to Paris, she became Superioress of the First Monastery (1655-1658), ending her days there on July 3, 1674, at the age of seventy-eight. (Cf. *Année Sainte,* vol. VII, pp. 249-254.)

[2]The Compiègne Monastery had opened on June 13, 1648.

will make. May God fill you ever more with His spirit, my very dear Sister!

I am, in His love, your most humble servant.

VINCENT DEPAUL

Paris, September 3, 1648

1063. - TO SAINT LOUISE

Paris, September 5, 1648

Blessed be God, Mademoiselle, for the solicitude He has given you for your dear daughters and me during these public disturbances.[1] Here we are, all of us, by God's grace, not considered by Our Lord worthy of suffering something for Him on this occasion.

Rest assured, moreover, that I have not left unsaid anything I thought should have been said, by the grace of God. I say this regarding everything. The trouble is that God has not blessed my words, although I think that what is being said about the person to whom you know I am referring is false.[2] It is true that I am trying to speak the way the good angels do. They give suggestions but are not upset when people do not make use of their insights.

That is the lesson the blessed Cardinal de Bérulle taught me, and

---

Letter 1063. - Archives of the Mission, Paris, original autograph letter.

[1]Saint Vincent is alluding here to the events of August 26, 27, and 28. News of the arrest of Broussel, Councillor of the Grand Chambre, senior chamber of the Parlement of Paris, had aroused the people's indignation against the Court. Barricades had been erected in the street. The civilian militia, mobilized to restore order, was in sympathy with the rebels. The Queen, Anne of Austria, was obliged to yield and to recall Broussel, who was then on his way to Sedan.

[2]It is difficult to say to what Saint Vincent was alluding here. Is it perhaps the relationship between Mazarin and Anne of Austria? The rumor was spread by members of the Fronde that the Queen and her Minister were bound in a marriage of conscience, some adding that Saint Vincent himself had blessed their union. There was talk about this at Saint-Lazare, and Brother Robineau did not hesitate to question the Saint, who replied: "That is as false as the devil."

my own experience is that when I act otherwise I do not succeed but rather spoil everything.

If you want to stop at Madame de Saint-Simon's[3] house, why not?

Things are going along peacefully here. Your patients everywhere are beginning to feel better.

I shall try to have a word with the Comte de Maure,[4] but I am afraid of spoiling the affair by my wretchedness. However, I shall not go into detail. Our Lord will make up for what is lacking in me, if He so pleases.

I praise God for what you tell me about the visits to the Charities. Oh! how humiliated I am at not being able to make them! Our Lord will make provision for this in another way, if He so pleases.

I am, in His love, Mademoiselle, your most humble and very obedient servant.

VINCENT DEPAUL
i.s.C.M.

Paris. . . .

Addressed: Mademoiselle Le Gras, in Liancourt

(Manuscript notebook of Brother Robineau, p. 10, Archives of the Mission, Paris.) The question of this secret marriage has been studied by Jules Loiseleur (*Problèmes historiques. Mazarin a-t-il épousé Anne d'Autriche? Gabrielle d'Estrées est-elle morte empoisonnée?* [Paris: Hachette, 1867]), and by Victor Molinier (*Notice sur cette question historique: Anne d'Autriche et Mazarin étaient-ils secrètement mariés?* [Paris: A. Rousseau, 1887]). It seems an established fact that Mazarin had not received Sacred Orders. (Cf. Chéruel Adolphe, *Letters du Cardinal Mazarin* [9 vols., Paris, 1872-1906], vol. I, p. XVI, n. 2.)

[3]Louise de Crussol. Her second husband, the Marquis de Saint-Simon, became Lieutenant-General of the King's armies, Governor and Bailiff of Senlis, and Captain of the château of Chantilly.

[4]A relative by marriage of Saint Louise de Marillac. He took an active part in the disturbances of the Fronde. Was Saint Vincent trying to offer him some wise political advice?

1064. - TO JEAN DEHORGNY, IN ROME

Orsigny, September 10, 1648

Monsieur,

I received your letter of August 17,[1] whose purpose was to complete your reply to my letters concerning diversity of opinions, particularly regarding the book, *Communion.*[2] My reply to that letter, Monsieur, is that what you say about certain persons benefiting from this book in France and Italy may be true, but that for a hundred in Paris whom it has helped, by making them more respectful in the use of this Sacrament, there are at least ten thousand it has harmed, by causing them to abstain from it altogether. I praise God that you act as I do in not discussing these matters in our family and that things are progressing in Rome as they are here.

What you say is true, that Saint Charles Borromeo in his day stimulated the spirit of penance in his diocese and the observance of the canons on it, and that this incited people, even good Religious, to rebellion against him because of this innovation. However, he did not make penance or, if you wish, satisfaction consist in abstaining from holy Confession or the adorable Communion,

---

Letter 1064. - The original signed letter was formerly the property of the Edward Laurence Doheny Memorial Library, St. John's Seminary, Camarillo, California (USA). The Doheny collection, including this letter, was sold by Christie's Auction House, New York City, October 17-18, 1988. The present owner is unknown.

Coste's citation reads: "Departmental Archives of Vaucluse, D 296, seventeenth or eighteenth century copy. The footnotes indicate the variations found in the text published in March 1726 in *Mémoires de Trévoux* (p. 448). Neither the manuscript in the Departmental Archives nor *Mémoires de Trévoux* includes the postscript, which we have taken from the supplement to *Lettres et conférences de Saint Vincent de Paul* (p. 70). The editor of this supplement had access to the original, lent to him by Mademoiselle d'Haussonville; it cannot now be found."

[1]*Mémoires* gives the date as August 7. This seems reasonable because mail from Rome took at least a month to reach the person to whom it was addressed in France. This letter, therefore, could not have been written on August 17.

[2]Antoine Arnauld, *De la fréquente Communion, où les sentiments des Pères, des Papes et des Conciles touchant l'usage des sacrements de Pénitence et d'Eucharistie sont fidèlement exposez, pour servir d'addresse aux personnes qui pensent sérieusement à se convertir à Dieu, et aux pasteurs et confesseurs zélez pour le bien des âmes*, (Paris: A. Vitré, 1643).

except in cases stated in the canons. We, too, strive to observe them in cases of the proximate occasions of sin, enmities, and public sins. He is, however, very far removed from what is said about his ordering public penance for private sins and making satisfaction for them before absolution, as the book in question claims.

Let us get down to particulars now. Regardless of what you tell me about the book, *On Frequent Communion,* the truth is that it was written principally to revive the ancient penitential practice as a requirement for being restored to God's grace. Although the author sometimes pretends to propose this ancient practice only as something that is more useful, it is nevertheless certain that he intends it as something necessary, since throughout his book he portrays it as one of the greatest truths of our religion, the practice of the Apostles and of the entire Church for twelve centuries, an immutable tradition, and an institution of Jesus Christ. He never ceases to say that he is obliged to observe it, and to hurl abuse constantly against those opposed to the reestablishment of this type of penance.

Furthermore, he teaches clearly that in ancient times there was no other form of penance for any kind of mortal sin except public penance, as may be seen in the chapter 3 of part two, where he adopts as a truth the opinion stating that in the early Fathers, especially in Tertullian, only public penance is to be found, in which the Church exercises the power of the keys. From this it follows, as a very clear consequence, that M. Arnauld wants to establish public penance for all types of mortal sin, and it is not calumny to accuse him of that but a fact, easily deduced from his book, provided it is read without bias.

And you, Monsieur, tell me this is false. You are to be excused because you did not know what was at the bottom of the author's maxims and all these doctrines; namely, to lead the Church back to its primitive practices, saying that the Church has ceased to exist since that era. Two of those coryphaei[3] of these opinions told the

---

[3]Leaders of a party or of a school of thought. Was Saint-Cyran one of these?

Mother Superior[4] of Sainte-Marie in Paris, who they had been led to hope could be won over to their opinions, that there has been no Church for five hundred years. She herself told me so both verbally and in writing.

You tell me, in the second place, that it is false that M. Arnauld wanted to introduce for great sinners the practice of doing penance before absolution. I reply that M. Arnauld wants to introduce penance before absolution not only for great sinners but he makes it a general law for all those guilty of mortal sin, as may be seen from these words taken from part two, chapter 8: "Who cannot see how necessary this Pope considers it for the sinner to do penance for his sins, not only before receiving Communion but even before receiving absolution?" And a little further on he adds, "Do not these words clearly show us that, according to the holy rules this great Pope has given to the entire Church, after learning them from the everlasting tradition of the same Church, the order which priests must observe in exercising the power the Savior has given them to bind and to loose souls is not to absolve sinners until they have left them groaning and weeping and had them perform a penance proportionate to their sins?" We have to be blind not to realize, by these and many other words that follow, that M. Arnauld believes it necessary to defer absolution for all mortal sins until penance has been done. As a matter of fact, have not I myself seen this practiced by M. de Saint-Cyran? Is it not still being done with regard to those who place themselves entirely under their guidance? And yet, this opinion is an obvious heresy.

As for the question of declaratory absolution, you tell me that only his first book is needed to show the contrary, and you cite three or four authorities for that. My reply is that it is no wonder M. Arnauld speaks on several occasions like other Catholics. In that, he is merely imitating Calvin, who denied thirty times that he makes God the author of sin, even though he does his utmost in

---

[4]Hélène-Angélique Lhuillier.

other places to establish this despicable maxim, which all Catholics attribute to him.

All innovators do likewise; they sow contradictions in their books so that, if they are reproved on a certain point, they can escape by saying that they stated the contrary elsewhere. I heard the late M. de Saint-Cyran say that, if he had spoken certain truths in a room to persons capable of accepting them, and went into another where there were people who were not, he would tell them the contrary, and that Our Lord acted in this way and recommended that people do likewise.[5]

How can M. Arnauld seriously maintain that absolution really wipes away sins, since he teaches, as I have just pointed out, that the priest must not give the sinner absolution until he has done penance, and that the main reason why he wants this order to be observed is to give the sinner time to expiate his crimes by salutary satisfaction, as he sets out to prove in chapter 2 of part two? Can any discerning person who wants sins to be expiated by salutary satisfaction seriously believe, before receiving absolution, that the sins are expiated by the absolution?

You tell me that M. Arnauld says that the Church retains in her heart the desire that sinners might do penance according to the ancient rules, and M. Arnauld states that both the old and the new practices of the Church are good but the old is better, and the Church, being a good mother desiring only the greatest welfare of her children, always wants what is best for them, at least in her heart.

My reply is that Church discipline is not to be confused with

---

[5]In *La cabale des dévots*, Raoul Allier finds it hard to believe that Saint-Cyran made such a remark. He prefers the hypothesis that Saint Vincent misunderstood him. "Saint-Cyran," he writes, "realized so fully that his ideas ran counter to the customary teachings that, to avoid summary condemnation and useless scandals, he opened his mind only to friends on whom he could rely and who would understand him." This, according to Allier, is the explanation of what Saint-Cyran is supposed to have said to Saint Vincent. The Saint was in the presence of the Abbé when the latter made the remark, and we know that Saint Vincent was far more inclined to excuse than to accuse, to minimize the gravity of reprehensible deeds and words than to exaggerate them. His authority, in our opinion, carries far more weight than that of Raoul Allier.

disorders that may occur. Everyone blames these disorders; the casuists are always complaining about this and calling attention to them so people will recognize them, but it is going too far to say that not to practice M. Arnauld's type of penance is a form of laxity which the Church tolerates with regret. We have no great assurance about the Eastern practice you mention, but we do know that throughout Europe the Sacraments are approached in the manner condemned by M. Arnauld, and that the Pope and all the bishops approve the custom of giving absolution after confession and of doing public penance only for public sins. Is it not insufferable blindness, in a matter of such consequence, to prefer to the universal practice of all Christendom the ideas of a young man who, when he did his writing, had no experience in the direction of souls?

If, as you say, the practice of public penance continued in Germany until Luther's time, it was only for public sins. No one objects to this type of penance being reinstated everywhere, since the Council of Trent expressly ordains it.[6] What connection has the instruction of Saint Ignatius, which you also quote to me, with the conduct of those who keep everyone from Communion, not for eight or ten days but for five or six months, and not only great sinners but good nuns who live lives of great purity, as we have learned from the letter of the Bishop of Langres to the Bishop of Saint-Malo?[7] To call attention to such serious disorders, which tend toward the complete destruction of Holy Communion, is not merely to dwell on trifles. Honest people, far from having to put such dangerous maxims into practice, have good reason to disregard them and form a bad opinion of those who authorize them.

Saint Charles took good care not to approve them, since he recommends nothing so much in his councils and documents as

---

[6]Session XXIV, chap. VIII.

[7] According to Abbé L. N. Prunel (*Sébastien Zamet, évêque-duc de Langres, pair de France* (1588-1655) [Paris: Picard, 1612], p. 264, n. 2), the document sent by Sébastien Zamet, Bishop of Langres, to Achille de Harlay de Sancy, Bishop of Saint-Malo, was a reply to the questionnaire concerning Saint-Cyran, drawn up by de Harlay at Richelieu's command. It is given in full in Prunel's book, pp. 265-268.

frequent Communion. Several times he issues severe penalties against all preachers who, directly or indirectly, dissuade the faithful from frequent Communion. And never shall we find that he prescribed public penance or abstention from Communion for all kinds of mortal sin, nor that he wanted three or four months to elapse between confession and absolution, as is very often done by these modern reformers, and for ordinary sins. So, even though there may be some excess in giving absolution readily to all sorts of sinners, which Saint Charles deplores, it must not be concluded from this that this great saint approved of the extremes to which M. Arnauld has gone, since they are in total opposition to a number of regulations he made.

As for what is attributed to him in the book, *On Frequent Communion*, about keeping people away from the holy Sacraments, my reply is that this book is, in fact, strongly influencing everyone to refrain from frequent confession and Holy Communion, even though he pretends, the better to hide his cards, to be very far from intending this. On page 36 of his preface, does he not actually praise highly the piety of those who would wish to defer their Communion until the end of their lives because they consider themselves unworthy of approaching the Body of Jesus Christ? Does he not also assert that God is more satisfied with this humility than with any other kind of good works? On the contrary, does he not state in chapter 2 of part three that to say that the King of Heaven is honored by our Communions is to speak unworthily of Him and that Jesus Christ can receive only shame and outrage from our frequent Communions made according to the maxims of Father Molina, the Carthusian,[8] which he attacks all through his book as a work of pure fabrication? What is more, in chapter 4 of part one he uses Saint Denis as a proof, saying that those who receive Holy Communion should be entirely purified of the images remaining with them from their past life, by a pure, unalloyed, divine love,

---

[8] Anthony de Molina, author of the treatise *Instrucción de sacerdotes*, which was translated into several languages, died in 1612.

and must be perfectly united with God alone, entirely perfect and entirely irreproachable. In no way did he mitigate these lofty words so foreign to our weakness—far from it. After expressing them so bluntly, he has still maintained in his b[ook], *On Frequent Communion,* that they are the dispositions necessary for the worthy reception of Holy Communion. This being the case, how can a man who ponders these maxims and M. Arnauld's line of action imagine that he really wants all the faithful to receive Communion frequently? On the contrary, it is certain that a person cannot hold these maxims to be true unless, at the same time, he himself refrains from frequenting the Sacraments. As for myself, I admit frankly that, if I paid as much attention to M. Arnauld's book as you do, not only would I renounce Mass and Holy Communion forever in a spirit of humility, but I would even have a horror of the Sacrament. For, it is true that for those who receive Communion with the ordinary dispositions approved by the Church, he represents it as a snare of Satan and a venom that poisons souls. He also treats all those who approach it in this state as nothing less than dogs, pigs, and Antichrists.

Even if people were to close their eyes to every other consideration and remark only what he says in several places about the admirable dispositions with which he wishes Communion to be received, would anyone be found on this earth with such a high opinion of his own virtue as to feel he was in a proper state to be able to receive Communion worthily? Only M. Arnauld can do so. Having set these dispositions at such a height that even Saint Paul would have been afraid to receive Communion, he does not fail to boast several times in his apologia that he himself says Mass daily. In this, his humility is as much to be admired as his charity and the good opinion he has of so many wise spiritual directors, secular as well as religious, and so many virtuous penitents, who practice the devotion. Both groups are the butt of his customary invectives.

Furthermore, since the Church commands us to receive Communion once a year, I think it is heresy to say that it is a great act of virtue to want to put off Communion until death. It is also heresy to prefer this spurious humility to all kinds of good works, since obviously martyrdom, at least, is much more excellent. It is likewise heresy to say categorically that God is not honored by our Communions and receives from them only shame and outrage.

Because this author keeps everyone from Communion, he will not be concerned if all the churches are left without Masses. Venerable Bede says that those who fail to celebrate this Holy Sacrifice without some legitimate impediment deprive the Blessed Trinity of praise and glory, the angels of delight, sinners of pardon, the just of help and grace, souls in purgatory of refreshment, the Church of the spiritual favors of Jesus Christ, and themselves of medicine and a remedy. Knowing that, he makes no scruple, as we see in chapter 40 of part one, of applying all these admirable effects to the merits of a priest who stays away from the altar in a spirit of penance. He speaks even more favorably of this penance—more even than of confession—than he does of the Sacrifice of the Mass.

Now, who cannot see the great power of this discourse to persuade all priests to neglect saying Mass, since as much is to be gained by not saying it as by saying it? According to the maxims of M. Arnauld, it can even be said that much more is to be gained because, since he elevates abstention from Communion much higher above the reception of Communion, he must also think that abstention from Mass is more excellent than the Mass itself.

The moral of all this is that this new reformer keeps priests and the laity away from the altar only under the fine pretext of penance. However, to discover in what consists this great penance, which he believes is so advantageous to souls, read the very words of the preface, page 18. There, of all the rigors of the ancient practice of penance, he retains almost nothing but separation from the Body of the Son of God, which, according to the Fathers, is the most important part because it represents the privation of beatitude and, according to men, is the easiest because everyone is capable of it.

Could M. Arnauld demonstrate more openly that his book was written with the sole intention of causing serious harm to Mass and Communion, since he uses all of antiquity to preach penance to us (a single act of which I have never seen performed by the author of this doctrine, nor by those who assisted him in introducing it), and after all this fanfare, he contents himself with the fact that people are not receiving Communion? Those who read his book and do not see this intention in it are surely among those spoken of by the prophet: *Oculos habent et non videbunt.*[9] I do not understand how you, Monsieur, can accuse M. Arnauld's opponents of doing serious harm to penance since, on the contrary, people complain, and rightly so, that this author has gone to great lengths to prove that it is necessary to do long and rigorous penances before receiving Communion and absolution. At the same time, he has declared explicitly (so that no one can feign ignorance as an excuse), that the only thing he reserves from the ancient penance is absence from the altar.

This, Monsieur, is my reply to your letter, written in such haste that I have no time to reread it.

I am on my way at this very moment to celebrate Holy Mass that God may be pleased to make you understand the truths I am telling you, and for which I am prepared to lay down my life.

If I had the time, there are many other things I would say to you on this subject. I ask Our Lord Jesus Christ to tell you them Himself. Please do not send me any reply on this subject, if you persist in holding to these opinions. I am, in the love of Our Lord, Monsieur, your most humble servant.

VINCENT DEPAUL
i.s.C.M.

You will no longer be Master and Administrator of Saint-Esprit in Toul, if this Parlement does not accept the review of your lawsuit in the King's Council against Messrs. Thierry, Plainevaux, and . . . of which the latter has obtained permission to take possession.[10] Now,

---

[9]*They have eyes but see not.* Cf. Ps 115:5 or Ps 135:16. (NAB) Ps 113:5 or Ps 134:16. (D-RB)

[10]M. Dehorgny, as a matter of fact, lost the Saint-Esprit benefice in Toul. Saint Vincent subsequently asked for it in Rome for M. Edme Jolly, who intended to resign it in favor of the Congregation (cf. vol. V, no. 1664). Negotiations dragged on. On December 29, 1657, Saint Vincent wrote to M. Georges des Jardins, "We have not yet received the letters of union, but we are still working on this and hope in the end to receive them." (Cf. vol. VII, no. 2500.)

if your review is accepted, the person who is Chief Justice says that the Parlement is unwilling to do it, having refused it a second time and torn up the above-mentioned review. At least, the Advocate General has done so. So, if they abandon the latter and there is nothing more to be hoped for, I shall send word to salvage whatever we can of the furniture. They have taken advantage of the period of almost general revolt in our Parlements. Well, if they do not pass judgment on us before my letter arrives, it cannot be delayed beyond eight days. *In nomine Domini!*

Addressed: Monsieur Dehorgny, Priest of the Mission, in Rome

1065. - TO ETIENNE BLATIRON, SUPERIOR, IN GENOA

Paris, September 25, 1648

Monsieur,

The grace of Our Lord be with you forever!

Please excuse me for writing to you by a hand other than my own, but I am in a great hurry.

I praise God for the attitude of the Cardinal,[1] for whom I have the greatest sentiments of respect and reverence. I would be happy if he could see from where they proceed; he would know that no one has ever had greater esteem for another. I also bless God for the charity of those priests, our cofounders, and I ask him to bless the chapel in the house.

I am greatly consoled by His Eminence's determination to put good order in the seminary by having them make retreats. I beg Our Lord to sanctify them by His holy mercy.

Letter 1065. - Archives of the Mission, Turin, original signed letter. The last part of the letter, from the words: "In the love of Our Lord," etc., is in the Saint's handwriting.
[1]Stefano Cardinal Durazzo.

You are right to raise some objection about accepting that good monk. Please stay out of that affair and let Divine Providence act. If, however, you know that it might turn out well and he is very insistent, you could give it a try, please.

We shall send you Brother Claude[2] as soon as this can be done; he has gone to take the waters in Moulins. Had he been here, we would have sent him back to you. He wants to learn how to make bread and to let blood. To learn that will take him about two weeks. In the meantime, we shall send you two others so you will not be shorthanded. If you have too many, send them on to Rome.

In the love of Our Lord, with that fondness for you which you know is greater than I can express, I greet your Community, prostrate in spirit at their feet and yours, and I am, Monsieur, your most humble servant.

VINCENT DEPAUL
i.s.C.M.

I forgot to mention that I was very moved by what you told me about the accident that occurred in G[enoa],[3] which I related to the Company. Each of the priests has celebrated Mass to thank God that the damage was not as bad as we had been led [to fear] at first, and that God may be pleased to preserve that city from danger. Our Brothers will receive Communion for this same intention, God willing.

I am, in the love of Our Lord.

Addressed: Monsieur Blatiron, Superior of the Mission of Genoa, in Genoa

---

[2]Claude Le Gentil, born in 1620 in Berchères, Châlons diocese (Champagne), was received into the Congregation of the Mission in Paris on January 22, 1637, and took his vows on March 24, 1643. (Cf. *Notices,* vol. I, p. 494.)

[3]In the margin was written, "A tornado hit on the feast of Saint Augustine."

— 369 —

1066. - TO SAINT LOUISE

Saint-Lazare [October 1648][1]

Mademoiselle Le Gras is humbly thanked by her servant, Vincent, for the remedy she sent him, which he intends to use, God willing.

We shall work on the Monstrel[2] business and on the fair.[3]

I do not recall what was in the letter from the Pastor in Serqueux.[4] If you know it, I shall reply to him today.

I think the air might do me good; the little I had recently on our journey from Saint-Germain[5] made me feel better. If I do not go to Saint-Germain tomorrow, I could leave to go and see our dear Sisters in Fréneville.[6] I set great store by that air, which has always [benefited][7] me in our little infirmities.

Would it not do you good, Mademoiselle, to go and take the air somewhere in the region of Liancourt, Saint-Denis, or elsewhere? Please think it over; also, let me know the name of the root you sent me and how it should be used.

Letter 1066. - Archives of the Motherhouse of the Daughters of Charity, original autograph letter.

[1]Date of the reply to this letter (cf. no. 1067).

[2]Montreuil. In the XIIIth century it was called *Monsteriolum* or *Monsterolum* from *Monasteriolum*, "little monastery;" from this came the word *Monsterel* or *Monstrel*, still in use in the XVIIth century.

[3]The famous Saint-Laurent fair depended on the Saint-Lazare house.

[4]François du Marche. Serqueux is located in Seine-Maritime. Two Daughters of Charity were established there by Msgr. de Saint-Luc, squire of Taillefontaine, by a contract drawn up on November 13, 1645.

[5]Saint-Germain-en-Laye, where the Court was residing.

[6]The Daughters of Charity were established in Fréneville in 1647.

[7]This word was omitted in the original.

1067. - *SAINT LOUISE TO SAINT VINCENT*

[October 1648] [1]

Monsieur,

I do not quite recall the matter about which the Pastor in Serqueux wrote you. I have an idea, however, that it concerned some nuns near Forges, [2] *who are being accused of some serious fault; I think people are trying to take the abbey from the nun in charge because of this. He maintains that she is completely innocent of the accusation against her.*

What I sent you is licorice. Infusions are made from it; the small pieces make it easier to use, but it must be fresh and you should cut only as much as you need because it turns black. I would not dare boast that we have it in our garden because all we have seen of it so far are the flowers and leaves.

I had forgotten to send you word that the Prioress of Montmartre, Mademoiselle Channelin's sister, is very close to death from lung disease and asks for your holy prayers. She also asks for those of the members of your Company that God may be pleased to have mercy on her.

I am sending the enclosed letter back to you, lest you think it was delivered to the addressee.

I beg God that your journey will not be long and that you will return in perfect health.

Our Sisters are asking us for a certain syrup we do not have on hand; I shall send someone to see if Brother Alexandre [3] *could give us some.*

Since your charity allows me, I shall be able to go to Saint-Denis and perhaps to Bicêtre. I have no more to do in Liancourt this year. I also think that Monsieur and Madame are going to La Roche-Guyon for a month.

If you leave tomorrow, I shall not have the honor of seeing you beforehand. What will become of my poor conscience in the meantime? The state to which my negligence, laziness, and infidelities have reduced my soul would frighten Saint Catherine if she were on earth, since it would

---

Letter 1067. - The original autograph letter is the property of the Daughters of Charity in Châteaudun.

[1]Date written on the back of the original by Brother Ducournau.

[2]Principal town of a canton in the district of Neufchâtel-en-Bray (Seine-Maritime).

[3]Alexandre Véronne, infirmarian at Saint-Lazare.

appear loveless to her, void of the love which I should have in abundance and which, by His grace, has made me, Monsieur, your most obedient servant and very humble daughter.

L. DE MARILLAC

Friday

Addressed: *Monsieur Vincent*

1068. - TO RENE ALMERAS, IN ROME

October 23, 1648

Monsieur,

I received two of your letters at the same time, the one about M. de Fondimare's[1] departure, Brother Doutrelet's[2] reply, M. de Restal's opinion of our Rules, and especially the decision being made on the vows; the other one concerns your being relieved of your present duty.

I shall begin by replying that we must submit to the disposition of Providence with regard to entrances and departures from the Company, and imitate the acquiescence to God's good pleasure that we see in Our Lord's acquiescence to His Father's good pleasure in the desolation of His divine company. Depending on His own good pleasure, He always does and provides all things for His own glory and the welfare of the persons concerned. Accordingly, we should look upon the departure of these persons as a boon for the Company and perhaps for themselves as well.

Letter 1068. - Jean-Baptiste Pémartin, *Lettres de Saint Vincent de Paul* (2 vols., Paris: Dumoulin, 1882), vol. II, p. 121, l. 612.

[1]Pierre de Fondimare, born in Le Havre, entered the Congregation of the Mission on October 18, 1644, at twenty-three years of age.

[2]Michel Doutrelet, born in Rouen, entered the Congregation of the Mission on May 14, 1644, at eighteen years of age, and took his vows on May 14, 1646.

As for Doutrelet, you know from him the reason why he does not wish to renew his vows. If he persists in that, dismiss him as soon as possible, assuming that His Holiness approves. Furthermore, we must be submissive to the good pleasure of God, who only wills this means so that the Company may subsist. I think that this and all the various opinions given there on this matter should cause you to get this business approved as soon as possible.

The Pope,[3] it is said, does not like the religious state. Fine, but since our vows do not make us Religious, he will perhaps approve them, especially the matter depending on him—I mean, on his disposition. It will be well also to make him understand that it will be difficult to keep the Company in existence, given its varied, important, arduous, and far-flung works. The diversity is apparent in the fact that we are devoted to the service of the poor common people and of the clergy; to the latter through retreats for those preparing for Holy Orders, others for young boys aspiring to the priesthood, as in the seminaries of the Petit Saint-Lazare, Saint-Méen, Le Mans, and the two we are going to open in Agen,[4] and lastly those for ordinands. As for rural missions, you know the variety, difficulty, and importance of them. How to keep men free in the midst of such hard and important works!

Add to these Barbary, Persia, and Arabia Felix where Propaganda Fide is sending us,[5] and Madagascar. Note, Monsieur, how very difficult it is to be able to have the Company subsist in such demanding works. If His Holiness, or the Congregation to which he will refer this matter, does not approve these simple vows, may he do us the charity of giving us a means to that end. The Congregation is under the authority of His Holiness; it is up to him to give us the means to subsist, if he does not approve of the one we are proposing. If he does not give his approval after all that, we must

---

[3]Innocent X (1644-1655).
[4]The Agen Seminary did, in fact, open a few days later, under the direction of Guillaume Delattre, but it was not founded until 1650.
[5]No. 1046, n. 2, indicates that Propaganda Fide withdrew its request to the Congregation of the Mission to send Missionaries to Arabia Felix (present day Yemen).

assent to remain a simple Congregation under his laws. We shall submit to this; perhaps experience will cause them to recognize our need of them. If His Holiness makes provision for the above and approves what we have done, that will put an end to this whole little show of emotion and these pretexts for abandoning one's vocation.

I almost forgot to tell you, with regard to Doutrelet, that I do not remember whether he was given his title deed to the house. If so, we must consider what means are to be taken to get rid of it. M. [Carcireux][6] had us subpoenaed to pay him for his, together with the back interest . . .[7] under pretext of the recognizance we had assumed for it to release him from it—that is, to retain possessory rights to it for him. Observe this black ingratitude and what will have to be done with regard to Doutrelet.

Furthermore, I think you went too far in what you gave to M. de Fondimare. Why give handsome presents to those who desert the Company? It is enough for those whom we dismiss; does it not suffice for us to give them eight or ten écus at most? It will be well for you to make that clear to the Community, so that they know what to expect. The Jesuits do not give anything to those who leave, neither do the Oratorian Fathers nor any Order of which I am aware.

As for our Rules, Monsieur, I think you must begin to get them approved, at least the ones on the vows and on the perpetuity of the General's term of office, for the sake of those who will come in future. If it is so difficult to get all the Rules accepted, you should have them abridged to the summary form you sent me, adding the two points mentioned above. In the name of God, Monsieur, waste no time getting this done.

---

[6]Pémartin reads: "Curtivaux," but there was no Missionary by this name. Paul Carcireux, born in Beauvais, entered the Congregation of the Mission on July 27, 1640, at the age of twenty, took his vows on March 20, 1644, and was ordained a priest in 1645. He left the Congregation to assist his father in his financial difficulties. (Cf. vol. II, no. 781.) In September 1660 his sister, Françoise Carcireux, a Daughter of Charity, wrote to Saint Vincent asking that her brother be allowed to return to the Congregation of the Mission. (Cf. vol. VIII, no. 3265.) Saint Vincent did not acquiesce to this request.

[7]The ellipsis replaces a passage which Pémartin found illegible or which he misread. Here is his text: ". . . the back interest from the time we had made or anything whatever. M. Chomel has our priory and under pretext of the recognizance . . . ."

Let us now come to your little letter. I assure you that it has made me ponder over and over what might have prompted you to ask to be relieved of your office. At times I felt that you wanted to imitate Messrs. Dehorgny and Codoing who, like you, asked to be relieved of their office of Superior; at other times, that you thought your leadership was the reason why those men left; at other times, I felt that the real reason was not that at all but that you think I have some special understanding with M. Dehorgny, which I am not sharing with you, and that the packet of letters I have written to M. Dehorgny[8] leads you to think I have some business with M. Dehorgny, of which neither he nor I is informing you because of a lack of confidence in you.

Regarding the first point, I shall tell you that, if it is only for the reason I cited, I have no cause to worry but rather to praise God—I know of no superior who does not ask to be relieved of his office. As for the second, that thought never crossed my mind—far from it. I thank God for your fine leadership, asking Him to continue to grant it to you. And for the third, the business about which I wrote to him is of such a nature that I can discuss it with no one else on earth, not even Monsieur Lambert, my Assistant, in whom I have implicit confidence, as I have, and rightly so, in those with whom I share my thoughts. But I have not spoken to anyone whomsoever in the Company and have asked him not to mention it to anyone at all. It involves the salvation and reputation of a person who does not want me to speak of this to anyone else but him. That, Monsieur, is the nature of the matter I am discussing with him. In the name of God, Monsieur, rest assured that there is no one else in the world in whom God gives me greater confidence than in you, nor anyone I esteem more highly. After that, Monsieur, I beg you to put that thought in the same class as the one the evil spirit gave you when you were sick. I can assure you they both spring from the same source and tend toward the same end, and I assure you of this in presence of Our Lord, in whose love I am . . . .

---

[8]The letters of June 25, September 10, and perhaps others which we no longer have.

M. Brisacier[9] has an aversion for the vows. He has spoken with me previously in this vein about them. However, he was satisfied when I told him we had no intention of entering the religious state. He mentioned to me that his services might be requested there for the King's affairs. If this happens, deal cautiously with him. You might say something to him about this, as a thought that had occurred to you. The entire outcome must be in reference to the members of the Congregation. It suffices for you to direct all your energies along these lines and let the Ambassador[10] deal with His Holiness. There is already some new statement of fact from elsewhere with regard to us. If the Ambassador is not too highly esteemed by His Holiness, it will be sufficient for him to mention it once to begin with and for you to make your private entreaties, not so much with arguments as with recommendations to our Prelates, as best you can, with regard to our Frenchmen. *Mitte sapientiam et nihil deerit.* [11]

---

[9]Laurent de Brisacier was born in Blois on August 2, 1609. His brother, Jean, a Jesuit, made a name for himself by his controversies against the Jansenists. He was also the uncle of Jacques-Charles de Brisacier, future Superior of the Foreign Missions Society. He became Dean of Saint-Sauveur in Blois in 1632 and was tutor to Louis XIV around 1649, during M. Péréfixe's absence. The Court sent him to Rome to negotiate various affairs, and he was charged by the Queen to fulfill a vow she had taken during her son's illness, of funding a solemn Office every year on the feast of Saint Louis in the church of Our Lady of Loreto, if he were cured. Laurent de Brisacier also became State Councillor. His quarrels with the Chapter of Blois caused him many a lawsuit. He took an active part in the foundation of the Foreign Missions Seminary and died in Blois on February 15, 1690. (Cf. André Rebsomen, "Une famille Blésoise, Les de Brisacier," in *Mémoires de la Société des sciences et lettres de Loir-et-Cher* [June 30, 1902].)

[10]François du Val, Marquis de Fontenay-Mareuil, Seigneur de Mareuil, de Villiers-le-Sec, and de Jaguy-en-France, Marshal of Royal Fortifications, Councillor of the King in his Council of State. He was also French Ambassador in Rome (1640-1650) and died in 1665.

[11]*Use wisdom and nothing shall be wanting.*

1069. - TO ANTOINE PORTAIL, IN MARSEILLES

October 30, 1648

The practice of wearing the rosary on one's belt is always observed in this house. I ask you to see that it is observed there. Our other houses are faithful to it; it is a holy and edifying custom.

1070. - TO ETIENNE BLATIRON, SUPERIOR, IN GENOA

October 30, 1648

I beg God to inspire you with the most effective way of dealing with M. . . It seems to me that the best way will be the one that is most gentle and forbearing, which is more in conformity with the Spirit of Our Lord and more apt to win hearts. If you win his, he will give you great satisfaction. His present state is only a passing temptation, for which we must pray to God for him.

Please suspend the monthly retreats you would like your Community to adopt. We are in the process of examining whether or not it is advisable to continue those that are made here, because of certain inconveniences that have arisen from them.

1071. - TO A RECENTLY DESIGNATED BISHOP [1]

I was very sorry that my illness and many business matters prevented me from replying sooner by letter to the honor Your Most Ill[ustri]ous Excellency deigned to show me. I recognize my

---

Letter 1069. - Reg. 2, p. 104.

Letter 1070. - Reg. 2, p. 200.

Letter 1071. - Vatican Library, Barberini collection, *Latinorum* 2172, original signed letter in Latin, photocopy in the Archives of the Mission, Curia Generalitia, Rome.
[1]Probably Giovanni Battista Spinola, elected Bishop of Matera on May 14, 1648, transferred

inability to thank you adequately both for this favor and for the benefits you have lavished up to now on our confreres in Rome. But the Lord will pay this debt of gratitude for me, and Christ, who offered Himself as surety for the poor, has already superabundantly responded to my wishes by choosing for the episcopate a Prelate who wishes to make himself useful, knows how to govern, is remarkable for his prudence and the integrity of his character, and promises to be a worthy successor of saints.

How great [are] my joy and happiness at seeing that God has directed so well the [course of] events that, having made you grow from virtue to virtue, He now leads you from [honor] to honor! Trusting in the Lo[rd], therefore, we hope that [He who] has led you to do great things for the good of the Church, will raise you still higher. Along with our deep gratitude, we offer Him also our loving prayers. May He who has set you apart to instruct His people in salvation maintain your flock in doing g[ood] and preserve your Church without stain or wrinkle under y[our] guidance! We hope for this all the more because God has quieted [the disturbances] which were rising like tumultuous waves and has brought an end to the war which was breaking out. We are now enjoying peace, which we constantly implore Him to maintain.

As for the advice and benevolence with which you deign to favor our confreres, I tha[nk] you for them, not in the measure required by my duty, but according to my own strength; I shall respond with my best wishes and my prayers. What the powerlessness of my insignificance cannot of[fer] you, you will receive from the superabundant liberality of Him who gives all persons a share in the treasures of His ma[ny] graces.

In the meantime, if Your Most Ill[ustri]ous Excellency wishes to honor me with His orders, you will always find [me] disposed to obey most promptly.

---

to Genoa in 1664, then raised to the cardinalate. He died on January 4, 1704.

I am Your Most Ill[ustri]ous and Most R[everend] Lordship's most humble and very devoted servant in the L[or]d.

VINCENT DEPAUL
Unworthy Superior General
of the Congregation of the Mission

The nones of November,[2] 1648

1072. - *SAINT LOUISE TO SAINT VINCENT*

November 6, [1648] [1]

Monsieur,

A few days ago a person from Fontainebleau informed us that Sister Barbe Angiboust has had a fever since the September feast of Our Lady.[2] Yesterday someone from Saint-Germain-de-l'Auxerrois told us that her confessor had sent word to a lady in the parish that she was dying and they were going to give her Extreme Unction.[3] In view of this news, Monsieur, do you think it would be a good idea for us to send a Sister there today? We did write, and one of our Sisters left for there a week ago to be her companion, but we have had no news of her.

---

[2]November 5.

Letter 1072. - The original autograph letter is the property of the Daughters of Charity in Ans (Belgium).

[1]There is some confusion concerning the date of this letter and its reply (no. 1073). Coste states that it was written on November 6 and, citing *Lettres de Louise de Marillac,* L. 223, assigns 1658 as the year. *Saint Louise de Marillac, Ses Ecrits* (Paris: P. Kremer, 1961), L. 222, p. 304, indicates only the year 1648 in dating this letter to Saint Vincent. In letter 223 to Sister Anne Hardemont, in which she is asked to visit Sister Barbe, the date given is October, 1648.

Ecrits spirituels (Tours: 1983), on the other hand, dates the letter to Saint Vincent (L. 222, p. 178) "end of September 1646;" for the letter to Sister Anne Hardemont (L. 223, p. 179) October 1646 is given.

In the present edition, the order of letters followed by Coste has been maintained.

[2]September 8, Birth of the Blessed Virgin Mary.

[3]Sister Barbe recovered; she did not die until December 27, 1658.

Would your charity kindly give us a prompt reply? I also ask your blessing, for the love of God, and am, Monsieur, your most humble and very grateful daughter and servant.

L. DE M.

Please remember the Bishop of Beauvais' [4] *reply.*

1073. - TO SAINT LOUISE

[November 6 or 7, 1648][1]

FIRST DRAFT

Mademoiselle,

It would be a charity and an encouragement for the other Sisters if you sent a Sister[2] to visit our poor patient, by coach if there is one; if not, by water[3] as far as Melun, and from there on foot for the three leagues to Fontainebleau, with someone to accompany her.

---

[4]Augustin Potier.

Letter 1073. - The original autograph letter is the property of the Daughters of Charity in Ans (Belgium).

[1]This letter is the reply to the preceding one. At first Saint Vincent had written his answer on the same page as the letter of Saint Louise but, because it was not sufficiently legible, or did not quite convey his thought, he started it over on the page left blank.

[2]Saint Louise chose Anne Hardemont. At one time she had sent Sister Anne to visit Sister Barbe and to report on her health. It is uncertain whether Saint Louise's letter to Sister Anne (*Ecrits spirituels*, L. 223, p. 179) is in response to Saint Vincent's present letter.

[3]On the Seine.

SECOND DRAFT

I am deeply affected by the serious illness of our poor Sister Barbe. It would be an act of charity to send a Sister to her and an encouragement for the others. So please send one, Mademoiselle, by coach, if there is one, or by water as far as Melun, where there is a means of transport on Monday or Tuesday at the Saint-Paul port.[4] From there she will have to go on foot through the woods to Fontainebleau, where there is no danger now that the Court is not there. The coach is on rue de la Cossonnerie.[5]

1074. - TO MATHURIN GENTIL, IN LE MANS

Paris, November 7, 1648

Monsieur,

The grace of Our Lord be with you forever!

I am replying in haste to your very dear letter of the twenty-sixth of last month and am leaving for Saint-Denis, where I am making a visitation with the Visitation nuns.

We have received nothing of what is due to the late M. Le Bourgais,[1] except for one hundred livres, which were sent to him, as you know. There is little reason to hope for the rest, since we have no recognizance, and it is just that it revert to the relatives of the deceased. It seems to me that his father is still alive.

It will be well for you to terminate your business with M. Voseillan for the repurchase of the fish ponds. If he is unwilling

---

[4]On the Quai des Célestins opposite rue Saint-Paul. Wine, iron, coal, and spices were unloaded there.

[5]This street still exists; it runs from one side of the Boulevard Sébastopol to the Forum des Halles, site of the former central market of Paris.

Letter 1074. - Archives of the Mission, Turin, original signed letter.

[1]Jacques Lebourgais, born in Coutances (Manche), entered the Congregation of the Mission as a priest on September 17, 1645, at thirty-eight years of age.

to come down to 125 livres, you will have to give him something more rather than go to law.

It is true that our business with M. Rivière is all but concluded; you should act in whatever concerns his chapels as you do for the rest, except that it must be clear that you are acting as procurator for M. Rivière, while waiting for us to settle and finish completely with him.

We will do our best to send you some priests and Brothers.

It is not our intention that anyone in your house should offer the Holy Sacrifice for our deceased members to the prejudice of your obligations, which must be taken care of first. In place of the Masses, prayers could be offered for our deceased.

M. Bajoue is sending three books to M. Cornaire[2] and a set of regulations for the Charity to M. Roujon. They are all in one package wrapped in paper and sent by coach in your name. Please have it picked up and continue to pray for me. I am, with the affection God knows, in His love, Monsieur, your most humble servant.

VINCENT DEPAUL
i.s.C.M.

At the bottom of the first page: M. Gentil

1075. - TO LOUIS RIVET, SUPERIOR, IN SAINTES

November 15, 1648

We must be careful not to give the Vicars General any grounds

---

[2]Guillaume Cornaire, born June 4, 1614 in the Besançon diocese, was ordained a priest during Lent of 1639, entered the Congregation of the Mission on December 2, 1647, and took his vows in Le Mans on November 23, 1653, where he provided for the spiritual needs of the sick in the hospital. He died there, perhaps in 1660. Brother Chollier wrote his obituary, but it is no longer extant.

Letter 1075. - Reg. 2, p. 107.

for discontent. They are our masters; as far as possible we have to adapt ourselves to their wishes. Therefore, when they send you any priests, the Company must accept them willingly and keep them for as long as they request, even priests they send there to receive correction. You may, however, represent humbly to them that you are overburdened, if this is the case, or any other inconveniences that may arise. It is also quite fitting that the Company observe their intentions with regard to missions, not undertaking any without their consent nor without asking them where. We should take as a maxim never to be surprised at current difficulties, no more than at a passing breeze, because with a little patience we shall see them disappear. Time changes everything. I read in the history of the Jesuits that the Pope, who succeeded the one who erected their Company into a religious Order, obliged them to wear a hood.[1] That was rather hard for them, yet they had to endure it during his lifetime. Immediately after his death, however, they got rid of the hood. In like manner, if you are presently being obliged to do something you do not like, let a few days slip quietly by; the instability of things will soon free you from this constraint. God raises us up and humbles us, consoles and afflicts us, according as he sees us disposed to profit by these states.

**1076. - HENRI DE MAUPAS DU TOUR, BISHOP OF PUY,
TO SAINT VINCENT**

Monsieur,

Two matters, very important for the glory of God, oblige me to write you these lines.

(1) The disorders in the Benedictine Abbey of Monestier,[1] in this

---

[1]Choir dress. Pope Paul IV was eighty-three years old when he issued that order. He died the following year (1559).

Letter 1076. - Archives of the Mission, Paris, original autograph letter.
[1]Today Le Monastier, principal town of a canton in Haute-Loire.

*diocese, four leagues from Puy, which depends on the priests from Sans-
terre. The Fathers of the Reform of Saint-Maur, who live in the abbey of
Saint-Germain-des-Prés, can give you all the details of this. I returned
from there yesterday, where I demanded that the Prior punish one of the
monks who had his mistress in his room when I arrived; she is due to give
birth within the week.*

*(2) The acts of violence and the sacrileges that the soldiers in the
Languedoc regiment, commanded by the Sieur de Valon, committed in a
church in my diocese three days ago. I most humbly entreat you to inform
the Queen of this as soon as possible. I am writing about it in greater detail
to the Minister of Finance. I think he will show you my letter. The glory of
God is at stake here. The altars have been profaned and the sacred
ciborium stolen, along with the chalice used in the daily celebration of the
Mass. I fear that God may vent His wrath upon those who are in authority,
if they do not look after His interests. I shall send an express messenger to
the Court in a week to bring the information and the complaints.*

I am, Monsieur, your most humble servant.

HENRY,
Bishop of Le Puy

Le Puy, November 18, 1648

Addressed: *Monsieur Vincent, Superior General of the Mission, in
Paris.*

**1077. - TO TOMMASO TURCO, MASTER GENERAL
OF THE DOMINICANS**

November 26 [1648][1]

Vincent de Paul informs Tommaso Turco that, after listening to Fathers
Labat and Biarrotte and Brother Bernard, he advised them to return to their
Province, or rather, he sent them back, committing them to negotiate with

---

Letter 1077. - Archives of the Mission, Paris, copy made at the Generalate of the Dominican
Fathers, *Epistolae R. P. Turchi,*IV, 88, p. 20; the original is in Latin. This letter had been
previously published by Daniel Antonin Mortier, in his *Histoire des maîtres généraux de l'Ordre
des Frères Prêcheurs,* 1913, vol. VI, p. 513.
[1]Year required by the place of the document in the register.

a view to reconciliation. He awaits the results of the talks to enact the union and peace, if the proposed conditions please him. This measure will be most agreeable to the King, the Queen, and the Cardinal.

1078. - TO JEAN BARREAU, CONSUL OF FRANCE, IN ALGIERS

December 4, 1648

We cannot better assure our eternal happiness than by living and dying in the service of the poor, in the arms of Providence, and with genuine renouncement of ourselves in order to follow Jesus Christ.

1079. - *SAINT LOUISE TO SAINT VINCENT*

[December 1648] [1]

Monsieur,

We are having a very difficult time finding someone to go to the meeting at the Duchesse d'Aiguillon's house. The only instructions we can give the person is to put our papers in her hands. Since I believe that the interest of the others is similar to ours, I thought perhaps my son could go and do as the others do, unless, Monsieur, your charity thinks it well for us to give our papers to the person who is going there from your house.

We shall await the order it will please you to give us, asking God to grant you perfect health for His glory. I am, Monsieur, your most obedient and very grateful daughter and servant.

LOUISE DE MARILLAC

Addressed: *Monsieur Vincent*

Letter 1078. - Reg. 2, p. 34.

Letter 1079. - Original autograph letter, property of the Daughters of Charity, 3 rue Oudinot, Paris.
    [1]Date added on the back of the original by Brother Ducournau.

1080. - ETIENNE BLATIRON TO SAINT VINCENT

Genoa, December 10, 1648

Several bandits are converted in the course of a mission given in Lavagna.[1]

1081. - TO RENE ALMERAS, SUPERIOR, IN ROME

December 11, 1648

Blessed be God, Monsieur, that your Community is presently making good progress! Sometimes God allows Communities to fall into such desolation that it seems all is lost, but afterward he raises them up to a better state than before. Trials from on high are always salutary. I beg you to ask God for me, as I do for you, that our minds may never be surprised at seeing degeneration in our houses. He puts down and raises up people as He pleases, and His abasement of some [person] whom He intends to use is a portent of future elevation. Mistrust of your own way of governing is good, but should we not rely on Our Lord and allow Him to act, since it is He who governs and not we?

1082. - TOMMASO TURCO TO SAINT VINCENT

Rome, December 21, 1648

Monsieur and Very Reverend Father Vincent,

I feel greatly indebted to your zeal for the welfare of the affairs of my

---

Letter 1080. - Abelly, *op.cit.,* bk. II, chap. I, sect. IV, p. 71.
[1]Small town near Genoa, and birthplace of Pope Innocent IV (1243-1254).

Letter 1081. - Reg. 2, p. 229.

Letter 1082. - Archives of the Mission, Paris, copy made at the Generalate of the Dominican

Order and the care you have taken to put the older Fathers of the Toulouse Province back on the road to duty. Vanity and dissipation had led them astray and caused them to invent grounds for complaint where they themselves should have found their good and their peace of mind. I effected the union, about which they are complaining, Monsieur, only at their earnest entreaties and with their consent, to settle their quarrels and private disagreements. They had been like this for two years without a Provincial, in a state of confusion, and with factions and divisions into which the pretensions of some, including Fathers Biarrotte and Marrin [1] had thrown them.

In the course of my visitation there, I found the convents of that Province in a pitiful state on both temporal and spiritual levels: the collapse of houses fallen into ruin in Marciac,[2] La Réole,[3] Port Saint-Marie,[4] etc., due to poor financial management, lack of zeal for the common good, and the poor observance of the officers. Scandals were occurring everywhere, as in Bergerac, Agen, Marciac, Port Sainte-Marie, etc. The general complaint of the laity was that they were being neither served nor edified. In a word, the common entreaties of everyone, including themselves, seeing that they had no novices, no studies, and no means or hope of being able to have any because of the pettiness and poverty of their convents, forced me to apply this effective and unique remedy to the many present and future ills; namely, the union of this wretched Province, the second largest of the Order besides, to the Congregation of Saint-Louis beyond the Loire, whose convents have a fine reputation for both spiritual and temporal matters. They also have the means of training many novices in the observance and in learning so as to mend the breaches in this Province, which would otherwise be irreparable, and to introduce imperceptibly and lovingly the principles and practices of the regular life, the basis and the only mainstay of religious houses.

These considerations, Monsieur, which had confirmed this union, should have led them to foster and cherish it, if the ambition and vanity of certain priests and Doctors had not changed them. They saw themselves deprived of the office of Provincial because they had no inclination to

---

Fathers, *Epistolae R. P. Turchi,* IV, 88, p. 118; the original is in Latin. In vol. XIII, Coste makes the following addition: "For the rivalries between the Parisians and the Gascons, see Père Mortier, *Histoire des maîtres généraux de l'Ordre des Frères Prêcheurs,* 1913, vol. VI, in which this letter was published."

[1] This word could also be Martin.
[2] Principal town of a canton in the district of Mirande (Gers).
[3] Principal town of a canton in Gironde.
[4] Principal town of a canton in the district of Agen (Lot-et-Garonne).

regular observance, the only road to the welfare and preservation of observance in the convents where it already existed, and to oblige others to accept and embrace it, conformably to the orders and wishes of the most Christian Kings Henry IV and Louis XIII, of happy memory. These latter always insisted at General Chapters and with the Generals of the Order that the Provincials of France be of the observance, and that the novices be trained in houses of the strict observance. That is another of their grounds for complaint, and through the craftiness of Father Labat, their Procurator in this court at the time, they had the audacity here to extort surreptitiously, under false pretexts, Bulls of Committimus in partibus, contrary to the Brief of Pope Urban VIII of happy memory, the orders of the General Chapters, and the recently issued decree of the Congregation of Regulars obliging them to obey me, upon and after examination of all their complaints.

So, Monsieur, in this affair, conducted with such violence and boldness, contrary to the honor of this court, most indignant at having been taken by surprise; contrary to the authority of the College of Cardinals; contrary to the orders of the King, who has deigned to confirm the decree of union by his patents; contrary to the disposition of the Parlements of Toulouse and Bordeaux, who ratified it; lastly, contrary to the good intentions of the Cardinal, by whose advice I have brought this whole business to a head; I cannot yield in anything whatsoever, until they first have obeyed and made reparation by their obedience and submission for the bad seed of rebellion and irreverence their violence and sudden attacks have sown in the minds of the monks. The ensuing consequences and example would be very pernicious if I were to yield in the slightest, even if my duty and my conscience allowed me to do so. Consequently, Monsieur, I beg you to agree that they should obey me. Afterward I shall make them understand that I am their father, always ready to grant them free pardon when they are in a state to receive it, that is to say, in their duty.

I can do nothing else at present, since I am bound to the interests of this court and of my Order. I am much obliged to you for your willingness to incite them to their duty. God grant that they may believe you! From these difficulties you can see, Monsieur, how hard it is to please everyone, how many agonies and problems must be faced when the bishops insist on the reforms of convents, and how much easier it is to desire this good than to effect it. If I do not respond . . . their good desires as quickly as they would like, it is due more to a lack of means than of good will, since one of my greatest consolations is to see my Order in observance and in a state proper to its vocation.

I ask God to continue to bestow His graces on you and to bless your holy intentions. If I can do anything here regarding them, I beg you to

make use of me in this place with as much liberty as I have confidence in
your piety. I have already offered my services for anything I can do for
your good Fathers and sons who are here.

I beg you to believe me . . . .

1083. - TO ETIENNE BLATIRON, SUPERIOR, IN GENOA

Paris [Christmas 1648][1]

M[onsieur,]

[The grace of] O[ur Lord be with you forever!]

[Since God has been] p[leased to bless the works you have] done
and [to grant them success,] I ask Him to be Him[self your reward,]
and may all His creatures g[lorify] Him for this. He sees my
gratitude, and that consoles me, since it is beyond my power to
express it in words. May His Divine Goodness grant that the souls
you have assisted make a holy use of the lights they have received,
and may those whom you are going to assist experience the effects
of His mercy!

I do not mind the fact that you went from one mission to another
without returning to the house, except that you are depriving
yourself of a little rest, and I strongly fear that the excessive work
will be too much for you. In the name of O[ur] L[ord], Monsieur,
take care of yourself.

Last Tuesday Brother Ennery,[2] Brother Claude[3] and another

---

Letter 1083. - Archives of the Mission, Paris, original signed letter. The document is in very
poor condition.

[1]The date was on that part of the original damaged by humidity; it was rewritten on the back
of the letter.

[2]Jean Ennery [John McEnery], born in December 1616 at Castle Mak Ennery, today
Castletown [Castletown McEnery, Co. Limerick], entered the Congregation of the Mission on
September 23, 1642 and took his vows on October 11, 1645. According to Saint Vincent, he
was "a wise, pious, and exemplary man" (cf. Abelly, *op. cit.*, bk. III, p. 48). He taught theology
at Saint-Lazare (1652), aided the unfortunate people of Champagne impoverished by the war
(1653), and assisted his countrymen who had fled to Troyes (1654). Lastly, he was sent to Genoa
where he died of the plague in 1657.

[3]Claude Le Gentil.

good coadjutor Brother left here, all of them quite pleased to go
and render you their service and submission. They took the Lyons
coach with a priest and a cleric of [our Company], who are setting
off for Barbary. [The first, named] M. Dieppe,[4] [is going to A]lgiers
in place of M. Le Sage, and the o[ther to] Tunis to [act as] Cons[ul
of the] French [nat]ion. [In this capacity, he is respons]ible for
[fa]cilitating [the ransom of s]laves. [His name] is Huguier;[5] [he is
a] good businessman and a very God-fearing person as well.

God has been pleased to call to Himself good M. de Fargis,[6] who
had been with us for a year; he gave us great consolation because
he was very pious and exemplary. We shall have a conference on
him one of these days. I ask you to pray and have others pray for
his soul, without forgetting mine, which tenderly cherishes you and

[4]Jean Dieppe, born in Cancale (Ille-et-Vilaine), was received into the Congregation of the
Mission on August 5, 1647, at thirty years of age. On December 22, 1648 he left Paris for Algiers
where he died of the plague on May 2, 1649.

[5]Benjamin-Joseph Huguier, born in Sézanne (Marne) on March 10, 1613, was Attorney at
the Châtelet of Paris before his admission into the Congregation of the Mission on September
15, 1647. He served in Tunis (1649-1652), returning to France in May of 1652. He took his
vows that same year and was ordained a priest in February 1655. After ordination, he became
chaplain of the galleys in Toulon. However, he felt drawn to Barbary. So, on September 19,
1662 he was sent to Algiers with the title of Vicar Apostolic. While nursing the plague-stricken
there, he contracted the illness and died of it himself in April 1663. (Cf. *Mémoires de la
Congrégation de la Mission,* vol. II, pp. 221-230.)

[6]The family of Charles d'Angennes, Seigneur de Fargis, had made a reputation for itself in
military and diplomatic circles. By his marriage to Madeleine de Silly, Madame de Gondi's
sister, he became Comte de la Rochepot. Saint Vincent probably saw him more than once at the
de Gondi home when he was chaplain there. M. de Fargis was Ambassador in Spain (1620-
1626). On January 1, 1626 he signed the treaty of Monçon, which was disclaimed by Richelieu
and concluded on a new basis on March 6. The Queen Mother, dissatisfied with the politics and
influence of Richelieu, had surrounded herself with a certain number of important persons ready
to oust the powerful minister. Madame de Fargis, her lady-in-waiting, who belonged to the
opposition, was involved in the intrigues. In 1631 she was condemned to death, but she fled
abroad, dying in Louvain in 1639. Her husband was imprisoned in the Bastille for the same
reason on February 14, 1633. On June 2, 1640, he had the sorrow of seeing his twenty-seven
year old son killed in the siege of Arras. He still had one daughter, Henriette, then at Port-Royal,
who resisted the pressures of her father to have her marry, preferring to spend her life in the
monastery. She died there on June 3, 1691, after being Abbess for many years. M. de Fargis
entered the Congregation of the Mission on December 31, 1647. In the seminary his conduct
was so exemplary that Saint Vincent stated that "he never saw him commit a single venial sin."
He died on December 20, 1648. (Cf. *Notices,* vol. II, pp. 425-430.)

your little Community, whom I greet in a spirit of humility and affection.

If Brother Robert wants to become a monk, fine, let him do it, seeing that for so long we have been unable to rid him of his fancy to study. May Our Lord give us a share in His humility, patience and charity. I am, in His love, Monsieur, your most humble servant.

VINCENT DEPAUL
i.s.C.M.

Addressed: [Mo]nsieur Blatiron, Superior [of the Priests] of the Mission, in Genoa

1084. - TO A PRIEST OF THE MISSION

[December 1648 or January 1649]

Monsieur,

God has been pleased to take good Brother de Fargis from us a year after His goodness had given Him to us. He was Count of Rochepot and Seigneur of Fargis. He had married the sister of the wife of the General of the Galleys, our first foundress, and had been the King's Ambassador in Spain. He died on December 20. In death as in life, he appeared very detached and filled with God. While we had the joy of having him with us, he was assuredly a great example to us, so much so that I never saw him commit a single venial sin. I recommend his soul to your prayers, and I ask Our Lord to sanctify yours more and more. I do not doubt your courage to imitate him.

Letter 1084. - Lyons manuscript.

1085. - TO THE MARQUIS DESPORTES

December 31, 1648

Monsieur,

The letter you did me the honor of writing to me is worthy of a
truly Christian soul like yours. I cannot express to you, Monsieur,
how edified I am by your views regarding the office of bishop and
your dispositions regarding the pension, for which I shall do all in
my power for you. The good use you wish to make of it makes this
a twofold obligation for me. Nevertheless, I foresee two difficulties: first, that ecclesiastical pensions are given only to those who
are ecclesiastics, who wear clerical dress and actually live in
conformity with all that. I know, Monsieur, that you have the
ecclesiastical spirit and that this difficulty does not apply to you.
But here is a second one, which is greatly to be feared: the Queen
and the Cardinal[1] are so overwhelmed by petitioners of all sorts that
they have no freedom to consider which of them are the most
deserving. Pensions and benefices are being wrung from them, and
they are prevented from disposing of one and the other as they
would like. I shall not fail to speak to them of you, Monsieur, in
the circumstances and in the manner God knows. It is true that your
name is too illustrious and your merit too well known to need
recommendation, and perhaps the esteem Her Majesty and H[is]
E[minence] have for them will oblige them to give you some
satisfaction sooner than I dare to hope. I ask O[ur] L[ord] that this
may be so.

His Divine Goodness has been pleased to take good M. de
Fargis from us one year after He had given him to us; he died on

---

Letter 1085. - Reg. 1, f°30. The copyist notes that the letter was written by the secretary and
signed by the Saint.
[1]Jules Cardinal Mazarin.

the nineteenth of this month.[2] In death as in life, he appeared very detached and filled with God. While we had the joy of having him with us, he was assuredly a great example to us, so much so that I never saw him commit even a venial sin.

I recommend his soul to your prayers and ask O[ur] L[ord] to sanctify yours more and more. I do not doubt, Monsieur, your courage to imitate him in his withdrawal from the world, if this were possible for you, for I think you are living as piously and religiously in your own home as you would in a cloister. *O Dieu!* Monsieur, how good it is to prepare oneself in this way for a blessed eternity. I am, in His love, Monsieur, your . . . .

VINCENT DEPAUL

1086. - TO LAMBERT AUX COUTEAUX, AT SAINT-LAZARE

Fréneville, January 18,[1] 1649

Vincent de Paul writes that it is not expedient to put the wheat in the Saint-Lazare granaries up for sale. It is better to lend it at interest to God by distributing it as alms to the poor. If a setier[2] of wheat a day is not sufficient, let two be given.

---

[2]In the preceding letter it is stated that M. de Fargis died on December 20. The inconsistency here may be due either to an error of the copyist or to a lapse of memory on the part of Saint Vincent.

Letter 1086. - Letter mentioned by Brother Pierre Chollier in his deposition for the process of beatification.

Pierre Chollier, born in Unienville in the Troyes diocese on March 3, 1646, entered the Congregation of the Mission in Paris on October 26, 1668, and took his vows in November 1670. He served as personal secretary to a number of Superiors General. He had a talent for writing; we are indebted to him for the biographies of Brothers Alexandre Véronne and Bertrand Ducournau, and of Father Guillaume Cornaire. He died at Saint-Lazare on November 6, 1716.

[1]On January 18 Saint Vincent was still in Villepreux; consequently, there is an error either in the locality or in the date given here. The letter might well belong to January 28.

[2]An obsolete unit of measure equal to about twelve bushels.

1087. - TO ANTOINE PORTAIL, IN MARSEILLES

Villepreux, January 22, 1649

Monsieur,

The grace of Our Lord be with you forever!

I do not know whether you wrote me by the regular mail which arrived last week. I did not receive a letter from you but I did hear from M. Chrétien and from Tunis.

I did not write you last week; I think you know the reason why. I left Paris on the fourteenth of this month to go to Saint-Germain with the intention of rendering some small service to God, but my sins rendered me unworthy of this. After a stay of three or four days, I came to this place, which I shall be leaving the day after tomorrow to go visit our houses.[1] It is God's will that I be of no use now for anything else. I shall go straight to Le Mans and then on to Brittany. I sent you word that M. du Chesne[2] would go to

Letter 1087. - Archives of the Mission, Turin, original signed letter.

[1]Conscious that she was not safe in Paris, the Queen had gone to Saint-Germain-en-Laye, followed by most of the Court. Parlement, the nobility, and the people were ready to do anything to bring about Mazarin's dismissal. All Paris was mobilized. Moved by the impending disasters and by those which already afflicted the capital, Saint Vincent decided to go and see Anne of Austria who would willingly listen to him. He left before dawn on January 14, accompanied by his faithful secretary, Brother Ducournau, who has left an account of this journey, later used by Collet. In Clichy the people, armed with pikes and guns, rushed on the two travelers. The Saint might not have escaped the danger had not one of the assailants recognized him as his former Pastor, and calmed his companions. In Neuilly, where the Seine had flooded its banks, Saint Vincent courageously forded the river on his horse. He arrived at Saint-Germain between nine and ten in the morning, saw the Queen, and told her clearly that her duty was to dismiss her minister. When he was brought before Mazarin, he spoke to him just as frankly. The minister was taken aback for a moment, but replied that he would be happy to sacrifice himself, if such was the opinion of Michel Le Tellier, Secretary of State for War. As may be guessed, Le Tellier's advice was negative. Saint Vincent could not return to Paris, where news of his visit to the Court placed him in danger of arousing the wrath of the people, already in a state of commotion because of the rumor that Mazarin and the Queen were secretly married, and that Vincent himself had blessed the union. Three days later, furnished with a document of safe-conduct and protected by an escort, he took the road to Villepreux. (Cf. Collet, *op. cit.*, vol. I, p. 468; also no. 1063, n. 2 for Saint Vincent's reply when questioned by Brother Robineau.) The Saint's intervention took great courage because the Queen became angry with anybody who suggested that she should capitulate. (Cf. Guy Patin, *La France au milieu du XVIIe siècle, d'après la correspondance de Guy Patin* [Paris: Armand Brette, 1901], p. 11.)

[2]Pierre du Chesne.

Marseilles but he is, in fact, needed too much at Saint-Lazare. Please be patient, Monsieur, and do the best you can both for men and for resources. It is impossible for us to supply you with anything, nor can we do so for the other houses which are depending on the coaches for their income. The latter are no longer running and, to all appearances, it will be a long time before we get anything from them, not even what the tax-farmers owe us. They will not pay us from the *aides*[3] either, as long as these disturbances last. All this still cannot adequately describe to you the straits in which poor Saint-Lazare finds itself.[4] May God be praised! So, you will say to me, what will the Marseilles house live on? First of all, and without hemming and hawing, you must dismiss all your seminarians who do not pay sufficient fees; second, tell the Bishop of Marseilles[5] what is happening, to prompt him to give you some assistance; in the third place, try to get some Mass stipends. I regret saying this to you but necessity takes precedence over any other consideration. In a word, do your best not to put us in debt.

The men in Barbary must be notified of what is happening so they will watch their expenses. I am writing to M. Le Vacher[6] about this. And because he has sent me word that the Brother who is going as Proconsul[7] needs to give several gifts when he goes into office, and we cannot send him anything for this purpose, I think it would be well for him to postpone his journey; I ask you to delay it for a while.

I am concerned about the mistake made by M. Le Vacher in allowing a tax to be levied on French ships in order to pay off the

[3]Indirect taxes on consumer goods such as meat, fish, wood, and especially wine.

[4]When he wrote these lines, Saint Vincent was unaware that six hundred soldiers, lodged at Saint-Lazare, had pillaged and plundered the house, taken off the doors, sold part of the wheat, and set fire to the wood pile. (Cf. Abelly, *op.cit.*, bk. I, chap. XXXIX, p. 182; Collet, *op. cit.*, vol. I, p. 471.) At this news, the city ordered Colonel de Lamoignon to send soldiers daily to the Saint-Lazare house until further orders, for its "security and preservation." (Cf. Le Roux de Lincy and Douet d'Arcq, eds. *Registres de l'hôtel de ville de Paris pendant la Fronde* [3 vols., Paris: Jules Renouard, 1846-1848], vol. I, p. 204.)

[5]Etienne du Puget (1644-1668).

[6]Jean Le Vacher.

[7]Benjamin Huguier, seminarian of the Congregation of the Mission.

debts of a private individual. The Marseilles merchants are right to complain about this. Please see them for me and, after apologizing, find out what means there are to rectify this mistake. I will willingly make use of them. Right now, I am going to write to the Court to obtain a letter from the King to the Dey, asking that he not allow any tax to be levied on French vessels, so as to permit free trade. I shall also ask the Duchesse d'Aiguillon to urge that dispatches be sent both for the reversion and the commission of the Tunis consulate.[8]

The uncertainty about the mail going through and whether this letter will reach you oblige me to conclude. I assure you, Monsieur, that I am, in O[ur] L[ord], your most humble servant.

VINCENT DEPAUL
i.s.C.M.

Addressed: Monsieur Portail, Priest of the Mission, in Marseilles

1088. - TO SAINT LOUISE

Fréneville, February 4, 1649

Mademoiselle,

The grace of Our Lord be with you forever!
I am still here in Fréneville,[1] where this very cold weather took

---

[8]Martin de Lange, Consul in Tunis, had died at the end of July 1648. The Duchesse d'Aiguillon had already bought the consulate in Algiers. For the same reason, she acquired the consulate of Tunis, which she offered to the Congregation of the Mission, with the King's permission.

Letter 1088. - This letter was published from the original in the *Notice sur la conservation et la translation des reliques de saint Vincent de Paul,* p. 9.
[1]Obliged by snow and cold weather to stay in Fréneville, Saint Vincent did not remain idle. As the result of a sermon on the means of appeasing the anger of God and on the attitude to observe in the midst of the ruination that the civil war was causing, almost all the inhabitants

me by surprise, on the occasion of the feast I wanted to spend here.
I intended to help prepare these good people to give themselves to
God that He might grant them the grace of making good use of the
trials they are expecting.

Our dear Sisters[2] seem more and more united, loving their
vocation; they are carrying out their duties very well, thank God.
They give us some of their whole-meal bread, whereas the farmer
mixes barley in his. This has come from their charity; we shall give
them some wheat in return. They have also sent us some apples,
which the good people gave them. They go to confession to M. Le
Gros[3] during the time since they have been to one of us, and have
done the same with us since they have been to M. Le Gros. This
seems like a good practice to me.

I think you are quite courageous to stay in your house like that.
People have talked about the madman of old, and that is what made
me write you as I have written. I do not think things will go that
far.

Our Lord is giving you good health in the midst of all this. I
thank Him for it with all my heart and at Holy Mass where I see
you before God every day I ask Him to preserve you.

God willing, as soon as the good weather arrives, I hope to leave

---

of Valpuiseaux went to confession. (Cf. Collet, *op. cit.*, vol. I, pp. 472-473.)

[2]Sister Toussainte David and Sister Jeanne Fouré of Loudun. Sister Jeanne had been a nurse
for children in 1646, and had come to Valpuiseaux in 1649. In 1651 she returned to her family.
In 1644, Sister Toussainte was in Saint-Severin, then in Valpuiseaux in 1650, and in 1655 she
was in Paris, where she signed with a cross the Act of Establishment of the Company. She was
later sent to Sedan.

[3]Jean-Baptiste Le Gros, born in 1614 in the Coutances diocese, entered Saint-Lazare as a
priest on June 24, 1644, and took his vows on June 29, 1646. He was Procurator of the
Motherhouse (1648-1651), then Superior of Saint-Charles Seminary (1651). He was still at
Saint-Lazare in 1652 and 1653, and was Superior in Richelieu (1653-1655). Since he was in
Richelieu on February 6, 1654, he probably arrived there at the end of the preceding year. Le
Gros died in Montech, near Montauban (Tarn-et-Garonne) in 1655. (Cf. Lyons manuscript, f°
226-230.)

The variations regarding the date of the death of Jean-Baptiste Le Gros reveal the difficulties
caused by inaccurate record keeping and/or the work of copyists in past centuries. Coste gives
the date of his death as November 5. *Notices*, vol. III, pp. 146-148 gives December 31, while
Notices, vol. V, p. 370 gives January 7, all in 1655.

and go straight to Angers, where God knows how gladly I will visit your daughters.

M. Escart[4] spoke to me about one of them in Bicêtre, who is very troublesome to the others. It would be well for you to see what is to be done there.

That, Mademoiselle, is all I have to say to you for now, except to recommend myself to your prayers and to those of our dear Sisters. I am, in the love of Our Lord, Mademoiselle, your most humble servant.

VINCENT DEPAUL

Addressed: Mademoiselle Le Gras

1089. - TO JACQUES NORAIS [1]

[Fréneville,] February 5, 1649

Monsieur,

The grace of Our Lord be with you forever!

Mon Dieu! Monsieur, how grieved I was and still am at the loss you have suffered in the pillage of your house in Orsigny![2] I confess, Monsieur, that the damages we have sustained and may still have to sustain are nothing in comparison. Our sins have

---

[4]Pierre Escart, born in the canton of Valais (Switzerland) in 1612, entered the Congregation of the Mission on March 6, 1637 and was ordained a priest the following year. He was stationed in Annecy and later sent to Richelieu. At the beginning of his stay in Annecy, he made a good impression on Saint Jane Frances de Chantal, who said of him, "M. Escart is a saint." He was indeed virtuous, zealous, and very austere, and would have continued to please Saint Jane Frances if he had known how to moderate his zeal, to be more tolerant with the defects of others, and to judge his confreres, especially Superiors, with greater fairmindedness. His temperament carried him to extremes, and in a fit of misguided passion he killed one of his friends. He went to Rome to seek absolution for this murder and died there some time before 1659.

Letter 1089. - Reg. 1, f° 15, copy made from the autograph draft.
[1]Honorary Secretary to the King and co-owner with Saint Vincent of the Orsigny farm.
[2]Soldiers of the royal army had pillaged the Orsigny farm.

rendered us guilty of all these losses, but you, Monsieur, what have you done? What has good Mademoiselle[3] done, whom Our Lord has burdened with the heavy cross of her long and painful illness? He has visited you both by your own flesh and blood, by a long and trying illness, and by your loss of property. What name shall [we][4] give to this way in which God is dealing with you? Really, Monsieur, I see none more appropriate, in a certain sense, than what He used with Job, whom He overwhelmed in these three ways.[5] O Monsieur, what a happiness to be treated in this world like that great saint, who never said or did anything displeasing to His Divine Majesty, and whom God singled out as the model of the just! Add to that, Monsieur, that it is a God who did so, without whose orders nothing is done. His Divine Goodness, who loves you more tenderly than any father ever loved his child, has done so in order to be glorified in you both, to sanctify your dear souls more and more, and to reveal to heaven and earth His love for you and His esteem for your virtue, since He puts it to such a test. A pagan[6] teaches us that in these circumstances we must be submissive to Providence. The Son of God, who understood this better than he, tells us that it is a great happiness to suffer on such occasions and that His glory is the reward of those who do so for love of Him. It must be stated clearly: a spirit less experienced in the school of Jesus Christ than Monsieur and Mademoiselle Norais would [accept this,][7] since it is a necessity and there is no remedy, but I am sure that your piety, which knows so well that charity converts necessity into virtue by acquiescing to God's good pleasure in all the afflictions we inevitably suffer, will be quite capable of sharing in this blessedness and of drawing from it the merit of His glory. In line with that, Monsieur, it is true to say that what appears to be a loss for you according to the flesh is a great advantage according

---

[3]Elisabeth Merault, wife of Jacques Norais.
[4]Word omitted by the copyist.
[5]Cf. Jb 1:1 - 2:13. (NAB)
[6]Job.
[7]Word omitted by the copyist.

to the spirit and a strong motive for giving thanks to God.

1089a. - TO SAINT LOUISE

Fréneville, February 11, 1649

Mademoiselle,

The grace of Our Lord J[esus] C[hrist] be with you forever!

I have just received two of your letters by an express messenger whom M. Lambert sent to me, one which you wrote on the second of this past January and the other on the day before yesterday, which you addressed to me here. They both cause me to be in admiration of God's goodness in giving you good health in this severe weather and in the midst of matters which are a source of concern for you. I thank Him most humbly for this; I also thank Him every day at the holy altar, where I see you daily with your dear daughters.

I think you are right, Mademoiselle, to see those good Ladies for the reason you gave me, but I do not know if the . . . city air will be bad for your health, since you are coming from the clean, open air. That could be offset if you slept there only one or two nights, then returning on the last one with that good seminarian to your lodging. It seems also . . . something. So much for that, if he has separate lodgings and is exemplary in the parish. You did not tell me the name of the cloister.

I thank God for the courage with which He animates our dear Sisters in Bicêtre, especially Sister Geneviève.[1] *O mon Dieu,* Mademoiselle! what strong characteristics of the Spirit of Our Lord

---

Letter 1089a. - Archives of the community of Notre Dame de Charité, 5 rue Outrequin, Chevilly-Larue, Rungis (Val-de-Marne), original autograph letter. Raymond Chalumeau, C. M. has provided the editors with a copy of the letter. In some places the original is in poor condition and hardly decipherable.

[1]Sister Geneviève Poisson.

are present in hers! They will probably take into consideration the fact that it is a royal hospital. The men from Paris will do no harm to it and the others will not come that close to a town. I pray to God and will pray to Him every day for those dear Sisters and those dear children whom God is blessing.

So, we will have to see what to do about that poor Sister who is upsetting that house in this way. The expedient you suggest is not bad. We shall see if it is pleasing to God.

I am sending you an unsealed letter I have written to the Ladies of Charity. Have it delivered or hold it as you see fit. I would be inclined to let them . . . . I am afraid of not following the light of God to which prudence seems to have called me to render Him some small service. In short, please discuss the matter with M. Lambert and . . . Our Lord will advise you.

I am detained here in Fréneville by this bitter cold until the weather changes, which will not be very soon. In the meantime, if there is anything urgent, M. Lambert can send me an express messenger.

By the grace of God, I am feeling well in this place, where the charity of our dear Sisters, who give me some of their bread, bacon, and apples, makes up for your broth. Last evening I sent them that . . . . Sister Barbe told me that Sister Jeanne[2] was not feeling very well today; it surprised me to see her at Mass this morning upstairs in our little chapel. I did not intend for our Sisters to go up there, since I always speak to them downstairs in the place where the farmer's wife is staying. We . . . and that of her little children, except when they wanted to say something to me privately in the same room. They are still doing well and are very helpful, thank God. Since the Pastor[3] had complained of them to M. Escart about some trifle, Barbe waited for him the day before yesterday near . . . and asked his pardon on her knees. I praised her for this. He is sometimes ill with gout and would like them to visit him. I find it hard to advise them not to go, because

---

[2]Sister Jeanne Fouré.
[3]Could this be Guillaume de Lestocq, Pastor of Saint-Laurent?

this is a charity, and to advise them to go, because he speaks too freely
. . . . I thought of telling them never to go alone and to go two together.

I think, Mademoiselle, that this is all I have to tell you right now
except that I was consoled to receive regards from our dear Sisters
Julienne[4] and Helot,[5] and all the others in general, whom I would
mention if I remembered their names. I do pray for them daily
before God at the holy altar, where it is a consolation for me to see
them. I beg them to ask God's mercy for me for the many sins I
have committed and daily commit, particularly the misuse I make
of His grace. I am confident, Mademoiselle, that you do me this
same favor, which you began to do for me so long ago.

I am, in the love of Our Lord . . . .

Since writing this letter, I have received your latest one, which
mentions extraordinary confessors[6] for our dear Sisters. My
thought is that it will be well to do . . . . If all of them cannot go to
your house for the confessors, then we . . . two one day a week or
every two weeks to your house from Saint-Lazare and the other to
the cloister where you go for your hospice. For confessions it seems
to me they could go and confess two by two each day to your house
in the faubourg, or I could ask M. du Chesne to go and hear them
in your little oratory, and M. Lambert to go to the conferences or
have M. du Chesne go when he is unable. . . . Monsieur . . . while
waiting until you have an outside parlor, where you could . . . hear,
unless you set aside your new room near the door for this purpose,
which might be the best thing. It would seem that, since we cannot
go to serve those good girls in La Chapelle, there is question . . . in
the faubourgs. We have given up hearing confessions in the towns
but not in the faubourgs. Please talk all this over with M. Lambert.

Your daughters came back for Mass. I told them I was glad to
see them but that it is not advisable to keep this up. I also told them

---

[4]Sister Julienne Loret.
[5]Sister Elisabeth Hellot.
[6]Four times a year, during the Ember Season, confessors different from those who ordinarily
administered the Sacrament of Penance were provided for women religious by the Church.

I will go to their house tomorrow after Vespers to give a conference. The subject is that it is good to know whether there are virtues proper to Daughters of Charity in the country, in addition to . . . of the Sisters in towns. The second point is that they are . . . . I said they should find some upright woman of the parish assigned to the Charity. . . . . . . your most humble and obedient servant.

VINCENT DEPAUL
i.s.C.M.

1090. - TO THE LADIES OF CHARITY

[Fréneville,] February 11, 1649

Mesdames,

The grace of O[ur] L[ord] be with you forever!

Although the Providence of God has removed me far from you, I do not fail to see you often at the holy altar and to offer you and your families to O[ur] L[ord], confident that your charity is asking God's mercy for me. I most humbly entreat you, Ladies, to do me this favor and to rest assured that, if God is pleased to consider the prayers I offer and will continue to offer Him incessantly for you, you will be consoled and guarded by His special protection in the midst of the afflictions with which His Divine Majesty is pleased to try us all.

You must have heard, Ladies, that God has given me the opportunity to go visit the houses of our Little Company, which I am now doing, with the intention of returning home whenever the state of affairs will allow.[1] What shall we do in the meantime,

---

Letter 1090. - Reg. 1, f°27 v°.

[1]On January 14, 1649 Saint Vincent slipped out of Paris to travel to Saint-Germain-en-Laye to beg the Queen to dismiss Cardinal Mazarin as the only means to bring to an end the upheavals of the Fronde. Despite his efforts, Vincent was suspect in the eyes of Mazarin's enemies and, therefore, could not return to Paris. He used this opportunity to visit many of the houses of the

Ladies, about the works the good God has entrusted to you, especially the Confraternity of Charity of the Hôtel-Dieu and the work of the poor foundlings? In truth, it seems that private misfortunes are dispensing us from concern for public ones and that we would have a good excuse in the sight of others to distance ourselves from this concern. But, Ladies, I really do not know how this would stand before God, who could say to us what Saint Paul said to the Corinthians, who found themselves in similar circumstances: "Have you resisted yet to the point of shedding blood?" [2] or, at least, have you sold any of your jewels yet? What can I say, Ladies? I know that several of you—and I believe the same holds true for all of you—have given alms which would be considered very great not only in persons of your state in life but in queens. The stones would cry out if I were to keep silence about this,[3] and it is because of the preeminence of your incomparably charitable hearts that I am speaking to you in this fashion. I would be most careful not to act in this way with other persons less animated with the Spirit of God than you are.

But what, then, shall we do? It seems fitting, Ladies, to question whether it is expedient for you to hold the large meeting that had been proposed. Where, when, and how? There are reasons for and against this.

It would seem, in the first place, that it should be held because it is customary to have one around this time. In the second place, since the needs are extraordinary, it would seem that the means to remedy them must also be extraordinary, such as holding a general meeting.

On the other hand, it would seem that now is not the right moment for one because of the troubled state in which we are,

---

Congregation during the next five months. On the Queen's orders, he finally returned to Saint-Lazare on June 13, 1649.

[2]Cf. Heb 12:4. (NAB) Saint Vincent, writing in haste and without checking his sources, incorrectly attributes this to Saint Paul, but the quote cannot be found in either Letter to the Corinthians. It refers instead to the Letter to the Hebrews.

[3]Cf. Lk 19:40. (NAB)

which is upsetting people and causing charity to grow cold. Perhaps many Ladies are fearful of going to one, and perhaps those who go, unless they have unusual charity, will put a damper on one another. Furthermore, since the Princess[4] will not be there, nor their Ladyships d'Aiguillon and de Brienne,[5] it seems that things would not be as some might wish, especially if thought were being given to making some substantial change in the work.

These, Ladies, are the pros and cons that occur to me right now. Please come to a decision on this by a plurality of votes. When I was leaving Saint-Germain, the Duchesse d'Aiguillon told me, or has written to me since, that the Queen told her she would send something for the poor foundlings. I do not know if she has done so. I asked M. Lambert[6] to send them a little wheat, and I have written to Madame de Lamoignon, the President's wife, to be so kind as to use her influence with the city authorities to provide an escort for the wheat both inside and outside the city. I do not know what has been done about this either. If it has not been carried out, I beg both parties, by this letter, to do whatever is necessary for that purpose.

And because even that is not enough, Ladies, see if it is advisable, as officers of the Charity, to borrow the sum of two or three thousand livres to meet the most urgent needs. I am writing to ask M. Lambert to pledge himself in our name. If pledging is difficult, it would be advantageous for each one of us to make an effort to do so. In that case I am asking M. Lambert to do whatever will have to be done on our part. I admit, Ladies, that what I am saying is somewhat importunate but it would be even more so if I were saying it to persons less charitable than you. Lastly, I ask O[ur] L[ord], who presides over meetings such as yours that are held in

---

[4]Charlotte de Montmorency, Princess de Condé.

[5]Louise de Béon, wife of Henri-Auguste de Loménie, Comte de Brienne, Seigneur de Bassy, and Secretary of State for Foreign Affairs. As a Lady of Charity, Madame de Brienne took an active part in the good works of Saint Vincent and Saint Louise. The Daughters of Providence owed much to her. She died on September 2, 1665.

[6]Lambert aux Couteaux.

His name, to help you to understand what He desires of you on this occasion and to grant you the grace of carrying it out.

The extreme cold has kept me in this place[7] and will do so until the weather gets milder. I expect to leave then for Le Mans or Angers, or both. I hope to receive there the results of your meeting, unless M. Lambert sends them to me here by express messenger.

In the meantime, I ask God to bless and sanctify more and more your meeting and your own dear persons.

I am, in the love of O[ur] L[ord], Ladies, your . . . .

VINCENT DEPAUL

1090a. - TO LAMBERT AUX COUTEAUX,[1] AT SAINT-LAZARE

[February or March 1649]

. . . I was greatly consoled to learn from your letter that you and the whole Company are accepting cheerfully the carrying off of your possessions.[2] I assure you, Monsieur, that my only other distress at these great losses is to see you burdened with so much work. . . .

---

[7]Fréneville.

Letter 1090a. - Abelly, *op. cit.*, 2nd ed., bk. I, p. 293, reprinted in *Mission et Charité*, 19-20, no. 57, p. 76. This edition uses the latter text.

[1]Since 1642 Lambert aux Couteaux had been Assistant to the Superior General in the administration of the Motherhouse. At the time, Saint Vincent was still in the west of France making visitations of the houses of the Company, and Lambert aux Couteaux had written to inform him of the situation at Saint-Lazare.

[2]Saint-Lazare had been looted by soldiers in January 1649, during the troubles of the Fronde; the same happened some time later to the Orsigny farm which furnished Saint-Lazare with provisions.

1090b. - TO SAINT LOUISE

Fréneville, February 17, 1649

Blessed be God, Mademoiselle, for all you tell me and for all He has done for the poor foundlings.[1] O Jesus, my Savior, how good You are to these poor little abandoned creatures! How strongly that should encourage us, Mademoiselle, to continue the little services we are trying to render them.

I thank God that you are still well and that there is good reason to hope that this little spiritual assistance for your daughters will put them back where they were before the public calamity[2] threw them a little off balance. By God's grace they are good; I think this slight lapse has not disheartened them. So, come and go from your house to the city Hospice; I hope that will be helpful.

Last Sunday, we had the little conference with our Sisters here.[3] M. Escart and the two officers of the Charity were present for it. Everyone spoke up and said some very good things on the subject I sent you; namely, whether there were any particular virtues proper to the Daughters of Charity in the country, other than those which Our Lord asks of the Sisters of the same Company, who live in towns. . . . Barbe . . .[4] put her thoughts in writing. Both said no, but that it was true that many virtues should be present to a more outstanding degree in Sisters in the country than in those in towns—charity for the sick, for example, because of the distance between places where they are obliged to serve them, and because of their incomparable state of misery. They said the same for mortification, giving similar reasons, and furthermore that this was

---

Letter 1090b. - Archives of the Motherhouse of the Daughters of Charity, original autograph letter. It was discovered some time in 1984 and published for the first time in *Echos de la Compagnie* (February 1985), no. 2, pp. 61-63 [English edition, pp.59-61].

[1]In his letter of February 4 (no. 1088), Saint Vincent asked Saint Louise to visit Bicêtre, where one of the Sisters was causing trouble.

[2]The Fronde.

[3]Sisters Toussainte David, Jeanne Fouré, and Barbe. Nothing more specific is known of the latter besides her name.

[4]The handwriting is difficult to read.

true for love of purity, poverty, and simplicity for the Sisters in the country, and that perhaps, in future, experience will show that the most virtuous should be chosen for country places.

That, more or less, is the result of their thinking, which gave me great consolation. The doctor in this area came to see me yesterday and told me he wanted to put himself under their care for treatment during his illness but was dissuaded from doing so by the consideration that this might do an injustice to the surgeons in Messe.[5] Because he is well known there, that might imply that the latter were ignorant. He is urging me to buy a house for them [the Sisters]. I said we would try to do so in time. He also told me they did not have enough of the common remedies used to purge those recovering from an illness. That is why most of them have a relapse. I told him we would give them some; both are still a little short.

I hope to leave tomorrow, God willing, if the snow now beginning does not continue for very long. I hope that your prayers and those of your daughters will obtain God's grace for me and that my sins may not hinder the accomplishment of His designs on my journey. I am, in His love, Mademoiselle, your most humble and obedient servant.

VINCENT DEPAUL
i.s.C.M.

Addressed: Mademoiselle Le Gras, Superioress of the Daughters of Charity across from Saint-Lazare, in Paris

---

[5]Probably Mespuits, a hamlet near Valpuiseaux.

1091. - TO DENIS GAUTIER, IN RICHELIEU

Orléans, February 25, 1649

Monsieur,

The grace of Our Lord be with you forever!

The Providence of God has made you the refuge of the poor Mission in Paris. Monsieur Escart and our Brothers Jean Geneset[1] and Ambroise[2] are setting off now to take advantage of your charity at the seminary. All are familiar with the spirit of piety and exact regularity of Monsieur Escart and will be edified, I hope, by our Brothers.

Monsieur Lambert wrote me that you intend to develop the Bouchard woods on your own and that you asked him previously for some Brothers for this purpose. One of them was in charge of the horse-driven mill in Orsigny, where you got the horses Monsieur Testacy is bringing you. The other is a winegrower who can look after your vineyards.

As for me, I hope to leave tomorrow to open the visitation in Le Mans. God in His mercy has given me the time to do so. I left Paris for Saint-Germain-en-Laye more than six weeks ago and spent three or four days there. I had started out for Le Mans but was told that they were expecting that Orsigny would be pillaged and that I should tell our Brothers what to do. This obliged me to take the Fréneville route, where the harsh winter weather took me by surprise and I was forced to spend a month there. It has now been three days since I left there with a flock of 240 sheep which I was sending to you. The bad weather, however, has obliged me to leave

Letter 1091. - Collection for the process of beatification.

[1]Jean Geneset, a coadjutor Brother, born in Saint-Mihiel (Meuse) in Lorraine, was received into the Congregation of the Mission around 1643, at about twenty years of age, and died in September 1652.

[2]Ambroise Tumy, a coadjutor Brother, born in Argenteuil (Val-d'Oise), entered the Congregation of the Mission on August 10, 1644 in Paris, at the age of twenty, took his vows in December 1652, and died at sea, in the protected part of the harbor of the island of Aix, in January 1660.

them along the way with a lady I know. This is the flock we saved from the pillage of Orsigny.[3]

So, here I am on the point of setting out to begin the visitation in Le Mans. From there I hope to go on to Angers to try to get what the tax-farmer owes us and send you what was intended for you. From there I can head for Saint-Méen and Tréguier, returning from the latter to your house or to Luçon. God willing, I shall try to continue the visitation in Tours, if my strength allows.

O Monsieur, how grieved I am by the death of the late Monsieur du Coudray! I had thought of picking him up when I was passing through and taking him along with me; now Our Lord has arranged otherwise. Please, Monsieur, write me in Angers the details of how God took him. Address your letter to the Sisters of Sainte-Marie[4] if you find an opportunity, but not otherwise. I would ask you to go there if I were sure of the time I could be there.

I have not given you any news of Saint-Lazare nor of our little collèges[5] in Paris. M. Escart can tell you; he left there after me. What has happened since his departure is that they have emptied this house of everyone they could, so as to have the means of continuing for a longer time the distribution of alms to about two thousand persons. By God's grace, they have been doing this for them every day; at least four setiers of wheat, Paris measure, are needed daily. Crécy, Troyes, and Montmirail are looking after their own poor, prompted in this by the example you gave them. May Our Lord Jesus Christ grant that this support for the Company may be maintained for as long as it perdures, and may He grant the houses the grace of being able to subsist!

I embrace your Community, prostrate in spirit at their feet and yours. I ask both you and them to offer me to His Divine Goodness

---

[3]The Orsigny farm was the principal resource of the Saint-Lazare house. The soldiers of the royal army had pillaged it. "Cattle, wheat, all that belonged to the Brothers who looked after the place, were carried off, and even all the possessions of a rich private gentleman [Jacques Norais], who had placed them there for safety." (Cf. Collet, *op. cit.,* vol. I, p. 471.)

[4]The Visitation nuns.

[5]The Collège des Bons-Enfants and Saint-Charles Seminary.

— 410 —

that God may grant me the mercy and grace to serve Him better than I have done in the past. I am, in His love and that of His holy Mother, Monsieur, your most humble and obedient servant.

VINCENT DEPAUL
i.s.C.M.

Addressed: Monsieur Gautier, Superior of the Priests of the Mission, in Richelieu

1092. - *THE DUCHESSE D'AIGUILLON TO SAINT VINCENT*

Saint-Germain,[1] *March 2, 1649*

Monsieur,

I was extremely distressed at not having any news of you and of being unable to send you any from us. However, good Brother Mathieu [2] *has just arrived to get some wheat for the poor foundlings, and he gave me this news. I am taking advantage of it to tell you that God seems to be giving us grounds for hope that He, in His mercy, intends to grant us the settlement, since matters seem to be inclined in that direction. The members of the Parlement sent deputies to the Queen, who was kind enough to grant that grain be given them every day that the conference lasts, if they were willing to send persons to whom they would give absolute power to settle matters without further deliberation or recourse to the Parlement, after returning and reporting on this proposal. As desired, they ultimately*

Letter 1092. - Archives of the Mission, Turin, original autograph letter.
[1]Saint-Germain-en-Laye.
[2]Brother Mathieu Régnard was born on July 26, 1592 in Brienne-le-Château, now Brienne-Napoléon (Aube). He entered the Congregation of the Mission in October 1631, took his vows on October 28, 1644, and died October 5, 1669. He was the principal distributor of Saint Vincent's alms in Lorraine and also during the troubles of the Fronde. Because of his daring, composure, and savoir-faire, he was a great help to the Saint. His biography is in vol. II of *Notices,* pp. 29-33.

authorized the Chief Justice,[3] Messieurs de Mesmes,[4] de Nesmond,[5] and Le Coigneux;[6] President Viole,[7] Longueil,[8] Menardeau,[9] Le Cocq,[10] Bitault,[11] and Lefebvre.[12] The conference is to be held Thursday in Rueil, and Monsieur,[13] the Prince,[14] the Cardinal,[15] the Chancellor,[16] and M. de La Rivière [17] are supposed to go. We must ask God to preside over it so that peace will be made.[18] Today, the Te Deum was sung here for the peace with Germany, whose ratification has taken place.

---

[3]Mathieu Molé, born in Paris in 1584, became Attorney General in 1614 and Chief Justice of the Parlement of Paris in 1641. Appointed Keeper of the Seals on April 3, 1651, he lost the office ten days later because of political pressure resulting from the Fronde, but was reappointed on September 9. He held the position of Chief Justice until the Queen Regent, Anne of Austria, summoned him to the Royal Court outside Paris. He died January 3, 1656. (Cf. Amable-Guillaume-Prosper Brugière, Baron de Barante, Le Parlement et la Fronde. La vie de Mathieu Molé [Paris: Didier, 1859].)

[4]Henri de Mesmes, Comte d'Avaux, a Presiding Judge in Parlement, died in 1650.

[5]François-Théodore de Nesmond, Seigneur de Saint-Dysan, judge in the Parlement of Paris since December 20, 1636. He became successively the Superintendent of the house of the Prince de Condé and Presiding Judge of the Parlement. He died November 25, 1664, at the age of sixty-six. He and his wife, Anne de Lamoignon, sister of the famous magistrate, had four sons and one daughter. One of his sons became Bishop of Bayeux.

[6]Jacques Le Coigneux, a Presiding Judge in the Parlement, died August 21, 1651.

[7]Presiding Judge of the fourth Court of Inquiry in the Parlement. This judge examined written evidence of cases prior to litigation in the Parlement.

[8]René de Longueil, Marquis de Maisons, First Associate Chief Justice of the Parlement, later Superintendent of Finances, Minister of State, and Chancellor to the Queen Mother. He died September 1, 1677.

[9]Claude Menardeau, Councillor at the Parlement.

[10]Jean Le Cocq, Seigneur de Courbeville, Councillor at the Parlement.

[11]Councillor at the Parlement.

[12]Louis Lefébvre de Caumartin, Councillor at the Parlement.

[13]Gaston, Duc d'Orléans, brother of Louis XIII, was born in Fontainebleau in 1608, the son of Henri IV and Marie de Médicis. Gaston took part in the conspiracies against Richelieu and, during the Fronde, against Mazarin. He became Lieutenant-General of the kingdom in 1643 and died in 1660.

"Monsieur," in this context, is the stylized title used for the eldest brother of the French king.

[14]Louis II de Bourbon, Prince de Condé. The Great Condé, as he was called, was born in Paris in 1621, the son of Henri II de Bourbon and Charlotte-Marguerite de Montmorency. One of the great French generals, his reputation was marred only by his participation in the Fronde and his alliance with the Spanish against Mazarin and the Crown. Subsequent to the Treaty of the Pyrenees (1659) between France and Spain, he was given once again a command in the French army. Bossuet preached at his funeral in 1686.

[15]Jules Cardinal Mazarin.

[16]Pierre Séguier.

[17]Louis Barbier, Abbé de la Rivière. Born in 1593, he was Rector of the collège du Plessis. Later, befriended by the Duc d'Orléans, he became Minister of State in 1646. In 1665 he became Bishop of Langres; he died in 1670.

[18]The agreement between the Court and the Parlement was concluded on March 11; it was not ratified until April 1, after modifications by the Parlement.

I think it would be well for you to await the outcome of this conference in Orléans or Le Mans so that, if it is successful, as we desire, you need go no further. I will take care to let you know what happens.

I am sending you a letter from the Guardian of the Chinon Capuchins. You can see from it how he is complaining about the chaplain in Champigny.[19] M. du Rivau [20] has told me the same thing. Please let me know what to do because they are afraid he is carrying off the money belonging to the poor.

Please pray for me and believe that I am always your most humble servant.

1093. - TO ANTOINE PORTAIL, IN MARSEILLES

Le Mans, March 4, 1649

Monsieur,

The grace of Our Lord be with you forever!

I know you are too attached to God's good pleasure to be surprised at not receiving any letters from me for a month or two. This has really been in spite of myself because I would not have stopped writing to you if the mail coaches had not stopped running.

You knew about my departure from Paris and one of the purposes of it.[1] Since, because of my sins, that one did not succeed, I am trying to carry out the second, which is to visit our houses. I am beginning with this one, after a month's stay in Fréneville, where severe cold and snow hemmed me in. I intended to be there only two or three days to find room there for a flock of sheep and two horses, rescued from the pillage of Orsigny; but I think Providence kept me there so long to make me realize that they were not

---

[19]Champigny-sur-Veude, near Richelieu. M. Romillon was the hospital chaplain.
[20]Chevalier Jacques de Beauvat, Sieur du Rivau.

Letter 1093. - Archives of the Mission, Turin, original signed letter. The postscript and the words "the Consul of Algiers has enough to bear the expense" and "I do not know the details of M. du Coudray's death" are in the Saint's own handwriting. There is also evidence of some editing of the original.

[1]To persuade the Queen to dismiss Cardinal Mazarin so as to bring an end to the Fronde.

safe in that place. The soldiers came within a quarter of a league and stole the horses from one of the farms. That obliged me to leave there in very bad weather and have the sheep taken to a walled village near Etampes, about four or five leagues away.

As for the horses, I brought them here, where I arrived in good health, thank God, on the second of this month, notwithstanding the difficulties of the weather and the roads. I opened the visitation the next evening. Persons from the town, who have been calling on me, have prevented me from continuing it without interruption. I do not yet know how things are going but, from what I can see, all seems well. I hope to leave for Brittany in ten or twelve days, and from there go to Richelieu, then on to the other houses. If God is pleased to continue to give me good health, I hope to have the joy of seeing you in Marseilles. This would be a great consolation to me, after the troubles[2] of such a long journey and the afflictions we are now witnessing.

I think you are aware of the losses we are suffering, not only of the wheat we had in Orsigny and at Saint-Lazare[3] but also the deprivation of all our income. This is forcing us to empty Saint-Lazare and the Bons-Enfants, where there are now no more than seven or eight priests, eighteen or nineteen students, and a few Brothers. The rest have been sent to Richelieu, here, and elsewhere, and they, too, will be obliged to leave when there is nothing left. Of the little wheat there is, three or four setiers are distributed every day to two or three thousand poor persons. This is a great consolation and joy to us in our present extremity and causes us to hope that God will not abandon us, especially in the Marseilles house, although we are in no position to offer it any assistance.

Yes, Monsieur, to my great regret, I have already told you this, and you can see it for yourself. Inform the Bishop so he can give you some help for the seminary. You will have to send them [the seminarians] away, except for those who can pay adequate fees.

---

[2] "Turmoil" was the word first used.
[3] In this passage these words were crossed out: "which would last us nearly a whole year."

The matter speaks for itself; I am wondering if some members of the Company might not have to go to the galleys and serve as chaplains so as to get the salaries and, by this means, keep the house going.

In short, Monsieur, I beg Our Lord to show you how to do this and to give you an ever greater share in His patience and His manner of acting so you can continue to assist this poor Community in these trying circumstances. In the meantime, it does not seem advisable for Brother Huguier to go to Tunis, nor M. Dieppe to Algiers, unless the Consul in Algiers has enough to bear the expense,[4] since we can send them nothing from here. So delay them, if you think fit.

God has willed to take to Himself M. du Coudray in Richelieu and Brother Dumesnil[5] at Saint-Lazare. I am really sorry that I did not get to see the first man before he died. You know the obligations the Company has toward him. I recommend him in a particular way to your prayers and to those of the Community and ask that you pay the customary respects to both of them. The latter died as he had lived; I do not know the details of M. du Coudray's death.

I am in a hurry to end this, which I do by asking to be remembered in your Holy Sacrifices. I tenderly embrace M. Chrétien and his whole Community. I am, in the love of Our Lord, Monsieur, their servant, and yours in particular.

VINCENT DEPAUL
i.s.C.M.

If things quiet down, I am thinking about holding a meeting of all or some of the Superiors. Please tell me what you think about this, and address your letters to the Duchesse d'Aiguillon at the Court. Weigh carefully whether it is advisable for you to bother the

---

[4]The original wording was: "unless those who are there are able to support them, and themselves as well, from the revenues of the consulate."

[5]Jacques Dumesnil, seminarian, born in Nibas (Somme), in the Amiens diocese in 1622, entered the Congregation of the Mission in Paris on January 6, 1641 and died in February 1649.

Bishop with your needs and if, in the meantime, it would be advantageous for you to have some of the men work on the galleys, or to send some to Genoa if the Cardinal is in agreement.

Addressed: Monsieur Portail, Priest of the Mission,in Marseilles

1094. - TO SAINT LOUISE

Le Mans, March 14, 1649

Mademoiselle,

The grace of Our Lord be with you forever!

This letter is to give you news of me and to ask for yours. My news is that I am well, thank God, and in three or four days I hope to leave for Angers, where I shall see your daughters.

Monsieur Gautier has come here from Richelieu; he told me that God has taken poor Sister Elisabeth;[1] I was deeply affected by this. He thinks it advisable to recall the other Sister and to send two from Paris, but I find that very difficult to do in this bad weather, from which I am sure you are suffering, and your Community along with you.

I ask Our Lord Jesus Christ to be Himself your strength and consolation and to draw His glory from the public and private tribulations. I still rely on the prayers of your Community and especially on yours.

Letter 1094. - In 1881 the original signed letter belonged to Count Yvert of Saint-Germain-en Laye. The postscript is in the Saint's handwriting.

[1]Elisabeth Martin died in Richelieu.

I am, in the love of Our Lord, Mademoiselle, your most humble servant.

VINCENT DEPAUL
i.s.C.M.

Monsieur Gautier told me that he saw your good Sisters in passing in Angers, that things are going fairly well, that Sister Cécile² is doing wonders, and that two of them are a trial to the others;³ one of them is extremely scrupulous. I hope to see them in four or five days, God willing.

1095. - *EDMUND DWYER, BISHOP OF LIMERICK, TO SAINT VINCENT*

[1649 or 1650] ¹

I have often written to Your Reverence about the state of your Missionaries in the kingdom. Truthfully, before God, it is such that never, within living memory, have we heard that such great progress and advancement in the Catholic faith have been made as we have noted in the past few years. This has been done through their industry, piety, and assiduity, especially at the beginning of the year, when we opened the mission in this town, where no less than twenty thousand persons went to Communion. Such good results have been hailed by all the inhabitants that I am sure most of them, thank God, have been snatched from the clutches of Satan by the remedy applied to so many invalid confessions, drunkenness, swearing, adultery, and other disorders, which have been completely abolished. In this way, the whole face of the town has been changed, since it has been obliged to have recourse to penance because of plague, famine, war, and dangers closing in on us on all sides, which we accept as manifest signs of God's wrath. Nevertheless, although we are useless servants, His

---

²Cécile Angiboust, Sister Servant at the Angers hospital (1648-1657).
³Sister Jeanne from Loudun and Sister Barbe from Troyes.

Letter 1095. - Abelly, *op.cit.,* bk. II, chap. I, sect. VIII, p. 151. The original is in Latin; Abelly's translation has been used in the French.
¹In his account, Abelly makes it clear that the Limerick mission, of which this letter speaks, was given at the beginning of the year between August 16, 1648 and April 1650.

Goodness has willed to do us the favor of making use of us in this work, whose beginnings have in truth been difficult. Some persons even felt that we would not be able to succeed in it, but God has made use of the weak to confound the strong of this world.

The leading citizens of the town are so assiduous in coming to the sermons, catechism, and all the other exercises of the mission, that the cathedral is scarcely large enough to hold them. We could not better appease God's anger than by rooting out sin, the basis and cause of all evils. To be sure, if God does not stretch forth His hand to us, our fate is sealed. It is up to Him to grant mercy and to forgive.

Father, I confess that I am indebted to your children for the salvation of my own soul. Write them a few words of consolation. I know of no mission under heaven more useful than that of Ireland, for even if they were a hundred men, the mission would always be a big task for so few workers. Our sins are very serious. Who knows whether God may not will to pluck us from this kingdom and give the Bread of Angels to dogs, to our blame and confusion.

1096. - TO SAINT LOUISE, IN PARIS

Angers, March 23, 1649

Mademoiselle,

The grace of Our Lord be with you forever!

I received here one of your letters, dated March 3, sent in care of the Mother Superior of Sainte-Marie.[1] It consoled me greatly to see the good health Our Lord is giving you and how He is blessing your works, those of Madame and Mademoiselle de Lamoignon and, in general, of all the Ladies of Charity in the parishes in Paris.

You can well imagine, Mademoiselle, how gladly I thank God for all this, asking Him to grant them the grace to continue. I have

Letter 1096. - The original autograph letter is the property of the Daughters of Charity of 20 rue Mage, Toulouse.

[1]Mère Marie-Augustine Bouvard, Superioress of the Visitation convent in Angers. She was the daughter of King Louis XIII's chief physician. She had been professed at the Second Monastery of the Visitation in the faubourg Saint-Jacques, Paris, where she died on November 15, 1659, at the age of forty-eight, after twenty-eight years in religious life.

been deeply grieved, however, to hear how your poor daughters and your poor foundlings in Bicêtre are still surrounded on all sides by a large army.[2] I find my consolation in the hope that Our Lord, who has taken them under His special protection, will not allow anything to happen to them.

I have been at work here for three or four days, making the visitation of our dear Sisters of the Hôtel-Dieu. Last evening we had the final exercise for the closing of the visitation. I am now having my recommendations transcribed and will leave them with them. As for the rest, I can tell you that, by the grace of God, things are going well. You can certainly be the judge of this from my telling you that they observe their order of the day exactly, and their only failing in this is not keeping silence from eight in the evening until prayers. In a word, all is going so well that it fills my heart with consolation. There are, however, one or two Sisters whom I think we will have to change; we shall see. I am not going into detail about our Lord's guidance of them, as I am not sure about this note reaching you.

I hope to leave tomorrow for Saint-Méen and to stop by Nantes to see our dear Sisters there. I trust that God may be pleased that I may find them in as good a state as the ones here.

In the meantime I send greetings to our good Ladies of Charity and recommend myself to the prayers of our dear Sisters. I am, in

---

[2]Condé's soldiers, numbering from twelve to fifteen thousand, were scattered around the capital. Some were in Saint-Denis, quite near the Motherhouse, and in Bourg-la-Reine, near Bicêtre. A number of them tried several times to force their way into the Foundling Home, where the Sisters lived in a constant state of alarm. Saint Louise implored Geneviève Poisson and her companions to take the most rigorous precautions against the violence of the soldiers. "Be careful to keep all the Sisters together," she said in one of her letters, "and be very careful of the older girls, whom you must always keep under your eyes or locked in the school." (Cf. *Ecrits spirituels*, L. 234, p. 276.)

the love of Our Lord, Mademoiselle, your most humble and obedient servant.

VINCENT DEPAUL
i.s.C.M.

Addressed: Mademoiselle Le Gras, Superioress of the Daughters of Charity, in Paris

1097. - TO SAINT LOUISE

Saint-Méen, Easter Monday,[1] 1649

Mademoiselle,

The grace of Our Lord be with you forever!

The work of the visitation I am making here prevents me from writing to you in my own hand.

I praise God for protecting our Sisters in Bicêtre and Saint-Denis[2] and for the good state in which the others are. I especially thank His Divine Goodness for your good health and I thank you for the prayers you say for mine.[3]

I am deeply moved by the charity and perseverance of good M. Alain, as well as by the damage done in Bicêtre and the poverty of the children. May God be the reward of the first-mentioned, and

---

Letter 1097. - Archives of the Mission, Paris, original signed letter.

[1]April 5.

[2]The Saint-Denis foundation was due to Mademoiselle de Lamoignon and to Madame de Nesmond. Sisters Elisabeth Turgis, Françoise Noret from Liancourt, and Marguerite Le Soin from Arras, began serving at the hospital on August 22, 1645.

[3]At this point the following five lines were scratched out: "which was affected by a fever during the night as a result of a fall I took into the water; the horse lay down and, if someone had not spotted me, I would not have been able to move from there. Thank God, I am feeling much better at present." Collet, or rather Brother Ducournau whose account he follows, states that this happened about half a league away from Durtal (cf. *op. cit.,* vol. I, p. 474). The Saint was saved by one of his priests, who was with him. Drenched to the skin, he remounted his horse and went to a little cottage to dry off.

may He will to provide for all the rest! Since that place is unfit for habitation, we would like to hope that the Parlement or the town might provide another, but apparently they will not. Still, we must not stop asking for one, if this is the opinion of the Ladies, which we must follow in these circumstances. Please do so, through Madame de Lamoignon, who will speak to them about it. If the Princess,[4] the Duchesse d'Aiguillon, and Madame de Brienne can be consulted on this, it would be a good idea to find out their views. Mine is that they will go along with whatever the other Ladies decide.

I received only one of your letters in Angers and answered it from the same place. If I could remember some of the points, I would repeat here what I wrote you.

With regard to your desire to unburden yourself of useless Sisters, I do not quite understand the uselessness of which you are complaining. If you mean that of our Sisters who are not productive or who do not know what to do after being tried for a time and who, in fact, have no character traits that might give hope for improvement, you would do well to dismiss them. If, however, you mean those who are not yet sufficiently well trained for the duties of the Charity and therefore cannot attend to them, or who are prevented from doing so by some handicap of which they can be cured, I think, Mademoiselle, we must be as patient as possible with them.

The review[5] will be made during the retreat at Pentecost, God willing.

I am pleased about your stay in Paris. I am well aware that there has been good reason for it.

Among our Sisters in Angers, only two have spiritual difficulties, but even those are not serious and will amount to nothing, I hope. The rest are content, and all are most exact in their little duties. I cannot speak highly enough of Sister Cécile,[6] nor express

---

[4]Charlotte de Montmorency, Princesse de Condé.
[5]The annual confession, or at least one made several months after the preceding retreat.
[6]Cécile-Agnès Angiboust.

adequately the consolation they have given me, as I have already written you. If Sister Jeanne must be separated from them, she should not be sent straight home[7] but be given another try in Richelieu, where she would be close to home.

When I am in Nantes, I will see what is happening with Sister Marie from Tours[8] and will write to you about it.

If you think it advisable to send the Sister you mentioned back here, do it. As for Sister Mathurine,[9] please tell her not to worry about her relatives. M. Thibault[10] is supposed to see them and get from them what they may have for her.

I rely greatly on your prayers and on those of all our Sisters. I ask them, and you in particular, to continue. I am, in the love of Our Lord, Mademoiselle, your most humble servant.

VINCENT DEPAUL
i.s.C.M.

Addressed: Mademoiselle Le Gras

---

[7]She came from Loudun.

[8]Marie Thilouse, a Sister who presented problems. She had several assignments before being sent to Nantes.

[9]Mathurine Guérin, Saint Louise's secretary at the time, was born on April 16, 1631 in Montcontour, Brittany. She entered the Company of the Daughters of Charity on September 12, 1648, despite the opposition of her parents. After the time of formation, she was sent to Saint-Jean-de-Grèves parish and then to Liancourt. Recalled to the Motherhouse in 1652, she again became Saint Louise's secretary and the Seminary Directress. In 1655 she was made Treasurer; in 1659 she was sent to the newly acquired hospital in La Fère (Aisne), and in May 1660 Saint Vincent recalled her to work in the hospital of Belle-Isle. She was named Superioress General in 1667 and again at three other periods: (1676-1682, 1685-1691, 1694-1697). She died at the Motherhouse on October 18, 1704. A long sketch of her life and virtues was written in *Circulaires des supérieurs généraux et des soeurs supérieures aux Filles de la Charité et remarques ou notices sur les soeurs défuntes de la Communauté,* Paris, 1845, pp. 556-568.

[10]M. Thibault was Superior of the Saint-Méen house.

1098. - *SAINT LOUISE TO SAINT VINCENT*

April 6, 1649

Most Honored Father,

We are most anxious to know your whereabouts and the condition in which you are. I beg God in His goodness that your health and your Community business will allow you to come home soon. You are sorely needed for the works of charity in Paris. Madame de Lamoignon, the President's wife, especially begs you to return soon.

I shall let other persons tell you the news of the peace, since all I know is that it causes us to join the people in praising God for it.

Good Monsieur Alain has died, and our Sisters are preparing to return to Bicêtre one of these days to take possession of the place and plant the crops. God willing, they will be able to remain there for the length of time Providence has ordained!

Madame du Sault, the President's wife,[1] sends her most humble regards; she really hopes you will be back here before she leaves for home.

I most humbly entreat you, Most Honored Father, not to forget our poor Sisters, if you go near Nantes. See also if they can manage without changing any Sisters. As I told you in two previous letters, if your charity thinks Sister Marie from Tours[2] needs to be changed, at least have her sent to Tours rather than back here to Paris. We have tried her in several places and, when I sent her to Nantes, I told her this was our last attempt. Do with her whatever your charity sees fit, as Our Lord inspires you.

In the name of God, dear Father, pray for us. I had written to you and made known our needs, my own in particular, but I strongly fear that our letters[3] were not delivered to you.[4] I only hope God will be merciful to us

---

Letter 1098. - Archives of the Motherhouse of the Daughters of Charity, original autograph letter.

[1]A Lady of Charity.

[2]Marie Thilouse. Cf. no. 1097, n.8.

[3]Cf. Coste, vol. II, no. 823 and vol. III, no. 846; also, *Ecrits spirituels*, L. 122 p. 154 and L. 156, p. 168.

[4]Saint Vincent did not go to Nantes until the end of April; Marie Thilouse left the Company of the Daughters of Charity at the end of 1649.

*and give back what, in His justice, He has taken away from us! I am, in
His most holy love, Most Honored Father, your most obedient and very
grateful daughter and servant.*

LOUISE DE MARILLAC

Addressed: *Monsieur Vincent, General of the Priests of the Mission*

1099. - TO SAINT LOUISE

Saint-Méen, April 9, 1649

Mademoiselle,

The grace of Our Lord be with you forever!

I hope to leave for Nantes in three or four days and to write to
you from there about the state in which I shall find our dear Sisters.
Monsieur des Jonchères[1] wrote the Bishop of Saint-Malo[2] that he
was offering to put me up in his home and for me to let him know
what day I thought I would be arriving. The Bishop thinks it is
because of the disturbances. Our Lord will be our guide, if He so
pleases.

I heard with sorrow here of the death of good M. Alain. O
Mademoiselle, how that has grieved me! We must ask God to send
us someone else like him.

Somebody wrote me that the poor children have been moved
out of Bicêtre.[3] I am anxious to know where they have been taken.
Mon Dieu! what trouble this change must have given you!

I have to repeat to you in this letter how consoled I was by the
visitation of our dear Sisters in Angers. O Mademoiselle, what

---

Letter 1099. - *Etudes religieuses,* vol. VIII, p. 1875, pl. 284, taken from the original.

[1]Chaplain of the hospital in Nantes and Director of the Sisters.

[2]Ferdinand de Neufville (1646-1657).

[3]The foundlings were temporarily transferred to the Motherhouse of the Daughters of Charity because of the siege of Paris.

great reason for praising God for His adorable guidance of these good Sisters!

It seems to me that Sister Jeanne from Loudun and Sister Barbe from Troyes have calmed down a little, the latter almost completely. We must await the outcome.

I continue to be in good health, thank God. I took the opportunity here to be purged and bled. I feel sure you recommend me to Our Lord, and our dear Sisters as well. I see you [all] before God[4] at the Holy Sacrifice of the Mass.

If you see good Madame de Lamoignon and our good Ladies of Charity, please assure them that I do not forget them before God. In His love I am your most humble servant.

VINCENT DEPAUL

1100. - TO SAINT LOUISE

Saint-Méen, April 15, 1649

Mademoiselle,

The grace of Our Lord be with you forever!

This letter is to give you further news of me and to ask you for yours. I continue to keep well, thank God. I am plagued here by bad weather and flooding; otherwise, I would have left for Nantes this past Tuesday. As soon as this little deluge subsides, I shall leave here to go and visit our Sisters, as I did those in Angers, who gave me greater consolation than I have received in a long time. I have written you this but cannot refrain from repeating it. They need a Sister capable of teaching the mysteries to the poor when they

---

[4]In *Etudes religieuses* this reads: "I see you; you are before God." Coste is of the opinion that the correct text is the one given here.

Letter 1100. -Archives of the Daughters of Charity, original signed letter.

arrive, as the Ladies do at the Hôtel-Dieu. We will speak of this again, God willing.

Meanwhile, I shall continue to ask God to bless and keep you and your daughters, whom I greet. I am, in the love of Our Lord, Mademoiselle, your most humble servant.

VINCENT DEPAUL
i.s.C.M.

Addressed: Mademoiselle Le Gras, Superioress of the Daughters of Charity, in Paris.

1101. - TO SAINT LOUISE

Nantes, April 28, 1649

Mademoiselle,

The grace of Our Lord be with you forever!

It has been ten days since I arrived in this town; I hope to leave tomorrow for Luçon, God willing. I found the poor Daughters of Charity just at the end of a great persecution directed against them. They have been accused of an infinite number of things, the main one being that they are appropriating the goods of the poor. The three priests who live in the house and M. Valton de Lafosse (the husband of that woman to whom Sister Jeanne Saint-Albin[1] had said something which offended her), who was a Father of the Poor[2] this past year, started this persecution against them through the last-named. When he was leaving office, he went to thank the

---

Letter 1101. - Archives of the Mission, Paris, original autograph letter.

[1]Sister Jeanne Saint-Albin entered the Community as a widow. She was assigned to Nantes in June 1647, and recalled to Paris in December, 1650. She almost left the Community in October 1655 (cf. *Ecrits spirituels,* L. 457, p. 487). Her name is still on the list of the Daughters of Charity after 1660.

[2]Administrator of the hospital.

officials at the Town Hall[3] and told them that everything would be fine at the hospital without the Daughters of Charity, who were doing a very poor job in their duty and, what is worse, were ruining the hospital and feathering their own nest.[4] He also offered to donate the money to send them away. The Town Hall deputed the members of the Chapter and of the Presidial Court[5] to hold a meeting so that the three bodies could send a delegation to verify this accusation and determine whether to dismiss or keep the Sisters. This was done but, by the grace of God, the present Administrators saw clearly that the charges were false and deputed the Dean[6] to tell the Sisters so and to encourage them.

All that, however, did not [make][7] the accusers give up. They went to see the Bishop of Nantes[8] on his return two days ago and said some astounding things against those poor Sisters. Now today I was told that the Bishop of Nantes, who has always objected to this establishment, wants a new investigation of all the complaints made against them. I had the honor of seeing him before this latest complaint, and I told him I had seen those good Sisters of the hospital and found a number of things that they could improve on but, by the grace of God, they were innocent of the things of which they were being accused. He replied rather graciously that they were good Sisters. I am now wondering whether I should go back to see him to speak to him at greater length about this affair. I realize, however, on the one hand, that no matter what I say to him he will not change his mind about his decision to investigate these charges, and that regardless of what I say to him, I will not be able to rid him of his dislike for this work. There are also a few other

[3]The Aldermen.
[4]That is, taking what did not belong to them.
[5]Presidial Courts were royal courts established in the sixteenth century to relieve the pressure of appeals to the Parlements. In certain cases they also served as courts of first instance.
[6]The Dean of the Chapter.
[7]A word omitted in the original letter.
[8]Gabriel de Beauvau de Rivarennes.

particular reasons which I will tell you. I think, therefore, that it is not advisable for me to see him. Nevertheless, if the des Jonchères brothers[9] think I should, I will do so. So much for the persecution of those poor Sisters.

I made the visitation and saw them every day except one or two. I must confess that they are not in a very satisfactory state: (1) they have become careless in the observance of regularity; (2) they have not been exact with regard to prayer, reading, examens, or silence; there was no charity—or very little—among themselves, no obedience, forbearance, nor was there, to tell the truth, the requisite devotedness to the care of the sick.[10]

Jeanne, the Sister Servant,[11] is a very fine, sensible, and gentle Sister. Some of the others feel she has not shown enough foresight.

Henriette[12] is a Sister full of zeal and charity but is not very respectful or submissive—or not at all—to the Sister Servant. She is also troublesome to the doctor and to many persons and does not keep the Rule. I think she is the cause of most of the Sisters' infractions.

I cannot continue describing the state of each of the others; I will do it in person, God willing. I am in a hurry right now. By the grace of God, they are in a better state now, and are determined to do well.

It is absolutely necessary to recall Henriette and to send someone who knows pharmacy to replace her. Marie[13] must be sent to Richelieu; once she gets there, we will figure out a way to send her home. The situation is such that this cannot be done from here, nor can she even be removed until the Sister you name to replace her arrives. An eighth Sister is needed. If there is any way to do so,

---

[9]M. des Jonchères, confessor of the Daughters of Charity, had a brother who was Presiding Judge of the Presidial Court of Nantes.

[10]We still have the autograph rough draft of the advice the Saint left to the Sisters of Nantes at the end of the Visitation. (Cf. vol. XIII, no. 148.)

[11]Jeanne Lepeintre, Sister Servant at the Nantes hospital.

[12]Henriette Gesseaume, who was in charge of the pharmacy, had been in Nantes since 1646.

[13]Marie Thilouse from Tours.

please send two suitable ones. When I get back to Paris, we will decide what to do about everything else.

I have been approached about another establishment in the Vannes diocese. I told M. des Jonchères not even to think about it, at least not so soon.

I hope to leave for Luçon tomorrow, then return to Richelieu, God willing, and from there to Paris, unless something urgent requires me to proceed further; in which case, it takes only a month to go and return to Richelieu. When we are in Paris, we will discuss all that is needed here.

In the meantime, Mademoiselle, take care of your health, for the love of Our Lord. In His love I am, Mademoiselle, your most humble servant.

VINCENT DEPAUL
i.s.C.M.

Addressed: Mademoiselle Le Gras, in Paris

1102. - TO ANTOINE PORTAIL, IN MARSEILLES

Richelieu, May 11, 1649

Monsieur,

The grace of Our Lord be with you forever!

I found two letters from you waiting for me in this house. I do not recall your proposing anything for which you need to consult someone else if you do not have my opinion, as you say you are obliged to do on the twentieth of this month. I just read the points of four or five of your letters, written to me before the latest ones,

---

Letter 1102. - Archives of the Mission, Turin, original signed letter. The postscript is in the Saint's handwriting.

and I could not find anything about that. If the matter cannot be put in writing or is so urgent that you cannot give me information on it and await my reply, seek the advice of the house councillors and M. de la Coste,[1] and I will ask God to grant you the grace to follow His eternal plans in all things.

God knows how much I want to make the visitation of the houses where you are, and I deeply regret not being able to do so, since the Queen has commanded me several times to return to Paris. Now, I do not see how I can do God's Will by not obeying, since I myself have always believed and taught that Princes, even wicked ones, must be obeyed, as Scripture says. All I can do is to have someone ask Her Majesty, as I am doing, to allow me to continue my journey, not as far as Marseilles but only to Cahors. I shall await the answer here.

When I am back in Paris, we will try to send you M. du Chesne or someone else, along with a Brother. I do not know if it could be Brother Jean Parre.[2]

Speaking of Brothers, I heard from Genoa that you have kept Brother Claude,[3] who was on his way back there. This surprises me, since you know how much they need him. They are very insistent in asking me for him; please send him back.

All your other letters, six or seven of them, require nothing of me but a thousand thanks to God for everything you tell me, in particular the success of the ordination, the Fréjus mission, the conferences for secular priests, M. Brunet's zeal, M. de la Coste's satisfaction, his charity for the Community, and, lastly, the blessings God is showering upon it. So, I beg His Infinite Mercy to be His own thanksgiving and to sanctify your souls more and more,

---

[1]Gaspard de Simiane de la Coste, Administrator of the hospital for convicts in Marseilles.

[2]Born in Châtillon-en-Dunois (Eure-et-Loir), Jean Parre entered the Congregation of the Mission on April 16, 1638, at twenty-seven years of age, took his vows in 1643, and died after 1660. Parre and Brother Mathieu Régnard were two of the most intelligent and active instruments which Divine Providence placed in Saint Vincent's hands. Parre traveled all over Picardy and Champagne assessing and remedying needs.

[3]Claude Le Gentil.

particularly your own. I am, in the love of Our Lord, Monsieur, your most humble servant.

VINCENT DEPAUL
i.s.C.M.

Since, by the grace of God, there is now peace,[4] it seems there is nothing to prevent us from holding the meeting of the Superiors of the Company in Paris.[5]

Addressed: Monsieur Portail, in Marseilles

1103. - TO SAINT LOUISE

Richelieu, Day after the Ascension [1649][1]

Mademoiselle,

The grace of Our Lord be with you forever!

M. Lambert[2] must have informed you of my arrival here. The following morning, when the mail was leaving, I was too busy with visits to write to you and have been so taken up with our visitation since then that I still have not been able to talk with our good Sister.[3] I shall do so, God willing, at the first opportunity.

---

[4]Early in March the peace of Rueil was concluded between the Court and the Parlement, ending the first phase of the wars of the Fronde.

[5]This General Assembly was not convoked until 1651, lasting from July 1 to August 11. It was the second assembly held during Saint Vincent's lifetime; the first had met in 1642.

Letter 1103. - The original autograph letter is on display in the Saint Vincent de Paul Society hall in Metz.

[1]The contents of the letter and the place from which it was written leave no doubt about its date. In 1649, the day after the Ascension was May 14.

[2]Lambert aux Couteaux.

[3]The two Daughters of Charity in Richelieu were Sister Françoise Carcireux and Sister Charlotte Royer.

Sister Françoise Carcireux, born in Beauvais, entered the Company of the Daughters of

I am writing to M. Lambert and sending a note to the Duchess to thank her for her horses.[4] I am giving them my reasons for wanting to go as far as Notre-Dame de la Rose and to three or four houses we have in that direction. However, I abide by their wishes since they, like you, see the needs there. Any fear of travel on horseback or in the sun will be banished by my using the carriage that was sent to me.

The most urgent business is housing the foundlings. I gave the Duchess the reasons, which I am not repeating here to you. She or M. Lambert must have told you what they are. It is only a question of a month or so. To put it briefly, I am suggesting to her a general meeting of the Ladies to decide whether to present the matter to the Queen, to ask for a general collection, or to petition the Parlement to provide for the needs, in the name of the officers; this will carry more weight than your name alone. I said also that M. Lambert could do this, if it is inconvenient to wait for me, and that, in the final analysis, I shall do whatever I am told.

I have written you about the state of our Sisters in Nantes. Abbé de Vaux wrote me that the Angers Sisters are doing well, for which I thank God.

M. Gautier told me that a number of girls here are asking to be

Charity around 1640-1641. Stationed first at Saint-Germain-l'Auxerrois, then with the foundlings at Bicêtre, she was sent to Richelieu in 1648. She left there in September 1659 for the hospital in Narbonne. From 1672 to 1675 she filled the important role of Assistant of the Company.

A native of Liancourt, Sister Charlotte Royer was sent to Richelieu in 1648, after having served the poor in Saint-Jean parish. She was still there at the time of Saint Louise's death in 1660.

[4]For the Saint's return, the Duchesse d'Aiguillon had the thoughtfulness to send two horses harnessed to the carriage she had already given him. When Saint Vincent wished to give them back, the Duchess told him to keep them. He could not refuse, and was obliged, on the Queen's orders, to use the horses. (Cf. Abelly, *op. cit.*, bk. I, chap. XXXIX, p. 186.)

admitted into the Charity. God grant that we may be admitted into His company, and may He keep you in good health!

I am, in His love, Mademoiselle, your most humble and obedient servant.

VINCENT DEPAUL
i.s.C.M.

In the name of God, Mademoiselle, do not worry about the bailiff.[5] Do you not see the extraordinary care Our Lord is taking of Him, almost without you? Let His Divine Majesty act; He is quite capable of showing the mother, who takes care of so many children, His satisfaction in this, by the care He will take of her child, and that she could never anticipate or surpass Him in goodness. Remember what I told you before about good blessed Madame de Chantal[6] regarding her late son.[7]

Addressed: Mademoiselle Le Gras, in Paris

---

[5]In order to provide Saint Louise's son with a position, Saint Vincent had appointed him bailiff of Saint-Lazare. In this capacity, Michel Le Gras was responsible for dispensing justice in the dependencies of the property. He kept this post until 1656. His mother, concerned mainly about the salvation of his soul, wanted to see him married, and was not succeeding as quickly as she wished. He finally married Gabrielle Le Clerc on January 18, 1650 in Saint-Sauveur Church. Saint Vincent witnessed the marriage contract.

[6]Saint Jane Frances Frémiot de Chantal was born in Dijon on January 23, 1572. Married to the Baron de Chantal, she was the mother of four children, but was widowed at a very early age. She placed herself under the guidance of Saint Francis de Sales, and with him established the Order of the Visitation. The foundation of the First Monastery in Paris brought her to that city, where she remained (1619-1622). There she became acquainted with Saint Vincent, whom she requested of Henri de Gondi, Bishop of Paris, as Superior of her nuns. Until her death in Moulins on December 13, 1641, while returning from a trip to Paris, she kept in close contact with this holy priest, whom she consulted for spiritual direction and the business affairs of her community. (Cf. Henri de Maupas du Tour, *La Vie de la Vénérable Mère Jeanne-Françoise Frémyot* [new ed., Paris: Siméon Piget, 1653].)

[7]Her son, Celse-Bénigne de Chantal.

1103a. - TO SAINT LOUISE

Richelieu, May 19, 1649

Mademoiselle,

The grace of Our Lord be with you forever!

People here are talking to me about many girls whom I have yet to see. I think you told me that the girls from this area are not very suitable and that you have made due allowance for them, considering the times. I would really like a reply to these two points before my departure, if possible. If I can leave ahead of time, this will not hold me up.

I expect the decision on what I wrote to M. Lambert in about two or three days, God willing.[1]

I am feeling well, by the grace of God. I am worried about the state of your health. If, as I am hoping, Our Lord continues to grant you good health, it is a very special mark of His goodness. I ask Him to do so and to bless your works more and more.

I have played the sick man a little these days to free myself from a large number of visits, which were hindering me during the visitation I am making. This has prevented me from seeing your Sister. I shall do so at the first opportunity.

Good day, Mademoiselle. I am, Mademoiselle, your most humble and obedient servant.

VINCENT DEPAUL
i.s.C.M.

Addressed: Mademoiselle Le Gras, in Paris

Letter 1103a. - The original autograph letter is the property of the Jesuits in Aix. Coste inserted it in his supplement, vol. XIII, no. 3321, p. 843. Its date prompts us to insert it here.

[1]There are no letters extant on this matter, neither to Lambert aux Couteaux, nor from him to Saint Vincent, giving the response the Saint was expecting.

1104. - *CHARLES NACQUART TO SAINT VINCENT*

[Fort-Dauphin, May 27, 1649] [1]

Monsieur and Most Honored Father,

Your blessing, please!
Since the memory of the just person must be eternal, the least of the duties I am obliged to render to my dear deceased brother and companion, M. Gondrée, is to send you an account of his last days and the virtues he practiced during the illness which snatched him from me in the springtime of his life and in the hope I had of seeing this good laborer at work.

This, then, will be just a sample to add to the conference to be held concerning him, so that you will not miss any of his final actions, which crowned all the preceding ones.

I shall not repeat here the virtues he practiced on the way, in La Rochelle and during our sea voyage of six and a half months because he practiced the virtues of a good Missionary: humility, mortification, charity, gentleness, simplicity, and zeal, letting no opportunity to do so pass by. There is also everything that was done during the six months he lived here, as you have seen in the journal I wrote, the better part of which is due to him.

Leaving aside piety, modesty, gentle conversation, and the exactness and care he took with the French as well as with the natives on every occasion he had to serve and instruct them, I come to the first journey he made to Fanshère with Monsieur de Flacourt to visit Andian Ramach, [2] *King of the region where we live. It was the Friday before the Rogation Days. I let him go because I had already been there twice. Since he could not say Sunday Mass there, he conducted a public prayer service for the French, who had accompanied Monsieur de Flacourt. This took place in front of the house of the King, who, along with a number of the natives, assisted at it in profound silence and repeated the promises he had made to me of becoming a good Christian, once there were priests with him and a church was built there. This journey was made during a time of abstinence, and no fish and vegetables, such as people want in this country as in France, were available. But even though he had given a dispensation to the French, he himself wanted to observe abstinence, and ate only a*

Letter 1104. - Archives of the Mission, Paris, original autograph letter.

[1]This date was added on the back of the original. Fort-Dauphin is located in the southern part of Madagascar, on the east coast.

[2]The modern spelling is Andriandramaka.

little boiled rice. Added to the heat of the journey, this brought on the illness from which he did not recover.

Let us observe how Our Lord refined this gold in the furnace and revealed his patience during his illness. On Wednesday, eve of the Ascension of Our Lord, although he was feeling very ill, he wanted to celebrate Mass, which he was barely able to finish. Despite this, he still went to hear the confession of a dying Frenchman, who had asked him to do so. He returned home with chills and went to bed, telling me he had been disturbed by dreams during the night; among others, he had imagined that he was making a large number of crosses. This, he said, was an omen that he would soon be needing one for himself.

I asked him what caused his sickness. He told me it was due in part to the journey, which had made him constipated. Then, when he returned home, he became nauseated from the stench of a sick man we had taken in because there was no other place to put him.

Next, his fever rose so high that by afternoon he was delirious and very agitated. This caused him to get out of bed and make frantic efforts to go out, and he was unable to speak. I ran to him, embraced him, and put him back to bed. For a quarter of an hour, he still could not speak, although he tried hard to do so. Something like red foam was coming out of his mouth, a sign that his lungs were affected. He also would be short of breath and had a hard time singing in church. When he recovered his speech, he had no recollection of what he had just done. The first thing he requested was to go to confession.

On Friday, the fever abated a little but only so it could muster renewed strength to flatten him because by evening it was twice as violent. After being so constipated, he had a fierce attack of diarrhea, which made him so weak all of a sudden that he could no longer stand on his feet. All his joints ached so badly that he said he could not bear the pain any more. Yet, his loudest cries were "Blessed be God! May God be glorified! If it is Your Will to see me suffer so much, I gladly do so. If you increase my pain, increase my patience as well." I said to him, "Courage, dear brother! Our good God sees your struggle. He is trying you in the fire of this fever. Is it not better, as one of the Lenten prayers states, ut temporaliter maceremur in corpore quam suppliciis deputemur aeternis?"[3] *"How right you are,"*

---

[3]*That we may discipline our body here rather than suffer eternal punishment.* This prayer is taken from the Mass for the Friday after Passion Sunday as celebrated at the time of Saint Vincent; it is not contained in the Mass for this day in the *Sacramentary* in use since Vatican II.

he replied. *"Ah! how good God is and how much He loves me! I am not worthy of His love."*

The pain he was enduring obliged me to look for some remedy. Fortunately, I found some oil, which the natives make from a fruit called bloodwort,[4] and use very hot. We applied it to the spot that was painful, and this gave him some relief. After that, he continually thanked the Creator. This relief was short-lived, however, for the same pain began again, preventing him from getting any rest. I told him he could say, Deus meus, ad te de luce vigilo,[5] *and he said to me, "I can also truly say,* De nocte vigilo.[6]*

The day after the Ascension, I told him he should place himself in manu Domini [7] *and receive the Sacraments, the divine remedies when human ones can do nothing. "Gladly," he replied, "I leave that up to you," so obedient was he to whatever was recommended.*

Preferring to anticipate rather than to put off things until it was too late, I brought Our Lord to him and, in presence of most of our Frenchmen, who devoutly accompanied the Blessed Sacrament, I said to him with a heart full of emotion and words moved by tenderness, "Well, dear brother, the Great Doctor of soul and body has come to visit you! Now is the time for you to practice what you have so often preached to the sick; namely, to make acts of faith, humility, contrition, and charity." "That is what I want," he replied. Next, I told him that, since the outcome of his illness was uncertain, I was giving him Holy Viaticum and he should give himself entirely to Him who was giving Himself entirely to him. To this he replied generously, "I do not belong to myself; let Him do with me whatever He wills; I belong entirely to Him." He then received Him with great devotion.

From then on his strength diminished, but his mind was still sound enough to be occupied with God by aspirations too long to describe here. Nothing was spared to improve his condition, and for his part he did not refuse anything we asked him to take for love of our good God.

The feast of Pentecost came and I exposed the Blessed Sacrament for the Forty Hours devotion, asking everyone, in their concern for his health, to beg the heart of God to restore it, if it was necessary for him. For my part, I said the prayer of the Apostles, Ne derelinquas nos orphanos,[8] *with the twofold intention of not being deprived of the graces of the Holy Spirit*

---

[4]A red resin extracted from a species of palm, used to check bleeding.
[5]*My God, I seek you at break of day.* Cf. Ps 62:2. (D-RB)
[6]*I watch in the night.*
[7]*In the Lord's hand.*
[8]*Do not leave us orphans.* Cf. Jn 14:18. (NAB)

and of not being left the orphan of my spiritual father. *"Did You not say, Lord, that it was not good for a person to be alone, without a companion to stimulate his fervor in his coldness, or to lift him up when he falls?"* However, after I let these groans arise from my heart and asked for the preservation of a worker who was so essential in a country needing him so much, I returned to the house. The only reply I received was of death, since I saw that his illness had advanced. He was so weak that he was continuously delirious, although his wanderings were all pious, such as saying Mass, or instructing someone. Thereupon, I took the opportunity to help him raise his heart to God by reciting a verse of the Psalms or some other prayer. I reflected how true it is that the mill produces flour only from the wheat that has been put into it, and the mind turns naturally to the things and thoughts that we have often presented to it. However, it was no delirium when he said to me and to those who came to see him, *"Oh! how good it is to serve God when we are in good health because, believe me, it is very difficult in sickness, which weakens our poor minds."* At other times, he would say with feeling, *"We think we are badly off when our body is suffering; still, it is a great happiness to put up with the pain for love of God. A moment of tribulation buys an eternity of glory."*

It was quite obvious that he was in the habit of suffering with love. Although, as I mentioned above, the pains in all his joints had caused him to say in the beginning that it was impossible to suffer more; although, I repeat, these pains were increasing, he said, *"I am not suffering so much, for I feel a force within me and a grace which causes all this pain to seem like almost nothing."* *"Well,"* I replied, *"this confirms that* Juxta est Dominus iis qui tribulato sunt corde; [9] cum ipso sum in tribulatione.[10] And nearly always he would softly reply to all these verses, *"Ah! how right you are, dear sir; how true that is."*

When he had slipped into his delirium again, he began to mumble, *"How can these Huguenots be converted?"* And I answered, *"By gentle conversation."* What is remarkable here is that it was, in fact, shortly after his death that, of the ten who were here, five were converted, coming back, one after the other, after he had conversed gently and humbly with them. Possibly I was wrong in thinking he was dreaming when he spoke about the conversion of these Huguenots; perhaps it was a prayer he was saying for this very purpose and which was answered at that moment in his heart, although it was not put into effect until later.

It had been ten days since he had received Holy Communion, and I

---

[9]*The Lord is close to the brokenhearted.* Cf. Ps 34:19 (NAB) Ps 33:19 (D-RB)
[10]*I am with him in distress.* Cf. Ps 91:15. (NAB) Ps 90:15. (D-RB)

asked if he would like to do it again, to receive Him who had sent the Holy Spirit upon the Apostles. "Oh! most willingly!" he said. On Pentecost, however, I was busy with chanting Matins and High Mass and reconciling those making their devotions; after Vespers in the evening, there was the exhortation to the Frenchmen and instructions for the natives. So, it was on the following day that I brought him Our Lord, whom he received with the same devotion as the first time. Since almost all the Frenchmen were present, he lovingly recommended to them devotion to the Blessed Virgin, although he himself found it difficult to speak and begged me to recommend it to them.

I cannot help saying here what I think will be remarked in the conference on his life, that his devotion to the Blessed Virgin was so fervent that he has left here in writing a number of practices, which I think he formulated during his retreat. I also think that he and three or four seminarians from Saint-Lazare had come together to encourage one another and to talk about it during recreation and spiritual discussions.

After he had received Communion, I found him so exhausted that I suggested he receive Extreme Unction, hoping that the Sacraments might do more for his health than remedies. I brought it to him immediately and he received it so devoutly, presenting each member to be anointed, and answering the prayers, that I was moved to tears, as were all those present. When this was over, I went to celebrate Holy Mass, at the end of which I baptized a young woman who was going to marry a Black man baptized in Nantes, France. He was the companion of the one baptized in Paris who, shortly after, also married a Black woman from here, whom I had baptized. Returning from Church and having nothing with which to console this poor, listless friend, close to death in his illness, I told him what I had just done in Church: "Well, dear friend! we have just begun Our Lord's work by baptizing a woman, and we shall soon have another when I complete the instruction. Are you not pleased about this?" He punctuated his reply by saying, "O bon Dieu! who would not be happy about this? Is it not why we were sent here? But my greatest regret now is that I have to leave these poor people who are so well disposed. O bon Dieu! what a great honor! Ah! will You not grant me the grace of being of service to You in this?"

These sentiments and his zeal for the salvation of the inhabitants of this country can be more easily imagined than expressed. He often used to talk to me about this when he was in good health, and he spoke of our mission in this country only in terms of gratitude to God for the great honor He had bestowed on us. Just recalling his fervor in speaking of this brings tears to my eyes, even as I write, and I experience great humiliation at carrying out my duty so poorly.

To return to our patient: after saying such beautiful words in a strained voice in such a short space of time, he immediately relapsed into drowsiness. During this period, his zeal for the conversion of these poor infidels became even more obvious. He had applied himself to learning the native language, and he said in his delirium, "Yes, that is a fine expression Aka alino," which means, "Do not forget." Does not this phrase alone indicate how zealously he had tried to instill Christian doctrine in them? Then, with a start he said, "Yes, gentlemen, I call you as witnesses that I have left everything in France and traveled six thousand leagues over the sea before reaching here with so much difficulty, all for the conversion of these poor people!" I told him we had begun to till the soil and, now that the seed had been planted, the harvest would come when Our Lord willed it. "Yes," he said, "but that will take a long time." "What!" I said, "Do you think that those who dispose themselves as best they can, and who likewise prepare for the future as we are trying to do, are doing less than those who make more progress because they will find the road cleared for them?"

On the last of the feast days, I perceived clearly that he could no longer withstand the violence of such a malignant fever, which for two weeks had almost devoured him, while the heat and severe pain in his head and in all the members of his poor body had exhausted him. Returning from services in church, I asked him, "In the event that God chooses to release you from this exile, what would you want to say to our good father, Monsieur Vincent?" "Tell him I thank him most humbly for having admitted and tolerated me as a Missionary, and especially for sending me to this country, instead of so many others who would have done a much better job than I." "What do you want to say to Monsieur Lambert and all the seminarians?" "Tell them to thank God for the same reason." "And to your mother and relatives?" "I beg them to have many Masses said for me for the same intention." "And if you leave me here alone, what is your last will and testament for me?" He asked me if I would be willing to say some Masses for him. "Yes, rest assured of that. You pray for me up there and I for you here below, and even if death separates us bodily it will not divide our hearts, which have been so closely united in one and the same purpose of serving God and having others serve Him. But is that all you have to say to me?" After reflecting a little, he said to me in presence of two or three Frenchmen, "My real will and testament for you is to warn you that you will have a great deal to suffer here" (and he repeated "yes, really suffer"), "not just a little but, I repeat, a great deal." I did not ask him why but was content to keep that dear testament in my heart, begging Our Lord that His Will be done in me, by me, and through me, and that all this might be for the glory of God.

I cannot tell you how true this last will and testament proved to be; the *physical suffering to be endured here from the heat and the lack of many things that are plentiful in France is only a small part of it. But I bless God for the grace He has granted me of overcoming much mental suffering at seeing myself alone in terra aliena,[11] deprived of the good company of the deceased and the hope of having anyone else for a long time to come, of receiving the Sacraments, and of being unable to make progress (being alone and involved with the French) in a work that requires laborers right away.*

Finally, after benediction in the evening, everyone assembled in a last attempt to implore Our Lord to cure the illness of the person He and all of us loved. I came back to tell him this. Since he seemed to be losing consciousness, I asked him if he knew who I was. "Yes, your name is Nacquart." In an effort to cheer him up, I asked if he knew his own name. With a little smile he gave me an answer revealing his habitual humility: "As for me," he said, "I am a person who is not worth much." I replied, "Blessed be God who has given you these sentiments; you will not be any less before Him." Although his mind was wandering with regard to temporal matters, he was constantly concerned about spiritual ones, and from the very depths of his humility he ascended to trust in the Divine Mercy. Clasping his crucifix, he mumbled, "Yes, God will forgive me; otherwise I would be lost." When I simply touched his crucifix, he held it tighter, as if he had said interiorly Inveni quem diligit anima mea; teneo et non dimittam.[12]

Foreseeing that he did not have long to live and that I would not have the opportunity much longer to be reconciled with Our Lord, I asked him if he could give me the Sacrament of Penance and concentrate long enough to hear my confession and give me absolution. "Yes, yes," he said, and immediately bared his head and gave me the Sacrament without hesitation. He also exhorted me to sorrow for my sins. Then I received his last blessing.

I remained with him to encourage him in his last moments. He was preparing himself also, for he turned again to his crucifix and, after looking at it, removed his cap with difficulty because he was so weak. Holding the image of his Master in his trembling hands, he kept trying to recite the Litany of the Holy Name, but his memory failed him so I said the words and he answered them devoutly. I tried to calm him down and make him take a little rest because he was somewhat agitated. Around ten that evening, I encouraged him again, although I was worried about that night,

---

[11]*In a foreign land.* Cf. Ps 137:4.
[12]*I have found him whom my heart loves; I take hold of him and will not let him go.* Cf. Song 3:4. (NAB)

so I got two people to stay with him. Because I was a little fatigued myself, having been up almost day and night, being in church for the feasts, and having lost my appetite because I felt so sad, they told me to go and rest and to keep up my strength for the people. So I gave in, after asking those staying with him to take good care of him and to come and get me at the slightest change. I said good night to the patient and asked him to do his best to rest; then, I threw myself on the bed.

In the meantime, a high wind came up, making a rustling noise among the leaves with which the hut was covered, like the others in this country. The Frenchmen staying up with him had moved back a little, and often he could be heard repeating the words he had in his head from the onset of his illness, Deus, Deus meus, ad te de luce vigilo.[13] *His crucifix was beside him, fastened to his straw mat and, with the aid of a cord that had been suspended there to help him move, he would put his hand on it and utter many words that were incomprehensible.*

Oh! what a lazy coward I am to have allowed them to persuade me to go take a rest, while my brother kept repeating that he stayed up with Our Lord during the night as well as during the day! Who could doubt that the weak hand he so artfully placed on the corpus of the crucifix was simply searching for what the Apostle Saint Thomas wanted to touch, and that he was saying with him, Deus [sic] meus et Deus meus,[14] *and that the heart which had so tenderly loved and faithfully served the Lord, and struggled so valiantly, seeing himself at the end of his earthly career which he had hoped to begin in this country, might cry out,* Cupio dissolvi et esse cum Christo.[15]

But it is better for me to let people imagine for themselves what he might have said and thought in those last moments when, being closer to his center, these movements were undoubtedly much more violent, and when the attendants suddenly asked him if he wanted something, they received no answer. When they awakened me, about a quarter after midnight, all I found was the corpse of him whose soul had gone to receive the reward for the services he had rendered and the virtues he had practiced toward God, his neighbor, and himself. You can imagine the state of my poor heart, which even now trembles as I write, and the overwhelming grief I felt in burying this blessed body, which had served not only to acknowledge Our Lord before others but had also suffered the martyrdom of so many

---

[13]See n. 5.

[14]*My God and My God.* "Thomas said in response, 'My Lord and my God'." Jn 20:28. (NAB) The reference to John is obvious, even though the Latin in the letter is inaccurate.

[15]*I long to be freed and to be with Christ.* Cf. Phil 1:23. (NAB)

mortifications voluntarily chosen and endured with admirable patience, especially during this ultimate trial in which he had been refined, and the finishing touches had been put on his being purified like gold in the furnace.

I realize, however, that I cannot express the sorrow I felt with such tenderness and regret while performing the funeral rites, chanting the Office of the Dead, and celebrating the Mass; even more so when I had to place in the ground the person whom I would have been willing to ransom with my own life. Oh! how many sobs interrupted the chanting of the Office, obliging me in the end to ask those present, who could not hold back their tears, to pardon my weakness for something for which Our Lord Himself had been excused, when it was said to Him at the raising of his friend, Lazarus, from the dead, Ecce quomodo amabas eum! [16]

Not only the French had their faces covered in mourning, but the natives as well, who were just getting to know him. A good number of them could not refrain from weeping at the death of a person of whom they used to say during his lifetime that they had never seen men like us who did not get angry and annoyed, and who spoke to them lovingly of matters pertaining to their salvation, as we tried to do in instructing them.

I am well aware that my own death, which will occur whenever God wants, will not affect me so deeply as did his, and that the reasons for sadness were so deeply embedded in my soul that they would have overwhelmed me if I had not thought that he was not dead but asleep and that I must be silent, since God had done this for the best. Still, the thought went through my mind that He was meting out to me a harsh punishment for not profiting by his good example while he was alive. Little by little, however, my sadness was swallowed up in resignation to the Will of God and abandonment to Divine Providence. I asked for the share of grace He had prepared for such a faithful servant. Whenever I speak of him now, it is only to console myself and the whole Company by the words which would serve to canonize the deceased, Beatus ille servus quem, cum venerit Dominus ejus, invenerit vigilantem, etc.[17]

I think that everyone who knew him in Paris and elsewhere will testify that he was always on the watch in prima vigilia[18] *of his seminary, in* secunda vigilia,[19] *when he was in Saintes, and* in tertia vigilia,[20] *when he*

---

[16]*See how much you loved him.* Cf. Jn 11:36. (NAB)
[17]*That servant is fortunate whom his master finds watching when he returns.* Cf. Lk 12:43. (NAB)
[18]*At the first watch.*
[19]*At the second watch.*
[20]*At the third watch.*

returned to Paris to receive priesthood. You will see that, in the time I had the happiness of being in his company, I noticed how careful he was to keep his body and soul in an incomparable and angelic purity, and his heart faithful to the practice of all the virtues of a good Missionary. In a word, he did much good and no evil, as far as I could see, going straight to God in his actions and leading so many others to Him. He ended his days with the regret of not being allowed to work for the conversion of this new kingdom so easily to be won over for Our Lord. He endured joyfully in his illness all that a body can suffer, which was all the more praiseworthy in one who was by nature sharp but who had perfectly mastered this and turned it into a cordial gentleness. Lastly, he watched day and night, right to the end, as he often repeated during his illness. Who, therefore, could have any doubt that he was found watching for this Lord who, at cockcrow when he died, after midnight, doubtless brought him immediately into the light of His glory and the possession of all His goods? If I may not say he is a saint, yet, in view of all of the above, I can be sure that he is among the blessed, according to Scripture.

I shall never forget a remark that, immediately after his death, there was a lunar eclipse lasting a good three hours. This made me think that the heavens were sharing with us in mourning the person who was needed so much to help dissipate the night and the darkness of ignorance on this earth. With this I shall close. I conclude that, if such a beautiful heavenly body can be eclipsed, then no one is so just that he may not sin and need, after death, the prayers and suffrages of the Church. I am sure that the entire Company and all our houses will not delay to pay their respects, offering the usual prayers for him, as soon as they are notified. I think you will do this in a circular letter which I hope will include how he began and all the progress people have remarked, to be joined with the ending I am now sending. I hope this blessed will and testament of sufferings, which has been left to me, may be executed in me as a sure sign of the choice made of me to carry to this country or elsewhere the name of Him in whose love I desire to end my life, as did the deceased, and to remain forever, Monsieur and Most Honored Father, your most humble and obedient servant.

NACQUART,
i.s.C.M.

1105. - TO SAINT LOUISE

Richelieu, May 29, 1649

Mademoiselle,

I received your letter, which grieved and consoled me at the same time by informing me at the same moment of your illness and your cure. I thank God for this and ask Him to strengthen you more and more.

My little fever has left me, thank God. I am completing my visitation and hope to leave in four or five days, God willing. I have not yet left this house to pay my visits, nor have I seen our Sister. I shall do so tomorrow or the next day, God willing. I praise God for the favor the Chancellor's wife[1] did for you.

I am deeply grieved at the loss of our good Sister who returned ill from Saint-Denis, but I bless God for the departure of those whom He has not called.

If the Saint-Germain business is not settled, we will discuss it on my return, God willing.

It seems to me that it is better at first for the Bailiff to go very slowly rather than put everything he has into this office;[2] perhaps it will be sold at a higher price.

I shall observe more closely the girls who present themselves from here. In the meantime, I recommend myself to your prayers. I am, in the love of Our Lord, Mademoiselle, your most humble servant.

VINCENT DEPAUL
i.s.C.M.

Addressed: Mademoiselle Le Gras, Superioress of the Daughters of Charity, in Paris

---

Letter 1105. - Original autograph letter, now at the Miséricorde in Agen.

[1]Madame Séguier.

[2]In 1649 steps were taken for Michel le Gras, bailiff of Saint-Lazare, to procure a position in the Mint, but he did not yet have sufficient funds to purchase this office.

1106. - *A MISSIONARY IN BARBARY TO SAINT VINCENT*

[Between 1645 [1] and 1660]

Our Lord has granted us the grace of recovering two of our precious stones which had been lost. They are quite valuable and have a celestial brilliance. I was very pleased about this.

1107. - *BENJAMIN HUGUIER TO SAINT VINCENT*

Tunis, June 5, 1649

Monsieur,

Your blessing!

Monsieur Le Vacher [1] read me a letter today, which he had just received from Monsieur Barreau, informing him of the death of good Monsieur Dieppe on May 2. I thought that, since I lived a long time with him in the seminary and was sent to Barbary on the same day, it was my duty to write you about the virtues he practiced, of which I was aware and which his humility could not hide.

First, his zeal for his own sanctification, for God, and for the relief of poor Christians, became apparent to me when, two days before we left Paris, he expressed to me his joy at being chosen. He foresaw, as God permitted, that in his work among the sick slaves or amidst the difficulty of carrying out his functions among the Turks, he would shortly be consumed as a holocaust.

This caused him to endure generously the hardships of the journey to Marseilles, during which he was ill most of the time. Nevertheless, he never missed celebrating Holy Mass and reciting his Office, even though, because of his motion sickness in the coach, he was obliged to devote to this the time we used for rest. During the time he seemed to be recreating, he entertained us with hymns and Spanish lessons, always working and resting in this way.

Monsieur Portail had asked him to instruct a poor heretic, who wanted

Letter 1106. - Abelly, *op.cit.*, bk. II, chap. I, sect. VII, §10, p. 135.
  [1]The year the Barbary Mission began.

Letter 1107. - Lyons manuscript, f° 212ff.
  [1]Jean Le Vacher.

to convert. The man had been sent by the Bishop of Marseilles.[2] The whole house witnessed his great gentleness and charity in this. The same was true when the opportunity happily arose, at the end of a mission on a galley, to hear general confessions; he accepted all the fatigue involved as a great source of joy.

He had such devotion to the Blessed Virgin that when he received instructions to prepare for the journey, the only visit he made—and I accompanied him—was to Notre-Dame des Vertus,[3] where he celebrated Mass afterward. By a certain exterior joy, proceeding, I think, from an interior joy, he indicated that, in the midst of all future storms, this Mother would give him a haven of refuge in her Son.

M. Barreau calls him a peaceful man, a true Israelite without guile. That is what I observed in the seminary, during the entire journey, and afterward.

You quite rightly appointed him our Superior on the journey, but he never seemed to act as one, although he observed and had us observe all that we had prescribed. He did this so pleasantly and with such conde-scension that he set himself and his own privileges aside when he saw that we were following your orders. He took care of our needs with a kindness seasoned by that salt Our Lord requires. We remembered this in Lyons, for example, when on an unforeseen occasion we were at supper with three or four laymen. After remaining there the length of time which honor and courtesy might require, he left the table before the end of the meal because a German Huguenot captain, previously a stranger to us, began telling a story that put a monk in an unfavorable light. We left along with M. Dieppe, to the embarrassment of the heretic who on another occasion might be more discreet.

He knew that covetousness is the queen of vices, and embraced its opposite, practicing poverty in every way he could. I will not mention what I observed in him in the seminary, since my brothers also observed it, but I saw him when he was leaving it, and this was to my great confusion because I was all dressed up in new clothes when one of our priests, to make me realize that I had to look after him, pointed out to me that he was still wearing his old hat, and his everyday shoes and clothes. All he brought away with him, besides the three little books we had in the seminary, was an old breviary, and a discipline which I caught sight of when we were on the way. He kept this same spirit during the journey, where he was unwilling to take advantage of his authority by buying things in the few

---

towns through which we passed, but he did use it to go on foot from Avignon to Marseilles. It was not that we were short of money, but to imitate the journeys of Our Lord in one way at least.

I praised and thanked God, in the solemn service we had soon after, for having willed to call good Monsieur Dieppe to Himself in this way, at the beginning of his career. This death has been a powerful sermon for me. God grant that I may profit by it and that, not content simply to die in Barbary, I may die as a true Missionary, servant of God and imitator of O[ur] L[ord] J[esus] C[hrist]!

I ask this of God through your holy prayers, and am, Monsieur, in O[ur] L[ord] J[esus] C[hrist], your obedient

HUGUIER
i. s. C. M.

1108. - TO MICHEL THEPAULT DE RUMELIN,[1] IN TREGUIER[2]

Paris, June 7, 1649[3]

Monsieur,

The grace of Our Lord be with you forever!

This is just a little note of thanks for the many benefits our Missionaries in Tréguier are constantly receiving from you, Monsieur, by way of housing, alms, advice, and the patronage you extend to them. My thanks, however, are prompted by a heart filled with gratitude and respect for you, a living image of the charity of God. M. Tholard[4] could not contain his feelings of gratitude for this

---

Letter 1108. - Archives of the Mission, Paris, original signed letter, tracing made from the original.

[1]Messire Michel Thépault, Sieur de Rumelin, Licentiate in civil and canon law, Rector of Pleumeur-Bodou and of Plougasnou, then Canon of the Tréguier Cathedral and Penitentiary of the diocese. He was a great benefactor of the Missionaries and founded the Tréguier Seminary. He died on August 30, 1677. (Cf. lecture of Canon Daniel in *Annales de la Congrégation de la Mission*, vol. LXIII [1908], pp. 191-201.)

[2]Although no house had yet been founded in Tréguier, the Missionaries had, in fact, gone there in response to the request of the Bishop, Grangier de Liverdi.

[3]Saint Vincent did not return to Paris until June 13 (cf. no. 1110). Either the letter is incorrectly dated or it was not sent from Paris. The first hypothesis seems more probable.

[4]Superior of the Tréguier house.

and has poured them out to us so we could join our thanks to his and our prayers to those he offers for your greater sanctification. So, Monsieur, we shall ask God, as I am now doing, to be Himself your thanks and your reward, and to make us worthy of being of service to you. His Divine Goodness knows how readily we will do so. As for myself, Monsieur, I offer you my obedience with all possible humility, entreating you most humbly to make use of it whenever the occasion arises, and to continue your paternal patronage of Monsieur Tholard and his confrere so that they may correspond to the holy instructions of the Bishop and be of help to the souls to whose salvation you zealously contribute so much.

May Our Lord grant me a share in your virtues and prayers and make me worthy of the honor I have of being, in His love, Monsieur, your most humble and obedient servant!

VINCENT DEPAUL
i.s.C.M.

Addressed: Monsieur de Rumelin, Canon of the cathedral church of Tréguier, in Tréguier.

1109. - TO RENE ALMERAS, SUPERIOR, IN ROME

June 18, 1649

I have seen from two of your letters the state of things where you are. You must not be discouraged because success does not seem very likely. This is a passing cloud; the day will come when the Company will have greater credibility and support, and those who can do good for it will have greater charity for it than they do now. When the Jesuits were beginning, their plans were somewhat thwarted during the pontificate of [Paul IV],[1] who obliged them to

---

Letter 1109. - Reg. 2, p. 230.
[1] The name was omitted in the copy.

wear a hood.[2] They did, in fact, wear it while he was alive, but after his death they discarded it because the new Pope was more favorably disposed toward them. Let us be submissive to Providence; He will see to our affairs in His own time and in His own way.

1110. - TO GABRIEL DELESPINEY,[1] IN TOUL

Paris, June 19, 1649

Monsieur,

The grace of Our Lord be with you forever!

I returned here Sunday in good health, thank God. I just received your letters, and am consoled and very grateful to the Divine Goodness for the fine governance He grants you and for the care and diligence with which you are acting. I ask Our Lord to draw from this His own glory and the sanctification of your dear soul.

The Governor of Toul has not yet arrived. When he does, I shall express to him the thanks we owe him. I will see how he feels about the evocation.[2] I am awaiting the final decision Messrs. Trélon and Midot[3] are to take on this question. I am writing to the former in reply to his letter. We really must follow their advice. So, what should we do? Is it not better to fail after asking advice than to risk acting on our own? I have been told that Plenevaux is here. I instructed someone to take care that he does not surprise us at Council by initiating some proceedings. I think it is useless to write

---

[2]As mentioned in no. 1075, n. 1, wearing the hood signified a choir obligation to which the Jesuits had not committed themselves.

Letter 1110. - Archives of the Mission, Turin, original signed letter.

[1]Born at Grandchamp (Calvados), Gabriel Delespiney was received into the Congregation of the Mission on August 5, 1645, and took his vows on January 25, 1656; he was Superior in Toul (1648-1652) and in Marseilles (1659-1660).

[2]Act by which a matter under discussion in one jurisdiction is removed to another jurisdiction.

[3]Cauchon, Seigneur de Trélon, and Jean Midot, Vicar-General of Toul.

to M. Midot; his charity prompts him sufficiently to do us good, and he knows we will be eternally grateful. Please express all possible gratitude and obedience to him on my part and tell your dear Community that, prostrate in spirit before them, I embrace them with all the tenderness of my heart and earnestly entreat Our Lord to shed His consolation and His light upon them more and more. I also recommend myself to their prayers and yours.

I am, in the love of Our Lord, Monsieur, your most humble servant.

VINCENT DEPAUL
i.s.C.M.

I am, nevertheless, going to write to M. Midot.

Addressed: Monsieur Delespiney, Superior of the Toul Mission, in Toul.

1111. - TO BROTHER JACQUES RIVET[1]

June 19, 1649

God knows that the consolation I received from your letter goes beyond anything I can say. You can be sure that all those I receive from you are very dear to me, since you are aware of the special affection God has given me for you. If it were not already complete, as it is, it would have increased considerably when I saw in your

---

Letter 1111. - Reg. 2, p. 297.

[1]Jacques Rivet, a coadjutor Brother, was born in Houdan (Yvelines) on September 11, 1620, entered the Congregation of the Mission on December 16, 1641, and took his vows on April 22, 1646. Saint Vincent had lent him to the "Bishop of Condom to be his major-domo during the absence" of the person who ordinarily filled that duty. The Bishop was so satisfied with him "that he wanted to retain him permanently. In the end he was urged to get married." (Note of Reg. 2.) Mention of him as late as September 23, 1657 (cf. vol. VI, no. 2391) assures us that he chose to remain in the Company.

letter the sincerity of your heart and its fidelity to God, for which I thank His Divine Goodness.

Oh! I certainly believe, dear Brother, that you would prefer to die than to leave God for others because, in the end, others pass away but God remains. This is a test Our Lord is making of your steadfastness, in order to give you a greater share of His love.

I have been told that you are needed in La Rose, so I ask you to return there when you receive this letter, and please notify me of your arrival.

I think you heard about my journey to Brittany and Poitou. I was hoping to go and see you but Providence arranged things otherwise and, by the Divine Goodness, brought me back to Paris a few days ago in good health. Our houses I visited gave me good reason to praise God for the regularity observed and the union which is apparent in them.

Those in Paris are still doing well, thank God, as, in general, is the whole Company, according to what I have been told. This does not mean that here and there no fault is to be found with someone, but that should not surprise us, since there were failings among Our Lord's own disciples.

The affection of my heart has caused me to speak this way to yours, although I had no intention of saying so much to you.

I rely on your prayers. Adieu, dear Brother, let us stay close to Him.

1112. - TO A PRIEST OF THE MISSION

[Around June 1649][1]

I was overjoyed at the remembrance of good Monsieur Dieppe, who died in Algiers. I never think about him without sensing the

---

Letter 1112. - Lyons manuscript.

[1]Date of the death of Jean Dieppe (May 2, 1649), and the date of Benjamin Huguier's letter (June 5, 1649), dictate the choice of the date of this letter. (Cf. no. 1107.)

fragrance of his virtue. Brother Barreau wrote to me about him in his last letter with renewed sentiments of esteem and regret, so grateful was he for his good intentions and his suitability for the work he had undertaken. May God be pleased to give the Company men who are equally zealous in our dear vocation!

I beg Our Lord to be your strength to continue until His eternal plan for you is carried out.

1113. - TO BROTHER JACQUES RIVET

June 27, 1649

To God be the glory, dear Brother, and to you a thousand blessings from heaven for your steadfastness in your vocation, in which His Infinite Goodness undoubtedly wishes to sanctify your dear soul! Alas! how greatly consoled you will be at the hour of death for having thus overcome difficulties! I ask Our Lord to strengthen you more and more with His own Spirit, so that you will remain always faithful to Him.

I have already asked you to go back to La Rose, and perhaps this letter will find you there. In this case, I praise God in advance, but if you are still in Condom, politely take leave of the Bishop[1] as soon as you can, no matter what he says. He will have greater respect for you when he sees you determined to follow the voice of God who is calling you to La Rose.

I assure you, dear Brother, that your brother[2] is in Saintes and is living there contentedly as a very good Missionary. Your

Letter 1113. - Reg. 2, p. 298.
[1]Jean d'Estrades.
[2]Louis Rivet, Priest of the Mission.

younger brother[3] is now with him; we sent him there for a change
of air because he was not feeling well here.

Adieu, dear Brother. Please pray for me.

1114. - TO MOTHER JEANNE-MARGUERITE CHAHU[1]

[Around June 1649][2]

I thought, dear Sister, that I would have the long-desired consolation of seeing your dear self in person, instead of in the letters
you have sent me. I must confess to your dear heart that they have
greatly saddened me, seeing that the one person in the world whom
I have always regarded as being among those most submissive to
God's Providence is having difficulty deciding whether she should
consent to the choice O[ur] L[ord] has made of her for the guidance
of His dear spouses and your daughters in Meaux. It would seem,
dear Sister, that this election is a true call from God; first, because
it was held canonically, having all the requisite conditions. It was
held in presence of the Superior, with the mutual consent of the
Community, your Superioress, and the Superioress of your dear
house here, which, before it consented, was entreated several times

---

[3]François Rivet, born in Houdan (Yvelines) on July 28, 1628, entered the Congregation of
the Mission on October 12, 1647, took his vows on November 6, 1650, and was ordained a priest
on April 1, 1656.

Letter 1114. - Reg. 1, f° 6, copy made from the autograph draft.

[1]The name of the recipient can be deduced from the contents. This letter was written to a
professed Visitation nun of one of the monasteries of Paris, after the death of Saint Jane Frances
de Chantal. Of the four Sisters who became Superioresses at the regular elections between 1641
and 1660, Mother Jeanne-Marguerite Chahu is the only one whom Paris lent to Meaux.

She was received into the First Monastery of the Visitation in 1621 and left it in 1627 to make
a foundation in Dol (Brittany), which was transferred to Caen in 1631. A vote of the Sisters in
Riom took her from the monastery in Caen a year after the completion of her second three-year
term of office. She was Superioress in Riom (1636-1642), Dijon (1642-1648), Meaux (1649-
1652), and Caen (1653-1659). After leaving Dijon, she spent six months at the Conception
Convent, rue Saint-Honoré, in Paris, with the mission to establish the reform there. She died on
January 27, 1660, at sixty-three years of age. (Cf. *Année sainte*, pp. 785-802.)

[2]Mother Chahu was elected Superioress of the monastery in Meaux on May 20, 1649.

to let them have you. You are free and not needed where you now are, as you have told us several times. All of this is in conformity with the holy Council of Trent, the recommendations of our blessed Mother de Chantal, and with the customs. Furthermore, I have never heard that any member of your holy Order refused to obey God in similar circumstances, although several have raised objections at first, and this caused our blessed Mother to say, in her answer to those who might raise similar objections, what she states in Constitution 47, *On the election of Superioresses,* at the bottom of page 647. To be sure, dear Sister, it is not so much our blessed Mother who says that but the Holy Spirit, who states in the ninth session, Canon 7, that if no Sister in the same monastery can be found with the qualities requisite for a canonical election, another member of the same Order may be elected. In the name of God, my dear [Mother],[3] allow me to ask you how you will answer God, at the moment of death when you go to render an account to Him, if He asks you why you did not obey your holy Book of Customs, the recommendations of our blessed Mother, the unchanging traditions of the Order, and, what is more, the Holy Spirit Himself, who speaks to you through the mouth of the holy Council. If you say you were not consulted before consenting to have your name put on the list, you have me to blame. I took no notice of that, never having heard that it was customary to ask such permissions of the Sisters involved. But my lack of politeness, if there is any, dear Sister, will not excuse you before God. If you tell me that your dear monastery needs you, my reply, dear Sister, is that it is true that in her answers our blessed Mother wanted the Superioress of the Sisters to take that into consideration, but I have seen from the letters you wrote me this past year that your dear Sisters could get along without you. Some of your recent letters say the same thing.

For all these reasons, dear Mother, I ask you to make this the subject of your retreat in order to obtain from the Divine Majesty

---

[3] A word omitted by the copyist.

the courage to obey Him on this occasion, or at least please make an hour's mental prayer on this subject, spending an hour on the following points: (1) the reasons you have for doing on this occasion what you would wish to have done at the hour of death; (2) to learn if there is any reason to doubt that God's Will lies in what is set down for you in your holy Book of Customs, recommended by our blessed Mother and confirmed by the traditions of your holy Order and the holy Council of Trent; (3) before God to look into the depths of your soul and see whether you have any other motives than that of [obeying]⁴ your own feelings rather than God. In that case, dear Sister, I beg you to overcome your feelings and to give God the glory that a true daughter of Sainte-Marie is bound to give him in these circumstances. My hope is that you will do so and that I shall have the constant determination to be, all my life, in the love of Our Lord . . . .

You say in your last letter, dear Sister, that you are ready to leave but that the peasants there are preventing you from doing so. In the name of God, dear Mother, exert yourself and do not tolerate this pretext of disobedience to your holy Order. The Bishop is too good to stand in your way; M. Duvergier is too reasonable not to give his consent and, lastly, even if the city gates should be closed against you, the Governor and his wife will be discreet enough to have them opened for you. Our blessed Mother disapproved of these practices and used herself as an example, saying that even if Superiors of houses where she might be sent should lock her up in a tower, she would find, with God's help, a means of escape in order to obey her superior.

---

⁴A word omitted by the copyist.

1115. - TO BERNARD CODOING, SUPERIOR, IN RICHELIEU

June 30, 1649

When I was in Richelieu I forgot to leave you in writing the topics you should discuss during recreation. I just remembered this and am enclosing the list. The best way of using it is for the Superior or whoever represents him in his absence, such as the Assistant or the oldest member, to propose a difficulty and for each one to give frankly and simply his opinion on the subject, without responding to what the others have said. Then, the person who proposed the question may give his opinion and draw the conclusion according to a majority vote. We readily did that here formerly and it was most helpful.

I do not know whether I asked you to assign someone to accompany M. . . when he goes to see the nuns. In case you have not done so, please do it and do not allow anyone whomsoever to leave the house without a member of the Company as companion, not so much because of the danger as for the sake of example.

1116. - TO LOUIS THIBAULT, SUPERIOR, IN SAINT-MEEN

Paris, July 3, 1649

Monsieur,

I have been back for about two or three weeks but am still having a hard time getting my bearings and finding the time to write to you. I am doing so, nevertheless, to respond to the letter you wrote to M. Lambert.

Letter 1115. - Reg. 2, p. 263.

Letter 1116. - Original signed letter, Congregation of the Mission, Toulouse; Archives of the Mission, Paris, photocopy.

We are going to let you have a priest and a seminarian. If they are not exactly what you want, at least they are the most suitable men we have. They will leave in a week or two. When they arrive at your house, please send Messrs. Beaure[1] and Le Blanc[2] back to us, and Brother Joseph along with them, if you have enough Brothers without him.

As for [Brother] Pascal,[3] I strongly hope that you find him satisfactory, or that you will bear with him for a while and try to get him to settle down to his duty. If, in the end, he is incorrigible, he will have to be dismissed.

I told Mademoiselle Le Gras how distressed you are about that girl she dismissed. She will in future follow your advice and write to the parents of those who are not suitable, before they leave. Although she did not do so for this girl, she hopes you will put right her mistake and gradually calm her brother down. To tell the truth, she is a fine girl but lacks common sense in certain things, and this is a great handicap for Sisters who have dealings with their neighbor. That is why good Mademoiselle was obliged to have her leave. This, Monsieur, will not prevent those who are postulating from being received whenever you think it is time and can assure us of their good qualities.

I am filled with gratitude to God's Goodness for the strength He gives you after so much work, for the graces He is bestowing on your Community, and for His blessings on your missions. I thank Him for this with all my heart, imploring Him to continue them and to sanctify all of you more and more.

My most affectionate greetings and salutations to Messrs. Serre,

---

[1]Coste had written "Bureau;" according to Fr. Raymond Chalumeau, C.M., former Archivist at Saint-Lazare, this is a copying error and should be "Beaure". Jean Beaure, born in August 1609 in Englesqueville (Calvados), entered the Congregation of the Mission as a priest on October 7, 1639.

[2]Georges Le Blanc (George White).

[3]Jean-Pascal Goret.

de Beaumont, Le Blanc,[4] Turbot,[5] and the others, and most tenderly to you, Monsieur. I am, in the love of Our Lord, your most humble and obedient servant.

VINCENT DEPAUL
i.s.C.M.

Now that I think of it, it will be difficult to send you a priest and, in that case, we shall send you two Brothers. I shall be consoled to hear the number of persons in your two seminaries.[6]

1117. - TO HUGUES PERRAUD, IN RICHELIEU

July 4, 1649

I am pleased to know that you are preparing for your journey to take the waters. God grant that they may be beneficial to you and that He Himself may be your strength in your coming, your going, and your good use of the difficulties His Providence may place on your path. Fine! Go then, Monsieur, not to try to recover your health but to accomplish God's Will, and come back just as content to be ailing as if you were cured, in the hope that Our Lord will be no less glorified by this.

---

[4]According to Fr. Chalumeau, C.M., his name should be "Le Boysne." Léonard Le Boysne, born in La Chapelle-Janson (Ille-et-Vilaine), was received at Saint-Lazare on May 6, 1638. He was sent to Luçon and then to Richelieu. In September 1645 he went to Saint-Méen, where he died on February 25, 1670. As a priest, he was very edifying; Father Alméras, Superior General, praised him highly in his circular of March 13, 1670: "We have just lost a hidden treasure of grace and holiness. . . . He excelled in piety, meekness, mortification, regularity, obedience, and good example, but especially in humility and charity. I consider myself fortunate to have made my seminary with him. . . . He was a very virtuous Missionary and one of the most talented in the Company." His biographical sketch is extant in the Lyons manuscript, pp. 234-237.

[5]Jean Turbot, born in Beaumesnil (Eure), entered the Congregation of the Mission on March 8, 1644, at twenty-three years of age, took vows in July 1646, and was ordained a priest in March 1648.

[6]The last paragraph is in Saint Vincent's handwriting.

Letter 1117. - Reg. 2, p. 298.

I do not know why you are afraid that the Superior will not give you, within reason, whatever you need. He would not want you to go begging, although neither does he want to deprive you of the opportunity of honoring the poverty of Our Lord in your expenditures. Let us truly belong to God, Monsieur; He will be ours entirely, and in Him we shall have all things.

1118. - TO A PRIEST OF THE MISSION, IN GENOA[1]

You are fortunate, Monsieur, to be so busy with your duty and, consequently, to be doing God's Will that you have no time to think of yourself. He thinks about you enough and looks after the affairs of your soul while you look after those of your vocation, in which I ask Him to bless you more and more.

1119. - TO RENE ALMERAS, SUPERIOR, IN ROME

July 9, 1649

Please, Monsieur, let us consider as of no account the present difficulties of your work. What does not get done at one time gets done at another, particularly in Rome. You may ease up in your efforts but do not discontinue them.

I see clearly that nothing more is to be expected regarding the house you had in mind. Look elsewhere, and if another opportunity presents itself, do not lose it, but neither should you be too hasty in trying to find one. What surprises me more, Monsieur, is that those good Fathers,[1] who formerly wanted to be incorporated with us,

---

Letter 1118. - Reg. 2, p. 350.
[1]There is no proof of accuracy for the date of February 5, 1649 given in *Recueil des Exhortations et Lettres de Saint Vincent,* part II, p. 132; in fact, it even seems most improbable.

Letter 1119. - Reg. 2, p. 230.
[1]The priests of the Congregation founded by Authier de Sisgau.

have thwarted your plans. I can hardly believe it, but even if it were true, we must not lessen in any way the respect and service we owe the great servants of God, which they are. As far as you can show them esteem and affection, please do so.

1120. - TO ETIENNE BLATIRON, SUPERIOR, IN GENOA

July 9, 1649

There is no remedy, Monsieur; so now, you are ill, and you are ill outside of Genoa, far from any help in a place where illnesses are serious and dangerous because of the foul air, as you yourself have written me. Blessed be God! However, you have been hiding your illness from me and, if M. Martin had not informed me about it, my only fear would be to learn that you are in danger. But God did not want me to be without distress while He keeps you suffering, and the holy union of our hearts did not permit it.

After receiving this news I presented your sufferings and mine to God, asking Him, for you and for me, acquiescence to His good pleasure. Lastly, I asked Him for your good health, if it is for His greater glory, or else a perfect use of His visitation. I have also asked the Company, with all the affection I could, to pray for you, and I think everyone has done his duty well before God, who knows how dear you are to us all and how consoled we shall be if He sees fit to preserve you.

1121. - *ALAIN DE SOLMINIHAC TO SAINT VINCENT*

Mercuès, July 9, 1649

Monsieur,

Having learned from M. Cuissot that you were now in Paris, I did not want to delay writing to you, and would have done it long ago, if opportunities had arisen, but the disturbances,[1] which have troubled the State in recent times, deprived me of them. I daresay that, if I have not had the joy of communicating with you by letter, I did not fail to do so in spirit. True, when I heard that you had gone to the country to visit our houses, I feared that your poor health might suffer from this season and the severe weather we have had this winter. Blessed be God for having preserved you for His service!

Our two deputies from Chancelade [2] filled me with joy and consolation on their arrival here, when they told me you had said in Richelieu that you would do us the favor of visiting your house in Cahors. I could not express the joy and consolation this news gave me. I was planning to keep you here a while, where we have some of the best air in the kingdom, to restore you to perfect health, and to discuss many things with you. Blessed be our Good Master, who has deprived us of this consolation! I also thought you would have been consoled to see our seminary, where you would have found thirty-five seminarians who would have given you satisfaction. Your men who have seen it say that it is the finest in the kingdom, and someone recently told me that good order is observed there even better than in Paris. M. Cuissot is doing his job well; it is important that you leave him there.

I think he must have told you that the Grand Archdeacon of my church has willed to our seminary a small holding, one league from Cahors. It is one of the most beautiful spots in the area and has a detached building, quite fit for habitation and furnished with everything necessary.[3] This

---

Letter 1121. - Archives of the Diocese of Cahors, Alain de Solminihac collection, notebook, a copy made from the original.

[1]The Fronde, an upheaval (1648-1652) against Mazarin during the minority of Louis XIV. It was brought on by the unpopularity of the Cardinal and his financial demands, and by the desire of the nobility to dominate the monarchy, similar to the English nobility. The revolt was finally checked, and the monarchy emerged from this period greatly strengthened.

[2]Fathers Vitet and Parrot.

[3]By his will of February 1, 1649, Claude-Antoine Hébrard of Saint-Sulpice, Grand Archdeacon of Cahors, had bequeathed to the seminary a farm in Cayran, near Cieurac.

property is easily worth eight thousand livres, and they are already in possession of it. True, they are obliged to educate a young man for the Church, etc.

ALAIN,
Bishop of Cahors

1122. - TO BERNARD CODOING, SUPERIOR, IN RICHELIEU

July 25, 1649

I am persisting in what I told you with regard to persons coming to and going from the house; namely, that it is good to keep to the custom of Our Lord when He used to send out His disciples two by two. While you have the internal seminary, it is easy for you to assign a companion to those who go out to the town or the environs; this will also be a diversion for the seminarians, who need it occasionally. Even if you did not have the seminary, the matter is sufficiently important for you to be given someone to serve expressly as a companion, as far as possible, or to do in the house what someone else would be doing at the time he accompanies people here and there. I am talking here about those who go on foot; for those who go further, on horseback, a servant can accompany them.

We should in no way be surprised at little misunderstandings that arise. The angels and the Apostles had their differences, and Our Lord permits this both inside and outside of Communities for a greater good, but it is up to us to avoid the painful consequences and to be reconciled as soon and as closely as possible. How would it be, Monsieur, if everyone approved of our way of acting in all things and if we never found fault with the conduct of others? God would have to change human nature. I know that those two men mean well and that close union among themselves will be main-

---

tained if they are willing, which I do not doubt, to concede something to the gentleness and forbearance recommended so highly by Our Lord.

1123. - *ALAIN DE SOLMINIHAC TO SAINT VINCENT*

Mercuès, July 28, 1649

Monsieur,

I wrote you a long letter in the last mail. This one is just to tell you that, since a priest with the requisite qualifications cannot be found in this area to be Director of the Ursuline Monastery in Cahors, and knowing how you never tire of working for the glory of God, I am turning to you to beg you, as I do by this letter, to find me someone capable of directing this monastery. I have such confidence in you that I believe you would not send me any other kind of person. Please work on this as soon as you can and, when you find someone, let me know the qualities you observe in him. . . . I would really like someone at least forty years old, who is experienced in the direction of nuns and is a man of prayer.

ALAIN,
Bishop of Cahors

1124. - TO FRANCOIS FOURNIER, SEMINARIAN, IN AGEN [1]

August 1, 1649

My dear Brother,

The grace of Our Lord be with you forever!
I am delighted to hear that you went to visit the Cahors Seminary

---

Letter 1123. - Archives of the Diocese of Cahors, Alain de Solminihac collection, notebook, a copy made from the original.

Letter 1124. - Italian manuscript of François Fournier's obituary. Archives of the Mission, Provincial House, Rome.

[1]François Fournier, born in Laval (Mayenne) on February 2, 1625, entered the Congregation

and that, edified by the good order you observed there, you have decided to have it established in the Agen Seminary, where you are. For that and for the sanctification of all your actions, I beg Our Lord to animate you with His Spirit. Seeing your heart so filled with enthusiasm and good intentions, I have conceived in my own a far greater esteem for you than I already had. So continue, dear Brother, to give yourself entirely to God to procure His glory and the salvation of your neighbor and to work for the poor people by forming good seminarians, who will be the light of the world and the dispensers of the treasures of heaven and earth.

For goodness sake, consider your obligations to God, who has elevated you to such a sublime work. Remember that the means for acting in a useful manner in your office are mistrust of self and confidence in the Lord, who, if He needed the help of men for the successful outcome of His plans, would have put in your place a Doctor and a saint.

1125. - TO ANTOINE PORTAIL, IN MARSEILLES

Paris, August 6, 1649

Monsieur,

The grace of Our Lord be with you forever!

I am writing to you more grieved than I have been in a long time. I just learned of our loss of good M. Brunet,[1] that fine worker of

---

of the Mission on August 12, 1644, took his vows on September 24, 1646, and was ordained a priest on September 25, 1650. He was professor of theology at the Agen Seminary (1649-1658) and in Cahors (1658-1663), Secretary General of the Congregation (1663-1677), and Assistant General from 1667 to April 4, 1677, the day he died. The life of Saint Vincent, commonly and correctly attributed to Abelly, was erroneously thought to have been written by Fournier. It is quite possible and even probable that, as Secretary General, he helped prepare the material, but that is the extent of his role. There is good reason to believe that Brother Ducournau contributed much more than he. (Cf. *Notices*, vol. I, pp. 247-267.)

Letter 1125. - Archives of the Mission, Turin, original signed letter.
[1]For details of his death see the following letter.

the Lord, that great friend of the poor and light of the Company. Ah well! since it is God who has taken him from us, we must adore His way of acting and remain at peace. What has increased my sorrow is the fear that the Company there may be in danger from the contagion or even suffering from it, God forbid.[2] The help we can give you, Monsieur, in these trying circumstances is to ask His Divine Goodness, as I do and as we all do, to be your light and your strength. We cannot offer you any advice since we do not know your present state or the progress of the disease since it began. Also, before you receive this letter, I hope you will have everything under control, not only for the preservation of the Company but also at the hospital and in the other works. If the galleys have left the port of Marseilles, as we have been told, it is easy to look after the rest, with God's grace. I recommend you once again to Him that He Himself may be your consolation and that of the whole Community.

The Duchesse d'Aiguillon is supposed to be sending you five hundred livres, of which four hundred are for Masses celebrated or to be celebrated, according to the instructions you have already received, and one hundred for other Masses she is requesting for the soul of the late M. de la Coste.[3] If you need more money, let

---

[2] In 1649 the plague, brought to Marseilles by ships from Algiers and the Levant, and lasting until the beginning of 1650, claimed more than eight thousand victims there, but only one Priest of the Mission.

[3] He died on July 24. As soon as he fell ill, M. de la Coste put his conscience as well as his business affairs in order. He found the strength to dictate his will, in which we read the following: "I bequeath to the house of the Priests of Mission of France . . . the sum of sixteen thousand livres . . . that the income may be used annually and perpetually by the above-named Priests of the Mission of France for the upkeep of the seminary they wish to establish for the instruction of the clergy in all matters pertaining to the perfection of their state. . . . If the above-mentioned seminary is not fully established at the time of my death, they shall use . . . the income from these sixteen thousand livres, partly to give missions and remedy the most urgent needs they find in this area, and partly for the maintenance of the seminarians who will accede to Holy Orders at each ordination." (Cf. M. de Ruffi, *Vie de M. le chevalier de la Coste* [Aix: David, 1659], pp. 198-199.)

me know; we shall send some immediately and, if need be, we shall sell our crosses and chalices to assist you.

I think you must have already left for Annecy, along with M. Chrétien, in conformity with what I told you, and have left M. Le Soudier [4] in charge, unless some particular reason caused you to act otherwise. In the event that you are still in Marseilles and can get away, I ask you to do so and to take care of the above. I am writing to you in Annecy by this same mail so that you will have news of me, wherever you are. May God give us more news of you soon, and may it be as good as I am hoping for!

I was going to finish without even mentioning the thought that came to me about good M. de la Coste, whom God has taken. I cannot speak of him without inexpressible sentiments of esteem and reverence because of his piety, zeal, and the many heavenly graces with which he was filled. Oh! how fortunate he is and how astonished I should be to see the loss of these two great servants of God while I, who am so useless, am still in this world! And indeed, I even have reason to fear that my sins may be the cause of this tribulation. Please, Monsieur, ask for mercy for me. I am, in the love of Our Lord, Monsieur, your most humble servant.

VINCENT DEPAUL
i.s.C.M.

Ask M. Le Soudier to send us a notarized power of attorney, in conformity with the statement I am sending you.

Brother Alexandre [5] requests that you bring him one or two

---

4 Jacques Le Soudier.
5 Alexandre Véronne.

pounds of scorpion oil,[6] and Brother Jean Besson[7] is asking you for something else. If you, or whoever reads this letter in your absence, can do both things, please do so.

Addressed: Monsieur Portail or, in his absence, the Superior of the Mission of Marseilles, in Marseilles

1126. - TO ETIENNE BLATIRON, SUPERIOR, IN GENOA[1]

[Around August 6, 1649][2]

We are deeply grieved by a considerable loss the Company has just suffered in the person of Monsieur Brunet, about whom you wrote me such good things. Indeed, too much good can never be said of him. God took him to Himself on July 24 and, along with him, the Chevalier de la Coste, a great servant of God. He was responsible for the hospital for convicts in Marseilles and was, as it were, its founder and patron. This is how it happened. A ship with the plague aboard had come in from Algiers and was quarantined in the roadstead. During this time all the sailors died, and their belongings and the rigging were thrown into the sea. Some fishermen came across a mattress that was afloat; they took it, dried it out, used it, and died of the plague. Then their neighbors caught it. Monsieur Brunet went to hear their confessions and as soon as they

---

[6]Fable has it that scorpions carry with them an oil which is a remedy against their stings. The oil was extracted from the flesh and given to the sufferer as a medicine; it was supposed to be very useful to bring away the descending stone of the kidneys. Cf. *Brewer's Dictionary of Phrase and Fable,* Harper, 1981.

[7]Jean Besson, a coadjutor Brother, who was born in Carisey (Yonne) on November 30, 1611, entered the Congregation of the Mission on December 8, 1635, and took his vows on October 21, 1646.

Letter 1126. - Lyons manuscript.

[1]The Lyons manuscript does not give the name of the recipient. The words, "Monsieur Brunet, about whom you wrote me such good things," clearly indicate that it is Etienne Blatiron, whom Jean Brunet had just left to go to Marseilles.

[2]If this letter was not written on the same day as no. 1125, it followed it very closely.

received absolution they died in his presence. He went to the hospital to dine with Monsieur de la Coste and told him what he had just done; immediately the disease struck both of them. It was the feast of Saint Mary Magdalene, and both of them died two or three days later, almost at the same time.³ O Monsieur, what a loss for us, for the hospital, and for the whole city! But then, it is God who called them; may His Holy Name be blessed!

1127. - TO A PRIEST OF THE MISSION

[Around August 6, 1649]¹

Before I reply to your letter, allow me to convey to your heart the bitter sorrow of mine. We have just lost in Marseilles good Monsieur Brunet who, after assisting at the death of some plague-stricken persons on the feast of Saint Mary Magdalene, caught the disease himself and died of it two days later. The sad news was sent to the Duchesse d'Aiguillon by an express messenger. What adds to our grief is the uncertainty about the state of that poor Community, which is suffering in the midst of the common affliction and is more exposed to danger than the rest of the people, who are escaping or keeping out of the way as best they can.

---

³There are a few discrepancies in the details of this letter and in the account given by Ruffi, *op. cit.*, pp. 185-186. Ruffi wrote that on July 19 "M. Brunet, . . . who lived at the hospital . . . was requested to go to the islands to hear the confessions of some persons who were in quarantine." He "went there, . . . and on his return . . . also heard the confession of a poor woman, who died as soon as she had received absolution. Hardly had he performed this duty, than he was seized with a fever so violent that he barely made it back to the hospital. M. de la Coste personally took him to his room." Ruffi added that M. de la Coste, with no regard for the risk he was running, nursed Jean Brunet and caught the plague at his bedside.

Letter 1127. - Lyons manuscript.
¹This letter must have been written shortly after no. 1125.

1128 - SAINT LOUISE TO SAINT VINCENT

Saturday, [August, 1649] [1]

Monsieur,

The suggestion made by the Duchess to have the children fed on goat's milk has made me think of another solution; if it works, we could feed them for an écu. But we would have to try it out before proposing it, then give it to them whenever your charity wishes. I will tell you how but it would be too long to put it in writing.

I most humbly entreat you, Most Honored Father, to remember the request I made you yesterday [2] and kindly let me know if your charity is granting Sister Françoise,[3] the gardener, what she asked of you yesterday. Also, please offer to God at the holy altar the renewal of several other Sisters and give us your holy blessing. I am, Most Honored Father, your most obedient and very grateful daughter and servant.

L. DE M.

1129. - SAINT LOUISE TO SAINT VINCENT

[August, 1649] [1]

Monsieur,

Since writing the enclosed letter,[2] I thought it better to address it to your

---

Letter 1128. - Original autograph letter at the hospital in Evreux (Eure).

[1]Date added on the back of the original by Brother Ducournau.

[2]Sister Françoise had requested permission to take vows.

[3]Sister Françoise Fanchon, born on June 25, 1625 in Conche-les-Pots (Picardy), entered the Daughters of Charity on August 9, 1644. She remained at the Motherhouse, where she became first the gardener then the cook. She took her vows in 1649. Not knowing how to write, she signed with a cross the Act of Erection of the Company in 1655. Later she became Sister Servant in Saint-Médard parish. She died on May 12, 1689.

Letter 1129. - Archives of the Motherhouse of the Daughters of Charity, original autograph letter.

[1]Date added on the back of the original by Brother Ducournau.

[2]Letter of Saint Louise to Sister Julienne Loret, which she had asked Saint Vincent to deliver. (Cf. *Ecrits spirituels*, L. 256, p. 297.)

charity because this business needs to be settled promptly. For this reason I am sending you the letter for Sister Julienne, who will explain everything to you. Monsieur Lambert knows about it; all the trouble has arisen because of attachment to confessors. We really have to reflect on what could be done to avoid these unfortunate incidents.

I am very sorry to cause you so much anxiety by my poor leadership. Will your charity please recall that I already spoke to you about that poor young Sister,[3] and you suggested sending her home. However, she is determined not to go back, and the advice Renée gave her is to allow herself to be put in the coach and to get off shortly after they leave her. These are bold persons, capable of doing great harm; that is why they are to be pitied. My thought is that this misfortune befalls them because they have the audacity to receive the sacraments with such bad dispositions. May God have mercy on us and grant me the grace of being always, my very dear Father, your most obedient servant and grateful daughter.

L. DE MARILLAC

Addressed: *Monsieur Vincent*

1130. - SAINT LOUISE TO SAINT VINCENT

August 30, [1649][1]

Monsieur and Most Honored Father,

I suspected that I needed to come to this place,[2] but I cannot give you an account until I have the honor of seeing you. Monsieur de la Hode, chaplain in Chantilly,[3] came to see me to give me some advice. Apparently the whole family is being attacked from all sides. I do not know what our good God is telling us by this. I most humbly entreat your charity kindly

---

[3]Sister Anne-Marie. Saint Louise's letter to Sister Julienne speaks of Sister Anne-Marie's scandalous conduct.

Letter 1130. - Archives of the Motherhouse of the Daughters of Charity, original autograph letter.
 [1]Year added on the back of the original by Brother Ducournau.
 [2]Liancourt, where Saint Louise had arrived on Saturday, August 28.
 [3]The Daughters of Charity had been there for two or three years.

to let me know if I should stop in Chantilly because of the situation; I think it might be necessary.

I heard that Madame de Romilly⁴ has learned that the family of Monsieur Portier, who lives across from Saint Paul's, is all we could want it to be.⁵ She is supposed to speak to you on their behalf. I most humbly beg you, my very dear Father, not to mention the estate to her unless she mentions it to you, because the people who discussed this with my son told him that the parents are satisfied with the property. Under such circumstances it is better not to declare too openly what one has because that can be prejudicial if things do not materialize.

Hopes for the future, for property as well as employment, are quite good. Not that I intend or wish to deceive anyone—God forbid—but it seems to me that in the past the expense of preparing a man for a post was considerable. Then there is his intention not to squander what he has but to work to acquire more. This is what I strongly hope he will do, once he is settled. I most humbly entreat your charity to commend this matter and all the needs of our Company to our good God, to draw his graces and blessings upon it. I ask you to give me your blessing for love of Him, in whom I am, Most Honored Father, your most obedient servant and very grateful daughter.

L. DE MARILLAC

Addressed: *Monsieur Vincent*

1131. - TO N***

August 31, 1649

In this letter Vincent de Paul speaks of reparation to be made because of the desecration of some hosts by troops in the areas surrounding Paris.¹

---

⁴Louise Goulas, wife of Pierre Sublet, Seigneur de Romilly. She was a Lady of Charity who devoted herself to the foundlings in a very special way.

⁵There was question of a marriage plan for Michel Le Gras, but negotiations were unsuccessful.

Letter 1131. - Collet, *op. cit.,* vol. I, p. 479.

¹During the blockade of Paris, sacrilege and profanations were quite frequent in the environs of the capital. Unruly soldiers had broken into churches, stolen vestments, smashed the

1132. - TO SAINT LOUISE, IN LIANCOURT

Paris, September 2, [1649][1]

Mademoiselle,

The grace of Our Lord be with you forever!

You are a little too sensitive about the departure of your Sisters. In the name of God, Mademoiselle, work at acquiring the grace of acceptance in such situations. Purging the Company in this way is an act of mercy Our Lord is granting it and will be one of the first things Our Lord will let you see in heaven. Meanwhile, you have the assurance that not one of those whom Our Lord has called to the Company will abandon her vocation. Why worry about the others? True, Renée and Mathurine have left, and apparently Anne-Marie will not stay much longer. Let her go; you will not lack Sisters. M. Thibault writes that he has three or four ready to go, if we want him to send them. I told him we would decide that on your return and you might pass through Chantilly on your way home; so please do so.

We had a general meeting yesterday; I have never seen the Ladies so enthusiastic about this good work.

Madame de Romilly mentioned to me the matter of which you are cognizant. She says that fifteen thousand livres will be given to that good girl, and she can expect the same amount after the death of her father and mother. I gave her the particulars of the bailiff's[2] estate in presence of Madame d'Aiguillon[3] who, like you, thought

---

tabernacles, and carried off ciboria containing hosts. Limeil, Croissy, Férolles, Villabé, Antony, and Châtillon-sur-Marne were especially victimized. The Company of the Blessed Sacrament reacted, ordered an investigation, and urged its members and even the public to make amends to Our Lord. Missionaries, sponsored by the above-mentioned Company, were sent to places that had been most severely ravaged by the soldiers. (Cf. René Voyer d'Argenson, *Annales de la Compagnie du Saint-Sacrement*, ed. Blauchet-Filleau [Marseilles: Léon, 1900], pp. 106ff.)

Letter 1132. - Original autograph letter, property of the Daughters of Charity, 20 rue Mage, Toulouse.

[1]Saint Vincent is answering letters 1129 and 1130; the year, therefore, is 1649.

[2]Michel Le Gras, Bailiff of Saint-Lazare.

[3]The Duchesse d'Aiguillon.

that only the broad outlines of things should be given. This good lady was responsible for making enquiries on the girl's behalf about the person and his estate. I saw Father Delahaie afterward and entrusted the affair to him; he on his part is supposed to inform me about it.

That, Mademoiselle, is all I can tell you at present, so it seems to me, except that I ask you once again to thank God for purging your Little Company in this way. I ask Our Lord to bless it, and I am, in His love, Mademoiselle, your most humble servant.

VINCENT DEPAUL
i.s.C.M.

Addressed: Mademoiselle Le Gras, in Liancourt

1133. - TO MONSIEUR DES VERGNES, IN PERIGUEUX

Paris, September 4, 1649

Monsieur,

The grace of Our Lord be with you forever!

I received your packet[1] with the respect and joy I owe both to your person and to the reasons for consolation it contains. You can well imagine, Monsieur, how gladly I have thanked God for the graces He is granting to the Bishop of Périgueux[2] and for the remarkable service he in turn is rendering to His Divine Majesty. I am much obliged to you, Monsieur, for sending me the enactments of his synod. I have found them worthy of their author and a great presage of blessings on his diocese. His incomparable piety

---

Letter 1133. - This original signed letter was most recently the property of the Augustinian Sisters of the Assumption, Paris.
[1]The first redaction had "letter."
[2]Philibert de Brandon (1648-1652).

and zeal have always led us to hope for such actions. May God preserve him for the Church for an entire century!

I make no reply, Monsieur, to the congratulations you offer me in his regard, except that I do not in any way deserve them. It is quite apparent that his calling is purely from God and is not the work of men.

I did not delay long in sending the journalist your note on the conversion of the nobleman, of which you are aware. May God be pleased to bless more and more the works of that great Bishop so that they may bear similar fruits!

You know, Monsieur, that we are all devoted to the service of the bishops. If the Bishop of Périgueux orders us to take charge of his seminary, we shall send him some of the best men we have, whenever he wishes. If you think it advisable to assure him of this, please do so—I mean in the event that he wishes it, but not otherwise. It is to be hoped that such questions will be resolved solely by the inspiration of God rather than by human persuasion.

I beg Our Lord to make us worthy of the honor of your benevolence and make me worthy of the honor I have of being, in the love of Our Lord, Monsieur, your most humble and obedient servant.

VINCENT DEPAUL
i.s.C.M.

In the event that His Excellency does wish to make use of us, would he kindly inform us two months before the establishment so that we may prepare as many workers as he desires.

Addressed: Monsieur des Vergnes, Officialis of Cahors, presently at the residence of the Bishop of Périgueux

1134. - TO BROTHER JACQUES RIVET

September 5, 1649

I have received your letter with consolation on the one hand because it was your letter, and with distress on the other because there is good reason to fear that you may succumb to the allurements enticing you to abandon your vocation. Seeing you in this danger, I am bound to extend a hand to extricate you from it, as I do by my prayers and letters. I have already written you twice,[1] and this is the third time, that you should return to La Rose or Agen.

I asked the Bishop of Condom[2] if this was agreeable to him and he consented to it, once his major-domo had returned. Now, I know he is back with him at present and you, Brother, are not in your own house. Why is that? Do you not remember the lights God has so often given you in your prayer, causing you to take the resolution before His Divine Majesty and to testify publicly to the whole Company that you would rather die than leave it? And now, on the slightest pretext, when it is a question of neither death, nor blood, nor threats, you are surrendering without the resistance merited by such a promise made to God, who is constant and jealous of His honor, and who wishes to be served as He wills. He has called you to the Company; you have no doubt of that. He has even preserved you in it despite the efforts of your own father, who wanted to have you near him; and you preferred to follow the Gospel rather than please him.

You have lived among us in such an edifying manner that Our Lord has always been honored in your person. Do you want to go back on your word to Him now, misuse His grace, make light of His goodness, and fall into the regrets into which others have fallen through disorderly living? I have never seen anyone, to whom God has granted the grace that you have received from His goodness, leave any Community without having his conscience bothered a month later by the reproaches of God, and his life by a thousand vexations.

"But," you will tell me, "I intend to please God always." Alas! fine pretexts are never lacking, and if you examine yourself carefully, you will discover that it is not to make yourself better, more submissive, more detached from the world and your comforts, more humble, more mortified, and more clearly united to your neighbor by charity, as you should be in order to become more pleasing to God. Nevertheless, dear Brother, you think you are serving Him and working out your salvation by departing from the way of perfection; this is an illusion. If you had not already entered on the way of the perfect, fine; but Saint Paul says that if those who have once been enlightened and have savored the Word of God fall back, it will be very difficult for them to be renewed by repentance.[3] How can you be convinced that you can preserve yourself by returning to the world, since you have such a hard time overcoming yourself when you are not in it? I am not calling the house of the Bishop of Condom the world, but you would not be far from it, and perhaps you would not be long getting there.

God allows us to go from bad to worse when we leave the state in which He has placed us. One day the late Queen Mother [4] ordered Cardinal de Bérulle to send back to her a page who had entered the Oratorians. This holy man replied that he could not take from God a young man who had given himself to Him and that he did not want to be responsible for his salvation. I have used this example with regard to the Bishop of Condom so that he will excuse me if I cannot consent to your leaving. No, dear Brother, I cannot consent to this for the simple reason that it is not God's Will, and your dear soul would be at risk in it. If you believe the contrary, at least leave only by the same door through which you entered the Company. That door is a spiritual retreat, which I ask you to make

---

[3]Cf. Heb 6:4-6. (NAB)
[4]Marie de Médicis, mother of Louis XIII. She died on July 3, 1642.

before deciding on such a major separation. If you do not want to
go to the La Rose house nor to Agen, then go to Richelieu; you will
be welcome everywhere. The goodness of your heart has won all
the affection of mine, and this affection has no other aim than the
glory of God and your sanctification. I know you believe this to be
true, and you also believe that I am in Our Lord . . . .

1135. - TO THE SUPERIORESS OF THE SECOND MONASTERY OF THE VISITATION, IN PARIS

Saint Lazare, Feast of the Nativity of the Blessed Virgin[1]

I request our dear Mother Superior of the Visitation Sainte-
Marie in the faubourg Saint-Jacques to permit a single entry into
her monastery to Reverend Mothers de Saint-Jean and de Saint-
Joseph of the Montmartre Abbey.

VINCENT DEPAUL
i.s.C.M.

1136. - TO RENE ALMERAS, IN ROME

Paris, September 11, 1649

Monsieur,

The grace of Our Lord be with you forever!
You have good reason to protest as you do, seeing the services
of M. Ferentilli[1] so little acknowledged in France, but the C[ardi-

Letter 1135. - Original autograph letter, property of the Daughters of Charity, rue des Bourdonnais, Versailles.
[1]September 8.

Letter 1136. - Archives of the Mission, Turin, original signed letter.
[1]A Roman Bishop very devoted to Saint Vincent and his Congregation.

nal][2] should be somewhat excused because of the difficulties the troubles[3] have caused him, as well as those he has to face for the reasons I have written you. This is certainly not for lack of good will. I have always found that he has a great deal of it for that good Prelate, but he is powerless to express it to him.

M. de La Haye-Aubert's dispensation for the Aumale vicariate will be sealed on the first day the seals are done, I hope. I will let you know what it will cost.

We are patiently awaiting the Pope's blessed reply, and we believe in faith that God's Will will be made known to us in it; therefore, we shall conform ourselves to it without question, with the help of His grace. I am delighted that you are opposed to giving money for the success of this affair [4] and that you want to leave the outcome to Providence alone.

Mon Dieu! Monsieur, how ardently I desire that the Company be firmly established on this maxim, which is founded on faith! I only wrote you that crooked proposition to tell you that it had been suggested to me by C[ardinal] Gr[imaldi], and I assure you once again that I am most edified that you are rejecting it.

I am even more so by the Stations you made at the seven churches because of the dishonor to the Blessed Sacrament here, and I thank you for this.[5]

M. Duiguin, who was in Ireland, has been here for a few days; he left Brother Patriarche in Saint-Méen. The latter has not yet recovered from his mental illness, which is why M. Brin sent them back to us, even though he is much better. I have been told that this good Brother greatly edifies the Company in his present state because he is so cordial, gracious, active, and totally given to God. We have just lost another man very much like that, who died here

---

[2]Jules Cardinal Mazarin.
[3]The Fronde.
[4]Probably the question of the vows. The vows of poverty, chastity, obedience, and stability were optional for the members of the Congregation of the Mission. Saint Vincent was working toward making them obligatory for all those who would subsequently enter the Company. Six years were to elapse before his desire was accomplished.
[5]Cf. no. 1131, n. 1.

in this house only three or four days ago, eighteen or twenty months after being received. The whole Community regrets his loss; I am still grieved by it, although in this as in all else I adore the ways of God with my whole heart. This good boy's name was Simon, and he came from Le Mans.[6] Please pray and have others pray for his soul and for mine also. I am, in the love of Our Lord, Monsieur, your most humble servant.

VINCENT DEPAUL
i.s.C.M.

Addressed: Monsieur Alméras, Superior of the Priests of the Mission of Rome, in Rome

1137. - TO A PRIEST OF THE MISSION, IN ROME

[1649][1]

The Congregation is growing in numbers and virtue, by God's mercy, as was apparent to me during the visitations and as everyone recognizes. Only I, wretch that I am, still go on burdening myself with new evil-doing and abominations. O Monsieur, how merciful God is to bear with me so patiently and for so long, and how weak and miserable I am to make such poor use of His mercy! I beg you, Monsieur, to offer me frequently to His Divine Majesty.

---

[6]Simon Busson, born in the town and diocese of Le Mans, entered the Congregation of the Mission as a coadjutor Brother during Lent of 1648, when he was about twenty-two years of age. He died on September 6 or 7, 1649.

Based on the date of this letter to René Alméras, Coste (cf. vol. XI, no. 106, p. 153) corrected the errors in *Notices,* vol. II, pp. 431-438, and the citation in *Notices,* vol. V, p. 102.

Letter 1137. - Abelly, *op.cit.,* second ed., part 2, p. 146.
[1] This date is called for by the Saint's mention of the visitations he had just made.

1138. - TO ETIENNE BLATIRON, SUPERIOR, IN GENOA

September 17, 1649

If you are finally being housed other than in rented rooms, there is good reason to believe that this is due to the powerful hand of God and His special goodness; for who could overcome so many great difficulties without Him? And who, without a special grace from heaven, could persevere constantly in this undertaking as your incomparable founders are doing? If, after so much effort and prayer, the matter is not successful, it will be a clear sign that God does not will it. Therefore, Monsieur, let us await its outcome with great indifference.

I admit that it is difficult for our Brothers to keep their temper when they are so overworked; we have some elsewhere who do little and complain a great deal, and who try the patience of their superiors. I praise God for the patience you have practiced toward your men, particularly with Brother . . . , when you overlooked his outburst. I am sure he recognized his fault, for forbearance brings that about better than reproofs which, nevertheless, must be given at the appropriate time and with the prudence God has given you. *O Dieu!* Monsieur, how necessary forbearance is for everyone and all things in general, and how gladly I thank God for the forbearance he has given you! Please ask Him for it for me, as much as is needed to merit the forbearance I have caused Him to practice during the sixty-nine years He has put up with me on this earth.

1139. - TO CLAUDE DUFOUR, IN SAINTES

September 18, 1649

God knows that the letters I receive from you give me very great

---

Letter 1138. - Reg. 2, p. 200.

Letter 1139. - Reg. 2, p. 300.

consolation because of the disposition He has given you toward
slaves and convicts. This is a grace so precious that none greater
can be seen on earth. What makes me doubly grateful to God for
this is the fidelity of your heart, which bends and stands firm in
accordance with the Divine good pleasure. Now, since the service
of these poor people is an extraordinary vocation, you must reflect
carefully on it and ask God to make known to us whether you are
called to it. I ask you on your part to do this and I intend on my part
to do so, not that I have any doubts about your determination, but
in order that I may be more certain of God's Will. Furthermore,
now is not the time to go there: the plague in Marseilles has driven
away the galleys and left the hospital without patients, and the
plague in Barbary will make us put off sending anyone there. So,
here is an opportunity for a little patience in this delay. It is also an
occasion to merit better the happiness of such a holy work, by the
good use of the lesser works to which you are devoting yourself,
and these are still very great since in God's house everything is
supreme and royal.

1139a. - MARTIN LEVASSEUR,[1] TO SAINT VINCENT

[Rome, September 29, 1649]

Monsieur,

*These few lines are to inform you of the most remarkable things I noted
in the life and death of M. Dunots and what was said in the conference*

Letter 1139a. - Municipal library of Lyons, Ms. 1285. The text used in this edition was printed
in *Mission et Charité,* 19-20, pp. 76-81.

[1]Could this name have been misread? According to *Notices,* vol. I, p. 479, and vol. V, p. 385,
Martin Levasseur was born on January 5, 1630 in Eu (Seine-Maritime), entered the Congregation
of the Mission on March 7, 1651, and was not ordained a priest until Holy Week of 1654. On
September 29, 1649 he was neither a member of the Congregation of the Mission nor a priest.
During Saint Vincent's lifetime there were no other Levasseurs who were priests. Charles and
David Levasseur were coadjutor Brothers.

"Le Vazeux" could perhaps be the proper reading. Achille Le Vazeux, born in Bonneval

held on this subject. There would be too much to relate if I tried to describe for you in detail the virtuous actions of this good servant of God. I shall mention only what seems most noteworthy and edifying to me.

We can reflect on this good servant of God both as a priest and as a Missionary. As a priest it can be said that he was a true epitome of the picture Saint Paul gives us in the Letters to Timothy and to Titus, and I think it would be very difficult to find a priest his age, in the active life in common like ours, who better put into practice what this Apostle directs us to do.

First of all, his devotion was sincere, straightforward, and solid, with no great indiscretion. It was not superficial and inconstant like that of many persons, which has more flame than heat. His meditation was almost continuous, except for the time he spent at Holy Mass and in the recitation of certain vocal prayers which he used to say daily. He was more concerned with prayer than with speculation. You know, Monsieur, how attentive and fervent he was in reciting his Office, and before he died everyone said he seemed like an angel in choir with the others.

As for Holy Mass, he never celebrated it until he had made a long preparation and, when possible, heard another Mass. His thanksgiving always lasted half an hour or three-quarters of an hour, and if he had not heard Mass before going to the altar, he heard it after he had said his own. On Sundays and feast days he usually heard three.

Piety and respect were obvious in his great care for the cleanliness of the church and the priestly vestments. He often used to sweep the church and the sacristy and was unwilling to let anyone else do it or help him, thanking those who tried to relieve him. He kept this up until the time of his illness, even though he was no longer sacristan. It was also he who washed the corporals and purificators. He was most careful to see that the ceremonies were observed and that we kept our hands clean because, he said, they were the instruments of the sacrifice of the Mass.

In his studies his only object was to rouse himself to the love of God and to the other virtues, as is clearly manifest in the writings found after his death. Except for a compendium of scholastic theology and one of philosophy, which he had copied with a few additions of his own, he had saved nothing from his time in Rome, except a synopsis of the Scripture Com-

---

(Eure-et-Loir) on June 22, 1620, was admitted to the Congregation of the Mission on August 24, 1639, received the priesthood on April 3, 1649, and shortly after ordination was sent to Rome, where he remained until 1653. He directed the Annecy Seminary (1653-1659), then was recalled to Paris and was sent to the Collège des Bons-Enfants; from there he returned to his family a few days before Saint Vincent died.

mentaries of Menochius which he had written during his first few months in Italy, and a few notes he had made on a Latin synopsis of sermons on the Mission and the Instructions of Murcantius. This is all that was found among his belongings, along with the rhymes based on Thomas à Kempis and a few litanies. Yet, he told me before he died that he had read all the books that are here, except for Ara, which he read only in part because he found it difficult. In all his own remarks there is nothing subtle or curious; everything in them is affection, devotion, and common things.

As Missionary

(1) A very great and extraordinary attachment to his vocation. He always spoke about it with appreciation. I found the following, written in his own hand: "Beware of imagining that you could do better elsewhere."

(2) His exactness is well-known and, to put it quite simply, he was the soul of good order in the house because of his good example and his carefulness to ring the bell exactly on time for the daily exercises.

(3) His fervor. He was never idle but was either praying, reading, sweeping, or working in the garden. For an entire year he awakened so punctually that, regardless of how cold it had been and even if the clock stopped during the night, he got up right on time. Once, beside himself, he said to me, Homo Dei apprehendo vitam aeternam.[2] His conversation was usually about God or about virtue.

(4) His mercy toward the poor. He often said to me that it was very hard to stay here because the poverty of the good people was painful to him and made him very sad, when he saw that they could not be helped as they needed. He was always after me to see how we could assist them.

(5) His love of God. He often used to say, "We have to die; what are we doing in this world?" and he longed to be in heaven. One day, when a certain person did something wrong, he told me he was unable to see God being offended and that this caused him a pain similar to what he would suffer if someone tore out his heart. He often asked me to warn others of their failings. Once, when I told him that this was a waste of time, he replied that at least I should do it so as not to be responsible before God, and he strongly agreed with the maxim of the Jesuits, "Either good order or the door."

As a consequence, he was very careful in the confessional to give absolution only to those whom he felt were entitled to it. One day, when some priests of the Company questioned him about the opinion of certain

---

[2]*As a man of God, I am taking hold of everlasting life.* Cf. 1 Tm 6:11-12. (NAB)

authors regarding necessary and presumed involuntary proximate occasions and relapses, he replied coldly that it could never be like that for him. Speaking to me one day of the ease with which a certain person gave absolution and light penances, he said, "O Monsieur, how difficult it is to have genuine faith regarding what takes place in the Sacraments of Penance and Holy Eucharist and not be more careful that they are not profaned." When I shared with him one day that people were complaining about his penances and delay of absolution, he told me that we should let them talk and should consider God alone. He was fully persuaded that the compliance of confessors is one of the greatest reasons for the disordered state of the people. He could not hear the opposite being said without expressing his feelings. I know from experience what that did for certain souls in great spiritual distress who, by God's grace, were delivered from it.

When the cavalier, Santi, was sick, he asked me to send him [Dunots] to him, but the former was already dead. When someone else went he refused to go to confession to him. When I went to see him, he said he deeply regretted the loss of this good priest and that it had been a great consolation to go to confession to him. He said he had several confessors in Rome and elsewhere, but had never found any who had given him more enlightenment and consolation.

As for himself, he made his confession with such humility, compunction, and holy fear that while I was hearing him, there often came to my mind this passage of Holy Scripture, Ad quem respiciam nisi ad pauperculum et trementem sermones meos,[3] *and never have I given absolution with such joy and fullness of heart, for I seemed to see grace in him, so externally visible was it in this great servant of God.*

Although it was almost always absolutely necessary for him to follow the custom of the Company to confess some sin of his past life in order to ensure the Sacrament, his soul was so pure that, in addition to the penance I would give him, he nevertheless often asked me to add to it some arduous discipline. Those are his own words.

His obedience was quasi modo geniti infantis,[4] *with never any objection. He often told me he was surprised that there were people who had trouble obeying. He said he had learned from experience that he had always been mistaken when he followed his own opinion, but when he followed that of superiors he always recognized the truth of the words,* Qui

---

[3]*Whom shall I respect but the poor and those who tremble at my words.* Cf. Is 66:2. (NAB)
[4]*Like that of a newborn child.* Cf. 1 Pt 2:2. (NAB)

vos audit, me audit.[5] *He often used to repeat the words of Saint Bernard, "He who follows his own opinion, follows a false teacher."*

Whenever he went some place, even for half an hour, he would kneel down and ask my blessing, most often at the door in the presence of lay persons. He did so with such humility and respect that those who saw him were moved. One person who happened to be there said to me, "O Monsieur, in your house you know what virtue is; as for us, we live like animals."

When he had some scruple, he would seek me out and ask if there was any sin in that and whether he should confess it. When I told him no, he would go to the sacristy and vest for Mass.

As for his meekness, he never offended anyone and, even though he was sharply reproached on certain occasions, he never showed any sign of being humiliated or sad but always humbled himself.

His mortification is more to be admired than imitated. If I were to write you what he suffered for chastity, it would be a long story. Besides the ordinary discipline for which he had permission, he often came to ask my permission to take others. For a long time he used certain belts made of branches from the gooseberry shrub which he had twisted and adjusted for this purpose and applied to the flesh. The thorns from this type of bush are a horrible sight because he would use year-old branches. Just imagine that, Monsieur; and people think it is great, as indeed it is, that Saint Teresa disciplined herself with nettles. For a long time he slept on the bare ground. True, he did not practice these extreme mortifications the last two years of his life because he was forbidden to do so. He told me that the saints were honored with good reason because virtue was difficult to acquire and one really had to suffer before acquiring even a little.

As a reward God gave him great purity of body and mind. In his most recent communications he told me he no longer felt any of his past temptations, and for more than a year God's mercy had aided him in that regard. Nevertheless, he was very prudent in conversations with women and never looked them in the face.

Lastly, the constancy with which he always followed virtue, and the perseverance with which he sealed all his good works. When he fell ill, he asked me not to leave him; the following day he went to confession and asked for Communion as Viaticum, after which he asked me to give him Extreme Unction as soon as possible.

He showed very great patience, never grumbling or complaining. He

---

[5]*He who hears you, hears me.* Cf. Lk 10:16. (NAB)

— 486 —

*said he would not recover, and the morning before he died, he told me he
had suffered extraordinarily during the night and that God had made him
experience a sampling of all the pains the saints had endured, "even those
of the holy martyrs," he added a little later. I dared not question him in
great detail but I thought that this was some vision of the devil. He died in
great peace, like an infant in the cradle. After his death I found among his
papers a little piece of paper with protestations to God written in his own
blood and carefully sealed so that it might not be read. I am sending it to
you, Monsieur, along with the verses he wrote on Gerson and on the Gospel
which I think are well worth saving. A Capuchin had asked me for some
of them but I excused myself saying I wanted to send them to you. They are
incomplete because he was unable to revise them and was doing this only
for his own consolation. M. Blosquelet is asking me for his scholastic
theology notes, and someone else for what he did on Sacred Scripture, and
for a synopsis of the instructions of Menochius and of the sermons on the
Mission, the points of which he wrote briefly in Latin. They ask that you,
Monsieur, allow me to give these to them, if you deem it proper.*

*This, Monsieur, is what I had to tell you about the late good M. Dunots,
but I think his humility has deprived us of the knowledge of many of his
actions, which would serve as examples and give us much edification. I
can say in all truth and simplicity that, in my poor judgment, it would be
very difficult for a man to attain greater purity and innocence in this life
than this good servant of God. That is why I believe he is in heaven,
according to the words of Our Lord,* Beati mundo corde, quoniam ipsi
Deum videbunt.[6] *Please pray to God for me, Monsieur, that He may
pardon me the poor use I have made of the example of this good servant
of God and grant me the grace to imitate him in some way.*

*I will just add a few more things here: (1) he always rose around
midnight to say some little prayer on his knees. He did this with permission;
otherwise he never would have done it, regardless of his great devotion;
(2) he was extremely careful not to speak unfavorably of his neighbor, and
he could not bear to hear people speak ill, even in general, of vices or
disorders in certain provinces or towns, or of certain professions; (3) it
was his custom to say, "Fathers, Brothers, let us do good; we will find it;"
and when he was teaching some of our men, scarcely a day would go by,
either in class or at repetition of prayer which he sometimes held in the
absence of the superior, without his saying at the end, "Let us do good;
we will find it;" (4) often—quite often, in fact—he used to say, "I want to*

---

[6]*Blessed are the clean of heart, since they will see God.* Cf. Mt 5:8. (NAB)

die, I want to die," which showed how detached he was from the world and how he was thinking of eternity. But how can I mention everything? His life was one of constant dedication to God or to charitable works for the neighbor; therefore, it is impossible for us to express how much he is missed by lay persons as well as by the members of the house.

I am, Monsieur, your most humble and obedient servant.

LE VASSEUR
i.s.C.M.

San Salvatore, September 29, 1649

1140. - TO FATHER FRANCOIS BLANCHART[1]

Saint-Lazare, Feast of Saint Jerome,[2] 1649

Reverend Father,

The bearer, Monsieur de Saint-Paul, is a monk of your holy Order and the brother of Monsieur de La Bourlerie, assistant tutor of the King. He wishes to spend a month in your house in order to see your holy observances and put into practice those which are in conformity with his intention to live and have others live in a small Community, observing the Rules of Saint Augustine, not in the exact manner of your holy Congregation but as best it can, short of

---

Letter 1140. - Property of the Daughters of the Charity, Provincial House, Mill Hill, London.

In 1857 this authentic letter of Saint Vincent was given by Monsignor Weld to Henry Granville, 14th Duke of Norfolk. It was later given by Henry, 15th Duke of Norfolk, to his sister, a Daughter of Charity, Sister Mary Howard (Lady Etheldreda Fitzalan Howard), who gave it to the Central House of the Sisters of Charity, Saint Vincent's, Mill Hill. The letter was sent by Sister Howard to Saint-Lazare in Paris to be examined, and was declared to be authentic.

[1]François Blanchart was born in Amiens in 1606. After a short stay at Saint-Acheul Convent (1624), then at Saint-Vincent Abbey in Senlis, he came to Sainte-Geneviève Abbey, which he left to introduce the reform and take the position of Superior at Sainte-Catherine Convent in Paris, then at Saint-Denis in Rheims. His attainments caused him to be chosen for more important positions: Assistant, Visitor, Coadjutor General (December 14, 1644), and lastly, Abbot of Sainte-Geneviève and Superior General (February 1645). The Congregation of Canons Regular of Sainte-Geneviève had him as Superior (1645-1650, 1653-1665, 1667-1675).

[2]September 30.

that. I have assured him that you in your goodness will grant him this favor.

I entreat you most humbly, R[everend] Father, to consent to this. In so doing you will contribute to the sanctification of his soul and to the salvation of the souls entrusted to him; you will also be doing a service to a deserving person and to Monsieur de La Bourlerie, his brother. I assure you, Reverend Father, that I too shall be as much obliged to you as if you had granted this favor to me. I am, R[everend] Father, your most humble and obedient servant.

VINCENT DEPAUL
Unworthy Superior of the Congregation of the Mission

Addressed: Reverend Father Abbot of the Congregation of Sainte-Geneviève

**1141. - TO PHILIBERT DE BEAUMANOIR DE LAVARDIN,
BISHOP OF LE MANS[1]**

October, 1649

Excellency,

I venture to write you this letter to assure you, with all possible humility and respect, of my perpetual obedience. I beg you most humbly, Excellency, to accept it and allow me to inform you that there are many priests here, even some of a certain rank, who are

---

Letter 1141. - Reg. 1, f° 10, copy made from the original autograph letter.

[1]This Bishop still resented the fact that Saint Vincent did not feel he could recommend him for the episcopate. He had taken up residence in Le Mans even before receiving his Bulls. Thus, Saint Vincent was very surprised, on his arrival in Le Mans on March 2, 1649, to find the Bishop there. Through two of his own priests, the Saint asked his permission to remain in the seminary for a week or so. Philibert de Lavardin, flattered by this request, consented willingly and even added that he would be very pleased to receive Saint Vincent in his own house. The latter was preparing to go and thank the Bishop, when he heard that he had left. Philibert de Lavardin was not a model Bishop. After his death, when it was rumored falsely that, on his own admission, he never had the intention of ordaining anyone, a number of priests believed this, and had themselves reordained. (Cf. Collet, *op. cit.,* vol. I, p. 473.)

asking for benefices which were vacant and which you have granted since your consecration, including the archdeaconry and canonry. Owing to your failure, Excellency, to register your oath of fidelity in the *Chambre des Comptes,* it is being alleged that you, Excellency, could not dispose of these benefices.

The last person to bring pressure to bear on me in this matter is one of the King's chaplains, who is making the request for one of his brothers. He brought me a Doctor of the Sorbonne, very knowledgeable in the question of benefices, to try to persuade me that it is up to the King to grant these benefices. By the grace of God, however, I stood my ground, and rightly so, I think. Nevertheless, because there are a large number of petitioners and because they might obtain these benefices by some other means, I have thought, Excellency, that since we make special profession of obedience to the Bishops and particularly to those who so kindly allow us to be in their dioceses, as you so kindly do in yours, Excellency, I feel I should inform you of this so that you might have your oath of fidelity registered, in order to dismiss the pretext of these persons here and of any others who could stir up trouble in that regard.

I found it difficult to summon the courage to write to you, Excellency, for fear that you might not be open to this. However, the importance of the matter and the fear of failing in my duty toward you have caused me to prefer falling into rashness than to fail in fidelity in the service I owe you, Excellency. I am, in the love of Our Lord, Excellency, your most humble and obedient servant.

VINCENT DEPAUL
i.s.C.M.

1142. - TO JACQUES CHIROYE, IN LUÇON

Paris, October 3, 1649

Monsieur,

The grace of Our Lord be with you forever!

I am glad you have received payment for the bill of exchange I sent you for fifteen hundred livres and consequently that you have paid back the amount you had previously taken, thinking we would pay it here.

However, I certainly am more surprised to learn that the Bishop[1] never tires of giving you something. *Seigneur Dieu,* what charity! I had the happiness of speaking with the late Bishop of Geneva[2] several times when he was alive. He was so good that God's goodness was clearly visible in his own. But I have never met anyone before or after him in whom this same Divine Goodness was more apparent than in the Bishop of Luçon. I am sending him a note of thanks for his most recent acts of generosity, more to avoid being ungrateful than to express my gratitude to him, which is so great that I cannot put it into words. May God grant us the grace of rendering to the Luçon diocese the services this distinguished Bishop expects of us and which we owe him for so many reasons! I am consoled to hear that you are striving to render him all possible reverence, submission, and obedience; it would, moreover, be unpardonable for you to fail in such a just duty.

I am writing to Richelieu to ask them to send you by coach a priest for M. Thouvant's[3] mission. I hope he will be with you two or three days after this letter is delivered to you. Before the close of this mission, we shall consider your proposal concerning M. L., and I will write to you about it. May God be pleased to bless your

---

Letter 1142. - Archives of the Mission, Turin, original signed letter.

[1]Pierre Nivelle, Bishop of Luçon.

[2]Saint Francis de Sales.

[3]Claude Thouvant, Canon and Archdeacon of Aizenay. (Cf. no. 907, n. 6.)

work and leadership and to grant me a share in the merit of your prayers and Holy Sacrifices! I cordially greet your little Community for whom, and for you in particular, I am in the love of Our Lord, Monsieur, your most humble servant.

VINCENT DEPAUL
i.s.C.M.

Addressed: Monsieur Chiroye, Superior of the Priests of the Mission, in Luçon

1143. - TO RENE ALMERAS, SUPERIOR, IN ROME

October 8, 1649

M. Ferentilli spoke to you as a Roman and certainly as a friend, when he advised you to have presentable men. *Mais quoi!* what would M. . . and the likes of him do in Rome? You are not allowed to preach there or hear confessions in the house or teach the ordinands in public; *cui ergo fini?* [1] Only to have fine looking men at the altar and in the refectory and to take them from their work here! This display of men, Monsieur, would certainly cost the Company dearly, and I am not sure whether there might not be something undesirable in this before God. To say that they will appear in the parish—if you ever get one—again, *cui fini?* And then, unless I am mistaken, there are very few sermons given and liturgies performed in the parishes of the city. If indeed Providence provides us with some work in Rome, you will soon have with you, not any of our older men but those who will contribute most to the welfare of the Mother of Churches. *O Jésus!* Monsieur, you would

---

Letter 1143. - Reg. 2, p. 230.
[1]*Then, for what purpose?*

really have to be well matched.[2] The poor, who do not know where to go or what to do, who are suffering already and who increase daily, are my burden and my sorrow.

1144. - TO MATHURIN GENTIL, IN LE MANS

Paris, October 12, 1649

Monsieur,

The grace of Our Lord be with you forever!

We already had the Chancellor's[1] word and a decree signed by the rapporteur to halt Hossard's proceedings until the verification of our establishment in the Parlement.[2] However, when I spoke to the Chief Justice,[3] he told me that this same Parlement would annul anything that might come from the Council, that in two weeks he would ask the Procurator General[4] to come and see him, and that he would try to persuade him to hand down his verdict, which he has been withholding from us for two or three years. You can see, Monsieur, that this means you will have to drag out the affair with M. Hossard.

How can I have M. Aubert[5] paid the twenty livres the farmer owes him, if he does, since we ourselves cannot get anything of what he is obliged to hand over to us? Please ask him to excuse us.

I am really distressed that the ordination has been turned down,

---

[2]The Coste text did not have the sentence that follows. Father Raymond Chalumeau, C.M., former Community Archivist in Paris, has informed us that it belongs here. It is found in context in Collet, *op. cit.,* vol. I, p. 479.

Letter 1144. - Archives of the Mission, Turin, original signed letter.

[1]Pierre Séguier.

[2]On January 15, 1650 the Parlement registered the letters patent by which the King, in August 1645, had united to the Congregation of the Mission the direction or provostship of the collegial and royal church of Notre-Dame de Coëffort in Le Mans and the benefices dependent on it.

[3]Mathieu Molé.

[4]Blaise Méliand.

[5]A merchant in Le Mans.

and I ask God to grant you the grace of rectifying this error at the first opportunity. I shall write about it so that they will find the means of having it—in fact, I think I have already done so—and also that everything possible be done[6] for the growth of the minor and major seminaries. I am not writing to him now because I do not think he has returned from his journey.

I greet and embrace cordially your dear soul and the whole Community, for whom, and for you in particular I am, in the love of Our Lord, Monsieur, your most humble servant.

VINCENT DEPAUL
i.s.C.M.

I have just learned that you have not been well. I am certainly very sorry about this and would be even more sorry if I did not hope that you are now feeling better. I ask this of Our Lord with all my heart, and I ask you, Monsieur, to do all you can to recover, sparing nothing that might contribute to that. I await more recent news on the state of your health.

Will you have room and could you find one hundred beds for a group of the ordinands? Please let me know about this in writing; they are obliged to pay their own expenses.[7]

At the bottom of the first page: M. Gentil

---

[6]First redaction: "May God forgive M. L. if he turned down the ordination, and may He grant him the grace of rectifying this error at the first opportunity! I shall write him to dispose himself to do this; in fact, I think I have already done so, and also that he should do all he can." The correction was made in the Saint's own handwriting.

[7]The last paragraph, which begins with "Will you have room," is in the Saint's handwriting.

1145. - *CARDINAL MAZARIN TO SAINT VINCENT*

October 13, 1649

Monsieur,

I am much obliged to you for your good advice and for all you wrote me in your letter of the fourth of this month.[1] I have received all this with the confidence and esteem it deserves, and truly a wiser argument or one more full of affection for me cannot be found. I thank you a thousand times, asking that I might continue to benefit from your dutiful attention in similar circumstances. In the meantime, to repay you for this, I shall seek opportunities for expressing to you, better than by these lines, that I am . . . .

1146. - *ETIENNE BLATIRON, SUPERIOR IN GENOA, TO SAINT VINCENT*

October 19, 1649

Monsieur,

Some time ago I wrote you regarding the virtue I had remarked in Monsieur Brunet's life. Now I would like to be able to recall that and many other [acts of virtue] I saw him practice, which I should have noted and tried to imitate if I had been mindful enough of my own good. We held a conference on this subject and I had intended to send you a summary of it right away; however, our constant work does not allow us to do anything leisurely but always in haste, as I am now doing. More than my work, however, I beg you to accept my good will.

Anything I could tell you about this good servant of God is but a shadow in comparison with the truth. I had asked Monsieur Portail to write a summary of his principal acts of virtue, but he told me that this was too difficult a request, and that his acts of virtue were so numerous and excellent that a ream of paper could not contain them. He added that his virtues could be better admired than written down because they were

Letter 1145. - Archives for Foreign Affairs, Mémoires et Documents, France, Ms. 264, f° 487, copy.
[1]This letter is no longer extant.

Letter 1146. - Lyons manuscript, f° 223ff.

sound and hidden, and his life was not showy and pompous but solid and interior.

"Among other things," he said, "I admired his deep humility, his admirable gentleness, and his resignation and most perfect conformity to the Will of God. What was most outstanding, however, was his constant, unvarying perseverance in these virtues, so much so that, even though he was old and a senior member, he did not make a show of this and act like an emeritus miles,[1] but seemed rather like a child or a seminarian in the practice of humility and obedience, as in all else." Up to this point, I am quoting Monsieur Alméras.

Following are some of the things our priests in Genoa remarked about this good servant of God:

A very profound humility, always considering himself as the least. He took special pleasure in working at the lowliest duties and sought every opportunity to perform them. When there was sweeping to be done, he was usually the first on hand and often cut short his recreation to go to the kitchen and wash the dishes. He considered himself fortunate when no one could be found to serve the Masses because then he could serve them himself. If at times he made a little error in serving them, he immediately humbled himself and knelt at the feet of the priest to ask his pardon. If he noticed that anyone had muddy shoes, he would watch for a time when no one was looking and would clean the shoes on the quiet. He very humbly accepted the clothes that were brought to him and personally returned those he took off, not wanting to inconvenience the Brothers who were supposed to come and pick them up. He never complained about a cassock being too long or too short or badly made. When he went out with a member of the Company, he always tried to give the right side to his companion, even if the latter were younger; if he could not take the lowest place, he became embarrassed and would blush, making it clear that he was not just being polite in what he did but was doing it through a genuine sentiment of humility.

This same virtue was the reason why we never heard him argue with anyone. If in conversation he at times encountered someone who had an opinion different from his, he immediately condescended with a gracious smile, submitting his judgment to that of the other person. One day, while he was traveling on foot from Alet to Marseilles, he hurt his leg near Narbonne. After staying a week there with his companion in the hope of getting on a boat, they were obliged to go by land. Since they could not go on horseback because they were short of money, and in addition good

---

[1] *Veteran.*

Monsieur Brunet was no longer able to walk, they bought a donkey to carry him and their coats, without saddle or stirrups.

He traveled one hundred and twenty leagues in this manner. I could never convey to you the joy in his heart, which he also manifested exteriorly at seeing himself on that animal, even though he was often taunted and followed by children who pointed at him and shouted after him. During missions, although he had a bad leg, as we know, he was unwilling to go on horseback unless everyone else did the same. In that case he would choose the worst and the least comfortable horse, and delighted in riding without saddle or bridle through places where he was very well known. Those who saw and knew him were astonished and in admiration of him.

His great obedience was apparent in his perfect resignation at remaining wherever he was assigned and in doing whatever duty or work people wanted him to do. He was sent from Notre-Dame de la Rose to Alet, where he was indescribably happy with the conversation of the Bishop of Alet [2] and the great good he could do for souls. He was there only three months, and when he received instructions to leave, he was not in the least upset. Having been sent later from Rome to Genoa, he had no sooner arrived than there was talk of sending him back to Rome. He was always indifferent and ready to go wherever obedience might call him. One day he was assigned as companion to a priest who was going out. He immediately got ready to accompany him despite the fact that he had been suffering from diarrhea for three days. His companion remarked this and asked him why he had not told him about his ailment. He replied that he did not think he should excuse himself when obedience was calling. In this he showed how obedient and mortified he was. He was extremely mortified in everything, and what was most admirable was that he tried so hard to conceal his virtue that we are aware of only the smallest part of it.

His mortification made him so punctual and obedient to all the house regulations that he seemed to have no other desire except to obey, so much so that the following Scripture text cannot apply to him: Proni sunt sensus hominis ad malum ab adolescentia.[3] *He was so mortified in speech that he was never found talking out of time, and followed closely the counsel of the wise man,* Os sapientis in corde suo.[4] *If necessity obliged him to speak, he did so in a low tone and in few words. He was abstemious at table; when unusual fruits or dishes a little better than usual were served, he would*

---

[2]Nicolas Pavillon (1597-1677).

[3]*The desires of man's heart are prone to evil from his youth.* Cf. Gn 8:21. (NAB)

[4]*The source of wisdom is in his heart.* Cf. Sir 21:26. (NAB) Eccl 21:29. (D-RB)

not touch them, and on such occasions the Brothers used to say to one another that Monsieur Brunet's share would remain intact. What they had thought they often saw come to pass.

He wore a small iron chain against his flesh and said he was the slave of Jesus Christ. Around his neck he wore a six-inch figure of the Crucified but with no cross; it had three rather long, sharp nails which he often put next to his bare skin to share and honor the sufferings of Our Lord Jesus Christ, mortificationem Jesu Christi in corpore circumferens,[5] *in accord with Saint Paul's advice. He never complained of cold, heat, weariness, food, drink, sleeping quarters, or the inconvenience of his room. He was lodged in a little cubbyhole under a stairway where there was just a small window and not even a chair on which to sit, and nobody noticed this. He never said a word about it and was unwilling to get a chair for himself, until someone in the house found him on his knees writing and brought him one.*

If paradise is the reward of the poor in spirit, Monsieur Brunet will have a large share in it, since he had no attachment for the things of this earth; that was quite evident. Whenever he received a medal, booklet, rosary, or something similar for his own use, he would accept it only on condition of being able to give it away when charity demanded it. In fact, he used to give whatever he had to the first person who asked for it. When he was asked why he gave these things away so easily, he replied that an act of charity was worth more than all the possessions in the world. If, by chance, he forgot or lost something, he was not at all upset but would say that if someone found it that person would make better use of it than he did. As for clothing, his practice was to ask or refuse nothing, and he showed the greatest joy when he was given old clothes.

He was extremely punctual and exact in observing the Rules. Although he lived in the most distant rooms, he was always among the first at Divine Office and the other Community exercises. He never let the month go by, whether he was in the country or at home, without presenting himself to the Superior for spiritual communication, although very often he did not know what to say because his life and his soul were so well-regulated. As soon as he heard the clock strike, he would kneel down and leave what he had begun, to run where obedience was calling him.

His simplicity was extraordinary, neither put on nor hypocritical, so that anyone who saw or heard him could sense what was in his heart. He did not know how to equivocate, and avoided exaggeration in anything he had seen or heard.

---

[5]*Carrying about in our bodies the mortification of Jesus Christ.* Cf. 2 Cor 4:10. (NAB)

But who could describe his gentleness, kindness, and cordiality? If someone was angry and saw this good servant of God, he would have to calm down. In him were verified these words of Jesus Christ, Beati mites, quoniam ipsi possidebunt terram,[6] *meaning, according to Saint Augustine,* possidebunt corda hominum vel subjugabunt.[7]

He had a great love of solitude, causing him to be quite at home with prayer and meditation. He was never seen running here and there in the house; anyone who needed him had no great trouble finding him, since he was usually in his room and almost always kneeling or standing, reading and praying in this place of solitude and retirement. He had acquired close union with God, with whom he conversed so often and so lovingly that we would see him with his eyes bathed in tears and his face radiant, and this moved us to devotion. We never saw him looking sad or melancholy, although occasions for being so often presented themselves in the order of fallen nature. Instead, by the grace of God, he constantly practiced virtue. He did not get upset about things but remained cheerful, conforming himself to God's Will in everything and accepting from His hand both adverse and favorable events.

I shall close here because they are taking the pen from my hand. I am sure that what I have said is very little in comparison with all that could be told. I ask this good servant of God to pray for us in heaven, where I believe he is enjoying unending glory. I am, in the love of God, Monsieur, your most humble and obedient servant.

ETIENNE BLATIRON
i.s.C.M.

1147. - TO GUILLAUME DELATTRE, SUPERIOR, IN AGEN

October 23, 1649

I cannot see that things in La Rose are as bad as they make them out to be. True, something did get into M. . . but he has been freed of that. Let me say, not just for this but for all the other disagree-

---

[6]*Blest are the meek, for they shall possess the land.* Cf. Mt 5:5. (NAB)
[7]*They will possess or subjugate the hearts of men.*

Letter 1147. - Reg. 2, p. 300.

ments, that I am afraid some troublemaker is giving you unchari-
table reports in order to introduce divisiveness into our houses and
among our Brothers. If this is the case, Monsieur, give yourself to
God so as not to listen to that person. You will then experience a
consolation similar to one I had. One day I had forbidden a servant,
whom I had before the Company came into being, to report
anything to me that was prejudicial to anyone. I did this because I
recognized this tendency in him and because he had already tried
to give me a bad impression of an upright man with whom I was
living. After that, he no longer dared to bring me such news.
Whenever I think of this my heart is touched with gratitude to God
for that grace. Scandal often does as much harm to the listeners as
to those who devise it, even if it were to do no other harm than
disturb the mind, as it does, and give rise to temptations to speak
or write about it to others.

I really think that frugality has enabled you to survive. I know
you have very little income, that boarders' fees help you in only a
small way, and that, with the high cost of living this year, you will
have a hard time managing, but I am also well aware that, if you
knew how powerless we are to assist you, you would be sympa-
thetic about this and not even dream of asking us for anything. The
recent wars and present famine in almost the entire kingdom
prevent us from being paid and from providing for our own little
necessities. I would indeed be more surprised than ever, if God had
not given me a little confidence and submission to His Providence,
when I see our poverty on the one hand and on the other the heavy
expenses we have to shoulder. You must regulate yours according
to your possibilities and take on only as much as you can handle. I
say this with regard to poor priests passing through, whom you
might want to assist. True, this would be excellent, if you could do
it, but you must attend instead to what is necessary. It is not
advisable for you to ask the Bishop's permission to extend this
hospitality; he will gladly approve the suggestions you make him
for the good of his seminary, but he is not in any mood to accept
others that do not concern him. If, however, you think you should
write to him about your needs, I leave that to your own discretion.

1148. - TO BISHOP MASSARI [1]

Paris, November 5, 1649

Excellency,

Words cannot express my joy and respect upon receiving the letter you did me the honor of writing, coming from someone so dear to me and whom I honor so highly. If previously I had esteem for Your Most Illustrious Lordship, based on what I had heard of your virtues, I am now obliged to have love and gratitude toward you, to which I add the renewed offer of my perpetual obedience. I entreat you most humbly to accept it, Excellency, along with that of our little Congregation which is entirely yours.

In conformity with your wishes, I have asked God with all my heart to bless the important duty in which His Providence has placed you. And because I have learned from our men there that when Your Most Illustrious Lordship entered the College of Propaganda Fide you had the piety to have a general Communion made for this purpose, I also had one here to correspond with it on our part; all the priests in the house offered Mass for your intention. Please God we shall offer these same prayers again from time to time because I cannot think of a better intention for which to pray.

Please allow me, Excellency, to ask for the assistance of your prayers for me. I assure you that I am and always will be, Excellency, your most humble and very obedient servant.

VINCENT DEPAUL
Unworthy Superior of the Congregation of the Mission

Letter 1148. - Archives of Propaganda Fide, II Africa, n° 248, f° 120, original signed letter.
[1] He had just succeeded Bishop Ingoli as Secretary of Propaganda Fide.

1149. - TO MATHURIN GENTIL, IN LE MANS

November 9, 1649

I have news from one of our houses[1] that the poor food being served there is having a harmful effect on bodies and minds. If the person in charge of the pantry, thinking he is saving money, is inclined to this excessive frugality and does not provide better meals after the warning I am giving him and the letter I am writing him about this, I shall be obliged to replace him with someone who will supply adequately what is needed to feed the Community the way we do at Saint-Lazare and elsewhere because, for want of this, several men have become ill. I tell you this, Monsieur, because you are in a similar duty and so that you will please be careful to avoid such unpleasant consequences. Make an effort to serve good bread and good meat and not to sell the better wine so as to serve what is inferior, nor to expose the Community to complaints of miserly treatment. I have been so affected by the ones made to me by the house of which I am speaking that I strongly fear others may give me the same cause for distress. I hope it will not come from you; please be attentive to this.

1150. - *ETIENNE BLATIRON, SUPERIOR, TO SAINT VINCENT*

Genoa, November 1649

His Eminence, the Cardinal,[1] spent a week with us and made retreat with ten of the Missionaries. Oh! what a great servant of God he is! His exactitude and punctuality in observing the order of the exercises was incredible, although he looks very frail and is fifty-six years old but appears older because of his constant labors, both spiritual and corporal.

Letter 1149. - Reg. 2, p. 131.
    [1]This house was probably the Le Mans Seminary, where Mathurin Gentil was Treasurer!

Letter 1150. - Abelly, *op.cit.,* bk. II, chap. IV, p. 291.
    [1]Stefano Cardinal Durazzo.

*In the morning, he would make his prayer on his knees in common with
the others, motionless from beginning to end, even though some of the men
stood up. For the other meditations, which each one made in his room, he
made them kneeling or, if he was sometimes a little tired, he would ask me
if he could stand up. I had already told him he could and that it would even
be all right if he sat down for a while so as not to tire himself too much,
but he never failed to ask me each time so as to have the merit of obedience.*

*When he shared his thoughts and the good sentiments he had during
prayer, he did so as simply, humbly, and devoutly as any one of us. As soon
as he heard the bell for the Office or the other Community exercises, he
dropped everything and was one of the first in chapel. At table he wanted
to be treated like everyone else. I begged him to allow us to treat him
differently, and he finally gave in. He was upset that we gave him separate
washing facilities, since he wanted to be the same as everyone else.*

*Toward the end of the retreat, I asked him to give us all his blessing to
obtain perseverance from God. He did not want to do this; on the contrary,
he insisted that I give it myself. Still, after much persistence, he blessed us.
Oh! dear Father, what an example of virtue we have before our eyes!*

1151. - SAINT LOUISE TO SAINT VINCENT

[Between 1647 and 1649] [1]

Most Honored Father,

*Forgive my too violent apprehension of what I have always most feared
in the person about whom I spoke to you. My reflections on this subject,
which increase my sorrow, are the reason why the consolation God has
given me through your charity has not been apparent to you. If you believe
in the guidance of Divine Providence in my life, in God's name, my very
dear Father, do not forsake me in this need; if not, do me the charity of
pointing out my self-deception so that I may not die impenitent.*

I forgot to entreat you most humbly, for the love of God, to say Holy

Letter 1151. - Archives of the Motherhouse of the Daughters of Charity, original autograph
letter.
[1]Before 1647, Saint Louise always wrote "Monsieur" in the salutation of her letters to Saint
Vincent; after 1649, she always addressed him as "Monsieur and Most Honored Father," or
"Most Honored Father," or "Very Reverend Father." In this instance we have "Most Honored
Father" at the start and "Monsieur" at the end; this indicates the period between 1647 and 1649.

Mass for my son tomorrow and do whatever God chooses to inspire you to help him out of the great distress in which I think he now is. This would really arouse your compassion if you saw it as I do.

I am doing my best to understand the thoughts you so kindly gave me. I ate my supper better than I thought I would. I want to try to give God what He is asking of me on this occasion, which I hope to know through the advice your charity will give me. I have great need of this and of being, as God wishes, Monsieur, your most grateful daughter and humble servant.

L. DE M.

Addressed: *Monsieur Vincent*

1152. - TO BROTHER JACQUES RIVET, IN LA ROSE

November 13, 1649

I have received your letters, and they gave me the inexpressible consolation of knowing that you have returned to La Rose. I am sending this letter there to tell you how welcome back you are. Indeed, no matter what was written to me about you, I always believed you would do what you have done. The situation was truly dangerous, but God's grace was strong and you have been faithful to your vocation. For this, I bless His mercy a million times.

You would have done some good in that good Bishop's[1] house, but you will do incomparably more by remaining in the original state in which you know God has placed you. Although this Bishop is very virtuous, you would nevertheless have been obliged to associate with people who are not as virtuous as he, and whose example and conversation might have been perhaps too harmful to you. Our business is to gain heaven; everything else is a sheer waste of time. So let us take the shortest and safest routes to it, such as a

---

Letter 1152. - Reg. 2, p. 301.
[1]Jean d'Estrades, Bishop of Condom.

hidden life, the acquisition of the Christian and evangelical virtues, and lastly the observance of our little Rule.

So then, dear Brother, I ask Our Lord, who preserved you in the midst of such danger, to accomplish in you His eternal designs. He doubtless wants to bring you up in His house and make you entirely His in time and eternity. Amen.

1153. - TO MARC COGLEE, SUPERIOR, IN SEDAN

November 15 [1649][1]

As for the eternal covenant you wish to make with Our Lord in the Company, *O Jésus!* Monsieur, I consent to it with all my heart, which loves yours more than I can tell you.

1154. - *SAINT LOUISE TO SAINT VINCENT*

[November 1649] [1]

Most Honored Father,

I am very sorry for being so insistent, but the impossibility of continuing to take in the little children weighs too heavily upon us. Right now our two wet nurses have seven of them who refuse to drink from the bottle, and we do not have a double [2] *to put them out to nurse, no reserve of sheets or linen, and no hope of being able to borrow any more.*

Do us the charity, Most Honored Father, of telling us whether, in

Letter 1153. - Reg. 2, p. 18.
[1]The manuscript dates the letter 1645. Quite probably the copyist mistook a 9 for a 5. On November 15, 1645, Marc Coglée was, in fact, in Marseilles, not in Sedan. Furthermore, he did not take his vows until December 13, 1649.

Letter 1154. - Archives of the Motherhouse of the Daughters of Charity, original autograph letter.
[1]Date added on the back of the original by Brother Ducournau.
[2]A small copper coin worth two deniers.

conscience, we can watch them being put in a situation in which they will die, for the Ladies attach no importance to giving us any relief. I am sure they think we are making our fortunes at their expense, which is absolutely contrary to the truth because we kept only one hundred livres of the money allocated to us for the wet nurses' food. I know of only one way to help all those who are suffering in this work; namely, that we, in the name of our Company, should petition the Chief Justice [3] to have us relieved of taking the children and to give this responsibility to whomever he wishes. However, the Ladies would have to agree to this course of action so that no one will be offended; otherwise, it seems to me that we are in continual mortal sin.

Yesterday four children were brought in. Besides the seven who are nursing, there are three who have been weaned—all recent foundlings—and one of them is just skin and bones. They should be put with a wet nurse again, if possible. If we could bear this trial without involving you, I would most gladly do so, but our helplessness does not allow it. These good Ladies are not doing what they can; not one of them has sent anything, nor has anything come in from those in the group because most of them have paid their annual dues in advance.

I beg God to have mercy on us. I am beginning to fear that all this misery is due to me who am what I am, Most Honored Father, your most obedient and very grateful daughter.

L. DE MARILLAC

I think a general meeting should be held. The Hôtel-Dieu lunches are also falling off.

Addressed: *Monsieur Vincent*

---

[3]Mathieu Molé.

1155. - *SAINT LOUISE TO SAINT VINCENT*

[November 1649] [1]

Most Honored Father,

I most humbly entreat your charity to give me about a quarter of an hour tomorrow so I can make up for what I seem to have lost yesterday in the opportunity Divine Providence was giving me. I do not know whether I should put the blame on fear or my pride, which always makes me reluctant to speak about myself.

Enclosed is Madame de Romilly's reply. I beg you to take the trouble to let me know whether I should send your letter to the President, Madame de Lamoignon, [2] even though the Princess [3] is not coming, and whether it is advisable to invite Madame de Brienne, who is back in town.

Enclosed also is a short report I have done. If you see fit, you might take the trouble to talk about it at the meeting. Please let us know where the latter will be held so Mademoiselle de Lamoignon can be notified.

Will your charity please let us know whether we should tell our Sisters in Serqueux to send us the girl they mentioned to us? Enclosed also is a letter from Messieurs de Gien. What shall we tell them? Cannot the Duchesse de Ventadour [4] be more insistent?

Yesterday one of our Sisters, wearing her habit, went off without saying a word; she is the one from Saint-Cloud. What does this mean? Are not strong measures required for some of them so that this practice will stop? Once before this Sister asked us if she could leave; we gave her the

---

Letter 1155. - Archives of the Motherhouse of the Daughters of Charity, original autograph letter.
[1]Date added on the back of the original by Brother Ducournau.
[2]Madame de Lamoignon was President of the Ladies of Charity (1643-1651).
[3]Charlotte de Montmorency, Princesse de Condé.
[4]The Duchesse de Ventadour, née Marie de la Guiche de Saint-Gérand. On February 8, 1645, she married Charles de Lévis, Duc de Ventadour, widower of Suzanne de Thémines de Montluc, who had bequeathed forty thousand livres to Saint Vincent for the foundation of a mission in Cauna (Landes). After her husband's death (May 19, 1649), Marie de la Guiche sought consolation in works of charity. She was one of Saint Louise's principal auxiliaries and best friends. The eve of Saint Louise's death, the Duchess came to be with her, caring for her with all the devotedness of a Daughter of Charity. She spent part of the night with her and, after a short rest, returned to stay by her bedside until the end, holding the blessed candle herself. (Cf. Gobillon, *op. cit.,* pp. 178, 181.) In 1683 the Duchesse de Ventadour was elected President of the Ladies of Charity. She died in her château, Sainte-Marie-du-Mont, in Normandy, during the night of July 22-23, 1701, at the age of seventy-eight. Thanks to her generosity, this locality had an establishment of Daughters of Charity as early as 1655.

permission and she stayed on of her own free will. I think God is speaking to us through these events, either to destroy the work or to strengthen it. Will your charity please reflect on this and tell me honestly if I am the Jonah who should be removed from it?

I belong to God for anything He chooses and am, Monsieur, your most obedient servant and very grateful daughter.

L. DE MARILLAC

Addressed: *Monsieur Vincent*

1156. - *SAINT LOUISE TO SAINT VINCENT*

[November 1649] [1]

Most Honored Father,

I am too insistent, but we have absolutely reached the point where we must get help without delay or abandon everything. Yesterday we had to use all the money in reserve here—nearly fifteen to twenty livres—to buy wheat for the children at Bicêtre, and we had to borrow some to have at least four setiers. Furthermore, no income is in sight for the next month.

There are twelve or thirteen children here and no change of diapers for them. Something must be done at the meeting of the Ladies tomorrow, please, such as a decision to take up a collection in the parishes every Sunday, placing small baskets in prominent places and having the pastors and preachers promote this; also, have the collection taken up at the Court, as proposed. If someone went to speak to the Princess [2] about these dire needs, I think she would make a donation. It is shameful that the Ladies are going to so little trouble. They must think we have more than enough to live on, or else they want to force us to abandon everything. For these reasons I think they have made up their minds to do nothing at all.

Will your charity please let us know if we should send out notices for

---

Letter 1156. - Archives of the Motherhouse of the Daughters of Charity, original autograph letter.
[1]Date added on the back of the original by Brother Ducournau.
[2]Charlotte de Montmorency, Princesse de Condé.

the meeting, and whether you think it is a good idea to send Madame de Schomberg[3] and Madame de Verthamon[4] to it?

The other things I had to tell you would take too long. I can do that tomorrow, if I have the honor of seeing you. I have great need of God's very special assistance, since in all that concerns me I see only wretchedness and affliction. Blessed be God for this! It is sufficient to reveal my need to you; I have no other hope of assistance and consolation except from your charity, of whom Providence has willed that I be, Most Honored Father, your most obedient daughter and very grateful servant.

L. DE MARILLAC

Will your charity please let us know if the subject for the conference[5] is indeed the one you gave me when I was complaining about Sisters who are asking to be changed?

I am afraid you are going to the country.

Addressed: *Monsieur Vincent*

1157. - TO JEAN GICQUEL, IN LE MANS[1]

December 5, 1649

Your difficulty in keeping the accounts for the mission expenses obliges me to ask you to give yourself truly to God to accept any kind of duty. You must believe you are doing His Will when you carry out the orders given you and be convinced that we deviate

[3]Anne de la Guiche, Duchesse de Schomberg, a Lady of Charity.
[4]Marie Boucher d'Orsay, wife of François de Verthamon, Master of Requests.
[5]On November 28, Saint Vincent gave a conference entitled "On The Love of Work" (cf. vol. IX, no. 42).

Letter 1157. - Reg. 2, p. 301.
[1]Jean Gicquel, born in Miniac (Ille-et-Vilaine) on December 24, 1617, was ordained a priest during Lent of 1642, entered the Congregation of the Mission on August 5, 1647, and took his vows on May 6, 1651. He was Superior of the Le Mans Seminary (1651-1654) and of Saint-Lazare (1655-1660) (cf. vol. V, nos. 1908, 1912 and vol. VI, no. 2157), and Director of the Company of the Daughters of Charity (1668-1672). An interesting diary of the last days of Saint Vincent, attributed to him, is preserved at the Motherhouse of the Congregation of the Mission.

from this Divine Will when we follow our own choosing. It would be sufficient to tell you that with regard to the ceremonies, but it should also be added that they are highly recommended in Holy Scripture, where they go almost hand in hand with the divine commandments. This leads us to think that God is honored as much by the ceremonies, when they are performed in His Spirit, as He is by the observance of His law. You can conclude from this the importance of this practice and whether there is not a temptation to be excused from it.

In God's name, Monsieur, let us remain indifferent; let us strive to be equally attached to whatever obedience marks out for us, be it agreeable or disagreeable. By the grace of God, we belong to Him; what else should we desire except to please Him? No wonder we are contradicted; what merit is there if we are not? And who can protect himself from this? For some petty contradiction should we stop doing good, and a good such as glorifying God? The person about whom you wrote me, who finds fault with your ceremonies, is very wrong in acting as he does, but I hope he will not do it any more. I have sent him a note about this, and perhaps I will make him see his fault even more clearly at the first opportunity.

We shall send you someone soon, God willing, in order to agree on the same ceremonies as we have here, so that we can try to be uniform in this as in everything else.

I praise God for the good that people are telling me about you; you serve as an example there. This fills my heart with consolation.

1158. - TO LOUIS RIVET, SUPERIOR, IN SAINTES

December 8, 1649

If M. . . writes to me, I will take the opportunity of letting him know in my reply that he is not giving us the satisfaction he led us

---

Letter 1158. - Reg. 2, p. 108.

to hope for. I will also try to give him a hint that he should show a little more submission and indifference than he now does. However, since this is the work of the Holy Spirit rather than that of men, who can say things but not move the person, we shall pray to God for that. I ask you to do so also, Monsieur, that He may attract him strongly to the practice of the virtues, above all, of humility and condescension. Your good example will also contribute to this. His correction will probably take a long time because of the impetuosity of his age and his vivacious spirit, but be patient! These very things should cause us to bear with him gently, in the hope that the idle dreams of presumption and the force of desire usually found in young people will diminish with age.

I know well, Monsieur, how much you have to endure in your present duty, and I ask Our Lord to strengthen you in your difficulties. It is in such circumstances that we acquire virtue; where there is no suffering, there is little merit. My wish is that God may grant us great indifference with regard to duties. O Monsieur, how sure we would then be of doing His holy Will, which is our sole aspiration, and how much peace and contentment we would enjoy, or so it seems to me! I beg you to ask Him earnestly for this grace for me and for the whole Company. I often offer to Him your own soul, which is very dear to me because it is so good and precious to Our Lord, in whom I am your . . . .

1159. - TO RENE ALMERAS, SUPERIOR, IN ROME

December 10, 1649

I cannot give you a definite answer about Brother [Doutrelet],[1] until I know what he has decided to do and how far his good intentions regarding the Company may go, if he really is deter-

---

Letter 1159. - Reg. 2, p. 268.
[1]As is known from no. 1068, Brother Doutrelet did not wish to renew his vows.

mined to remain in it. Nevertheless, Monsieur, I shall tell you that if his conversion is real and sufficiently extensive to include a definite intention to die in his vocation and to live in it according to our customs, complete submission to superiors, indifference with regard to places and employments, and, in a word, the desire to work unceasingly at the acquisition of virtue; if, I repeat, all this seems genuine enough to you, I consent to your keeping him and giving him a try for a while. If he decides to leave, I have nothing to say except *in nomine Domini*, and that, at the time he leaves, he must be notified of the revocation of his title. If he still wants to sit on the fence between two extremes, bargaining with God and with the Company, limping along on one foot, wanting to do one thing but not another; in short, barely belonging to us as he has been for some time, I think you should wait no longer but try to persuade him gently to leave and, if you can, get from him a written declaration that, since he was given the title only to provide him with the means of working in the Company, he does not intend to use it nor to ask for anything from it, given the fact of his departure.

If he is unwilling to do this, please do not hesitate to dismiss him. In that case, inform him that we are revoking his title and, to prevent him from being admitted to Orders, give notification of this to those to whom he might go to have himself ordained. It is also advisable that you compile at the same time an official report of his misconduct, indicating his present state and the most scandalous acts he has committed. Have this signed by some of your priests who have witnessed his disorderly behavior. Obtain some advice as to how this document should be drawn up. If I cannot do so today, I will send you at the first opportunity the Company's power of attorney to make the above-mentioned revocation.

1160. - *SAINT LOUISE TO SAINT VINCENT*

[December 1649] [1]

Monsieur,

Enclosed is a letter from Mademoiselle de Villenant in which you will see what I have learned about the matter. [2] *What bothers me is the difficult time widows have in being freed of their responsibilities after the death of their husbands. We are having trouble finding the money needed in order to be received and to pay the commissions, or to obtain the gift of this, which I have been told can be done.*

Furthermore, the good woman who is managing this affair told me today that the most urgent matter to be resolved is that the person who had been handling the discussions for us had returned to his own region and would be glad if, on his return, he found the business concluded by someone else. This makes me somewhat fearful that they may be thinking of breaking off with us. If that is the case, I would not know what else to say.

All the above-mentioned difficulties are only with a view to my son's lack of experience. However, he needs to be spurred on to work seriously and somehow to attend to matters on his own. Like me, he has a lazy disposition, and in order to accomplish anything we have to be pushed either by necessity or by our inclinations which, through bursts of enthusiasm, lead us to undertake even some rather difficult things.

When Monsieur de Marillac [3] *examined the clauses,* [4] *he saw clearly that there was something to be desired in them. Nevertheless, he did not advise me to break things off, even though they may not have granted me what he advised me to ask, because he sees great advantages for us in this affair.*

If your charity is coming to this neighborhood Saturday morning, I most

---

Letter 1160. - Archives of the Motherhouse of the Daughters of Charity, original autograph letter.

[1]Date added on the back of the original by Brother Ducournau.

[2]On the eve of Michel Le Gras' wedding day, his mother was trying to ensure a respectable position for him. Since the plan she mentions in this letter was unsuccessful, some other solution had to be sought. René-Michel de la Rochemaillet, uncle of Michel's fiancée, agreed to appoint him Counselor at the *Cour des Monnaies,* the court concerned with minting, counterfeiting, and devaluation of currency and cases arising therefrom.

[3]Michel de Marillac, Counselor in the Parlement, cousin of Michel Le Gras.

[4]The clauses of the marriage contract.

humbly ask you to let me know. That is the day the uncle [5] *and the young lady* [6] *are supposed to come, and I think everything will have to be settled. Your valuable good advice will be a big help to me in making a decision. I beg you most humbly to give it to me as coming from Our Lord. I am, in Him, Monsieur, your most humble daughter and very grateful servant.*

L. DE M.

Addressed: *Monsieur Vincent*

1161. - TO SIMON LE GRAS, BISHOP OF SOISSONS

Paris, December 15, 1649

Excellency,

I received your letter and your orders as if they had come to me from Our Lord. I had shared your views on the Abbess of Biaches,[1] Excellency, with those who spoke to me on her behalf, and with her, too, before I learned them. I had also used nearly the same arguments you did me the honor of writing me, in order to get her to relinquish Saint-Jean-des-Bois[2] and to accept Argensolles.[3] She has finally made up her mind to do this, Excellency, provided Madame d'Argensolles and her nuns give their consent. I told her I would work on this, and soon after that I did, in fact, make the proposal to M. de Montmaur,[4] the brother-in-law of Madame d'Ar-

[5]René-Michel de la Rochemaillet.

[6]Michel's fiancée, Demoiselle Gabrielle Le Clerc, daughter of the Seigneur de Chennevières and the late Dame Musset de la Rochemaillet.

Letter 1161. - Sainte-Geneviève Library, Ms. 3251, f° 323, copy. The spelling in the copy indicates that the original was written by Saint Vincent himself.

[1]Blanche d'Estourmel. She governed the Biaches Monastery in the Noyon diocese (1614-1664).

[2]In Oise near Compiègne. Saint-Jean-des-Bois and Argensolles were both in the Soissons diocese.

[3]Argensolles is about one league from Epernay. At that time the monastery there was governed by Claude de Buade (1630-1681). Like Biaches, it belonged to the Cistercian Order.

[4]Henri-Louis Habert, Seigneur de Montmaur, Master of Requests.

gensolles. I explained to him in detail the merit of the affair so that he might act as an intermediary with her; he led me to hope that he would be willing to do so. Since then he has told me that he discussed it with one of the nuns of the Order, who looks after Madame's business affairs, and that he asked her to go to Saint-Germain to talk to him about it. We are awaiting the reply.

Among the objections M. de Montmaur foresees that the Argensolles nuns will raise with us, the main one is their fear that, if they give their house over to nuns of such an Order, they may want to pass from a position of occupant to that of proprietor someday, and in this way, their property might be contested by those who have no right to it. My reply to that, Excellency, was that the agreement drawn up will be so incontestable that this claim will never arise, and that the agreement will be confirmed in the Parlement and wherever else this may be necessary. In it they will declare that they are entering this monastery simply as guests and will place themselves under the obligation of leaving whenever it pleases God to grant us peace.

I shall do myself the honor, Excellency, of informing you of the outcome of these negotiations, which are a special blessing for me because they give me the opportunity to ask for your blessing. I do this now, Excellency, prostrate in spirit at your feet. I entreat you to believe that no priest in your diocese will render you obedience with greater submission and joy than I shall do, whenever it pleases you to give me the opportunity to do so. This, Excellency, is what I await. I am, in the love of Our Lord, your most humble and obedient servant.

VINCENT DEPAUL
i.s.C.M.

— 515 —

1162. - TO BERNARD CODOING, SUPERIOR, IN RICHELIEU

December 15, 1649

I read the letter you wrote to M. Lambert, and I take this opportunity to tell you that we must not meddle in the Duke's[1] affairs because: (1) this arouses the jealousy of his officials there; (2) it would make us troublesome to Madame,[2] who will be very edified if we leave it alone; (3) since your predecessor[3] gave people grounds for thinking that he took a little too much advantage of Madame's benevolence, he drew upon himself and upon the Company the ill will of the people and the envy of the leading citizens of the town; (4) our profession should lead us to avoid any involvement in secular affairs. Besides, if am not mistaken, the attorney you mention came to see me when I was in Richelieu and wanted me to give him the same assistance. However, I discovered that there were certain reasons why his request should not be granted. You also mention this, Monsieur, as though it were a simple proposition, and merely so as not to offend him by a refusal to write on his behalf. I am telling you all this not so much for its own sake as for other occasions which might arise. When we are new to a place and duty, we always need a few words of caution.

I would also like to tell you, Monsieur, that now is not the time to complain about feeding the preacher, and still less to shift responsibility for it to the inhabitants, for fear lest their opinion of our being stingy will be borne out, and they will reproach us with the fact that the house is well endowed and that, since we receive other persons for retreat free of charge, we certainly can do an act of charity for a poor Capuchin. In time we shall see if the church council could provide some funds for that and for the other things. Meanwhile, I ask you once more to leave things as they are, without

---

Letter 1162. - Reg. 2, p. 178.

[1]Armand-Jean du Plessis, Duc de Richelieu, nephew of the Duchesse d'Aiguillon.

[2]The Duchesse d'Aiguillon.

[3]Denis Gautier.

changing anything or making innovations, and all that for a good reason.

This will serve as a reply to your idea of having papers drawn up on the land, division into lots, etc. Not that this should not be done, but not for some time yet; first, we have to obtain the Seigneur's document of amortization.

1163. - *ALAIN DE SOLMINIHAC TO SAINT VINCENT*

Mercuès, December 15, 1649

Monsieur,

After having thanked you a thousand times for the trouble you took to speak to the Chancellor [1] *and to explain so clearly to him the reasons that might prompt him to grant me the favor I am asking, and after entreating you to render me the same service with the Queen, I must tell you that my evocation* [2] *is as certain as if I already had it in my hands because all it requires is an order from Her Majesty to the Chancellor. Since she has never refused anything I have asked her and it has always been for other persons, how could I have any doubt that she would refuse me this favor, which I am requesting for my dear Spouse, after having acted and suffered as I have done for the service of the King and Her Majesty?*

I can say truthfully that since the onset of this trouble until now, I have not let pass any opportunity which I could make the most of and use for that purpose. I have not even waited for occasions to present themselves but have sought them out and strongly and constantly opposed anything that I knew was contrary to the service of Their Majesties. After all that, now that I find myself in this critical situation, I would find it hard to believe that she would refuse me her patronage.

You will receive from the deputies a copy of our conference, which I have not yet sent to any of the Bishops who were present, except for the

---

Letter 1163. - Archives of the Diocese of Cahors, Alain de Solminihac collection, notebook, copy made from the original.

[1]Pierre Séguier.

[2]Act by which a matter under discussion in one legal jurisdiction is removed to another jurisdiction.

Bishop of Périgueux, because I have not had time to review and study it.
I shall do so after my retreat, which I am now making. After sending it to
you, I added at the beginning of the article about the visitation the words
you will see on the enclosed piece of paper. I thought it appropriate to
insert them because they are in line with the Councils and holy decrees.

You will see that it has been decided to establish seminaries and that
those who cannot do so will send the clerics of their dioceses to the one
nearest them. As for the direction, we have always agreed that it should
be given to your men. We also agreed that a collège or house should be
established to receive those who will dedicate themselves to God's service,
so that they will be trained in piety and the spirit of the Church during
their studies. That is why I stated that the direction should be entrusted to
your men and I gave a number of reasons for this. So, this suggestion was
approved by the whole assembly, etc.

ALAIN,
Bishop of Cahors

1164. - SAINT LOUISE TO SAINT VINCENT

[December 1649] [1]

Monsieur,

I think your charity will recall my speaking to you about that good girl
from Saint-Cloud. The enclosed letter is for her; please take the trouble to
read it. Divine Providence has not made it possible for her to sell what she
has inherited, but she is renting it to her sister, who is well-off and will
pay her thirty écus a year for it. Our Sisters are fond of her and find no
difficulty accepting her, provided your charity approves.

We would really like to know if the poor wet nurses will get any money
for these feast days. We would also like to know if the children who are
still nursing, and whom they are bringing back because they are not being
paid, will be put out to nurse again with the money given for putting the
new foundlings there. We will do our best to get them to take them back,

Letter 1164. - Archives of the Motherhouse of the Daughters of Charity, original autograph letter.
[1]Date added on the back of the original by Brother Ducournau.

if we have any money. However, some have already been left with us. We are very much in need of God's guidance in the business of my son.[2] *I think he will have the honor of discussing this with you, since he has taken the liberty of staying at your house tonight, for fear of something unpleasant. He will tell you the distressing difficulties in this affair which I think he has always submitted to God's Will. In this Will I have the honor to be, Monsieur, your most obedient and grateful daughter and servant.*

L. DE MARILLAC

Addressed: *Monsieur Vincent*

1165. - *SAINT LOUISE TO SAINT VINCENT*

[December 1649] [1]

Monsieur,

I most humbly entreat your charity to recommend our concern [2] *to God. I found the de Marillacs* [3] *quite willing to please us. However, the nun thinks it advisable for me to see Mademoiselle d'Atri* [4] *to remind her of the services the late M. Le Gras rendered to her late mother* [5] *and to try to have her, like the Comte de Maure,* [6] *arrange something for my son. In view of this, I entreat you to allow me to go to Port-Royal with her daughter, who is willing to take me there tomorrow or the next day.*

---

[2]The position Saint Louise was seeking for him before his impending marriage (cf. no. 1160, n. 2).

Letter 1165. - Archives of the Mission, Paris, original autograph letter, which in 1990 belonged to Abbé Lorenzo, curate of Saint-Dominique Parish, Paris.

[1]Date added on the back of the original by Brother Ducournau.

[2]The position Saint Louise was seeking for her son.

[3]The cousins of Michel Le Gras: Jeanne Potier, wife of Michel de Marillac, and Marie de Creil, widow of René de Marillac. Marie de Creil had become a Carmelite nun.

[4]Marie-Angélique d'Atri, one of the daughters of Geneviève d'Attichy. She was a nun at Port-Royal. Saint Louise's husband had done a great deal for the d'Attichy children after their parents' death. He "had used up everything," writes the Foundress, "his time and his life, in the affairs of their house, completely neglecting his own." (Cf. *Ecrits spirituels*, L. 96, p. 97.)

[5]Geneviève d'Attichy, wife of the Duc d'Atri.

[6]Husband of Anne d'Attichy, who was Mademoiselle d'Atri's aunt.

I am really afraid Madame de Herse may have discouraged the Ladies from coming to the meeting by suggesting they bring money with them. I think she should make it clear, Monsieur, that she does not mean it should come from their own purses nor that we are trying to oblige anyone to do this.

The more I think of what we owe, the more I fear that the affair is going to be left on our hands. The wet nurses are beginning to threaten us and to bring back the children; the debts are accumulating so quickly that there will be no hope of paying them. That will be more detrimental to the Company in the countryside than if we had used counterfeit money.

I am thinking about that poor pregnant woman. I believe she could be accepted now. If you would like me to speak about it to the Reverend Mother Prioress [7] and Madame Le Vacher for you, I will be very glad to do so.

I did not have time to see M. Desbordes,[8] as I had planned. M. de Marillac enlightened me on what was most urgent. If this business were not under the guidance of Divine Providence, I would be very apprehensive about it.

You know my need to obtain from our good God the means of drawing down His grace so as to carry things out. I think He still wants me to place in your charity's hand my will and my limited power of acting in order to offer Him everything. This is what I am doing, most particularly in this matter and in all else, for the accomplishment of His holy designs on me. I am, by His grace, Monsieur, your most obedient servant and very grateful daughter.

LOUISE DE MARILLAC

Addressed: *Monsieur Vincent, General of the venerable Priests of the Mission*

---

[7]Prioress of the Augustinians of the Hôtel-Dieu.

[8]Vicomte de Soudé and Commissioner of Audit. He was also a friend of the Marillac family.

1166. - TO SAINT LOUISE

Saint-Lazare, Thursday, at eleven o'clock [December 1649] [1]

Mademoiselle,

You are right in fearing something about the kind of financial arrangements connected with that post. What makes me say this is that it has been vacant for a long time, perhaps because they have not found any merchant willing to buy it. Most likely they had to sell it since it belongs to several persons. I do not know if it is one of those newly-created, which few people want to buy; it is advisable for you to find out about this. Mademoiselle Lunis' late husband has a nephew named M. Cocquerel, who is at the *Cour des Monnaies*. Through Mademoiselle Lunis, he could tell you what kind of post it is, what it is worth, how many pledges they have, if they have been paid, and if there is any seizure for debt or resistance to confirmation.[2]

The work of the foundlings is in the hands of Our Lord. Friday we shall see what effect Madame de Herse's proposal has.[3] As for the insults the Company will have to suffer, it will be most happy since this comes from doing good.

I will be very glad if you speak to these good nuns of the Hôtel-Dieu on behalf of that poor creature, who is not yet in town and will not be here for another ten or twelve days.

Letter 1166. - Archives of the Motherhouse of the Daughters of Charity, original autograph letter.

[1]This letter is an answer to the preceding one.

[2]The purchase of an office required confirmation by the government, which raised money by such sales.

[3]According to Baunard (cf. Louis Baunard, *La Vénérable Louise de Marillac* [Paris: C. Poussielgue, 1898], p. 399), it is in the speech delivered at this meeting that the touching appeal, so often and so justly quoted as a model of eloquence, was made: "Come now, Ladies; compassion and charity . . . ." (Cf. vol. XIII, no. 196, for this conference to the Ladies of Charity. In n. 1 to this conference, Coste has questioned Baunard's assumption.)

It will be good for you to see Mademoiselle d'Atri.

I ask Our Lord to bless your labors and your business. I am, y[our] s[ervant].

V. D.

Addressed: Mademoiselle Le Gras

1167. - TO BERNARD CODOING, SUPERIOR, IN RICHELIEU

December 18, 1649

I thought Brother Admirault[1] would abide by what I already told M. Benoît[2] to tell him; namely, that we practice the Gospel counsel of not returning to our parents' home once we have left them to follow Our Lord. You know what He said on this subject and how He dissuaded His disciples from going back to their native place. He saw a disadvantage in this for them, and we have always found it the same for our men in such circumstances. If you ask me, Monsieur, why then did we send you to your home, I reply that it is because you did not ask for this and, in fact, you went there only through obedience. And then, there is a big difference between you and a young man. You are a senior member and are, so to speak, confirmed in the Company. He, on the contrary, is weak and a beginner. So I ask you please to dissuade him from making this visit and to dispel any hope of it from his parents.

Letter 1167. - Reg. 2, pp. 302, 178. The second excerpt begins at the words, "Is there no way, Monsieur, to send back to M. Cuissot . . . ?" We do not know whether, in the original, it came before or after the part we have placed at the beginning.

[1]Claude Admirault, born in Chinon (Indre-et-Loire), entered the Congregation of the Mission on September 20, 1648, at sixteen years of age, took his vows in 1651, was ordained a priest in December 1656, and was placed in the Agen Seminary. He was Superior of the Montauban Seminary (1665-1675, 1686-1690), and the Agen Seminary (1690-1694).

[2]Benoît Bécu.

Is there no way, Monsieur, to send back to M. Cuissot³ the
Brother he lent you? Does not the word "lend" oblige one to return
something? And if you promised him to do so, are you not doubly
obliged to keep your word? There is no point saying that you left
him Robin,⁴ since he keeps asking for Bernard.⁵ We must be sincere
with one another. Regardless of how much the Richelieu house
needs this Brother, the fact is that he still belongs to Cahors which,
furthermore, has a great deal to do. You know there are about forty
people there and only three or four Brothers, whereas you have at
least five. If you need more, hire a servant and send this Brother
back as soon as possible, I beg you. Good order demands that
Brothers, no less than priests, cannot leave one house to go to
another or remain in another house by their own choice or that of
the local superiors, unless the General has decided it this way. I
wrote this recently to Cahors, Agen, and La Rose, where quarrels
have arisen because of the changing of Brothers.

1168. - *SAINT LOUISE TO SAINT VINCENT*

December 20 [1649] ¹

Monsieur,

*I have been assured that the post belongs to those in possession of it
and that no one can purchase it unless they resign. Our business continues.*

---

³Gilbert Cuissot, Superior of the Cahors Seminary.

⁴Jacques Robin, born in Mortiers (Charente-Maritime), entered the Congregation of the
Mission as a coadjutor Brother on March 8, 1644, and took his vows on September 7, 1648.

⁵Bernard Gazet, born in Sainte-Livrade (Lot-et-Garonne), entered the Congregation of the
Mission as a coadjutor Brother in La Rose on February 26, 1647, at the age of twenty-two.

Letter 1168. - Archives of the Motherhouse of the Daughters of Charity, original autograph
letter.

¹Year added on the back of the original by Brother Ducournau.

I found the person I mentioned to you yesterday quite calm, and this morning he did well what he was supposed to do. I most humbly beg your charity to continue to recommend him to God.

Mademoiselle de Villenant requests most humbly that you allow her to talk to you before Thursday; and if so, would you please tell her, Monsieur, where she will have the honor of meeting you. If this is possible, kindly let me know through our Sister who is the bearer of this note. It is an urgent matter of importance for the glory of God.

I am very sorry for not having stopped by Monsieur Desbordes' house. The coachman did not know the way and took the wrong road.

Enclosed is the clarification of the doubt we had. Will your charity please see that it does not get lost and continue to do me the honor of believing that I am, Monsieur, your most obedient and very grateful daughter and servant.

L. DE MARILLAC

Addressed: *Monsieur Vincent, General of the venerable Priests of the Mission*

1169. - TO ETIENNE BLATIRON, SUPERIOR, IN GENOA

New Year's Eve, 1649

I had clearly foreseen that your journey to Rome would be made at the wrong moment if you undertook it in the present state of your affairs, and I told you to postpone it, if you judged it advisable. Your Community was also right to desire this but proceeded wrongly in the way of holding you back because: (1) they should defer to the leadership of the Superior and the orders of the General; (2) they did not contact me to point out the inconveniences of your absence; (3) they had recourse to outside means to prevent it, asking the help of persons who are not members of the Congregation. Although we owe obedience to the bishops in what concerns our work for the neighbor, our internal direction belongs nevertheless to the Superior and to the Officers of the Company; (4) in a family, people see only the special reasons that concern it; we see not only these but also the general reasons why orders must be given. Since these are not known by the individual members, they should not then interfere with matters outside their competence.

In short, Monsieur, at its beginning the Company has fallen into the disorder in which others do not find themselves until several centuries later, and the road to dissension lies open when subjects criticize what Superiors do. I want to believe that your men did not reflect on that and, therefore, I excuse them. Do not fail, however, to inform the Visitor, who will soon be with you, of what I have just written you, so that he may speak so clearly to them about it that they will not fall into the same fault again.

You tell me there is a spy in the house, who remarks and reports what goes on. Please tell me if he is a Frenchman and what his name is, in veiled terms. I know you are all leading a life in which there is not only nothing blameworthy but which is, rather, most edifying. Nevertheless, I admit that it is most annoying to be criticized in this way because persons inclined to that never judge things objectively but according to what they are themselves.

1170. - *ALAIN DE SOLMINIHAC TO SAINT VINCENT*

Mercuès, January 5, 1650

Monsieur,

My most humble thanks for offering to assist me both with the Chancelade affair and with our evocation. My assurance that you would do me this kindness has caused me to act as I now do toward you, and since I am as devoted to your service and your dedicated Congregation as I am to my own affairs, I have no difficulty making use of your services on occasion, as I am now doing.

Letter 1170. - Archives of the Diocese of Cahors, Alain de Solminihac collection, notebook, copy made from the original letter.

If the Chancellor refuses to grant me what I am asking of him, and the Queen does not command him to give it to me, this will really dash the enthusiasm of people in this area in the service of the King, once it becomes known, because if they abandon me, after the risks I have taken, what will others think will happen to them? We shall be awaiting the outcome.

The approval you give to our conference will make me appreciate it all the more. Many other matters were decided, which have not been put into writing; among others, one that concerns you and which I shall perhaps add, if you think it advisable. It is to entreat our Holy Father not to grant any more rescripts de promovendo a quocumque episcopo, *on the virtues of the Ordinary, nor any* extra tempora.[1] *The Bishop of Périgueux is responsible for writing about this to the Cardinal Datary, in the name of the assembly. I have written to the latter in advance, telling him the serious trouble it is causing in our dioceses and that it is the ruination of our seminaries, which are established mainly to test the vocation of clerics, as has been so highly recommended by the holy canons. All the bishops in the kingdom should unite with us in this.*

There is fighting every day in Bordeaux,[2] and the terrible desolation in that part of the country is unbelievable.

I never complained about the refusal of Father Faure, the Jacobin,[3] to preach in our pulpit. I could not have done so because I had never seen, spoken to, or written him. It was about his Provincial, to whom I had promised our pulpit and who had assured me that Father Faure was coming to preach.

It is not the curate of Puy-l'Evêque[4] who is asking to enter your Company; it is another man, who is serving in one of the annexes of that parish. He is a native of that place, and the people there are very different from the people of Gourdon. This man is gentle and virtuous and has studied theology. He has only one good eye but is not deformed. Moreover, he obtained a rescript from Rome for a dispensation because it is in Canon Law, and I gave him Orders. Monsieur Cuissot told me he had not gone to him but to Monsieur Water about his plans. I shall tell him or have him notified that he should go and see him to examine his vocation and then

---

[1]*To be ordained by any bishop . . . outside the times.* The sense of this statement is that no general permission should be given to any bishop to ordain men without sufficient training and outside the normal time for administering the sacrament of Holy Orders.

[2]Cf. Antoine Saintmarc, *Bordeaux sous la Fronde (1650), d'après les Mémoires de Lenet* (Bordeaux, 1856).

[3]Dominican. "Jacobins" was the name popularly given to the Dominicans whose Paris house was on rue Saint-Jacques.

[4]Principal town of a canton in the district of Cahors.

let you know what he thinks, to see if you want us to send him to you. We shall do this gladly, wishing to express to you, on this occasion and on any others that will arise to serve you, that I am, etc.

ALAIN,
Bishop of Cahors

1171. - TO MARC COGLEE, SUPERIOR, IN SEDAN

January 7, 1650

Regarding the incident with the gentlemen of the Sedan bureau, who want control of the receipts of the Confraternity of the Rosary, it is advisable, in similar public rivalries involving the Company, for you to notify us immediately. In the meantime, in order to pacify them and to remain on good terms with them, it will be well for you to comply with the request of those gentlemen regarding these receipts, since you see that they are determined not to allow the pastor to maintain such absolute control that they are not aware of what is going on. Furthermore, what they are asking is justified, given the regulations. The people, who contribute to these alms, must want this. The monk who made the establishment could not deviate from the rules of the parish by his own regulations or by what is done in other places where this confraternity is established, unless the churchwardens of the time consented to it.

1172. - TO JACQUES CHIROYE, SUPERIOR, IN LUÇON

January 9, 1650

I have been told here that La Motte[1] does not bring in an income

---

Letter 1171. - Reg. 2, p. 144.

Letter 1172. - Reg. 2, p. 160.
    [1]This appears to be a piece of property known as "La Motte," which Jacques Chiroye wanted to add to the Community's holdings in Luçon.

of fifty écus, as you wrote me; far from it. Even if it should bring in more, does that justify your maintaining two households or the expense involved in the purchases and furnishings this demands? I have already written you my thoughts on this. I greatly fear that what the Bishop[2] is doing, according to what you say, is through your explicit or tacit inducement rather than on his own initiative. This being the case, I ask you to delay carrying out this plan, which could be more burdensome than advantageous.

In the name of God, Monsieur, let us be more careful to extend the empire of Jesus Christ than our own possessions. Let us take care of His affairs and He will take care of ours. Let us honor His poverty, at least by our moderation, if we do not do so by total imitation.

1173. - TO LOUIS SERRE, IN SAINT-MEEN

January 11, 1650

You have consoled me greatly by reporting the state of your house to me. What you tell me about M. Thibault,[1] however, distresses me. He is risking his health too much; he did not feel well and yet he went to work. I fear he will fall victim to this in the end. In the name of God, Monsieur, look after him and see that he rests and takes better care of himself. You will be doing a service to the Company and to the many persons who have need of his services for their salvation. Please do the same with regard to any others who need to restrain themselves.

---

[2]Pierre Nivelle, Bishop of Luçon.

Letter 1173. - Reg. 2, p. 173.
[1]Louis Thibault.

1174. - TO A BISHOP [1]

[Between 1643 and 1652][2]

Who would not acknowledge that it is a very clear blessing of God on the diocese of . . . to have given it a Bishop who brings peace to souls in places where neither bishops nor visitations had been spoken of for a hundred years? Consequently, Excellency, can I ever conceive a high enough esteem for your person or pay you sufficient respect? Must I not declare that you are a God-given Bishop, a Prelate of grace, and a truly apostolic man who, through Jesus Christ, has become well-known to people in greatest distress? May His Holy Name be forever blessed for this! May He preserve you for many years to come! May you be rewarded in the end with an eternity of glory and be recognized in heaven among a very great number of blessed souls who will have entered this abode of glory through you and will acknowledge you there as their second savior after Jesus Christ!

1175. - TO MOTHER ANNE-MARIE BOLLAIN, SUPERIORESS OF THE MADELEINE CONVENT

My dear Mother,

The grace of O[ur] L[ord] be with you forever!

What you ask me about having that good priest for the direction of the house[1] raises two difficulties: first, with regard to authority, he will want to assume too much, and this is not advisable because he will consider himself a born Superior, and perhaps his succes-

---

Letter 1174. - Abelly, *op.cit.,* bk. III, chap. XI, sect. IV, p. 138.

[1]Abelly states that the letter is addressed to a bishop of great merit, appointed through the influence of Saint Vincent. This bishop had reported to the Saint the first fruits of his labors.

[2]The period when Saint Vincent was a member of the Council of Conscience.

Letter 1175. - Reg. 1, f° 62 v°, copy made from the original autograph letter.

[1]The Madeleine convent.

sors will claim the same thing as a right; second—and I place this last—there is the man himself. Since he is somewhat delicate and sickly, at first he would find the responsibility for your house a problem. It is better to see how things will go in the beginning.

I told our Brother who takes care of business matters to return to you today the papers you sent me, which are only copies. You suggested to me that we should have recourse to arbitrators and that you would take M. Defitta[2] for yours. I told you that we will gladly abide by his decision. M. Pepin is the only one I have found who thinks we could not lease Verneuil. M. Blavet said in his presence that we could. All those to whom I have spoken about it since then, and who know the coach business, think it is unjust for your Dreux coaches to prevent the establishment of some in Verneuil as well as in Lisieux, Bayeux, Coutances, and Valognes farther on, where the owners of the Rouen coaches in which you have shares have the right to put some, and throughout Normandy. Judge for yourself, dear Mother, what right Dreux has to exclude all these other towns, which have no coaches, from having some for their convenience, when they wish. Moreover, there are many examples of that: the coaches from Abbeville and Calais still use the Beauvais route where there are already some established. "Yes," you say, "but the owners will get less from their tolls." Even if this were to be the case, should your private interest be prejudicial to the other towns farther on, since the establishment of coaches is a question of public transport? One thing that is unjust is for the other coaches to pick up persons in Dreux; if they did, the Dreux coach should be allowed to seize the other coaches.

These, dear Mother, are my humble thoughts, which I write to you in all simplicity. The pen is being taken from my hand and I must finish. If M. Defitta judges otherwise, I defer to his decision. I am in the love of O[ur] L[ord], your most humble servant.

VINCENT DEPAUL
i.s.C.M.

2A Paris lawyer and one of the Saint's friends.

January 15, 1650

Monsieur,

The grace of Our Lord be with you forever!

You know that all things in this world are subject to change, that man himself is never in the same state, and that God often allows some falling off in the holiest Companies. This has happened in some of our houses, as we have observed for some time now in the visitations that have been made, although at first we did not know the cause. It has taken a little patience and attention on our part to discover it, but God has finally shown us that the liberty some have taken to sleep longer than the Rule allows has had this bad effect. Not being at prayer with the others, they were being deprived of the benefits of making it in common, and often they prayed only a little or not at all in private. The result was that these persons were less careful of themselves, their actions lacked energy, and the Community was irregular in its practices. To remedy this disorder, the cause has to be eradicated; therefore, exactness in rising must be recommended and enforced so that gradually each house will be changed and become more attached to the Rule, and each member in particular will be more attentive to his spiritual welfare.

This led us to hold our first spiritual conference of the new year on this first action of the day, to strengthen all of us more in the resolution to rise without fail at four o'clock, and thereby to participate more fully in the happy consequences of this fidelity. Since this, along with the inconveniences that arise from the contrary, served as a motivation for us in our conference, I thought it my duty, Monsieur, to share it with you, together with the objections and replies that may be given and the means that may

---

Letter 1176. - Reg. 2, p. 302. Other authentic concordant copies are extant, including one in the Departmental Archives of Vaucluse, D 296.
[1]According to Collet, *op. cit.*, vol. II, p. 295.

be used. You can make your Community aware of this, to maintain it in the same custom, or to enter into the spirit of it, if it is not already doing so, in order to share in the same happiness.

(1) The first benefit of rising at the sound of the bell is that we are observing the Rule and, consequently, the Will of God.

(2) Since the obedience practiced at that hour is all the more pleasing to God because it is prompt, it also draws down blessings on the other actions of the day, as we see in the promptness of Samuel who, having risen three times in one night, was praised by heaven and earth for this and highly favored by God.[2]

(3) The first fruits of good works are the most honorable. Now, since all honor is due to God, it is only right to give Him this one. If we refuse, we are giving the first share to the devil, preferring him to God. The result is that this lion prowls around the bed in the morning to seize this action so that, if he cannot get anything else from us during the day, he might at least be able to boast that he got the first of our actions.

(4) We form the habit when we accustom ourselves to a particular time. The result is that afterward we are prompt in rising. This even serves as a clock in places where there is none, and we have no difficulty jumping out of bed. On the other hand, nature takes advantage of what we offer it. If we stay in bed one day, it demands the same satisfaction the next day and will demand it as long as we do not deprive it entirely of any hope.

(5) If Our Lord left paradise for us and was reduced to such poverty in this life that He had nowhere to lay His head, with what greater reason should we not get out of bed to go to Him!

(6) Well-regulated sleep is beneficial to health of body and mind, but a person who sleeps a long time becomes effeminate; furthermore, temptations occur at those times.

(7) If man's lifetime is too short to serve God worthily and to make up for the bad use made of the night, it is a pity to want to shorten still more the little time we have for that purpose. A

---

[2]Cf. 1 Sm 3: 2-9.

merchant rises early to become rich; every minute is precious to
him. Thieves do the same and spend the nights waiting to take
passers-by by surprise. Should we be less diligent for good than
they are for evil? People in society pay their calls in the morning
and take great care to be present at the rising of an important
personage. *Mon Dieu!* how shameful if laziness causes us to lose
the time assigned for conversing with the Lord of Lords, our
support and our all!

(8) When we are present at prayer and at repetition, we share in
the blessings of Our Lord, who reveals Himself generously there,
being, as He says, in the midst of those gathered together in His
name. Morning is the best time for this action and the quietest part
of the day. The ancient hermits and the saints, in imitation of David,
used it for prayer and meditation. The Israelites had to rise early to
gather the manna, and why should not we, who lack grace and
virtue, do likewise to attain them? God does not dispense His favors
equally at all times.

Indeed, since the time He has granted us the grace of rising all
together, we have observed greater punctuality, recollection, and
modesty in this house. This leads us to hope that, as long as this
beautiful harmony lasts, virtue will go on increasing and each man
will become stronger in his vocation. Carelessness has caused
many to leave: not being able to coddle themselves at whim, they
could not grow in love for their state. How can we go gladly to
prayer if we rise only grudgingly? How can we meditate profitably
if we are only half in church, and then merely out of propriety? On
the contrary, those who are zealous in rising usually persevere,
hardly ever grow lax, and make good progress. The grace of
vocation depends on prayer, and the grace of prayer depends on
rising. If then we are faithful to this first action, if we come together
before Our Lord and present ourselves all together to Him as the
first Christians used to do, He will give Himself in turn to us, will
illumine us with His lights, and will Himself accomplish in and
through us the good we are bound to do in His Church. Lastly, He
will grant us the grace of attaining the degree of perfection He

desires of us so that we may be able one day to possess Him fully in the eternity of the ages.

See how important it is, Monsieur, for the whole Company to rise exactly at four o'clock, since prayer derives its worth from this first action, and all other actions are of value only to the degree that prayer makes them worthwhile. The person who said that he could gauge from his prayer how the rest of the day would go really knew what he was talking about.

But since the softness of some will not yield without protest because it is only an excuse, I foresee being told that the Rule of rising should not apply in the same way to persons of a weak constitution and to those who are more robust, and that the former need more rest than the latter. To this I oppose both the opinion of doctors, who all agree that seven hours suffice for all sorts of persons, and the example of every religious Order in the Church, whose hours of sleep are limited to seven. None of them takes more, some of them do not have even that much, and most of them have their sleep interrupted because they get up once or twice during the night to go to choir.

What condemns our cowardice is that women religious have no greater privilege, even though they are weaker and have been raised more tenderly. But do they not sometimes sleep longer than usual? No, I have never heard this said, and I am certain of it with regard to the nuns of Sainte-Marie,[3] with the exception of the sick in the infirmary.

Someone else will say, "What, Monsieur, do we have to get up when we feel sick? I have a bad headache, a toothache, and an attack of fever, which kept me awake almost all night." Yes, my brother and friend, you must get up if you are not in the infirmary or have not been told to stay in bed longer. If seven hours of rest have not given you relief, one or two hours more, taken on your own volition, will not cure you. But even if you were, in fact, helped by this, it is advisable for you to give glory to God like the others

---

[3]The Visitation nuns.

by going to the place set apart for prayer, and there you can explain your need to the Superior. Otherwise, we would always be starting over because often several persons may not feel well, and others might pretend they do not in order to coddle themselves, and this would be a constant source of disorder. If we miss some sleep one night, nature will be quite capable of making up for it another night.

"Monsieur," someone else will protest, "do you also mean to deprive of any kind of extra rest those who return from a journey or have just finished some hard work?" Yes, as far as the morning is concerned, but if the Superior thinks that the fatigue is such that it requires more than seven hours of sleep, then he will have them go to bed earlier than the others in the evening.

"But they arrive very late and quite exhausted." In that case there is no harm in having them sleep longer in the morning because necessity serves as a rule.

"What! you mean we must always rise at four o'clock, with, as is the custom, one late sleep until six once a week or at least every two weeks, to recover a little of our strength? That is very difficult and could cause us to fall ill!" This is the language of self-love and here is my reply to it. Our regulations and even our customs require all of us to rise at the same time. If there has been some laxity in this, it has occurred only recently and in just a few houses, through the abuse of certain individuals and toleration on the part of Superiors. In other houses the practice of rising has always been faithfully observed, and these houses have been blessed. To think that a person could fall ill from not allowing some interruption in this exactness is an illusion; experience proves the contrary. From the time that we have all been rising, no one in this house, who was not sick before, has become ill, and we know of none elsewhere. We do know, however, and the doctors have said so, that too much sleep at night is bad for the sinuses and the digestive system.

Finally, if the objection is made that some business may arise, preventing a person from going to bed at nine or even ten o'clock, and that it is only reasonable for him to take in the morning the rest he lost in the evening, my reply is that we should avoid these complications, if possible, in order to retire on time. If we cannot do so, this happens so rarely that the loss of one or two hours of sleep is of little importance compared to the scandal given by staying in bed while the others are at prayer.

Am I not wrong, Monsieur, to have dwelt so long on pointing out to you the utility and importance of rising, since your Community is perhaps one of the most fervent and regular in the Company? If that is the case, my aim is not to persuade them to tender, humble gratitude to God for the fidelity He has given them; if, however, they have fallen into the fault we are combatting, I think I have good reason to invite them to reform, and to ask you, as I do now, to see that this is done.

Here briefly are the means for you and them to do so. For the Community:

(1) Be convinced that exactness in rising is one of the most important practices in the Company and that as the day begins so the rest of the day continues; (2) give yourselves sincerely to God on going to bed in the evening, asking Him for the strength to overcome yourselves in the morning and to obey His voice without delay. For this end, kneel and invoke the protection of the Blessed Virgin by an *Ave Maria,* and recommend yourselves to your Guardian Angel. Many have been helped by this; (3) consider the bell as the voice of God. As soon as you hear it, jump out of bed, make the Sign of the Cross, prostrate yourself on the floor and, kissing it, adore God in union with the rest of the Community which is adoring Him at the same instant. When you fail in this, impose some penance on yourself. Some have used the discipline for as long a time as they have lost fighting with their pillow. The last means for each member is never to waver from this exactness because the longer you put it off, the harder it becomes for you.

The general means, which depend on your solicitude, Monsieur, and of the Officers of the house, are: first, that there always be someone appointed to go from room to room, carrying a light, when necessary, who says aloud *Benedicamus Domino,* repeating it until he gets a response. After that, another man should make the rounds, even a second one when the Community is large. Those named for this duty must be exact in carrying it out. Second and lastly, those in authority should stand fast and never allow anyone to remain in bed after four o'clock in the morning, under any pretext whatsoever, outside of the infirmary—if there is one—except in a case of great necessity.

Speaking of authority, exactness to rising has been found so beautiful and beneficial that it has been decided that those who have not been faithful to it should never be given positions of authority in the Company. Their example would soon be followed in this relaxation, and it would be bad form for them to take for themselves what they would be obliged to refuse to others. May God be pleased to forgive our past failings, Monsieur, and grant us the grace to correct them so that we may be like those fortunate servants whom the master will find watching when he comes. "Amen I say to you," says Our Lord, "he will make them sit down at table and proceed to wait on them. And if he shall come in the second watch, or come in the third watch, and find them so, blessed are those servants. Amen I say to you that he will place them in charge of all his property." [4]

That is enough for one letter, Monsieur. Please offer me to God and to the prayers of your little Company, of whom and of you in particular I am, Monsieur, the most humble and devoted servant.

VINCENT DEPAUL
i.s.C.M.

---

[4] Cf. Lk 12:37-38.

— 537 —

1177. - TO SAINT LOUISE

[January 1650][1]

I understand no more about those kinds of things you are proposing to me, Mademoiselle, than about the clauses you showed me. If you feel that the Prior[2] and I should be named in the contract, he should be named before me. I beg Our Lord to bless the newlyweds[3] and give you the dispositions he gave the Blessed Virgin when she was present with her Son at the wedding of Cana.

Your good daughter from Vienne came to pressure me this morning for the foster parents. I told her we are doing our best but she has to be patient for a while and do the least harm possible. However, since that is not ready money, I think she was a little disappointed.

1178. - TO RENE ALMERAS, SUPERIOR, IN ROME

February 4, 1650

I sent your letter to M. . . . What you wrote him about Florence

---

Letter 1177. - Archives of the Motherhouse of the Daughters of Charity, original autograph letter.

[1]The contents of this letter dictate the assignment of the date. Michel Le Gras was married on January 18, 1650.

[2]Adrien Le Bon, former Prior of Saint-Lazare. He died on April 9, 1651, in his seventy-fourth year.

[3]At last Saint Louise was seeing the realization of her fondest dreams. On January 13, 1650, she wrote to Sister Jeanne Lepeintre, Sister Servant in Nantes, "I beg you and all the Sisters to offer your Holy Communion for my son who, I believe, will receive the sacrament of Matrimony one day soon. It would seem that God has chosen for him a very virtuous young lady, who is not from Paris." (Cf. *Ecrits spirituels*, L. 275, p. 311.) Michel Le Gras was married to Gabrielle Le Clerc in Saint-Sauveur Church in Paris on January 18. His bride was the daughter of the Seigneur de Chennevières and of the late Dame Musset de la Rochemaillet. The following year a little girl, Renée Louise, was born, whom the Daughters of Charity called "the little Sister." She later became Mademoiselle d'Ormilly. Renée-Louise was still living in 1696, the year her father died.

Letter 1178. - Reg. 2, p. 60.

is very much to the point. God has granted us the grace up to this time not to seek out any establishment, either directly or indirectly. If the Company takes my advice, it will always be preserved through this maxim, for if we are good, we will not lack any, and if we are not, we already have too many houses anyway, and can hardly fill the few we have.

I have been told that the Archbishop of Toulouse[1] has been waiting for a long time for me to give him some indication that I would like the Company to work in his diocese, so he could establish us there and put us in charge of his seminary, but I have been careful not to give him the slightest sign of this. His brother was here a few days ago; he skirted the issue with me for a long time, but I deliberately refrained from discussing it. Providence must call us and we must follow it, if we are to go forward confidently.

1179. - CHARLES NACQUART TO SAINT VINCENT

Monsieur and Most Honored Father,

   Your blessing!
   Since the vast expanse of sea which separates us does not allow me to be able to give you verbally an account of my mission, I have recourse to this letter. It will serve for your charity and, by the same token, for the Sacred Congregation of Propaganda Fide, as the report the latter requests of an explorer sent to this land to find out if it is promising and worth encouraging evangelizers to win it over for Our Lord Jesus Christ. I am well aware that humility should cover the face with shame and close the mouth of such a poor instrument as I, since I am engaged in a work of such great consequence, and I acknowledge that I am both unworthy and incapable of it. However, my duty and charity, together with the expecta-

---

[1]Charles de Montchal.

Letter 1179. - Archives of the Mission, Paris, seventeenth century copy; Arch. Nat. M 214. Saint Vincent had copies of this letter sent to the houses of the Company and even to persons outside of it.

tions of the Sacred Congregation, oblige me to imitate the simplicity of those who have put in writing what God had accomplished in and through them in similar work, as I note that the great Saint Francis Xavier did in his wonderful letters. I realize, besides, that I am obliged to walk in his footsteps, since he was my predecessor, not in actual fact but in desire, for he ardently longed to come to this island but was driven away from it and led elsewhere by adverse winds or, rather, by the Spirit of God.

I shall describe simply and plainly to you our occupations before we boarded ship, and on land and sea, with a brief description of the country, its inhabitants with their customs and superstitious ceremonies, and what God in His goodness has done through us in this country. May the glory for the good be to God, and to me pardon and mercy for the evil done and the good omitted!

(1) What happened before we set sail.

On April 18, 1648, Monsieur Gondrée, my companion, and I left Richelieu, where we were living, for La Rochelle. Along the way, as is customary in our Congregation, we taught Christian doctrine in front of inns and elsewhere, whenever the opportunity presented itself.

We reached La Rochelle on Good Friday and, finding that the ship was not ready, we stayed there almost a month. But we were not idle; for, when we presented ourselves to the local Ordinary,[1] he gave us permission to work in town or country at whatever we felt to be most expedient for the glory of God. Gratefully accepting this, in imitation of Saint Francis Xavier, whom you gave us as a model on our journey, we chose the hospitals. Although we were not lodged in them, we spent a good part of the morning visiting and serving the sick there, with the permission of the Fathers of Charity, who did us the favor of letting us work with them.

The prisoners were our parishioners during the Easter season. After administering the Sacraments, we acted as feet for them, going in their place to see those who, they hoped, would obtain their release.

(2) The most noteworthy events of our voyage.

Early in the morning of May 21, feast of the Ascension of Our Lord, we weighed anchor. At the Mass celebrated immediately after that, I exhorted the congregation to entrust our voyage to Divine Providence, who would make sea and wind favorable to our ship in proportion to the care we would take to keep our hearts in the purity of grace and fidelity to His service.

Since the feast of Pentecost was near, I prepared our flock of one hundred and twenty persons to receive the Holy Spirit through Penance,

---

[1]Jacques-Raoul de la Guibourgère (1646-May 15, 1661).

and I opened the Jubilee which His Holiness had granted the faithful for peace. Everyone made the Easter duty by a general confession. This kept us busy until the feast of the Blessed Sacrament, since we preferred to do this ahead of time because of the dangers of the sea, rather than await the uncertainty of our arrival at the place we were trying to reach.

On the eve of the feast of Saint John the Baptist, a small ship from Dieppe, on its way to Saint Christopher,[2] dropped anchor at Saint Vincent,[3] Cape Verde, where we had stopped to take on a water supply. A number of the passengers gained the Jubilee on land, where we celebrated Mass.

The next day, feast of Saint John the Baptist,[4] twelve black Portuguese, good Christians, came to hear Mass. At the end, they sang the Te Deum laudamus *and asked for the Sacraments, which we were unable to administer because we did not understand their language. I wrote you from that island, Monsieur, explaining to you the need for priests in the country of Senegal, near Cape Verde, where the inhabitants, who are black, seem very open to the reception of the Gospel. There is no danger except that in one season the air there is a little unhealthy.*

If anyone would like to know the ways and means of becoming established in this country, he should contact M. Rozée, who lives in Rouen. He is one of the directors and seigneurs who have land granted in this country and who send ships there.

After remaining there six days to take on provisions, we put out to sea. The winds were against us from early July until August 16 and we almost had to give up, although we were close to the equator. But we had recourse to Him who draws the winds from His storehouse, and to the Blessed Virgin, Star of the Sea. In her honor we made a public vow to God to go to confession and communion during the week preceding her glorious Assumption, and to build a church in Madagascar under the patronage of the Queen of Heaven. A good will collection was taken up for this. As soon as each one had thrown his Jonah into the sea of Penance, the storm abated and the wind changed in our favor so that, on the eve of Our Lady's feast, we crossed the equator.

We experienced the same heavenly assistance around the September feast of Our Lady.[5] The wind, which had been against us, became favorable

---

[2]An island of the Lesser Antilles; also known as Saint Kitts.
[3]An island of the Cape Verde archipelago.
[4]June 24.
[5]September 8, Feast of the Nativity of the Blessed Virgin Mary.

immediately after our public prayer in honor of the Blessed Virgin, whose help we experienced on several other occasions.

When we were in sight of the Cape of Good Hope, God preserved us from the danger of being dashed against a submerged rock, about two leagues from land. A sailor spotted it and we promptly avoided it. As we neared the shore to drop anchor, our ship ran aground on another rock; we stayed there for six or seven hours in the fear of having to remain in a barren, unknown land. Finally, however, the tide floated the ship without any damage to it, and we went on to drop anchor at the port named the Bay of Saldanha.[6]

(3) The Bay of Saldanha and its inhabitants.

Because of the lengthy voyage, and the use of salted meat and water that went bad with time, several persons had contracted an illness called scurvy, affecting the nerves and joints. The land cures this disease. When we went to fetch water in this place, we saw some black people, inhabitants of the country, dressed in animal skins, and armed with bows and arrows, which they used for hunting. They were very thin and so famished that they rushed like dogs on the meat we threw to them. I was deeply moved to compassion, seeing those poor people who did not know their Creator. Prostrate on the ground, I asked Him who wills that everyone be enlightened and saved, to provide them with the means necessary for salvation. They noticed this action and said to one another, "These are Saterons," *meaning high priests. This made me think they had among them certain persons destined for some kind of worship, although I had not seen any sign of this, except that the men are circumcised and the women cut a joint of their finger when their first and second children come into the world. But I think these things are done more through custom than for any religious reason. I noticed a certain order among them because the men, women, and small children were all separated at meals, each eating with his or her own group. It seems to me that the way to help these poor uncivilized people would be to try, in passing, to win over through friendship one or two boys of twelve to fifteen years of age and teach them our language. In this way we could gradually learn their customs and some means of instructing them. If any of our men pass through there, I beg them to try this method or something else better.*

After remaining a week at the Cape of Good Hope, we left and took to the open sea. Suddenly an adverse wind forced us to drop anchor. Perhaps God was punishing us for our negligence or coldness in thanking Him for

[6]Saldanha Bay, located on the southwest coast of the Republic of South Africa. The copyist mistakenly wrote "Sardinia" for "Saldanha".

the provisions we had just picked up on land because, once we had celebrated Holy Mass for this intention, we had such a good wind that in a short time we passed Cape Agulhas,[7] which usually is very difficult and dangerous.

I greatly admired the Divine Wisdom during our voyage, in the countless number of various kinds of fish, very similar to land animals. Among others we saw some which Wisdom had equipped with wings by which they escaped when they were pursued by almost all the other fish. Some even landed on our ship.

Finally, after sailing for six months, we sighted Madagascar. I then exhorted the entire crew to forget all the minor offenses that had occurred among them during such a long, tiresome journey. Everyone promised to do so. On December 4 we cast anchor in the port so long and so ardently desired.

When we reached the port, I was one of the first to go ashore. As my feet touched land, I knelt on the ground to offer myself to God to carry out His plans and to take spiritual possession, in His name, of this island and all the others, by the authority of our Holy Father the Pope, in order to establish there the empire of Jesus Christ and to destroy that of the prince of darkness. I went straight to the Chapel in the fort to celebrate Mass, which had not been said there for five months, for lack of consecratable matter. The next day, December 5, M. de Flacourt, our leader and the mandated Governor of the country, together with M. Gondrée, my companion, and the entire crew, came to the fort, and I celebrated a high Mass of thanksgiving. The Te Deum laudamus was sung, as we had vowed to God on the ship. The French whom we found welcomed us with great joy. When everyone was housed, we moved into a little hut that was vacant.

(4) Our work aboard ship.

No doubt you are interested, Monsieur, in knowing how we tried to procure God's glory during the six and a half months we spent at sea. That is why I shall report it quite simply here. From the day we embarked until we landed in Madagascar, we said Mass and had morning and evening prayers publicly, weather permitting, in the way our Congregation does during Missions. I had some leaflets printed for this purpose, which I distributed to the crew.

We prepared them to gain the Jubilee and arranged for them to make their general confession to this end. We left Cape Verde a few days after the feast of Saint John the Baptist. Reflecting that with us now were people who had been picked up, sailors as well as passengers, in need of

_____

[7]The extreme southern tip of Africa.

instruction, we gave talks three or four times a week on the principal mysteries of faith and on other essential matters, as we do during our missions in Europe. After the introduction, we would question the young people on the points presented in the preceding instruction, concluding with an uninterrupted talk on some other point important to salvation. We continued this for six weeks with good results, but then we stopped for fear of tiring people, and to give them a little break. Our daily schedule was arranged much the same as in our own houses, except that sometimes we had to adapt ourselves to weather, place, and persons.

After mental prayer and the Divine Office, we read a chapter of Holy Scripture and shared our thoughts on the moral lessons which had impressed us, to be used for our own benefit as well as for that of our neighbor. Since there are always some sick persons on a crowded ship, one of us would visit them in the morning and another in the afternoon.

About nine-thirty we would read together Saint Francis Xavier's letters and note what applied to us. Our conferences were on how we could remedy our own needs and those of the ship.

In order to make good use of time, which is boring in idleness, we had our people meet in groups of three or four. One person would read to the others from the Introduction to a Devout Life *by the servant of God, Bishop Francis de Sales, and from the* Imitation of Christ. *This was done in an edifying manner. We even succeeded in persuading a good number of our people to hold spiritual conferences two or three times a week on various subjects, especially on the occasions of offending God and the particular means of resisting them. From the responses of the passengers and sailors, we were keenly aware that Our Lord was among us in this. At the end, summing up what had been said, we would add a few simple words of our own and conclude with a story from Holy Scripture or some example from the lives of the saints.*

After supper we would each go with a separate group on deck to contribute to good conversations and discourage bad or useless ones. In the same vein, when anyone had sworn or said something indecent, it was the practice for him to hold out his hand and receive a rap on the knuckles after he had promised to make amends. This was done without severity and by common consent. Having given sufficient time to conversation, we returned to our little cabins, where five or six little boys would often come to visit us for spiritual discussions of the stories we had been telling them, applying them to their own benefit. Then we would recite the rosary, one group answering the other.

That, Monsieur, is how we used our time during the journey. However, if God granted us the grace of following this little program during our voyage, you should know that the zeal of M. de Flacourt, our very wise

Governor and Commander, contributed greatly to it, since things could not have gone so smoothly if we did not have the support of his authority. We certainly owe to his piety the better part of the joy of our journey.

(5) A brief description of the island of Madagascar and its inhabitants.

Before reporting what we have done in this country, I think it is necessary to give a short description of the island, its inhabitants, and their customs and mores, so that you can see the state in which we found religious matters.

The island of Madagascar is also called Saint-Laurent because it was discovered on his feast day. It is six hundred Italian miles long, two hundred miles wide in some places, and four hundred in others. It is fourteen hundred miles in circumference. It is very hot but not unbearable.

It is divided into several regions separated by very high mountains. People who have seen much of the country assert that it has more than 400,000 inhabitants. Our hut is on the tip of the island in a place called Taolagnaro. We are near the Tropic [of Capricorn] at 25° latitude; consequently, our seasons are the opposite of those in France.

In each region there is an influential person, acknowledged as the chief, and he is like its little king. The vassals of these petty kings number three to four thousand men. Their wealth consists in three to four thousand head of cattle, which belong to them, and in the tribute paid by their vassals, which is one-fifth of their food supply of rice and roots. The title of king does not really fit because they are not truly absolute monarchs, and also because they live so poorly that the most insignificant seigneur in France lives better than the most influential person in Madagascar. Royalty is not inherited by the children, if they are not adults when their father dies. There are other influential persons under these petty kings, who are almost as powerful and rich as they. All these important persons are carpenters.

There are two types of inhabitants. Some are black and have kinky hair, like the man baptized in Paris, who works for the French and is still a Christian; these are the original inhabitants of the country. Others are white and have long hair like the French; they came from Persia about five hundred years ago. In some regions they have made themselves the masters of the black men, as they are here where we live; in other parts they are under the black men, as in Matatanes and elsewhere. They say that their genealogy can be traced back to a man named Ramini, begotten from the foam of the sea, and that this great person was a friend of Mohammed.

Throughout the island, most of the people live in villages at the foot of the mountains, from which water falls in such quantity that rivers are formed and empty into the neighboring sea. There are some wanderers called Ombilambo, who are rather wild and live in the woods, stealing *whatever they can; they run away as soon as they see a stranger. There are no towns, fortresses, or inns. All the houses are built of wood and covered with leaves, and are very low. The doors are so small that a person can barely get in and out through them. The fire is lit and the cooking done in the house, which has no chimney. They have no beds or chairs except the wooden floor on which they sleep. They eat and drink on a mat made of rushes.*

The food of the country consists of rice, beef, mutton, and goat in rather small quantity. In our area there is plenty. Farther on, where we go to trade, poultry is common. There is no wheat or wine, but they make a certain drink out of honey. Roots, beans, watermelon, lemons, and oranges are plentiful. There are no animals for hunting, except for a few wild boar and bulls, and there are very few waterfowl.

The rivers abound in fish, but almost everywhere it is very risky to cross them because there are so many crocodiles, and they are dangerous.

Almost all the inhabitants go bareheaded and barefoot. They wear no underwear, and their clothing is different from ours because they wear a pagne, which is a piece of cloth around one and a half aunes [8] *long and three-quarters wide. The women also wear pagnes that are sewn together and hang from shoulder to feet. Although the shape of the robe is similar, the quality, however, is different, for each one dresses according to his or her class: influential persons wear silk; the others, cotton. Children go naked until they are seven or eight years old. They all have their ears pierced, and they fill the very large holes in them with a piece of wood shaped especially for this purpose, which they embellish with gold or an oriental shell, depending on their social rank. They also adorn themselves with* harais, *out of which they make bracelets.*

They live a long time. There are many elderly persons around, and they say they are so old that their years cannot be counted.

(6) The sect or religion of the country and their superstitious observances.

Although these people have no specific, structured religion, since nowhere on the island can any temple or priest be seen, there are, nevertheless, certain superstitious ceremonies and observances. These were introduced around five hundred years ago when the white people, who are really Kafirs, came from the coasts of Persia to win over the natives. They found them simple by nature, having no laws or religion, and they easily attracted them to the superstitions of Mohammedanism. Certain

---

[8]French measurement of 1.88 meters, or 3.92 feet. These pagnes were about six feet long and three feet wide.

people still practice some of these, such as not eating pork, offering cattle in sacrifice before eating them, and others which I shall mention later. A certain kind of idolatry still persists.

First, they say that Zanahary, that is, God, is master of all, but they confine him to heaven where, they say, he is like a king in his kingdom. In some places, however, since they know God and the devil by name only, they give preference to the devil in their sacrifices, offering him the first share. "This is for Andian Rabilo," they say, meaning his lordship the devil, "and this part is for Zanahary," meaning God. I do not know the reason for this, unless they fear one more than the other, because they say that some persons among them are possessed or at least beaten by Zachare and Drimi, which are the names of devils in this country.

The important people allow themselves to be called gods, and when they want to praise the French they call them Zanahary, but the French do not permit this. The most intelligent among the white people have a limited knowledge of matters concerning the creation of the world, the sin of our first parents, and other similar things. They say that the wicked, generally speaking, will go into the fire, but they do not know where or for how long.

Then there are the Ombiasses. This word means writers, and they are so called because they know how to read and write in Arabic. They are respected as are priests among us. They are the masters of the ceremonies, customs, and superstitions of the country. The people fear them because of their handwriting and their books, in which there is not much development, reason, or doctrine, but only here and there that God is great, and something from the Koran, which they call Ala Koran. The remainder of the contents of these books is composed of illegible scribbles, which these writers make the people believe are capable of curing illnesses, foretelling future events, and finding lost articles.

The custom of circumcising children is general all over the island, not for religious reasons but for purely human motives. It is not done when the child is a week old; in some places they wait a year, in others two, three, four, five, six, or even seven years after their birth.

This ceremony is performed by the Ombiasses at a public gathering. Fathers and mothers bring their children, along with food, such as steer and capons, to be given to these writers. As soon as the child is circumcised, . . . blood from the slaughtered steer and capon is put on the wound. The great general circumcision takes place in the Friday year. They distinguish years as we do the days of the week, and we are now in the Friday year.

The white men observe a kind of fast in two different months; it consists of not eating between sunrise and sunset, but they eat enough all through the night to last for the whole day. They abstain from eating beef and drinking wine, but capons and brandy are not forbidden. If anyone does not wish to fast, he can be exempted by having someone else fast in his place. They cannot give any origin or reason for this superstition, except that it is a custom of their ancestors, and it is stated in their books that those who fail to observe it will go into the fire.

They practice another superstition, called Missanath, *meaning the banquet gathering, which is held when an important person has a new house built or an old one restored. This is one of their principal feasts, and I will describe it here for a better understanding of what follows. This is what happens at that ceremony: when the time fixed for entrance into the new or restored house arrives, the important person's subjects assemble and present him with gifts. Some bring cattle, others bring honey wine, earthen pots, and other household utensils characteristic of the country. The chief has the gifts accepted by one of his men, who points at them one at a time, indicating to him who gave what. Then the chief, standing on the threshold, makes a speech, wishing them temporal happiness so that they might prosper and live for a long time, and he encourages them to go on living and to keep up their services and gifts. The other Roandries, or chiefs, who are of lesser rank than the king but the most important chiefs in the region, also come on this occasion, accompanied by some of their subjects, to present their gifts. When they arrive, they hold maneuvers with halberds and iron-tipped spears, the weapons of the country. Then the master of the house steps forward and, pointing a javelin at their heart, embraces them, while both shout with gladness.*

After two or three days have passed receiving the people and their presents, and the day arrives that has been fixed for entrance into the house, fifteen or sixteen cattle are brought in and the men grab hold of them, no matter how enraged they may be. They are brought down, their feet are tied together, and their horns are stuck into the ground. The men hold them ready to be slaughtered, while stroking their necks. In the meantime, three or four Ombiasses advance gravely, dressed in fine robes with rich belts whose ends they put over their shoulders. Holding a big knife, they go towards the place where the cattle are being held, and they circle them three times. On the first round they throw sand from the sea on them; on the second, grass taken from the seashore; on the third, sea water. Then they slaughter them quickly and collect the blood in wooden bowls, to be presented to the chiefs, who will mark their foreheads and chests with it, praying that it will bring them happiness and long life. Next, the master of the house, holding a large knife, walks at the head of a procession, followed by the important guests. They go around three times, passing above the blood of the animals, and all enter the house, where they go around three more times, shouting with joy and stamping their feet loudly on the floor to show that the house is solidly built and safe to live in.

After that, the Ombiasses, with wax torches carried before them, come forward solemnly bearing their soratra, that is, their books, which I have already mentioned. As they pass, they strike fear into the people, making them give place to them, threatening them with some catastrophe that will befall them if they do not move back fast enough. I was present at this extravaganza, which caused me to smile. They tried to make me move back like the others. "No," I said, "I am not afraid of your books; they are only paper and ink and cannot hurt anyone, no more than the dust at your feet."

They were amazed at my words and contempt of their ceremony, but they never explained anything to me, as has happened on many other occasions where I criticized their fraud, by which they deprive the people of their possessions. Those present said that the Ombiasse of the Vazaha, meaning the French priest, far surpasses their writers in knowledge and doctrine, and that most of the French surpass the black people in ability. When these book bearers reach the house, they circle it three times, sprinkling it with blood so that it will last longer and nothing will harm those who live in it. Then the Roandrie goes to the door and, seated on the floor, preaches to the people to encourage them to go on serving him. He goes around distributing about four to five hundred cattle to feed four to five thousand persons. The skin is eaten along with the meat, as we do with pork in Europe. That is how the morning is spent, and everyone goes off to boil or roast his share of meat.

Meanwhile, the wives of the Roandries prepare the banquet for the chief's household, and have slaves bring three or four hundred portions of rice and meat on leaves that they hold in their hands. Other larger portions on large leaves of various shapes are brought in by some men; these leaves are made from red bark.

Finally, around two o'clock in the afternoon, everyone assembles once again in front of the chief's house. They dance to the sound of a drum, made from a hollowed-out tree trunk and covered with skin. The drum is beaten on one end with a stick and on the other by hand. With grotesque movements, they sing of what has happened in the country. In the meantime, a large quantity of honey wine is brought in and distributed to the crowd. In this drunken confusion the day and the ceremony ends, and the next day everyone returns home.

I inquired of an Ombiasse the reasons for each detail, and the only answer I received was that it was the custom of their ancestors. They have other festivals or gatherings which include a banquet; for instance, before and after the rice harvest.

To the preceding ceremony I will add what they do to deliver possessed persons. Some time ago I went to a place thirty or thirty-two miles from here to give instructions in a rural area. Someone came to tell me there were two possessed women there. I saw no sign of possession, just sad faces. I was also told that they could not speak. I wanted to see how they acted on this occasion, which was as follows: someone ran to get an Ombiasse, who immediately had a javelin handed to those present and to the two women. Then this exorcist took the lead in a dance, which was performed with such gestures that it looked like they were trying to fend off with their feet and hands something that horrified them. Once they were all in a frenzy from the dancing, the old faker of an Ombiasse pretended to throw his javelin into a container filled with water and had the women drink from it. Then he struck them with his knee to chase away the devil, who had never been there; for this was, in my opinion, only a case of melancholy, which this strapping fellow dissipated by the liveliness of his dance.

That is how they perform their miracles, to make people respect them, not forgetting to be well paid, especially when the patients are wealthy. The following shows how they cure people: first, they put on a worried and puzzled air and, taking a plank, they spread sand over it, on which they make a large number of dots at intervals, which they call Sakilo, and they frequently count them to learn the outcome of the illness. They sell some of this sand inside a piece of wax, which they make the person wear around the neck to obtain good health. Then they send for a large number of cattle and capons, and they say that this one should be taken instead of that one. The important thing is that they always choose the best ones, with the thought in mind of eating their share. After that, they do some writing on leaves, entwining the letters, and they have the sick person take a drink of water. If the sick person recovers his health naturally, the cure is attributed to this foolishness. Who would not pity the simplicity of these people, who allow themselves to be deceived in this way at their own expense? Who could refrain from a just indignation against these cheats, who are well aware that these things are futile and irrelevant?

What is more directly contrary to the honor of God, and which will be more difficult for us to eradicate, is an equally ridiculous and damnable kind of cult that the chiefs of the country and their subjects render to certain idols which they call olis, or ointments. The Ombiasses make and sell them. These little idols are fashioned from a piece of wood or a hollowed out root, which they attach to a belt. They put powder and oil in them. Some they shape like little men, pretending they are alive and capable of granting them everything they wish, such as good weather or rain, and preservation from diseases and enemies. They do not fail to feed them, sometimes honey *or the heart of a special fowl. Since I often showed them that these olis were inanimate objects which cannot eat and have no more powers than any stone picked up at random, this makes them angry; and since they cannot prevent me from pointing out their abuse to them, they try to change the subject. When they are pressured, they admit in private that this is true but that, if those objects are dead, their souls are with God. Everybody has some in their house and they carry them with them to the country; they have recourse to them in their needs as we do to God. When in doubt, they never do anything without seeking their advice. Then they believe that the first thought that comes to mind has been suggested to them by their olis. When they sow their rice and other vegetables, they take their olis to the fields, sacrifice an animal to them, sprinkle their field with the blood of this victim, and pray to their olis to give them a bountiful harvest of good rice.*

When they want to cross rivers, they first turn to their olis, asking them to protect them from the crocodiles. Then they address the crocodiles themselves and make a speech to them saying aloud, "Listen, you know very well that neither my family nor I have ever done any harm to your father and mother, or to you yourself. I beg you not to do any harm to me." Then they accuse themselves of any evil they have done saying, "It is true that I stole this and that but I will make restitution." Then they throw water and sand to the four winds and cross confidently. Whenever someone is caught, they say that his olis were no good. I tell them that, if they abandon this abominable superstition, they need only have recourse to God, who is all-powerful, and attribute to His goodness what they attribute to this idol.

Thanks be to God, most of the people around here have been undeceived of this. God Himself, who is always jealous of His own honor, does not let these abominations go unpunished; for, as He formerly did in Egypt, He sends such an extraordinary swarm of locusts that they fill and darken the air at the same time, like the thickest flakes of snow seen in winter in the northern regions. Even as I write, the land is covered with them, et comedunt fructus terrae eorum et omne faenum;[9] *afterward, the ground looks like fire had swept over it. The Ombiasses and some of the chiefs, far from acknowledging that this is a chastisement by which God is punishing their idolatry, make the people believe that they have the power to cause the locusts to come and to keep them away, and when they are not given what they demand, such as rice and other things, they threaten*

---

[9]*And they devour the fruits of the earth and every plant.* Cf. Ps 105:35. (NAB) Ps 104:35. (D-RB)

to summon the locusts. If they do arrive after that, they say to these simple people, "Did I not tell you so?" And when the insects have devoured everything and go elsewhere, they boast of having chased them away. There is good reason to hope that God in His goodness will deliver these poor people from this plague, if they submit to the yoke of faith and the observance of His Commandments.

(7) The secular customs of the country.

They make war among themselves to have one another's cattle.

The chiefs keep their slaves like dogs. They sell the men at the same price as cattle, and children for the price of calves.

Wherever the white people are the masters, they reserve the right to slit the throats of animals they want to eat, so a black man is not allowed to slaughter his own animals. These slaughterers are usually Ombiasses, who get a share of the animal that is killed, and it is not the smallest share that they take. In places where the black people have remained the masters, the whites would not dare to slaughter the animals. This custom is one way to prevent theft and to assure that the chiefs have more cattle when their subjects die because they take everything, leaving nothing for the children of the person who worked all his life to accumulate something.

The stratagem used by the chiefs to keep the lowly always in subjection is that they have seized the best lands, where they sow their rice, vegetables, and other crops, and they deprive them more and more of their remaining possessions, impoverishing them and obliging them to have recourse to their [the chiefs'] storehouses, which are well stocked.

Thieves are punished in different ways: if they are chiefs or heads of a village, they may buy their way out by giving cattle; if they are poor, they are killed or, if they are spared, they, their wives, and their children become the slaves of the man who was wronged.

The most common vice of the country is sexual indulgence. Not all forms of it are considered dishonorable, but if a man is caught in adultery, he is given the same punishment as a thief: if he is rich, he can buy his way out; if he is poor, he is put to death or becomes a slave.

A murderer can also buy his way out: if he is poor and friendless, he becomes a slave or is put to death, but even if the son of a chief were to kill his father, he would not be put to death.

Relatives may intermarry, except in the first degree. Marriage is not permanent; couples may separate by mutual consent and each may marry someone else, as often happens. Polygamy is permitted, although it is not widespread, but a large number of the chiefs practice it because they can afford to feed several wives.

Among the black people, no great ceremony is attached to marriage, except that the choice is up to the couple and not the parents. The husband usually purchases his wife, giving the parents a few cattle or something else for her. But the chiefs have a big gathering of relatives, friends, and subjects on both sides, and frequently the agreement and promise of marriage is arranged by the parents at the birth of the boy and the girl. They marry very young. Cattle are killed on the wedding day, as on their Missanaths. In the presence of the relatives, the Ombiasses wish them all kinds of temporal goods. Their hair is tied together and, while they hold hands, the husband puts his knee on that of his bride. Then a banquet follows and the ceremony ends with dancing.

The older Frenchmen tell me that mothers abandon their babies born on a Saturday between sunset and cock crow, and these poor exposed children die unless, by chance, someone finds them, as sometimes happens here. The excuse these unnatural mothers give for this inhuman act is that this period of time is unlucky, and if these babies were to live, they might kill their fathers and mothers. Still, they sometimes let them live, but they make them serve their brothers and sisters.

It is also said that mothers on Saint-Marie Island, at the tip of this one, likewise abandon their babies born on the three days of the week they consider unlucky, but I have no firsthand knowledge of that because it is done in secret, as do unnatural mothers in Europe in order to preserve their honor. They say that is common in this country too, when the mother is from the upper class and has conceived by a slave.

No name is given to children before the age of six or seven, except amboa *(puppy) or* lambo *(piglet) for the boys because at that age they are more like animals than people. When they are a little older, however, an Ombiasse observes the planet under which the child was born and gives the boys the name of Radama, which means Adam, or names of the prophets Raby, Ramose, Elijah, or Moses. Girls are given the name of Rahona, which means Eve; or Ramary, or Mary, or other names indicating that they are beautiful, very rich, and will live a long time.*

Funerals are held according to the rank of the deceased. If the person is an important Roandrie, he is buried in a beautiful robe. His face is left uncovered and adorned in the custom of the country with a necklace made of coral and beads of gold and silver. Relatives and friends of the deceased meet to pay their respects, and all of a sudden they throw off their weapons and shields, go over to the corpse with their heads lowered, and weep sincerely while singing mournful chants. Perfumes and aromatic wood are burned; then they carry the corpse to the place destined for the burial. Once they arrive, they redouble their cries and groans, and bury him. After that, some cattle are slaughtered, and they rejoice far more than they had grieved. Immediately the carpenters, who are all chiefs in this region, start building a sort of house over the pit, and a large group of slaves bring in a huge stone in the shape of a pyramid, which they raise in front of the burial place. On top of this pyramid they place a steer's horn.

This same ceremony is generally observed at the death of all kinds of persons, except that the pomp of the funeral increases or diminishes according to the rank of the deceased. Rich and poor alike bring the first fruits of their harvest to their father's grave and leave fruit trees around the burial place. No one dares to pick the fruits there. When they have a bad dream, they have an animal slaughtered for the intention of their dead father.

In the region where we live, they have been ignorant until now of what becomes of the soul at death and whether it is separated forever from the body. Now that we are telling them what faith teaches us, they are truly amazed, especially to hear us talk of a blessed or wretched eternity.

So that is what we have been able to learn about their mores and superstitions, both from asking questions and from observing most of them. There are many other areas at the tip of the island, of which we have no knowledge. It is said that there are Portuguese in one place and Dutchmen in another. When we have traveled all over the land and gone around the island by boat, we will give you all the details of this. But even if there were no areas or people other than the ones we know, would not this vast number of sheep without a shepherd, exposed to the fury and cruelty of the wolves, be enough to soften and move anyone to Christian compassion? Bear in mind especially that they are well disposed and that the nets of a poor fisherman and sinner like me are incapable of holding such a large number of fish, unless some zealous and astute workers come to my aid. This will be evident from what I shall say in the following pages.

(8) The state in which we found matters pertaining to the Christian religion.

Having spoken about the country, the inhabitants, their customs and superstitions, it is fitting to describe to you the state in which we found matters pertaining to our holy religion, since we have come here to propagate it. The gentlemen of the Company of the Indies had heard about this island from some heretic, who had the aptitudes necessary to establish himself here. The first time, they were obliged to entrust to him the leadership and instruction of those they were sending here. With the exception of nine or ten heretics, these men were all Catholics, whom the commanding officer had brought there. These gentlemen have always had some priest to serve the spiritual needs of the French; we came across one named M. de Bellebarbe. He worked there as best he could but made little progress because he did not have the support of the commanding officer who, allowing Mass to be said for the Catholics, had the sermons preached in his own home. This, coupled with some domestic disorders, kept the unbelievers from going either to the prayers of the Catholics or of the commanding officer because they were surprised to see two kinds of religion among persons of the same country. These gentlemen have removed for me this obstacle to the advancement of God's glory by recalling this commanding officer and forbidding any heretic to board the vessel for the crossing. M. de Flacourt, one of these gentlemen, was put in charge and proceeded on this voyage as much for the glory of God as for the service of that company; it is to be hoped that the blessing of heaven will be on both. And God, in His great mercy, has chosen us as workers to look after the souls of the Frenchmen in this country and to work for the conversion of the unbelievers.

We found in this region only five children who have been baptized: a little girl who had been abandoned in the woods, the illegitimate son of a Frenchman, and three little slave girls brought back from the war and saved from the massacre. The latter were baptized by a deacon, who has died.

(9) Our occupations in this country.

We first tried to edify and win people over by gentle, pleasant conversation. God in His goodness has been pleased to make use especially of this means for the conversion of five heretics. Our first task was to prepare the French we found here to gain the Jubilee for peace. Next, we applied ourselves to learning the language of the country. We had great difficulty in this because the dictionary we were lent on the ship contained very few words and was neither well-prepared nor correct, and there is a big difference between the pronunciation and the written word. Also, it is one thing also to know the meaning of an isolated word and understand how it is being used in the construction, and to recognize and understand it in the speech of the natives. That is why we were obliged, with great difficulty, to bring together the interpreters, who had a hard time finding words to explain our faith in a country where people never speak of religion. We have tried to train two men, whose names are Claude Hastier and François Grand-Champ. The latter does a better job at explaining things.

As soon as we were able to stammer a few words, we began to instruct the unbelievers. The black men among them are much more docile than the white men, who consider themselves very intelligent and do not listen when matters of faith are mentioned. If they do listen, it is only through curiosity and with indifference. In exactly the same way, the Roandries confirm in themselves the words of Our Lord, Vae vobis divitibus,[10] *and*

---

[10]*Woe to you rich.* Cf. Lk 6:24. (NAB)

Abscondisti haec a sapientibus et prudentibus et revelasti ea parvulis [11] because, after these good black people listen carefully, they say to one another, "So, we must not swear any more, nor work on Sunday, nor steal."

These chiefs say that their slaves are incapable of learning how to serve God; they would like to prevent us from instructing them, and to keep them in ignorance for fear lest their own malice be revealed.

But because you, Monsieur, perhaps want me to describe here a few particular cases by which you may understand more clearly the way we want to instruct these poor barbarians, and how they, on their part, correspond with God's grace, I shall recount some of them here.

(10) Some details about the instruction of the islanders from December 15, 1648 until after Easter 1649.

I had heard that the chief of this region, named Andian Ramach, had spent three years in Goa and was brought back here by the Portuguese when he was seventeen; he is fifty now. Six days after our arrival, M. de Flacourt sent me and a few Frenchmen to see him in Fanshere, where he lived, a journey of one and a half days from here. He gave us a good welcome, made three Signs of the Cross on his forehead, mouth, and lips saying, Per signum sanctae crucis de inimicis nostris libera nos,[12] and said the Pater, Ave, and Credo in Portuguese. Through the interpreter I asked him why he was the only one in the region who knew how to pray to God, and why he had not taken care to have his subjects instructed. He replied that they were incapable and that there was no priest to instruct them. I answered him that I had come to see him because I wanted to serve him and all his subjects as well and that they would be capable of learning, once they were taught as he was. He told me he was happy about this and would come to prayers whenever I had them in his village. Other chiefs there told me the same and asked me to come and instruct their children. This petty king said he had been baptized in Goa, in a college where there were several priests; he had been ill and Baptism restored him to health, after which he made his confession and received Communion once. Then he was brought back here by a Portuguese trader, accompanied by two priests who lived on a little island about two leagues from here. Still to be seen there are the walls of a house, built by the Portuguese more than a hundred years ago, as attested by the inscription on a marble cross. One of these priests died, and the other returned with the trader after baptizing

---

[11]You have hidden these things from the wise and the prudent and have revealed them to children. Cf. Mt 11:25. (NAB)

[12]Through the Sign of the Holy Cross, deliver us from our enemies.

just one man, as I mentioned, who has three crosses tattooed on his stomach. Eight years later, Andian Ramach reverted to his superstitions.

After more conversation on both sides, I made much of the young people, extending my hand to them, in the custom of the country, while stammering a few words of their language. Then I gave them little presents of glass bead bracelets, which delighted them. They called me their father, and I said they were my children. Each one scrutinized me closely, and when I went to recite the Divine Office, they came to watch me pray and stayed around me.

This first journey filled me with joy and hope. On my return, I consoled my dear companion with all the good news. We spent Christmastide by gaining our Jubilee, administering the Sacraments, and preaching to the French, as we are accustomed to do. When the feast of the Epiphany arrived, we began to baptize the children, in order to correspond with the mystery of the vocation of the Gentiles. M. de Flacourt named the first one Peter, and thus he became the first stone in our spiritual Church.

About this time, a ship left carrying twelve Frenchmen sent to live at Sainte-Marie, a little island two hundred leagues from here, where a Roandrie is the lord. There are fourteen villages and around six to seven hundred inhabitants, who are very sociable. They speak about the same language as here. This region is unhealthy and, although the land is good for farming, it is difficult to clear because the woods are so thick. M. de Bellebarbe had been sent there to look after the people, and I asked him to prepare the way there as best as possible for Christianity, but he did not stay long and now he has gone back to France.

Some time later, when we had learned a little of the language, we spoke to the natives about learning how to pray to God. They were ashamed and excused themselves saying they were incapable. Taking their hands, we had them make the Sign of the Cross and say the words. After that they were delighted to have said and done what they had formerly believed was impossible. We did the same with the young people, and on Sundays we would teach them a little Christian doctrine through our interpreter. In a short time they were freed of the mistaken idea they had of being incapable of learning.

Several Roandries from the environs came to see the commanding officer and gave him some small gifts in the hope of receiving better ones, as is the custom of the country. We took advantage of the curiosity of these chiefs to entice them, along with their slaves and vassals who were accompanying them, to come and see our chapel. There, through an interpreter, we spoke to them about our faith. They said that these were beautiful things and they wanted to learn about them. Some had gone to the High Masses and were asking what they were, and why, when the priest finished chanting, all the Frenchmen answered with one accord. We replied that we were all of one mind in presenting our needs to God and in singing His praises together. Someone told us that formerly in this land their ancestors had large houses, where they used to assemble as we do in our churches, and that on Friday, after singing as we do, they slaughtered cattle, sheep, and goats for a public banquet. However, wars had done away with these things a hundred years ago.

I took the opportunity from this to tell them that we would teach them a more excellent way to pray to God than that of their ancestors, which was only worldly, and how to serve Him as He commands us to do, without having to have banquets.

The most knowledgeable of the Ombiasses in this region, who was fifty years of age, was here with the others. We asked him, through the interpreter, how he was serving God. He told us that Ramofamade, meaning Mohammed, was their prophet, and Moses was ours; that we did well to follow the law of Moses, and they, that of Mohammed. He told us the story of our first father, Adam, almost as it is in Genesis, except for one irrelevant detail, namely, that there was one river of milk, another of honey, and a third of wine, and that the reason God became angry was because of the stench that arose when Adam and Eve emptied their bowels in the garden. He added that some of the children of Adam were white and were great lords from whom the French and the white men in this country were descended; the others were black and were slaves from whom the black men trace their origin. We spoke to him about Jesus Christ, Son of the Incarnate God. He replied that their books made reference to a prophet named Raissa, who had come to earth directly from God, without being born among men, and that he was greater than Mohammed, who had yielded to him. When we told him that this person was Our Lord Jesus Christ, the Son of God, whom we adore, he replied that God had no son and was alone, but that they, like us, also hoped to get to heaven by observing their ceremonies. However, none of the interpreters were capable of explaining the mystery of the Trinity, as I hope we will be able to do with time, using the similes and manner of speaking of this country.

At the conclusion of our visit, he said he was pleased to learn about our beliefs and to leave his fifteen-year-old son with us so he could learn from him later. I gladly accepted his offer, but that little rake was unwilling to stay. He told me his father would not allow him to drink wine until he had learned their superstitions.

That is what I learned from the most knowledgeable man in the country. However, he never says a word about God to the black people, but is content to dupe them with his olis and salis. If anyone could win over an Ombiasse like him and divert his attention from the small profits he draws from his frauds, everything else would soon follow. But good interpreters are needed who can understand and convey the reasons on both sides. This can be done only through long practice because the language has no rules of grammar, and the French have not been living in this country for long. I hope, with time, that God will grant us the grace of overcoming these difficulties.

My first visits to the rural areas were made during Lent to some sick Frenchmen three or four leagues from here. As we passed through the village, the natives gathered out of curiosity to see a little watch I had borrowed. They admired it and thought it was alive, and they were saying that we were gods. This obliged us, like Paul and Barnabas, to tell them that we were men like themselves. From this I took the opportunity to speak to them as best I could about God. These poor people likewise said that they were incapable of learning, and when I tried to have them make the Sign of the Cross, they ran away. When one of the braver ones, the village chief, had made it and pronounced the words, each of the others then asked to do so.

(11) Visits made to the rural areas from Easter time 1649 to the month of June.

When the Easter feasts were over, I learned that Andian Ramach was having a Missanath at his house, which had been repaired. I thought it a good idea for me to be there to see what went on in this ceremony and take the opportunity to speak about the faith to such a large crowd, in the presence of the king and other chiefs who would be there. I brought an interpreter with me in order to speak more easily to them. I asked the king to tell them himself what he had learned, since they had greater confidence in him. He promised me this several times but did nothing, and by waiting for him we lost the opportunity because of the great confusion of the banquet. However, I spoke to the local chiefs and the Ombiasses who were in his house, and I had another advantage in this visit because the people saw that I was always near their king and thought I was in good standing with him. Since then, this has been very useful to me because I was able to say to them in all truth that their king had asked me to instruct them. He himself entreated me to come and live permanently with him and to give him the Office in Portuguese, and he would pray to God as he used to do. On leaving, he told me to write to Louis de Bourbon to give him a fine gift. I told him that the latter would not fail to do so, if he would become a good Christian again and do his part, along with us, for the salvation of his subjects. I also said that, if we came to live with him, we would not be a burden to him. The people here are so parsimonious that it would be better to give them something than to take anything from them.

On my way home, one of the village chiefs, named Ramanore, had someone ask me to come into his home and to ask God to restore his health. He was, after the white men, one of the most influential men in the country and, in the past, had come to the instructions given in our house, after trying all the superstitions of the Ombiasses to no effect. When I explained to him that God often permits bodily ills for the salvation of our souls and that He was all-powerful and could cure him, if he abandoned the superstitions of his country and was willing to serve God as we do, he immediately asked us to instruct him. I assembled the villagers to come and listen. Through the interpreter I had brought with me, I told them the essential elements of the faith most necessary to salvation. After listening to everything, the sick man said that his heart was relieved and that he believed everything he had just heard. He also said he had great compassion for the Son of God, who died for us, that he would thank Him for this, and would never forget it. He asked if Jesus Christ was powerful enough to restore him to health. "Yes," I said, "if you believe with all your heart and that your soul will be cleansed of all your sins by holy Baptism." He sent for some water and urged me to baptize him. However, fearing that he was seeking bodily health more than spiritual—which later happened—I put him off saying that proof was needed that his desire to serve God was genuine and that it would be apparent if he would see that both he and his whole family were thoroughly instructed, once his health was restored, as I was hoping Our Lord would do for him.

When his wife heard the Commandments of God explained, she said that for a long time they had had recourse to God in everything, especially in planting and harvesting their rice, when they would raise their eyes to heaven and say to God, "You are the One who can make what I am harvesting grow; if You needed it I would give it to You, and I shall give some to those in need, like the Frenchmen who come to my house, and the poor slaves." That made me think of Cornelius, but I had not had any vision telling me to baptize the man.

Everyone present was delighted with what they had been told, and said that these things were worth more than gold and silver, which could be taken away from a debtor—"But who could take this from us? We shall still find it in our hearts when we awake from sleep." In these conversations I perceived that, even though the Holy Spirit had not visibly descended on them, He was nevertheless making Himself clearly felt by the light He was shedding on their souls. I said good-bye, leaving to the sick man the hope of a cure and to everyone that of being instructed. Shortly afterward, I heard that this simple man had recovered his health, but was in no hurry for me to give him instructions as he had promised, although he still professed to have this desire. I think that human respect and the fear of being on bad terms with the chiefs whom he serves are the cause of his putting it off. He is leading a good moral life, and I have baptized two of his children since. Some later said that I should have baptized him, and his good health would have given credence to his baptism, but I felt he would have given more if he sought it earnestly when he was in good health.

(12) Some visits we made during June and July, and the death of Monsieur Gondrée.

Around the Rogation Days, M. de Flacourt was going to Fanshere and wanted one of us to go with him. M. Gondrée went and suffered a great deal from the heat and the journey on foot, and from abstinence also, since he had eaten only a little boiled rice, which left him in a weakened condition. He came back with a fever and unbearable pains in every joint. At the height of all his ailments he showed great constancy and truly Christian sentiments.

During the feast days around Pentecost, although I was greatly distressed by the illness of this good servant of God, Our Lord gave me the strength to satisfy the devotion of the French and of our catechumens, hearing confessions, preaching and saying Mass in the morning, having Vespers in the afternoon, and instructing the islanders.

I baptized two young women, who were married to two black men. One of the men had been baptized in Paris by the Nuncio, and the other in Nantes. This consoled our patient, who received Extreme Unction with great devotion. He said his great sorrow was to abandon these poor unbelievers. Then, with great fervor, he exhorted the French to the fear of God and devotion to the Blessed Virgin, to whom he himself was very devoted. He asked me to write and thank you most humbly in his name, Monsieur, for the favor you had done him in admitting him among your children and bearing with him, and especially for having selected him from among so many others more capable, to be sent here. He also requested that the members of our Congregation thank God for this in his name. Then he said to me, "I leave you this warning as my last will and testament: that you will suffer much in this country, and not just a little but a great deal." He spent part of the night making continuous aspirations to God and, with a smile, gave up his soul to Him on the fourteenth day of his illness.

He was buried the next day amidst the tears of all the Frenchmen and of the unbelievers. The latter said that, until we arrived, they had never seen men who were not angry or irritable, and who taught them heavenly things with as much ardor and gentleness as we were doing.

Please pause here to imagine the sentiments of my poor heart in the loss of the person whom I loved as myself. Everything about him was pleasant and he was, after God, my sole consolation in this country.

I asked Our Lord Jesus Christ for the deceased's share of the grace needed to do alone the work of two. After his death I experienced the effect of his prayers and a double strength of mind and body to work for the glory of God. Then the fear of dying before I had put the work of God in order spurred me on to do what was most necessary: to write instructions in the native tongue on what must be believed and done, in order to familiarize myself with them and to leave them for those who will come after me, in the event that God should take me. After great difficulty trying to express religious matters in a country without religion, I finished what was most necessary and sent a copy to M. Bellebarbe at Sainte-Marie so he could use it, but he was unable to do so because he had no interpreter.

Once I had the instructions written down in order, I assembled the faithful of our congregation on Sundays and holy days. They were amazed to see me speaking their language in such a short time, even though I could only stumble through the most elementary things I had learned. The children of one of the chiefs, named Andian Panole, who lived about two hundred leagues from here, had come here on some business. They came to see us and stayed for the instructions. When it was time to leave, they said they wanted to be instructed also and would report to their father what they had heard about our religion. I gave them the hope that in time we would go there. We would profit greatly there because that area is better and more thickly settled than our region, and the inhabitants are very interested in coming to the prayer service of the French who go there to trade.

I lose no opportunity to announce Jesus Christ, either personally or through someone else, to the black people who live in the distant places where the French go. After exhorting the latter to go to confession and Communion before leaving, I recommend to all of them the fear of God and tell them to give good example to the unbelievers. I instructed the most intelligent among them not to lose any occasion to speak about our faith, and I gave them in writing the necessary instructions for this.

In June I went to the country to see if the celestial seed I had sown in the villages was beginning to spring up. I learned that a solemn assembly was being held in Fanshere for entry into the house of Andian Sero, who people think should succeed Andian Ramach. He had heard that the village chief, Ramanore, whom I mentioned previously, had been cured immediately after I had visited him, so he pleaded with me to go to his house to pray for the health of his grandson. "What do you want me to do?" I asked. "Do you think that God can cure him without the olis of this region?" (because it is one of the most superstitious.) "Do and say whatever you want," he said, "provided my boy is cured." Lifting my heart confidently to God, I went to see Andian Ramach and said to him, "You are well aware of what Baptism is and how you received health of soul and body from it.

Now your grandson is ill. If you want me to baptize him, send for your son-in-law, your daughter, and the child. I will explain Baptism to them, and you can give him whatever name you choose. " So he did this and called him Jerome, and he told me to pronounce carefully the words, which he pronounced also. I indicated through the interpreter that the child would be bound to live as a good Christian, and the father said to me, "I give him to you and, when he grows up, I want you to be his father and mother. " Then I baptized him, explaining to the Roandries present that, although children were baptized without any preparation on their part, adults, nevertheless, had to be instructed beforehand.

Shortly afterward the child regained his health and, by the grace of God, none has died here after Baptism, as has happened in Canada. That is why the pagans are not opposed to our baptizing their children, believing that this will keep them healthy, after what happened to a black man, whom I told that his child would die if he had him circumcised, which is what happened. Later, he came to me with his wife and said to me in tears, "You were right in what you said. " These poor people wept for the loss of their child's body, and I for his soul.

Before I left, Andian Ramach spoke to the people about the Command- ments of God. I confirmed what he said and offered to instruct them. The Roandries who had come to the celebration said that they wanted to be baptized before leaving. I entered the new house, which I found filled with the Roandries' wives. I spoke to them about the faith. They replied that the Ombiasses of the area exempted women from learning because they were incapable. But when I told them that the women in France are as well taught to serve God as the men, they said they really wished there were some here to instruct them.

(13) Other visits made during August, September, October, November, and December.

Since the death of my dear companion, on whom I was relying and to whom I entrusted the care of our house and the surrounding area, I am unable to go as far afield as before. I have to be home on Sundays and feast days to celebrate Holy Mass and the Divine Office, and preach to the French and give instructions to the unbelievers in the environs. That is why my rounds last only six days.

In August I went to the mountains closest to us. During the day I gave instructions to the villagers and, in the evening by moonlight, in addition to them, to the others who were returning from work. I was greatly consoled on the one hand to see that they believed with all their heart, and with tears in my eyes I would say, Quid prohibet eos baptizari? [13] *However,*

---

[13]*What is to prevent them from being baptized?* Cf. Acts 8:37. (NAB)

fearing that they might make a wrong use of Baptism, since they had no priest to maintain them in Christian piety, I put everything in the hands of God's adorable Providence. I would have baptized some children but I was afraid we could not tell them apart from the others, especially since the pagans change dwellings quite frequently. I think also that it is advisable to give them some kind of distinguishing mark.

Those I have baptized in our neighboring villages are recognizable, and in their area they are called by their baptismal names of Nicolas, François, Jean, etc.

It would be too long and boring for me to try to list the names, journeys, villages, and people to whom I have announced Our Lord Jesus Christ, and the details of what took place. I can tell you that we could not wish for any greater openness to the reception of the Gospel. All are complaining that, since the French have been in their country, they have never mentioned the faith to them, and they have a holy envy of those who live near our house.

I shall report only what took place on a few particular occasions. At the end of November I went to visit the villages on the other side of Fanshere. I had brought with me a large picture of the last judgment, and of heaven and hell. In each village I declared that I had come so that their eyes might see and their ears might hear things for their salvation. After explaining what they had to believe and the Commandments of God, I showed them the dwelling places of eternity and urged them to choose the one above or the one below—heaven or hell. "Tsiary aminy Rabilo; aminy Zanahary tiako andeha," they cried out. (That means, "I will be careful not to choose to go with the devil; I want to live with God.")

They told one another that their Ombiasses made no mention of God to them and visited them only through self-interest and to deceive them, whereas I taught them free of charge. They admired the way we were able to make figures on paper. When they heard about the sin of our first parents, some of them cursed them saying, "Oh! how wonderful it would have been to remain as God had created us, without having to work or be subject to the ills of this life and to death!" Others were angry with the devil, saying that if they could catch him, they would burn him. When someone would arrive late, after the picture had been folded up, they would say to him, "Ah! you have not seen the treasure!" And we had to unfold it and explain all over again.

On my way home, I passed through Fanshere and showed my pictures to the king, who was familiar with them and explained them. Then I asked to be allowed to baptize the children in his village and to forbid circumcision. He told me he would not stand in the way of Baptism, but that I should let them perform circumcision. A little patience is needed to set them straight with time. If we can reconvert this petty king to his pristine state of being a Christian, the other chiefs will follow him, and our arms will be dropping with fatigue from baptizing. Since the white men are the least disposed to accepting the Gospel, and among them are the chiefs and the Ombiasses, I tried not to lose any opportunity to speak to them about the faith because if they can be won over to God, the rest will be easy.

That is why, when I went to the tip of the island, two days' journey from here, where I was extremely consoled to see the people so well-disposed, I went to see Andian Madamboro, the king's elder brother, who had been displaced by his younger brother. This chief is an Ombiasse and is very superstitious; people attribute to him the power to summon and to dispel locusts. He first asked me for a remedy for gout, from which he was then suffering. After I had told him that God alone could cure him, or give him patience in his pain, I evangelized him about Jesus Christ. I told him he had to believe in the One whose picture he was holding; he took it and kissed it, placed it on his head and heart, and asked me to stay and instruct him. All I could give him was some hope. I wanted to see his books, which were all blackened with smoke. All those present took hold of my cassock and cried out, "What are you doing? You will bring us bad luck; wash your hands and your mouth." Scoffing at their fear, I picked up those books, in which I saw only some poorly sketched figures. When I asked him the meaning of the writing, he said it was the names of the planets. I told him that all those superstitions and deceits by which he was deluding the people had to be abandoned. He replied that he knew no evil and did not intend to serve the devil but to observe the customs of their ancestors. He said that I should teach him something better and he would leave all that aside. He told me to come and see him often, provided it was not on a Friday. On that day he spoke to no one because he had observed that anyone who spoke to him on that day came to some harm as a result of some catastrophe. I told him I would try to come precisely on that day, on which Our Lord Jesus Christ had redeemed us by His death. I had him make the Sign of the Cross and left him in these good dispositions.

Next, I went to visit Andian Machicore, the king's son-in-law, in another village. (People attribute to him the power of summoning the rain; one time it did rain, and they presented him with some cattle in thanksgiving.) In my conversation with him, in the presence of several inhabitants of the locality, he asked me if it would rain soon because their rice was all burnt up for lack of water. I noticed that the moon was pale and the sky was clouding up. I told him that, in my opinion, it would rain soon but that I really knew nothing for certain because that was up to God alone, who sends and holds back the rain as He pleases. "But you," I said, "if you have the power to summon the rain, why do you let the country's rice and

*your own rice dry up and be lost?" He attributed this power to his olis,
who all have their own names. I remember one whom he called Andian
Valotomboko, meaning "the Lord who is eight feet tall." I was a little
incensed and rightly indignant against these pieces of deceit, and said that
it was devils whom they were honoring in these ridiculous figures, the
inventions of magicians to transfer to demons the honor belonging to God
alone.* Et loquebar de testimoniis tuis in conspectu regum et non confun-
debar.[14] *There is no danger in telling them the truth, since they would not
dare harm a Frenchman, still less me, who converse gently with them
without, however, flattering them when it concerns the glory of God.*

*The greatest difficulty will be to convert these arrogant men, who are
incapable of reasoning. There is no learning in this country; custom and
temporal interest triumph over reason. Still, this should not surprise us in
persons who have only a spark of knowledge, since some persons in Europe
who are highly enlightened find it just as difficult to extricate themselves
from vice.*

*Some time ago, I went to a place on the other side of the mountains,
called the valley of Ambolo, where there is only one chief. He and all his
subjects, around four thousand in number, are black. There is no Ombiasse, but they go there to sell their olis. While I was at the king's house, I
showed him the picture of the last judgment, saying that this is how God
would burn polygamists, including him and his wives (he had five of them).
His expression changed; he begged me to come and instruct him, and said
he would oblige his vassals to accept the Gospel.*

*At Christmastide I visited the region of Anossi, where there are around
ten thousand people. I have only two more visits to make in order to set
ways right,* in omnem locum in quem est ipse Dominus venturus.[15] *I shall
go as soon as possible so that those who come after me will at least find
the land cleared. This has been done at the cost of great fatigue, but He
who gave the Evangelists* nivem sicut lanam [16] *makes the heat here seem
like a gentle dew to those who are in the furnace of charity.*

---

[14]*And I spoke of your decrees before kings and I was not ashamed.* Ps 118:46. (D-RB) Cf.
Ps 119:46. (NAB)

[15] . . . *into every place to which the Lord Himself intended to come.* Cf. Lk 10:1. (NAB)

[16] . . . *snow like wool.* Cf. Ps 147:16. (NAB)

Conclusion

The ship is ready to weigh anchor now, after time has been given me to make these remarks. In conclusion I shall tell you, Monsieur, that all these poor persons who are pining away await only the aquae motum [17] *and the hand of a few good workers to plunge them into the pool of Baptism.*

How often, while evangelizing in the rural areas, have I not wept on hearing these poor people cry out, "Where then is that water you promised us, which cleanses souls? Have it brought here and say the prayers." But I am holding off, fearing that they are asking for it for material needs, like the woman who, so as not to have to go to the well, asked Our Lord for the water that quenches thirst, but was not yet familiar with that which extinguishes the fire of concupiscence and gushes forth to eternal life.

I mentioned at the beginning that we found five baptized children. Our Lord has been pleased to add to this fifty-two others. Although there are many adults who are adequately prepared, I am delaying until we can marry them immediately after Baptism, to remedy the vice of the country, as we did with those who had been baptized in France. Meanwhile, I will be careful to see that none of those who are well enough disposed will die without Baptism. Some time ago, I baptized an old woman who was seriously ill; God had made manifest in her the effects of His grace by the deep sentiments of His goodness which He suddenly gave her. She was the first in this country to go to a blessed eternity, and her body was the first to be buried in the French cemetery.

On the feast of the Purification,[18] we blessed and laid the cornerstone of the church we are going to build for our dwelling, after thanking God for choosing us to erect a temple to His Divine Majesty in such a large kingdom, where there is no trace of a church, even though there are more than four hundred thousand souls, who can be hewn as living stones of the spiritual edifice we hope to erect to His glory.

I shall await help and orders from you and from the Sacred Congregation for the Propagation of the Faith. In the meantime, if I cannot make much progress, I will try not to let what has already begun be lost. Where are all those Doctors, as Saint Francis Xavier used to say, who waste time in Academies, while so many poor unbelievers petunt panem, et non est qui frangat eis? [19] *May the Master of the house provide for this! Unless there is a large number of priests to give instructions and maintain the*

---

[17] . . . *movement of the water.* Cf. Jn 5:1-9. (NAB)

[18] February 2, Feast of the Presentation of the Lord.

[19] . . . *look for bread, and there is no one to break it for them.* Cf. Lam 4:4. (NAB)

good results, we can advance little; even though the people are ready to believe and are easily attracted to the bosom of the Church, their attachment to transitory things may, like thorns, stifle the seed sown in their hearts. And although they receive it joyously, cito arescit, quia non habet humorem.[20] *I feel sure, Monsieur, that all the members of our Congregation tremble with joy at the news so agreeable to their zeal, and desire to cooperate with God in the conquest of this new kingdom for Jesus Christ. Out of compassion at seeing me alone in such a distant country, able to administer the sacraments to others but incapable of receiving any others myself except the Eucharist, they will, I am sure, beg God's goodness to strengthen me in His grace.*

What could console me the most after God would be to learn the most important events that have taken place in our Congregation for the good of the Holy Church and the glory of God. I shall continue to pray for you, Monsieur, that before He calls you to Himself, He may be pleased to have you see your children multiplied like the stars in the firmament, and that all of them may be the fathers of several generations for heaven, where I hope to see you, through the merits of Our Lord Jesus Christ and the assistance of your prayers and those of all our confreres. I am, Monsieur, your most humble and obedient servant.

CHARLES NACQUART, *i.s.C.M.*
Apostolic Missionary on this island

Fort-Dauphin, Madagascar, from Taolagnaro, residence of the French, February 5, 1650

1180. - TO GUILLAUME DELATTRE, SUPERIOR, IN AGEN

February 6, 1650

I feel certain that what was imputed to you about the Jesuit Fathers is simply calumny and that you would not wish to offend a Company that is so holy and useful to the Church of God. I praise God that people have also recognized the truth. I hope that what

---

[20]*It soon withers because it has no moisture.* Cf. Lk 8:6. (NAB)

Letter 1180. - Reg. 2, p. 125.

happened will serve only to bind you more closely to these Fathers, toward whom I wish you to manifest great esteem, affection, and deference, as I am endeavoring to do here, and I do so with much consolation.

1181. - TO A PRIEST OF THE MISSION[1]

... And I—the most uncouth, the most ridiculous, the most stupid of men among these persons of rank to whom I could not say six consecutive words without letting it be seen that I have neither wit nor judgment—how have people put up with me until now, if that is the case, in the position I hold? But what is worse, I have no virtue that even comes near the person in question.

1182. - TO MATHURIN GENTIL, IN LE MANS

February 9, 1650

No one has complained to me, as you seem to think, about the room in which you had the floor leveled. All I know about it is what you yourself have written me, but that is enough to make me think that the Superior[1] is not happy with this renovation nor with the others done in his absence. This gives me good reason to ask you not to do anything of importance without consulting him. If he does not agree to the matter, but you think it is necessary or very useful,

---

Letter 1181. - Manuscript of Brother Robineau, pp. 22, 61.
[1]This Missionary had complained about his new Superior, saying that he was not refined enough. After praising the Superior as he deserved, Saint Vincent added the above words. If, as seems probable, the Superior is Pierre Watebled, then the letter was written in 1650. Cf. nos. 1190, 1191 and 1202.

Letter 1182. - Reg. 2, pp. 307, 132. The second fragment, which was perhaps the first in the original, begins with the third paragraph, "I am glad. . . ."
[1]Antoine Lucas.

let me know your reasons and his; we will decide whether it should be done or put off.

I rarely receive letters from M. . . and he has never mentioned you, at least not in the way you think. Furthermore, I would not allow such persons to attempt to inform me of what goes on within the Community, which is none of their business. Besides, you are too wise and discreet for people to find much fault with your actions. But if someone were to criticize them without good reason, should you not be glad to suffer something for justice sake, since Our Lord has said that those persecuted in this way are blessed? Please keep your heart in peace, Monsieur; you belong to God, by His grace, and are determined to live and die for His greater glory. Is not that a great happiness and a reason to rejoice unceasingly, whatever troubles you may have?

I am glad you have anticipated the intention of the Bishop of Le Mans[2] regarding the tax on your chapels. I see clearly that this could be settled some day in a court of law. For now, I see a certain risk to be feared in that. This is why I ask you to pay this tax, without prejudice to your rebate. For several years we paid the one levied from the beginning on Saint-Lazare, while awaiting an opportune time to get ourselves exempted from it, as we have done since. At first we were satisfied with registering a complaint, sometimes with the Bishop of Paris, sometimes with the commissioners of the Clergy, and sometimes with others, trying to influence them in this way to relieve us of this burden at their convenience. Perhaps a good mission, which will satisfy the Bishop, is all you need to win his benevolence and, through his favor, rid yourself of this excessive tax because your claim is indeed just.

---

[2]Philibert de Beaumanoir de Lavardin.

1183. - CHARLES NACQUART TO SAINT VINCENT

Monsieur,

Your holy blessing, please!

Fearing that the letters might be read and diverted, I am keeping this one from the packet and am entrusting it to a friend to have it delivered to you in person because of what you will find in it, which I did not think advisable to include in my journal. This letter is a kind of spiritual communication to ask your advice with regard to situations that have arisen, so that I may know how to act in them. It will also reveal to you what sort of person one must be to live in this place. I recall that you wished me a share of O[ur] L[ord]'s patience, and I shall tell you here the little difficulties I have encountered, giving me cause to exercise it.

You told me that these Gentlemen would provide us with what was necessary not only ad victum [1] but also ad vestitum.[2] However, according to what M. de Flacourt has told me both in La Rochelle and here, he has no intention of furnishing any clothing. So, in order not to upset him, I spent for fabric, linen, and other small necessities in La Rochelle about two-thirds of the money you had sent us. Otherwise I would no longer be wearing anything indicating that I am a priest, no more than does M. de Bellebarbe, who is now dressed in grey. Except for the ten écus I have left, I spent the remainder here for necessities and to supplement the inadequate amount given me to go and visit the sick in the rural areas. Please have this clarified, if you are sending anyone here, and get everything spelled out in detail to avoid any misunderstanding. I preferred to spend everything rather than have the slightest disagreement, and I borrowed one hundred francs from the captain of our ship, as I shall tell you in an express letter for him.

I have found it very difficult to practice what you wrote me about being gentle and respectful in conversation, while remaining faithful to the interests of God and not betraying my conscience. As you are aware that the conversations of people of the world are all too often about things that should not be heard by a priest, when impurity and scandal, usually aimed at priests or others, form part of the talk, I have tried my best to change the subject as gently as I could. By trying to be faithful to God and my conscience, I have made myself obnoxious; but, of the two, I have chosen

---

Letter 1183. - Archives of the Mission, Paris, seventeenth century copy.
[1] Food.
[2] Clothing.

to please God rather than others, for fear of losing the prerogative of servant of Jesus Christ. Only M. de Flacourt has criticized this; the others were glad and were grateful to me for it. Innocentes et recti adhaeserunt mihi, quia sustinui te, Domine.[3]

When people work here on Sundays and holy days without permission and before Mass, I have told them that the custom of the Church has to be followed, which is that this is not to be done without necessity or without a dispensation, and after Mass. For doing this, I am considered as someone who wants to lay down the law and to infringe on the temporal through ambition.

When, to remedy the complaints and murmuring of several people, I notified the person who could put an end to them, I was looked upon as the cause of all this.

When, out of compassion, on hearing the sick who were complaining of dying for lack of food and medicine, I went respectfully to the father of the family on their behalf, I was dismissed in only God knows what way, as if I had made them say those things. It is a shame to see so little organization in this that those who had been promised in France remedies during their illness have to sell their shirts, made from cloth brought from France, for some poultry, which cost less than a sou in the money of this country; or, if they have sores to dress, they have to tear up their underwear. How can we stand by and watch this? You will find enclosed a letter addressed to members of the Company in Paris. Please read it, but do not show it to them [4] unless I am calumniated. I have reason to fear that this may be my payment for the small services I have rendered to these Gentlemen, after risking my life on land and sea. Nothing, however, is lost in the sight of God.

What will have to be done with regard to these wretched wars which I mention to these Gentlemen? People here say that many excuses will be found for the past and for the future. I am well aware that only false pretexts exist, capable of destroying the work of God and of jeopardizing the salvation of those who perpetuate them. If war is waged, it is only to put by a few commodities. There is not much to be done for religion in this country, with a Governor pious in appearance only, who thinks of nothing but temporalities. Not only words are needed but a person who, both by example and authority, contributes effectively to the designs of God, which are of such great consequence, as [you] can imagine.

---

[3]*The innocent and the upright have adhered to me because I have waited on you, Lord.* Cf. Ps 25:21 (NAB) Ps 24:21 (D-RB)

[4]This letter was published in *Mémoires de la Congrégation de la Mission*, vol. IX, pp. 94ff., taken from a copy preserved in the Archives of the Mission, Paris.

Saint Francis Xavier accomplished much by his virtue and zeal, but the authority of those who supported him and supplied him liberally with necessities contributed a great deal to this. There is no punishment here for Frenchmen who are scandalous, nor for those sordid men and women who service the settlement. The French simply say, "I will not go to confession." And people say that the others are dogs. Is there no way for these Gentlemen to establish some sort of justice?

I have no cause for complaint about my food, which, if anything, is too good. But if a native or some little children have to be enticed with presents, people say that this is being too indulgent. Because of this pretext of avarice, I have no bait to fish for men, and yet it would cost very little to supply amply what is needed, as you will learn better from those who have lived here rather than from what I could explain to you in writing.

Because I accepted a piece of glass from one of the natives, I am being suspected of wanting to establish trading in this country. And I was only planning to use it for a small cross to be put in the church! The workmanship would have cost more than the material was worth, and it would not have been even four fingers long and two wide. I gave it away when someone asked me for it because I care about as much for precious stones as I do for straw.

When Monsieur had not had his beard trimmed on Sunday, Mass had to be delayed. He complained to me about being inconsiderate in not notifying him so he could take his time, and said that some day there would be other priests here. I explained to him that I had told his servant to be careful to inform me before the last bell if he was not ready. After everyone has assembled and the priest is vested, it is too late to let me know.

He has often repeated that there are monks who have offered to pay their own way and to take care of all their own expenses here and that he would tell the Company that there was no danger in allowing all sorts of them to come! I do not know if he is doing this as a reproach to me or has something else in mind. I replied that all I wanted was that God would send those who would render Him the best service. Others would meet as many obstacles as we do, and their number and diversity would only cause confusion.

All this, joined to the difficulty I find with the conduct of the French, causes me to suggest that you consider whether it is advisable for us in future to be responsible for the French who, from now on, will be placed in several settlements that are disorganized and in unhealthy districts, at a great distance from one another. How can we manage all that and the natives? Would it not be better for these Gentlemen to have some good secular priests on salaries, and that there be enough of us to establish a Community, live in places where the chances for winning souls seem more *likely, and work only with the natives? It is futile to talk about the Rules of the Mission or about recollection to one lone priest—or even if there were two of us—in a settlement where the French make a racket of drunken brawls, songs, and their work, and all the confusion involved in the care we must take in our life and conversation with lay persons.*

Certainly, you will do whatever you think best about this; as for me, however, I am very weary of it all, and I do not think we can do anything much for the natives unless we are completely disengaged from these Gentlemen in order to work only at giving missions. Furthermore, it is against our Rule to have parishes, and we cannot do both well. You know what confusion this has caused in Richelieu, even though there is a large Community to do the work in both of these. In addition, I think that in future the French will marry native women and go to live in distant, isolated places. How can we take care of all that?

Andian Ramach has often told me that we should go and live with him in Fanshere. That is the place to make a settlement of six priests to give missions in this region. With the aid of a good interpreter, we could do this little by little in the villages. A school could be opened there for children, of whom we would have a large number of an age when they would be capable of learning, and it would not cost much to feed them. No linen or clothing are needed as in France; they go around completely naked, except for a loin cloth, made of drugget, with which they cover themselves. They are used to sleeping on the ground and living on rice and roots native to the country.

I do not know what to tell you about the girls; some virtuous widows or young women from France would be needed to take care of them. However, that would be one more problem for us because you know the obtrusiveness of this sex. Daughters of Charity who are well-grounded in virtue would be suitable, but they should not live in the same place as we do, ne crederentur uxores sacerdotum [5] *by these naturally suspicious people and by the French. But it is imperative to instruct them and to help curb the dissolute ways of sexual excess by instilling modesty in the girls, who even from childhood are everywhere as shameless or even more shameless than the little boys.*

From this younger generation good marriages could be made, and their children would be even better Christians than their parents. We will have to do here what is done to reform a Community; we will do what we can with the older people, but it is the children who will instruct their parents

---

[5] *Lest they be suspected of being the wives of the priests.*

and reform the country. People say the same to me everywhere: "We are too old; come and instruct our children." The children would like nothing better, even though they are very undisciplined. Their parents love them so much that they spoil them and let them do as they please without punishing them.

Four coadjutor Brothers would be needed; one of them should be a pharmacist and know surgery, with some experience in caring for the sick. He should bring a supply of the necessary medicines because there are none at all in this country. The other should be a tailor and should bring linen and other cloth for us, drugget [6] *for the little boys, and colored cassocks if we are going to have a school. The third one should be able to instruct young people, with the aid of an interpreter, and have classes to teach them to read and write in the French characters so as to introduce the custom. Here they read and write in Arabic, which is too difficult. For this purpose you can have printed just one hundred copies of the catechism I am sending in that language, while waiting for a better one or until strongly bound prayer books with large type can be printed. The fourth Brother should be a steward and should bring all the supplies needed for our Communities because all we have here is what is imported, except for beef, rice, and edible roots. In addition, we need enough money to buy everything, until the time when we can take as much land as we need to plant crops, with the permission of Her Majesty and the Gentlemen. This can be done without detriment to the Gentlemen from France or to anyone else because there is plenty of land.*

Boiled rice, as it is eaten in this country, is not very nourishing, and it is not easy to get used to it. Honey wine is not good for the health and is very rare. Pure wheat flour can be brought from France. It keeps for three or four years and can be used for consecratable matter, for making bread at sea, and for baking it here in a small oven. Good-keeping wine is needed for Mass and for preserving one's health in this country where, without proper nourishment, medicines, and other provisions, people are very subject to serious illness and death, as you can learn from persons who have been at sea and from those who have lived in this country. To trust fine promises, as we did, makes it disagreeable to have to purchase things from the French at four times what they would cost in France. Sometimes even things that could easily be brought from France cannot be found here at any price and yet are necessary, so I have had to do this to stay in good health, without however pampering myself. What would be even better is

---

[6] A fabric woven from wool, cotton, or silk, and used at times for clothing.

to have something to offer some relief to the sick French or to the natives. It is so sad not to be able to help those who are doubly afflicted by illness and poverty, when it would take so little to save their lives. There should be a well-run hospital established here by those Gentlemen; it would save many lives, to their own advantage.

Besides what can be shipped from France, a sufficient stock of local products should be procured; you can get information about this only from someone who has experience with this country. I was hoping to send you a person who knew the language of the country to inform you about matters, but he was refused passage, even though he is one of the oldest residents. I do not know the reason for this or if he is suspected of something, but he is our best interpreter and has willingly given himself to God to remain with me until he can get away, which will be at the arrival of the first ship, after this one returns.

I think it would be well for us to have permission to accept some Frenchman here after his term of service is up, if he feels called to the service of God; there are two or three here who have requested this of me. They are all well-disposed and have a basic knowledge of the language and lifestyle of the country. With so much work to be done, we can never have enough; many die and we have had fifty-seven deaths among us in twelve or thirteen months. Even though those who are truly called present themselves, unless we have this permission people will say we have corrupted them. They think I have done so with this interpreter, who volunteered on his own and has always continued through devotion, although he has been offered wages, which he has refused in order to work with me. I could do nothing unless he was with me all the time; one cannot have two masters, so one must choose the better one, which is God.

Two good carpenters and a joiner are also needed to build churches and wooden houses, and they should bring from France locks, padlocks, and nails, all ready made. In a word, they should bring whatever is necessary for housing and furnishings in this country, where as much can be found as in a desert. It would be a good idea as well to bring whatever can be planted and grown in France, such as wheat, vines, grains, seeds and kernels, legumes, etc. However, everything must be kept airtight because the sea air spoils many things, but should be exposed to the fresh air occasionally in good weather.

When I have gone to the country, I have always had a Frenchman with me, interpreter or not, who carried a gun, for no other purpose than self-defense, if we are attacked by thieves or drunkards. I think it would not be a bad idea to have some lay persons with us in the settlement, if we make one, so we can defend ourselves in case of necessity. The fear of our weapons keeps everyone in check, and they will not dare approach if they *see a firearm, no matter how large their number. Some of the French have been massacred for lack of vigilance.*

That is what is most necessary for making a settlement, and I think there is no other way to subsist. I am ashamed at having specified so many things which, in France, we can do without and mortify ourselves; but since we have bodies to serve as instruments in the service of God in this country, where there is such a great need of workers, we must procure the wherewithal to survive, since it is so hard to come by.

Matatanes is the best place to make a settlement as soon as possible, in order to spread our religion effectively. It is in the center of the island, where the French resided, and is a very pleasant place in which to live. All the best people are there, and the Ombiasses come from there. In addition, it is easy to go all over the country from there. Presently no Frenchman has Her Majesty's permission to settle there. With regard to spiritual matters, that is where the best harvest in the whole country and those most capable of instruction are to be found. About a dozen priests would be needed, along with the interpreter I mentioned who has lived there, because there are slight differences in language according to the region, as in France we have the dialect of Picardy, Normandy, etc. One of our men who knows Arabic, or who can at least read and write it well, would be most necessary. I am going to try to learn to read and write it from an Ombiasse who will teach me, so I can understand what is in their book and write out something for them by way of instruction. I do not know, however, if I shall succeed in this.

The means of subsistence in Matatanes are the same as mentioned above. The problem is that only three or four persons at a time can come on the boat, and it takes a long time to recover a dead person such as I have been, left all alone.

If you ask what qualifications are needed in workers for this country, you will be a better judge of that than I, who am unworthy to be included among them. I shall simply give you my own opinion, which is that the qualifications are those required by Saint Francis Xavier; that is, persons are needed who excel more in virtue than in knowledge. The knowledge required is that which God gives to the saints. If there are no good preachers, no matter, except that the French have to be taken care of. In that case someone potens in opere et sermone [7] *is needed to control these undisciplined people who have been thrown together, most of them sent to this country by their parents, who do not know what to do with them, or who came here on their own because of dissolute living or curiosity. When*

---

[7] *. . . mighty in deed and word.* Cf. Lk 24:19. (NAB)

they see that their hopes of finding a good country here are dashed, all they do is curse the day they came. Even when their time is up, they have to remain just as long again because there is no ship to take them away, as they had been promised. I leave you to imagine what sort of life they lead in such desperation in a country where it is so easy to yield to corrupt nature. Nothing would give us greater pleasure than not to have to take care of such persons, on whom we often only waste our time and are repaid by ingratitude and calumny. They act like madmen toward the doctor who is trying to cure them, becoming annoyed with him instead of taking his remedies.

If we had only the natives to instruct, all we would need are a few catechists, even someone with a good memory who might not want to be a priest but who had a facility for languages and was capable of learning this one quickly. This is easy for a person who has nothing else to do because the pronunciation is not difficult. All that is required is a good memory for retaining the words, which are neither declined nor conjugated and which, in time, can be compiled into a dictionary and a grammar, I hope.

This can be done when we have our own interpreter and are living away from this place of confusion, where we are under orders to those who are always suspicious. Rather than helping matters they hinder them and would think they had done themselves great harm in giving us an interpreter, whom they put to work at trifling tasks instead. I mean that a layman, guided and formed by a priest, will be able to do the teaching until such time that the priests, who are occupied more with the Office and other things, will be able to teach on their own, without using interpreters. I could never learn the language perfectly here without living among the natives. I know a little of the vocabulary of the catechism, which I have studied, but I cannot completely understand their arguments without an interpreter. Long practice is needed in the beginning for a thorough understanding of the true meaning of the words.

Good health and strength are required of those who will be working here, both because of the fatigue of the long sea voyage and because of the lack of conveniences here in the rural areas. We have noted that the youngest and most robust are the ones who die rather than those who are of average strength but are in good health. Persons thirty-five, forty, or fifty years of age are healthier than those who are younger, because the country is so hot.

The danger to chastity is not so great as people think. We should not go out alone and should be serious-minded and on our guard, although the solid practice of chastity is required on many occasions when we are exposed to losing it.

Impatient natures like mine are not very suitable, even less are those persons who ask to come here through caprice and who might act accordingly; bene patientes ut annuntient,[8] *especially here where the people are unaided in understanding these new subjects.*

It is hardly possible for someone to live alone, as I do, without a companion. I recall that Saint Xavier asked for persons of extraordinary virtue for such a situation, and you know that this does not apply to me.

There is no reason to fear persecution or danger when we have an armed Frenchman with us, but there is little security in being alone, particularly if we were to go to places where these poor people have been pillaged and burned. They will always be distrustful and difficult of approach; at the sight of one lone Frenchman they flee like a large flock of sheep before a single dog.

Toward the center of the country, some chiefs were killed when war was waged on them, and women and children as well. It is also said that, without waging war, it will be impossible to get cattle to supply the settlement in future. Some people say that the only way to master the people is to slay the leaders and that this is the best way to establish religion, as the Portuguese have done. Quod si aequum est, judica.[9] *How can we remedy this if we remain here? I have always opposed to this the example of Our Lord, who did not command the Apostles to raise armies to establish Christianity, but to be lambs among wolves. Although the white people have become masters either by ingenuity or by force, all we have to do to destroy all the power of the influential persons is to live here and allow the black people to continue to enjoy their possessions and acquisitions. In truth, the former are rich only at the expense of children who have been deprived of their paternal inheritance. In addition, they make an advance of animals to the village mayors, and they profit from this after the latter's death, taking everything they find that belonged to the deceased.*

I can assure you that, if we open our school here or in Matatanes, there will be no need of wars to maintain it; we can trade things native to the country for all the animals and other victuals necessary which cannot be brought from France but which grow here. I myself bought six cows, costing me about one écu apiece, and a few hens so I could have eggs on Friday and Saturday, along with a little milk, so as not to be obliged to eat meat. Meat is eaten almost all the time, including during Lent, not only at the Governor's table but in the homes of all the French. In this they live like Huguenots because they are careless about getting fish and other

---

[8]*Very patient in order to teach.*
[9]*You be the judge whether this is just.*

things that pious persons could easily obtain. Most of them have no scruple about this, even though I have often made it clear to them that I dispensed only those who were ill, or who had done their best but could not make provision for this, or, lastly, those who in conscience had a legitimate excuse before God.

I am obliged to let all that go since I have been unable to remedy it. They all send me to the person in charge, and whenever I have discussed it with him I have been reproved; he says that if he has any commodities it is not for that purpose. It would not take much, if not for everyone, at least for his own table. It is only a lack of organization, and that would be easy to arrange. Up until now I have not broken abstinence, except that, because no one is willing to take the trouble to make butter, as I shall try to do when I can, I have permitted myself to use beef tallow, or oil from the fish which I myself have very often caught off the rocks. This causes me to reflect on the spiritual catch of the Apostles, who sometimes went fishing for a living, and our good God has provided me with what I need to live.

What should be done about fast and abstinence for the French and for the natives who will become Christians? Please give me a little advice on this because it bothers my conscience. All they have to do is to drop a net into the sea. I know that anyone who can do something but refuses is unworthy of absolution. There are some who are legitimately excused, but those who can fast and abstain are giving in to their appetites, lack of piety, and negligence, under false pretexts of being unable either because of the Company or for fear they may fall sick and die. What can we say to that?

Instead of preventing the natives from working on Sundays and holy days, trading is done on those days. They say it is better for them and for the Christians among them to work, and they need the French to oversee them. Most often their work is not necessary. If the French ask for time off to go away, they are given Sundays and holy days. They leave the day before and will miss Mass for trifling matters saying that, if they were given other days off, they would not use them. What can we do about that?

You can imagine from all this the disorder which exists, and the pain my poor heart has felt from the whole situation. This has caused me to say many times that, were I not here through obedience, usquedum dicatur mihi,[10] *I would have shaken off this yoke, too heavy for a pygmy, to transfer it to broader shoulders, especially because of M. de Flacourt's treatment of me, although he is beginning to see the truth and innocence of what he had imposed on me. Do not say a word to him about this, unless he*

---

[10]*Until I am told [otherwise].*

mentions it first (which I fear, even though he said pax, pax *to me). If he does not say anything, I can assure you on my part that I have drunk the bitterness of this chalice through that of O[ur] L[ord] and the Apostles, experiencing in this the prediction made to me by my dear companion in his testament shortly before his death. When I asked him what he was leaving me before dying, he replied, "Sufferings. Oh! how you will have to suffer! It will not be for a short time, but I assure you that all will be well." Oh! how happy I am about that. It is very little compared to what will perhaps have to be endured in future to imitate the vessels of election who were chosen to carry the name of Jesus to the Gentiles.*

If M. de Flacourt complains about me, I know he is alone in this because everyone else, even the most dissipated, would be ready to give me their hearts and their eyes. Ask pardon of him for me for the harm he will tell you I have done. I shall accept your reprimand for it because, even though my conscience does not reproach me except for my personal laziness in God's service, I have tried not to fail with regard to the neighbor. Still, I do not consider myself virtuous because I know I am a man and the weakest and the most at fault of anyone you could send. God knows that I am not lying. What I have always most dreaded has happened to me in the choice made of me, not in my being sent here, for I had no difficulty rising above the objections of flesh and blood to submit to obedience, once I knew God's Will, but because you have placed the responsibility on the weakest man.

I have always been convinced, and still am, that I was sent only as an explorer and that you will send the one quem missurus es,[11] *whom I shall not be worthy to obey, if you send some priests by the next ship. I am well aware that it is useless to anticipate what will not happen, that I might have no authority over anything, but do my utmost to be submissive and to carry out whatever is ordered me by those whom you will give me as Superiors. I know you are too sensible to give me the last place and not put me at the helm, and that, in the event you do establish a Community here, you will take good care not to remove an inferior member from his place, causing him to groan continually until he is put back there. You would also not want to be responsible for the faults I might commit in a work of such great consequence, since I have neither the knowledge, judgment, nor experience to guide me in such thorny matters. As people say, if the foundation is badly laid, many preposterous things will ensue. A skillful architect is needed to lay the foundations here; I have every reason to believe that I have been alienated from the others by my foolishness.*

---

[11]*Whom you will have sent.* In other words, "someone else."

I am not saying this through false humility so as to wheedle some authority out of you in any way, because nothing is more apt to discourage me than to find that I am not under the authority of a Superior. If you do not send me one, which I have no doubt you will do, I think I will have heart failure because I have already done too much harm, without adding to it my own loss and the loss of the salvation of many people; whereas, if someone gives me orders, I think I shall be saved from that death which is my own will. Then, with a joyful heart I shall run in the path of obedience with nothing to weigh me down, once I find myself freed from this burden, which I dread more than any difficulty imaginable. I see in it no possibility of working out my salvation, which I must prefer to that of everyone else; but I do not fear shipwreck in the vessel of obedience.

I ask you to summarize the main points of what I have written above and remedy the situation through the person you will send. You can inform him fully of it either verbally or in writing.

Regarding what is needed in temporal matters, if you send three or four priests and two or three coadjutor Brothers, that will be the most you could get through, and as many on another voyage. Make inquiries and see that those who are coming get information, not just from hearsay but from someone who has been here and knows what is needed. Above all, see if it is advisable to continue the care of the French. If there is one reason in favor of this, there are two against it. No matter how hard we try, nothing will ever be to their liking. Furthermore, of all the men, the one here is the most difficult to talk with and to satisfy because of rash judgments, suspicions, or unfounded reports.

If there can be no separation, and we have to remain in the settlement, give orders that things be made clear before the men leave France, without waiting until they get here, because we dare not open our mouths, no matter how gently we speak, lest we be dismissed in front of everyone. Furthermore, our Institute was not founded to be dependent on anyone or to live from hand to mouth as I do here, mixing with lay people who, at meals and in everything else, respect no other rules, time, or standard but their own appetite. All our time is wasted in this, and the mind languishes all too quickly with their frivolous conversation.

This letter is a mass of confusion, written in fits and starts. I had hoped to put it into better order, if the ship had not been ready to leave. Extract an antidote from all this poison and tell me what to do about all my mistakes, if you are still going to have me stay in this country. Possibly, if God had kept M. Gondrée alive, I might have given you this report in person, not with the intention of leaving the country but to return to it in a better frame of mind. If you think it advisable for me to make a trip to France by the next ship, it will take four months to get there, as much time in France, and the same to come back, never to leave again because we would be firmly established here. May God's Will be done in everything and everywhere!

M. de Flacourt is staying another three years, and when I wrote this I thought he was on his way back. He had made preparations but suddenly changed his mind. I did not ask if he would send any more priests or if schools would be opened here. I did tell him, however, not too long ago, everything I felt about this and the means I thought necessary. Since he listened to me coldly, however, I leave it up to him to tell those Gentlemen whatever he pleases. They will notify you, as you will notify them, of whatever you think most necessary in what I am writing you, leaving out what is superfluous.

I realize I will not be able to go too far away, but I will try to dispose the fathers in the villages around here to have their children baptized and, when I can, I will visit those I have already seen. Are we going to have a Portuguese interpreter for Andian Ramach, and what will be needed to build a church there, and will God grant me the grace of bringing him around? Could we give him some presents to win him over, such as some olive-shaped cut glass, some silk, a silver cup, or some silver trinkets and a few gold beads, false pearls or coral for a rosary he asked me for, and an Office book in Portuguese? We would give him these things little by little to remain on friendly terms with him and to entice him to listen more closely and be receptive to the ways of salvation both for himself and for many others. Might we also have something similar to win over an Ombiasse and, when we have instructed him and dissociated him from his olis, make use of him to attract those whom he had formerly deceived? One or two hundred livres would go a long way for this purpose, both for the king and for the Ombiasses.

God knows what could come of all this and how many souls we would gain, one of which is worth more than all the treasures on earth. Those Gentlemen will have difficulty approving this method, but I think it is quite appropriate for persons attached to their own interests, as are the people here. I am really afraid that the hue and cry will be raised that we are incurring heavy expenses for ourselves and for religion, which is the principal reason for making land grants on this island. I also fear that they will report all this in order to be exempted from import duties on ships and merchandise arriving in France, and are not sufficiently concerned about contributing in some small way to God's work. May He grant that this be not so!

I do not know whether you will send any Missionaries to Sainte-Marie, where there are some French, but there is no way to communicate between here and there except by sea. It is very unhealthy there, and good food is *essential in that place because of the poor air and frequent rainfall. The language is somewhat different and, with the help of a few French here who have lived there, I will try to use the vocabulary of that region in the catechism already compiled in the language used here. People say that the French will be making several settlements, including two large ones. One of them will be at Antavares, near Matatanes, a three-day journey from here. You can decide, from what I have suggested, whether you will entrust the care of the French to some Priests of the Mission or to secular priests. May everything be for the greater glory of God, in whose love I am, with all my heart, Monsieur and Most Honored Father, your most humble and obedient son.*

CHARLES NACQUART, *i.s.C.M.*
Mission of Madagascar

Fort-Dauphin, February 9, 1650

1184. - TO THE DAUGHTERS OF CHARITY, IN VALPUISEAUX [1]

Paris, February 10, 1650

My good Sisters,

The grace of Our Lord be with you forever!

I was consoled greatly to receive your letter. I beg Our Lord to restore Sister Perrette to health and to keep Sister Marguerite well so that together you can continue the services you are rendering to God.

Thank you for your charity toward us in watching out for our little possessions, and for the trouble Sister Marguerite has taken to check the books and linen. If some have gone astray, we must have patience and try to save the rest. Yesterday morning that poor man came to the door to pick up his belongings, without entering the house or speaking to anyone except the porter. You can rest

---

Letter 1184. - Archives of the Mission, Paris, original signed letter.
  [1]Commune in the district of Etampes (Essonne). The Daughters of Charity had been established there in 1648.

assured, Sisters, that you will never see him over there again with my consent, and if he is so inconsiderate as to return, please let me know immediately so I can see that he goes away. I do not think he will come to see me any more, and I will be glad of that.

I beg Our Lord to give you His peace and His Spirit, and to grant me a share in your prayers. I am, in His love, my good Sisters, your affectionate servant.

VINCENT DEPAUL
i.s.C.M.

Addressed: To the Sisters of Charity, Servants of the Sick Poor, in Val de Puiseau

1185. - TO RENE ALMERAS, SUPERIOR, IN ROME

February 11, 1650

I am distressed but not surprised by M. . .'s manner of acting. Those who have once faltered in their vocation rarely return to the point where they should be. There is usually a certain basic resistance to regularity in those persons, causing them to lose heart at every turn. The worst of it is that they have a bad influence on others so that, since misery loves company, they have grounds for presuming they are right. For a long time now I have been determined not to accept any more of them. Recently we have dismissed two, who are begging to return, but God has granted me the grace to stand firm. What you tell me about M. . . strengthens me in this resolution, and to that I shall add that it is better to let him go a second and last time than to keep him, if you are not morally certain that he will change his ways.

Letter 1185. - Reg. 2, p. 266.

1186. - *SAINT LOUISE TO SAINT VINCENT*

[February 1650] [1]

Most Honored Father,

I think the Bailiff [2] informed you yesterday of the state of that unpleasant business, which seems to depend entirely on how Monsieur Lesguier will explain to Monsieur d'Emery [3] the Queen's wishes in this matter, in keeping with a new order he received from Her Majesty. I most humbly entreat your charity kindly to let me know whether someone should speak to him, and who should do it. It should, however, be done today. What compels me to leave no stone unturned is that, in addition to this fee, twelve to fifteen hundred livres will be required for the expenses of his reception—even two thousand livres, we have been told.[4]

In the name of God, Most Reverend Father, reflect a little on whether thought should not be given to persuading these Ladies to stop taking in new foundlings, so we can pay the debts and bring back from the country all the babies who have been weaned. I assure you in conscience that we can no longer withstand the pity these poor people arouse in us when they ask us for what is justly owed them, not only for their services but for having advanced their own money, and then seeing themselves faced with dying from hunger. Three or four times they have been obliged to come from great distances without getting their money. We owe a large amount for the wet nurses' food and often for seven or eight babies who have been weaned, as well as for money we have borrowed! Still, it is not self-interest that causes us to speak up, although, if this continues, we will be obliged to use up what we have because we cannot refuse to give them something, however little it may be.

Letter 1186. - Archives of the Motherhouse of the Daughters of Charity, original autograph letter.

[1]Date added on the back of the original by Brother Ducournau.

[2]Her son, Michel Le Gras, Bailiff of Saint-Lazare.

[3]Michel Particelli, Sieur d'Emery, Comptrollor General of Finances (1643-1648). Born in Lyons, he died in Paris in 1650.

[4]Michel de la Rochemaillet, uncle of Michel Le Gras' bride, had relinquished his office of Counselor at the *Cour des Monnaies* to his brother, René-Michel de la Rochemaillet, who in turn had given it over to Michel Le Gras, a lawyer at the Parlement. The letters confirming the appointment were signed on June 13, 1650. After the customary investigation of his "life, morals, and religion," the new Counselor was authorized on July 14 to take the oath. (Cf. Arch. Nat. Z1b 566.)

Please forgive me for badgering you as usual, and do me the honor of believing always that I am, Most Honored Father, your most humble and very obedient daughter and servant.

L. DE M.

Addressed: *Monsieur Vincent*

1187. - *ALAIN DE SOLMINIHAC TO SAINT VINCENT*

Mercuès, February 15, 1650

Monsieur,

After thanking you most warmly for the trouble you have so kindly taken for us in the Sainte-Geneviève affair, and asking you most humbly, as I now do, to continue your care and assistance for us in this matter, allow me now to tell you confidentially and in all confidence that Father Vitet, syndic of Chancelade, is so strongly determined to see this business [end] quickly that there is nothing he will not do or risk for this purpose. Since he sees that Rome is opposed to it and that an appeal by writ of error to the Parlement is one way to proceed, he has decided to take it that far at any cost. That is why, first of all, the monks of Sainte-Geneviève gave us notice of the appeal lodged by them against the Beauvais decision and had a writ issued against Grosbois. He sent it to me along with several reports containing various cases of appeal by writ of error, and wrote me that an appeal had to be presented to the Parlement to obtain a brief addressed to the Abbot of Grosbois,[1] *together with orders from Cardinal de La Rochefoucauld.*[2]

Letter 1187. - Archives of the Diocese of Cahors, Alain de Solminihac collection, notebook, copy made from the original.

[1]Grobosc or Grosbois, a Cistercian monastery in the Angoulême diocese, near the Périgord border. Jean de la Font had been its Abbot since May 18, 1641.

[2]François de la Rochefoucauld was born in Paris on December 8, 1558. He became Bishop of Clermont on October 6, 1585, Cardinal in 1607, Bishop of Senlis in 1611, and Commendatory Abbot of Sainte-Geneviève in Paris in 1613. He resigned his bishopric in 1622 to dedicate himself entirely to the reform of the abbeys dependent on the Benedictines, Augustinians, and Cistercians. With that end in view, he obtained from Pope Gregory XV on April 8 special powers and the title of Apostolic Commissary. Supported by such men as Saint Vincent, Father Tarrisse,

I sent the copy of this brief and the above-mentioned reports to Paris to have them examined by Messrs. Camus and Montelon, and had them examined again here by my lawyer from Cahors, who is a reputable person. His advice concurs with that of Paris; namely, that there are no grounds for an appeal by writ of error in the brief obtained by the monks of Sainte-Geneviève addressed to the Abbot of Grosbois, but that, because it was misstated and contained omissions, His Holiness had to be petitioned to have it declared null and void. In addition, an appearance had to be made before the Abbot of Grosbois to require him to refer us to His Holiness, given the invalidity of the said brief. . . . who may appoint him and, in case of a refusal, to declare solemnly that we were appealing it, and list the nullities of this brief.

I sent Father Vitet the opinion of the above-mentioned lawyers in Paris and Cahors, along with the act that had been drawn up, with an order to follow this opinion exactly. He replied that he had received it but persists in saying that an appeal by writ of error to the Parlement is necessary. By my order, my Vicar-General wrote to him and to the Prior of Chancelade that I found the proposal very strange and was surprised that he did not follow the orders I sent him. These had instructed him, among other things, not to produce any documents before the Abbot of Grosbois, following the advice of the Council. He went off and made that demand of the Abbot, who refused to comply with the referral but ordered that the parties produce the documents within three days, whereas, at the same time, Father Vitet was supposed to have made the act of protest of appeal, following the orders he had about it and the advice of the lawyers. He produced our decree from the Council, contrary to the specific prohibitions he had, and from there went to the Crown to have notice given to the monks of Sainte-Geneviève of the protest of appeal, in the event that the said Abbot of Grosbois should disregard it. Then he went back to Grosbois, where he found that the Abbot had already handed down the decision.

On his return to Chancelade, the Prior wrote to me here. I replied that I was quite surprised at the proceedings of Father Vitet, who ignored the opinion of the Council in order to follow his own opinion and produce the documents, contrary to the specific prohibitions he had. He excused himself in a letter, saying that things could not have been done otherwise

and Father Charles Faure, he restored order and discipline in the monasteries. The Cardinal died February 14, 1645; Saint Vincent was with him to prepare him to appear before God. He was buried at Sainte-Geneviève but his heart was given to the Jesuits. (Cf. M. M. La Morinière, *Les vertus du vrai prélat représentées en la vie de l'Eminentissime cardinal de la Rochefoucault* [Paris: Cramoisy, 1646]; Lallemand et Chatonnet, *La vie du Révérend Père Charles Faure, abbé de Sainte-Geneviève de Paris* [Paris: J. Anisson, 1698].)

because the monks of Sainte-Geneviève, rather than the said Abbot, should have been given notice of these protests. This is most impertinent and quite ridiculous.

I sent him word to come and see me here. When he did, I asked him why he said that notice of the protests should have been given to the monks of Sainte-Geneviève instead of to the Abbot of Grosbois and why he had not followed our orders. The only answer I received was that he shrugged his shoulders and bowed his head. Because he alone has fostered this affair and is the only person we have who understands it well, I did not want to reprimand him as he deserved. I treated him very gently for such a fault and told him he had to go to Paris to appeal to the Privy Council against the above-mentioned decision. During the time he remained here, his appeal by writ of error was always on his mind and he spoke of it from time to time, as well as of the decisions handed down by the Abbot of Grosbois and Cardinal de la Rochefoucauld.

I refuted all these propositions and reminded him of what he had reported to me on his return from Paris after he had obtained our decree of July 1647; namely, that all our friends in Paris had told him not to appeal to the Parlement because the monks of Sainte-Geneviève had close contacts with it, due to the large number of their monks and boarders related to those who might be our judges. This is only too true.

Before he left here, I had orders and some advice written out for him, which I gave him to be used in the prosecution of this affair and told him not to do anything without seeking counsel and following it. At the same time I added that he should not take this matter to the Parlement where, as he himself had told me, our friends in Paris were advising us not to go. I also put forward some personal reasons of my own, which compel me not to take it there.

When he arrived in Paris, he consulted with Messrs. Camus and Montelon, according to our orders. They found that we had solid grounds for appealing to the Council against the decision of the Abbot of Grosbois. By the next mail he wrote to the contrary that M. Montelon was of the opinion that an appeal should be made to the Parlement and that M. Camus had not yet made up his mind. By another mail he wrote me that everyone was in agreement about an appeal by writ of error to the Parlement of Paris, both against the decision of Grosbois and the orders of Cardinal de la Rochefoucauld. He also stated that he was having letters of appeal drawn up to that effect and even in anticipation of a writ which the monks of Sainte-Geneviève had him give to this same Parlement.

I leave you to imagine my surprise at this news. Immediately I sent my Vicar-General to Cahors to consult with our lawyer about what we had to do. I cannot tell you how amazed he was at these proceedings. Within the hour he drew up an act of repudiation of them which I sent to Monsieur Lefèvre, my attorney in Paris, to have notice of appeal given to the monks of Sainte-Geneviève. I also wrote a long letter to Father Vitet, telling him how astonished I was that he had brought this affair before the Parlement against our orders. He wrote back to me excusing himself, saying I had my Vicar-General write to him three times to say he should follow the Council's advice and that I had even told him this myself. This is true, but he said nothing of his being expressly forbidden to take this affair to the Parlement.

He has written a letter full of complaints to my Vicar-General, and he wrote it in a troubled frame of mind because it contradicts what is in his other letters. After a long outburst, he told him to send him a little money so that he will be able to retire at the same time because, after the repudiation I made, he would no longer dare to show his face.

Please note that the letters he had decided to present to the Parlement on appeal and anticipation have not yet been presented, since the Council's advice was to wait until the writ served by the monks of Sainte-Geneviève had expired. Therefore, there is no repudiation and revocation, since no action has yet been taken by the Parlement.

Instead of keeping the said repudiation quiet, however, he went and made it public. He also showed my letter and those of my Vicar-General to Messrs. Camus and Montelon and sent word that they thought it a very bad thing that I had their decision reversed by a lawyer from Cahors. I had written him and sent him the repudiation, asking him to get quarterly letters from the Parlement for a four-month delay in our petition before His Holiness, prohibiting the parties from attempting anything in the meantime, and to notify the monks of Sainte-Geneviève of this. He gave us no reply to the above, so that I now find myself very much at a loss and I greatly need your advice and assistance because, as I have already told you, I have no one who understands this business as well as he does. Father Parrot, his companion, is as much deputized as he is but does not understand it as well. The other man always conducted the business alone, without allowing Father Parrot to get involved, and also has all the documents in his possession.

I beg you, in the name of God, to work at bringing this person around and, if possible, make him dismiss any further thought of going to the Parlement, or even to the Council at this time because the latter would refer us back to the Parlement. Get him to go through Rome instead, following my express order to him about this, pending the time when the Council will recover its authority.

He took you by surprise in leading you to believe that the decree of registration of the erection of the Congregation of Sainte-Geneviève stated that the Congregation could be established in other houses only with the consent of the diocesan bishops, together with that of the abbots and monks in them, as you wrote me. As you can see from the wording of the enclosed decree, please note that this is not what is said with regard to the houses which are presently under that Congregation. Now, by the decision of the Abbot of Grosbois, our houses are included in this and, although we are appealing, this decision holds good until we have it suspended, and our lawyer from Cahors, who is very clever and prudent, has always believed that this was just the beginning.

As for me, I must confess that I have always felt that this decree was very prejudicial to us, and everyone else to whom I have shown it has the same opinion. Yet, Father Vitet acts as if this decree is a triumph and noises it abroad as a victory for us, and under this pretext wanted to constrain me to consent to bringing the affair to the Parlement. If he had not given, as he did, the decision of the Abbot of Grosbois, it seems that the above-mentioned decree could be favorable to us. But in the present state of affairs he will never convince me. Nevertheless, even if the Grosbois decision should not stand, I would be very cautious about the going to the Parlement because, since these are clauses inserted in the said decree proprio motu,[3] the Parlement will remove or interpret them as it sees fit, both in general and with regard to details.

He also took you by surprise by telling you that we had made an appeal by writ of error. This is not so because it is only a simple act of declaration for appeal. Were it not up to the Council, a petition would be required for that and a decree to have the parties subpoenaed. Were it up to the Parlement, letters would be required. Now, none of this is the case, so we have full liberty to lodge an appeal in Rome, as must be done, which I told him to do before and which I ask you to give him strict orders to do, forbidding him explicitly to go to the Parlement. If you want to give him the reasons for this, here they are: the monks of Sainte-Geneviève have such close contact with a good number of monks or boarders that we would have all their relatives petitioning against us because of problems arising from the nature, circumstances, and ramifications of this affair.

Most of our statements of grounds of appeal are on spiritual matters, observances to be regularized, or the spirit of the Rules. No lawyer in France is capable of pleading this case, not even the Assistant Public Prosecutor, and I do not think that even the lay judges can hear the case. It would take more than two hearings to plead it properly because the

---

[3]*On his own initiative.*

monks of Sainte-Geneviève would do all they could to magnify it and get it into a muddle.

I have some very strong reasons for not going to the Parlement: (1) you know about the censure of the book, Libertés de L'Eglise gallicane; [4] *I was one of the members of the commission who had it condemned, along with the Archbishop of Sens [5] and the Bishop of Uzès; [6] (2) the way I have acted in this area for the service of the King; (3) an intendant of finance wrote me from Paris that everyone had heard of me. There are also many other personal reasons. If, after all that, you cannot bring this person around, please let me know and, in the meantime, send for young Lefèvre, my attorney at the Great Council, to get from the Parlement as soon as possible the quarterly letters mentioned above and send them on to Rome.*

I would like very much to be able to tell you what is driving that man to see a quick end to this affair, for better or for worse, and to risk everything for that purpose, but it is a mysterious secret which was told me confidentially and which I have repeated only to my Vicar-General, who is writing this to you under my authority. I cannot put it in writing but would like very much to be able to whisper it to you; it originated only about two years ago. So please be wary of this man and inform yourself from time to time of what he has done in this business. Do not give him permission to leave until he has compiled the quarterly letters and sent them to the Court of Rome to obtain the brief, get the commissioners I indicated to him, and wait a little longer to see if the monks of Sainte-Geneviève will stir up anything in the Parlement.

I am writing you another letter through Father Vitet. When he brings you my letter, please tell him whatever the Holy Spirit inspires you to say. Be careful in speaking to him not to let him know that I gave you any reports.

I have been assured that the most renowned Doctor and Regent of the University of Toulouse has begun to teach the doctrine of Jansenius, starting with the first article of his errors. I was told also that the Bishop of Comminges [7] preached there three times on this doctrine. The following day, an anonymous person wrote him a letter refuting everything he had said.

---

[4]Pierre Dupuy, *Traitez des droits et libertez de l'Eglise gallicane* (2 vols., n. p., 1639). This work justified all the intrusions of secular power over the power of the bishops and of the Pope. It was censured on February 9, 1639 by a large number of the bishops.

[5]Octave de Saint-Lary de Bellegarde, who died in 1646.

[6]Nicolas de Grille.

[7]Gilbert de Choiseul.

One of the Oratorian Fathers preached recently that Jesus Christ did not die for the damned and reprobates. That town will cause us trouble. I pray God to have mercy on His Church. I cannot sufficiently admire God's goodness toward my diocese; with all the dealings we have with people in Toulouse, those who return from there or from Paris are not tainted in any way and simply say that there is some new religion that is setting people at variance. Then, it is hushed up in such a way that, by the grace of God, I do not see a single person in my diocese who is upset by it, nor speaks about it, nor does not follow my opinion entirely in matters of faith and the teaching of the Church. I praise God for this and ask Him kindly to bestow on you all the graces I wish for you.

I am embarrassed at having written you such a long letter but necessity has obliged me to do so. I feel it my duty to tell you confidentially that Father Vitet's great passion for seeing our business settled quickly, for better or for worse, is not because he has any love for the monks of Sainte-Geneviève—on the contrary, he has a strong aversion for them— but it is so that, if the outcome is successful, as he sincerely hopes, he can act upon the mystery I mentioned to you, which I cannot put on paper and which would require a great deal of time. If he does not succeed, he is assured of retiring on a good benefice. That is why he is risking everything to terminate matters. When you have read my other letter, which Father Vitet will give you, I think it is advisable for you to show it to him or to read it aloud to him, and use this opportunity to speak to him.

I am, Monsieur, etc.

ALAIN,
Bishop of Cahors

1188. - *CHARLES NACQUART TO SAINT VINCENT*

Fort-Dauphin, February 16, 1650

Your holy blessing, please!
After all the letters I have written you, this one will inform you that a big change almost took place. You will learn that during Mass on Septuagesima Sunday, as I was reading the Gospel of the workers sent into the

---

Letter 1188. - Archives of the Mission, Paris, seventeenth century copy; Arch. Nat. M 214.

vineyard, this vineyard to which I have been sent seemed so vast to me, and I saw such a great need of workers, that all during Mass I felt deep in my heart that it must not be left to wither for want of workers, since so long ago the Master reproached the lazy saying, quid hic statis tota die otiosi? Ite in vineam meam.[1] *This caused me to reflect that assuredly God was asking something more of me than I had given to this in the past.*

Now, I think that, apart from the fact that I received this as an inspiration, begging O[ur] L[ord] that it might have its effect, this stemmed from the sadness I felt at having made so little progress and from seeing that I would do even less in future. But, examining the reason why I had been sent—for the French and for the natives—working for the former with very little success and unable to do more for the latter because I was alone; in addition to my negligence, ignorance, and incompetence, I found that I was lacking the necessary temporal assistance which could be given. I felt this was because M. de Flacourt was so occupied with temporal administration that he scarcely bothered to contribute to spiritual advancement, since he was on the eve of his departure or, when he changed his mind about going, to write to France.

He mentioned nothing to me, although when I had proposed to him my idea about reestablishing the baptized king, making a settlement at Fanshere, and opening a seminary, he said that it would be very costly for the Company and that it was an undertaking fit for a king. Furthermore, although he and all those Gentlemen in Paris wanted to contribute to this to the exclusion of anyone else, I saw no sign of that, other than the small instances of aversion he had manifested in my regard for no reason. He was unwilling to give me an interpreter to work exclusively on a translation of the instructions, which we had to do by fits and starts, and even took away the man who was so eager to remain with me free of charge and without a salary from anyone. What is more, I felt I could not do without him, so that at least, since I was alone, I could do my best to prepare with him the instructions to be put in writing in this language, not only for myself but for posterity.

This boy is the one who speaks it best, and God has given him the grace to make himself clearly understood in these matters. In the beginning he found them difficult because he was not accustomed to them. He had never spoken about them and could hardly ever go to the country or leave the settlement any more. Without a good interpreter, not only would I be unable to instruct the natives of the settlement, who are quite familiar with

---

[1] *Why have you been standing here idle all day? . . . Go to my vineyard.* Cf. Mt 20:6-7. (NAB)

the mysteries but need an explanation of other matters necessary to salvation, but I could not tell them things clearly nor understand their arguments.

All that made my heart ache very much, seeing that I would be only useless on my own. I was even apprehensive about my letters being considered suspect and being withheld, to prevent all that I proposed to do in this country from being carried out. Indeed, I felt we needed something like a lightning bolt, enclosed in the cloud that surrounds it, which causes a stir by breaking it up in a rain of tears and flashes of prayer and groaning, as I am experiencing right now. For a long time I held back, afraid of vexing the person to whom, through cowardly deference, I dared not express my feelings freely. I was fearful of spoiling something in such an important matter, and sometimes of losing the honor of continuing such a beautiful work for the entire Company, as has happened with the good Capuchins on Saint-Christopher Island. So, I saw only two or three ways to remedy these two extremes. They came to me in the presence of O[ur] L[ord], and I shared them with three persons whom I thought would give me the best advice.

I took as my intermediary Captain Le Bourg, who prepared everything for the peace that follows. This is what I did, immediately afterward, with a heart filled with confidence that God would make everything turn out for the best. I prepared with all possible respect to tell M. de Flacourt, whose decision I promised to obey in the way he would give it, saying to him, "Monsieur, you know the plan of God, of your Gentlemen, and of my Superiors regarding this mission. It has a twofold goal toward which I must work: first, to render you and the entire French settlement the service of my profession; and second, to win over the natives and the other inhabitants of the country. We must have the means to attain these two goals. If the first one is not as it should be, you can see that I am doing all my limited power allows, although quite badly, and I cannot complain of anything in that except of my own negligence and inefficiency, which lead me to wish for someone else more worthy.

"As for the second, although I have the good will to do all I can to accomplish it, I am new here and do not know the language. I cannot do it without an interpreter who would be assigned to do only that, without being interrupted as I have been until now. The person best suited to this work has been sent to milk the cows and to labor in the fields, even though he would like nothing better than to give himself to God for the other work. He has told me many times that he could not serve two masters. You can get other persons to take care of your temporal needs, but he is the only one I can find whom God has disposed to do to this work. Otherwise, I shall waste my time while waiting for some priests, who will find nothing

ready. I thought about sending them many things on the first returning ship but I have not been able to do so. Besides, those who might be sent are not informed about the needs of this country, and this cannot be put into writing as well as it can be said. When I write, I shall perhaps be suspect; nevertheless I must express my sentiments freely to my Superior, to whom I must communicate my interior state, and whose advice I must ask regarding our behavior and that of the persons entrusted to my care.

"There are only two ways to do this, and you will tip the balance to whatever side you think best: either I make a trip to France to say what I think before God is necessary for His glory in this country, or I write with the assurance that I am not suspect; or else, if I remain here, that I have the simple necessities which are in your power to grant me; that is, since I have to trust you, you must trust me; your influence should sustain mine and vice-versa. In a word, allow me to take the interpreter and go far enough from the fort, away from the noise, where I can live on my own and carry out the duties of the profession of a wretched Missionary such as I am."

His conclusion at that time was that I should go to France. Although that other good priest [2] was very anxious to return home, knowing that my intention was to advance matters and to recruit as many workers as I could for the good of everyone, he gave his consent before M. de Flacourt, who was satisfied with this. So it was all settled that he would remain behind. I left everything at his disposal and packed my bag as lightly as possible.

M. de Flacourt asked me to say farewell to the French after Vespers on Septuagesima Sunday, which I did, telling them why I was going. They had mixed feelings about this and so did I because I was finding it difficult to leave and to undertake the round trip, which is so long and dangerous. The crew was happy to have my company; the people in the settlement wanted, on the one hand, to keep me to render them service; on the other, they gave their consent because of the Gospel, which required workers promptly, and I was going to recruit some who would have what it takes to cultivate this vineyard, while bearing the burden and the heat of many days.

So, here was this poor priest, torn in several directions by his own mixed emotions and those of others. Still, even though the decision had been taken and accepted by all parties, I remained indifferent, entreating the Master of the vineyard to tell me to go in the morning or wait until noon, so as not to lose the value of obedience to His Will alone. Deus scit quia non mentior,[3] and that I held nothing for certain, except that He would do

---

[2] M. de Bellebarbe.
[3] *God knows I do not lie.* Cf. 2 Cor 11:31. (NAB)

everything for the best and that He had ways and means to assure the outcome of the designs of His Providence, which were infallible and irresistible.

The following day I offered Holy Mass for that intention. No answer. I sent my bag to the ship and was prepared to be the bearer of my own letters. And suddenly, all the plans were changed: I was told that I had to stay behind to satisfy those who were not happy with the priest who was remaining, although he was quite capable of doing a decent job of looking after the needs of the settlement. The natives themselves came to me and said, "What! you are going away! Who will help us pray to God?" And that shackled my will, which remained a prisoner of the Will of God voiced by the people.

However, my other request, to live alone with the interpreter, was granted me, without any prejudice to M. de Flacourt's respect and friendship. Rather, it increased them and gave the latter less reason to find so much fault with him. So, our hearts are united again, with a mutual promise that this will be for God's greater glory. They are going to build a little rectory for me near the church. Now, however, that poor companion, who is to act as my tongue, is ill with pleurisy, which he said was a result of sadness at the thought of being separated from me. However, the desired news that I am staying, plus the bloodletting and the good treatment I am giving him, has already half cured him of his illness, since he says that the cause of it has been removed.

God grant that there will be no changes! I do not know if this country is the cause, but we see many chameleons here who change color less often than certain persons change their mind and mood. Sometimes we are in favor; sometimes not; but we are more often out of favor than in. Despite the fact that things seem good, I am not above suspicion of having led that interpreter astray for some purpose disadvantageous to those Gentlemen. But what else could I do except spend all my time with him learning the language and instructing the natives? The honor for this will redound to them, as it did to M. de Montmagny [4] in Canada. Oh! if only someone like him were here!

I greatly fear that, to all appearances, those Gentlemen will be satisfied with making fine suggestions for the conversion of this country and cause us to waste our time by putting off too long what could be done without delay. If you see no probability of one or two settlements being maintained, as I mentioned, either by them or by someone else, is it worth the trouble to unsettle some poor priests and go to such pains to send them off to die

---

[4]Charles Huault de Montmagny, Knight of Malta, Governor of Canada. He was very zealous for the propagation of the faith.

so far away, in order to serve such undisciplined settlements? Do we not have enough French on our doorstep? Does it not suffice for them to have a priest, whom they could maintain and whose wages they could pay, without our being captives and held back from working properly for the conversion of the natives, who ask only for that?

Look at my recent letter addressed to those Gentlemen, in which I propose means to them that are perhaps too much to their advantage and too onerous for you. Do what you please with it; my conscience is clear now that I have said what I know and have done all I can.

If you take the trouble to write to Madame Gondrée, address the letter to Captain Le Bourg in Dieppe. If you want to write a little note to my poor father, if he is still alive, the address is on my letter to him.

Do not let God's plan for this country grow cold, even if these Gentlemen look on that as unimportant. Providence will furnish you with the means of carrying it out in other ways, which you will find out from Captain Le Bourg. That would perhaps be best, if it is possible.

Will not everything I have reported about this country suffice to put the entire Company, and especially our seminarians, into the plan of learning Saint Peter's trade of making and repairing nets suitable for fishing so many souls? You sent me to cast the nets, but only fifty-seven fish have been caught, and they are all small except for three big ones. Yet, there are so many to be caught that I am sure you will put to sea persons who will succeed in filling the nets to the breaking point.

I shall not mention M. Maillard, who has asked so often to come. He has the requisite dispositions of spirit and he is healthy. I think his voice is a little weak, and he is subject to constipation, but he is well-suited to teaching small children; he is also a good steward. I leave all that to you, wishing to have only those persons whom O[ur] L[ord] has prepared well to become fishers of men, who know what to do in the organization of this work, and who can resolve the difficulties that arise here, where it is not easy to write for guidance concerning them.

I have every reason to cast myself at the feet of O[ur] L[ord] as a poor fisherman and a great sinner. Please cast yourself there so that He will not withdraw from me, although I give Him only too great reason to do so. When you choose to relieve me of this crushing burden, if it is necessary for me to go and do penance for my faults, let me go to the seminary, where this monster will be reformed by the example and fervor of those at whose feet I may humble myself, in order to obtain, through them and through you, hope in the grace and mercy of O[ur] L[ord]. In His charity, I pray that our hearts may be impelled to carry out His plans for the Company.

In His love I am, Most Honored Father, your most humble and obedient son.

CHARLES NACQUART, *i.s.C.M.*
Mission of Madagascar

1189. - *CHARLES NACQUART TO SAINT VINCENT*

Fort-Dauphin, February 16, 1650

Monsieur,

Your holy blessing, please!
Blessed be God if the person for whom I am writing this letter is himself the bearer, as he promised me.[1] *Besides my obligations toward him for being the recipient of so much pleasure, honor, and affection, and for the gift of so many commodities both on his ship and for more than a year during which he had to reside on the coast, taking compassion on me, as a good father does for his son in need, he has also urged me to accept one hundred francs for any needs I might have in this country. If I had to repay him a hundredfold or if he was willing to accept it, who could doubt that you would not give it to him? But he will accept just the amount given, which I shall use only for what I need and to avoid what you are aware of and which he can tell you.*

O Monsieur, warm my heart by welcoming him, not as he deserves and as I would wish, but with all possible cordiality. Assure him that, if the opportunity arises of rendering him any service, you will do it or have someone else do it as if it were for my own father. I am so well acquainted with his natural goodness that I know only too well how much he has contributed to the work of God in this country, and not only in spiritual matters. I have discussed them with him and have accepted his opinions with the respect due to a man who has been my best advisor in this country and has acted as my intermediary, as I mentioned elsewhere. But if he were to be the one in charge of the next ship to come, since he is quite capable of doing so, I know of no one better suited to explain everything to you and to fulfill the promise he made of furnishing some small temporal provisions, if he returns. Even if he is not the one, he would not fail to give someone else advice on this, and even a report. If he were in Dieppe, he would acquit himself faithfully of furnishing whatever he could.

Letter 1189. - Archives of the Mission, Paris, seventeenth century copy.
[1]Captain Le Bourg.

So much for singing his praises. Since he is so deserving, may God grant that someone might procure for him a commission as King's Captain, which would only take a word to request that it be granted by Her Majesty, Regent and guardian of the kingdom. If you can do anything for this loyal man, in this matter or in anything else, you will be doing a favor for a man who will not be ungrateful, and I will consider it as done to one who is, in the love of O[ur] L[ord] who will be his reward and yours, Monsieur and Most Honored Father, your most obedient servant and very affectionate son.

C. NACQUART,
i.s.C.M.

In the event that he is not the bearer, I know that you will thank him by letter and will see that he receives the amount mentioned, without being any less zealous in doing him a favor whenever the occasion arises. Please God, I shall see him again in this country at the next embarkation, accompanied by four priests and three coadjutor Brothers! Et sic deinceps diu usque impleatur numerus fratrum nostrorum.[2]

1190. - TO LOUIS RIVET, IN SAINTES

February 20, 1650

Thank you for the advice you gave me. I am writing[1] to the person and I hope he will reform his manner of acting. This is a passing storm, stirred up by age and passions. Thank God he is fundamentally good and deserves to have us bear with the weaknesses of nature, as you are doing. I thank Our Lord for this; you honor His patience by the patience you exercise with regard to the failings of others, putting up with them as He put up with the boorishness of His disciples and puts up daily with the greatest sinners like me. O Monsieur, how consoled I am that you are

---

[2]*And so for a long time to come, until the number of our brothers is complete.*

Letter 1190. - Reg. 2, p. 108.
[1]The letter referred to here is most probably no. 1191. See also no. 1202.

working constantly at the acquisition of virtue! Your love for it is apparent in the distress you experience because others are not working hard enough at it. When, in addition, I reflect on your constant zeal in the ministry of the Gospel in order to win souls to Jesus Christ, I cannot esteem and cherish your own soul highly enough. The tender affection I conceived for it long ago leads me to offer it frequently to God that He may sanctify it more and more and, through you, save the people whom you serve.

It certainly is very difficult, Monsieur, to find accomplished superiors. True, yours[2] is inexperienced and not very prepossessing exteriorly, but he is wise and virtuous, as you yourself acknowledge. This has always led me to hope that Our Lord would supply the rest until, through practice, he has acquired part of what he lacks. I ask you, Monsieur, to do whatever you can, by word and example, so that the Community will have confidence in him and be attentive to our little observances. I will recommend to him that, on his part, he act more humbly and gently. It seems to me that this will be easy for him, since he is very much inclined to do so.

1191. - TO A PRIEST OF THE MISSION, IN SAINTES

February 20, 1650

I cannot refrain from telling you how consoled I am that you are devoting yourself almost continually to the salvation of souls, that your own soul is advancing in the love of God by this means, and that His Infinite Goodness is pleased to bless your labors. I certainly thank Him for this with as much gratitude as he has given me esteem and tenderness for you.

I am also writing to you for another reason. I am wondering whether I answered the letter you wrote me some time ago. On the one hand, I know I intended to do so, and only the great pressure of business could have caused me to omit this obligation. On the other hand, however, seeing that, no matter how hard I try, I am late at least with certain replies, I fear I have committed this fault in your regard. If this is the case, Monsieur, I ask your pardon, and if it is not, please let me know.

You made your interior communication to me in that letter. It gave me good reason to praise God for the zeal He gives you to correct the faults within your Community, and particularly for the good dispositions He has granted you in serving Him. Because man's state changes every day, especially in persons like you, who are striving for their own advancement, I ask you, if you still want to continue to make your communication to me, to make it according as you find yourself right now. I assure you that I will reply each time you write, not only for what concerns your interior life, but for anything else. Thanks be to God, I try to do so for everyone. How much more, then, for you, who are for me what Our Lord alone knows. In Him I am at your service as much as I can be. Please have no doubt about that.

If, nevertheless, you prefer to open your heart to M. Watebled, so as not to deviate from the common way, I shall be consoled by this and you, I hope, will be satisfied because, since Our Lord approves of the trust you have in your Superior as the representative of His Divine Person, He will inspire him to say whatever is most appropriate for you. Although he may not have the experience I have nor all the other good qualities desirable in a person in authority, do not, on that account, Monsieur, neglect any part of such a holy practice nor of any of those God is pleased to prescribe for us in our state. They have great value if they are performed in a spirit of love and obedience, and you know the danger of following other lights.

I mention this to you only to excite us to gratitude for the grace God has bestowed on us, in giving us the determination to walk in the path traced out for us by Our Lord and the saints. Let us ask Him for the grace of persevering to the end. I am inclined to believe that human nature inspires you with many thoughts contrary to the esteem and deference you owe to M. Watebled, but I am also inclined to believe that you rise above these base feelings and profit from this repugnance, and this increases the merit of your fidelity. True, he is still new in the office and does not have the demeanor or perhaps the gentleness it requires, but I can assure you that he is one of the souls closest to God that I know, and we have always remarked great virtue in him. It is not easy to find perfect men in whom there is nothing to criticize. What is lacking in this servant of God is little in comparison to what he possesses, and Our Lord will compensate for what he lacks in your regard, if you see Our Lord in him and him in Our Lord, as I beg you to do with all my heart.

1192. - TO SISTER JEANNE LEPEINTRE, IN NANTES

Paris, February 23, 1650

My good Sister,

The grace of Our Lord be with you forever!

I was greatly consoled to receive your letter but, on the one hand, it distressed me to see you continually inconvenienced by your restricted living accommodations. If God Himself does not provide some solution to this, it must not be sought elsewhere. Nevertheless, go see M. d'Annemont[1] and tell him the inconveniences arising from living in such close quarters and having so many patients. He can bring this to the attention of the Administrators and consult with them to see if some place might be adapted for use nearby or above the wards to give you a little more freedom.

I was also consoled by your earnest request to be relieved of authority; it is good for anyone in charge to ask, from time to time, to be relieved, even though the person must remain indifferent,

---

Letter 1192. - Archives of the Motherhouse of the Daughters of Charity, original signed letter.
[1]Chaplain of Maréchal de la Meilleraye.

which is what you are doing, thanks be to God. Continue to be firmly grounded in this practice, always entrusting yourself to the care of Providence, who will remove you from this office whenever it is expedient. While you are in it, He will give you the necessary graces to carry it out well. Yes, Sister, rest assured that, when you remain thus in the state in which obedience has placed you, the merit of this same obedience extends over everything you do, giving each action inestimable value, even when things do not turn out as you wish.

It is true, Sister, that spiritual direction is very useful. It is an occasion for advice in difficulties, encouragement in weariness, refuge in temptation, and strength in dejection; in a word, it is a source of well-being and consolation, when the director is truly charitable, prudent, and experienced. But are you well aware that where men are lacking, the help of God begins? It is He who instructs and strengthens us; He is our All and leads us to Himself by Himself. If He does not allow you to have a spiritual father to whom you can have recourse in every circumstance, do you think it is to deprive you of the benefit of the direction of such a father? Not at all. On the contrary, it is Our Lord who takes his place and in His goodness directs you Himself. It would seem that He has done so until now, and you can be sure He will do so until He provides otherwise. I have always noticed this particular attention of Providence for many pious persons deprived of similar help from men. I could quote you many beautiful examples of this and tell you some wonderful things on this point, but this is not necessary for you, who have no doubt of it and who have daily experience of the effects of the divine protection.

We are not yet able to recall Sister Henriette; please be patient with regard to her.

It is much to be desired that you all have one and the same confessor. I think M. Cheneau is quite capable of this and is a very upright man. So, from time to time, continue to try and persuade this Sister to go to confession to him so that, if she goes to someone else, the Bishop of Nantes[2] will know that it was neither on your orders nor with your consent.

I see clearly that what has kept you from making your little regulations and from following the recommendations I left for you are the little troubles you have endured up until now. I hope that God in His goodness will give you in future more peace and grace to be very exact, and that you will give the example in this to our Sisters.

If admitting boys into your kitchen is a necessary evil, you must bear with it for the love of God, who permits it. If it can be avoided, wait for the Administrators to take care of it, and for this purpose ask M. Truchart about it from time to time. Nevertheless, be submissive to whatever the outcome will be.

You say they have given you a spy, who is upsetting you. I admit that this is painful, but after the effort you have made to free yourself from this servitude, you must be patient. Alas! my Daughter, I do not know anyone who does not have someone watching him. The most influential persons have them even in their bedrooms, and the world is in such a wretched state today that for almost everyone we see, there are as many spies. This should be a reminder to us that we should act with great reserve and in the presence of God. I would like to believe that you and our Sisters act in this way and that this will cause those very persons who spy on your actions to proclaim your virtue abroad.

Have you had set up in your room the enclosure to be used for your little meetings, as we found advisable when I was in Nantes? If you have, can you not have a little recreation there every day? Please enlighten me on this. Meanwhile, I approve of your tact in giving a little liberty to our Sisters to laugh and talk when the occasion presents itself, if you are not taking an hour or so to recreate together; you need a little relaxation from your constant work.

---

[2]Gabriel de Beauvau de Rivarennes.

I praise God that your sick Sister is better and that all the others, you in particular, are in good health.

I greet each and every one of you with all possible affection. Please ask God to have mercy on me. On my part, I often offer you to Him that He may give you the strength and generosity of spirit to overcome the difficulties to be encountered in the service of God and of the poor. May He be in the end your eternal reward in heaven. I am, in His love, my good Sister, your affectionate servant.

VINCENT DEPAUL
i.s.C.M.

Addressed: Sister Jeanne Lepeintre, Servant of the Poor and of the Daughters of Charity of the Nantes Hospital, in Nantes

1193. - TO BERNARD CODOING, SUPERIOR, IN RICHELIEU

Paris, February 23, 1650

Monsieur,

The grace of Our Lord be with you forever!

I asked the Duchesse d'Aiguillon for the canonry that is vacant, or about to be vacated, in Champigny,[1] for your doctor's son. She told me she had promised to give it to a young man from Tours, but that she will be glad to oblige the doctor on another occasion. I will be on the alert for this, hoping to be able to render him service, as I am bound to do. I greet him most humbly.[2]

I told you that the Lady[3] highly approves of the change to be made at the Champigny hospital, the withdrawal of the chaplain,[4]

Letter 1193. - Archives of the Motherhouse of the Daughters of Charity, original signed letter.
[1]Champigny-sur-Veude, commune in the district of Chinon (Indre-et-Loire).
[2]These words, from "as I am bound to do," are written in the Saint's hand.
[3]The Duchesse d'Aiguillon.
[4]M. Romillon.

the establishment of our Sisters, and all the other things you pointed out to us for the sake of order and the good of the poor. Make arrangements for all that, while waiting for Mademoiselle Le Gras to prepare two of her Sisters for you, which I already mentioned to her. We will let you know when they will be able to leave. The Lady will approve of what you say should be done with that girl who is staying at the hospital. Still, before putting her out, please wait until I talk to her once more to find out exactly what she wants.

Since writing the above I spoke to the Lady again. She agrees that the girl should be removed from the house, and even that she should not go near it, on account of her disorderly life.[5]

When you wrote to M. Drouard, I do not know if you suggested the vacant land in Richelieu for the building. If you see that the inhabitants and the interested parties are disposed to accept that, write to Monsieur Drouard, if you have not already done so. As for me, I do not want to broach the subject with the Lady. It is advisable for you to send me the letters unsealed.[6]

I shall find out from Mademoiselle Le Gras and let you know whether she is willing to accept the girl from there, who is asking to come to the Charity.

I received the copy of the Bois-Bouchard lease. I must confess that I cannot understand the terms of it. That house with its dependencies has an estimated income of between one thousand and eleven hundred livres, and your lease is drawn up for only one hundred ninety-five livres. So the reserves you have set aside would have to give you eight or nine hundred livres a year, which I cannot believe. If that were the case, was it necessary to draw up a lease of the rest for such a trifle? There must be some misunderstanding about all that. Please, Monsieur, clear it up for me as soon as as possible.

With regard to this, I repeat the request I made you not to change anything or start anything new in matters of importance. Well-

---

[5]This last phrase is written in the Saint's hand.
[6]This last sentence is written in the Saint's hand.

regulated Societies, particularly the Jesuits, have as a maxim that, when a new Superior goes to a house, he should leave things the way his predecessors left them, especially if the Visitor has been there. If you tell me that you acted in that way in Richelieu, as you have already written me, and that I allowed you to draw up that lease, I would like to remind you, please, that it is true that I actually gave you that permission, but this lease is drawn up quite differently from what you proposed to me. I await word from you on that matter, as also on the state of the Community, whom I greet along with you, Monsieur. I am *in Domino* your most humble servant.

VINCENT DEPAUL
i.s.C.M.

At the bottom of the first page: M. Codoing

1194. - TO MATHURIN GENTIL, IN LE MANS

Paris, February 23, 1650

Monsieur,

The grace of Our Lord be with you forever!

I am glad you are exempt from that clergy tax this year because of the payment you made; we shall see about another year.

Since the eight hundred or one thousand livres you want to borrow are to be used to pay off your debts, and since the ordinations are approaching and you are making no preparations, for lack of funds, I think you should borrow another thousand livres to buy beds and the other things you should have. Perhaps M. de Beaugé could give you both these amounts at the same time, or you could go elsewhere to get whatever he refuses you. I will have a power of attorney drawn up for you for this purpose and send it to you

---

Letter 1194. - Archives of the Mission, Turin, original signed letter.

right away. If M. Beaugé were willing to accept as payment, or as part of it, the modest revenues you mention, I approve of our giving them to him, but I strongly doubt that he will.

Let me know how much money M. Planchois wants from you to give up half of his pension, and the amount of the pension. Even if you come to an agreement on that, I do not think the first settlement made with him should be dropped in drawing up the new one, as you say, because it must be affixed to the King's patents verified by the Parlement,[1] and nothing in it should be touched, especially since these patents mention it.

I will have our ledger checked to see if M. Planchois is right in saying that he gave two receipts for the sum of eighteen livres and that you are counting them twice, so that if he has received them only once, we are not doing him a wrong. I am waiting to hear from M. Lucas[2] about his mission.

I wish all of you perfect health and many blessings on you and your work.

I am *in Domino,* Monsieur, your most humble servant.

VINCENT DEPAUL
i.s.C.M.

At the bottom of the first page: M. Gentil

1195. - TO SAINT LOUISE

[Between 1645[1] and 1660]

If Mademoiselle Le Gras wishes me to go to the parlor, I shall

---

[1]January 15, 1650. (Arch. Nat. MM 535.)
[2]Antoine Lucas, Superior of the house.

Letter 1195. - Archives of the Motherhouse of the Daughters of Charity, original autograph letter.
[1]Brother Ducournau, mentioned in this letter, became Saint Vincent's secretary in 1645.

gladly do so, although I have chills, and experience has taught me not to go out in the air in this condition or I will get chills again, which are followed sometimes by fever. Nevertheless, I shall do whatever Mademoiselle pleases. If she chooses to write me what she wants to tell me, I shall receive it in the spirit Our Lord has given me to do whatever she thinks I can do for God. I shall soon send you Brother Ducournau.

1196. - *A PRIEST OF THE MISSION TO SAINT VINCENT*

1650

I must give you a report of the results your prayers and Holy Sacrifices have produced both in Joigny and in Longron [1] *where we are now giving the mission. I have nothing to say about Joigny, except that I admire the regularity of the inhabitants in going to hear the sermons and catechism lessons and their diligence in rising early, for sometimes we began ringing the bell for the sermon at two o'clock in the morning, yet the church was full.*

I must admit in all frankness, however, that I find that things go better in the rural areas than in the towns, and that I see there more signs of genuine, sincere repentance and of the uprightness and simplicity of early Christianity. These good people usually are in tears when they come to confession. They consider themselves the worst sinners in the world and ask for greater penances than are imposed on them. Yesterday a person who had made his confession to another Missionary came and begged me to impose on him a greater penance than the one given him and to order him to fast three days a week for this entire year. Another asked me to give him the penance of walking barefoot on the ground during the time it was frozen. Yesterday, also, a man came to see me and said, "Monsieur, I heard in the sermon that the best way to stop swearing was to kneel down immediately before those in whose presence one had sworn. That is what I have just done because as soon as I realized I had sworn, upon my word, I got down on my knees and asked God's mercy."

Letter 1196. - Abelly, *op.cit.*, bk. II, chap. I, sect. II, §7, p. 46.
[1]Grand-Longueron, a hamlet in the commune of Champlay near Joigny (Yonne).

1197. - TO SAINT LOUISE

I do not have a fever, Mademoiselle, I have only the congestion I had but it is much less now, thank God. I have just taken a purgative for the fourth time and I think that is enough.

I did not forget you today. God has granted me the grace of celebrating Mass for your intention.[1]

I am pleased with what you tell me about the Chancellor's wife.[2]

It would be well for you to be at the meeting[3] here tomorrow and to see Madame de Marillac[4] in the morning. If you cannot do both things, please postpone the visit to this good Lady until Tuesday.

Good morning, Mademoiselle. I am. . . .

V. D. P.

Addressed: Mademoiselle Le Gras

1198. - TO MATHURIN GENTIL, IN LE MANS

Paris, March 16, 1650

Monsieur,

The grace of Our Lord be with you forever!

I am sending you the two documents you requested. The first is a copy checked against the original of the verification of your establishment.[1] The second is M. Planchois' receipt for the last sum

---

Letter 1197. - Archives of the Motherhouse of the Daughters of Charity, original autograph letter.

[1]It was probably Saint Louise's feast day or the anniversary of some memorable event in her life.

[2]Madame Séguier.

[3]The meeting of the Ladies of Charity.

[4]Either Marie de Creil, wife of René de Marillac, or Jeanne Potier, wife of Michel de Marillac.

Letter 1198. - Archives of the Mission, Turin, original signed letter.

[1]Cf. Arch. Nat. S 6707.

of money, amounting to twenty-four livres, which I had him given in two installments, on what you owe him. I told him we will give him nothing more and that he should see you. As for the arrangements he suggested to us for half of his pension, we did not come to any agreement on that, as you can imagine. On the contrary, I informed him that we could not possibly consent to that, and he is no longer expecting it.

M. Pousset has not written me to assist him with any business in the Parlement. Besides, I cannot render him any service of that sort because I never apply to the judge for anyone, and I am not permitted to do so. If, however, I could be of some help to him on another occasion, I would gladly do whatever I can.

We have two seminarians qualified to render service to the Church, which they are actually already doing; one, whose name is [Louis] Champion, teaches ethics at the Collège des Bons-Enfants and the other, [François] Fournier,[2] at the Agen Seminary. The first one is from Châteaudun and the other is from Laval, in the Le Mans diocese. Both of them are the right age and are working at the acquisition of virtue. They have received only tonsure. Would you or M. Lucas please ask the Bishop of Le Mans for dimissorial letters[3] *ad omnes*[4] for them, if possible? I am afraid I cannot send you today their letters regarding tonsure but will do it some other time.

Be very careful, Monsieur, not to remove the locks the Administrators have put on the granaries, as you proposed to me, nor have a key made to open them. You must not on any account go to court against them but live on the best possible terms with them, even if they might be planning to deprive you entirely of those granaries. If you live on peaceful terms, they will not do so. Peace is worth

---

[2]The secretary left a space for their first names, which he did not know or had forgotten.

[3]Dimissorial letters are statements giving a subject permission to be ordained by a bishop other than his own Ordinary. Exempt religious cannot be ordained by any bishop without the dimissorial letters from their own major Superior.

[4]*For all [Orders]*. Saint Vincent appears to want the Bishop of Le Mans, where Champion and Fournier were born, to furnish letters attesting to their freedom to receive Orders at that time and in the future.

more than all worldly possessions; in addition, God rewards it even in this life. I ask you to work at this and do not even think about giving any revenues as payment, nor sell or exchange or do anything else with them, so as not to break up the house in any way. Instead, take the necessary steps yourself to prevent these insecure revenues from being lost.

I am so busy that I have no time to write to M. Lucas. I have just about enough time to embrace him, and the whole Community along with him. The Community here is getting along fairly well.

I am *in Domino*, Monsieur, your most humble servant.

VINCENT DEPAUL
i.s.C.M.

At the bottom of the first page: M. Gentil

1199. - TO ANTOINE LUCAS, SUPERIOR, IN LE MANS

March 23, 1650

Your proposal about the Laval Priory is contrary to our maxims and our custom of not seeking any establishment, directly or indirectly. Providence alone has called us to all those we have, through persons having the right to do so. If the Company has faith in what I say about this, it will be inviolably preserved through this reserve. If that gentleman brings it up again, tell him that I gave you this answer.

I have asked the procurator[1] of your house to leave things as they are with the Administrators and to beware of touching the locks on the granaries, still less to initiate any lawsuit. Peace is

---

Letter 1199. - Reg. 2, pp. 58, 123. The second part, which begins with the words, "I have asked," may have been the first part in the original.
[1]Mathurin Gentil.

worth far more than anything they might take from you. If we bring
it about in others, is it not only right to preserve it among ourselves,
so as not to be rebuffed with that reproach which we read in
yesterday's Gospel, "Physician, cure yourself?" [2] In the name of
God, Monsieur, let us bear with losses like that rather than give
scandal. God will take up our cause, if we practice Our Lord's
counsel.

1200. - TO RENE ALMERAS, SUPERIOR, IN ROME

March 25, 1650

If the house in Rome has been orphaned, as you say, by the
absence of M. Dehorgny, Our Lord will be its Father, Counselor,
and Protector. Have no doubt about this but redouble your trust in
His goodness and let Him act. He Himself will be that energetic
man of grace who you think should be put in your place. You know,
Monsieur, that the outcome of matters depends entirely on Him,
and I know that, if it had depended on us, what you had undertaken
would have been very successful, especially since you brought to
it all the prudent foresight, care, and diligence one might expect of
a virtuous man. The works of God are not accomplished when we
wish them, but whenever it pleases Him. Do you think that the
Jesuits neglected anything when they came to Paris to obtain a
prompt permission to establish themselves here? Not at all. Yet,
they went four years without seeing any results from their applica-
tions and their cleverness. The Oratorian Fathers have been in
Rome a long time. Have they been able to get permission for some
small establishment of their own? No, they are at Saint-Louis but
are subject to the Confraternity.[1]

---

[2]Cf. Lk 4:23. (NAB)

Letter 1200. - Reg. 2, p. 232.
[1]Beginning in 1618, of the twenty-four priests who constituted the corps of chaplains for

God often delays the conclusion of a holy endeavor so that those involved in it might merit its grace by the length of the work, their patience, and their prayers. This is why I beg you not to grow weary in yours. Although He may delay, He will reveal that it is pleasing to Him, if it is done, nevertheless, in a spirit of resignation regarding the outcome.

1201. - TO FATHER BLANCHART

Saint-Lazare, March 26, 1650

The R[everend] F[ather] General of the Congregation of Sainte-Geneviève is most humbly requested by his servant, Vincent, to give a favorable reception to this gentleman, who wishes to speak to him of an affair pertaining to his salvation.

VINCENT DEPAUL
i.s.C.M.

1202. - TO A PRIEST OF THE MISSION, IN SAINTES [1]

March 27, 1650

I am answering your letter of March 16. I am too greatly distressed for having put off writing to you before this to fall into this same fault again. I ask your pardon for this right now, most humbly prostrate in spirit at your feet.

It does not surprise me that you have been tempted because that

---

Saint-Louis-des-Français, six were chosen from among the Oratorian Fathers of France. (Cf. Msgr. Pierre La Croix, *Mémoire historique sur les institutions de France à Rome* [Paris: Victor Groupy, 1868], p. 47.)

Letter 1201. - Sainte-Geneviève Library, Ms. 2555, copy.

Letter 1202. - Reg. 2, p. 308.
[1]The confrere to whom the letter of February 20 was written. (Cf. no. 1191.)

is the distinctive characteristic of those who are trying to serve God. Our Lord Himself was tempted and, since He was, I do not know anyone who can be exempt from this. I would be amazed to know someone who was. The great benefits of grace, like those of fortune, are preserved only with difficulty, and the devil takes great care not to leave you in peace. He will not fail to turn you aside from your holy resolutions, if he can do so, because they involve the salvation of a great multitude of souls, whom you could free from his tyranny by the strength of the holy Word you proclaim to them and by the grace of your vocation.

God has great plans for you, directed toward helping you do what Jesus Christ did when He was on earth. This requires you to resist temptation vigorously, with special confidence in the assistance of His Divine Goodness. Courage then, Monsieur. Be faithful to Him, and the Divine Goodness will be favorable to you. I beg Him most humbly to grant you this grace and to make known to you the esteem and affection I have for you, assuring you that they are far greater than you can imagine.

As for your difficulty in making your interior communication to M. Watebled, it is good for you to make the effort to overcome yourself, bearing in mind the communication the Son of God had with the Blessed Virgin and Saint Joseph, and later with the Apostles, and even with the Scribes, Pharisees, and magistrates. If God has not endowed this good priest with much external grace, he has enriched his soul with great virtue, as you yourself acknowledge. If some persons in the town are surprised that others submit to him, they are persons who feed their eyes on corporal grandeur. You, however, penetrate more deeply into things and know how precious and worthy of veneration is a pure soul who is the temple of the Holy Spirit, totally dedicated to God's service. You must not stop at these material externals, nor even submit to a man because of his virtue, regardless of his sanctity, but to God alone, whom you see in him. This is what I ask you to do with regard to M. Watebled and to whoever may succeed him.

I really think, Monsieur, that a sedentary life is harmful to you.

This comes from being hot-blooded and quick-tempered, and these are moderated with age and not by any change of residence. We take our temperament with us wherever we go, and this impetuosity and hastiness are sources of boredom and unrest. There are some persons who are content with everything and others who are scarcely content with anything. These latter need patience to bear with themselves.

I think this letter will reach you when Lent is almost over, so it would be useless to offer you any remedy for the indisposition it [Lent] is causing you; besides, you do not want to be dispensed from its obligation.

I beg Our Lord, Monsieur, that we may be able to die to ourselves in order to rise with Him, that He may be the joy of your heart, the end and soul of your actions, and your glory in heaven. This will come to pass if, from now on, we humble ourselves as He humbled Himself, if we renounce our own satisfaction to follow Him by carrying our little crosses, and if we give our lives willingly, as He gave His, for our neighbor whom He loves so much and whom He wants us to love as ourselves.

I have the utmost confidence in your prayers.

1203. - *BALTHAZAR GRANGIER,[1] BISHOP OF TREGUIER, TO SAINT VINCENT*

1650

I want to thank you for the faithful ministry of your four priests during my mission here. Their ability, zeal, and assiduity in preaching and hearing confessions were so great that the results have been very successful. I can say that all the inhabitants of this place, of every age, sex, and rank, have been converted, and I have good reason to praise God for

---

Letter 1203. - Abelly, *op.cit.*, bk. II, chap. I, sect. II, §6, p. 45.
[1]Balthazar Grangier de Liverdi.

having given me, through your instrumentality, such good workers. M. . .
is gifted with a moral vigor in the pulpit that is irresistible. I have already
booked him for the mission in . . . next year.

1204. - TO A BISHOP

[Between 1646 and 1652][1]

Excellency,

Since a member of a religious Order in this city has written a
thesis in which he has put forward a proposition that savors of
Jansenism and has been condemned by the Sorbonne, the Chancellor [2] has banned the meeting and discussions that were supposed
to be held on this subject. The Superior raised some objections
about this, so he sent for him and told him that, if he acted contrary
to this, he knew how to recall him and all his men to their duty. He
ordered him to go and see the Nuncio, who severely reprimanded
him for not preventing this thesis from appearing, and he threatened
to have him chastised, along with all his men who were promoting
this doctrine, and to write to the Pope and the General about it. This
Superior and his whole Community then punished this religious
themselves, declaring him incapable of holding any position of
authority in the Order and deprived of active and passive voice.
Then, they expelled him from their house. This leads us to hope
that, henceforth, if matters are controlled in this way to prevent
such ventures, this pernicious doctrine could finally be dispelled.

Letter 1204. - Abelly, *op.cit.*, bk. II, chap. XII, p. 417.

[1]Saint Vincent speaks here of Jansenism in a very decisive and dogmatic manner—unusual
for him before 1646. On the other hand, the letter would seem to date from the time he was a
member of the Council of Conscience (1643-1652).

[2]Pierre Séguier.

1205. - TO A BISHOP

[Between 1643 and 1652][1]

A year or so ago, I had the honor of writing to you about the election of . . . as Abbot of . . . so that you might take the trouble of coming to Paris to inform the Queen of the qualifications of the person and the needs of the abbey. However, because of some inconvenience which prevented you from coming, you were good enough to point out to me in a letter the just reasons for preventing this election from taking place. The matter has dragged on since that time, because of the opposition of two monks among the electors, called to the election a day later than it took place. This opposition has just been dismissed unexpectedly by the Parlement, to the satisfaction of the person elected. This has put him in even hotter pursuit of his confirmation, and he is pressing hard to have his letters patent sent.

Because he has the support of many powerful persons, there is reason to fear that he may succeed. That is why your presence here is greatly to be desired, so you can say a few words to the Queen about the matter and add some weight to the reasons for preventing this wrong. I know that Her Majesty, who has great respect for you, will approve of this. The Keeper of the Seals thought it a good idea for me to entreat you, as I humbly do now, to come as soon as possible, for the love of God. I trust you will do so, knowing how much you have His interests at heart. Perhaps it is on this occasion, as you have done me the honor of writing me, that the reform of that house and of those affiliated with it depend, and that Our Lord wills that the merit of such a desirable outcome be imputed to you, who are one of the Prelates in the kingdom with the greatest zeal for the glory of His Church.

Letter 1205. - Abelly, *op.cit.*, bk. II, chap. XIII, sect. VII, p. 457.
[1]The period during which Saint Vincent was a member of the Council of Conscience.

INDEX

This index proposes to facilitate reference to the biographical data used in this volume and to the explanation of places and terms which recur frequently in the text and which have been explained in the footnotes when first used. Names of persons are in bold print, those of terms or places appear in *italics*. The accompanying numbers indicate the letters to which the reader should refer for the desired information.

A

SEGUIER, Pierre: 1043
SENAUX, Nicolas: 879
SENECEY, Marie-Catherine de la
    Rochefoucauld, Baronne de: 1026
SERRE, Louis: 967
SETIER : 1086
SKYDDIE, John: 876
SOLMINIHAC, Alain de: 843
SPINOLA, Jean-Baptiste: 1071

T

TESTACY, Charles: 870
THIBAULT, Louis: 897
THILOUSE, Marie: 1098
THOLARD, Jacques: 903
THOUVANT, Claude: 907
TRAVERSAY, Anne Petau: 998
TREFFORT, Simon: 870
TRUMEAU, Marie-Marthe: 836
TUMY, Ambroise: 1091
TURBOT, Jean: 1116
TURGIS, Elisabeth: 973

V

VACHEROT, M.: 833

VAGEOT, Philippe: 1022
VALENCAY, Léonor d'Etampes de: 1021
VALOIS, Patrice [WALSH, Patrick]: 958
VAUX, Abbé de (LASNIER): 833
VENTADOUR, Marie de la Guiche
    de Saint-Gérand, Duchesse de: 1155
VERONNE, Alexandre: 918
VERTHAMON, Marie Boucher
    d'Orsay, Dame de: 1156
VILLEQUIER, Antoine de (AUMONT):
    883
VILLEROY, Ferdinand de Neufville de:
    862
VIOLE, Madeleine: 915

W

WALSH, Patrick [VALOIS, Patrice]: 958
WALSH, Thomas: 1060
WATEBLED, Pierre: 995
WATER, Jacques: 870
WHITE, George [LE BLANC,
    Georges]: 842

Z

ZELAZEWSKI, Casimir: 887